1977 YEARBOOK

EVENTS OF 1976

FUNK & WAGNALLS NEW ENCYCLOPEDIA 1977 YEARBOOK

LEON L. BRAM
Vice-President and
Editorial Director

ALBERT BENNETT
Editor

Funk & Wagnalls, Inc., New York

Frontispiece:
**Elections 1976—President Gerald R. Ford,
right; President-elect Jimmy Carter.**

TABLE OF CONTENTS

MEMBERS OF THE STAFF

FOREWORD TO THE EVENTS OF 1976 YEARBOOK

In the United States the year 1976 was punctuated by two main events. In July the people celebrated their country's Bicentennial. In November they elected a Georgia peanut farmer to be their next President.

For the rest of the world it was a year of continuing, if not continuous, excitement. In 1976 the emerging nations of Africa and Asia became increasingly vocal, and their voices became increasingly effective. Some countries of southern Africa fought fiercely for independence, while the oil-producing countries of the world fought for unanimity in their confrontations with the oil-consuming countries.

These and all the other dramatic events of the year are chronicled in the pages of this Yearbook.

The editors are particularly proud of the new ways in which the year's developments in science and technology have been covered in the pages that follow. Just a glance at the titles introduced this year—Communications, Earth and Planetary Sciences, Energy, Environment, Life Sciences, Transportation—will demonstrate the reason for our pride. We feel that the accessibility of this vitally important and absorbing material has been vastly improved.

Other notable articles of the year cover the world's three new nations (Seychelles, Transkei, and the Socialist Republic of Vietnam), the highly influential Organization of Petroleum Exporting Countries (OPEC), and, of course, the quadrennial Olympic Games.

THE EDITORS

Every Border Has Two Sides

a look at Canada-U. S. relations

by Robert MacNeil

Flying from San Francisco to New York City, I look off on the left to the northern horizon. The plains dissolve upward into a gray mist, a luminous cloud layer diffusing into the clear blue of the stratosphere. Somewhere in that mist, on the rim of the earth, Canada begins. I look into that mist and remember the words I sang as a child: "O Canada, the true north, strong and free." Strong, yes. But how long free, I wonder.

The sky darkens as we fly into the eastern evening. Ahead of us is a dark blue band tinged with pink from the sunset behind us. For a few moments, slipping north of Detroit and across Lake Saint Clair, we bite off a small piece of Canada before sweeping out across Lake Erie and down over Pennsylvania. My vestigial "Canadianness" feels that this boundary crossing should be marked, noted somehow. If this were the irritable Middle East or paranoid Eastern Europe, we would have violated air space, scrambled MIGs, caused incidents. But American Airlines Flight 16 treats a piece of Ontario as though it were a chunk of Michigan. And so did most Americans, until Canadians began to wake up.

The result of the awakening has been a decade of ferment, extraordinary for a people as phlegmatic as Canadians. Psychologically, this bustle of self-discovery may be as important as the equivalent decade for Americans two centuries ago. A little late, perhaps, but Canadians do not like to rush into

Opposite page: On an Arctic shore in northwest North America, an obelisk marks the Canada-Alaska boundary.

In the Strait of Juan de Fuca between Washington and British Columbia, a sailor changes the flag each time the ferry crosses the international boundary.

anything. What has emerged is a country that might be a little harder for Americans to live with—if they were paying any attention. Unfortunately, they are not. In 1976 American schoolchildren probably learned more about the physiognomy of the planet Mars than of their vast, beautiful neighbor to the north.

Canada is the delicate preserve of the State Department specialist (in 1972 State created the position of Deputy Assistant Secretary for Canadian Affairs), the professors of political science, and expansionist corporations. It would not hurt the average American to know something about the country, now trying in a gentlemanly way to pry a little of its future away from the determined American embrace.

There are questions to be asked about the flash of nationalism on the other side of the border: Is it too late? Can it hurt the United States? Has it stopped the erosion of Canada's economic independence? Or has it just stayed this erosion temporarily, until the resumption of what may be inevitable—the steady absorption of Canada by the U.S.?

Canada, of course, had no revolution. The Americans tried to get the Canadian colonists to join them but failed. Canadians opted for obedience to authority, law, and order—qualities which have marked their character ever since. They opted for colonial dependence and, in a certain sense, that lasted until after World War II. Great Britain permitted greater and greater self-determination during the 19th century, but the last fiber of the umbilical cord was not severed until 1949, when Canada ceased to use the Privy Council in London as the highest court of appeal. There was little overt quarrel with this gradual, decent evolution. But it affected our Canadian psyche, stunting the growth of a Canadian identity. All our symbolism was imperial symbolism: red ensigns and royal coats of arms, authentically Canadianized by the Royal College of Heralds in London. We looked to England for political inspiration.

Culturally we were castaways on the beaches of Britain and the U.S. Even the books we read as children, called *Stories for Canadian Boys* or the like, were written and published in England. We grew like

The Saint Elias Mountains tower along the border between the Yukon Territory in Canada (foreground) and southeastern Alaska (background).

Storm clouds brood over a field of ripening wheat in Saskatchewan. The province grows nearly two thirds of Canada's wheat.

Sam Dixon on his potato farm in Alberta. Both Canada and the U.S. import and export potatoes across the border.

trees in a prevailing wind: the Anglophile bent toward England, the more republican toward the U.S., few straight up. As if these forces were not enough, the professional and economic pull was just as strong. Making it in many professions meant going abroad. It was the archetypal colonial situation, only we didn't know enough to call it that.

After the war, as millions of Europeans streamed in, seeking material abundance, thousands of Canadians went abroad to escape what they regarded as the confining provincialism of so much of Canadian life in the 1940's and 1950's: no newspapers on Sundays, dreary bars that invested even the consumption of beer with the decadence of a Dostoevskian vodka shop, and piercingly cold winters. We fled, some to England, some to the U.S.—writers, scientists, teachers, doctors, journalists, actors, engineers, musicians, and filmmakers. I don't know how many thousands. Many, attracted by the renaissance of the Canadian spirit (naissance would be more accurate), have gone back. Many have not and, especially in the U.S., have assimilated inconspicuously.

Unnoticed by most of us, another colonial reality was working on Canada. Immigration swelled the work force, capital flowed in, and seemingly limitless resources were opened up. Canada had everything everybody wanted: a 20th-century Aladdin's cave of riches—aluminum, nickel, platinum, uranium, asbestos, iron, pulp, oil, gas, and water. The Canadian standard of living climbed dramatically on the international charts, and Ottawa began to play a slightly less timid world role. Under Lester Pearson, Canada became the perfect member of the United Nations, ready with troops for duty in trouble spots.

Successive Canadian governments played polite games with American administrations from that of Harry S. Truman to that of Lyndon B. Johnson. The inherited furniture called Canadian-American relations was ritually polished; the pleasant speeches called attention to "the longest undefended border in the world." Visits were exchanged, ceremonial trees planted, and trade lubricated.

But vague uneasiness began to surface in government reports in the 1950's, and in the 1970's it broke the surface of our complacency. The truth was that Canada was buying its standard of living by selling itself to the U.S., selling not just exhaustible resources but its political independence. The inflow of American capital was not monitored politically. It became obvious that economic decisions fundamental to Canada's existence as a sovereign nation were increasingly being made by Americans.

An international airstrip and road extend along the border between Sweetgrass, Mont., and Coutts, Alberta.

The Trailcreek border crossing, in northwestern Montana, is on a road used only during the summer, mostly by loggers.

Pierre Elliott Trudeau, the first prime minister to notice and exploit the facts politically, put it simply in 1974: "Canada, of all the industrialized nations of the world, is most subject to foreign control. And that control is mostly American."

The U.S. held 85 percent of all foreign investment in Canada, more than $35 billion—the backbone of the Canadian economy. Americans owned or otherwise controlled roughly half of what Canada produced industrially. To Canadians that was devastating, but it was hard to convince Americans that it mattered.

At the same time, an older reality was rediscovered: Whatever indigenous Canadian culture existed was rapidly being displaced by American culture. To Abraham Rotstein of the University of Toronto, "In Canada, we may still own the cupboard, but little of the contents." He musters these statistics for "foreign control": more than half the university professors in the humanities and social sciences; 85 percent of magazine circulation; 83 percent of book sales; 71 percent of the publishing industry; 96 percent of films; and so on through television, the theater, and the arts. About four fifths of "foreign" means American.

Opposite page: The CN tower in Toronto, Ontario, 1815 ft. high, is the tallest free-standing structure in the world. On clear days this communications antenna can be seen from New York State, 30 mi. across Lake Ontario. It houses a restaurant and bar.

Above: A pulp mill in Fort Frances, Ontario. Fort Frances, across the Rainy River from International Falls, Minn., was once a fur-trading post of the Hudson's Bay Co. It is now a mining and pulp center.

Below: Flags on Peace Bridge mark the Canada-U.S. boundary over the Niagara River between Buffalo, N.Y., and Fort Erie, Ontario. Technically, the boundary is an abstract vertical plane that cuts from underground through the air to the edge of outer space.

Niagara Falls in winter. The Canadian, or Horseshoe, Falls (right) are 162 ft. high. The American Falls are 5 ft. higher but discharge only about one ninth the volume of water.

Niagara Falls, Ontario, like its counterpart on the New York side of the river, is a resort city catering to the honeymoon trade.

With great foresight, that danger was recognized in the very beginnings of broadcasting. The Canadian Broadcasting Corp. (C.B.C.) was established to promote Canadian culture. It was assumed that the narrow ribbon of Canadian population, running 3000 miles from east to west, would be far harder to influence along its length than at any point from south to north across the border. The assumption was correct, and the C.B.C. labored faithfully to nurture Canadian writers, musicians, actors, and other creative people. But Canadians cannot be stopped from liking American television, movies, books, plays, sports, politics, newspapers, cars, and life-styles.

Thoughtful Canadians began to reconsider this cultural displacement just as the decade of America's greatest problems—assassinations, riots, crime, Vietnam, and Watergate—caused a certain distancing. "At least we don't have those things here," was a common and understandable emotion in a nation with a well-established national inferiority complex. Something in Canada must be right. Was it the Queen? Or were Canadians just nicer? Whatever, that essence must be preserved; something intrinsic and different about the Canadian way of life must be guarded. Canadians were helped in these emotions by

the migration, briefly, of those who determined international chic. Livable Toronto replaced swinging London as the sociological/journalistic cliché of the moment. It became exotic to say you'd had a weekend in Montréal. Less exotic Canadian cities, upon learning that they had achieved livable dimensions—a human scale, safety, and wholesomeness—began to primp. And abetting this new self-respect were the Vietnam expatriates, Americans escaping the war, propagandizing about how civilized Canada was. According to Keith M. Glazier of the University of Calgary, it was "the Vietnamization of America that finally brought about the Canadianization of Canada."

Law enforcement agencies in the Buffalo-Fort Erie area include the New York State Police, the U.S. Border Patrol, the Buffalo Police Department, the Ontario Provincial Police, the Niagara (Ontario) Regional Police, and the Royal Canadian Mounted Police.

All of these strands are visible in the new Canadian nationalism. Compared with the ranker growths that fall under that name, the Canadian variety is mild and tentative. But the sight of even a few hairs sends the teenager for a razor. He has the right to call it a beard. Most importantly, it *feels* like a beard.

There is one other strand to be mentioned: French Canada. In a way, the French started it. Their historic frustration with second-class citizenship erupted in the early sixties. Some terrorist violence shocked Canada into a stampede of measures to reassure the French quarter of Canada's population that they were equal. To the pain of many Anglophile Canadians, the French language was officially rehabilitated, federal revenue sharing was revolutionized to aid Québec Province, and a new Canadian flag was born—all to stop Québec from breaking away from Canada. But for many the flurry of those years created a new perspective: It was Québec, after all, that made Canada *most* different from the U.S., now that the British role had dwindled.

The Dundee Line Hotel straddles the border between Fort Covington, N.Y., and Dundee, Québec. Bar customers buy their cigarettes in the U.S. and their liquor in Canada.

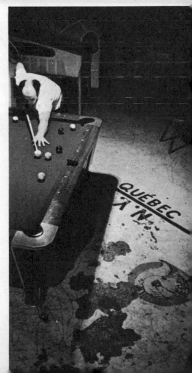

Lyle Hurtubise's farm lies partly in Québec, near Abercorn, and partly in Vermont, near Rich-ford.

A snow-defined swath through the woods divides Maine from Québec near Estcourt Station, Maine's northernmost point. Road veers shy of the border.

Enter the charismatic Trudeau, whose historic mission was to be to gather these strands and weave a new fabric of Canadian nationalism. How you evaluate his success depends on perspective. Active nationalists in Canada believe he pussyfoots and changes nothing fundamental in Canada's neocolonial relationship with the U.S. American opinion runs the gamut from indifference to the conviction of the conservative *National Review* that Trudeau is leading Canadians into Marxist socialism.

What has he done to reassert Canada's interests and to affect American interests?

To extract more "significant benefits" for Canada, his government established the Foreign Investment Review Agency in 1974 to screen projected takeovers and expansions by foreign firms. A study published in July, 1976, by the prestigious Canadian-American Committee thought the impact of the act difficult to determine. The report speculated that the effect on investment might come less from decisions of the agency than from "the spreading belief in U.S. business circles that U.S. investment is now unwelcome in Canada."

Trudeau has attempted to establish closer relations with the European Economic Community, the only economic unit in the Western World with resources resembling those of the U.S. But this effort is not expected to result in any dramatic diversion of trade or investment patterns.

Of less significant economic impact, but more irritating to the American concerns involved, are the Canadian government's measures to resist cultural domination. *Time* magazine was forced to end its Canadian edition when Canadian advertisers lost tax exemptions for space they bought in the magazine. The *Reader's Digest* was similarly affected, but the publishers decided to continue the Canadian edition. The government's object is to divert Canadian advertising into Canadian publications. The same was true of a rule adopted by the Canadian Radio and Television Commission that requires cable–TV operators along the border to delete commercials from American programs they pick up. The U.S. network programs, received from cities such as Buffalo, are very popular, and Canadian advertisers pour millions of dollars into spots so they can be seen in Canada. In addition, radio and TV broadcasts originating in Canada must include a stated percentage of Canadian content, and efforts are being taken to make movie theaters show a certain proportion of Canadian films, many of which are made with government subsidy.

Few people in the arts and communications believe this effort will ultimately succeed, although it will keep some Canadian talent employed. Mordecai Richler, the Canadian novelist, has observed that the effort, "in effect, licenses mediocrity."

The most dramatic act of economic nationalism by Trudeau was his decision during the Arab oil embargo of 1973 to consider Canadian needs first. Some Americans protested, "They're cutting off our oil," and the double irony underscored Canada's position. The oil came out of Canadian soil but 75 percent of the capital that produced it was foreign.

In 1973 Canada imposed an export tax on oil exported to the U.S. In 1974 it announced that it would phase out crude oil exports to the U.S. by the early 1980's. The reasons: Canadian consumption was rising, known reserves were dwindling, and new exploration was disappointing. Canada itself was going to become a net oil importer.

Many American users depend on Canadian natural gas. In 1970 Canada's National Energy Board began refusing applications for additional gas exports. The board may eventually reduce exports under existing licenses.

Although these measures have caused nervousness and some outrage in the U.S., they are mild compared with what more extreme nationalists would like Canada to do to seize the power inherent in its

The boundary near North Troy, Vt., and Highwater, Québec, where it follows the 45th parallel.

Georges and Cécile Béchard live in a house built on the Québec-Maine line in Estcourt Station. They are U.S. citizens.

An early morning mist rises from the waters of the Lubec Narrows in Passamaquoddy Bay between New Brunswick and Maine.

resources. Some would like to reduce gas exports to the U.S. drastically. There are calls on the federal government to nationalize parts of the oil industry. In the last resort, Canada, which has come to think of itself as playing the role of a developing country, could follow the example of some Third World countries and simply nationalize by expropriation. But the economic situation would not permit such drastic measures, and a description of that situation reveals how little has actually changed.

Canada has been running a growing trade deficit with the U.S.; purchases far outstrip sales. The current account deficit was $1.5 billion in 1974 and $4.6 billion in 1975. Such a drain must undermine the value of the Canadian dollar, so high interest rates have been maintained to attract capital. Net capital movements from the U.S. to Canada show surpluses of $2.5 billion and $4.9 billion, respectively, in 1974 and 1975. The Canadian position is aggravated by relatively higher wages and lower productivity than exists in American industry, making a greatly improved export performance unlikely. To push exports will mean continuing reliance on exporting raw materials, thus perpetuating the pattern Trudeau wants to change.

So, given the ever-present specters of inflation and slow recovery from recession, Canada seems trapped in a pattern it can break only by accepting a much reduced standard of living. If austerity is the price Canadians are willing to pay for independence, that is not evident now; and the federal government is pushing its vision very cautiously.

What Canada is trying to do, economically and culturally, may seem a doomed attempt to cultivate something unnatural, continually resisted by natural forces, if the ever-burgeoning American economy is to be regarded as a "natural force." To many the natural state is a continental North American economy. If it makes sense in Europe, why not in North America? Economically, it may make sense. Politically and emotionally, it makes no sense, at least for the foreseeable future.

To bring it closer to home: My brothers' children are growing up in Canada. Will they become American citizens in their lifetime if they still live in Nova Scotia or Ontario as they now do? No! Will they grow increasingly like American children in their tastes and visions? Yes! And that is more important than whether they sing "The Star Spangled Banner" or "O Canada."

The question is whether there is something vitally distinct in the Canadian spirit, some élan that can survive all the formidable forces coming to erase it, something more than the difference between Maine and California. If that élan is not there, it is too late to invent it. But it's going to be a rather touchy few years between our countries while Canadians try to find it— or invent it.

As part of the Canadian observance of the U.S. Bicentennial, Prime Minister Pierre Elliott Trudeau presents President Gerald R. Ford with a copy of a new book entitled Between Friends/Entre Amis. This handsome volume, designed and edited by Lorraine Monk, was produced by the National Film Board of Canada. It "chronicles and captures the land and, more especially, the people" along the international boundary between Canada and the U.S. All the photographs on the preceding pages appear in that volume and have been reproduced with the kind permission of the film board.

Amateur Sports on Trial

by Dick Button

As a participant in two Olympics, I have a special feeling for the Games. This past winter at Innsbruck the competitive sap once again rose in my veins as I covered the figure-skating competition for ABC–TV. I watched America's Dorothy Hamill shake off nervous tears moments before skating onto the ice arena and clinching a gold medal, and I stood by admiringly as Jim Millns and Colleen O'Connor of the United States created a glorious dance program that showed what the new Olympic sport of ice dancing is all about. And the Summer Games? I was as thrilled as most viewers by American performances in Québec: by 16-year-old platform diver Greg Louganis, by 33-year-old hurdler Willie Davenport, by the electrifying young American boxers and male swimmers, by the fiery basketball team on a mission to reclaim some national pride.

But at Innsbruck, as well as in my day-to-day contact with skaters and other amateur athletes, I was conscious of other feelings among those who did not win gold medals. They are feelings of frustration with the U.S. sports establishment as it is presently run—and mythologized. For too many years, Olympic medals won by our athletes have represented more than victories over foreign competitors and over "oneself." They have also represented bitter triumphs over the hardships and the stale mystique of amateurism. The frustrations of American athletes are growing and becoming more vocal. Fortunately, testimony before the President's Commission on Olympic Sports (established June 19, 1975) has helped to bring some crucial questions out into the open. Does amateurism still mean anything in today's athletic world? Must rival U.S. sports federations continue in a state of virtual war—with the individual athlete as hostage? Do our athletes deserve more autonomy? How can U.S. sports best be financed? Are the modern Olympics top-heavy, moribund, dead?

Dick Button, U.S. men's figure-skating champion in 1946, knows the problems of amateur athletes at first hand. He appears (below) on ABC-TV describing the figure-skating competition at the 1976 Winter Olympics. Hearings on amateur sports were conducted during the year by the President's Commission on Olympic Sports, shown (opposite page) meeting in Washington, D.C., with President Gerald R. Ford.

DONNA deVARONA

The President's Commission on Olympic Sports heard testimony from many prominent American athletes, including tennis star Billie Jean King (center). Former Olympic decathlon winner Rafer Johnson and swimmer Donna de Varona served as members of the commission.

I do not have all or even many of the answers. But I am optimistic about American sports (and, the doomsayers notwithstanding, about the Olympics), if only because we are learning from other nations. Most of us are well aware that foreign world-class athletes—particularly in the Iron Curtain countries—are generously subsidized, whether as sport club members, athletic-institute "students," or privileged military personnel. But these countries also have truly national programs. For example, the Soviet Union's *Spartakiade,* a kind of Russian national Olympics held every year, includes all Olympic sports. Moreover, the coaching and competition start at village level, and by the time of the finals at the Moscow stadium, some 50,000,000 athletes have participated! East Germany, too—which won more gold medals than the U.S. at Montréal—has a *spartakiade.* The sports progress of such relatively small nations within the past fifteen years has been breathtaking. And it has been largely due to national programs that the U.S. could readily imitate.

Or take the sport closest to my heart, figure skating. The Soviet Union had not since World War I entered international skating competitions until 1960. Yet the Olympic Pair champions in 1964 were Russian, and the U.S.S.R. has won all the World and Olympic pairs titles since 1965. In their system, the Russians do not dally or compromise in their headlong pursuit of being first. Not long ago, their top-ranked figure skater was abruptly "removed" from the international circuit. Could it have been because full support was being concentrated on another as a better gamble?

Other nations reward their amateur champions well, as American Frank Shorter reflected in reference to his Olympic marathon victory in 1972. "Had I been a Finn," said Shorter in testimony before the President's commission, "my town would have built me a house. Peugeot would have given me a free car, all of this tax free, and I could have done endorsements. Every time I would have gone to a shopping center I would have gotten $2000 for cutting a ribbon. I could have demanded $2000 every time I set foot on the track for the rest of the summer. . . ."

The Montréal Games showed again the admirable strides made by smaller nations in international sports. Is it because these countries send professionals, whereas we Americans hold to the ethics of amateurism as expressed by the founder of the modern Olympics, Baron Pierre de Coubertin: "The important thing is not victory, but the struggle"?

The answer, unfortunately, is not quite so tidy. And for U.S. athletes, the true struggle seems to be against the bureaucracy and factionalism of the National Collegiate Athletic Association (N.C.A.A.), the rival Amateur Athletic Union (A.A.U.), the U.S. Olympic Committee (U.S.O.C.), and, indirectly, the venerable International Olympic Committee (I.O.C.).

The Israeli tragedy at Munich in 1972 impressed painfully on the world that the Olympic Games are anything but above politics. But since long before 1972, U.S. athletes, peculiarly, have had internal, organizational politics to contend with. They have seen as much red tape as white tape in the locker room. Too often they have been the pawns in administrative squabbles. Both the N.C.A.A. and the A.A.U. have been criticized for being authoritarian, exploitive, and—perhaps most seriously—inconsistent and hypocritical in regard to money and the shibboleth of pure amateurism.

The two federations and other feuding sports organizations and sponsors control many major amateur meets and championships in the U.S. Accusations fly fast. The A.A.U. has been accused by athletes of playing politics in selecting coaches and competitors, "blackmailing" athletes who appear in N.C.A.A. meets, and stinting on paying expenses for competitors. Another complaint is that a former wrestler or gymnast, say, may have decision-making power over skaters or track-and-field athletes.

More to the point, the handling by the A.A.U. and N.C.A.A. of many individual cases has been questionable, if not nationally embarrassing. One example, in 1959, was the curious response by the A.A.U. to a Swedish basketball team that hoped to play some games in the U.S. against American college teams. Having received a letter promising cooperation, the Swedes arrived—and left the U.S. without being allowed to play a game. This rug-pulling display of American hospitality was pivotal in widening the breach between the A.A.U. and N.C.A.A.

Organizational regulations often create difficulties for American athletes anxious to compete at the international level. Many Europeans, Asians, and Africans, not so hampered, get better seasoning before the Olympics. In California, a so-called renegade club, the Pacific Coast Club, has been formed largely because of frustration at paralyzing edicts. With the A.A.U., according to distance runner Francie Larrieu, "you're lucky to appear in one or two good invitational meets."

Sportscaster Howard Cosell (top) and marathon runner Frank Shorter testify before the President's Commission on Olympic Sports, on which decathlonist Bill Toomey served. "Had I been a Finn," said Shorter of his 1972 Olympic victory, "my town would have built me a house."

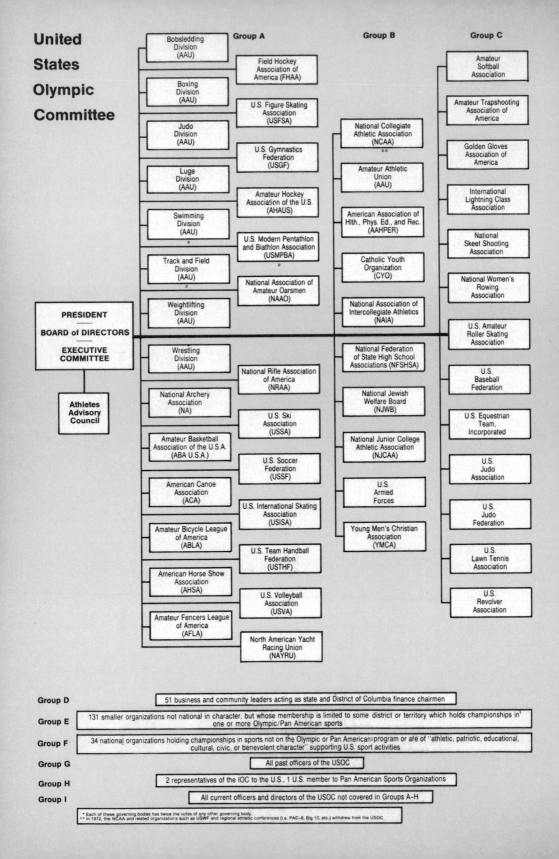

United States Olympic Committee

PRESIDENT — **BOARD of DIRECTORS** — **EXECUTIVE COMMITTEE**

Athletes Advisory Council

Group A

- Bobsledding Division (AAU)
- Boxing Division (AAU)
- Judo Division (AAU)
- Luge Division (AAU)
- Swimming Division (AAU) *
- Track and Field Division (AAU) *
- Weightlifting Division (AAU)
- Wrestling Division (AAU)
- National Archery Association (NA)
- Amateur Basketball Association of the U.S.A. (ABA U.S.A.)
- American Canoe Association (ACA)
- Amateur Bicycle League of America (ABLA)
- American Horse Show Association (AHSA)
- Amateur Fencers League of America (AFLA)
- Field Hockey Association of America (FHAA)
- U.S. Figure Skating Association (USFSA)
- U.S. Gymnastics Federation (USGF)
- Amateur Hockey Association of the U.S. (AHAUS)
- U.S. Modern Pentathlon and Biathlon Association (USMPBA) *
- National Association of Amateur Oarsmen (NAAO) *
- National Rifle Association of America (NRAA)
- U.S. Ski Association (USSA)
- U.S. Soccer Federation (USSF)
- U.S. International Skating Association (USISA)
- U.S. Team Handball Federation (USTHF)
- U.S. Volleyball Association (USVA)
- North American Yacht Racing Union (NAYRU)

Group B

- National Collegiate Athletic Association (NCAA) **
- Amateur Athletic Union (AAU)
- American Association of Hlth., Phys. Ed., and Rec. (AAHPER)
- Catholic Youth Organization (CYO)
- National Association of Intercollegiate Athletics (NAIA)
- National Federation of State High School Associations (NFSHSA)
- National Jewish Welfare Board (NJWB)
- National Junior College Athletic Association (NJCAA)
- U.S. Armed Forces
- Young Men's Christian Association (YMCA)

Group C

- Amateur Softball Association
- Amateur Trapshooting Association of America
- Golden Gloves Association of America
- International Lightning Class Association
- National Skeet Shooting Association
- National Women's Rowing Association
- U.S. Amateur Roller Skating Association
- U.S. Baseball Federation
- U.S. Equestrian Team, Incorporated
- U.S. Judo Association
- U.S. Judo Federation
- U.S. Lawn Tennis Association
- U.S. Revolver Association

Group D	51 business and community leaders acting as state and District of Columbia finance chairmen
Group E	131 smaller organizations not national in character, but whose membership is limited to some district or territory which holds championships in one or more Olympic/Pan American sports
Group F	34 national organizations holding championships in sports not on the Olympic or Pan American program or are of "athletic, patriotic, educational, cultural, civic, or benevolent character" supporting U.S. sport activities
Group G	All past officers of the USOC
Group H	2 representatives of the IOC to the U.S., 1 U.S. member to Pan American Sports Organizations
Group I	All current officers and directors of the USOC not covered in Groups A–H

* Each of these governing bodies has twice the votes of any other governing body.
** In 1972, the NCAA and related organizations such as USWF and regional athletic conferences (i.e. PAC–8, Big 10, etc.) withdrew from the USOC.

Nor has the U.S.O.C. escaped criticism. The committee is perched at the top of the organizational pyramid of U.S. amateur athletics. Various divisions of the A.A.U. are represented on it, but the N.C.A.A. and related bodies withdrew in 1972, and the individual athlete is underrepresented. Nevertheless, the committee dictates the terms of U.S. Olympic participation with a tradition-bound absoluteness under which many athletes chafe. Lamented American decathloner Bruce Jenner just before his gold medal performance at Montréal, "In Europe, they want the athlete and the country to do well, and if it means giving the athlete some money, they give it to 'em. Here, they're only interested in upholding some archaic, idealistic amateur code."

As for the I.O.C., it has traditionally promulgated the code of Olympic amateurism—in spirit, at least. But the I.O.C. for years has been less than perfect in resolving problems. At the 1936 Olympics, for instance, when Canada protested the presence of Canadians on the British hockey team, the I.O.C. first disqualified the British team, then reinstated the expatriate players and declared the hockey competition "non-Olympic," and then ruled that it was official after all. I personally found the I.O.C.'s handling of the Taiwan-or-Republic-of-China controversy deplorable, as did many people who regret the poisoning of sports by politics.

Few would quarrel that the Olympic-American ideals are worthy precepts. But amateurism today is, if not a bankrupt standard, a bankrupt definition. We very much need to put our money where our mouth is. There is no getting around the fact that all athletes need time, facilities, and coaching in order to train properly. How can these be provided without support? Amateurism is relative, not absolute. Is a Swiss skier

Many noted athletes have fallen afoul of the rules governing amateur competition. Jim Thorpe, shown practicing the discus throw at the 1912 Olympics, later had to return his two gold medals. Austrian skier Karl Schranz (right) confers with his employer, ski manufacturer Franz Kneissl, at the 1972 Olympics. Schranz was disqualified for appearing in advertisements for Kneissl's skis.

Following pages: Sports programs in the Soviet bloc countries stress mass participation and special facilities for the gifted. Clockwise from upper left: A gymnastics room for the children of workers in a Leipzig, East Germany, factory; men in their seventies run a cross-country race in Moscow; Olga Korbut, who was a 17-year old lieutenant in the Soviet army at the time of her gymnastic triumphs in the 1972 Olympics, browses in the Moscow Sports Institute library; a track in the Sports Palace of a Moscow automobile plant; students at a sports club in Novorossiysk, U.S.S.R., learn "art gymnastics" a spartakiade, or national Olympics, in Sofia, Bulgaria; a pool at a sports club for railwa workers and their children in Khar'kov, U.S.S.R.; a Soviet army volleyball club practices in Kiev; a children's soccer school in Tbilisi, U.S.S.R.; a world-champion Soviet figure skating pair, Oleg Protopopo and Ludmilla Belousova, perform at the 1964 Olympics.

Great amateurs who excelled in later careers: Swimmer Johnny Weissmuller (above) became Hollywood's Tarzan; decathlonist Bob Mathias (below) was elected U.S. Congressman; (opposite page, top to bottom) track star Jesse Owens prospered in public relations; swimmer Buster Crabbe played Flash Gordon in motion pictures; and the late all-around athlete Babe Didrikson Zaharias scored as a professional golfer.

who is paid for endorsing his favorite brand of ski a professional? Is a Russian speed skater—a student—who is groomed and subsidized by his government an amateur? The issue is as old and older than the controversial case of Jim Thorpe, the great American Indian athlete who had to return his two Olympic gold medals and other trophies in 1913 after the A.A.U. discovered he had played professional baseball while attending college. But the issue of amateurism should not, I think, be an issue at all.

American athletes have had to play a hypocritical role: that of virtuous amateur and more and more often that of virtuous professional. Both on and off the record, they have had much to say about the pro forma canons of amateurism.

"I think we are all professionals now," stated Frank Shorter in a bitter mood of exaggeration before the President's Commission on Olympic Sports. Shorter also referred to twenty-five specific "rules" of amateurism which, if strictly observed, would mean that nobody at all could show up at the Olympics.

As a member of that commission, former Olympic decathlon champion Bill Toomey said, ". . . an athlete shouldn't have to lose money because he is in the sport. . . . It is obvious that the rules that the I.O.C. have set down are flagrantly being abused by many of the countries. . . . If, in fact, all of this is happening, why do we pretend to have these rules? Why don't we address ourselves to the fact and why not at least be realistic?"

So let us be realistic. The real problem is reorganization. The organization of American athletics is unique in one respect: It is grounded in our educational system. "Who produces and trains most of our Olympic-quality athletes?" asks James Michener in his recent book *Sports in America* (Random House, 1976). "Our colleges and universities. Who provides the scholarships, the skilled coaches, the competitive meets and the stadiums in which they are held? The colleges and universities."

As the first report (Feb. 9, 1976) of the President's Commission pointed out, most other nations have a "highest sports authority" ruling over a club system that affords uniformity in programs and facilities, year-round participation, and specific, targeted funding where it is most needed. Some even launch one-year or multi-year "plans" for given sports that need development nationally. Equally important, sports "consciousness" is displayed by business and industry in many countries. Factories have their own sports programs—and I don't mean bowling—and less absenteeism because of them.

The U.S. system, on the other hand, is in effect decentralized, a "shake-the-tree" system. Its ruling body, the U.S.O.C., lacks the power to deal effectively with many policy and funding disputes of the 1970's. Even the N.C.A.A. and A.A.U. agree that reforms of the existing structure of U.S. sports are needed. Especially, the creation of a strong "higher sports authority," be it governmental, coalitional, or new and private, is called for. With a so-called vertical system, all sports—all Olympic sports—can receive proper attention and encouragement. And support entails not only dollars but good coaching, good sports medicine, good nutritional programs.

But let's not gloss over those dollars. American athletes are wearying fast of having to choose between penury and hypocrisy. I think it is most regrettable that money is made a hobgoblin. The promotion of sports events for financial gain, whether the participants are amateurs or pros, generates more interest, more informed fans, and above all more participants. Television coverage of the events, in addition to enriching promoters and advertisers, has multiplied sports spectatorship by the thousands. It has made the Olympics a truly worldwide event. Some critics feel that U.S. sports have become too spectator-oriented. Yet how else does a sport grow nationally, attract newcomers, gain exposure and financing? It is foolish to vilify the medium: For all its commercialism, TV has given us the second look, the time-slowed beauty of an end run or a platform dive, the proof, grace, and agony at the finish line. All are brought into our living rooms by means of expensive technology. Money is the fuel of sports, and yet it is kept away from young amateurs as though it were a poison.

"You can sing a record at fourteen," noted U.S. tennis star Billie Jean King before the President's commission, "and make a million dollars. Everyone says, isn't that wonderful. But if you're an athlete, oh, no. Oh, no. For God sakes, don't make any money so maybe you can go train the rest of the year without having to have your parents work three jobs. My parents worked three jobs so my brother and I could be in sports."

After better organization and financial support, the next crying need for amateur sports, it seems to me, is that of an open—to all—Olympics. Why *not* open the Games up? Why not make them truly the summit

For 20-year-old Dorothy Hamill, the grueling years of training paid off in 1976. Clockwise from above: Dorothy takes to the ice at age 10; she wins a trophy at a Toronto, Canada, skating school at 14; the Hamill family (left to right): father Chalmers Hamill, daughters Marsha and 18-year-old Dorothy, and mother Carol in their Riverside, Conn., home; Dorothy receives a gold medal for figure skating at the 1976 Winter Olympics; she yields her amateur standing to appear in ads that feature her now-famous freckles and hair style; she rehearses with Gene Kelly for her first TV special in November.

meeting of the best athletes in the world, professional and amateur? (An open Olympics does not mean that cash prizes will replace gold medals.) It is a fallacy and an absurdity to imagine that permitting money-earning athletes to compete in the Olympics—and they already are competing in them—will be the end of amateurism. What are eager young athletes before they become professionals if not amateurs? It is from the ranks of aspiring and hard-training youngsters that superathletes must come, however swift their rise.

The Olympics are unquestionably the beacon of international amateurism. They are the very essence of sports-for-sports' sake. By opening up the Games to professionals and semiprofessionals and quarter-professionals, the I.O.C. will also paradoxically be strengthening amateurism: creating a more democratic stage for the world's best athletes, regardless of race, creed, or income, and thereby inspiring all the more youngsters on the way up. By having no restrictions on entrants in the Games, might we not also finally lay to rest all of the talk and confusion about under-the-table money and over-the-hill purity?

As for American sports, some form of higher or "highest" authority is obviously needed. But I would prefer that it not be a U.S. governmental body or that our sports be federally subsidized. Instead of a federal sports authority, why not a U.S. Commissioner of

Sports? Or perhaps an overseeing body of a judicial type, a "Supreme Court of Athletics," to which not only disputing organizations but individual athletes could have recourse? And while I have no ready answers for the mutual wounds of the A.A.U. and N.C.A.A., I believe one way to defuse their rivalry might be to create other organizations, other championships.

Our young athletes desperately need their way eased for competing often against the subsidized men and women of other countries. Could our athletes not receive loans from the American government for their training and travel expenses? Cannot the business sector play a role with grants? Can we not allow our skaters, runners, and fencers to accept needed earnings from commercial endorsements (but not for competing in the Olympics)? Could not Olympic funds be raised through lotteries, taxes on professional sport tickets, or other means surer than tree-shaken contributions? And cannot parents of promising athletes and athlete-hiring firms be favored with tax write-offs? Such realistic steps can be taken. Has not the U.S.O.C. for several years obtained contributions from businesses which, in return, are allowed to use the Olympic emblem in their advertising?

That professionalism, subsidization, or commercialization might kill the amateur spirit is utter nonsense. When I turned professional, two decades

Since ancient times, the crowds have demanded and exalted athletic heroes. The Greek discus thrower (above) was idealized as a model of physical perfection.

ago, it in no way tainted my love for skating or for excelling (today I am a decidedly amateur squash player who does not at all enjoy losing). The fervor to compete, the charting of self-improvement, the oneness with the moment of truth—these feelings are too deeply rooted in man and woman to be bought off by all the dollars and cents of our 20th century. The professional circuit has not made Chris Evert any less of a tennis champion, and TV commercials have hardly turned athletes such as O.J. Simpson, Pete Rose, or Pelé into performing robots. If there is a "germ" at the heart of an athlete, it is less the urge to win than the compulsion to try to win. It is also the quest for one's individual potential, a kind of imperative that we will probably never fully understand. It is the determination that made a Japanese gymnast at Montréal complete a high-bar routine with a broken leg and which made a Finnish runner try his first marathon less than a day after he had won a 10,000-m race.

A famous poster shows contemporary idol Mark Spitz with the seven gold medals he won as a swimmer in the 1972 Olympics.

All these issues and errors are being aired and, little by little, ironed out. At the close of 1976, American amateurism was less of a stadium divided against itself. It was a year for optimism, possibly a turning point for all sports in our country. The President's Commission portends an earnest stock-taking at the top level, one which would pay dividends at the 1980 Olympics and thereafter.

WHO CARES FOR YOUR HEALTH?

by Jonathan Spivak

The medical care system of the United States is fast approaching a crisis that threatens to break down its capacity to serve the public. There are many strains on the system. The most urgent, according to a recent report of the U.S. Public Health Service, are runaway costs that, if not controlled, will place "severe restrictions on health care delivery and other public services—restrictions our nation should not tolerate."

A few disturbing statistics dramatize the extent of the problem. Medical expenditures for the nation soared from $35 billion in 1965 to $119 billion in 1975 and were expected to reach $135 billion in 1976. Hospital charges in 1975 rose 13 percent, 50 percent faster than for the consumer price index as a whole; in many cities the cost of a day's stay in a major hospital now approaches an astonishing $200. Physicians' fees, largely uncontrolled, are also soaring. Americans now spend an average of 10 percent of their income on medical costs, or $547 a year for each person.

Much of the increase in medical expenditures comes from rising costs rather than from more or better service to patients; indeed, the quality of health care delivery has simultaneously come under growing attack. Government agencies, Congressional committees, academic societies, and professional organizations have flooded the news with reports of such disturbing defects in the medical sphere as incompetent physicians, needless surgery, poorly tested and wrongly prescribed drugs, unsafe medical devices, and outright fraud against government-backed health care programs. And a steadily deepening public dissatisfaction with the quality of medical care has been reflected in the continuing rise of malpractice suits which, in turn, have inflated the cost of services by stimulating enormous increases in liability insurance rates and by provoking physicians to engage in more elaborate and expensive medical procedures.

Some observers have regarded the financial near breakdown as only a surface indicator of the system's deeper problem: the failure of the privately controlled and financed health service professions to assure high-quality, readily accessible care to all citizens. "Double-digit inflation is but one of several problems troubling the existing health care delivery and financing system," the Council on Wage and Price Stability stated in a report to the President. "Many of the poor, aged, and those living in rural areas still do not receive, or cannot afford, adequate medical attention. Catastrophic medical expenses continue to strike

Since 1929, when Norman Rockwell painted "Doctor and Doll" (opposite page) for a Saturday Evening Post magazine cover, the public image of the average American doctor and his duties has undergone dramatic changes. One knowledgeable observer of these changes is Jonathan Spivak (below). As a staff correspondent for the Wall Street Journal, specializing in health, education, and welfare, and as a member of the prestigious Institute of Medicine of the National Academy of Sciences, Spivak occupies a unique vantage point from which to report on the health care scene.

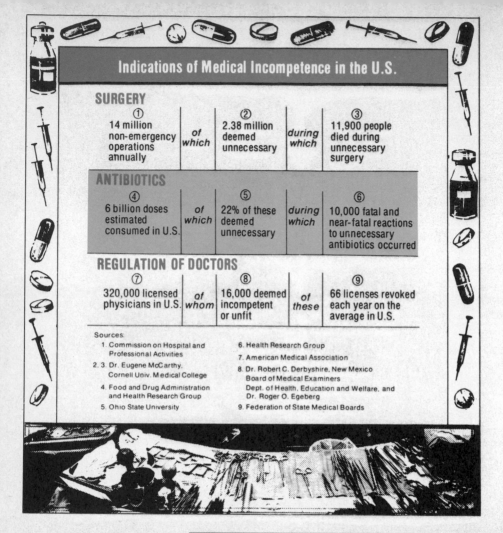

Charts published in The New York Times in January, 1976, indicate the alleged extent and effects of medical incompetence. The charts illustrated a controversial five-article series that found that some 5 percent of U.S. doctors are unfit to practice and "perhaps 30,000" people die each year through faulty drug prescriptions.

Medical Licenses Revoked in U.S., 1971-1974

(1) 320,000 licensed physicians in U.S. (2) 16,000 deemed incompetent or unfit   72 licenses revoked each year on the average in U.S.

	1971	1972	1973	1974
Alcoholism	3	0	0	0
Extreme incompetency	1	1	1	3
Narcotic violations	7	13	7	11
Obtaining license by fraud	0	0	0	1
Conviction of crime	7	4	1	9
Unprofessional conduct	10	3	6	9
Mental reasons	1	0	0	2
Allowing unlicensed persons to practice	1	0	0	0
Voluntarily surrendered license while under investigation	9	12	8	38
Reasons not given	10	14	5	14
Revocations for non-disciplinary reasons	40	30	9	1
TOTALS	**89**	**77**	**37**	**88**

(1) American Medical Association
(2) Dr. Robert C. Derbyshire, New Mexico Board of Medical Examiners
    Dr. Roger O. Egeberg. Dept. of Health, Education and Welfare
Source: Federation of State Medical Boards

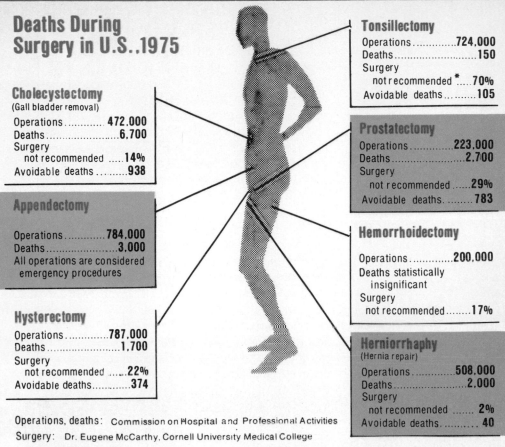

Deaths During Surgery in U.S., 1975

Tonsillectomy
Operations.............724,000
Deaths..........................150
Surgery
  not recommended *.....70%
Avoidable deaths..........105

Cholecystectomy
(Gall bladder removal)
Operations............472,000
Deaths.........................6,700
Surgery
  not recommended.....14%
Avoidable deaths.........938

Prostatectomy
Operations.............223,000
Deaths........................2,700
Surgery
  not recommended......29%
Avoidable deaths.........783

Appendectomy
Operations............784,000
Deaths........................3,000
All operations are considered
  emergency procedures

Hemorrhoidectomy
Operations.............200,000
Deaths statistically
  insignificant
Surgery
  not recommended........17%

Hysterectomy
Operations.............787,000
Deaths........................1,700
Surgery
  not recommended.....22%
Avoidable deaths.............374

Herniorrhaphy
(Hernia repair)
Operations.............508,000
Deaths........................2,000
Surgery
  not recommended.......2%
Avoidable deaths...........40

Operations, deaths: Commission on Hospital and Professional Activities

Surgery: Dr. Eugene McCarthy, Cornell University Medical College

Avoidable deaths: U.S. projections of avoidable surgical deaths based on percent of operations not
                    recommended by consultants. Cornell study and The New York Times projections.

* Estimate of various experts, not reflected in Cornell study.

Percent of Doctors Scoring 80%* or better on Test of Their Knowledge of Antibiotics

*The average score for university-affiliated doctors

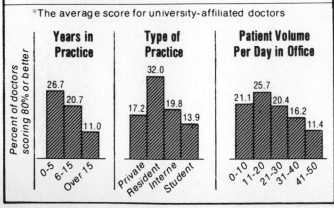

Percent of doctors scoring 80% or better

Years in Practice
26.7 | 20.7 | 11.0
0-5 | 6-15 | Over 15

Type of Practice
17.2 | 32.0 | 19.8 | 13.9
Private | Resident | Interne | Student

Patient Volume Per Day in Office
21.1 | 25.7 | 20.4 | 16.2 | 11.4
0-10 | 11-20 | 21-30 | 31-40 | 41-50

A spokesman for the American Medical Association called the conclusions of the Times articles "unjustified," and drug manufacturers contended that patients' confidence would be dangerously undermined. But many physicians praised the series, which also included a checklist of criteria for selecting a doctor.

numerous households every year, and are a constant concern for all."

Mounting attention has also been focused on the fact that contact with the American health care system has made many patients sicker than they were to begin with. Of the 35,000,000 patients hospitalized each year, an estimated 2,600,000 were held to have suffered an avoidable injury or infection during their hospital stay. It was also estimated that 10 percent of the drugs prescribed in hospitals produced serious adverse reactions. And a committee of the House of Representatives, probing the issue of surgical care, concluded that in a single year 2,400,000 unnecessary operations were performed "at a cost to the American public of almost $4 billion." The committee estimated that these unnecessary surgeries "led to 11,900 unnecessary deaths."

Leaders of the American Medical Association (A.M.A.) bitterly disputed the committee's conclusions. Dr. James H. Sammons, executive vice-president of the A.M.A., charged that the committee, headed by John Moss (D, Calif.), was deliberately biased and bent on proving that surgeons' decisions to operate were influenced by potential income. "Overwhelmingly surgeons operate—and physicians recommend operations—because they believe it is the best method of solving the patient's specific medical problems," Dr. Sammons maintained. Nevertheless, many medical experts privately endorsed the committee's findings.

Commenting on the deterioration in physician-patient relations, health experts pointed to several dramatic developments. Doctors are increasingly unavailable. Their fees are escalating. They are afraid of malpractice suits; consequently they practice "defensive" medicine, which subjects patients to unneeded, costly, and perhaps hazardous tests. (Critics

Recent scandals have focused attention on the problems of medical incompetence and inadequate policing of physicians. From top: Dr. Mario E. Jascalevich, a surgeon called "Dr. X" in early news reports, was indicted in 1976 on charges of murdering five patients in a New Jersey hospital a decade previously; Dr. Max Jacobson, who had his license revoked in 1975, allegedly prescribed the amphetamine "speed" for dozens of celebrities; Drs. Stewart (left) and Cyril Marcus, twin gynecologists on the staff of New York Hospital, died in 1975, apparently as a result of barbiturate addiction.

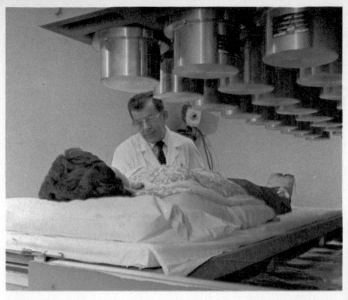

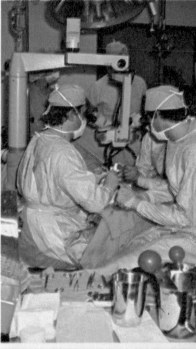

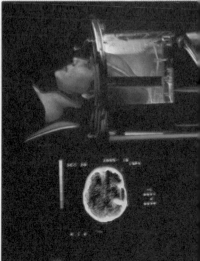

The latest technological advances in medical diagnosis and surgery, although widely publicized, are sometimes available only at a few locations and at prohibitive cost. Left: The "full body counter" at Brookhaven National Laboratory, Long Island, scans the body for differences in radiation density that might indicate diseased organs. Below: Using a microscope to magnify tiny blood vessels, surgeons at Jewish Hospital, Louisville, Ky., attach a severed finger to a patient's hand. Bottom: An X-ray scanner projects a cross-sectional picture of a patient's head on a TV screen.

charge that physicians order extra tests, frequently involving doses of radiation, only to afford themselves legal protection.) But some problems are not within the physician's control. Successful new techniques in medical science have led the public to unrealistic expectations; some patients have become convinced that no medical problem is beyond the capabilities of the profession. Sophisticated new drug and radiation therapies, complex intensive-care equipment, kidney dialysis and transplant centers, and coronary bypass surgery have all been brought within reach of a significant portion of the population. But these difficult procedures carry considerable risks. More patients than ever before are being benefited, but physicians and surgeons are also working with more severely ill patients, and as a consequence patient injuries are rising.

Malpractice claims began to climb steeply in the early 1970's. Now physicians in many states are unable to obtain insurance coverage at realistic prices. Some insurers have canceled liability coverage altogether. Physicians have staged strikes to call attention to their plight. Some have even given up private practice to join the Veterans Administration or the military services as protection against high insurance rates. Administrators of group-practice plans are finding that recruiting is easier for the same reason.

Attempts to solve the malpractice crisis fall into two broad categories: One sets limits on the current liability system; the other replaces it with a "no-fault" system that provides payment for medical injuries without attempting to determine who is to blame. Currently, most attention is directed to reforming the existing system by curbing excessive settlements and the costly defensive medical practices that result. Many states have established or are planning to establish insurance pools to make sure that coverage is available. Some have also passed laws limiting the maximum amount of malpractice settlements; but these limits, set at $500,000 in some states, have been challenged in the courts on the ground that they deprive an individual of the right of redress.

Another proposed corrective would be to limit the fees that lawyers receive—now as much as one third the amount of the settlement. Critics contend that a smaller percentage would lead to fewer suits. On the other hand, experts say that one of the glaring gaps in the system is its failure to compensate for minor injuries. They recommend the establishment of arbitration courts to handle small claims that malpractice attorneys find uneconomical to pursue.

Medical experts are becoming increasingly attracted to the concept of an indemnity system, like workmen's compensation insurance, that would provide a set payment for any medical injury. There would be no trial and no attempt to determine whether the physician was at fault or had failed to meet the prevailing standards of medical care. Instead, any person who suffered harm from contact with the medical care system would be compensated.

The difficulty, of course, is in establishing this payment schedule. Should it be a fixed amount according to injury, or should it vary according to the impact of the injury on the individual's future earnings? What allowance should be made for the normal hazards of a surgical procedure and for the age and medical condition of the patient? And, most problematic of all, who would pay? The cost could run into billions of dollars a year.

Malpractice problems have also become increasingly severe for hospitals. Judgments have been large, particularly for incidents arising in emergency rooms. In many areas of the country, hospitals have been reducing and even eliminating their emergency-room coverage, much to the dismay of the surrounding communities. Hospital administrators defend the practice by pointing to their urgent need to reduce malpractice insurance costs, which now average as much as $15 a day for each patient.

Hospitals are also adopting positive protection programs to increase their efficiency and reduce their vulnerability to suit. These range from simple safety checks, such as ensuring that bed rails are raised around weak and disabled patients, to the special training of cardiac-arrest teams. Some hospital experts argue that good relations with patients is the key to holding down malpractice suits, and several hospitals are concentrating their efforts in this area. At Baylor University Medical Center in Dallas, Texas, patients are immediately informed of mistakes and prompt corrective action is taken wherever needed. By

Socialized medical systems reduce costs, often at the expense of individualized care. Clockwise from upper left: A British doctor writes a National Health Service prescription for a patient; a British district nurse makes a home visit; a dental clinic in Wellington, New Zealand; a publicly run school for the handicapped outside Stockholm, Sweden; and a home for chronically sick elderly people in Sweden, where care for the aged is free.

In its heyday in the 1930's and 1940's, Hollywood found that films about doctors were good business. Right: Jean Hersholt, behind his desk on the set of Five of a Kind, a 1935 movie in which he played the kindly doctor who delivered the world-famous Dionne quintuplets.

Below: While Jean Hersholt was appearing as the all-wise Dr. Dafoe, Lionel Barrymore (left) could be seen as Dr. Gillespie, dispensing wisdom to Lew Ayres (right), who played an intense young intern in the Dr. Kildare series.

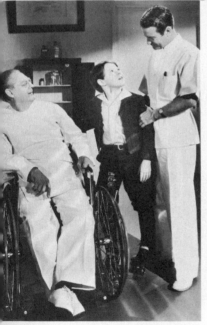

diligently pursuing this policy for the past several years, the hospital has been able to avoid costly suits, paying only minor amounts in claims, while other hospitals' payments have climbed steeply. But such attempts at greater efficiency and cost reduction unfortunately require additional staff time, and the accelerating cost of hospital labor already constitutes 70 percent of hospital operating expenses. Traditionally low-paid hospital workers—aides, orderlies, kitchen and maintenance staffs—have been gaining large wage increases through union activity, a result of hospitals having recently been made subject to the collective bargaining procedures of the National Labor Relations Act. As their earnings rise, more highly skilled personnel have been demanding and gaining proportional increases. Add to all this the costs of increasingly more complex equipment and procedures, with their potentially higher accident risks, and prospects are not too likely for halting the rise in hospital bills.

During 1976 the federal government and its agencies became deeply embroiled in the malpractice problem. First, the national swine flu immunization program was delayed because of the unwillingness of insurance firms to provide liability coverage to the producers of swine flu vaccine. Public dispensers of the vaccine were also affected; county health officials in California reported rates of more than $1 per vaccination for malpractice protection. As public health officials and drug companies turned to the government for help, members of Congress voiced suspicion that the companies were seeking to avoid their responsibilities.

An impasse developed that was broken only by the outbreak of the so-called Legionnaires disease in July. The symptoms of the malady initially appeared to resemble swine flu. The Administration came up with a solution: Include the national swine flu program in an existing statute that permits the government to be sued for errors committed by its employees. Congress agreed, stipulating that the government could in turn sue the pharmaceutical companies for any proved negligence on their part.

The ability of the Food and Drug Administration (F.D.A.) to protect patients against unsafe drugs and devices was also reexamined during 1976. The F.D.A. launched an investigation into the adequacy of the animal tests relied on by one manufacturer, resulting in agency orders that warning labels had to be displayed on two widely sold drugs. The agency also barred a new sweetener from being placed on the market. It then received a special appropriation from Congress to begin a broad examination of testing practices throughout the industry. A similar crisis arose over the safety of medical devices permitted on the market without government approval. Investigations by the General Accounting Office revealed that thousands of heart pacemakers were subject to failure because of moisture penetrating their circuitry. Evidence of other faulty devices was also accumulated. A law enacted in the spring of 1976 gave the F.D.A. power to set testing standards for medical devices and to keep off the market those that fail to measure up.

The toughest part of the health care system to bring under control has been the Medicare and Medicaid programs. Begun in 1966, these programs represented the first large-scale attempt to distribute medical services more equitably by extending to aged and

Above: For many years TV, too, profited from series about the medical profession. On the small screen, Raymond Massey (right) was Dr. Gillespie to Richard Chamberlain's Dr. Kildare.

Left: One of the last doctor series to be telecast during the cynical 1970's was "Marcus Welby." It starred Robert Young (right) in the omniscient title role, with James Brolin as his not-always-wise young apprentice.

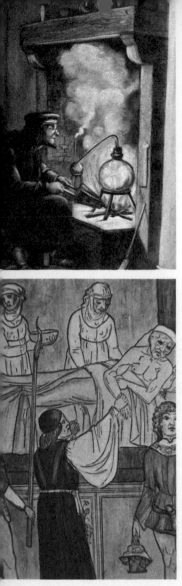

needy citizens, formerly dependent on free clinics and charity wards, full access to private physicians, hospitals, and nursing homes. Medicare, which is funded through Social Security payroll taxes, covers most of the medical costs of those over 65 and the disabled. Medicaid, administered by the states and funded through state and local welfare funds (50 to 73 percent of which is reimbursed by the federal government), covers medical costs of the poor, some of whom are also eligible for Medicare coverage. Now serving an estimated 30,000,000 people, the programs have become far more costly than anyone had envisaged. Under Medicare, physicians' and hospital fees jumped 25 percent in the first year of operation and have gone on climbing ever since. Federal costs for 1977 are budgeted at an astronomical $39.9 billion. The problem of cost regulation has become so alarming that many federal and state officials are recommending that health care for the poor be removed from the free market, in which the provider decides what the costs will be; these officials want the fees regulated like those of the public utilities.

The programs have also proved to be expensive to administer. Governor George Busbee of Georgia complained in his recent Congressional testimony that "The present Medicaid program is the most complex, confusing, duplicative, and administratively wasteful system ever conceived by man—one that will surely bankrupt the states and the federal treasury unless substantial reforms are undertaken."

Worst of all, Medicare and Medicaid have been subject to abuse by unscrupulous doctors, nursing homes, and other health care providers. By such

Through the ages physicians have been honored and feared as persons with special, even occult, powers. Top: The legendary Dr. Faust, in a 19th-century illustration, probes the secrets of life and death. Above: A 15th-century Venetian illustration shows a doctor at a sickbed holding a sponge in front of his nose to protect himself from infection. Right: A barber-surgeon, for centuries the average man's doctor, is shown operating on a peasant's head in this mid-17th-century Flemish painting.

means as increasing the frequency of visits and referrals among themselves, "treating" nonexistent diseases, prescribing unneeded drugs and therapies, and directly inflating or falsifying bills, these "Medicaid mills," as they have come to be called, have realized greatly swollen profits for themselves at the expense of the poor and at a loss to the federal, state, and local governments of perhaps $1.5 billion. Debt-ridden New York City alone has lost at least $340,000,000 to fraud and abuse.

The Medicaid scandals had a sobering effect on Congress, long engaged in a debate over extending medical insurance coverage to the entire population as a public right, like free education. Most other nations have adopted some form of universal coverage, but even the strongest supporters of a health insurance plan in the U.S. recognize the strong sentiment in this country against massive new federal outlays. Senator Herman E. Talmadge (D, Ga.) has been among those taking the lead in proposing legislation to deal with the cost problem before new benefits are extended to the public. His key reform: Hospital budgets would be established by the government a year ahead of time and the institutions would be required to live within these limits. Hospitals would be classified by size and type of service and subjected to performance comparison; those that proved most efficient would be allowed to keep some of their savings. Wilbur Cohen, former U.S. Secretary of Health, Education, and Welfare, has outlined a step-by-step plan that has many supporters. The Cohen plan would begin by covering the cost of catastrophic medical expenses and the health care needs of children. Then, as

Folk medicine still thrives in many parts of the world, often in combination with or in preference to scientific medicine. Top: a medicine man at work in a village of central Africa. Above: a shaman of the Huichol tribe in Mexico treating a patient. Left: Charts show points for insertion of needles in acupuncture; this ancient technique for killing pain and treating disease is still widely practiced in China.

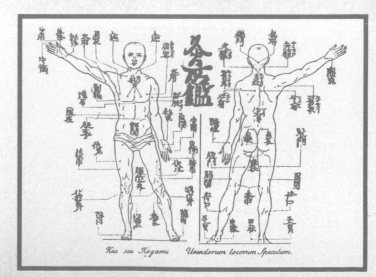

Kiu siu Kagami   Urondorum locorum Speculum.

administrative kinks are eliminated, cost controls are intensified, and the supply of doctors is increased, the national scheme would be expanded to cover almost all types of medical expenses for everyone. Political experts on Capitol Hill believe that cost controls and a comprehensive national medical plan will eventually be made compatible. The resultant program should have three components: vigorous restraints on the freedom of physicians and hospitals to raise charges faster than the general increase in consumer prices; government assurance that no American family would be made destitute by the costs of catastrophically expensive health care; and a new federally subsidized health insurance plan for the poor, replacing the Medicaid program. The major uncertainty is whether private health insurers would be allowed to administer the comprehensive program or whether it would be taken over by the government itself.

Adoption of a national health insurance plan is probably the most emotional issue remaining on the nation's agenda of domestic reform. Ideological disputes are still raging among liberals and conservatives, the A.M.A., private insurers, unions, and consumer groups. But a new willingness by all parties to compromise in the face of the impending crisis has left many observers hopeful. Perhaps the lawmakers in Washington are finally preparing to come to grips with the most urgent of the nation's health care problems.

Legislators, concerned about the quality and cost of the health care received by their constituents, are devoting more and more time and energy to the conduct of official investigations. And such investigative bodies as the Subcommittee on Long-Term Care of the U.S. Senate Special Committee on Aging (below) are getting more and more attention from the news media.

1977 YEARBOOK

EVENTS OF 1976

CHRONOLOGY FOR 1976

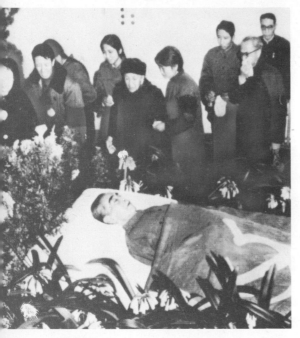

JAN. 8
FEB. 4

JANUARY

1 • A Lebanese jetliner crashes in the Saudi Arabian desert; all 82 persons aboard die.

8 • Chou En-lai, premier of the People's Republic of China, dies in Peking at 78.

15 • A federal judge in California sentences Sara Jane Moore to life imprisonment. She had been convicted of attempting to assassinate the President of the United States, Gerald R. Ford, in San Francisco on Sept. 22, 1975.

22 • A political and military agreement is announced in Beirut, apparently ending Lebanon's nine-month-old civil war. (Within two months full-scale warfare was again under way.)

30 • The U.S. Supreme Court, ruling on the Federal Election Campaign Act of 1974, upholds public financing of Presidential campaigns and limits on individual contributions to candidates for federal office.

FEBRUARY

2 • Daniel P. Moynihan's resignation as chief U.S. representative at the United Nations is announced. (Moynihan's resignation took effect Feb. 29.)

4 • An earthquake in Guatemala claims the lives of 22,934 persons; more than 1,000,000 are left homeless.
 • The twelfth Winter Olympic Games open in Innsbruck, Austria. (The games ended Feb. 15.)

7 • A dispatch by Hsinhua, the official news agency of the People's Republic of China, discloses that Hua Kuo-feng is serving as acting premier.

11 • The Organization of African Unity formally recognizes the Soviet-backed People's Republic of Angola, as forces of two dissident Angolan factions retreat into guerrilla warfare.

Daniel J. Haughton and A. Carl Kotchian re- • 13
sign as chief officers of the Lockheed Aircraft
Corp. (On Feb. 4 a Senate subcommittee had
revealed that Lockheed had made illegal payments to its agents in several foreign nations.)
Murtala Ramat Muhammed, Nigeria's head of •
state, is assassinated during an unsuccessful
coup. The next day Lt. Gen. Olusegun Obasanjo was appointed to succeed Muhammed.

U.S. Secretary of State Henry A. Kissinger visits • 16–24
six Latin American nations. In Costa Rica on
Feb. 24 he conferred with the foreign ministers
of five additional nations.

President Ford announces a reorganization of • 17
U.S. intelligence agencies, giving added management authority to the director of the Central Intelligence Agency.

Former U.S. President Richard M. Nixon and • 21–29
his wife visit the People's Republic of China.

FEB. 21

The U.S. Senate votes to grant commonwealth • 24
status to the northern Mariana Islands, a part
of the U.S.–administered Trust Territory of the
Pacific Islands. (The House had voted approval
in 1975.)

Spain withdraws the last of its official repre- • 26
sentatives in its erstwhile colony of Spanish
Sahara. At the same time, the Saharan assembly ratified the division of the territory into
two parts, annexed by Morocco and Mauritania.
Political and military leaders sign an agree- •
ment in Lisbon paving the way for an end to
military rule in Portugal and the establishment
of a parliamentary democracy there.

MARCH 20

MARCH

Former Gov. William W. Scranton of Pennsyl- • 3
vania is confirmed as U.S. ambassador to the
U.N.

Harold Wilson, leader of the Labour Party of • 16
Great Britain, announces his resignation as
prime minister.

The Thai government orders the U.S. to re- • 20
move almost all its military personnel from
Thailand by July 1.
A federal jury in California convicts newspaper •
heiress Patricia Hearst for armed robbery. (See
Sept. 24; Nov. 19.)

MARCH 24

24 ● President Isabel Martínez de Perón of Argentina is deposed; a three-man military junta led by Lt. Gen. Jorge Rafael Videla takes over the Argentine government.

APRIL

4 ● Prime Minister Kukrit Pramoj of Thailand loses his seat in parliamentary elections. (On April 24 he was succeeded as prime minister by his brother, Seni Pramoj.)

5 ● An estimated 30,000 Chinese take part in violent demonstrations in Peking's Tien An Men Square. (On April 7 it was announced that Hua Kuo-feng had been named premier and that Deputy Premier Teng Hsiao-ping had been deposed.)

● James Callaghan is elected prime minister of Great Britain and head of the British Labour Party.

19 ● The U.S. Department of Commerce reports that the real gross national product rose at an annual rate of 7.5 percent during the first three months of 1976.

25 ● The first free parliamentary elections held in Portugal in fifty years prove inconclusive. The Socialists won 35 percent of the vote; the Popular Democrats, 24 percent; the Social Democratic Center, 16 percent; and the Communists, 14.5 percent.

28 ● The Senate Select Committee on Intelligence issues a report of its fifteen-month investigation of domestic spying by government agencies.

MAY

6 ● Secretary of State Henry A. Kissinger ends a two-week trip to six African nations with an address before the U.N. Conference on Trade and Development in Nairobi, Kenya.

● More than 900 persons die in a major earthquake in northeastern Italy.

8 ● A 39-day strike by 1770 municipal craft workers in San Francisco ends. During the work stoppage the city's public transportation system had been shut down.

● Elias Sarkis, a conservative Christian, is elected president of Lebanon as the civil war continues. (See Sept. 23.)

MAY 6

Jeremy Thorpe resigns as head of Great Brit- • **10** ain's Liberal Party. Recent allegations of his having had a homosexual relationship in the 1960's had aroused public controversy. (Two days later Jo Grimond became interim leader of the party.)

A severe earthquake strikes a largely desert re- • **17** gion of Soviet Central Asia; casualties are few.

An Ethiopian army of 25,000 peasants begins • **22** forays against a secessionist guerrilla movement in Eritrea Province. (On June 19 the government halted the peasant advance when negotiations with the guerrillas showed signs of success.)

At Zamboanga airport a Philippine Air Lines jet • **23** explodes during a gun battle between the plane's Muslim-separatist hijackers and Philippine troops. Three of 6 hijackers and 10 of 89 remaining hostages were killed.

Two British-French Concorde jetliners arrive at • **24** Dulles International Airport, outside Washington, D.C., as limited supersonic commercial passenger service between the U.S. and Europe begins.

An estimated 2000 Syrian troops move into • **31** Lebanon to intervene in the civil war there.

JUNE

The U.S. Department of Labor announces that • **4** the national unemployment rate in May was 7.3 percent; this is the lowest figure since December, 1974. (The unemployment rate increased later in the year, however, reaching 8.1 percent in November.)

JUNE 5

JUNE 16

JUNE 20

5 ● Rep. Carl Albert (D, Okla.), Speaker of the House since 1971, joins Senate majority leader Mike Mansfield (D, Mont.) and Senate minority leader Hugh D. Scott (R, Pa.) in announcing plans to retire in January, 1977.
  ● A recently completed dam on the Teton R. in eastern Idaho bursts. Resultant floods killed 14 persons and left 40,000 people homeless.

9 ● In Madrid the Spanish parliament approves a bill legalizing the existence of some political parties in addition to the rightist National Movement.

11 ● The twelve-day U.N. Conference on Human Settlement ends in Vancouver, British Columbia. The 450 delegates from 131 countries approved more than 100 measures, including a declaration calling for restrictions on the private ownership of land.

15 ● Charles O. Finley, owner of the Oakland A's baseball team, sells three star players: Vida Blue (to the New York Yankees for $1,500,000) and Joe Rudi and Rollie Fingers (to the Boston Red Sox for $1,000,000 each). Three days later Commissioner Bowie Kuhn nullified the sales.

16 ● U.S. ambassador to Lebanon Francis E. Meloy, Jr., his economic counselor, and their Lebanese chauffeur are kidnapped and murdered in Beirut.
  ● In Soweto, a black township near Johannesburg, South Africa, a peaceful student protest escalates into violent clashes with government forces. (The disorder spread to other black townships, leaving an estimated 176 persons—almost all Blacks—dead.)

19 ● In Stockholm's Saint Nicholas Church, King Charles XVI Gustavus of Sweden, 30, marries a 32-year-old West German commoner, Silvia Renate Sommerlath.

20 ● The U.S. Navy evacuates 110 Americans and 166 other foreign nationals from Beirut, Lebanon. (See July 27.)

20-21 ● Italian parliamentary elections are held, with no party gaining a majority in the 630-member Chamber of Deputies. Communists won 228 seats, a gain of 49; Christian Democrats won 263, a loss of 3.

26 ● Indonesia's Irian Jaya Province (on western New Guinea) is struck by a major earthquake. It left about 3500 persons dead.

Gen. António Ramalho Eanes is elected pres- •**27**
ident of Portugal.

At Dorado Beach, Puerto Rico, President Ford •**27–28**
and the leaders of Canada, France, Great Britain, Italy, Japan, and West Germany hold an
economic summit meeting. They announced
their determination to stimulate economic expansion without inducing a new wave of inflation.

Seychelles, eighty-six islands in the Indian •**28**
Ocean, become an independent republic (and
a member of the Commonwealth of Nations)
after 182 years of British rule.

A long-delayed conference of European Com- •**29–30**
munist leaders is held in East Berlin. The
twenty-nine leaders taking part issued a document calling for the autonomy of each national Communist Party.

JULY

The Socialist Republic of Vietnam is pro- •**2**
claimed. Hanoi was named the capital of the
new nation, which reunited the former countries of North Vietnam and South Vietnam.

King Juan Carlos I of Spain names Adolfo Suá- •**3**
rez González to succeed Carlos Arias Navarro
as premier. Arias had been dismissed on July 1.
Israeli commandos in three airplanes land at •
Entebbe airport, Uganda, and forcibly free 103
hostages. The hostages were among the more
than 250 passengers on an Air France jet that
had been hijacked June 27 by pro-Palestinian
guerrillas.

The U.S. celebrates the Bicentennial of the •**4**
signing of its Declaration of Independence.

JULY 12

JULY 17
JULY 31

- José López Portillo is elected president of Mexico.

12-15 • The national convention of the Democratic Party is held in New York City; former Gov. Jimmy Carter of Georgia and Sen. Walter F. Mondale of Minnesota are nominated for President and Vice-President, respectively.

14 • An earthquake kills more than 500 people in northern Bali, Indonesia.

17 • Twenty-six schoolchildren, kidnapped in their school bus 36 hr. earlier, are reunited with their families in Chowchilla, Calif. (Three men were charged with the crime: Richard Schoenfeld, who turned himself in July 23, and James Schoenfeld and Fredrick Woods, arrested July 29.)
   • The twenty-first modern Summer Olympics open in Montréal, Canada. Taiwan, denied permission to compete as the Republic of China, withdrew from the games July 16. In a separate protest, thirty-one other nations, mostly African, withdrew later. (The games ended Aug. 1.)

20 • The Viking I landing vehicle makes a successful touchdown on Mars. Soon after, it began transmitting photographs of the planet back to earth.

21 • Christopher T. E. Ewart-Biggs, British ambassador to Ireland, is killed near his residence outside Dublin when a land mine is detonated under his car.

27 • Former Prime Minister Kakuei Tanaka of Japan is arrested for allegedly having accepted illegally imported money from a Japanese agent of the U.S. Lockheed Aircraft Corp. (On Aug. 16 Tanaka was formally indicted on charges that he received $1,600,000 to influence All-Nippon Airways to purchase Lockheed aircraft.)
   • In a second major maneuver (see June 20), the U.S. Navy evacuates 160 Americans and 148 other foreigners from Beirut, Lebanon.

28 • The first of a series of earthquakes strikes Tangshan and other cities of northeastern China. (In 1977 it was reported that 655,237 people were killed and approximately 700,000 were injured in these quakes.)

31 • A flash flood in the Big Thompson R. canyon in northern Colorado causes 139 deaths.

AUG. 16

Clarence M. Kelley, director of the Federal Bureau of Investigation, announces plans for an extensive reorganization of the bureau. The action followed criticism by Congress and private citizens of illegal and abusive domestic intelligence activities by F.B.I. agents. • 11

After a night of violence, Detroit officials declare a 10 P.M. curfew for all persons under 18. • 16

The national convention of the Republican Party is held in Kansas City, Mo.; President Ford and Sen. Robert J. Dole of Kansas are chosen as the party's candidates for President and Vice-President, respectively. • 16–19

AUG. 18

In Colombo, Ceylon (Sri Lanka), representatives of 84 so-called nonaligned nations meet to discuss their mutual problems. • 16–20

An earthquake and resulting tidal wave strike Mindanao and other nearby islands in the southern Philippines, leaving an estimated 8000 dead. • 17

At the P'anmunjŏm truce site in Korea, North Korean soldiers attack a tree-pruning detail of U.S. and South Korean troops, killing two American officers. • 18

An emergency session of the British cabinet is held to discuss the country's worst recorded drought. Britons were asked to lower their daily consumption of water by 50 percent. • 24

AUG. 30

SEPT. 3

SEPT. 9

領袖和导师毛泽东主席永垂不

25 ● President Valéry Giscard d'Estaing of France names Foreign Trade Minister Raymond Barre, an independent, to replace Jacques Chirac as premier. Chirac, a Gaullist, had resigned a few hours earlier.

26 ● The deaths of two persons who attended the International Eucharistic Congress in Philadelphia earlier in the month are announced. This brought to 28 the number of fatalities attributed to the mysterious Legionnaires disease. (An additional person was later listed as having succumbed to the illness.)
 ● Prince Bernhard of the Netherlands resigns almost all his military and business posts, following criticism by a Dutch government commission of his relationship with the Lockheed Aircraft Corp.

30 ● La Soufrière, a volcano on the Caribbean island of Guadeloupe, explodes; three scientists are injured. Two weeks earlier, 72,000 local residents had been evacuated.

31 ● In Los Angeles William and Emily Harris are sentenced to prison for eleven years to life. On Aug. 9 the Harrises, members of the Symbionese Liberation Army, had been convicted of armed robbery, kidnapping, and auto theft.

SEPTEMBER

1 ● Rep. Wayne L. Hays (D, Ohio) resigns his seat in the House, effective immediately. Hays, chairman of a powerful Congressional committee, had been involved in a sex and payroll scandal.

3 ● At 6:38 P.M. Eastern Daylight Time the Viking II lander sets down safely on Mars.

6 ● Seeking asylum in the U.S., Lt. Viktor I. Belenko of the U.S.S.R. lands at Hakodate airport, Hokkaido, Japan, in a MIG-25, one of the Soviet Union's most advanced jet fighters. On Sept. 7 Lt. Belenko was granted asylum; he arrived in the U.S. on Sept. 9.

9 ● Mao Tse-tung, chairman of the Chinese Communist Party, dies in Peking at 82.

10 ● Two jetliners, a British Airways Trident and a chartered Yugoslav DC-9, collide in the air near Zagreb, Yugoslavia; all 176 passengers and crew members are killed.

Four men and a woman arrive in police cus- ● 12
tody at Kennedy International Airport, New
York City, to face charges of murder and air
piracy. The five, advocates of independence
for Croatia (a part of Yugoslavia), had hijacked
a TWA jetliner bound from New York to Chicago on Sept. 10; the plane eventually was
flown to Paris. Meanwhile, on Sept. 11, a New
York City policeman was killed when a bomb
left by the hijackers exploded as he attempted
to deactivate it.

A strike by the United Automobile Workers ● 14
against the Ford Motor Co. begins at midnight.
(The walkout ended after the 170,000 striking
Ford workers ratified a new three-year nationwide contract on Oct. 12.)

In Philadelphia, President Ford and Jimmy Car- ● 23
ter, respectively the Republican and Democratic Presidential candidates, engage in the
first of three scheduled debates. (The second
and third debates were held Oct. 6 and 22.)
Elias Sarkis is inaugurated president of Leba- ●
non in the Syrian-held town of Chtaura.

Newspaper heiress Patricia Hearst is sentenced ● 24
to concurrent terms of 7 years for armed robbery and 2 years for using a firearm while committing a felony.
Prime Minister Ian D. Smith of Rhodesia an- ●
nounces his acceptance of a plan calling for a
temporary biracial government for his country,
to be succeeded within two years by a black-
majority regime.

OCTOBER

The federal government's swine flu inocula- ● 1
tion program begins.

West German voters return Chancellor Helmut ● 3
Schmidt's Social Democratic Party to power,
but with only a shaky 8-seat majority for his
coalition government in the lower house. (Parliament reelected Schmidt as chancellor on
Dec. 15.)

Earl L. Butz, under fire because of what he ● 4
terms "a bad racial commentary," resigns as
U.S. secretary of agriculture.

In Federal District Court, Richmond, Va., the ● 5
Allied Chemical Corp. is fined $13,375,000 for
polluting the James R. with Kepone, a highly
toxic insecticide.

SEPT. 14

OCT. 1

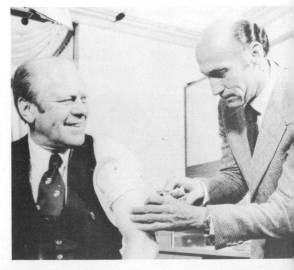

59

OCT. 6

OCT. 28

6 • After a series of bloody riots between Thai students and police, Defense Minister Adm. Sangad Chaloryu announces that Thailand will henceforth be ruled by a military Administrative Reform Committee.

12 • In Peking an official spokesman confirms the appointment of Premier Hua Kuo-feng as chairman of the Chinese Communist Party. He was also named chairman of the powerful Military Affairs Commission.

15 • Senators Walter F. Mondale (D, Minn.) and Robert J. Dole (R, Kans.) participate in the first debate by Vice-Presidential candidates, telecast nationally from the Alley Theater in Houston, Texas.
  • The Center for Disease Control, a federal agency, announces that no evidence was found linking the deaths of 35 inoculated individuals with the swine flu vaccine. (See Dec. 16.)

21 • The 1976 Nobel Prize in literature is awarded to the novelist Saul Bellow. Thus for the first time since the prizes were established citizens of one nation (the U.S.) won all Nobel awards. No Peace Prize was awarded.

22 • Hsinhua, the official Communist Chinese press agency, announces that the Central Committee of the Communist Party, under the leadership of Chairman Hua Kuo-feng, has shattered an attempted rebellion. Four leftists, including Chiang Ch'ing, the widow of Mao Tse-tung, were named as leaders of the revolt.

26 • The Republic of Transkei is proclaimed. The first of a series of independent black homelands to be carved out of the Republic of South Africa, it was recognized by no other country.
  • A two-day conference of 14 heads of state and other leaders of the 21 members of the Arab League ends in Cairo. They approved the general proposals for peace in Lebanon that were agreed to at a previous meeting of six Arab leaders (held in Riyadh, Saudi Arabia, Oct. 17–18).

28 • In Geneva a conference on the political future of Rhodesia opens under the chairmanship of Ivor Richard, a British diplomat. In attendance were Rhodesian Prime Minister Ian D. Smith and four black nationalist leaders: Robert Mugabe, Abel Muzorewa, Joshua Nkomo, and Ndabaningi Sithole.

NOVEMBER

Former Gov. Jimmy Carter of Georgia, the ● 2
Democratic Party candidate, is elected President of the U.S. with 50 percent of the vote.
President Ford, the Republican, won 48 percent; independent candidate Eugene J. McCarthy, 1 percent; and other candidates shared the
final 1 percent.

Syrian tanks and combat troops peacefully en- ● 10
ter Beirut, beginning the final phase of the
Arab League-approved pacification of Lebanon. (The occupation of Beirut was completed
Nov. 15; the civil war ostensibly ended.)

Japan began loading for return to the U.S.S.R. a ● 12
MIG-25 jet fighter flown to Hakodate airport
Sept. 6 by a Soviet pilot defecting to the U.S.

The Parti Québécois, which favors separation ● 15
of the province of Québec from Canada, wins
a majority of seats in the provincial legislature.

Newspaper heiress Patricia Hearst is released ● 19
in the custody of her parents upon the posting
of $1,500,000 in bail.

A major earthquake strikes eastern Turkey. Es- ■ 24
timates of the number dead ran to more than
4000.

The three largest U.S. steel corporations— ● 29
United States, Bethlehem, and Republic—announce a 6 percent increase in the price of
their products.

DECEMBER

José López Portillo is sworn in as president of ● 1
Mexico.

President-elect Jimmy Carter announces his ● 3
choice of Cyrus R. Vance, an experienced diplomat, to be U.S. secretary of state.

In a remarkable setback, the Liberal-Demo- ● 5
cratic Party of Japan wins only 48.7 percent of
the vote in national elections.

Democratic members of the House of Repre- ● 6
sentatives elect Thomas P. O'Neill, Jr., of Massachusetts as Speaker of the House and James
C. Wright, Jr., of Texas as majority leader of the

NOV. 2

DEC. 1

DEC. 8

DEC. 15

DEC. 21

95th Congress, scheduled to convene Jan. 4, 1977.

8 • Kurt Waldheim of Austria is elected to a second five-year term as secretary-general of the U.N.

14 • The conference on the future government of Rhodesia adjourns in Geneva. It was scheduled to reconvene in January, 1977.

15 • In Provo, Utah, Gary Mark Gilmore is sentenced to be executed by a firing squad on Jan. 17, 1977. (No condemned criminal had been executed in the U.S. since 1967.)

16 • Suspension of the federal swine flu immunization program is ordered because of a possible link between the vaccine and 94 cases of paralysis.
• The 13 members of OPEC announce a compromise agreement on oil-price increases. Saudi Arabia and the Union of Arab Emirates agreed to increase prices by 5 percent; the other countries agreed to a 10 percent increase to be followed after July 1, 1977, by an additional 5 percent increase.

20 • Prime Minister Itzhak Rabin of Israel resigns and dissolves parliament. Rabin also called for national elections to be held in May or June, 1977.

21 • The *Argo Merchant,* a Liberian tanker, after running aground on Dec. 15, splits in half off Nantucket Island, spilling approximately 7,500,000 gal. of crude oil into the Atlantic Ocean.

24 • Takeo Fukuda, a Liberal-Democratic Party leader, is elected prime minister of Japan.

A

ACCIDENTS AND DISASTERS. The National Safety Council (N.S.C.) estimated in December, 1976, that 67,800 Americans had died in accidents during the first eight months of the year, a decrease of 1600 from the same period in 1975. According to the N.S.C., accidents at home had resulted in 16,700 deaths (compared to 17,500 during January–August, 1975); in public places, 15,200 (16,000); at places of work, 8100 (8500); and in motor vehicle traffic, 30,420 (30,100). As in 1975, motor vehicle fatalities for the eight months were slightly higher than in the previous year, but remained far below the 37,013 deaths recorded in 1973. The relatively low level of fatalities was attributed by experts mainly to the reduced speed limits enacted as a result of the energy crisis of 1973–74 and to improvements in the nation's highway system.

The N.S.C. calculated that the total cost of the accidents that occurred in 1975 was approximately $46.2 billion (an increase of about $2.9 billion over 1974). Among the major categories of costs were lost wages because of personal injuries, $14 billion; insurance settlements and administrative charges, $8.1 billion; damages to motor vehicles, $6.9 billion; medical expenses, $6.1 billion; and property losses in fires, $4.1 billion.

Major Events. The following were among the notable accidents and disasters of 1976.

Jan. 1, Saudi Arabia: All 82 persons aboard a Middle East Airlines Boeing 707 perish when the aircraft crashes in a desert region.

Jan. 10, Nebraska: Eighteen people are killed and 60 injured by an explosion and resulting fire in the Pathfinder Hotel in Fremont.

Jan. 30, Chicago: A fire in the Wincrest Manor Nursing and Rest Home takes the lives of 18 elderly residents.

Feb. 4, Guatemala: A major earthquake centered near Guatemala City, plus aftershocks in the following 5 days, kill an estimated 22,934 persons and leave more than 1,000,000 people homeless.

March 9, Italy: In Europe's worst ski-lift disaster to date, 42 of 43 persons inside a cable car are killed when the conveyance falls into a ravine at Cavalese in the Dolomite Alps.

March 9 and 11, Kentucky: Fifteen miners are killed March 9 by a methane explosion in a coal mine in Oven Fork; a second methane blast in the same mine on March 11 takes the lives of 8 miners and 3 federal inspectors.

April 13, Finland: Forty-five workers are killed and 70 injured when a gunpowder explosion destroys an arms factory at Lapua (near Vaasa).

May 6, Italy: In the Friuli Region a severe earthquake, plus aftershocks in the next 5 days, kill about 920 persons, injure thousands more, and leave more than 200,000 people homeless.

May 21, California: Twenty-eight members of the Yuba City High School choir die and 20 persons are seriously injured when their bus plunges 30 ft. after smashing through a guardrail of a ramp of the Martinez-Benecia Bridge over San Francisco Bay.

May 20-23, Philippines: Rains caused by Typhoon Olga produce floods that take about 215 lives, render approximately 630,000 people homeless, and extensively damage rice crops.

June 5, Idaho: The collapse of the Teton R. Dam results in the flooding of 180 sq.mi. of land during the following 2 days. Fourteen persons are killed, and losses of about $400,000,000 are reported as 4000 homes and businesses and 50,000 acres of farmland are affected.

June 26, Indonesia: The worst earthquake in the country's history, plus consequent mud slides, devastate part of Irian Jaya Province (western New Guinea), destroying 20 communities and causing an estimated 3500 deaths.

July 14, Indonesia: A relatively mild earthquake shakes the northern tip of heavily populated Bali, killing more than 500 persons.

July 28, China: Two severe earthquakes strike Tangshan and other densely populated areas in the north. (January, 1977, reports showed 655,327 people dead and 700,000 injured.)

July 31, Colorado: Heavy rains and a resulting flash flood in the Big Thompson R. canyon cause 139 deaths and much damage.

Aug. 17, Philippines: Southern Mindanao and nearby islands are devastated by an earthquake and subsequent tidal wave; an estimated 8000 persons die, and damage is put at over $130,000,000.

Sept. 8-13, Japan: Typhoon Fran batters the southern part of the country with 100-m.p.h. winds and up to 5 ft. of rainfall. About 150 persons are killed, and more than 320,000 people are left homeless.

Sept. 10, Yugoslavia: In the worst midair collision on record, 176 persons are killed when a British Airways Trident collides with a Yugoslav DC-9 charter jet near Zagreb.

Only the capsized hull of the George Prince remains above water on Oct. 20 as rescue teams search for the ferryboat's passengers. The craft sank after colliding with a tanker on the Mississippi River near Luling, La.; some twenty survivors were pulled from the water.

Sept. 13, Pakistan: At least 140 people are killed when a six-story apartment building collapses in Karachi.

Sept. 19, Turkey: All 155 persons aboard a Turkish Airlines jet are killed when the craft crashes into a mountain near İsparta.

Oct. 1, Mexico: Strong winds and heavy rains accompanying Hurricane Liza destroy a dam on the Cajoncito R. at La Paz; resulting floods kill at least 630 persons.

Oct. 13, Bolivia: More than 100 people, most of them children, perish when a cargo jet crashes into a schoolyard at Santa Cruz.

Oct. 20, Louisiana: The ferryboat *George Prince,* crossing the Mississippi R. from Destrehan to Luling, capsizes and sinks after colliding with the Norwegian tanker *Frosta;* at least 78 persons aboard the ferry are killed.

Oct. 24, New York City: Twenty-five persons attending a function at a Bronx social club die when an early morning fire destroys the second-floor establishment.

Nov. 24, Turkey: A severe earthquake in Van Province near Mt. Ararat levels about 134 communities and causes more than 4000 deaths. Approximately 250,000 persons are left homeless.

Dec. 15, Atlantic Ocean: The Liberian tanker *Argo Merchant* runs aground near Nantucket Island, Mass., and its cargo of 7,500,000 gal. of fuel oil begins to leak into the ocean, threatening an important nearby fishing area. (After the vessel split in half on Dec. 21 the remaining oil, about 5,000,000 gal., spilled into the sea.)

Dec. 21, France: Seventeen handicapped children are killed when their bus plunges into the Rhône R. at Lyon; 9 persons survive the mishap. L.A.S.

ADVERTISING. Violence on television, rising costs and advertising volume, and the return of the "hard sell" were the prime topics of conversation in advertising circles in 1976.

Violence on Television. Advertising people became increasingly restive about violence in the media, especially in television programming. Early in the year agency executives expressed concern over mounting public pressures against excessive sex and violence on home television screens. Some advertisers, notably the General Foods Corp., suggested that clients attempt to curb these alleged excesses by refusing to sponsor unsuitable programs. The country's largest advertising agency, the J. Walter Thompson Co., unveiled a 40-min. presentation called the "Desensitization of America," an audiovisual show that was produced, said the agency, out of social concern and in the interest of advertisers, who needed to know more about the effects of media on their advertising messages.

In November the "family viewing" period initi-

Jingle, Jangle, Jingle

Quadrangle, the book publishing adjunct of The New York *Times,* brought out a collection of sheet music in 1976. Why is this event noteworthy? Because all the tunes in the soft-cover collection are for advertising jingles. Now we can gather around the Steinway and sing such old favorites as "If You've Got the Time We've Got the Beer" or "I Wish I Were an Oscar Mayer Wiener."

The "N" Justifies the Means

On New Year's Day, 1976, the National Broadcasting Co. observed its 50th anniversary by displaying a new corporate symbol, an abstract, red-and-blue "N" that had cost $750,000 to design. But six months earlier, the Nebraska Educational Television Network had adopted an almost identical logo. To get itself out of an embarrassing lawsuit (and avoid having to bring the peacock out of retirement), NBC gave the Nebraska network $500,000 worth of television equipment, plus $55,000 to find a replacement for the NETV "N"—which had originally cost less than $100.

The new NETV logo (top); the NBC logo (bottom).

ated in 1975 by the networks was found by a federal court in California to constitute censorship and a violation of the First Amendment right to free speech. The family hour was an evening time period during which the depiction of sex and violence in entertainment programs was sharply restricted. The National Association of Broadcasters decided to appeal the decision.

Actress Mae Questel is Aunt Bluebell in the ScotTowels television commercials. The "weigh-it-for-yourself" campaign won a 1976 Effie award for effective advertising.

General Foods, meanwhile, called for the creation of a fourth commercial television network, suggesting that the availability of additional television time might have the effect of putting advertisers in a stronger position to oppose violence.

Rising Media Cost. The General Foods proposal, which would probably have the effect of relieving advertising cost pressures, was widely discussed because demand for television commercial time had helped push the price of prime-time advertising to record levels. In fact, rising media prices were a yearlong concern for advertisers and agencies. A number of advertisers grimly continued to buy television time; others either moved or threatened to move into other media—which were not cheap, either. In December Robert J. Coen reported in *Advertising Age* that total spending on television ads would increase from $5.3 billion in 1975 to $6.6 billion in 1976. Television's share of total advertising volume increased from 18.6 percent in 1975 to an estimated 19.7 percent in 1976.

Trends and Styles. Rising costs made agencies especially anxious to get their money's worth. Thus the trend away from arty or clever commercials and toward a more "hard sell" approach continued in 1976. The essence of this approach was Aunt Bluebell's pitch for ScotTowels, a J. Walter Thompson campaign that won an Effie, the annual award for effective advertising given by the New York chapter of the American Marketing Association.

A special case of the hard sell was the new emphasis on comparative advertising. In major campaigns a Bufferin ad attacked Tylenol by name, TWA claimed that its on-time record was better than American's or United's, and the makers of Coca-Cola and Pepsi-Cola downgraded each other's soft drink.

Political Advertising. In the 1976 election campaign U.S. President Gerald R. Ford spent more than $12,000,000 for advertising, and his opponent Jimmy Carter spent about $11,000,000. Edward Ney, head of the Young & Rubicam agency and a critic of political advertising, conceded that the candidates' commercials had "good quality, good honesty, and definitely improved over the levels of the last fifteen years." The emphasis on television coupled with the new federal restrictions on Presidential campaign spending resulted in an absence of buttons, bumper stickers, and other traditional preelection paraphernalia.

Mergers and Acquisitions. Large-scale mergers were a feature of 1976. First came an agreement under which Penton Inc. was acquired by the Pittway Corp. for $18,000,000 in cash. (Pittway publishes eighteen magazines, Penton six.) CBS, Inc., announced its intention to buy Fawcett Publications; some estimates put the price in the $60,000,000 range. In another agreement S. I. Newhouse acquired Booth Newspapers Inc.; see PUBLISHING. In the area of advertising agencies, Ogilvy & Mather agreed to purchase the much smaller Scali, McCabe, Sloves agency for $10,000,000 in cash.

Advertising Volume. Data released in 1976 indicated that in 1975 national advertisers spent an unprecedented $15.4 billion in all media. The top 100 such advertisers alone spent a record $6.4 bil-

When Pepsi-Cola launched an aggressive campaign designed to show that Coca-Cola drinkers really preferred Pepsi, the first shot in the 1976 "cola war" of comparative advertisements had been fired.

lion. The biggest single advertiser, as always, was Procter & Gamble, with a $360,000,000 expenditure. Next came General Motors and Sears, Roebuck, with $225,000,000 each. The J. Walter Thompson Co. again led all U.S. agencies in billings, with $900,100,000. Thompson was followed by Young & Rubicam ($800,900,000) and McCann-Erickson ($775,100,000).

People. Elected to the Advertising Hall of Fame in 1976 were David Ogilvy, William Bernbach, and Victor Elting. Ogilvy (of Ogilvy & Mather) created the Commander Whitehead campaign for Schweppes and the "Man in the Hathaway Shirt" campaign. Bernbach (Doyle Dane Bernbach) led a creative revolution, fostering uncluttered advertising built on honest, striking ideas. Elting (Quaker Oats Co.) first proposed the industry self-regulatory plan that led to the National Advertising Review Board.

Deaths during 1976 included those of Arnold Gingrich (*see* OBITUARIES); Milton Biow, creator of "Call for Philip Morris" and "Bulova Watch Time" (Feb. 1 at 83); William Steers of Needam, Harper & Steers (Feb. 23 at 69); and John Orr Young, co-founder of Young & Rubicam (May 1 at 89).   J.V.O'G.

AFGHANISTAN. During 1976 Afghanistan remained politically stable. In April President Mohammad Daud submitted the secret draft of a promised constitution to a twenty-member study panel, but no date was set for the document's promulgation.

The economy did fairly well during the Afghan year ending March 20, 1976. Agricultural production increased slightly, and inflation was held within reasonable limits. Owing to continuing foreign aid, mainly from the Soviet Union and Iran, the balance of payments showed a small surplus. The private industrial sector, however, was stagnant. The new Seven-Year Economic Development Plan—scheduled to begin in March, 1976, but not yet published—reportedly envisaged total development expenditures of about $3.5 billion. State development expenditures for 1976–77 were set at $309,000,000, of which $195,000,000 was to come from foreign grants.

Afghanistan and Pakistan made a new effort to improve their relations, long disturbed by conflicting border claims and by Afghan support for a secession movement among Pathan tribesmen in northwestern Pakistan. In June Prime Minister Zulfikar Ali Bhutto of Pakistan paid a five-day visit to Kabul, and in August President Daud visited Pakistan for four days. The two leaders promised to continue their talks and agreed to suspend the propaganda war between the two nations.

See STATISTICS OF THE WORLD.   W.J.G.

AFRICA

The attention of the rest of the world was often drawn to Rhodesia and South Africa, trouble spots during most of 1976. Blacks tried to eliminate—or at least weaken—the last strongholds of white rule on the continent.

The winds of political change, stilled for many years in southern Africa, blew with increased force in 1976 and appeared to shake Rhodesia and South Africa, the last strongholds of white domination on the continent. At the same time, the frail bonds holding the other nations of Africa together appeared to loosen: Secessionist movements and border disputes strained relations between some states; and ethnic rivalries and the pressures of economic frustrations brought rebellions and military coups to other states. On the whole, 1976 was marked by increased violence and the threat of yet more violence to come.

Southern Africa. The collapse of the Portuguese empire in Africa brought independence to both Angola and Mozambique in 1975. In Angola ethnic and ideological rivalries erupted in a bloody civil war. The United States and the Soviet Union backed rival factions, supplied arms and money, and reintroduced power politics in Africa. Their surrogates, South African and Cuban troops, respectively, spearheaded the fighting. After the Soviet-supported Popular Movement for the Liberation of Angola (M.P.L.A.) routed its two Western-backed rivals in January and February, the South Africans withdrew, leaving the M.P.L.A. and its Cuban allies to put down an ongoing guerrilla war and to prepare for stepped-up fighting in Namibia (South-West Africa), where the South-West African People's Organization had been attempting, with little success, to oust the South African administration. Mercenaries were harshly dealt with by the M.P.L.A. In July four were executed, including one American, and nine others were given long prison terms; see ANGOLA.

After independence, Mozambique was quickly drawn into the conflict that erupted when black nationalist Rhodesians early in February intensified their efforts to topple the white-minority government of their country. White Rhodesians, who had declared their independence from Great Britain in 1965, firmly opposed the guerrilla attacks. Their policy of "hot pursuit" led to deep and bloody incursions into Mozambique in 1976. Faced with escalating guerrilla attacks from three

sides, worsening economic conditions, and intense diplomatic pressure from the U.S. and South Africa, Rhodesia agreed to negotiate with black nationalist leaders under a plan, initiated by U.S. Secretary of State Henry A. Kissinger, that called for black majority rule in Rhodesia within two years. Negotiations, begun in Geneva late in October, quickly bogged down, and on Dec. 14 the talks were adjourned with no hope for a settlement until their resumption in mid January, 1977. In the meantime, Rhodesian nationalists called for and received large supplies of arms and munitions, and they and the governments of Angola, Mozambique, Tanzania, and Zambia prepared for the possibility of a full-fledged war. Botswana announced in December that, despite pressure from these governments, it would not be a haven for guerrillas fighting against Rhodesia or South Africa. Although South Africa declared in May that it would not go to the military rescue of Rhodesia, it was faced with the probability of increased guerrilla warfare in Namibia and continued violence in the aftermath of the June riots in Soweto, brought on by a government regulation that made Afrikaans the official language of the nation's schools. In October Transkei (q.v.) became the first Bantustan (Bantu homeland) to achieve its independence from South Africa. At the year's end, however, no foreign country had recognized the new nation.

Eastern Africa. While Tanzania was serving as a training ground for Rhodesian nationalists and preparing for the possibility that it would be drawn into an all-out war in southern Africa, its fellow members in the East African Community, Uganda and Kenya, appeared in 1976 to be nearing the point of hostilities. When Kenya insisted on cash payment for goods delivered to Uganda, and when it permitted Israeli commandos to refuel in Nairobi after their July raid to rescue hijacked passengers at Entebbe airport, Uganda's Idi Amin threatened to unleash his Soviet-equipped army; see UGANDA. Although a potential conflict was averted through the August meeting of Amin and Kenya's President Jomo Kenyatta, Kenya

Left: Two white African leaders, deeply involved in the racial confrontations of 1976, meet in Pretoria on Sept. 14: South African Prime Minister Balthazar J. Vorster (right) greets Prime Minister Ian D. Smith of Rhodesia. Right: Two Rhodesian nationalist leaders, Robert Mugabe (left) and Joshua Nkomo (right), are joined by an information officer, George Silundika, at a Dar es Salaam conference in September. The meeting brought together representatives of five African countries concerned with the explosive Rhodesian situation.

moved ahead with plans to acquire American arms to offset the Soviet-supplied armies of Uganda and Somalia. The Somali people, divided among five separate nations and colonies, reiterated their claim to portions of Ethiopia and Kenya and reportedly considered annexing the French Territory of the Afars and Issas, scheduled for independence in 1977. It was feared this would lead to a renewed conflict with Ethiopia, long dependent upon the French territory's port, Djibouti, for the bulk of its foreign trade; Ethiopia has long resented the support Somalia has been providing to the Eritrean liberation movement in its fourteen-year struggle against the central government in Addis Ababa.

The new Tanzam railroad, linking Tanzania's port city of Dar es Salaam with the copper mines of Zambia, began limited operations in 1976. Built with Chinese financing and labor, the 1155-mi. line was transporting about 1200 tons of freight each day, far less than had been expected.

Northern Africa. Sudan, Ethiopia's western neighbor, continued to bind the wounds of the long civil war between the Muslim north and the Christian and animist south. In July the government of President Gaafar Mohammed al-Nimeiry survived another attempted coup, this one allegedly supported by Libya. In 1976 Libya was also accused of fomenting unrest in Tunisia, Egypt, and Chad. In the western Sahara, Algeria and Mo-

rocco appeared on the brink of war over Algeria's continued support of the guerrilla Polisario movement, an indigenous Saharan group that was contesting the partition of the former Spanish Sahara between Morocco and Mauritania. During 1976 the Polisario claimed to have killed some 6500 Moroccan and Mauritanian troops, and in June it launched an attack on Nouakchott, the Mauritanian capital.

Western Africa. Dahomey (Benin) closed its border with Togo after accusing Togolese officials of aiding rebels in an October, 1975, coup attempt. Although the border was opened late in March, relations between the two countries remained tense. To the east, the military government of Ghana was faced with the ongoing Ewe secessionist movement, which wanted union with Togo. In July five persons were sentenced to death

for participation in the abortive coup against Ghanaian leader I. K. Acheampong in December, 1975. In Guinea President Sékou Touré received Cuban Premier Fidel Castro for a three-day visit in mid-March. In May Touré survived an assassination attempt and accused Senegal and the Ivory Coast of planning a joint invasion. Although many of the wounds of the Nigerian civil war had healed, ethnic rivalries and quarrels over the division of the country's wealth remained. Gen. Murtala Ramat Muhammed, who overthrew the government of Gen. Yakubu Gowon in 1975, was himself assassinated in February. In March the government of Niger survived a coup attempt by

In a bleak March landscape "somewhere in Western Sahara" a band of guerrillas, calling themselves the Saharan Arab Democratic Republican Army, guard their prisoners. The guerrillas had skirmished with Moroccan and Mauritanian troops that had moved into their recently partitioned homeland.

dissident military officers, and in July, Equatorial Guinea rebels reportedly launched an abortive invasion by sea from Gabon. In Liberia U.S. Secre

On Aug. 5 hundreds of students from the South African township of Soweto try for the second day to march on Johannesburg, 10 mi. away. They were protesting the two-month detention by police of their comrades, seized during earlier student riots.

tary of State Henry A. Kissinger declared during an April 30 visit that Cuban troops would have to be withdrawn before the U.S. could consider the normalization of relations with Angola.

Central Africa. In Burundi the ten-year reign of President Michel Micombero ended on Nov. 1, when the military staged a bloodless coup in an attempt to stem the country's political and economic deterioration. Taking his place was Col. Jean-Baptiste Bagaza, who announced that the nation's constitution had been suspended and that power was being assumed by a thirty-member Supreme Revolutionary Council. In the Central African Republic, President Jean-Bedel Bokassa survived a Feb. 3 grenade attack. Later in the year Bokassa converted to Islam and assumed the name of Salah Eddine Ahmed Bokassa. On Dec. 4 he announced that he had changed the name of his country to the Central African Empire and proclaimed himself Emperor Bokassa I. The republic was to become a parliamentary monarchy with all power residing in the emperor.

The Organization of African Unity (O.A.U.). An emergency meeting of the O.A.U. in January failed to agree on a single resolution concerning the Angolan civil war. The annual O.A.U. meeting, held in Mauritius in July, was marked by no less than five national complaints of aggression. One of the few points of agreement was to deny membership to Transkei when it became independent of South Africa in October. The O.A.U. also agreed to grant membership to the Seychelles Islands, which became independent on June 28 after more than 180 years of British colonial rule. Other efforts at unity were only somewhat more successful. An April meeting in Dakar, Senegal, brought together African and Arab diplomats in an effort to draw the O.A.U. and the Arab League closer together. Delegate nations promised mutual support and noninterference in each other's internal affairs, but ratification of the agreements was postponed until the African-Arab summit conference, to be held early in 1977.

Economics. With the international economy depressed, with prices for raw materials low, with the costs of oil and consumer imports rising, most African nations suffered from balance-of-payments problems and rising unemployment throughout 1976. In May representatives of nineteen African states met in Paris and agreed to work together for price stabilization of raw materials. But efforts to reduce government expenditures were resisted by vested interests and by the general citizenry, which seldom could feel satisfied with the level of educational, housing, or health facilities. A buildup of these frustrating socioeconomic conditions helped create an explosive mixture. Observers stated that one means of igniting the mixture might well be the approximately $1.5 billion in arms and munitions imported into Africa in 1976, chiefly from the Soviet Union and the U.S.

See individual articles on many of the countries mentioned above.   J.T.S.

AGRICULTURE. World farm production in 1976 was generally good to excellent, even though some important agricultural areas were hard hit by drought. The United States, the Soviet Union, and Canada all enjoyed bumper grain harvests.

United States. The overall output of U.S. farmers in 1976 was good, and in several commodities they achieved record high levels, despite adverse weather conditions in some regions, notably a drought in Nebraska and other states of the Great Plains. News reports in December indicated that total U.S. farm income in 1976 would be about $24 billion, a significant increase from the 1975 total of $22.7 billion.

In October the U.S. Bureau of the Census estimated the nation's 1975 farm population at 8,900,-000, or about 4.2 percent of the aggregate U.S. population; in 1970 farmers had made up 4.8 percent of the total population. In 1976 U.S. agriculture maintained its long-standing trend of increasing output per man-hour of labor. By midyear, productivity was 42 percent higher than in 1967, an amazing improvement. The gains were due primarily to increased mechanization and to the better care given livestock.

Wagging Their Tails Behind Them

In 1976 Anette van Dorp, a West German agriculture student, founded her own business. She called it *Gesellschaft für Schafsverleih.* (In the U.S. it would probably be known as Rent-a-Sheep, Inc.) Anette bought 300 sheep in the spring, rented them to clients at a fee of $7.80 per sheep for the summer, and made a good profit selling them to butchers in the fall. The sheep, nicely fattened, had spent their summer grazing on (and mowing) the lawns of Anette's clients.

There Will Always Be a Smokey
The wide-brimmed forest ranger hat and the oft-repeated "Only You Can Prevent Forest Fires" were the unmistakable trademarks of Smokey Bear, who died in November at a bear's old age of 26. From 1950 until his retirement in 1975, Smokey, an American black bear, was the official symbol of the U.S. Forest Service's fire-prevention program. Both Smokey and his successor, Little Smokey, age 5, were rescued when they were cubs from forest fires in New Mexico.

Little Smokey (left) and Old Smokey grin and bear it at the National Zoo in Washington, D.C.

The U.S. Department of Agriculture (U.S.D.A.) in December estimated the 1976 American wheat harvest at a record 2.147 billion bu. (compared to 2.135 billion bu. in 1975). The nation's wheat supplies in late 1976 were about 10 percent larger than a year earlier, indicating that a considerable amount of the cereal was available for use as animal feed. This, in turn, helped reduce the price of fodder, and thus would probably lead to lower meat prices for consumers in early 1977. Pressure on fodder prices also was reduced by an unprecedented corn crop of roughly 6.06 billion bu. (up

from 5.77 billion bu. in 1975). Production in 1976 of another important fodder crop, soybeans, was down 16 percent from 1975, however, mainly because farmers seeded 8 percent fewer acres to the crop as a result of a big carry-over in supplies and consequent lower prices for the commodity.

Other crop estimates for 1976 by the U.S.D.A. included the following: barley, 377,000,000 bu.

A farmer tosses a handful of bone-dry earth in a drought-ravaged Kansas wheatfield in April. Despite low rainfall in the Great Plains during the first half of the year, the U.S. produced a record wheat crop in 1976.

Acting U.S. Agriculture Secretary John A. Knebel announces a large wheat sale to the U.S.S.R. at a news conference on Oct. 13. Ten days earlier Agriculture Department head Earl L. Butz had been forced to resign because of public reaction to a widely quoted racially disparaging joke he had made; Knebel was his replacement.

(compared to 383,900,000 bu. in 1975); oats, 562,000,000 bu. (657,600,000 bu.); rye, 16,700,000 bu. (17,900,000 bu.); rice, 117,000,000 hundredweight (128,000,000 hundredweight); and fall potatoes, a record 302,800,000 hundredweight (288,700,000 hundredweight).

Cotton output for the year was calculated by the U.S.D.A. at 10,260,000 bales, compared to 8,300,000 bales in 1975. Growers increased cotton acreage in 1976 as a result of higher prices, but yields were somewhat lower than in the previous year because of poor weather.

Farmers produced large numbers of livestock, especially cattle and hogs, and as a result wholesale prices were relatively low during most of the year. Because moderate grain prices allowed producers to purchase large quantities of cereal to fatten cattle in feedlots, the average dressed weight of steers was about 620 lb., up from a low of less than 575 lb. in 1974–75. Consumer spending for red meat topped $200 per person in 1976, well ahead of the $137 per capita spent in 1970. The percentage of income spent on meat continued its long-term decline, however.

U.S. Farm Exports. In the fiscal year ended June 30, 1976, foreign sales of U.S. agricultural goods totaled about $22 billion, the highest amount on record and an increase of approximately 3 percent from fiscal year 1975. Export tonnage increased by 22 percent over the previous year, thereby more than offsetting the effects of lower world prices for some leading commodities.

During fiscal year 1976 approximately 25 percent of American feed-grain production was sold abroad, earning $5.6 billion. About 55 percent of the U.S. wheat crop was exported, at an aggregate return of $4.9 billion. The U.S. gained $4 billion from foreign sales of more than half of its soybean harvest. Thirty percent of U.S. tobacco production went abroad, bringing income of $917,000,000, and foreign purchasers paid $881,000,000 for 40 percent of the American cotton crop.

The Soviet Union continued in 1976 to be a major purchaser of U.S. grain, although because of its excellent harvest it bought far less than in 1975. As of early October the U.S.S.R. had purchased some 6,350,000 metric tons of U.S. corn and wheat, compared to about 10,300,000 metric tons for the same period in 1975.

World Agriculture. Because a number of leading grain-producing countries enjoyed bumper harvests, global cereal output in 1976 outdistanced the previous year's total, despite poor weather conditions in several areas. Experts estimated in November that 1976 world wheat production would total a record 409,500,000 metric tons, compared to 352,000,000 metric tons in 1975.

Late in October, Leonid I. Brezhnev, head of the Soviet Communist Party, said that the U.S.S.R. had already harvested 216,000,000 metric tons of grain and that by year's end the country's record crop of 222,500,000 metric tons in 1973 would be equaled or broken. In 1975 the Soviet Union had produced only about 140,000,000 metric tons of grain.

Canada also had an excellent year. Statistics Canada reported in December that the country's wheat harvest was a record 864,300,000 bu., up almost 40 percent from 1975. Yields were 31.4 bu. per acre, compared to 26.8 bu. per acre in 1975. In November Argentina announced that it expected to have produced a near-record 13,000,000 metric tons of wheat when its harvest concluded in January, 1977. The People's Republic of China reported a record summer wheat harvest (estimated at 35,000,000 metric tons by the U.S.D.A.).

The 1976 harvest is helped to mature in these unique circular Nebraska wheatfields. The center-pivot irrigation system, which is becoming popular because it saves water and labor, waters each field from sprays attached to a series of interconnected wheeled towers that turn around a central pumping complex.

Much of Europe was devastated by a drought lasting from late spring through most of the summer. The European Economic Community calculated in late summer that its nine members would have to import up to 18,000,000 metric tons of corn during the year because corn crops were running 30 percent below the 1971–75 average. The National Farmers Union of Great Britain estimated in September that annual farm income in Britain would fall more than 30 percent from the previous year. The government of France calculated in early fall that the drought had cost French farmers $2 billion, mainly in lost income.

Grain and livestock production in southern and western Australia was reduced sharply by another severe drought. In October Australia's 1976 wheat crop was estimated at 8,400,000 metric tons, down more than 25 percent from harvests in recent years.   D.T.A.

ALABAMA. *See* STATISTICS OF THE WORLD.

ALASKA. *See* STATISTICS OF THE WORLD.

ALBANIA. Addressing Albania's 7th Communist Party Congress in November, 1976, party chief Enver Hoxha declared that a top-level purge he had conducted in recent years was aimed at removing eight officials who were conspiring with foreign enemies. Hoxha did not specify, but it was evident that the enemies he referred to were Soviets.

Albania's domestic purge appeared to leave the 68-year-old Hoxha in firm control. Throughout the year he persisted in his policy of isolating Albania from all outside contacts except the People's Republic of China. In November Hoxha even suggested that Albania's economic dependence on China would have to be reduced. Repeated calls by the Soviet Union for restoration of normal relations with Albania were rejected.

During 1976 the Albanian government stressed "unity between intellectual and physical labor." Salaries of government officials, managerial personnel, and "intellectuals" were reduced by up to 25 percent, and artists' and writers' royalties by up to 50 percent. In addition, officials and white collar workers were required to spend a month in a factory or on a farm. These measures did little to relieve continuing economic stagnation.

A draft constitution published on Jan. 21 called for resistance to "bureaucratization and liberalism" and for the abolition of all taxes and private property. Economic cooperation with "capitalist or revisionist monopolies or states" was forbidden.

See STATISTICS OF THE WORLD.   F.W.

ALBERTA. *See* STATISTICS OF THE WORLD.

ALGERIA. Despite criticism at home and abroad, in 1976 President Houari Boumédienne consolidated his power, and Algeria stabilized its government.

Three referendums were held during the year. On June 27 a new national charter was approved;

on Nov. 19 a new constitution was approved; and on Dec. 10 Boumédienne was elected to a renewable six-year term as head of state, commander in chief of the armed forces, head of government, and head of national defense. Still to come, in January, 1977, was an election for a new National Assembly.

The national charter was released in draft form on April 27. In its final form, it proclaimed Algeria to be a one-party state with a socialist economy and an Islamic state religion. It declared that economic development was to be accomplished through public ownership of the means of production and that popular education was to concentrate on Arab-Islamic and socialist principles. On July 5 Boumédienne signed the charter into law.

The first open political criticism of Boumédienne in several years came to light with the publication and distribution of a manifesto denouncing the so-called totalitarian rule and personality cult of the president. The document bore signatures of four leaders of the period before independence, including two presidents of the government-in-exile during the war against France. All four were placed under house arrest on March 11, and Boumédienne countered their charges in a speech on March 18. Parallel protests against the regime published by exiles in Europe, however, suggested that the protest was against the concentration of power, but that support for socialist policies remained strong.

The charter's emphasis on economic development echoed the major thrust of the national budget for 1976, announced on Jan. 2. Of a total expenditure of $5.8 billion, nearly 14 percent was devoted to investments in public sector companies. The military budget jumped by about one quarter from 1975, reflecting a heightened concern with defense. Total receipts were estimated at $6.5 billion, with earnings from oil and hydrocarbons estimated at $4 billion—over $500,000,000 more than in 1975. Algeria was unique among developing nations because of its immense oil revenues; but it was also unique among Arab oil producers because of its large population. Although a small surplus was anticipated in the national budget, most of the country's receipts would be needed to keep pace with its vigorous public-sector development campaign.

Algeria continued to support the Polisario, the independence movement in the former Spanish Sahara, known as the Western Sahara after February. The fiercest battles with Moroccan troops were fought before the formal Spanish withdrawal on Feb. 26, but sporadic clashes were reported throughout the year. Morocco and Mauri-

Victorious but exhausted, a young soldier sits on a doorstep in Huambo, Angola's second largest city, occupied by M.P.L.A. forces on Feb. 8. Above him is a picture of Agostinho Neto, president of Angola and head of the M.P.L.A.

tania both broke relations with Algeria on March 7 after it recognized the Saharan Arab Democratic Republic formed by the Polisario. Algerian and Polisario leaders warned that a prolonged guerrilla war might be forthcoming.

See STATISTICS OF THE WORLD. *See also* AFRICA; MIDDLE EAST.   S.C.

ALI, MUHAMMAD. *See* PEOPLE IN THE NEWS.

ANGOLA. The civil war in Angola reached a turning point in January, 1976, and by the second anniversary of independence, in November, the Popular Movement for the Liberation of Angola (M.P.L.A.) under President Agostinho Neto was in control of the country. The United States, which backed the opposing movements, the National Front for the Liberation of Angola (F.N.L.A.) and the National Union for the Total Independence of Angola (U.N.I.T.A.), attempted to persuade the Organization of African Unity (O.A.U.) to press for the withdrawal of a Cuban expedition supporting the M.P.L.A. When the O.A.U. met in January, votes of the members were evenly divided between the M.P.L.A. and the F.N.L.A.-U.N.I.T.A. coalition.

In early January the M.P.L.A., aided by some 15,000 to 18,000 Cuban troops, had blunted the offensive of the F.N.L.A. forces that were moving from the north toward the capital, Luanda, and of the U.N.I.T.A. troops that were moving up from the south. The Cuban forces, aided by Soviet arms and planes, spearheaded the counterattack and quickly routed the F.N.L.A., whose members fled into neighboring Zaire. The U.N.I.T.A., in the south, was aided by 4000 to 5000 South African troops, but when the U.S. Congress in late January blocked further aid to the F.N.L.A.-U.N.I.T.A., South Africa began to withdraw its forces, seriously weakening the U.N.I.T.A. The F.N.L.A.-U.N.I.T.A. capital of Huambo (formerly Nova Lisboa) was captured by the M.P.L.A. on Feb. 8, and by March 27 the M.P.L.A. was in effective control of Angola's main cities, roads, and communications. Some pockets of U.N.I.T.A. resistance continued in southern Angola, but these were largely wiped out by an M.P.L.A.-Cuban offensive mounted in early November. At the year's end only sporadic guerrilla activity continued, near the Zambian border.

Diplomatic support and recognition of the Neto government accelerated with the collapse of the rival coalition in late January. On Feb. 11 the O.A.U. recognized the M.P.L.A. government and admitted Angola as its forty-seventh member. Although most Western European governments recognized the M.P.L.A., the U.S. in June protested the continued presence in Angola of Cuban armed forces by vetoing Angola's request for membership in the United Nations. A subsequent vote was taken, however, in which the U.S. abstained, and on Dec. 1 Angola became the 146th member of the U.N.

On June 11 the M.P.L.A. government put 10 British and 3 American mercenaries on trial in Luanda for crimes against the Angolan "people's revolution." The verdict, delivered on June 28, condemned to death 1 American, Daniel F. Gearhart, and 3 Britons. Nine others—2 Americans and 7 Britons—were given prison terms ranging from 16 to 30 years. Despite pleas from U.S. President Gerald R. Ford and Great Britain's Queen Elizabeth II and Prime Minister James Callaghan, the 4 were executed by firing squad on July 10.

As 1976 ended Angola was desperately short of food, largely because the war had decimated its methods of transportation and distribution. Factories were operating at a mere fraction of capacity, although efforts were under way to rebuild the economy. Oil had begun to flow once more from the Gulf Oil Corp. wells in Cabinda, and trade relations were being cautiously reestablished with a few Western nations. (Angola has some of the world's richest deposits of iron ore, in addition to copper, uranium, and other minerals; and before the guerrilla war it was the fifth largest exporter of diamonds.) But tremendous problems remained, not the least of which were a primitive transportation system and a population that was 90 percent illiterate.

See STATISTICS OF THE WORLD. *See also* AFRICA.   J.T.S.

ANTARCTICA. Armed with their new knowledge of craters on the moon and Mars, scientists in 1976 turned their attention to a possible meteorite crater beneath the Antarctic ice, which may prove to be the world's biggest. First hypothesized in 1960, the crater lies some 2400 mi. south of Australia, beneath the mile-thick ice of Wilkes Land. Scientists estimated the crater to be 150 mi. across and ½ mi. deep. They conjectured that 600,000 to 700,000 years ago—before the emergence of modern man—a giant meteorite at least 2½ mi. across and weighing 13 billion tons crashed onto the

Scientists from the U.S. make gravity measurements on the Ross Ice Shelf, Antarctica. During 1976 other investigators on the ice shelf and nearby coasts drilled core samples for analysis of minerals and life forms.

Antarctic earth. Scientists speculated that such a colossal impact would account for the presence in southern Australia of tektites, glassy rocks the size of walnuts.

Studies by R. H. Thomas of the Ross Ice Shelf Project of the University of Nebraska indicate that the ice shelf is thickening in some places at the rate of 1 m (39.37 in.) a year. The edge of the ice sheet in at least one locality is advancing 1 km (3281 ft.) a year. A possible conclusion of the findings is that the Antarctic ice is advancing steadily northward. One aspect of the project, an attempt to drill through the ¼-mi.-thick ice to study the sea life beneath it, was abruptly halted on Dec. 14. Within hours of a breakthrough, scientists said that newly formed ice had choked off the drill assembly, making further efforts useless at that time.

Towing Icebergs. On Nov. 1 Saudi Arabia announced that it had commissioned a French engineering firm, the Cicero Co., to study the feasibility of towing icebergs from the Antarctic to its shores for use as drinking water and in irrigation. A preliminary report on the project indicated that a large iceberg—one weighing around 85,000,000 tons—could be towed across the 5000-mi. expanse of ocean in six months to a year at a cost of some $90,000,000.

At least six powerful tugboats would be required to complete the task, and in order to reduce melting of the iceberg due to water friction, the boats could not travel at speeds greater than 1 knot. To protect the iceberg against the sun's rays, the entire mass would first have to be encased in an 18-in.-thick wrapping of plastic. Despite these precautions, it was estimated that there would be about a 20 percent loss from melting by the end of the trip. Once anchored, however, near the Red Sea port of Jidda, the ice mass could be utilized gradually over a period of up to eighteen months before it had completely melted.

The French engineers estimated that the final cost of such drinking water would work out to 50¢ per m³ (cubic meter), which, despite the magnitude of the undertaking, is just half the present cost in Saudi Arabia of desalting seawater.

See EARTH AND PLANETARY SCIENCES: *Oceanography.*

ANTHROPOLOGY. Meetings of anthropological societies during 1976 reflected a growing trend toward expanding the science to embrace study of the ways in which people of modern cultures cope with and reason about the world. Reports were presented on such contemporary matters as strategies for coping with life in the urban ghetto voodoo practices may overcome feelings of plessness), warlike cultural values (combative

Margaret Mead, renowned anthropologist, at the American Museum of Natural History, New York City, on Dec. 16—her 75th birthday. To honor the occasion and her 50 years with the institution, the museum established a Margaret Mead Chair and a $5,000,000 Margaret Mead Fund for the Advancement of Anthropology.

sports do not release aggressive drives but rather help to condition society to an acceptance of war), and cultural factors in medical care (Westerners reject hypnotism and psychic manipulation because they expect physical or drug intervention). Other reports dealt with contemporary educational practices, the status of women, even "boom town" culture. At the 1976 annual meeting of the American Anthropological Association, outgoing president Walter Goldsmith endorsed the new trend. "Anthropology," he said, "should help in the formulation of policies affecting our own social order, rather than leave these matters to the economists and political scientists." Many of those present called for a redefinition of anthropology, and a committee was formed to assess the current status of the field.

Primate Matriarchies. In 1976 the widely held belief that dominant males in a group are assured greater access to females, presumably thereby ensuring vigorous offspring, was called into question for primate societies. In those societies, parallels to human behavior have been rather freely drawn. A feature article by staff writer Gina Bari Kolata in the Jan. 9 issue of *Science* magazine described a number of recent investigations of rhesus monkeys in which dominance in males (as well as in females) was seen to derive from the status of their mothers rather than from physical prowess. Females had choice in the matter of mating, and high-ranking females did not necessarily choose dominant males; low-ranking, even adolescent, males fathered as many offspring as the highest ranking males. Rhesus males usually leave their own group at adolescence; if they are well received by the females in the new group, they are able to remain long enough to achieve dominance by age and seniority. Observations of savannah baboons showed similar matriarchal patterns. Dominance ranks among female baboons were quite stable, with females inheriting ranks from their mothers; males, however, changed ranks frequently during their reproductive years.

In the opinion of some researchers mentioned in the article, previous investigations reporting the greater reproductive success of aggressive males were either based on conditions that did not occur in nature, such as forcing a noncohesive group of animals to compete for access to food, or were unintentionally biased by concentration on the activities of dominant males, who are more visible.

***Homo Erectus* in Africa.** At a news conference in March in Washington, D.C., the Kenyan paleontologist Richard E. Leakey reported the discovery of a 1,500,000-year-old *Homo erectus* skull at Lake Rudolf in Kenya. The skull was almost identical to that of Peking man, which was discovered in 1927 and dated at about 500,000 years. Leakey suggested that either Peking man was wrongly dated and is much older, or else *Homo erectus,* the direct ancestor of the modern human species, was remarkably uniform in physical characteristics over a long time span and across a vast geological range.

The new Leakey skull also clearly established that early humans coexisted with rather than descended from *Australopithecus,* the near humans that inhabited Africa between 3,000,000 and 1,000,000 years ago and had been believed to be our evolutionary ancestors. Other findings announced by Leakey were a 3,000,000-year-old skull of an earlier form of the *Homo* genus (similar to his "1470" skull found in 1972) and an almost complete pelvic bone of the same period, showing characteristics of upright walking.

At the same news conference, described by anthropologists as "historic," Donald C. Johanson described a find perhaps equal in importance to any previous discovery. He had unearthed in the Afar region of Ethiopia a large collection of 3,500,-000-year-old remains of a *Homo* group. (The oldest previous group was dated at 100,000 years.) The group included two children and at least three adolescents and adults, apparently victims of a flash flood. The Johanson find affords anthropologists an opportunity to trace the stages of development in humans of the earliest known times. A composite adult hand that Johanson constructed from thirty-five bones was of the same size and apparent dexterity as a modern hand. A pelvic bone clearly pointed to upright walking. The suggestion of tool use and other advanced capabilities in such ancient humans was entirely unanticipated, and it supported the controversial view that the human lineage goes much farther back in time than had been supposed, perhaps as far as 6,000,000 years.

Earliest Americans. In recent years, evidence from stone tools in the southwestern United States, Mexico, and South America has challenged the assumption that the peopling of the New World occurred in a single migration about 12,000 years ago when a land bridge existed between Asia and Alaska. In June modern dating methods were applied to a site in Santa Rosa Island off California, where tools were found near a human hearth that contained charred dwarf mammoth bones. The investigation yielded firm evidence that the island was inhabited at least 40,000 years ago.

Many scientists now believe that human migrations could indeed have occurred 40,000 years ago, as well as 70,000 and 100,000 years ago—periods during the Ice Age when enough water was locked in glaciers to lower sea levels and open the Bering Strait land bridge. In September an unusually large expedition, jointly sponsored by the National Geographic Society and the National Park Service, was formed to search for early signs of human presence in the Dry Creek area 75 mi. south of Fairbanks, Alaska. Dry Creek lies along a north-south corridor from the Bering Strait that remained ice-free during glacial times and is known to have been inhabited by humans 11,000 years ago.

See also ARCHEOLOGY.   E.A.C.

ARAB LEAGUE. The role of the Arab League in the mediation of regional disputes, representation of Arab interests in the world community, and coordination of Arab economic policies had been expanding in recent years. In 1976 Secretary-General Mahmoud Riad was one of the Arab world's most visible and widely respected figures.

Internal Affairs. On Sept. 9 the league unanimously voted to accept Palestine, represented by the Palestine Liberation Organization (P.L.O.), as its twenty-first full member. Created by the league in 1965, the P.L.O. had previously enjoyed observer status, without voting rights or full membership privileges. In May, 1976, Egypt formally proposed the admission of "Palestine" as a member-state, citing the 1974 Arab summit resolution recognizing the P.L.O. as the legitimate representative of all Palestinian people and the organization's growing acceptance in international circles. The granting of full league membership led to widespread speculation that the P.L.O. would soon declare a government-in-exile.

Finance ministers convening in Rabat, Morocco, at the end of April established an Arab States Monetary Fund (A.S.M.F.) with an initial capital of $900,000,000. The outlines of the fund had been established in November, 1975. To be based in Abu Dhabi, the fund was to establish Arab Accounts Dinars, similar to the Special Drawing Rights of the International Monetary Fund. The A.S.M.F. was to extend credits to Arab states with balance-of-payments deficits up to twice the amount of the individual state's annual contribution to the fund, for up to seven years. Its purpose was to stabilize individual Arab currencies and ensure their convertibility. Eventually, it was planned to establish a single Arab currency through the league. Initial pledges to the fund included $38,000,000 each from Saudi Arabia and Algeria; $25,000,000 from Iraq, Kuwait, and Egypt; and $15,000,000 from the Union of Arab Emirates.

Mediation Efforts. Riad traveled several times to Algeria, Morocco, Mauritania, and the Spanish (later Western) Sahara to try to reduce tensions over the future of the Sahara. By far the most pressing breach of peace in the Arab world, however, was the Lebanese crisis. From January until May Riad's repeated calls for a summit on Lebanon went unheeded. The league requested medical assistance for the wounded from the International Red Cross and the United Nations Children's Fund and pledged medical and hospital facilities, but little diplomatic progress was made.

After an urgent request from the P.L.O. on June 2, the Arab League did meet in Cairo a week later to discuss the worsening situation in Lebanon. In an overnight session the participants decided to send a multilateral security force to separate the warring factions. The league contingent was to replace Syrian forces that had entered Lebanon in

April. Riad persuaded President Suleiman Franjieh of Lebanon to accept the security force, but its mission was not honored by fighting units on either side. The peacekeeping force itself came under fire early in September, and special envoy Hasan Sabri Khóuli threatened to withdraw the league contingent.

In mid-October a limited summit meeting was convened in Riyadh, Saudi Arabia, by representatives of Lebanon, Syria, Kuwait, Egypt, Saudi Arabia, and the P.L.O. On Oct. 18 an accord was signed calling for expansion of the league security force from 2300 to 30,000 men. The league force, composed largely of Syrian units already in Lebanon, was to be stationed between front lines and was asked to confiscate all heavy weapons and report all violations of the peace. By the end of the year, an uncertain peace had been enforced, and Beirut was occupied by the force.

External Relations. Fifty-nine nations were represented at an Arab League–Organization of African Unity ministerial conference in Dakar, Senegal, April 18–22. The conference published an eight-point charter to be approved at the Afro-Arab summit in 1977. The charter bound signatories to promises of nonalignment and mutual nonaggression and noninterference and condemned "imperialism, colonialism, neocolonialism, Zionism, apartheid, and all other forms of discrimination and racial and religious segregation." Plans for closer cooperation between Arab and African communities were discussed.

Arab League discussions with the European Community were less successful. A conference in Luxembourg in May failed to reach agreement either on economic or political issues. Among the points of conflict were questions of oil prices, economic cooperation and assistance, the Arab boycott of Israel, recognition by European nations of the P.L.O., and pressure for Israel to relinquish occupied territories.

The boycott of Israel and of firms doing business with Israel continued to cause friction between Arab nations and the West. Mohammed Mahgoub, head of the boycott office, warned on July 24 that oil companies assisting with Israeli prospecting in the occupied Sinai would be blacklisted. The United States attempted to undermine the boycott by denying tax advantages to corporations honoring it, and both American Presidential candidates denounced the blacklisting system and called on companies to reject the boycott's conditions. The U.S. Commerce Department reported, nonetheless, that 94 percent of American exporters were complying with boycott demands.

See MIDDLE EAST; ORGANIZATION OF PETROLEUM

EXPORTING COUNTRIES; and articles on individual countries mentioned.   S.C.

ARCHEOLOGY. In 1976 clay tablets providing important information about Biblical times were found in Syria, an impressive collection of ancient gold was discovered in Bulgaria, the earliest known Maya monuments were uncovered in Guatemala, and bronze artifacts from Thailand tested traditional theories of the origin of the Bronze Age.

Ebla Tablets. The recovery of 15,000 clay tablets at Tel Mardikh in northern Syria, by a team of Rome University archeologists led by Paolo Matthiae, caused tremendous excitement among Biblical scholars and archeologists. Identified as ancient Ebla, the site is located 30 mi. south of Aleppo. The cuneiform tablets were buried in two small rooms of what may have been a palace library. Inscribed about 4500 years ago in a Semitic tongue closely related to the Biblical Hebrew spoken more than 1000 years later, the tablets contain significant references to "Daudum" (David), "Urusalim" (Jerusalem), a King "Ibrium" (the root word for Hebrew), and other Biblical names. The expedition's language expert, Giovanni Pettinato, reported that the Ebla tablets "establish the patriarchs and their names as historical realities."

Among the tablets are reports from ambassadors, administrative documents, key vocabulary lists containing "Eblaite" and Sumerian words, military reports, descriptions of rites and sacrifices, and texts concerning creation and the great flood. The tablets firmly place ancient Syria in the chronicles of civilization as a power rivaling Egypt and Mesopotamia. Conquered in 2250 B.C. by King Naram-sin of Akkad in Mesopotamia, the city of Ebla is mentioned only occasionally in Akkadian, Egyptian, Hittite, and Sumerian texts. It now seems clear that Ebla flourished between about 2400 and 2250 B.C. and served as an important center of a vital empire.

Gold from Bulgaria. The city of Varna, located on the Black Sea coast of Bulgaria, is the site of a sensational treasure trove of gold, copper, marble, and shell artifacts dating to the fifth millennium B.C. The finds were made public at the 9th International Congress of Prehistoric and Protohistoric Sciences held in Nice, France, in September. Eighty-one graves of a prehistoric civilization were opened to reveal masses of gold jewelry placed in the ground. Although the jewelry was arranged as if bodies had been present, no human remains were found. Other graves, also devoid of corpses, contained life-sized clay masks with gold details. One of the most important finds at Varna was a bowl painted gold, the first known example of gold painting on clay to be found in the Old

In the ruins of Ebla in northern Syria archeologists found thousands of 4500-year-old clay tablets. Stored in chambers of the royal palace, they describe an empire equal to ancient Egypt or Mesopotamia.

World. The amount of gold, marble, copper, shells, and graphite amassed in these graves is unprecedented for their early period, and indicates that Varna was a prominent trade center in ancient Europe.

Maya Stelae. The earliest known recorded inscription for the ancient Maya civilization was discovered on a large stone stela bearing the hieroglyphic inscription for June 3, 126 A.D. John A. Graham and Robert F. Heizer, both of the Anthropology Department of the University of California at Berkeley, unearthed the monument at Abaj Takalik in the Pacific highlands of Guatemala. The carved stone predates the oldest known lowland Maya sites by 166 years. The fifty stone stelae uncovered indicate that the powerful Mayans were not always confined to the lowlands, as had been previously believed. Monuments produced by the Olmec peoples, a group primarily from Mexico and thought to be older than the Maya, were found side by side with the stelae at Abaj Takalik. This was the first time that extensive Maya and Olmec carvings had been found together.

Bronze Age in Thailand. The traditional dates for the beginning of the Bronze Age (3500–3000 B.C.) have been brought to question by artifacts found at Ban Chiang, a farming village located on the Khorat Plateau in northeast Thailand. Bronze spearheads, anklets, and bracelets uncovered by Chester F. Gorman of the University of Pennsylvania and Pisit Charoenwongsa of the National Museum of Bangkok were dated by radiocarbon and thermoluminescence to 3600 B.C. They point to a people who mastered the metallurgical process thought to have originated in the Middle East. The finds also predate the appearance of bronze in China by two millennia. The sophistication of the artifacts undermines the traditional theory that the art of bronzeworking spread from northern China. It is now speculated that Southeast Asia played a more prominent role than China in the development of bronze metallurgy.   B.R.

ARCHITECTURE AND CITY PLANNING. Economic forces continued to weigh heavily on the architectural profession in 1976. Tight mortgage money and staggeringly high construction costs combined to enforce severe limits on both new commissions and completion of construction under way.

Construction Crisis. The year was characterized by heated debates and lengthy discussions about the causes of the economic slump, though few solutions to the current crisis were offered. Housing starts were at their highest peak since early 1973, but continued at a relatively low level; *see* CONSTRUCTION. The realization emerged that without new federal intervention the housing industry

The two towers of the newly completed Pennzoil Place rise above the Houston, Texas, skyline. Trapezoidal in shape, the 38-story structures are covered with a grayed-bronze skin of modified mirror glass. The towers were the work of two architects, Philip Johnson and John Burgee.

would not revive, since the cost of home building had begun to exceed anything affordable by the young families who made up the traditional home-buyers' market. Toward the year's end President-elect Jimmy Carter revealed a keen awareness of these problems and of the boost to the economy as a whole that a revived construction industry could give. Carter promised to seek ways to stimulate the industry, including such measures as tax abatements that would make new housing starts feasible.

Rehabilitated Housing. The trend toward the rehabilitation of old buildings continued to gather

Student housing is combined with shops in an original design developed for Pembroke College in Providence, R.I., by Lyndon Associates, Inc. Residential and shopping areas are differentiated through the use of vibrant colors.

Below: The Omni International, a $70,000,000, 14-story, multipurpose complex in downtown Atlanta. It combines a 472-room hotel with a convention center, sports coliseum, office towers, restaurants, motion picture theaters, luxury shops, and ice-skating rink.

ARCHITECTURE AND CITY PLANNING

momentum. Many historically important buildings were refurbished in honor of the Bicentennial and helped to remind Americans of the importance of their architectural heritage. Philadelphia accomplished a major renewal of its historic center, which brackets the mall at Independence Hall. Elsewhere, mounting costs prompted young families to consider renovation as a solution to their housing needs, and the movement to rehabilitate older, central-city row housing gained new impetus. The high cost of energy (q.v.) and the widespread publicity given to its increasing scarcity over the last few years gave new urgency to the search for alternative energy sources to provide heat and to cool and light buildings. Much research and development work continued to be done on solar energy systems for buildings. Architects were reassessing traditional construction forms in an effort to make them less wasteful of energy.

The most immediate impact of these efforts was visible in a number of private homes throughout the country that were using solar energy collection and storage systems to provide a substantial part of their energy needs. Such systems had a relatively high initial cost, and manufacturers, along with some architects and engineers, were working hard to make them not only more efficient but also less expensive.

The Kemper Memorial Arena in Kansas City, Mo., winner of an A.I.A. award for architectural excellence in 1976. The multipurpose arena housed the Republican Party convention in August.

New Trends. A tendency in architectural design that had been gathering momentum for some time became apparent. The clean-lined, spare look of the contemporary buildings of the last four decades had lost ground to a new unabashed proclaiming of the ordinary, a celebration of the popular culture. The best works of this new movement reflected a profound awareness of the requirements of those who would occupy the structures. At the same time they nourished the users' aesthetic needs through a witty deployment of strong colors. Thus, the student housing for Pembroke College in Providence, R.I., by Lyndon Associates, Inc., with participation in initial design by Charles Moore, made imaginative use of a site at the edge of the college campus by integrating both housing and shopping at the street level. The mass of the building was broken up so as to acknowledge the essentially residential nature of the street it fronted, while stressing the fact that the students were to live in houses, not dormitories. The facades of the houses were made of brick in flat planes, enlivened by the use of color to define the separation of the shops from the housing. The whole was constructed of familiar, readily available materials, assembled so as to reinforce the existing pattern of the streets. At the same time the concept developed a sense of place, of belonging, and of individual identity for its residents.

Several major developments that promised to have significant impact in the future took form during the year in both architecture and city planning. The Omni International in Atlanta, Ga., a set

Finlandia House, the conference and concert center of Helsinki, designed by Alvar Aalto, who died in 1976. Completed in 1971, the hall was perhaps the most ambitious and successful of the world-renowned Finnish architect's public structures.

of linked structures designed for many uses, represents one direction that privately financed inner-city redevelopment has taken over the last few years. The concept for the Omni was a business and convention center equipped with the facilities of an in-town family vacation resort—a sort of miniature Disney World in the midst of a city with other attractions.

The success of such redevelopment proposals has depended in part on their ability to combine several related functions (in this case office, hotel, convention, and trade-fair facilities with recreational outlets) while at the same time permitting an intensive 24-hour-a-day use. The various functions must not only be mutually sustaining and supporting but must generate activity, and therefore revenue, for each other.

Competitions. Judging took place in Vancouver, British Columbia, in early February of entries in the International Design Competition for the Urban Environment of Developing Communities. A total of 476 entries had been submitted from architects throughout the world. The competition was sponsored by the International Architectural Foundation and received strong support from the Philippine government, which offered to build at least one 500-family community to the design of the first prizewinner. This was to be erected along the shore area at Dagat-Dagatan in the Philippines. The purpose of the competition was to make architects and planners aware of the problems created in developing countries by the rapid pace of urbanization. Many of the people who were moving to cities in these countries had become squatters and paid no rent or taxes; therefore they received few public services. Their communities were becoming vast pockets of squalor and disease. It was hoped that useful solutions could be found not only for housing design but also for area planning to relate housing to neighborhood, to community, to city, and finally to region. The plans were to suggest various directions of self-help, first in the design of actual dwelling units, then in the areas of work, food production, schooling, and medical care.

First prize was awarded to Ian Athfield, a young architect from New Zealand, for his design integrating housing and work space. The work area would be the first component of the design to be built. Its initial occupancy would be by a building cooperative, to be controlled by the immediate neighborhood. This cooperative would supply components for the construction of individual dwellings on nearby sites prepared by the government. As the neighborhood developed there would be less need for the cooperative, so space it had occupied could be leased to private non-polluting industries. The brilliance of the solution lay in its sensitivity to the needs of its future occupants, giving them a goal and providing a flexible and manageable framework for their lives.

The 1976 awards for excellence in architecture were announced by the American Institute of Architects (A.I.A.) in midsummer. From nearly 500 entries submitted, 10 winners were selected by the 5-man jury from projects across the nation. Six of the winners were new constructions and 4 were renovated buildings. They included the Waterside apartment complex in New York City, the Kemper Memorial Arena in Kansas City, Mo., the Old City Hall in Boston, and the Center for Creative Studies in Detroit. A special award went to the twin apartment towers on Chicago's Lakeshore Drive designed by Ludwig Mies van der Rohe. Judges said that the glass skyscrapers retained their "newly minted appearance even after 25 years."

I. M. Pei & Partners. Prominent in architectural news was the New York City firm of I. M. Pei & Partners. On Aug. 12 it was announced that the John F. Kennedy Presidential Library, formerly slated to be built on Harvard Square in Boston, would be erected by the firm at Columbia Point, overlooking Boston harbor. The site, a commuter campus of the University of Massachusetts, would provide the architects with greater room to realize their original concept than would have been possible on the Cambridge campus; see LIBRARIES. Also in Boston, the John Hancock Tower, a 790-ft. parallelogram of greenish-blue glass, was finally dedicated on Sept. 29. Since its completion in 1972 it had been beset by a series of ills. Not the least of these was the repeated fall of glass panels

from the structure's sides, due to some as yet undetermined cause. But the New York *Times* said that the tower, with most of its problems solved, could now be called "Boston's finest high-rise structure and the best piece of skyscraper design to have come from . . . I. M. Pei & Partners."

Deaths. The great Finnish architect Alvar Aalto, regarded by many as the last of the giants of modern architecture, died on May 11 at the age of 78; see OBITUARIES. Other important leaders in the field who died during 1976 were Sir Basil Spence of Great Britain, the architect of the 1962 rebuilding of Coventry Cathedral (Nov. 18 at 69), and Antonin Raymond of the United States, who worked with Frank Lloyd Wright on the Imperial Hotel in Tokyo and later designed the American Embassy there (Nov. 15 at 88).   A.K.R.

ARCTIC. See ENVIRONMENT.

ARGENTINA. The year 1976 marked a turning point for Argentina, politically and economically.

Politics. On March 24 military authorities overthrew the government of Isabel Martínez de Perón, who had become president on July 1, 1974, following the death of her husband, Gen. Juan Domingo Perón. The military engineered the bloodless coup to prevent the country from plunging into further economic and social chaos under Isabel Perón's ineffective leadership, after she refused to step down at the military's request. The president, who suspended congress in February, had also resisted demands from her own party to reorganize the cabinet.

To consolidate its power, the military immediately installed a three-man junta with Lt. Gen. Jorge Rafael Videla as president, dissolved congress and municipal assemblies, suspended political activities, and dismissed the supreme court. By mid-April more than 3000 former government ministers, politicians, and labor leaders had been arrested, including Isabel Perón herself, who on Oct. 25 was found guilty of embezzling Peronist Party funds.

The military regime soon began to wage a violent and repressive campaign against left-wing guerrilla groups. In July government forces killed most of the leaders of the People's Revolutionary Army, a Marxist group. Then, in October, a raid by the government forces against the Montoneros, the other major leftist guerrilla group, had some success. Nevertheless, violence continued to disrupt the country, and right-wing guerrilla activities went unchecked. One rightist group, the so-called Death Squad, reportedly kidnapped and killed a number of foreign political exiles in Argentina, including former President Juan José Torres Gonzáles of Bolivia (q.v.).

The Economy. With Finance Minister José Alfredo

President Jorge Rafael Videla (center) leads the way as Argentina's new three-man military junta participates in holiday festivities on May 25. Adm. Eduardo Emilio Massera is on Videla's left, and Air Force Gen. Ramón Agosti is on his right.

Martínez de Hoz at the helm, the new administration moved rapidly to deal with the rampant inflation, severe recession, and general economic anarchy existing at the time of the takeover. Price controls on all products except pharmaceuticals were removed, strikes were banned, and some labor benefits were revoked. Other measures undertaken included the passing of a new law designed to stimulate foreign investment, the formulation of plans for the return of many state enterprises to private control, and significant adjustments in foreign exchange policies, designed to stabilize the peso.

The new economic program met with considerable success, and the monthly inflation rate was held to 10 percent or below (still very high, but an improvement over the 28 percent a month average in 1975). The economy registered some positive growth during the fourth quarter of 1976; nevertheless, the gross domestic product, adjusted for inflation, fell between 4 and 5 percent during the year. The improvement in the external accounts was more dramatic. After recording a $1 billion trade deficit in 1975, Argentina's trade account was in surplus for most of 1976.

Foreign Affairs. After showing its determination to cope with economic problems, the new regime was able to negotiate a $1.3 billion loan package with the International Monetary Fund and European, Japanese, and United States banks. This financing permitted a restructuring and renegotiation of the estimated $10 billion in foreign debt outstanding.

The harassment of foreign political refugees in Argentina drew a strong protest from the Office of the United Nations High Commissioner for Refugees. The U.N. agency urged other Latin American governments to offer the political exiles asylum.

See STATISTICS OF THE WORLD.   A.K.M.

ARIZONA. See STATISTICS OF THE WORLD.

ARKANSAS. See STATISTICS OF THE WORLD.

ARMSTRONG, ANNE. See PEOPLE IN THE NEWS.

ART. The discovery of several new works apparently by the Italian Renaissance master Michelangelo and important exhibitions celebrating the United States Bicentennial were among the highlights of 1976 in the art world.

Michelangelo Drawings. On Oct. 21, 1975, Paolo Dal Poggetto, art historian and director of the Medici Chapel State Museum in Florence, Italy, announced the discovery of a group of large-scale wall drawings in a washroom chamber located off the chapel, which is in the Basilica of San Lorenzo. Dal Poggetto attributed ten of these drawings to the great Michelangelo, who worked on the Medici Chapel from 1520 to 1534. In early 1976 fifty-five additional (and more imposing) mural drawings were discovered in a small basement cell beneath the choir of the same building; many of these drawings were also attributed to Michelangelo.

It is thought that Michelangelo may have used the well-concealed basement room as a place to hide from the Medici family in 1530 when a republic which the artist had supported collapsed. If the attributions are proved correct, the discovery would be one of the major art events of this century. Several other Michelangelo scholars, however, were not as firmly convinced as Dal Poggetto about the validity of the find.

Major Exhibitions. Art museum exhibitions in 1976 were topped off by the November opening of "Treasures of Tutankhamen" at the National Gallery of Art in Washington, D.C. After years of delicate negotiations, the Egyptian government allowed fifty-five of the most beautiful and representative treasures from the tomb of "King Tut," who ruled Egypt in the 14th century B.C., to travel to the U.S. After Washington, this lavish show was scheduled to be seen in museums in Chicago, New Orleans, Los Angeles, Seattle, and New York City between April, 1977, and April, 1979. Another Egyptian pharaoh, Ramses II, was

Completed in September, "Running Fence," an environmental sculpture of billowy white nylon, stretches 24 mi. through Sonoma and Marin counties in California. It was designed and constructed by the controversial Bulgarian-born artist Christo.

featured in a midsummer show at the Grand Palais Museum in Paris.

The Tate Gallery in London paid tribute to Great Britain's great 19th-century landscape artist John Constable with an exhibition of 335 paintings, sketches, and drawings; almost all the major Constable works were included. Another important exhibition, "The 'Wild Beasts': Fauvism and Its Affinities," was organized by the Museum of Modern Art in New York City for showing there, at the San Francisco Museum of Modern Art, and at the Kimbell Art Museum in Fort Worth, Texas. This unusually beautiful show presented over 100 paintings by Henri Matisse, André Derain, Maurice de Vlaminck, and others borrowed from collections throughout the world. In October the Metropolitan Museum of Art in New York City opened, to mixed reviews, a major retrospective of works by the popular American realist painter Andrew Wyeth.

U.S. Bicentennial Celebrations. During 1976 a large number of important exhibitions were developed by American art museums to celebrate the Bicentennial. "The World of Franklin and Jef-

ferson," an official exhibition assembled by the American Revolution Bicentennial Commission, included artifacts and memorabilia reflecting the

Art collector and oil magnate Armand Hammer displays a prize acquisition, Rembrandt's "Juno," which he purchased in September for $3,250,000.

The Spirit of 76

At the age of 76, artist Louise Nevelson seemed to be just getting started. Born in Russia and raised in Maine, where her father owned a lumberyard, Nevelson was noted for the richly geometrical sculptures she makes using curious pieces of metal and wood, some of them rescued from junk heaps. To help celebrate America's 200th birthday, she went to Philadelphia, where the latest Nevelson, a construction called "Bicentennial Dawn," was unveiled by First Lady Betty Ford. In the meantime, other recent works were on display in such varied locales as Cambridge, Mass., Scottsdale, Ariz., and New York City, where her post-1969 output filled two floors of a large gallery.

Louise Nevelson and her "Bicentennial Dawn."

lives and times of those early patriots. The show was produced by designer Charles Eames and his wife Ray; it was seen by large crowds in Paris, London, and Warsaw before it began its tour of the U.S. The U.S. Department of the Interior produced the touring exhibition "America 1976," which offered eighty paintings of national wilderness areas by many of the country's best-known living realist artists.

Other noteworthy exhibitions of unusual interest included "America as Art," developed by the National Collection of Fine Arts in Washington, D.C., to show that U.S. arts and social development are inseparable. "American Art: An Exhibition from the Collection of Mr. and Mrs. John D. Rockefeller 3rd" opened at the M. H. De Young Memorial Museum in San Francisco; "Two Hundred Years of American Sculpture" occupied the Whitney Museum of American Art in New York City for six months; and "The American Presidency in Political Cartoons, 1776–1976" was presented by the University Art Museum, Berkeley, Calif.

A major cooperative effort called "Heritage and Horizon: American Painting, 1776–1976" brought together important American paintings from the collections of the Cleveland Museum of Art, the Detroit Institute of the Arts, the Toledo Museum of Art, and the Albright-Knox Art Gallery in Buffalo. The depth and diversity of these collections made the exhibition unusually rich.

Sales and Acquisitions. The art auction market in 1976 was unusually successful, with a number of records broken both for collections and for individual works. This success was attributed, in large part, to the uncertainties of world currency and commodity markets and to fears of political instability in the non-Communist world. In such times wealthy individuals are inclined to invest as much as 20 percent of their free income in fine arts and antiques.

Especially notable was the sale of 13th-century

The Cooper-Hewitt Museum exhibition "Man Transforms" featured this eye-catching display of the shapes of bread—more than 100 of them. The museum, an adjunct of the Smithsonian Institution, moved into the old Andrew Carnegie mansion in New York City during the year.

An abiding testament to the acknowledged genius of Alexander Calder is his steel-plate stabile "El Sol Rojo," standing 80 ft. high near Aztec Stadium in Mexico City. The American sculptor died Nov. 11 at 78.

Sienese master Duccio di Buoninsegna's wood panel "Crucifixion" at just under $2,000,000. Sales of impressionist and postimpressionist pictures proved excellent to mixed, with Paul Gauguin's "Still Life with Japanese Woodcut" reaching a record price of $1,400,000. The Gauguin was sold during an auction to settle the estate of Josef Rosensaft, an American collector who died at least $5,000,000 in debt on Sept. 10, 1975.

Sales of contemporary art were less regular. Although a high percentage of works did not reach expected prices, new price records were set for paintings by American artists Mark Rothko, Arshile Gorky, Roy Lichtenstein, and Larry Rivers and by the British painter Francis Bacon. One of the nine known early impressions of Pablo Picasso's etching "Le Repas Frugal" sold for more than $107,000.

The Japanese print market showed real improvement as well-to-do Japanese invested in their heritage as a hedge against the serious inflation in that country. Prices generally were 20 percent over estimates.

The sale of two major paintings took place outside the auction houses during the year. Oil magnate and art collector Armand Hammer purchased Rembrandt's "Juno" from an anonymous New York collector for $3,250,000, said to be the highest price ever paid for a Rembrandt. The Hammer collection, including the new Rembrandt, has been bequeathed to the Los Angeles County Museum of Art. In the second major acquisition, the National Gallery of Art in Washington, D.C., purchased Jackson Pollock's "Lavender Mist" (1950) from artist and collector Alfonso Ossorio and his associate Edward Young for a price rumored to be in excess of $2,000,000.

New Museums. New York's Cooper-Hewitt Museum of Design, established in 1897, moved to new quarters in October. The museum, which has one of the world's finest collections on the decorative arts, relocated to a neo-Georgian mansion built in 1901 by the steel magnate Andrew Carnegie and donated to the Cooper-Hewitt by the Carnegie Corporation in 1972. The museum reopened with a new show called "Man Transforms: Aspects of Design."

In Paris the Centre National d'Art et de Culture neared completion. The first show, a Marcel Duchamp retrospective, was scheduled for January, 1977, and the center was to open formally the following April.

Deaths. The art world mourned the loss in 1976 of Josef Albers, Alexander Calder, Max Ernst, Man Ray, and Mark Tobey; *see* OBITUARIES. Other notable deaths included those of American painter

Leonid Berman, known as Leonid (Oct. 1 at 80); Daniel Catton Rich, former director of the Art Institute of Chicago (Oct. 15 at 72); Russian abstract painter Yevgeny Rukhin (May 24 at 32), in a suspicious fire in his Leningrad studio; and German-born international art dealer Justin Thannhauser (Dec. 26 at 84). H.T.H.

ASTRONAUTICS. *See* SPACE TECHNOLOGY.

ASTRONOMY. Many clues to the nature of the sun were gathered in 1976, but they served to make this nearest star more puzzling than had been imagined. New objects were found in the universe, from nearby "bursters" to free-floating intergalactic clouds that could affect the theory of how the universe will end.

Irregularities Found on the Sun. Several discoveries made during the year upset the long-held assumption that the sun is a relatively predictable star that gives off its energy at a constant rate. A study linking changes in the earth's climate to the sun's behavior (*see* EARTH AND PLANETARY SCIENCES: *Climatology*) showed that the corona has disappeared at times in the recent past and the eleven-year cycle of sunspots has varied. The finding raised severe doubts about the regularity of the solar constant, the supposedly fixed rate at which the earth receives solar energy.

Oscillations of the sun's surface, like the sound waves that reverberate outward from a struck gong, were reported in April, 1975, by Henry A. Hill of the University of Arizona. The sound waves peaked at periods from 6 min. to 1 hr. and rose as high as ¼ mi. Subsequent measurements by British, French, and Russian astronomers confirmed the oscillations and found that they had widely varying periods and amplitudes of up to perhaps 250 mi. According to Hill, the oscillations result from great storms set off by an instability in the two outer zones of the sun's sphere, where first helium atoms and then hydrogen atoms lose their electrons and become ionized.

Clues to the organization of the sun's magnetic field were discovered through signals from spacecraft Pioneer XI as it rose above the orbital path of the earth on its way to Saturn. The sun's magnetic field, roughly similar to that of the earth and Jupiter, is oriented outward in its northern hemisphere and inward in the southern hemisphere. The two opposite fields are separated by a thin warped sheet of "mixed-field" electric current along the sun's equatorial plane; this sheet of current flaps up and down like the brim of a floppy hat according to the strength of the solar winds above and below it. Solar winds are fast-moving streams of hydrogen and helium ions that rise up as holes are opened in the sun's corona (this is another recent finding); these winds carry the magnetic fields with them to the outer reaches of the solar system. A planet such as the earth, whose orbital plane is aligned with the sun's equatorial region, will experience the sun's northern magnetic field when the planet is above the equatorial current sheet and the reverse southern magnetic field when below it. Pioneer XI was well above the current sheet and recorded only the northern magnetic field. All previous satellites had had abrupt field reversals every few days; these reversals had mystified scientists. Many astronomers are now of the opinion that when the variable solar winds stream past the earth, the disturbances that are set off in the earth's own magnetic field cause changes in the earth's high altitude region and these changes in turn change the course of the weather in the lower atmosphere.

Mysterious Bursters. A new class of celestial objects of an unknown nature appeared to have been detected in our own galaxy, the Milky Way. Satellite instruments indicated their existence in 1974 by picking up intense, periodic bursts of X rays from an unknown source. By 1976 sixteen sources had been found and designated "bursters." These were apparently scattered throughout

A photograph of Comet West, taken from outer space on March 5, 1976. One of the brightest comets to be seen in a decade, it measured 50,000,-000 mi. from head to tail.

Gas ions possibly of the pregalactic universe of 15 billion years ago were detected by this 36-ft. radio telescope of the National Radio Astronomy Observatory at Kitt Peak, Ariz. Constituents of star formation, the deuterated formyl ions were found to be more abundant at the edges of galaxies than at the centers—and this finding supports the theory that they were left over from the "big bang."

the galaxy. Slow bursters ejected the most powerful radiations, at intervals of up to 4 hr., and rapid bursters gave off lower intensity radiations in periods as short as 6 sec. Sudden, sharp X-ray bursts were also detected from other galaxies in all parts of the sky during the year; they seemed to be associated with globular clusters.

Is Comet West a Planet Fragment? The controversial theory that a giant planet existed in our solar system until it exploded 6,000,000 years ago received support in 1976 from a study of the orbits of sixty comets that have been seen only once in the past 150 years. Thomas C. Van Flandern of the U.S. Naval Observatory calculated that the extremely long orbits of these comets (each takes at least 1,000,000 years to swing around the sun) all intersect at a common starting point in the asteroid belt between Mars and Jupiter, where the planet is believed to have exploded. Van Flandern concluded that the comets, the asteroids, and many of the meteorites that fall to earth are probably fragments of the lost planet. Comet West, a spectacular comet that was seen in the early morning sky during the month of March, has a 1,000,000-year orbital cycle. According to Van Flandern, the comet may also be a planetary fragment.

Fate of the Universe. Just as most scientists had concluded that the universe will expand forever because not enough matter exists to exert the gravitational force required to draw it back, evidence was found of substantial gatherings (clouds) of invisible matter among the galaxies. These clouds, which could have come from ex-

Carbon monoxide, important in the evolution of life, was found in the N159 region of the Large Magellanic Cloud, one of the galaxies nearest to the Milky Way. The discovery was made in 1976 by the new Anglo-Australian Telescope at Silver Springs, Australia, as it searched the southern skies.

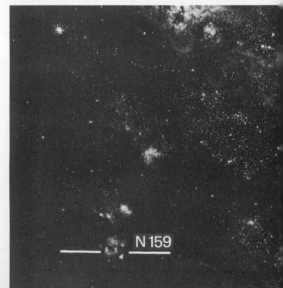

N 159

ploding galaxies, were discovered by Robert E. Williams and Ray J. Weymann of the University of Arizona while they were studying the light waves of quasars. (A quasar, an object at the outer edge of the universe, emits extraordinary amounts of energy.) The analysis by Williams and Weymann of the manner in which the clouds blocked off certain wavelengths of the quasars' light showed that the clouds were freely distributed in the space between galaxies. As a result of this discovery, a basis now exists for the theory that the universe might fall back in on itself and explode again in another "big bang," and that this explosion might be repeated endlessly.   F.C.H.

AUSTRALIA. Political tension ran high throughout 1976 as a result of the constitutional crisis that took place in Australia late in 1975. Labourites remained bitter about what they considered the illegal move made at that time by Governor-General Sir John Kerr, the representative of Great Britain's Queen Elizabeth II, who dismissed Labourite Prime Minister Gough Whitlam. Kerr had then called new elections that resulted in a parliamentary victory for a Liberal-Country Party coalition under Malcolm Fraser. For its part, the new Fraser government in 1976 began a systematic dismantling of the Whitlam program. Domestically, Fraser inaugurated his own program of conservative policies and fiscal austerity. In foreign relations he moved away from Whitlam's near neutrality toward closer ties with the United States.

Politics and Economics. Under Prime Minister Fraser, not even the national anthem remained unchanged. In May he announced that "Waltzing Matilda" would be played "at functions like the Olympic Games," replacing Whitlam's choice of "Advance Australia Fair." Of far more import, Fra-

ser was determined to combat Australia's severe economic problems by reversing Whitlam's policies. He announced that he would slash public spending, cut inflation, and encourage more foreign investment. With those ends in mind, he began 1976 by announcing that many government agencies would be abolished and that funds for health, pensions, and housing would be drastically cut. He indicated that he could not wholeheartedly support wage increases that were geared to rise automatically with rises in the cost of living.

In April Fraser announced new measures to encourage foreign capital to invest in Australian industry and mineral exploration, such investment having been blocked by the Whitlam administration. In May the government disclosed that it planned to alter Medibank, a program of national health services, so that it would no longer be free to all.

The political temperature rose immediately. In July powerful labor unions called the nation's first general strike. About half the 5,000,000-man work force joined the 24-hr. protest against changes in the Medibank plan, bringing transport and many industrial plants to a halt. A month later the prime minister was the personal target of an ugly demonstration at Monash University in Melbourne, where he was jostled and for a brief time virtually held captive by an angry crowd of student demonstrators.

The Monash incident was not the only sign that political passion was running high. All year long, Governor-General Kerr was subjected to insults and abuse during public appearances. His unpopularity, resulting from his role in the 1975 political crisis, was a source of worry to both the Australian

On July 11 students in Melbourne join Australia's first general strike, a protest against government cutbacks in Medibank, the national health services program.

A unique exhibition of Australian aboriginal art began a U.S. tour at the Museum of Albuquerque, N.Mex., on Aug. 15. Displaying art forms that took thousands of years to develop, the exhibition represented Australia's salute to the U.S. Bicentennial.

and the British governments. Queen Elizabeth was scheduled to tour Australia in 1977, but those in charge of planning her visit became concerned that if Kerr were to accompany her, the Queen herself might become a target of demonstrations.

The government budget, introduced in August, kept the control of inflation and the stimulation of business as top priorities. Despite that program, however, Australia suffered continuing economic difficulty. Unemployment exceeded 5 percent, and inflation was running at an annual rate of 12 percent. Shipbuilding was so hard-pressed by international competition that many economists predicted the industry would collapse within eighteen months unless it received government help. At the same time, a low birthrate and declining immigration caused concern about population trends. In an effort to encourage exports, the Fraser government on Nov. 28 devalued the Australian dollar by 17.5 percent.

In opposition, the Labour Party was slow to recover from the 1975 setback. Former Prime Minister Whitlam beat back challenges and retained the post of Labour Party leader in January balloting. Within a few weeks, however, there were allegations that late in 1975 Whitlam had discussed with two emissaries from oil-rich Iraq the possibility that their government might provide financial help for the Labour Party's campaign fund. But despite criticism by party colleagues, Whitlam was able to hang on to the party leadership.

Foreign Relations. The Fraser administration moved away from the nearly neutralist policies of its predecessor toward closer ties with the U.S. Fraser formally abandoned Whitlam's support for keeping Australia within a zone of neutralism and asserted his support for a strengthening of U.S. bases there. In February he stated that he supported a long-standing American request to build a new navigation station in southeastern Australia. In June he lifted Whitlam's ban on visits to Australia by American nuclear-powered warships.

Making a major foreign policy statement in June, the prime minister charged that the Soviet Union was engaging in a worldwide political offensive, and he strongly emphasized his nation's links with the U.S. This was followed in July with an official visit to Washington, D.C., where he and President Gerald R. Ford held a series of cordial talks. As a Bicentennial gift to the U.S., a Chair in Australian Studies at Harvard University founded by Whitlam, was inaugurated by Fraser.

See STATISTICS OF THE WORLD.   F.W.

AUSTRIA. Playing host to the Winter Olympic Games at Innsbruck was a highlight of the year in Austria. The games, which lasted for twelve days, brought Austria both world attention and a windfall in tourist revenues; *see* SPORTS: *The Olympic Games.*

Despite continuing economic difficulties throughout the world, the Austrian economy remained relatively healthy. After a 2.5 percent drop in the gross national product (G.N.P.) for 1975, Austrian economists expected a 1.5–2 percent G.N.P. gain in 1976. The inflation rate had been cut to 6–7 percent, and unemployment was down to 1.1 percent, lower than that of most other industrial nations. In announcing the federal budget for 1977, Finance Minister Hannes Androsch stated in July that the government would give priority to stabilization measures.

Politically, Austria spent a relatively quiet year following parliamentary elections in October, 1975. Chancellor Bruno Kreisky revamped his cabinet in August, appointing new ministers for foreign affairs, agriculture, and social welfare.

One source of domestic controversy was the claim by Austria's Slavic minority that it was the target of discrimination and "statistical genocide." Specifically, the Slovenes charged that they were being intimidated by German-speaking nationalist organizations, intent on removing Slovene as an official language. Consequently, they were apprehensive about the results of a census held in November to ascertain the number of Austria's non-German-speaking citizens.

The Slovene question led to friction with Yugoslavia, where Slovenes are a major ethnic group. But in line with Austria's stated foreign policy of "activist neutrality," Chancellor Kreisky worked to broaden relations with other socialist nations, among them Czechoslovakia, which he visited in February. He also welcomed a number of Communist leaders for talks in Austria, including Henryk Jabłoński of Poland, György Lázár of Hungary, and Manea Manescu of Rumania. Kreisky also took an active interest in Mideast affairs. In March he led a delegation of socialists on a fact-finding tour of the area. The next month, Egyptian President Anwar el-Sadat and a delegation of his cabinet ministers visited Vienna and conferred with Kreisky on joint Austro-Egyptian development projects in Egypt.

See STATISTICS OF THE WORLD.   F.W.

AUTOMATION. See TECHNOLOGY.
AUTOMOBILE. See TRANSPORTATION.
AVIATION. See TRANSPORTATION.

B

BAHAMAS. See STATISTICS OF THE WORLD.
BAHRAIN. See STATISTICS OF THE WORLD.
BANGLADESH. Bangladesh, seemingly on the brink of total collapse in 1975, made a surprising recovery during 1976.
Political Affairs. Under the leadership of Maj. Gen. Ziaur Rahman, the dominant member of the ruling three-man military junta, corruption at high levels was greatly reduced. The government rehired capable civil servants dismissed when Sheikh Mujibur Rahman held power (he was assassinated in an August, 1975, coup). Law and order were restored in the cities; murders by dissident elements continued in the countryside, but on a reduced scale. Many political figures jailed by Mujibur Rahman were released, and in July the resumption of political party activities was permitted. But in December, Ziaur Rahman assumed the title of martial-law administrator and ordered the arrest of more than 100 persons, including former President Khandaker Moshtaque Ahmed. These actions placed in doubt the government's pledge of new elections in February, 1977.
The Economy. For the second year in a row, good rainfall and the absence of any major natural disaster permitted a bumper harvest. At the same time, the government succeeded in reducing smuggling to India and continued to receive large food imports under international aid programs; consequently, the price of rice fell rapidly. However, large amounts of food went to waste because of inadequate storage facilities and the lack of an effective rationing system outside the cities.

According to official figures, the economy grew by 12 percent during the year ending June, 1976. Nevertheless, the gross national product was only about $70 per capita, or less than in 1969–70. The reason for this decline was the nation's rapid population growth, a problem to which the government assigned top priority. A comprehensive population control program, the country's first, was launched in September. Thousands of workers were sent out to the villages to provide instructions and devices, while strong incentives were offered for sterilization.
Foreign Relations. Relations with Pakistan continued to improve, but tensions with India rose markedly. Bangladesh accused India of lending support to guerrilla groups operating in the north (India denied the charge). The government also complained in May that India had been diverting too much water from the Ganges R. at the new Farraka barrier, 11 mi. above the border, thus causing extensive damage to agriculture and industry in Bangladesh.

See STATISTICS OF THE WORLD.   W.J.G.
BARBADOS. See STATISTICS OF THE WORLD.
BELGIUM. Belgium suffered severe hardship during 1976 as a result of the worst drought Europe had experienced in more than 200 years. The Belgian franc reflected these conditions and remained weak throughout most of the year.

Domestic Affairs. Poor weather had caused serious failures in Western Europe's 1975 potato crops. By January, 1976, Belgium, whose potato consumption was Europe's second highest, was reported to be in serious difficulties. Black-marketing sprang up as potatoes disappeared from stores. The government on Jan. 21 banned potato hoarding and specified strict penalties of high fines and prison terms of up to five years for dealers charging more than the top wholesale price of 11¢ a pound fixed by the administration.

Belgium, which had received no substantial rain after January, took drastic action during the summer to conserve water. The government announced on Aug. 20 that it would impose fines and jail terms on those who violated the regulations against watering lawns, filling swimming pools, and washing cars and sidewalks.

Germain Baudrin, former head of Belgium's telephone and telegraph system, received a nine-month prison sentence on Feb. 23. He had been convicted of accepting bribes from a Belgian unit of the International Telephone and Telegraph Corp. Premier Léo Tindemans promised on March 9 that the administration would investigate charges that the Lockheed Aircraft Corp. had bribed other Belgians.

In July King Baudouin completed twenty-five years on the Belgian throne. The popular monarch had been able to unify the French- and Flemish-speaking factions that formerly divided the country, and the Belgian monarchy had become as stable as any in Europe.

Foreign Affairs and Finance. Belgium continued to play a major role in European unity affairs. Premier Tindemans on Jan. 7 delivered a report on European unity that the heads of the European Community governments had ordered in 1974. The Tindemans report emphasized procedures for increased cooperation in specific areas rather than the goal of complete economic and political union by 1980. Tindemans proposed a "two-tier" approach in which more advanced community members could progress faster toward economic and social integration than those less well advanced.

Belgium took action during 1976 to halt the declining value of the Belgian franc. The Belgian National Bank raised the discount rate from 6 percent to 7 percent on March 17 and then to 8 percent on July 23 in an effort to bolster the franc's position in the joint float of European currencies. This float, known as the "snake," permitted currencies to fluctuate against each other by no more than 2.25 percent. Belgium's franc had dropped on July 22 to the "floor" level of $0.025145 in United States currency. A few days later the government increased short-term interest rates in a further move designed to stabilize the franc and to attract investors.

One boost to the economy was the signing of contracts on Aug. 24 for the Belgian firm Fabrique Nationale to coproduce $400,000,000 worth of jet engines for F-16 warplanes being bought by Belgium from the U.S.

See STATISTICS OF THE WORLD.   L.A.S.

BHUTAN. *See* STATISTICS OF THE WORLD.

BICENTENNIAL. The United States ushered in its third century as an independent nation during 1976 with thousands of birthday celebrations. The Fourth of July, of course, was the culminating day:

Above: An 8-tiered, 51-ft.-high national birthday cake was displayed on the Fourth of July in Memorial Hall, Fairmount Park, Philadelphia. Opposite page: The Argentine frigate Libertad *passes beneath the George Washington Bridge during Operation Sail on July 4. Sixteen windjammers and hundreds of lesser sailing ships from thirty nations gathered in New York harbor for the Bicentennial spectacle.*

Margaret Henkel, president of the Westport (Conn.) Historical Society, displays a hand-appliquéd Bicentennial quilt produced by sixty volunteers.

craft circling Mars cut a ribbon to open the Smithsonian Institution's Air and Space Museum. A fireworks display at the Washington Monument attracted more than a million persons to the Mall to conclude the day's festivities.

Philadelphia's yearlong celebration included performances by the Philadelphia Orchestra of works commissioned for the Bicentennial. The Fourth of July was celebrated with picnics, sporting events, patriotic musters, and an eight-hour "parade of the states." Ceremonies at Independence Hall featured an address by President Gerald R. Ford. In nearby Valley Forge twenty teams of covered wagons completed a yearlong 17,000-mi. journey to the site where George Washington's army encamped for the bitter winter of 1777.

Baltimore's Fourth of July observance featured

Bicentennial festivities in Milwaukee, Wis., included a parade of tricyclists.

from Mars Hill, Maine, where the first rays of sunlight emerged at 4:33 A.M., to American Samoa, where festivities included copra cutting and spear throwing. More than 11,700 communities, in an outpouring of patriotic feeling, celebrated with fireworks, parades, rallies, rodeos, pie-eating contests, and wreath-layings.

City Observances. The most elaborate celebrations occurred in cities prominently associated with the young nation. In Washington, D.C. (which was not in existence in 1776), the nation's most revered documents—the Declaration of Independence, the Constitution, and the Bill of Rights—were placed on public display for seventy-six hours beginning July 2. On Independence Day a signal relayed from the Viking space-an all-night program at Fort McHenry, where a 400,000-slice birthday cake was lit and a fireworks display reenacted the British bombardment of 1814.

Other notable Bicentennial events during the year were a parade in Detroit on May 2, a youth fair in Houston in May, a folk-arts festival in Denver in June, and an international trade exposition in Chicago in July.

Operation Sail. Perhaps the most spectacular Bicentennial event took place in New York harbor, where 16 full-sized, mostly square-rigged sailing ships, about 230 lesser sailing ships, and 50 ships of war from 22 countries convened on the Fourth of July for an international naval review. This assembly was described by some as the largest gathering of ships since the Spanish Armada.

More than 10,000 smaller boats dotted the harbor, and about 6,000,000 spectators lined the banks of the Hudson R. and lower Manhattan to watch the stately "tall ships" pass in review. Many of the vessels continued on to other U.S. ports as part of the Operation Sail program. New York City also staged a giant fireworks display over the floodlit Statue of Liberty.

Local Celebrations. Small towns tried not to be outdone. Seward, Nebr. (pop. 6000), celebrated with a bicycle race, a pet parade, barbecue, band concerts, a firemen's water fight, an antique car show, and the sealing of "the world's largest time capsule" containing a full-sized Chevrolet, a motorcycle, cases of soft drinks, and 10,000 letters from residents to their future grandchildren.

The American Revolution Bicentennial Administration (A.R.B.A.) tabulated thousands of new cultural and educational programs, new constructions, and restorations of historic buildings in cities and towns throughout the country. There were also many touring exhibits. Millions of spectators visited a privately funded, touring "Freedom Train" that displayed historical memorabilia.

Appraisals. Not all the Fourth of July observances were festive, and some expressed criticism of the nation. The People's Bicentennial Commission sponsored several rallies protesting what it considered the pervasive influence of big corporations in American life. Dissenters on the left objected that no spirit of national self-improvement emerged from the festivities. Many observers also decried the commercial exploitation of the Bicentennial.

In his assessment A.R.B.A. administrator John W. Warner concluded, "Admittedly, the Bicentennial failed to meet the level of expectation of some—those who viewed it as a signal to push ahead with major needed social reform. . . . But for many it rekindled spirits. . . . It is my belief that

Family get-togethers, like this one in Knoxville, Tenn., were a popular way of celebrating the nation's 200th birthday.

the Bicentennial marks a major turning point for the United States of America and its people."

Worldwide reaction was generally cordial. The Soviet Union sent a lukewarm message of congratulations. The London *Observer* editorialized: "The Fourth of July cannot be our feast . . . but we can be a little proud that no other nation, not even Imperial Rome, produced so great and nobly independent an offspring."   T.D.

BLACK, SHIRLEY TEMPLE. See PEOPLE IN THE NEWS

BOLIVIA. In June, 1976, Col. Hugo Banzer Suárez, who became president of Bolivia following a 1971 military coup, was forced to impose a state of siege to cope with student and labor unrest. Student demonstrations broke out at the beginning of the month, after President Banzer refused to allow the body of former President Juan José Torres Gonzáles to be returned to Bolivia following his kidnapping and assassination in Argentina. The Bolivian government did offer to provide a state funeral for Torres, but would not permit Torres's widow and the miners' union to conduct a private service, fearing political disturbances. On June 3, a day of national mourning for Torres, the miners staged a one-day strike. Violence in mining areas escalated, and after the government sent in troops a two-week strike began. The miners, who had demanded wage increases of 130 percent, settled for 17 to 30 percent wage boosts.

Bolivia's economic and financial position improved considerably, because of rising tin prices and improvements in the oil and gas industries. Inflation in 1976 was only 6 percent, and real economic growth reached 7 percent for the year. With foreign reserves at record levels, the government was able to relax the import controls it had imposed earlier in the year.

In July Bolivia—which has no direct access to the sea for its mineral exports—obtained a large free port zone from Argentina at Rosario on the Paraná R. The free zone was to be used by Bolivia as a transfer terminal for cargo to and from the Atlantic. Negotiations with Peru and Chile for a corridor to the seaport on the Pacific Ocean continued throughout 1976.

See STATISTICS OF THE WORLD.   A.K.M.

BOTANY. *See* LIFE SCIENCES.

BOTSWANA. *See* STATISTICS OF THE WORLD.

BRAZIL. President Ernesto Geisel had some success in 1976 in his push for political liberalization and a more just social policy, but his military government was not so successful in bringing Brazil's major economic problems under control.

Politics. The local elections, the first elections in Brazil since 1974, took place according to schedule on Nov. 15, belying speculation that right-wing military elements might force their cancellation. Although the election process heavily favored the government-backed National Alliance for Renovation (ARENA), the Brazilian Democratic Movement, the sole legal opposition party, increased its share of local government positions, scoring especially impressive victories in the major cities. But ARENA's overall success—the party

won about 70 percent of all mayoralties and city council positions—was sufficient to bolster President Geisel's credibility. ARENA claimed a margin of 4,500,000 votes out of an electorate of 43,000,000. ARENA candidates were unopposed in many areas, and restrictions on party broadcasts and advertising worked to ARENA's advantage.

In conjunction with the liberalization process, army excesses were curbed and torture of political prisoners was reportedly stopped as of May. Although still applied in an arbitrary fashion, censorship was also eased. On the other hand, the National Conference of Bishops of Brazil denounced the Geisel regime in November for allowing police and vigilantes responsible for a series of murders to go unpunished. Clergymen had been among the targets of the assaults.

Two former presidents of Brazil, Juscelino Kubitschek and João Goulart, died during 1976 (*see* OBITUARIES).

The Economy. Keeping to the promise of a more just social policy, the Geisel government upped minimum wages at the end of April by 44 percent, the highest such increase in a decade, and expanded state health insurance and assistance to small farmers. The military regime, however, had difficulty dealing with Brazil's major economic problems—soaring inflation and large trade and payments deficits. In June the government introduced a number of restrictive monetary measures to curtail money supply growth and inflation. Reserve requirements for commercial banks were hiked from 27 to 33 percent, the date by which deposits had to be made was advanced, and the central bank discount rate was raised from 22 to 28 percent. Despite these measures, the inflation rate for 1976 was still about 45 percent.

To bring the trade and current account deficits

Supporters of the Brazilian Democratic Movement (M.D.B.) celebrate the party's November electoral success in Rio de Janeiro. The M.D.B. did well in all the major cities, but the government-backed National Alliance for Renovation (ARENA) won most of the races nationwide.

Smiles abound as Bulgarian Communist Party leader Todor Zhivkov greets Cuban Premier Fidel Castro in Sofia on March 9. Three weeks later the 11th Congress of the Bulgarian Communist Party reconfirmed Zhivkov's leadership.

under control, the government tightened the already restrictive import system by requiring importers to deposit in the central bank for 360 days a sum equal to the value of goods imported. New exchange restrictions were also imposed on Brazilians traveling abroad. At the same 'time, the government tried to encourage exports by introducing additional export incentives. Nevertheless, the trade deficit still reached $2.3 billion in 1976, and Brazil's international debt reached $28 billion (triple the 1973 total) by the end of the year.

The government waited until after the elections to announce further policy changes designed to deal with the deteriorating economic situation. The government disclosed that it would undertake a $3.4 billion cutback in its spending plans for 1977. This cut was expected to reduce real economic growth in 1977 from 8 to 4 percent.

The country's fifteen-year-old minidevaluation system was maintained throughout the year. By the beginning of December, the cruzeiro had been adjusted downward fifteen times, representing a 24.8 percent depreciation of the cruzeiro against the United States dollar since the beginning of 1976.

Foreign Affairs. On Feb. 21, during a visit by U.S. Secretary of State Henry A. Kissinger, Brazil signed a consultation agreement with the U.S. Under the terms of the agreement, the Brazilian foreign minister and U.S. secretary of state would meet at least twice annually, and at least one of those meetings would be in Brazil. The agreement implicitly recognized Brazil as the major power in South America, and thereby displeased Brazil's rivals on the continent. Brazil's diplomatic courtship of Peru also raised suspicions in the region.

Diplomatic and economic relations between Brazil and Peru had been frozen since 1968, when leftist President Juan Velasco Alvarado came to power. His successor, President Francisco Morales Bermúdez, met with Geisel in November and signed eight agreements on areas of mutual cooperation.

See STATISTICS OF THE WORLD. A.K.M.

BREZHNEV, LEONID. See PEOPLE IN THE NEWS.

BRITISH COLUMBIA. See STATISTICS OF THE WORLD.

BULGARIA. Continuity and allegiance to the Soviet Union remained the hallmarks of Bulgarian policy in 1976. In domestic affairs the regime sought to raise living standards and enforce Communist orthodoxy. In foreign relations Bulgaria followed the general path laid down by the authorities in Moscow.

The ruling Communist Party held its 11th Congress in Sofia, March 29–April 2. Todor Zhivkov, the head of the party since 1954, was unanimously reelected as its first secretary, but there were some personnel changes in subordinate positions. The number of party secretaries was reduced from 6 to 5, and of Politburo members from 12 to 9. The most surprising Politburo change was the ouster of Zhivko Zhivkov (no relation to Todor Zhivkov), a man once thought to be a future contender for power.

On the eve of the congress, the Communist Party published projections of living standards for the years 1976–80; the party envisioned that real per capita income would rise 4 percent annually during that period. The party also exhorted the public to progress toward "physical and moral perfection." In line with that campaign, the government opened a drive against smoking and the consumption of alcoholic beverages. It was a matter of official concern that per capita consumption of alcohol had doubled in fifteen years.

Parliamentary elections were held on May 30, and in June the new National Assembly reelected Todor Zhivkov chairman of the State Council, the nation's highest office.

In foreign trade Bulgaria continued to integrate its economy with that of the U.S.S.R. Diplomatically, Bulgaria's most notable initiatives involved its neighbors. Late in January and early in February, Bulgarian delegates attended a five-nation conference on Balkan cooperation, held in Athens. In April Zhivkov made his first official visit to Greece, and in June he conferred in Ankara with the Turkish president.

See STATISTICS OF THE WORLD. F.W.

BURMA. In his fourteen years of iron-fisted rule President Ne Win turned Burma into a poverty-stricken hermit state—inward looking and committed to the "Burmese Way to Socialism." But during 1976 Ne Win's long reign grew shaky, and Burma began to look outside its borders for assistance.

In March Ne Win fired Defense Minister and Chief of Staff Tin U, a general regarded as a possible successor to Ne Win. With Tin U shunted aside, pro-Soviet Gen. San Yu became the likely heir apparent. In response students rioted in the capital of Rangoon, demanding economic reform and an end to the Ne Win–San Yu clique. The government quickly crushed the demonstrations and closed the country's universities for the fourth time in two years.

Dissatisfaction with Ne Win also spread to the army, the main prop of his regime. In July a group of young officers—possibly supporters of Tin U—attempted a coup in which Ne Win and San Yu were to have been assassinated. The plot was exposed and fourteen ringleaders jailed; at the end of the year their fate was unknown.

The government's battle with ethnic and Communist rebels did not go well in 1976. February and March were marked by some of the heaviest fighting to date. The pro-Peking Communist rebels operating along the China border made steady gains in manpower and weaponry, some of which was said to be United States ordnance left behind in South Vietnam. In May nine ethnic groups, united only in their opposition to the Rangoon government, banded together in a National Democratic Front. In Rangoon itself, the state of martial law imposed since the student riots late in 1974 was lifted on Sept. 1.

Despite Burma's natural wealth, the economy continued to deteriorate. Inflation galloped at close to 40 percent annually, exports declined, and the black market flourished. To stave off total economic collapse, Ne Win asked the World Bank to form an international aid consortium and agreed to accept a degree of World Bank supervision over Burma's economy.

In foreign affairs Burma remained scrupulously nonaligned but appeared to be far more wary of China's influence than of Moscow's. Despite gestures of friendship from Ne Win, Peking continued to supply and befriend the Communist insurgents.

See STATISTICS OF THE WORLD. R.J.C.

BURUNDI. *See* STATISTICS OF THE WORLD.
BUSH, GEORGE. *See* PEOPLE IN THE NEWS.
BUTZ, EARL. *See* PEOPLE IN THE NEWS.

C

CABINET, UNITED STATES. Two members of President Gerald R. Ford's cabinet left under controversial circumstances during the Presidential election year of 1976.

The first to go was John T. Dunlop, who resigned as secretary of labor on Feb. 1 after President Ford vetoed a labor-supported construction-site picketing bill that Dunlop had helped to draft. Dunlop denied that his departure was a protest. He said, however, that after the veto, "the requisite communications, confidence and trust" among labor, management, and government were "no longer possible" if he remained as head of the Department of Labor.

The second resignation was that of Secretary of Agriculture Earl L. Butz, who left on Oct. 4 with an admission that he had committed a "gross indiscretion" in repeating an obscene joke denigrating Blacks. The racial slur, in what had been intended as an off-the-record witticism, created a storm of criticism at the height of the election campaign. President Ford administered a "severe reprimand" to Butz, and Butz made a televised apology. The furor failed to die, however, and Butz was forced out of the cabinet.

Dunlop was replaced as secretary of labor by the government's chief labor mediator, W. J. Usery, Jr. Usery took the oath of office on Feb. 10; a week before, the previously nominated Elliot L. Richardson had taken office as secretary of commerce.

In a series of announcements in December, President-elect Jimmy Carter named the cabinet members who would take office with him in 1977, subject to Senate confirmation. The Carter appointees were: Secretary of State, Cyrus R. Vance; Secretary of the Treasury, W. Michael Blumenthal; Secretary of the Interior, Cecil D. Andrus; Secretary of Agriculture, Robert S. Bergland; Attorney General, Griffin B. Bell; Secretary of Commerce, Juanita M. Kreps; Secretary of Labor, F. Ray Marshall; Secretary of Defense, Harold Brown; Secretary of Health, Education, and Welfare, Joseph A. Califano, Jr.; Secretary of Housing and Urban Development, Patricia Roberts Harris; Secretary of Transportation, Brock Adams.

The executive departments, the years of their establishment, and their heads during 1976 follow:

Department of State, 1789: Secretary, Henry A. Kissinger.

Department of the Treasury, 1789: Secretary, William E. Simon.

Department of the Interior, 1849: Secretary, Thomas S. Kleppe.

Department of Agriculture, 1862: Secretary, Earl L. Butz until Oct. 4.

Department of Justice, 1870: Attorney General, Edward H. Levi.

Department of Commerce, 1913: Secretary, Elliot L. Richardson after Feb. 2.

Department of Labor, 1913: Secretary, John T. Dunlop until Feb. 1; W. J. Usery, Jr., nominated Jan. 22, confirmed Feb. 4.

Department of Defense, 1949: Secretary, Donald H. Rumsfeld.

Department of Health, Education, and Welfare, 1953: Secretary, F. David Mathews.

Department of Housing and Urban Development, 1965: Secretary, Carla Anderson Hills.

Department of Transportation, 1966: Secretary, William T. Coleman, Jr.   L.A.S.

CALIFORNIA. See STATISTICS OF THE WORLD.

CAMBODIA, formerly called the KHMER REPUBLIC, now officially DEMOCRATIC KAMPUCHEA. During 1976 the rural revolutionaries who came to power in April, 1975, consolidated their hold over the country. Stories brought out of Cambodia by refugees and defectors seemed to substantiate earlier reports of a reign of terror against the middle class, the intelligentsia, and members of the defeated United States-backed army. Western analysts believed that from 200,000 to 1,000,000 Cambodians had died either by execution or because of government-imposed hardships. As the year progressed, however, there were signs that the worst of the bloodletting seemed to have run its course.

Political Developments. Political life in Communist Cambodia remained something of a mystery. In April Prince Norodom Sihanouk, who had returned from exile in China to become figurehead chief of state, either resigned or was forced from his post, along with the rest of his cabinet. He was not permitted to leave for exile in France, as he reportedly wished. When Sihanouk slipped from sight in July, his friends abroad feared for his life.

In mid-April the powers in Phnom Penh announced the formation of a new government; Samphan, the man regarded by some analysts as the real leader in Cambodia, was the new head of state. Other experts were convinced, however, that a leadership struggle was still raging. One Cambodian defector—a pilot who flew his helicopter to Thailand—reported that real power in Phnom Penh was wielded by a five-man group called "the organization," or *angka.* This group, he said, included Communist Party Secretary Saloth Sar, Foreign Minister Ieng Sary, and Defense Minister Son Sen. Another possible leader, Nuon Chea, the chairman of the Cambodian People's Representative Assembly, was named acting premier in September.

Economic Affairs. The government continued to eradicate all semblances of the old regime and to drag the country toward a primitive sort of agrarian communism. In March a Swedish diplomat, one of the few Westerners allowed to visit the country, described the countryside as in a state of "total mobilization." Former city dwellers labored in the fields with the peasants, and large work brigades built dams and dug irrigation ditches.

According to the Swede and other observers, all industry and land, down to the tiniest of peasant plots, had been nationalized. Money was outlawed, and workers were paid not in wages but in rice or other goods. (The government claimed to have produced a good rice crop in 1976.) There were no stores, no restaurants, no telephones, and no formal schools. With nearly the entire population working in the fields, the cities were drained of population. Phnom Penh, once a metropolis of 2,500,000, was inhabited by perhaps 20,000 workers in the state-owned textile plants, along with an army of security guards.

Foreign Relations. Foreign trade was minimal, although boat traffic on the Mekong R. was resumed and Chinese ships called regularly at the port of Kompong Som (formerly Sihanoukville). About 1000 Chinese technicians in Cambodia advised on agriculture and industrial development. The Chinese also operated Cambodia's only regular link with the outside world—twice-monthly flights between Phnom Penh and Peking.

While they remade their country, Cambodia's Communist leaders at first paid little attention to foreign affairs. But in June Cambodia and Thailand agreed to set up embassies in each other's capitals. Two months later relations with Great Britain were normalized. In September Cambodia received delegations from Egypt, Tunisia, and Senegal, and the following month Ieng Sary visited Rumania and addressed the United Nations General Assembly in New York City.

See STATISTICS OF THE WORLD.   R.J.C.

CAMEROON. *See* STATISTICS OF THE WORLD.

CANADA. During 1976 the popularity of Pierre Elliott Trudeau, in his ninth year as prime minister of Canada, dwindled steadily; *see* PEOPLE IN THE NEWS. The decline in the 57-year-old Liberal leader's political fortunes was attributable largely to a series of cabinet scandals, stringent wage and price controls, and the explosive issue of bilingualism. So serious did the split between English-speaking and French-speaking Canadians become over the year that the prime minister himself warned that the Canadian federation was in danger of collapse—a warning that seemed far from empty after a separatist party swept to power in November in the French-speaking province of Québec.

Politics. The year began on a note of trouble for Trudeau. Many Canadians took strong exception to his New Year's Day remarks calling for a "new society" in which the government would wield far more power over the economy. Then, during a January visit to Cuba, Trudeau praised Cuban Premier Fidel Castro as a man with "thought and feeling for Africa." Coming at a time when Castro's troops were intervening in Angola, the statement drew a barrage of criticism.

At the same time, cabinet ministers close to the prime minister came under fire. There were hints of ministerial impropriety in the award of concessions for duty-free shops at Montréal's airports. One cabinet minister was found guilty of leaving the scene of an accident, and two other ministers were accused of trying to influence the judgment of the courts. Trudeau accepted the resignation of Corporate Affairs Minister André Ouellet but rejected that of Public Works Minister C. M. Drury, to the outspoken disgust of the parliamentary opposition.

The Summer Olympic Games, which opened in Montréal in July, provided Trudeau with more problems. In refusing to allow the team from Taiwan to participate as the Republic of China (as it was recognized by the International Olympic Committee), the Trudeau government was accused of bowing to pressure from the People's Republic of China, a major purchaser of Canadian wheat. Critics also charged that the action set a dangerous precedent for future Olympic Games.

The Language Issue. Perhaps the most critical questions to confront the Trudeau government in 1976 were the related ones of language and national unity. Trudeau came to power in 1968 because many Canadians believed that he could heal the breach between the English-speaking and French-speaking populations. Hoping to un-

Celebrating a Nov. 15 election victory in the province of Québec are members of the French-speaking Québec Party (Parti Québécois) and, at the microphone, Premier-elect René Lévesque. The banner at rear proclaims: "Things can't go on like this. We need a real government."

Opposite page: Members of the Taiwanese Olympic team on their way to Montréal wait at the Detroit airport on July 9, uncertain whether they will be allowed to participate in the Games as representatives of the Republic of China. Their demand to do so was refused, and they returned home on July 16, amid angry protests on their behalf.

dercut separatist sentiment among French Canadians in Québec, the Trudeau government expanded the use of French in government operations and recruited French-speaking Canadians for the civil service, the armed forces, and government-operated companies. But in 1976 these policies generated an English-speaking backlash.

The issue boiled to the surface in June, when air traffic controllers, with massive support from English-speaking Canadians, walked off their jobs rather than accept a government decision to extend the use of French in air traffic control in the province of Québec. Canadian airline pilots supported the strike, which lasted nine days and ended only after the government promised the strikers that the use of French would not be expanded unless (1) a three-man commission of jurists unanimously agreed that it would not be a threat to safety and (2) parliament accepted that judgment. The government action, which was seen by English-speaking Canada as a triumph and French-speaking Canada as a sellout, led to the resignation of Environment Minister Jean Marchand, a close political associate of Trudeau.

In October Trudeau warned his countrymen that the language issue imperiled the future of the country. Shortly thereafter, Defense Minister James A. Richardson handed in his resignation in protest over Trudeau's plan to give French equal official status with English in a proposed new Canadian constitution.

Québec Election. The language issue turned hotter than ever on Nov. 15 when predominantly French-speaking Québec, the country's largest province, held elections for its legislature. The campaign was fought largely on local issues, but underlying it all was French-Canadian resentment. Québec voters swept the Liberals out of power and gave the *Parti Québécois*, or Québec Party, which favors an independent Québec, 69 seats out of a total of 110. It was regarded primarily as a protest vote against the Liberals rather than a vote for independence. But the new provincial premier, 54-year-old Québec Party leader René Lévesque, insisted that he would attempt to start negotiations with Ottawa on a gradual transfer of sovereignty. Lévesque did promise that he would not push for total independence without one or more referenda of the people of Québec.

The results in Québec were another blow to Trudeau. As the year drew to a close, the Liberals retained a safe margin in the national parliament. But Liberal morale was low, and the chief opposition party, the Progressive Conservatives, led by about 15 percent in national opinion polls. Under their new leader, 37-year-old Joseph C. Clark of Alberta, the Progressive Conservatives were looking forward with unconcealed optimism to the national elections of 1978.

The Economy. Canada's first peacetime wage and price controls, imposed in October, 1975, and tightened and extended in 1976, were fought tooth and nail by labor and backed halfheartedly by industry. Under the anti-inflation guidelines, wage increases were restricted to from 8 to 12 percent, while price rises were limited to an amount covering increased costs. In July the government

In August representatives of eighty-four nonaligned countries met in Colombo, Ceylon, for a summit conference. Egyptian President Anwar el-Sadat and Indian Prime Minister Indira Gandhi wait for opening ceremonies to begin.

survived a challenge from organized labor when the Supreme Court of Canada ruled 7–2 that it was within its rights to introduce controls to meet a "national emergency."

All things considered, Canada's economy began a slow but steady recovery from the recession of 1975. The year ended with unemployment at 7.5 percent and inflation reduced from 11 percent to 5.8 percent; it was estimated that the real growth of the economy would reach a reasonably healthy 5 percent or more.

Foreign Affairs. Relations between Canada and the United States remained somewhat strained, and Trudeau continued to try to put distance between Ottawa and Washington on the international scene. In January, between stops in Mexico and Venezuela, the Canadian prime minister made a controversial visit to Cuba, the first ever by a head of government of a member nation of the North Atlantic Treaty Organization. In October Trudeau traveled to Japan; he was criticized at home for apologizing to his hosts for the bad treatment Canada had given its residents of Japanese ancestry during World War II.

See STATISTICS OF THE WORLD.   R.J.C.

CANAL ZONE. *See* STATISTICS OF THE WORLD.
CAPE VERDE. *See* STATISTICS OF THE WORLD.
CARTER, JIMMY. *See* PEOPLE IN THE NEWS.
CENTRAL AFRICAN REPUBLIC. *See* STATISTICS OF THE WORLD.
CEYLON, officially the REPUBLIC OF SRI LANKA. During 1976 Prime Minister Sirimavo R.D. Bandaranaike continued to head a coalition govern-

ment consisting of her Freedom Party (with a majority of parliamentary seats) and the Communists. Nevertheless, she was under almost constant attack from the United National Party on the right and the Trotskyist Lanka Sama Samaja Party on the left. She also drew fire from the Tamil Federal Party, which continued to demand the formation of an autonomous state for the Tamil minority in the north.

The high point of the Sri Lanka year was the summit conference of eighty-four nonaligned countries in Colombo, Aug. 16–20. Construction of the conference hall was financed by the People's Republic of China, which emerged as Ceylon's leading trade partner and political ally.

The economy in 1976 showed little if any improvement. Agricultural production was hampered by unfavorable weather, the cost of living soared, unemployment exceeded 15 percent, and the chronic deficit in foreign trade widened still further. In May the government agreed to pay the equivalent of $13,700,000 in convertible rupees to the former owners (mainly British) of tea, rubber, and coconut estates nationalized in 1975.

Ceylonese diplomat Hamilton Shirley Amerasinghe became president of the United Nations General Assembly in September.

See STATISTICS OF THE WORLD.   W.J.G.

CHAD. The struggle between Muslim northerners and the southern Christian government of Chad continued unabated in 1976. On April 13, the first anniversary of the coup that brought Brig. Gen. Félix Malloum to power, the banned National Liberation Movement (Frolinat) attempted to assassinate him. Four were killed and seventy-two wounded in the grenade attack at N'Djamena, but Malloum was not injured. Despite Libyan aid, Frolinat scored few successes against the government's pacification program. In a move to rally northern support, Malloum in June appointed nine Muslims to cabinet posts; four were from provinces where Frolinat resistance was concentrated. This move and steady military pressure may have influenced the surrender of 298 Frolinat soldiers at Aeche early in July.

In 1976 the Chad economy showed some signs of recovery from the 1974–75 drought. Plans for irrigation and drainage projects were aided by a $5,000,000 loan from the International Development Association and a $2,000,000 loan from France.

Relations with France, strained over the 1974 Frolinat kidnapping of a French ethnologist, improved in 1976. Early in March French Premier Jacques Chirac visited Chad and signed ten civic and military cooperation agreements. Relations with Libya, however, deteriorated further when, in September, newly issued Libyan maps showed that some 37,000 sq.mi. of Chad were claimed by Libya.

See STATISTICS OF THE WORLD. *See also* AFRICA.   J.T.S.

CHEMISTRY. The chemists of the United States celebrated a centennial as well as a bicentennial in 1976. The 110,000-member American Chemical Society (A.C.S.), the world's largest scientific association devoted to a single discipline, was founded on April 6, 1876, by thirty-five chemists who met in a New York University building on New York City's Washington Square. (Formation of the society had actually been proposed two years earlier when a group of chemists gathered at the home and laboratory of Joseph Priestley in Northumberland, Pa., to mark the centennial of Priestley's discovery of oxygen.) In 1976, to commemorate its founding, the A.C.S. undertook to refurnish the Priestley laboratory with original pieces and replicas of the scientific equipment he had used there for the last ten years of his life. The rest of the house was being renovated by the Pennsylvania Historical and Museum Commission, which had acquired it in a state of disrepair in 1960.

In another commemorative gesture, the A.C.S. mounted an elaborate traveling exhibit depicting chemists' activities. Called "Taking Things Apart and Putting Things Together," it was seen during the year in New York City, Columbus, Ohio, and San Francisco, and was scheduled to visit many more U.S. cities during the next three years.

The U.S. Postal Service marked the occasion with a commemorative stamp, issued April 6. It depicted typical laboratory apparatus superimposed on computer tape. It is interesting to note that the stamp that marked A.C.S.'s 75th anniversary showed a chemical factory spewing dark clouds of smoke, a symbol decidedly unacceptable twenty-five years later.

Synthetic Leaf. A device that converts sunlight into electrical energy by means of photosynthesis was developed by chemist Joseph Katz and other researchers at the Argonne National Laboratory. The device, which is in effect a synthetic leaf, is composed of a glass tube, or cell, about 2 in. high, divided into two compartments by a plastic membrane. Chlorophyll molecules bound to water are infused in the membrane. One of the two compartments contains a chemical solution, such as sodium ascorbate, that can donate electrons (a reducing agent); the other compartment contains an electron acceptor (an oxidizing agent), such as tetraphenylene diamine. An electrode is wired to the cell to detect electrical events. When the synthetic leaf is illuminated with white light or with the red portion of the light spectrum that living plants select for photosynthesis, an electrical current is generated. Chemical end products, similar to or identical with those created in natural photosynthesis, were also detected by the researchers.

The device can greatly increase our understanding of how photosynthesis works. It may also be the forerunner of solar energy converters with far greater storage potential than the solar energy devices now available.

Viewing Atoms in Motion. In 1976, for the first time, a motion picture was produced that showed the behavior of single atoms over a period of time. Using a specially adapted scanning electron microscope with a magnification of 10,000,000, researchers A. V. Crewe and M. S. Isaacson at the University of Chicago documented 2 hr. of movement by uranium atoms on a thin carbon film. The motion, which is caused by thermal energy and atomic interactions, was much more lively than had been anticipated.

The limited resolving power of the apparatus dictated the choice of uranium atoms because of their large size; refinements of the apparatus should make possible the eventual viewing of smaller atoms in motion.

Laser-Beam Isotope Separation. During the year several research groups reported success with new laser techniques for separating isotopes. Isotopes, usually occurring together, are forms of an element that are chemically identical but differ in the number of neutrons in their nucleus; this gives them different atomic weights and certain differences in physical properties. The isotope that most concerns the researchers in their separation attempts is the fissionable uranium-235: This isotope must be increased, or enriched, in proportion to nonfissionable uranium-238 before it can be used as reactor fuel in nuclear energy production. Other isotopes are valuable as "tracers"; they make it possible to follow an element's activities in medical, biological, and industrial processes.

Separation of isotopes is not possible with conventional chemistry, and separation by atomic weight through gaseous diffusion or centrifugation is slow and expensive. But with the use of laser light of appropriate radiation, one isotope in a gaseous mixture can be selectively excited. It can then be removed either electrically or in combination with another substance, leaving only the unexcited isotope in the original mixture.

During the year researchers were able to separate the isotope uranium-235; the nonradioactive isotope sulfur-34, which has great potential value as a tracer; the heavy hydrogen isotope deuterium, also important as a nuclear fuel; and several other isotopes of the lighter elements.

The implications for chemistry in laser isotope separation are enormous, for it is a step along the way to the chemist's dream of breaking molecular bonds and creating new compounds with minimal effort and expense.

Deaths. Lars Onsager, one of the world's most noted theoretical chemists, and Leopold Ružička, who was awarded the 1939 Nobel Prize in chemistry, died during the year; see OBITUARIES.   T.W.D.

CHESS. Political considerations played a major role in international chess in 1976. Soviet grandmaster Viktor Korchnoi defected to the West, and the Soviet Union boycotted the Chess Olympiad held in Haifa, Israel. A rumored match between world champion Anatoly Karpov of the U.S.S.R. and former champion Bobby Fischer of the United States failed to materialize.

Korchnoi and Spassky. Viktor Korchnoi, the second-highest ranked player in the world and several times Soviet champion, sought political asylum in July after winning the Amsterdam international tournament. He lived in the Netherlands for the rest of the year.

Earlier in the year Boris Spassky, who had lost the world championship to Bobby Fischer in Reykjavík, Iceland, in 1972, began a one-year residence in Paris with his French-born wife. The Soviet government permitted Spassky to leave on the condition that he refrain from chess activities during the year.

Chess Olympics. In October the U.S.S.R., its Eastern European allies, and several Arab nations boycotted the 22nd International Chess Olympiad because the tournament was held in Haifa, Israel. The U.S. team won the Haifa event, achieving the first American victory in a chess olympics since 1937 by defeating forty-seven national teams. The six-man U.S. squad headed by grandmaster Robert Byrne scored 37 points, followed by Holland with 36½ and England with 35½. A women's olympiad, also held in Haifa, was won by Israel, whose team was composed entirely of recent Soviet émigrés. A sparsely attended "counter-olympiad" was held by the boycotters in Tripoli, Libya, concurrently with the tournament in Haifa.

Other International Events. As part of the procedure for selecting a challenger for the world championship in 1978, two interzonal qualifying tournaments were held during the summer in Biel, Switzerland, and Manila, the Philippines. Winners were Tigran Petrosian and Lev Polugayevsky of the U.S.S.R., Vlastimil Hort of Czechoslovakia, Bent Larsen of Denmark, Henrique Mecking of Brazil, and Lajos Portisch of Hungary.

Despite these events, most interest in the chess world centered on a nonevent—a possible match between Bobby Fischer and Anatoly Karpov. Fischer, who had not played since 1972, met secretly with Karpov during the summer, but the two men failed to come to terms on specifics of a proposed match for the world title.

U.S. Tournaments. American tournaments were dominated by two Soviet émigrés, grandmasters Anatoly Lein and Leonid Shamkovich. The two men, who became New York City residents, shared first place in the U.S. open championship held in August in Fairfax, Va. In July the two had tied with Norman Weinstein of Boston for first prize in a sixteen-player Manhattan invitational tournament.

For the first time in four years, the U.S. chess federation did not sponsor a national individual championship. Diane Savereide of Culver City, Calif., won the U.S. women's championship for the second year in a row. Mark Diesen of Potomac, Md., and Michael Rohde of South Orange, N.J., were co-winners of the U.S. junior championship.

A twelve-team national chess league tourney with moves transmitted by telephone was won by the Washington "Plumbers" in May.   A.S.

CHILDREN'S LITERATURE. In the spirit of the Bicentennial, the year 1976 saw the development of a new concern about social equality and children's rights in the United States.

Social and Literary Issues. Several publications in 1976 sought to bring key social issues into focus. *Human (and Anti-Human) Values in Children's Books,* published by the Council on Interracial

The imaginative illustrator Maurice Sendak was right at home in the strange night world of children's dreams and desires that is the subject of Fly by Night. Published in 1976, the work was the final collaboration between Sendak and the American author-poet Randall Jarrell, who died in 1965.

Books for Children, included guidelines for parents and educators on racism, sexism, ageism, and elitism, as well as a large collection of timely reviews based on those criteria. The *Wilson Library Bulletin* devoted its annual children's literature issue to a human rights problem: the balancing of free access to children's books against the need for a fair representation of diverse cultural and racial groups.

A simultaneous concern was the battle against mediocrity. A new aid in selecting worthwhile books for children was the semiannual *Children's Literature Review,* a digest of critical commentary covering about fifty authors in each volume. Valuable historical perspective was provided by Elias Bredsdorff's *Hans Christian Andersen: The Story of His Life and Work, 1805–1875,* which offered new insights into one of the most influential writers in the history of children's literature.

Picture Books. A major event in the picture-book genre was the publication of *American Pic-*

turebooks from Noah's Ark to the Beast Within, by Barbara Bader. Among new picture books, John Burningham's *Mr. Gumpy's Motor Car* for the youngest audience and Lucille Clifton's *Three Wishes* (illustrated by Stephanie Douglas) for grades 5–8 were noteworthy. Cartoon books which were comical in a fresh visual way included Jeffrey Allen's *Bonzini! The Tattooed Man* (illustrated by James Marshall) and Jack Gantos's *Rotten Ralph* (illustrated by Nicole Rubel). Melodrama combined with comical drawings gave a special appeal to Russell Hoban's *A Near Thing for Captain Najork* (illustrated by Quentin Blake) and Mary Rayner's *Mr. and Mrs. Pig's Evening Out.*

A poignant event was the posthumous publication of *Fly by Night,* by the poet Randall Jarrell, who died in 1965; the slim volume was illustrated by Maurice Sendak, one of whose earlier collaborations with the poet had received a Newbery award.

Fiction. In the field of fantasy, Zilpha Keatley Snyder's *And All Between* succeeded in bringing home to the middle elementary child the same themes contained in George Orwell's *1984. A String in the Harp,* by Nancy Bond, interweaves the history of Taliesin, a 6th-century Welsh bard, with the problems of an unhappy American child in Wales. In the adventure category, Joan Phipson's *The Cats* develops the relationships between kidnapped boys and their captors in the Australian scrub country.

For the gifted adolescent reader, Virginia Hamilton's experiments with style continued to pose an interesting challenge. In *Arilla Sun Down* a 12-year-old relates the problems in her interracial family in typical junior-high-school vernacular; several flashback chapters employ black English and a stream-of-consciousness mode of narration.

Poetry and Folklore. Poetry was well represented in 1976 by Myra Cohn Livingston's *4-Way Stop,* Eve Merriam's *Rainbow Writing,* and Judith Thurman's *Flashlight and Other Poems.* Contemporary poetry was also anthologized in *Zero Makes Me Hungry,* edited by Edward Lueders and Primus St. John. Good compilations of American and Asian folktales included Gerald Hausman's *Sitting on the Blue-Eyed Bear: Navajo Myths and Legends* and Cora Cheney's *Tales from a Taiwan Kitchen.*

Nonfiction. Those who prefer unadorned facts were drawn to such books as Michael Weiner's *Man's Useful Plants* or Martha Reeves's *The Total Turtle.* The same readers might want a new magazine, *Owl,* a collection of poems, articles, and comics published by the Young Naturalist Foundation in Toronto. Notable nonfiction for older readers included Carolyn Meyer's *Amish People*

From the left: Eeyore, Pooh, Kanga (watching over Roo), and Tigger strike a proper birthday pose. American publisher E. P. Dutton put on display the original toys on which author A. A. Milne had based his 50-year-old classic, Winnie-the-Pooh.

and Milton Meltzer's *Never to Forget,* an eloquent account of the Nazi persecution of the Jews during World War II.

Other Events. The children's books whose authors won the best-known prizes in 1976 were Susan Cooper's *The Grey King* (Newbery award); illustrators Leo and Diane Dillon's *Why Mosquitoes Buzz in People's Ears,* written by Verna Aardema (Caldecott Medal); Walter D. Edmonds's *Bert Breen's Barn* (National Book Award for children's books); and Ruth Hürlimann's *The Cat and Mouse Who Shared a House* (Batchelder award for the best foreign children's book published in the United States).

Vital Statistics. Paul Gallico, the popular author whose works included many children's books, Ernest Shepard, illustrator of A. A. Milne's *Winnie-the-Pooh* (which was first published in 1926), and Munro Leaf, an author and illustrator who created Ferdinand the Bull, died in 1976; see OBITUARIES. Other deaths included that of Robert L. May (Aug. 11 at 71), author of the original story of "Rudolph the Red-Nosed Reindeer." D.Mac.

CHILE. Chile's military regime relaxed some of its repressive political and economic policies during 1976, as international economic pressures were brought to bear on the government of President Augusto Pinochet Ugarte.

Human Rights. February and March brought fresh denunciations of the Chilean government's treatment of political prisoners from the United Nations Commission on Human Rights and the In-ter-American Commission on Human Rights of the Organization of American States (O.A.S.). Although Chile routinely denied such allegations, there were signs of a more accommodating attitude. Prior to the visit of U.S. Treasury Secretary William Simon in May, the government released 49 political prisoners. During his visit, another 49 prisoners were freed, and the total reached 305 by the end of the month. Simon was impressed and departed favoring continued United States aid to Chile. Of special interest were those political prisoners who were being held without charges under the state of siege in effect since September, 1973. By the time the U.S. Presidential election was held in November, the Chilean government claimed to have released all but 20 such prisoners. One of them, Communist Party leader Luis Corvalán Lepe, was freed in December after complex negotiations involving the U.S. and the Soviet Union; see UNION OF SOVIET SOCIALIST REPUBLICS.

At the sixth annual meeting of the O.A.S. General Assembly, held in Santiago, June 4–18, a mild resolution urging Chile to "continue adopting measures to assure the observance of human rights" passed by a vote of 19–1, with Chile and Brazil abstaining. The O.A.S. decision to meet in Santiago was itself a foreign policy plus for the Pinochet regime.

Politics. Early in the year differences of opinion over the government's political and economic policies led ten of Chile's leading generals to send an ultimatum to Pinochet demanding economic reform and the dissolution of the secret police. On March 5 the cabinet resigned, giving Pinochet a free hand to reshuffle his ministerial team. Subsequently, President Pinochet dropped three generals from his cabinet, including the ministers of labor and social welfare, health, and transport.

The Economy. Sparked by rising copper prices and production and by the government's successful efforts to stimulate nontraditional exports, the Chilean economy showed positive growth in 1976. Although still high, inflation was about half the 340 percent rate in 1975. Meanwhile, the trade account registered a surplus estimated at $338,000,000. Because of the improving economic situation, the government eased up on some of its highly restrictive economic policies and began to pay more attention to social welfare. In addition to lowering reserve requirements, the government instituted a minimum employment program and began to work on labor and social security reforms.

In November the Chilean government formally turned down U.S. aid after Congress refused to increase its appropriation beyond $27,500,000 or to remove certain human rights conditions. Chile did accept aid from the World Bank and the Inter-American Development Bank.

See STATISTICS OF THE WORLD. See also ORGANIZATION OF AMERICAN STATES. A.K.M.

CHINA, PEOPLE'S REPUBLIC OF. The deaths during 1976 of Communist Party Chairman Mao Tse-tung, father of the Chinese revolution, and Chou En-lai, master diplomat and statesman, marked the end of an era for the People's Republic of China; see OBITUARIES. Together with a series of devastating earthquakes in July and August, these changes ushered in a period of domestic turmoil and uncertainty from which a new moderate regime headed by Party Chairman Hua Kuo-feng emerged; see PEOPLE IN THE NEWS. Preoccupation with these internal developments resulted in a low level of international activity.

Politics. The death of 78-year-old Premier Chou En-lai on Jan. 8 gave impetus to a resurgence of left-wing politics which had begun late in 1975. Deputy Premier Teng Hsiao-ping, Chou's hand-picked successor, who had taken over most of the ailing premier's duties prior to his death, came under attack from the Left for overemphasizing stability and economic development while soft-pedaling class struggle. On Feb. 7, in a surprise move, Minister of Public Security Hua Kuo-feng, a man in his fifties, was named acting premier to succeed Chou—an appointment which it had seemed certain would go to Teng. Then, early in April, left-wing forces (which enjoyed the official protection of Mao's wife, Chiang Ch'ing) clamped down on demonstrators commemorating the death of Chou. Several days later the Politburo of the Chinese Communist Party officially condemned Teng, climaxing an extensive propaganda campaign against him; Hua emerged as premier and first vice-chairman of the party Central Committee.

When Hua took office, his political views were largely unknown. As the summer wore on, however, he appeared more and more moderate. Seasoned administrators and party professionals appointed by Teng and Chou were retained in office. In Hua's eulogy for Chu Teh, the military hero and chairman of the standing committee of the National People's Congress who succumbed on July 6 at the age of 90, he failed even to mention the leftists' campaign against Teng. Wu Teh, 68, mayor of Peking and the successor to Chu Teh

Comrade Teng Goes Full Circle
In the power struggle following the death of Chinese Premier Chou En-lai, the most likely successor to Chou was thought to be 73-year-old Teng Hsiao-ping. A wily politician, Teng had been denounced during the Cultural Revolution of the 1960's as a "demon" and an anti-Communist "capitalist roader," but he had miraculously returned to power in the 1970's as deputy chairman of the party, chief of staff of the armed forces, and first deputy premier. Then history repeated itself. Wall posters sprang up attacking the "old capitalist roader." By April Teng was back on the lonely road, stripped of all his titles but one: comrade.

Comrade Teng Hsiao-ping.

After Communist Party Chairman Mao Tse-tung died in September, demonstrations, denunciations, and brutal caricatures were part of the new Chinese leadership's campaign to discredit Mao's widow, Chiang Ch'ing, and several of her left-wing allies. (She is represented by the figure on the right.)

as National People's Congress chairman, was also considered a moderate by Western observers.

The differences between Hua and the left wing finally erupted after the death of 82-year-old Party Chairman Mao Tse-tung on Sept. 9. In October Hua was named to succeed Mao in the all-powerful post of party chairman. Leaders of the radical left wing, including Chiang Ch'ing and her fellow Politburo members Chang Ch'un-ch'iao, Wang Hung-wen, and Yao Wen-yuan, were arrested and charged with plotting against Hua and distorting the deceased Mao's directives. As the year drew to a close, it seemed that Hua was consolidating his leadership with the help of the military, which had figured prominently in his rise to power.

The Economy. The year opened with the heartening report that the fourth five-year development plan had been successfully completed in 1975 and that a new plan would begin in 1976. Although specific data on the 1975 harvest were not disclosed, official sources stated early in the year that state procurement of surplus grain was up 8 percent over 1974 and that surpluses were especially high in the Manchurian provinces.

Continued emphasis on the development of the petrochemical industry during the first half of the year produced mixed results. In January Peking reported the completion of two new oil pipelines connecting the rich Taching oil fields of northern Manchuria with an undisclosed location [in] North Korea and with the newly completed oil [p]ort terminal at Dairen. On the other hand, oil [expo]rts to Japan were reduced in February and [China], reportedly because of a sharp upturn in [domes]tic consumption resulting from the new

five-year plan. But it was also rumored that there had been major explosions at Taching. The growth rate for the petrochemical industry declined to 12.7 percent during the first quarter, a drop of almost 50 percent from the same period in 1975; growth at Taching fell off by a third.

Overall industrial production for the first half of 1976 increased 7 percent, down from an estimated 10–11 percent increase in 1975. This decline may have been the result of a new emphasis on agriculture: In February it was reported that more than 1,000,000 party recruits had been sent out to the countryside as part of a program to expand and mechanize agriculture. The economy also suffered early in the year from the leftists' campaign against Teng Hsiao-ping's alleged overemphasis on economic planning.

Earthquakes and Aftershocks. At midyear record wheat and rice harvests were forecast for 1976, along with large increases in natural gas, chemical fertilizer, electrical power, oil, and coal production. But the major earthquakes which hit the northeast and the western province of Szechwan in the summer removed all cause for optimism.

The first shock, registering 8.2 on the Richter scale, hit the industrial city of Tangshan, 105 mi. south of Peking, at 3:40 A.M. on July 28. A second quake struck 67 mi. to the north about sixteen hours later. Aftershocks registering between 5 and 6.2 on the Richter scale persisted for more than a week, hampering relief efforts. Estimates of those killed ranged upward from 600,000. Peking was less severely struck, although many buildings collapsed and rubble littered the streets. *See* ACCIDENTS AND DISASTERS.

The economic consequences were severe. Two large new power plants were destroyed, seriously affecting thermal power output. The Tangshan steel mill, one of China's largest, was reportedly demolished, and the coal and transport industries were badly disrupted. The quakes forced temporary closure of the nearby port of Tientsin, through which passes 25 percent of China's foreign trade.

A quake registering 7.2 on the Richter scale hit Szechwan on Aug. 16, followed by another of 6.5 intensity on Aug. 21. Damage and loss of life were less in this sparsely populated area.

Foreign Affairs. Peking's foreign relations in 1976 reflected the leadership's preoccupation with domestic turmoil and natural disasters. Rapprochement with the United States was stalled by Washington's refusal to take further initiatives on the delicate question of U.S.-Taiwan relations in an election year.

The Soviet Union remained the foremost object of China's hostility. Following Mao's death, the new Peking leadership reaffirmed China's anti-Soviet stance by swiftly rejecting Moscow's condolence messages.

New aid agreements were signed with Ceylon (Sri Lanka), Egypt, Ethiopia, and Laos. China's trade with Japan continued to increase dramatically, but the two nations made little progress toward a permanent peace treaty.

See STATISTICS OF THE WORLD. T.L.K.

CHINA, REPUBLIC OF. See TAIWAN.

CIVIL RIGHTS AND CIVIL LIBERTIES. In 1976 the United States Supreme Court ruled against restraints ("gag orders") on news reporting of trials. The general trend of recent court decisions, however, was running against individual liberties, according to civil rights groups. School desegregation made slow but steady progress during the year, and "reverse discrimination" against Whites was attacked by the courts. The National Association for the Advancement of Colored People (N.A.A.C.P.) lost a $1,250,000 lawsuit in Mississippi that threatened its existence.

The N.A.A.C.P. The judgment that threatened to bankrupt the N.A.A.C.P. stemmed from a 1966 boycott in the town of Port Gibson, Miss. Blacks withheld their business from a dozen of the town's white merchants as part of an effort to get local officials to oppose alleged discrimination. Chancery Judge George Haynes ruled in August that since the merchants had no direct say in granting the civil rights, the boycott was "secondary" and as such illegal. The N.A.A.C.P., which was ordered to pay $1,250,000 in damages, appealed the judgment, and an emergency fund-raising campaign brought in more than $1,000,000 in grants and loans by late 1976. See NEGROES IN THE UNITED STATES.

School Integration. The U.S. Civil Rights Commission reported in August that twenty-two years after the Supreme Court outlawed racial segregation in schools, "segregation remains a problem, particularly in large districts." A commission study showed that in districts with more than 100,000 students, 3 out of 5 Blacks in the North and 2 out of 5 Blacks in the South still attended schools that were more than half black. Nevertheless, the commission concluded that "on balance, progress is being made in the desegregation of our schools." The panel found that desegregation worked best where citizens agreed that "compliance with the law is in the best interest of their children and their communities."

Busing programs to achieve desegregation were put into effect in September, 1976, in a number of cities, including Dallas, Texas, and Omaha, Nebr., with less disruption than in previous years. Nathaniel R. Jones, general counsel of the N.A.A.C.P., expressed hope that getting over "the hurdle of violence" in 1976 would be a major step forward and would help ease the fears of both Blacks and Whites about sending their children to schools in unfamiliar neighborhoods. See EDUCATION.

Minority Rights. Civil rights groups in 1976 forced the U.S. Department of Health, Education, and Welfare (H.E.W.) to back down on its plan to cease investigating individual complaints of discrimination. H.E.W. had contended that the requirement that it promptly investigate individual complaints was too much of a drain on its resources. But civil rights groups argued that if H.E.W. ceased following up individual complaints, citizens would be left without an effective defense against discrimination. Finally, H.E.W. agreed to continue investigating individual complaints.

The movement for the rights of homosexuals suffered a setback in March when the U.S. Supreme Court upheld a state law forbidding homosexual acts committed in private by consenting adults. The Court affirmed a Virginia law that made sodomy by consenting adults in private punishable by up to five years in jail and a $1000 fine. Thirty-six states had laws against sodomy in 1976, but thirteen other states had repealed such prohibitions in recent years.

Reverse Discrimination. State and federal courts showed increasing concern in 1976 over "reverse discrimination." The U.S. Supreme Court ruled unanimously in June that the Civil Rights Act of 1964, which prohibits discrimination by employers, protects white as well as nonwhite employees. The Court said it was unlawful under the act

The Case of the Hidden Leak
How Daniel Schorr, 60, obtained a copy of a secret Congressional report on the operations of the Central Intelligence Agency remained a mystery at the end of the year, but not for lack of investigation. After the report was published in a New York City weekly, the *Village Voice,* a Congressional committee conducted a full-scale inquiry into the leak. But Schorr, a CBS newsman for twenty-three years, defended his right to protect his source, and no leaker came forth to confess. After Congress absolved him of wrongdoing, Schorr resigned from CBS—partly because he expected to get fired eventually—and accepted an appointment at the University of California at Berkeley as a professor of journalism.

Newsman-Professor Daniel Schorr.

for an employer to fire two white employees suspected of stealing company property, but not to discharge a black worker also suspected of stealing. In another case, university efforts to increase minority enrollment came in for censure. A U.S. District Court judge in New York ruled that City College of New York had discriminated against Whites and Asians in selecting candidates for a special program to train doctors. Then the California Supreme Court held that a program granting students from minority groups preferred treatment in admission to medical school was unconstitutional. The court held that the medical school of the University of California at Davis, by setting aside 16 of the 100 places in its freshman class for disadvantaged students from minority groups, had violated the constitutional rights of nonminority applicants.

Civil Liberties. Both gains and setbacks were reported during 1976 by groups concerned with constitutional rights and civil liberties.

The American Civil Liberties Union (A.C.L.U.) hailed a U.S. Civil Service Commission ruling eliminating all political loyalty questions on the standard application for federal jobs. A government spokesman said such questions as whether a job seeker belonged to any group advocating the forcible overthrow of the government were being deleted because of federal court rulings that the "questions were so overboard, that they encroach on rights protected by the First Amendment."

Civil liberties groups and newsmen also cheered a U.S. Supreme Court decision in June unanimously striking down a "gag order" imposed on the press in a 1975 Nebraska murder

trial. Many lawyers interpreted the ruling as a virtual ban on prior restraint of news reporting of judicial proceedings. The justices left open the possibility, however, that in exceptional cases a gag order was permissible to assure a fair trial.

Civil liberties groups expressed concern during 1976 over recent Supreme Court decisions limiting the ability of citizens to bring suit in federal court for relief of alleged violations of their constitutional or statutory rights. Officials of the A.C.L.U., the Consumers Union, and seven other legal and public interest groups issued a joint statement: "If the trend continues—indeed, if it is not reversed—we believe that the protection of constitutional rights and liberties will be imperiled, and people will be unable to defend themselves against arbitrary and unconstitutional actions of state officials or to secure effective relief against invalid state laws."

Many Supreme Court rulings during the year had the effect of limiting the rights of criminal defendants and strengthening prosecutions. For example, the Court ruled in cases heard in January and June that police could make arrests without warrants in public places and in the doorways of the homes of suspects. The Court ruled in April that bank records are not confidential.

Government Surveillance and Secrecy. The U.S. Senate and House of Representatives Select Committees on Intelligence concluded their work early in the year with reports detailing illegal government surveillance of U.S. citizens by federal agencies. In response to the disclosures, President Gerald R. Ford issued an executive order on Feb. 18 restricting the power of the Central Intelligence Agency to gather domestic information. Burglaries were banned, as was the infiltration of groups made up of U.S. citizens. Physical and electronic surveillance of Americans was limited by a set of regulations. After disclosures that the Federal Bureau of Investigation (F.B.I.) had as recently as 1973 committed burglaries against groups that the bureau regarded as radical, a similarly restrictive set of guidelines was imposed on the F.B.I. in August.

The February executive order also decreed that the government would henceforth demand "secrecy agreements" from executive branch employees with access to sensitive information. This was an attempt to prevent leaks to the news media. One such leak in 1976, involving newsman Daniel Schorr, raised the issue of freedom of the press. In January Schorr obtained a copy of a classified report prepared by the House Select Committee on Intelligence. After he arranged for its publication in February, he became the target of an investigation by the House ethics committee. In September Schorr refused to tell the committee where he got the report, arguing that the First Amendment justified the protection of his source.

Censorship. A star of pornographic movies became the center of a censorship *cause célèbre* in 1976. Harry Reems, who was paid $100 for his performance in the film *Deep Throat,* was convicted on April 30 by a federal court in Memphis, Tenn., of "conspiracy to transport obscene materials across state lines"—an offense that would cost him five years in jail and a $1000 fine if appeals failed. This precedent-setting trial, in which an actor was named a conspirator in the distribution of a film over which he had no artistic control, sent shock waves through the Hollywood community. The prosecutor in the case, 33-year-old Assistant U.S. Attorney Larry Parrish, promised more such prosecutions in the future and became a national hero to antipornography forces. "If you don't have actors and actresses, you don't have these films in the first place," he said.

A more widely used weapon against pornography was municipal zoning. A Detroit zoning plan, intended to curb "adult" bookstores, theaters, and massage parlors by allowing them only in small, defined areas of the city, was upheld by the U.S. Supreme Court in June. Similar ordinances were adopted or proposed in Indianapolis, Ind.; New York City; Los Angeles; Des Moines, Iowa; Portland, Oreg.; and Kansas City, Mo.

In another censorship development, the Chicago city council passed an ordinance in May prohibiting persons under eighteen from seeing "excessively violent" films.   M.R.B.

COIN COLLECTING, or NUMISMATICS.

Of special interest to collectors in 1976 were the United States Bicentennial coins and medals, the new $2 bill, a proposal to eliminate pennies, and a new book on ancient Greek coins.

Bicentennial Issues. In addition to the Bicenten-

The 1976 version of the $2 bill (bottom) shows part of John Trumbull's painting of the signing of the Declaration of Independence. Both the old form of the bill (top), issued in 1966, and the new have a portrait of Thomas Jefferson on the face. A significant difference: The 1976 $2 bill was worth $1.15 in 1966 dollars.

nial quarter, half-dollar, and dollar coins first issued in 1975, the U.S. mint produced a series of Bicentennial medals in 1976. Struck in gold, silver, and copper, they were a great success with the collecting public. In September Secretary of the Treasury William E. Simon ordered a return to traditional coin types in 1977.

The introduction in April of one "new" denomination, the $2 bill, provoked controversy when it was noted that the cropping of John Trumbull's painting of the signing of the Declaration of Independence had resulted in the elimination of six signers, including the entire New Hampshire delegation. Secretary Simon resisted pressure to order a change in the bill's design until a larger number had been produced, fearing that the creation of a numismatic "variety" might hamper the bill's assimilation into general circulation. Like the old $2 bills last issued in 1966, the new ones bore a portrait of Thomas Jefferson on the face. Demand for them was small, as Americans could not be induced to prefer them to the common $1 bills. Some critics blamed their unpopularity on a weak promotional campaign by the mint.

Recommendations for Future Coins. The future of the present system of denominations became doubtful when Mary T. Brooks, director of the mint, announced the results of a study of U.S. currency needs through 1990. Among the recommendations of the Research Triangle Institute were: elimination of the cent; introduction of a two-cent piece (last struck in 1873); end of production of the half-dollar for circulation; and creation of a smaller, easier-to-handle dollar coin weighing roughly one third of the present "silver" dollar. All these recommendations are consistent with the general trend toward larger-denomination coins and bills, which are particularly attractive in an inflationary economy because they are easier to use and cheaper to produce. Rep. Henry S. Reuss, chairman of the House Banking, Currency, and Housing Committee, indicated that Congressional action on the recommendations could be anticipated early in 1977.

Ancient Coins. A major numismatic event of 1976 was the publication of *Archaic Greek Silver Coinage: The "Asyut" Hoard,* by M. J. Price and N. M. Waggoner. The hoard, which was buried about 475 B.C., was discovered in 1969 about 200 mi. south of Cairo. It originally contained over 900 coins from more than 70 Greek mints extending from Sicily to Cyrenaica, some of them heretofore unknown. The hoard makes it evident that no gold or silver coins were minted before about 560 B.C. and that the height of archaic minting activity was between the late 6th century and 480 B.C.,

both dates later than had been previously supposed. W.E.M.

COLOMBIA. Although the Colombian economy staged a strong recovery in 1976, labor and student unrest and guerrilla terrorism became an increasing problem for President Alfonso López Michelsen's government.

Improving economic conditions led the government to lift the year-old state of siege in June, despite student disruptions which had caused the closing of Bogotá University on April 2 (the university reopened July 15). The government reimposed the state of siege in October, however, after a series of crises touched off by a strike of 7000 doctors and other health personnel. The strike, which began Sept. 6, was settled Oct. 26, but not before allied student demonstrations again forced the closing of the university. The root cause of the discontent was the cost of living, which was rising at an annual rate of over 25 percent.

President Michelsen's Liberal Party won the midterm elections, which took place on schedule in April. The turnout was below 25 percent. On the whole, the results indicated a rejection of extremism, with Michelsen's party taking 50 percent of the vote.

During the year the two active guerrilla groups, the Revolutionary Armed Forces of Colombia and the National Liberation Army, were joined by a third, calling itself M19. Guerrilla activities included kidnappings, executions, and even the brief capture and looting of the town of Sabana Grande in July.

The economy recorded strong gains during the year because of excellent coffee prices and strong performances in other agricultural sectors. At the same time, the premium prices for coffee, which accounts for about half the country's exports, increased inflationary pressures and forced various fiscal, trade, and foreign exchange adjustments.

See STATISTICS OF THE WORLD. A.K.M.

COLORADO. *See* STATISTICS OF THE WORLD.

COMENICI, NADIA. *See* PEOPLE IN THE NEWS.

COMMONWEALTH OF NATIONS. For the British Commonwealth, 1976 was a year of troubling divisiveness. The number of member nations increased to 36 with the admission of Seychelles, which became an independent republic on June 28. But more and more, the members of the Commonwealth tended to identify with other groupings—the Africans and Asians with developing nations, the older, predominantly white members with the West, and Great Britain itself with the European Economic Community.

All members of the Commonwealth cheered when Rhodesia seemed ready to accept a timetable for transition to majority black rule. To work

At midnight on June 28, 1976, Seychelles becomes the newest member of the British Commonwealth and an independent republic. Saluting, as the Union Jack is lowered for the last time, is the outgoing governor, Colin N. Allen, flanked by the new president, James R. M. Mancham (left), and the new prime minister, F. A. René.

out the details, Britain convened a conference in Geneva in October. But the African members of the Commonwealth wanted Britain to reassert its old colonial power over Rhodesia and guarantee—with troops if necessary—the turnover of power to the Blacks, including black control of the interim government. Britain refused, pleading that it had too many problems at home to become a caretaker for Rhodesia. On Dec. 14 the Geneva conference adjourned on this deadlock, and it seemed unlikely that any solution could be reached before mid-January, 1977, when the talks were scheduled to resume.

Once again, President Idi Amin of Uganda (q.v.) was the chief troublemaker in the Commonwealth. After the Israeli raid on Entebbe in July to rescue skyjacked passengers, Amin refused to explain what had happened to Dora Bloch, a British subject who was left behind and presumably murdered by Ugandan troops. When London got no satisfaction from Amin, it broke relations with Uganda—the first time it had severed ties with a Commonwealth nation.

Amin also had problems with his eastern neighbor, Kenya, another Commonwealth country. After accusing Kenya of complicity in the Entebbe raid, he laid claim to a third of Kenya and threatened "drastic action" to take it. However, after Kenya imposed an economic blockade on Uganda, Amin thought better of it and signed a nonaggression pact with Kenya in August.

At the Summer Olympic Games in Montréal, Commonwealth ties again were strained. With Queen Elizabeth II on hand to open the ceremonies, 11 Commonwealth countries joined 20 others in refusing to take part in the Games. The boycotting nations insisted that they would not compete against New Zealand, a fellow Commonwealth nation, because it had permitted a rugby team to tour South Africa, a country hated by the Africans for its racial discrimination.

In Asia important Commonwealth countries such as Malaysia continued to enjoy stable governments and thriving economies. In September Pakistan asked that Britain return to it the fabled Kohinoor diamond, an important element of the British crown jewels. The request was firmly rejected by London. But the Asian Commonwealth country that caused Britain the greatest dismay was India. Under the leadership of Indira Gandhi the country, once called the largest democracy in the world, strengthened its ties with the Soviet Union, was accused of using nuclear technology to make weapons, and methodically stamped out political freedom at home.

See articles on individual countries.　　R.J.C.

COMMUNICATIONS. Communication by light wave became a reality in 1976 with the testing of optical fibers in telephone and cable television systems. Other advances during the year included the laying of a more efficient undersea cable, the expansion of satellite transmission, and the use of the home television screen to display information on demand.

Controversies developed, one over the lobbying effort by the American Telephone and Telegraph Co. (A.T.&T.) to maintain the Bell System's monopoly position and another over the assignment of additional channels for citizens band (CB) radio use.

Messages by Light Wave. A fundamental change in communications technology commenced i 1976 with the transmission of messages by fib guided laser light. Early in the year Bell Labor

A new single-modular circuit board introduced during the year in General Electric color television sets. It detects the signals for correct tint and color intensity that are broadcast with each program and automatically adjusts the picture to conform to them.

ries successfully tested a light wave telephone link in Atlanta, Ga., with a 2100-ft.-long, ½-in.-thick cable carrying 144 hair-thin glass fibers. Pulsed laser light, flashing 44,700,000 times a sec. through a pair of the fibers, was able to transmit a simulation of 672 simultaneous two-way conversations. The ½-in. cable's capacity was 48,384 two-way conversations; comparable capacity with copper wire would require about 5 cables, each 3 in. thick. Replacement of the bulky and expensive copper cables in the Bell System was to begin with switching systems in crowded metropolitan areas, where messages were already being transmitted in a pulsed form.

An 800-ft. glass fiber was installed in July by Teleprompter Manhattan Cable Television to carry signals from receiving equipment on its skyscraper rooftop to its processing center 34 stories below. The single strand conveyed sharp, bright television pictures of all incoming channels; its carrying capacity was 167 channels. So it became evident that with an optical fiber system of sufficiently fast laser pulses, home television sets ould pick up thousands of channels.

In Japan testing began in November of an elaborate optical fiber computer-controlled network capable of providing every Japanese home with two-way services. These services might include selected entertainment, cashless shopping, computer-stored information, medical assistance, and even a telemetering system for reading gas and water meters.

New Undersea Cable. A sixth transatlantic cable, laid by the cable ship *Long Lines* between Green Hill, R.I., and Saint Hilaire, France, was completed in June. Ownership of its 4000 circuits was shared by 4 United States companies and the postal, telephone, and telegraph authorities of 16 European nations. The first undersea cable, put into service in 1956, cost $300 per circuit mile; it carries only 36 telephone circuits. The new cable cost about $13 per circuit mile and is also capable of transmitting data, telex, and other recorded communications.

Expanded Satellite Communication. The use of both domestic and international satellites for transmitting voice, television, and recorded data rose markedly during the year. In contrast with cable systems (which require extensive networks of wiring), or microwave systems (which need line-of-sight towers at 30-mi. intervals), satellite communication systems can be established as soon as the spacecraft is in place; they have no need of frequent signal amplifiers or further maintenance. Placed in orbit at an altitude of 22,300 mi. and a speed of 6830 m.p.h., a broadcast satellite is "geosynchronous" with the earth's rotation; it appears to be fixed in the sky, and it remains in line of sight over thousands of miles. (Usually, a pair of satellites is sent up, one serving as a back-up for the other.) The satellite is able through its "transponders" (receiver-transmitters) to receive signals from many ground broadcast stations and transmit them directly to any number of dish antennas. The greater the transmission potency of the satellite, the smaller the ground equipment needs to be.

In January, the launching of the world's most powerful broadcast spacecraft, the Communications Technology Satellite (C.T.S.), made technically feasible the use of low-cost sending and receiving stations small enough to sit on a rooftop. This advance was expected to have a profound effect on the distribution of television programs and other information within ten years: It would allow far greater freedom in local transmission and selection. For example, during the C.T.S.'s two-year test period, curriculum sharing was established between the University of Stanford in California and Carleton University in Manitoba; three-way cross-country seminars were being regularly scheduled among groups of scientists and engineers.

Several other important satellite launches occurred during the year. These included a new International Telecommunications Satellite Organization vehicle known as Intelsat IV-A, which linked 40 nations bordering the Atlantic Ocean via 100-ft. dish antennas tied into ground-based systems; and an Indonesian satellite called Palapa-A that instantaneously united some 3000 islands of the sprawling archipelago with telephone, radio, television, and data communication via 26 ground stations. Marisat, 3 maritime satellites placed over the Atlantic, Pacific, and Indian oceans, provided something new—instant communication by voice or code between land bases and ships at sea. (Ground-based radio-telephone links are on limited channels that are subject to interference and crowding, sometimes causing communication delays of up to 8 hr.)

In the U.S. domestic communications were expanded by four satellites. Two RCA Satcoms went into operation, joining the first two U.S. domestic satellites, called Westar, launched in 1975 for Western Union. Two Comstars launched later in the year were leased to A.T.&T. and a smaller concern, General Telephone and Electronics Corp., which thereby joined the competition for satellite services. Approval was granted for yet another pair of satellites to be launched in 1977. The pair will be operated by the new Satellite Business System, a joint venture of International Business Machines, Aetna Life and Casualty Co., and Comsat General Corp.

Challenge to A.T.&T. The Bell System seemed to be in trouble. With the very real prospect of several other giant corporations offering long-distance telephone service by satellite or microwave (and also offering such business services as the interlinking of a company's branch offices for computer exchange, conferences, and data or picture transmission), the controlled monopoly over communications lines that A.T.&T.'s Bell System had enjoyed for many decades seemed to be ending—although the home telephone monopoly seemed relatively safe. Arguing that Bell's home phone system was subsidized with the profits from its other services and that home phone rates would have to go up as much as 80 percent unless competition was held down, A.T.&T. lobbied in the U.S. Congress for a bill that would effectively extend its legal monopoly. Others argued that Bell's home telephone profits were substantial. The "Bell Bill," as it quickly became known, seemed certain to be the focus of a battle among communications carriers in 1977.

Television "Black Boxes." Dozens of companies

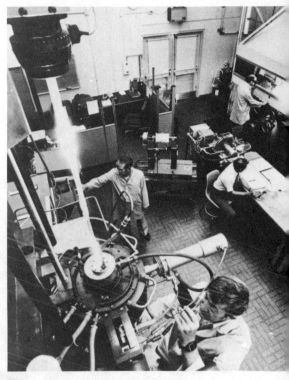

Fiber guides for light wave communication being produced at Western Electric's Atlanta works. Glass rods are prepared on a lathe (bright area, upper right), then heated and softened (glowing tube, left), and melted in a furnace (foreground). A technician pulls a strand of molten glass from an opening in the furnace and places it on a revolving drum (concealed below the furnace), which spins it into a continuous hair-thin thread.

recently introduced "black boxes" that by means of tiny programmed computers connect to the television screen and permit the user to play electronic games. An extension of the same technique, already being developed, could give the viewer access to "electronic libraries" of books, newspapers, catalogs, and other printed information. During the year the British Broadcasting Corp. tested a Texas Instruments system called Ceefax ("see facts") that displays sections of a newspaper at the punch of a keyboard on a decoder box. Mass production of the box was planned for 1977 at an expected cost of $100. *See also* TECHNOLOGY.

CB Radio Problems. The explosive growth of the CB radio in 1975 and 1976 (*see* RADIO AND TELEVISION BROADCASTING) caused serious problems of crowding and interference. Because of crowding, the effective range of the 23 channels on the low frequency band assigned to CB radio in 1956 (2 megahertz) was reduced from the intended 15 r to little more than 5 mi. Inferior design caused spillovers into other frequencies; these spillovers disturbed television channels, radios, public address systems, traffic lights, and even sewing machines. Many CB users made matters worse by illegally boosting their sets beyond the assigned frequency by means of linear amplifiers or directional antennas. In July the Federal Communications Commission (F.C.C.) released to CB radio the remaining 17 channels on the 27 megahertz band. Anticipating a fivefold growth over the next few years, the F.C.C. began to look further—for a part of the broadcast spectrum to accommodate as many as 200 channels. Any new assignment, however, was likely to bring strong opposition from other spectrum users. The F.C.C. issued regulations for the design of new CB sets to reduce spillover; Congress considered legislation that would require better shielding in other electronic equipment to protect against CB interference.

Further complicating the CB problem is the fact that low frequency bands of the spectrum are more vulnerable to sunspot activity. Government scientists predicted that CB broadcasting would become virtually ineffective for about three years starting in 1978, when the eleven-year sunspot cycle would begin to reach its peak period. R.G.G.

COMMUNISM. Two events of historic importance shook the Communist world in 1976. One was a virtual declaration of independence from Moscow by many of the Communist parties of Europe—and the Kremlin's apparent acceptance of the move. The other was the death of Mao Tsetung, founder of the People's Republic of China

and one of Communism's most influential theoreticians (*see* OBITUARIES).

European Communism. An international conference in East Berlin was the site of the amazing anti-Soviet revolt by many of Europe's Communist parties. As originally envisioned by Soviet Communist Party General Secretary Leonid I. Brezhnev in 1973, the conference was to proclaim Moscow's primacy in the Communist world and its role as the sole correct interpreter of Marxist doctrine. However, many of the European parties objected to Brezhnev's plan to use such a conference essentially as a forum to denounce China. Because of negotiations on that and many related issues, more than two years of talks were required before there was any consensus on what documents should emerge from the gathering.

In June, 1976, the leaders of twenty-nine European Communist parties finally met in East Berlin; only Albania and Iceland were not represented. The result was a unique display of Communist diversity. Soviet loyalists such as party leaders Todor Zhivkov of Bulgaria and Erich Honecker of East Germany spoke of the Soviet Union as first among Communist equals. But other Communists disagreed. Italy's Enrico Berlinguer, whose party (which is more liberal-minded than that of the U.S.S.R.) attained unprecedented influence in Italian domestic politics in 1976, criticized the 1968 Soviet invasion of Czechoslovakia, and spoke out for a "free debate of ideas" within the Communist world. Leaders of the French and Spanish parties echoed some of Berlinguer's sentiments. Rumania's President Nicolae Ceaușescu and

On June 29 in East Berlin Soviet Communist Party General Secretary Leonid I. Brezhnev addresses a conference of European Communist Party leaders. The conference was made memorable by a "declaration of independence" from Moscow by many European parties.

Yugoslav President Tito, both of whom continued to suppress dissent at home, demanded that whatever its policies, each party should be allowed to choose its own path without outside interference.

In the end, all twenty-nine parties signed a declaration on June 30 envisioning the "equality and sovereign independence of each party, noninterference in internal affairs, and respect for their free choice of different roads in the struggle for social change of a progressive nature and for socialism." The wording of the document made it a milestone in Communist history.

Evidently dissatisfied by the lukewarm Soviet acquiescence to the Berlin declaration, both Ceauşescu and Tito induced Brezhnev to make further promises of noninterference. During visits to Bucharest and Belgrade in November, Brezhnev pledged that relations between Communists would be based on "voluntary cooperation."

Change in China. Chairman Mao Tse-tung died in Peking on Sept. 9 at the age of 82. No sooner had the regime held a memorial service for Mao than factional infighting broke out among his heirs. Mao's widow, Chiang Ch'ing, and three top members of China's so-called radical faction evidently attempted to shunt aside Premier (later Chairman) Hua Kuo-feng and other more pragmatic party officials. The coup failed, and Chiang Ch'ing's "gang of four" was purged from the Chinese leadership and placed under arrest. Twice during the year—in April following the ouster of Deputy Premier Teng Hsiao-ping, and in December as the antiradical purge was under way—there were reports of fighting in Chinese cities.

After Mao's death the U.S.S.R. sought to lower the temperature of the long-standing Sino-Soviet dispute. Soviet leaders addressed friendly messages to the Chinese on several occasions during the autumn, and in November they dispatched a negotiator to Peking to resume talks on the dis-

U.S. Communist Party Presidential nominee Gus Hall (second from left) and Vice-Presidential candidate Jarvis Tyner (right) were introduced to the public in February by National Chairman Henry Winston (left) and Angela Davis (second from right). In November the Hall-Tyner ticket, on the ballot in 24 states and the District of Columbia, won 59,114 votes, or .07 percent of the U.S. total.

puted Sino-Soviet border. China's response was negative, however. At a Peking banquet on Nov. 15, Chinese Deputy Premier Li Hsien-nien accused the Kremlin of "creating false impressions of a relaxation" of Sino-Soviet tensions. Albania, long a close ally of China, was placed in an especially difficult position by the defeat of the Chinese radicals, with whom the Albanian leadership was ideologically in tune. Outspoken critics of the Soviets, the Albanians now found themselves on less-than-cordial terms with China as well.

Indochinese Developments. The Communist governments of South Vietnam, Laos, and Cambodia, all of which took power in 1975, consolidated their hold over the local populace during 1976. Tens of thousands of Indochinese were subjected to various kinds of thought-reform programs; purges were especially brutal in Cambodia. North Vietnam completed its takeover of South Vietnam on July 2, and henceforth, Hanoi proclaimed, the two were a single nation, the Socialist Republic of Vietnam.

See articles on individual countries mentioned; see also COUNCIL FOR MUTUAL ECONOMIC ASSISTANCE; WARSAW TREATY ORGANIZATION.   F.W.

COMORO ISLANDS. See STATISTICS OF THE WORLD.

COMPUTER. See TECHNOLOGY.

CONGO, REPUBLIC OF, in full PEOPLE'S REPUBLIC OF THE CONGO. Inflation and low export earnings began to have a serious political impact in the Congo late in 1975, when a report issued by the ruling Congolese Labor Party (P.C.T.) criticized the actions of its leadership. Prime Minister Henri Lopes and the cabinet were subsequently forced to resign, but President Marien Ngouabi announced a new P.C.T. cabinet late in December. In February, 1976, trade union leaders, hostile to the government's anti-inflation programs, including plans to establish a single wage-bargaining system for all state employees, began to mobilize for a general strike. The government responded with a wave of arrests in March, but in the subsequent trials union leaders were given light sentences. This action, it was believed, would blunt opposition to the government.

During the year efforts to improve communication and transportation systems were aided by a $10,000,000 loan from the Arab Bank and a $1,500,000 loan from France. At the same time $246,400,000 was allocated for exploiting the Loango-Marine oil deposits.

As civil war continued in neighboring Angola, Western sources warned of a Soviet arms buildup in the Congo, but evidence was scant. Ngouabi himself was instrumental in lessening regional tensions by organizing the Feb. 28 meeting in Brazzaville between Angolan President Agostinho Neto and Zairian President Mobutu Sese Seko. At the meeting Zaire officially recognized the People's Republic of Angola. (The Congo had recognized it in November, 1975.)

See STATISTICS OF THE WORLD. See also AFRICA.   J.T.S.

CONGRESS OF THE UNITED STATES. When the 94th Congress adjourned its 1976 session on Oct. 2, liberals and conservatives could agree with House of Representatives minority leader John J. Rhodes (R, Ariz.) in accusing it of "failure to deliver on its promises." While busy and argumentative (20,805 bills were introduced), the 94th session produced little significant legislation in spite of strong Democratic majorities of 290–145 in the House and 62–38 in the Senate. One major accomplishment was the creation in May of a permanent Senate Select Committee on Intelligence to oversee the Central Intelligence Agency. This had been a key recommendation of the Senate and House committees that wound up their investigations of United States intelligence agencies early in the year. Personalities, however—the retirement or scandalous downfall of powerful men—attracted the most attention on Capitol Hill during 1976.

Legislation. In 1976 the struggle continued between the fiscal conservatism of President Gerald R. Ford and the readiness of Congress to spend money to create jobs and achieve social and environmental goals. Ford vetoed fifteen bills during the session, and Congress overrode his vetoes only four times. The 1977 fiscal budget was approved at $413.1 billion (including a significantly increased $104.3 billion for defense), $13 billion above Ford's amended request. The budget featured a $4 billion appropriation, enacted in July over Ford's veto, to finance public-works jobs.

The most voluminous and painstaking piece of legislation enacted was a complex tax bill that extended the antirecession tax cuts of 1975 and made changes in the laws affecting gift taxes, estate taxes, and tax shelters. In April Congress approved the President's request for $135,000,000 for a national swine-flu immunization program. The Federal Election Commission was reconstituted in May to comply with a Supreme Court ruling.

Congress also extended federal revenue sharing through fiscal 1980, broadened unemployment insurance to cover 8,500,000 more workers, strengthened the antitrust laws, and revised the copyright laws. Many bills were debated at length but died in committee or in filibusters. Among

On Nov. 23 President-elect Jimmy Carter met in Washington with Republican Party leaders from both houses of Congress. Carter (left) is shown here with the Senate minority whip, Robert Griffin of Michigan (center), and the House minority leader, John J. Rhodes of Arizona.

them were measures concerning guaranteed full employment (the so-called Humphrey-Hawkins bill), gun control, the regulation of strip mining, national health insurance, lobbying reform, and auto emission standards.

Scandals. For five years, Wayne L. Hays (D, Ohio) was the chairman of the powerful House Administration Committee. In May a committee employee, Elizabeth Ray, claimed that she had been put on the payroll to have sexual relations with the chairman. Physically unwell and under pressure from Democratic leaders anxious to mute the scandal, Hays resigned his House seat on Sept. 1. Rep. John Young (D, Texas) was also accused of keeping a mistress on his payroll.

Meanwhile, in June, Rep. Allan T. Howe (D, Utah) was arrested on a charge of soliciting two Salt Lake City policewomen disguised as prostitutes. Convicted in July, he was defeated in his bid for reelection in November. The long dormant House Ethics Committee investigated Rep. Robert L. F. Sikes (D, Fla.) in May. Sikes, accused of using his position to enrich himself in real estate deals, was reprimanded for misconduct by the House in July and reelected in November.

The New Congress. Record numbers of legislators decided to retire voluntarily in 1976. Heading the list of forty-eight members of the House was Speaker of the House Carl Albert (D, Okla.). Among eight retiring Senators were majority leader Mike Mansfield (D, Mont.) and minority leader Hugh Scott (R, Pa.). These withdrawals resulted in major shifts of power toward younger

---

Sixth in the Stars of His Congressmen

On Oct. 19, 1976, President Gerald R. Ford signed a bill authorizing the promotion of an Army officer, even though he had been dead for 177 years. The U.S. Congress wanted Gen. George Washington to be raised above "all other grades of the Army, past and present" and voted to award him six stars and the rank of General of the Armies. (Some historians dispute Congress; they claim that John Pershing was awarded six stars after World War I.)

---

legislators. Some fifty committee and subcommittee chairmanships changed hands in the organization of the 95th Congress in December.

Victories in the November elections assured the Democrats of a gain of two seats for a 292–143 majority in the House. The Democrats caucused in December and chose Thomas P. O'Neill of Massachusetts to be the new Speaker of the House and James C. Wright, Jr., of Texas to be majority leader. Although 17 new Senators were elected, the Senate lineup remained 61 Democrats, 38 Republicans, and 1 Independent. The new Congress appeared eager to cooperate with President-elect Jimmy Carter. Said Speaker-designate O'Neill, ". . . we'll make him a good President." *See also* PEOPLE IN THE NEWS.   W.M.H.

94th CONGRESS, 2nd SESSION (Jan. 19–Oct. 2, 1976)

Senators	Term Expires	Senators	Term Expires	Senators	Term Expires
ALABAMA		**GEORGIA**		**MAINE**	
John J. Sparkman (D)	1979	Herman E. Talmadge (D)	1981	Edmund S. Muskie (D)	1977
James B. Allen (D)	1981	Sam Nunn (D)	1979	William D. Hathaway (D)	1979
ALASKA		**HAWAII**		**MARYLAND**	
Ted Stevens (R)	1979	Hiram L. Fong (R)	1977	Charles Mathias (R)	1981
Mike Gravel (D)	1981	Daniel K. Inouye (D)	1981	J. Glenn Beall, Jr. (R)	1977
ARIZONA		**IDAHO**		**MASSACHUSETTS**	
Paul J. Fannin (R)	1977	Frank Church (D)	1981	Edward M. Kennedy (D)	1977
Barry Goldwater (R)	1981	James A. McClure (R)	1979	Edward W. Brooke (R)	1979
ARKANSAS		**ILLINOIS**		**MICHIGAN**	
John L. McClellan (D)	1979	Charles H. Percy (R)	1979	Philip A. Hart (D)	1977
Dale Bumpers (D)	1981	Adlai E. Stevenson (D)	1981	Robert P. Griffin (R)	1979
CALIFORNIA		**INDIANA**		**MINNESOTA**	
Alan Cranston (D)	1981	Vance Hartke (D)	1977	Walter F. Mondale (D)	1979
John V. Tunney (D)	1977	Birch Bayh (D)	1981	Hubert Humphrey (D)	1977
COLORADO		**IOWA**		**MISSISSIPPI**	
Floyd K. Haskell (D)	1979	Dick Clark (D)	1979	James O. Eastland (D)	1979
Gary Hart (D)	1981	John C. Culver (D)	1981	John C. Stennis (D)	1977
CONNECTICUT		**KANSAS**		**MISSOURI**	
Abraham Ribicoff (D)	1981	James B. Pearson (R)	1979	Stuart Symington (D)	1977
Lowell P. Weicker (R)	1977	Bob Dole (R)	1981	Thomas Eagleton (D)	1981
DELAWARE		**KENTUCKY**		**MONTANA**	
William V. Roth (R)	1977	Walter Huddleston (D)	1979	Mike Mansfield (D)	1977
Joseph R. Biden (D)	1979	Wendell H. Ford (D)	1981	Lee Metcalf (D)	1979
FLORIDA		**LOUISIANA**		**NEBRASKA**	
Lawton Chiles (D)	1977	Russell B. Long (D)	1981	Roman L. Hruska (R)	1977
Richard Stone (D)	1981	J. B. Johnston (D)	1979	Carl T. Curtis (R)	1979

NEVADA
Howard W. Cannon (D) 1977
Paul Laxalt (R) 1981
NEW HAMPSHIRE
Thomas J. McIntyre (D) 1979
John A. Durkin (D) 1981
NEW JERSEY
Clifford P. Case (R) 1979
Harrison Williams (D) 1977
NEW MEXICO
Joseph Montoya (D) 1977
Peter V. Domenici (R) 1979
NEW YORK
Jacob K. Javits (R) .*....... 1981
James L. Buckley (C-R) 1977
NORTH CAROLINA
Jesse A. Helms (R) 1979
Robert Morgan (D) 1981
NORTH DAKOTA
Milton R. Young (R) 1981
Quentin N. Burdick (D) 1977
OHIO
Robert Taft, Jr. (R) 1977
John Glenn (D) 1981
OKLAHOMA
Henry L. Bellmon (R) 1981
Dewey F. Bartlett (R) 1979
OREGON
Mark O. Hatfield (R) 1979
Bob Packwood (R) 1981
PENNSYLVANIA
Hugh Scott (R) 1977
Richard Schweiker (R) 1981
RHODE ISLAND
John O. Pastore (D) 1977
Claiborne Pell (D) 1979
SOUTH CAROLINA
Strom Thurmond (R) 1979
Ernest F. Hollings (D) 1981
SOUTH DAKOTA
George McGovern (D) 1981
James Abourezk (D) 1979
TENNESSEE
Howard H. Baker (R) 1979
William E. Brock (R) 1977
TEXAS
John G. Tower (R) 1979
Lloyd M. Bentsen (D) 1977
UTAH
Frank E. Moss (D) 1977
Jake Garn (R) 1981
VERMONT
Robert T. Stafford (R) 1977
Patrick J. Leahy (D) 1981
VIRGINIA
Harry F. Byrd, Jr. (I) 1977
William Lloyd Scott (R) 1979
WASHINGTON
Warren Magnuson (D) 1981
Henry M. Jackson (D) 1977
WEST VIRGINIA
Jennings Randolph (D) 1979
Robert C. Byrd (D) 1977
WISCONSIN
William Proxmire (D) 1977
Gaylord Nelson (D) 1981
WYOMING
Gale W. McGee (D) 1977
Clifford P. Hansen (R) 1979

Representatives

ALABAMA
1. Jack Edwards (R)
2. William L. Dickinson (R)
3. Bill Nichols (D)
4. Tom Bevill (D)
5. Robert E. Jones (D)
6. John Buchanan (R)
7. Walter Flowers (D)

ALASKA
At large: Donald E. Young (R)
ARIZONA
1. John J. Rhodes (R)
2. Morris K. Udall (D)
3. Sam Steiger (R)
4. John B. Conlan (R)
ARKANSAS
1. Bill Alexander (D)
2. Wilbur D. Mills (D)
3. John P. Hammerschmidt (R)
4. Ray Thornton (D)
CALIFORNIA
1. Harold T. Johnson (D)
2. Don H. Clausen (R)
3. John E. Moss (D)
4. Robert L. Leggett (D)
5. John Burton (D)
6. Phillip Burton (D)
7. George Miller (D)
8. Ronald V. Dellums (D)
9. Fortney H. (Pete) Stark (D)
10. Don Edwards (D)
11. Leo J. Ryan (D)
12. Paul N. (Pete) McCloskey, Jr. (R)
13. Norman Y. Mineta (D)
14. John J. McFall (D)
15. B. F. Sisk (D)
16. Burt L. Talcott (R)
17. John Krebs (D)
18. William M. Ketchum (R)
19. Robert J. Lagomarsino (R)
20. Barry Goldwater, Jr. (R)
21. James C. Corman (D)
22. Carlos J. Moorhead (R)
23. Thomas M. Rees (D)
24. Henry A. Waxman (D)
25. Edward R. Roybal (D)
26. John Rousselot (R)
27. Alphonzo Bell (R)
28. Yvonne Brathwaite Burke (D)
29. Augustus F. (Gus) Hawkins (D)
30. George E. Danielson (D)
31. Charles H. Wilson (D)
32. Glenn M. Anderson (D)
33. Del Clawson (R)
34. Mark W. Hannaford (D)
35. Jim Lloyd (D)
36. George E. Brown, Jr. (D)
37. Shirley N. Pettis (R)
38. Jerry M. Patterson (D)
39. Charles E. Wiggins (R)
40. Andrew Hinshaw (R)
41. Bob Wilson (R)
42. Lionel Van Deerlin (D)
43. Clair W. Burgener (R)
COLORADO
1. Patricia Schroeder (D)
2. Timothy E. Wirth (D)
3. Frank E. Evans (D)
4. James P. (Jim) Johnson (R)
5. William L. Armstrong (R)
CONNECTICUT
1. William R. Cotter (D)
2. Christopher J. Dodd (D)
3. Robert N. Giaimo (D)
4. Stewart B. McKinney (R)
5. Ronald A. Sarasin (R)
6. Toby Moffett (D)
DELAWARE
At large: Pierre S. du Pont 4th (R)
FLORIDA
1. Robert L. F. Sikes (D)
2. Don Fuqua (D)
3. Charles E. Bennett (D)
4. Bill Chappell, Jr. (D)
5. Richard Kelly (R)
6. C. W. Bill Young (R)
7. Sam M. Gibbons (D)
8. James A. Haley (D)
9. Louis Frey, Jr. (R)

10. L. A. (Skip) Bafalis (R)
11. Paul G. Rogers (D)
12. J. Herbert Burke (R)
13. William Lehman (D)
14. Claude D. Pepper (D)
15. Dante B. Fascell (D)
GEORGIA
1. Bo Ginn (D)
2. Dawson Mathis (D)
3. Jack Brinkley (D)
4. Elliott H. Levitas (D)
5. Andrew Young (D)
6. John J. Flynt, Jr. (D)
7. Larry McDonald (D)
8. W. S. (Bill) Stuckey, Jr. (D)
9. Phil M. Landrum (D)
10. Robert G. Stephens, Jr. (D)
HAWAII
1. Spark M. Matsunaga (D)
2. Patsy T. Mink (D)
IDAHO
1. Steven D. Symms (R)
2. George Hansen (R)
ILLINOIS
1. Ralph H. Metcalfe (D)
2. Morgan F. Murphy (D)
3. Martin A. Russo (D)
4. Edward J. Derwinski (R)
5. John G. Fary (D)
6. Henry J. Hyde (R)
7. Cardiss Collins (D)
8. Dan Rostenkowski (D)
9. Sidney R. Yates (D)
10. Abner J. Mikva (D)
11. Frank Annunzio (D)
12. Philip M. Crane (R)
13. Robert McClory (R)
14. John N. Erlenborn (R)
15. Tim L. Hall (D)
16. John B. Anderson (R)
17. George M. O'Brien (R)
18. Robert H. Michel (R)
19. Thomas F. Railsback (R)
20. Paul Findley (R)
21. Edward R. Madigan (R)
22. George E. Shipley (D)
23. Melvin Price (D)
24. Paul Simon (D)
INDIANA
1. Ray J. Madden (D)
2. Floyd J. Fithian (D)
3. John Brademas (D)
4. J. Edward Roush (D)
5. Elwood Hillis (R)
6. David W. Evans (D)
7. John T. Myers (R)
8. Philip H. Hayes (D)
9. Lee H. Hamilton (D)
10. Philip R. Sharp (D)
11. Andrew Jacobs, Jr. (D)
IOWA
1. Edward Mezvinsky (D)
2. Michael T. Blouin (D)
3. Charles E. Grassley (R)
4. Neal Smith (D)
5. Tom Harkin (D)
6. Berkley Bedell (D)
KANSAS
1. Keith G. Sebelius (R)
2. Martha Keys (D)
3. Larry Winn, Jr. (R)
4. Garner E. Shriver (R)
5. Joe Skubitz (R)
KENTUCKY
1. Carroll Hubbard, Jr. (D)
2. William H. Natcher (D)
3. Romano L. Mazzoli (D)
4. M. G. (Gene) Snyder (R)
5. Tim Lee Carter (R)
6. John Breckinridge (D)
7. Carl D. Perkins (D)

LOUISIANA
1. F. Edward Hébert (D)
2. Corinne C. (Lindy) Boggs (D)
3. David C. Treen (R)
4. Joe D. Waggonner, Jr. (D)
5. Otto E. Passman (D)
6. W. Henson Moore (R)
7. John B. Breaux (D)
8. Gillis W. Long (D)

MAINE
1. David F. Emery (R)
2. William S. Cohen (R)

MARYLAND
1. Robert E. Bauman (R)
2. Clarence D. Long (D)
3. Paul S. Sarbanes (D)
4. Marjorie S. Holt (R)
5. Gladys Noon Spellman (D)
6. Goodloe E. Byron (D)
7. Parren J. Mitchell (D)
8. Gilbert Gude (R)

MASSACHUSETTS
1. Silvio O. Conte (R)
2. Edward P. Boland (D)
3. Joseph D. Early (D)
4. Robert F. Drinan (D)
5. Paul E. Tsongas (D)
6. Michael J. Harrington (D)
7. Torbert H. Macdonald (D)[1]
8. Thomas P. O'Neill, Jr. (D)
9. John Joseph Moakley (D)
10. Margaret M. Heckler (R)
11. James A. Burke (D)
12. Gerry E. Studds (D)

MICHIGAN
1. John Conyers, Jr. (D)
2. Marvin L. Esch (R)
3. Garry E. Brown (R)
4. Edward Hutchinson (R)
5. Richard F. Vander Veen (D)
6. Bob Carr (D)
7. Donald W. Riegle, Jr. (D)
8. Bob Traxler (D)
9. Guy Vander Jagt (R)
10. Elford A. Cederberg (R)
11. Philip E. Ruppe (R)
12. James G. O'Hara (D)
13. Charles C. Diggs, Jr. (D)
14. Lucien N. Nedzi (D)
15. William D. Ford (D)
16. John D. Dingell (D)
17. William M. Brodhead (D)
18. James J. Blanchard (D)
19. William S. Broomfield (R)

MINNESOTA
1. Albert H. Quie (R)
2. Tom Hagedorn (R)
3. Bill Frenzel (R)
4. Joseph E. Karth (D)
5. Donald M. Fraser (D)
6. Richard Nolan (D)
7. Bob Bergland (D)
8. James L. Oberstar (D)

MISSISSIPPI
1. Jamie L. Whitten (D)
2. David R. Bowen (D)
3. G.V. (Sonny) Montgomery (D)
4. Thad Cochran (R)
5. Trent Lott (R)

MISSOURI
1. William (Bill) Clay (D)
2. James W. Symington (D)
3. Leonor K. (Mrs. John B.) Sullivan (D)
4. Wm. J. Randall (D)
5. Richard Bolling (D)
6. Jerry Litton (D)[2]
7. Gene Taylor (R)
8. Richard H. Ichord (D)
9. William L. Hungate (D)
10. Bill D. Burlison (D)

MONTANA
1. Max Baucus (D)
2. John Melcher (D)

NEBRASKA
1. Charles Thone (R)
2. John Y. McCollister (R)
3. Virginia Smith (R)

NEVADA
At large: Jim Santini (D)

NEW HAMPSHIRE
1. Norman E. D'Amours (D)
2. James C. Cleveland (R)

NEW JERSEY
1. James J. Florio (D)
2. William J. Hughes (D)
3. James J. Howard (D)
4. Frank Thompson, Jr. (D)
5. Millicent Fenwick (R)
6. Edwin B. Forsythe (R)
7. Andrew Maguire (D)
8. Robert A. Roe (D)
9. Henry Helstoski (D)
10. Peter W. Rodino, Jr. (D)
11. Joseph G. Minish (D)
12. Matthew J. Rinaldo (R)
13. Helen S. Meyner (D)
14. Dominick V. Daniels (D)
15. Edward J. Patten (D)

NEW MEXICO
1. Manuel Lujan, Jr. (R)
2. Harold Runnels (D)

NEW YORK
1. Otis G. Pike (D)
2. Thomas J. Downey (D)
3. Jerome A. Ambro (D)
4. Norman F. Lent (R)
5. John W. Wydler (R)
6. Lester L. Wolff (D)
7. Joseph P. Addabbo (D)
8. Benjamin S. Rosenthal (D)
9. James J. Delaney (D)
10. Mario Biaggi (D)
11. James H. Scheuer (D)
12. Shirley Chisholm (D)
13. Stephen J. Solarz (D)
14. Frederick W. Richmond (D)
15. Leo C. Zeferetti (D)
16. Elizabeth Holtzman (D)
17. John M. Murphy (D)
18. Edward I. Koch (D)
19. Charles B. Rangel (D)
20. Bella S. Abzug (D)
21. Herman Badillo (D)
22. Jonathan B. Bingham (D)
23. Peter A. Peyser (R)
24. Richard L. Ottinger (D)
25. Hamilton Fish, Jr. (R)
26. Benjamin A. Gilman (R)
27. Matthew F. McHugh (D)
28. Samuel S. Stratton (D)
29. Edward W. Pattison (D)
30. Robert C. McEwen (R)
31. Donald J. Mitchell (R)
32. James M. Hanley (D)
33. William F. Walsh (R)
34. Frank Horton (R)
35. Barber B. Conable, Jr. (R)
36. John J. LaFalce (D)
37. Henry J. Nowak (D)
38. Jack Kemp (R)
39. James F. Hastings (R)[3]

NORTH CAROLINA
1. Walter B. Jones (D)
2. L. H. Fountain (D)
3. David N. Henderson (D)
4. Ike F. Andrews (D)
5. Stephen L. Neal (D)
6. Richardson Preyer (D)
7. Charles Rose (D)
8. W. G. (Bill) Hefner (D)
9. James G. Martin (R)

10. James T. Broyhill (R)
11. Roy A. Taylor (D)

NORTH DAKOTA
At large: Mark Andrews (R)

OHIO
1. Willis D. Gradison, Jr. (R)
2. Donald D. Clancy (R)
3. Charles W. Whalen, Jr. (R)
4. Tennyson Guyer (R)
5. Delbert L. Latta (R)
6. William H. Harsha (R)
7. Clarence J. Brown (R)
8. Thomas N. Kindness (R)
9. Thomas L. Ashley (D)
10. Clarence E. Miller (R)
11. J. William Stanton (R)
12. Samuel L. Devine (R)
13. Charles A. Mosher (R)
14. John F. Seiberling (D)
15. Chalmers P. Wylie (R)
16. Ralph S. Regula (R)
17. John M. Ashbrook (R)
18. Wayne L. Hays (D)[4]
19. Charles J. Carney (D)
20. James V. Stanton (D)
21. Louis Stokes (D)
22. Charles A. Vanik (D)
23. Ronald M. Mottl (D)

OKLAHOMA
1. James R. Jones (D)
2. Theodore M. (Ted) Risenhoover (D)
3. Carl Albert (D)
4. Tom Steed (D)
5. John Jarman (R)
6. Glenn English (D)

OREGON
1. Les AuCoin (D)
2. Al Ullman (D)
3. Robert Duncan (D)
4. James Weaver (D)

PENNSYLVANIA
1. William A. Barrett (D)[5]
2. Robert N. C. Nix (D)
3. William J. Green (D)
4. Joshua Eilberg (D)
5. Richard T. Schulze (R)
6. Gus Yatron (D)
7. Robert W. Edgar (D)
8. Edward G. Biester, Jr. (R)
9. E. G. (Bud) Shuster (R)
10. Joseph M. McDade (R)
11. Daniel J. Flood (D)
12. John P. Murtha (D)
13. Lawrence Coughlin (R)
14. William S. Moorhead (D)
15. Fred B. Rooney (D)
16. Edwin D. Eshleman (R)
17. Herman T. Schneebeli (R)
18. H. John Heinz, 3d (R)
19. William F. Goodling (R)
20. Joseph M. Gaydos (D)
21. John H. Dent (D)
22. Thomas E. Morgan (D)
23. Albert W. Johnson (R)
24. Joseph P. Vigorito (D)
25. Gary A. Myers (R)

RHODE ISLAND
1. Fernand J. Saint Germain (D)
2. Edward P. Beard (D)

SOUTH CAROLINA
1. Mendel J. Davis (D)
2. Floyd Spence (R)
3. Butler Derrick (D)
4. James R. Mann (D)
5. Kenneth L. Holland (D)
6. John W. Jenrette, Jr. (D)

SOUTH DAKOTA
1. Larry Pressler (R)
2. James Abdnor (R)

123

TENNESSEE
1. James H. Quillen (R)
2. John J. Duncan (R)
3. Marilyn Lloyd (D)
4. Joe L. Evins (D)
5. Clifford Allen (D)
6. Robin L. Beard (R)
7. Ed Jones (D)
8. Harold E. Ford (D)

TEXAS
1. Wright Patman (D)[6]
2. Charles Wilson (D)
3. James M. Collins (R)
4. Ray Roberts (D)
5. Alan Steelman (R)
6. Olin E. Teague (D)
7. Bill Archer (R)
8. Bob Eckhardt (D)
9. Jack Brooks (D)
10. J. J. (Jake) Pickle (D)
11. W. R. Poage (D)
12. James C. Wright, Jr. (D)
13. Jack Hightower (D)
14. John Young (D)
15. E (Kika) de la Garza (D)

16. Richard C. White (D)
17. Omar Burleson (D)
18. Barbara Jordan (D)
19. George H. Mahon (D)
20. Henry B. Gonzalez (D)
21. Robert (Bob) Krueger (D)
22. Bob Casey (D)[7]
23. Abraham Kazen, Jr. (D)
24. Dale Milford (D)

UTAH
1. K. Gunn McKay (D)
2. Allan T. Howe (D)

VERMONT
At large: James M. Jeffords (R)

VIRGINIA
1. Thomas N. Downing (D)
2. G. William Whitehurst (R)
3. David E. Satterfield, 3d (D)
4. Robert W. Daniel, Jr. (R)
5. W. C. (Dan) Daniel (D)
6. M. Caldwell Butler (R)
7. J. Kenneth Robinson (R)
8. Herbert E. Harris, 2d (D)
9. William C. Wampler (R)
10. Joseph L. Fisher (D)

WASHINGTON ·
1. Joel Pritchard (R)
2. Lloyd Meeds (D)
3. Don Bonker (D)
4. Mike McCormack (D)
5. Thomas S. Foley (D)
6. Floyd V. Hicks (D)
7. Brock Adams (D)

WEST VIRGINIA
1. Robert H. Mollohan (D)
2. Harley O. Staggers (D)
3. John Slack (D)
4. Ken Hechler (D)

WISCONSIN
1. Les Aspin (D)
2. Robert W. Kastenmeier (D)
3. Alvin Baldus (D)
4. Clement J. Zablocki (D)
5. Henry S. Reuss (D)
6. William A. Steiger (R)
7. David R. Obey (D)
8. Robert J. Cornell (D)
9. Robert W. Kasten, Jr. (R)

WYOMING
At large: Teno Roncalio (D)

[1] Died May 21.
[2] Died Aug. 3.
[3] Resigned Jan. 20; Stanley N. Lundine (D) elected March 2.
[4] Resigned Sept. 1.

[5] Died April 12.
[6] Died March 7; Sam B. Hall (D) elected June 19.
[7] Resigned Jan. 22; Ron Paul (R) elected April 3.

CONNECTICUT. *See*'STATISTICS OF THE WORLD.

CONSTRUCTION. In the United States construction continued to decline in 1976. The total construction bidding volume (accepted new projects) reached about $40 billion, a 16 percent decrease from 1975. The only markedly improved sector was multiunit housing, with a bidding volume total of nearly $3 billion, a 13 percent increase. Highway, heavy, and nonresidential construction bidding volumes fell 8 to 24 percent for the year, depending on the city reporting.

The costs of construction rose faster than the country's rate of inflation; by the end of the year, the major cities reported increases averaging 8.4 percent. Both common and skilled labor costs rose at a slower rate, 6.7 and 6.9 percent, respectively, and increases in the costs of materials were higher, averaging 12.2 percent. Dun & Bradstreet, Inc., a business information service, reported, however, that even with increasing costs, almost 25 percent fewer contractors failed in business than in the preceding year, when they accounted for one in every five bankruptcies.

Internationally, construction bidding volumes varied widely in 1976. Industrialized countries in general had further decreased volumes, while oil-rich developing nations maintained or increased volumes. Labor cost increases were moderate in countries with low rates of inflation but climbed as much as 49 percent in certain areas of Great Britain, 33 percent in Peru, and 55 percent in Brazil. Increases in the cost of materials followed somewhat the same pattern but at a lower percentage of increase.

Teton Dam Collapse. The dramatic collapse of the 310-ft. Teton Dam in Idaho on June 5, which

Welding flaws in the gigantic Alaska oil pipeline are detected by an automatic X-ray crawler. Here a crew inserts into the pipe a gas engine tractor that pulls the picture-taking equipment (foreground) from weld to weld.

killed 14 persons and left 40,000 homeless, set off new demands for tighter government regulation of dam sites and construction. The earth-filled irrigation dam on the Teton R., begun in 1971, had been opposed by environmentalists and some geologists who warned that the site was on porous rock in an earthquake zone. The embankment gave way as the dam was being filled for the first time, releasing 80 billion gal. of water over a 180 sq.mi. area. An official report of the cause of the collapse was to be released in January, 1977, after investigations by the U.S. Bureau of Reclamation, which was responsible for the dam, and by an independent panel of engineers named by the secretary of the interior.

Critics and legislators, citing many less publicized collapses (a break on Feb. 4 in Bear Wallow Dam in North Carolina killed four persons), pointed out that no safety programs existed for nonfederally supported dams in at least 25 states, and 10 states had no location and construction regulations for such dams. A federal law already on the books that requires the U.S. Corps of Engineers to inspect every dam in the country was ineffective because the U.S. Congress had not allotted funds for the corps to proceed.

Alaska Pipeline. Faulty welds in the Alaska oil pipeline also caused controversy in 1976. Alyeska

The Teton Dam in the Snake River valley of Idaho after the collapse on June 5 of its 310-ft. wall. The unleashed torrent of water rushed 100 mi. downstream, forcing 40,000 persons to flee from their homes.

Pipeline Service Co., the contractor, claimed that only an acceptable percentage of welds needed to be examined and that some welds classified as faults by inspectors did not need to be repaired. Environmentalists took the opposing view, leaving the federal Department of Transportation to work out further inspection and correction procedures. While awaiting a ruling, Alyeska repaired all but 34 of the 3955 welds in question, and the government exempted 3 faults as inconsequential. More than 90 percent of the pipeline was completed by the end of 1976, and the work force was reduced from 21,000 to 5000.

Nuclear Power Plant Construction. Despite environmentalists' cries to halt nuclear power plant construction, the 1976 tally sheet showed 184 such plants under construction around the world, at least 130 more on order, and an additional 325 planned. (Plants already in use numbered 164.) Proposals that would have restricted further development were defeated in all seven states of the U.S. where they appeared on election ballots during the year. The U.S. share of nuclear power plant contracts dropped in 1976, primarily

CONSTRUCTION

An engineer at the San Onofre nuclear power station, under construction in California, checks the results of the June 9 primary election. Proposition 15, designed to restrict further development of nuclear plants, was one of seven such measures defeated by the nation's voters during the year.

cause of competitive pressure from foreign contractors.

Arab Boycott Disclosures. Bidding by U.S. contractors on Middle Eastern projects did not show signs of being affected by a new law that required the contractors to notify the U.S. Department of Commerce if they received Arab requests to boycott Israel. On Oct. 6, when such a boycott became an issue in the Presidential election campaign, the Administration decided to make available to the public the contractors' disclosures to the Commerce Department. A California law, to go into effect Jan. 1, 1977, would make compliance with the boycott illegal in that state. Meanwhile, several Jewish organizations released documents during the year naming contractors and other firms that the organizations claimed had complied with provisions of the Arab boycott of Israel.

Construction Prospects. Industrial plant construction appeared to be the fastest growing segment of the industry in the U.S. and around the world. The main areas of activity were in the Middle East, North Africa, and Asia. Energy-related construction, including the building of power plants, gas and oil lines, processing plants, and synthetic fuel facilities, grew in 1976 and was expected to continue to be important.

The Export-Import Bank of the U.S., an independent federal agency, made moves in the fall to accelerate international construction starts. The bank began exercising its loan guarantee authority to obtain private funding for foreign projects. In the first project funded, $1.1 billion was raised, with $616,000,000 allocated for U.S. construction suppliers and contractors.

State and municipal bond sales for construction—a sound indicator of work to come—were mixed across the U.S., but increases showed in most areas. The best news for contractors was the passage of a federal bill in October providing $3.7 billion for construction projects in areas with high rates of unemployment. R.W.S.

CONSUMER EDUCATION AND PROTECTION. The year 1976 was one of political action for the consumer movement, with groups such as the Consumer Federation of America endorsing Congressional candidates for the first time and a coalition releasing an "indictment" of President Gerald R. Ford's record on consumer issues during the Presidential campaign. At the same time, the national goals of the movement shifted away from specific issue legislation, such as fair packaging and truth-in-lending, to more basic questions of government reform. Grass-roots consumer groups at the local level—fighting such diverse targets as high utility rates, confusing price tags, unfair property taxes, and questionable funeral costs—became more numerous and vocal. The chief legislative disappointment for the consumer movement was the failure to achieve enactment of a bill that would have created the Agency for Consumer Advocacy, an independent federal agency to represent consumer interests in the proceedings of government. The bill passed both the United States Senate and House of Representatives in 1975, but in 1976 Congressional leaders decided again not to take final action on the measure because they lacked the votes to override President Ford's anticipated veto. President-elect Jimmy Carter, who had sponsored a consumer protection bill as governor of Georgia, supported the bill to create the federal agency and was expected to promote its enactment in 1977.

Heavy industry lobbying did not prevent passage in September of the Antitrust Improvements

Act. The act contained a provision to allow state attorneys general to file suits on behalf of the citizens of their states in cases where federal price-fixing laws, for example, had been violated. The act also required large companies to give advance notice of mergers to federal antitrust enforcement officials. In other legislation the United States Congress passed a law in March requiring car-leasing companies to provide customers with advance notice of the full terms of their leases. The Consumer Product Safety Commission was given the right in April to seek immediate injunctions—without holding hearings—against products considered hazardous.

Presidential Politics. Spokesmen for the consumer movement generally supported Democratic Party candidate Jimmy Carter during the Presidential campaign. In his nomination acceptance speech in July, Carter spoke of "strong safeguards for consumers"; he later invited consumer advocate Ralph Nader to his home in Plains, Ga. Nader called the candidate's views "admirable," but stopped short of an endorsement. Carter, for his part, said that he intended to challenge Nader for the title of "top consumer advocate in the country." Also during the campaign, such consumer leaders as Bess Myerson, former New York City commissioner of consumer affairs, and Esther Peterson, former adviser to President Lyndon B. Johnson, joined together in a "Consumers for Carter" organization.

The Hazards of Living. The list of banned sub-stances grew in 1976, with a widely used food additive, Red dye number 2, being totally banned in January by the U.S. Food and Drug Administration (F.D.A.). The dye was found to cause cancer in laboratory animals. Later in the year, Red dye number 4, the coloring agent in Maraschino cherries, was banned in foods but not in cosmetics, and carbon black, a candy colorer, was banned in foods and cosmetics. The F.D.A. also acted to ban the use of chloroform in cough medicines, linaments, and toothpaste. Also a suspected carcinogen, chloroform was found to be present in certain toothpastes in levels as high as 2 percent by weight. Manufacturers said the substance was used to give a "tingle" to the brusher's mouth.

Prices. Although the 1976 rate of general inflation, as measured by the Consumer Price Index, held to 4.8 percent, or half the double-digit levels of 1974, dramatic increases in the prices of certain basic goods and services caused serious concern.

Coffee drinkers found that their habit, whether indulged at home or in restaurants, had become an increasingly expensive one. According to the National Coffee Association, green bean prices climbed more than 200 percent during the year, due largely to the 1975 frost in Brazil and to the continuing Angolan civil war.

All of these products, including the soft drink and the pills, contain Red dye number 2, a coloring agent banned by the U.S. Food and Drug Administration in January because of doubts about its safety.

New York City Consumer Affairs Commissioner Elinor Guggenheimer makes a cup of tea as she urges consumers to boycott coffee. Retailers supported the December campaign to bring coffee prices down after a year in which wholesale prices for the ground beans nearly doubled.

A sudden hike in auto insurance premiums forced more difficult budget adjustments. Premiums in many parts of the country doubled. At the same time, the auto insurance market for new drivers of all ages became very tight, with some companies refusing to write any new contracts at all, and others tightening their underwriting standards drastically. That situation was exacerbated by the near collapse of the Government Employees Insurance Co., one of the nation's largest insurers, which dropped all its customers in New Jersey and trimmed its lists elsewhere.

Other Events. On April 8 premiere showings of the film *All the President's Men* were held in sixteen cities to benefit the activities of local consumer groups. With the help of personal appearances by actor Robert Redford, a star of the film,

and his consumer-activist wife Lola, the premieres grossed about $200,000.

In May the consumer movement saw the fruits of an effort to work with the business community to solve consumer problems. The boards of directors of the two major trade groups of the supermarket industry voted to recommend to their members that they retain conventional price markings on individual items in stores converted to electronic checkout systems. In these systems a Universal Product Code of lines and spaces printed on each item is read by an optical scanner connected to a computer. The computer then relays the price of the item to the cash register. A study supervised by consumer representatives found that shoppers experience difficulty in comparing and remembering prices when items are not individually price-marked. As a result of the trade groups' recommendation, consumer groups eased their pressure for legislation to require individual pricing.

Progress was reported in the national campaign to discourage cigarette smoking. A study released in June by the Center for Disease Control showed that about 34 percent of U.S. adults smoked cigarettes in 1975, down from 36 percent in 1970. Smoking increased, however, among young women. The American Cancer Society, which in October began a five-year education campaign against smoking, also reported test results that for the first time clearly indicated the relative safety of smoking cigarettes low in tar and nicotine.   F.C.

COSTA RICA. Although Costa Rica's economic outlook improved in 1976 due to buoyant coffee prices, the government of President Daniel Oduber Quirós had to deal with increasing political and labor unrest and growing criticism from the private sector over its interventionist economic policies. In late summer and fall normally peaceful Costa Rica was rocked by strikes, violent antigovernment demonstrations, persistent rumors of takeover plots, and terrorist bombings. These disturbances occurred after a major confrontation took place in July between the government and workers of the autonomous but state-owned Costa Rican Institute of Electricity (I.C.E.). The discord reached crisis proportions after the courts declared that a strike by 2500 I.C.E. workers following the suspension of a previous wage increase was illegal. Faced with the threat of a national strike, I.C.E. granted the pay increase despite government opposition. Some of the general unrest was caused by continued high inflation; some of it was also attributed to infighting within the ruling National Liberation Party.

The private sector was agitated in 1976 by a new tax package. In addition to raising corporate taxes by 5 percent, the government imposed a levy on real estate transactions; later, coffee export taxes were increased. As of May 31 Costa Rica extended its offshore economic zone to 200 mi., as had most other Central American nations. Early in 1976 it was announced that two gold mines, closed since the 1940's, would reopen in 1977.

See STATISTICS OF THE WORLD.   A.K.M.

COUNCIL FOR MUTUAL ECONOMIC ASSIST-ANCE, known as COMECON, a Communist counterpart of Western European organizations aimed at achieving economic unity. Its members include the Soviet Union, most Eastern European countries, Cuba, and Mongolia.

The early 1970's saw a spectacular growth in trade between COMECON countries and the West. In 1976, however, Western nations became concerned about the resultant increase in Communist indebtedness. By the end of the year, COMECON nations owed an estimated $35–40 billion to the West. For this reason, the European Economic Community decided to move slowly on a request, submitted in February by COMECON Chairman Gerhard Weiss, for closer ties between the two trading blocs.

The thirtieth session of COMECON's ministerial council met in East Berlin, July 7–9. Although the talks themselves were secret (a communiqué was issued at the end of the session), Western analysts believed the ministers discussed a wide spectrum of problems. In addition to the COMECON debt, these included the steadily rising cost of Soviet oil imported by Eastern Europe and the problem of setting currency exchange rates in intra-COMECON transactions. A decision to work toward the integration of Soviet and Eastern European electric power grids was one concrete result of the meeting.

See also WARSAW TREATY ORGANIZATION.   F.W.

CRIME AND LAW ENFORCEMENT. The crime rate in the United States rose moderately during 1976. Among other developments the U.S. Supreme Court approved the revival of capital punishment, kidnappings again made news, and the last of the Scottsboro boys was pardoned.

The Crime Rate and the F.B.I. The number of serious crimes reported by the nation's police departments was up 2 percent during the first 9 months of 1976—an improvement over the 11 percent increase during the same period of 1975. In addition the Federal Bureau of Investigation (F.B.I.) reported that the number of violent crimes actually fell during the first half of 1976. According to the F.B.I. *Uniform Crime Reports,* murder was down by 10 percent, robbery by 10 percent, and rape and aggravated assault showed no change.

During the year the F.B.I. itself acknowledged

They Blamed It on the Computer

Early in the year the Springfield (Ill.) traffic department served notice on one Frank Gauss 4th, charging him with refusal to pay a parking fine dating from September, 1975. Cleared of the charge, he was set free in the custody of his father, Frank Gauss 3rd. The father had been nowhere near Springfield on the day in question, he testified, and as for the accused—he had not even been born. When he received the department's notice of his misdeed, Frank 4th was just 4 months old.

committing crimes, including burglary, politically motivated wiretapping, and harassment as recently as 1973 in the course of investigating radicals and dissenters. F.B.I. Director Clarence M Kelley publicly apologized in May, saying that the activities were "clearly wrong and quite indefensible." Kelley raised a minor Presidential cam-

Condemned murderer Gary Mark Gilmore leaves the chambers of the Utah Supreme Court on Nov. 10 after pleading to be executed without delay. Gilmore later attempted suicide in his prison cell. There were further delays and developments. Finally, in December, his execution was ordered to be carried out early in 1977.

Bus driver Franklin Edward Ray waves during a parade down the main street of Chowchilla, Calif., on Aug. 22. Ray and the accompanying children were kidnapped on July 15. Sealed in a buried truck trailer, they managed to dig themselves out some fifteen hours later.

paign issue on Aug. 31 when he admitted having received gifts and favors from subordinates. President Gerald R. Ford expressed confidence in Kelley, but Democratic candidate Jimmy Carter said he "would have fired him."

Capital Punishment. In July the U.S. Supreme Court upheld the capital punishment laws of Florida, Texas, and Georgia, and ruled that the death penalty was not inherently cruel or unusual. Prison officials began preparing their electric chairs and gas chambers for the 418 men and 5 women on death rows around the country. A grisly race soon developed between 2 condemned murderers for the dubious distinction of being the first person to be executed since 1967: Gary Mark Gilmore, 35, convicted by a Utah jury of the July murder of a motel night clerk; and Robert Excell White, 38, convicted in Texas in 1974 of killing a grocer and two customers during a robbery. The U.S. Supreme Court reviewed both cases and granted stays of execution to both men. But Gilmore's stay was vacated and his execution set for Jan. 17, 1977.

The Hearst Case. After fourteen months of confinement, newspaper heiress Patricia Hearst was freed on bail in November, pending appeal on her conviction in March for bank robbery; see PEOPLE IN THE NEWS. The last survivors of the revo-

lutionary group that kidnapped Miss Hearst in February, 1974, William and Emily Harris, were found guilty (Aug. 9 in Los Angeles) of theft, armed robbery, and kidnapping. The charges stemmed from events that occurred in May, 1974, at a Los Angeles sporting-goods store. Patricia Hearst awaited another trial for her part in those events.

Watergate Defendants. The 1972 break-in at the Democratic Party headquarters in the Watergate complex in Washington, D.C., continued to cast its shadow over those involved. John D. Ehrlichman, a top aide of former President Richard M. Nixon, began serving a prison sentence of at least thirty months in Stafford, Ariz., in October. Ehrlichman had been convicted for his role in covering up the break-in and for participating in the illegal activities of the so-called plumbers unit, a group assigned by the Nixon administration to stop security leaks. Another Watergate defendant, Robert C. Mardian, won a reversal in October of his conviction for conspiracy in the cover-up. Mardian was an assistant attorney general in the Nixon administration.

Kidnappings. A daring abduction followed by a resourceful escape occurred near Chowchilla, Calif., on July 15. A school bus was hijacked by 3 masked men who, after a long ride at gunpoint, forced the 26 children and their driver into a buried truck trailer and left them sealed within. The children, led by driver Franklin Edward Ray, dug themselves out. Within 3 weeks the police had arrested 3 suspects: Frederick Woods, James

Five Croatian nationalists who hijacked a New York City-to-Chicago flight on Sept. 10 arrive in custody at Charles De Gaulle Airport in Paris. Before surrendering, the hijackers had insisted that an appeal for Croatian independence be printed in four U.S. newspapers.

Schoenfeld, and Richard Schoenfeld, all of whom were later indicted.

In another case Samuel Bronfman 2nd, 23-year-old son of a wealthy liquor manufacturer, was the key witness in the trial of Brooklyn fireman Mel Patrick Lynch and limousine operator Dominic P. Byrne in White Plains, N.Y. The two were accused of abducting and holding Bronfman for ransom in August, 1975, but Lynch claimed that the young heir had been their accomplice in an extortion scheme. In December the two men were found guilty of grand larceny but not of kidnapping.

Organized Crime. A flare-up in Mafia gang wars seemed likely following the death in October of Carlo Gambino, the most powerful Mafia boss in the U.S.; see OBITUARIES. Another Mafia leader, John Rosselli, 71, met a traditional gangland end in August. His body was found in a drum floating in Biscayne Bay, Fla. Rosselli testified in 1975 that he had been recruited by the Central Intelligence Agency (C.I.A.) in 1960 for a plot to assassinate Cuban Premier Fidel Castro.

Assassination Probe. Thirteen years after the slaying of President John F. Kennedy and eight years after that of civil rights leader Martin Luther King, Jr., still another investigation was ordered into their assassinations. In September the United States House of Representatives established a twelve-member Select Committee on Assassinations to search for new information about the two killings. The inquiry was fueled by disclosures in recent years of facts and leads that the F.B.I. and the C.I.A. had apparently withheld from official investigators. Former Pennsylvania prosecutor Richard A. Sprague, assisted by a staff of 170, took charge of the inquiry.

Bolles and Letelier. In unrelated cases, apparently to silence them, two men devoted to causes were murdered by bombs planted in their automobiles. On June 2 in Phoenix, Ariz., a dynamite blast ripped through the car of Don Bolles, an investigative reporter for the Arizona *Republic*. Bolles, 47, a specialist in exposing land frauds and other forms of white-collar crime in the Southwest, died 11 days later. John Harvey Adamson, 32, a greyhound breeder, was subsequently indicted for the murder.

In the second case Orlando Letelier, former Chilean ambassador to the U.S. and an outspoken opponent of the current regime in Chile, was killed on Sept. 21 when a bomb exploded under his car in Washington, D.C.

Other Cases. Alabama granted a full pardon on Oct. 25 to Clarence Norris, the only survivor of the Scottsboro boys, 9 black youths convicted of rape in 1931 and later generally conceded to have been victims of racial injustice. Norris, 64, spent 15 years in an Alabama prison until his parole in 1946. He then left the state without authority and settled in New York City, working as a warehouseman. *See* NEGROES IN THE UNITED STATES.

The first successful hijacking of a U.S. domestic airliner since tight security measures were imposed in 1972 took place on Sept. 10. Five Croatian nationalists seeking to publicize their cause (the separation of the constituent republic of Croatia from Yugoslavia) hijacked a Trans World Airlines jet near New York City and forced the pilot to fly to Paris, where they surrendered to authorities. The five were returned to the U.S. and indicted on seven charges, including the murder of a New York City police officer. He was killed attempting to defuse a bomb allegedly left by the hijackers in Grand Central Station.   M.R.B.

CUBA. Cuba's political system underwent major reforms during 1976. On Feb. 15 the Cuban people approved a new constitution providing for a Council of State, to be elected by a National Assembly, which would itself be chosen by representatives elected at the local level. Elections were held as scheduled in November, and on Dec. 2 the National Assembly met for the first time. As expected, it chose Premier Fidel Castro to head the new Council of State. Constitutional reforms also included a government reorganization program raising the number of provinces from 6 to 14. These political changes reflected Castro's effort to institutionalize the revolution which he began twenty years ago.

During 1976 the Cuban people were forced to accept increased economic austerity measures. The reason was the fall in export income caused by a drop in sugar prices. The government reduced coffee rations (Cuba's coffee output had suffered a decline for several years), and it put telephone service, which had been free since 1964, on a paying basis once again.

Relations between Cuba and the United States were strained by the continued presence of Cuban troops in Angola (q.v.). In February U.S. President Gerald R. Ford said that Cuba was "acting as an international outlaw." At a rally commemorating the 15th anniversary of the Cuban defeat of the U.S.-backed invasion attempt at the Bay of Pigs, Castro seized on this point of contention and described Angola as an "African Bay of Pigs for American imperialism." Castro also used the occasion to warn the U.S. that he would not honor the antihijacking agreement between the two countries unless attacks on Cuban fishing boats ceased. Two Cuban boats had been machine-gunned and sunk by Cuban exiles in the Florida strait in April.

Although such key Latin American nations as Colombia and Venezuela did not approve of Cuba's military intervention in Angola, they did not alter their policy of seeking to normalize relations between all Latin American governments and the island nation. Chile and most of the other Central American countries were violently opposed to the intervention in Angola, so the region's position on Cuba was still unresolved after the sixth annual General Assembly meeting of the Organization of American States. At that June meeting the Inter-American Commission on Human Rights had re-

Cuban Premier Fidel Castro brings his message to a group of summer campers on Children's Day, July 18.

Another round of talks aimed at settling the question of control over Cyprus got under way Feb. 17 in Vienna. United Nations Secretary-General Kurt Waldheim (center) confers with Rauf Denktash (left) of the Turkish Cypriots and Glafkos Clerides of the Greek Cypriots.

ported that Cuba's treatment of political prisoners was "cruel, inhuman, and degrading."

See STATISTICS OF THE WORLD. A.K.M.

CYPRUS. The year 1976 passed with no measurable progress in ongoing attempts to find a solution to the enmity between the rival Greek and Turkish communities on Cyprus.

Further Talks. The fifth round of intercommunal negotiations got under way in Vienna on Feb. 17 between the leaders of the Greek and Turkish factions meeting under the auspices of United Nations Secretary-General Kurt Waldheim. The talks ended with no tangible results four days later.

Both negotiators were replaced in April after Glafkos Clerides, the Greek Cypriot representative, admitted that he had made a secret agreement to disclose Greek Cypriot proposals to the Turkish Cypriot negotiator before the Turkish Cypriots made their own proposals. Clerides resigned on April 8 and was replaced by former Labor Minister Tassos Papadopoulos. The Turkish Cypriot negotiator, Rauf Denktash, then charged that Papadopoulos was a former member of the EOKA (National Organization of Cypriot Struggle) guerrillas and refused to negotiate with him. Denktash was replaced on April 15 by Umit Suleiman Onan, acting president of the Turkish Cypriot assembly. Late in the year each side reaffirmed its position, and Waldheim was still unsuccessful in scheduling further negotiations.

On June 30 the Turkish Cypriot community elected Denktash president of the "Turkish Federated State of Cyprus." This independent "state" in northern Cyprus had been proclaimed in 1975. Denktash's National Union Party also won most of the forty seats in the legislative assembly of Cyprus, which was chosen in the same election. The Greek Cypriot community recognized neither the Turkish "state" nor the election.

Foreign Relations. With Turkish troops occupying 40 percent of Cyprus, the United States agreement on March 26 to resume military aid to Turkey enraged the Greek Cypriot community. Reacting violently to the U.S. promise of more than $1 billion in aid to that country over the next four years, some 2000 Greek Cypriots massed before the U.S. embassy in Nicosia on April 6 and again on April 12. They threw rocks and torches at the building and had to be dispersed by the police with tear gas.

In a nearly unanimous victory on Sept. 5, the coalition of parties supporting President Makarios won 34 of the 35 seats in the parliament controlling the Greek areas of Cyprus.

On Nov. 12 the U.N. General Assembly adopted a resolution calling on Turkey to remove its troops from Cyprus. But at year's end Turkey had taken no steps to comply.

Cyprus continued to provide refuge for many Lebanese Christians who fled their country during the civil war. By March 28 it was reported that more than 1000 were in Cyprus, many of them having made the 200-mi. voyage in fishing boats and small steamers.

See STATISTICS OF THE WORLD. L.A.S.

CZECHOSLOVAKIA. Beneath a facade of economic prosperity, Czechoslovakia continued in 1976 to suffer from the consequences of the 1968 Soviet invasion that ended political liberalization in Prague. The Czechoslovak government installed by the U.S.S.R. echoed Soviet policy closely in both domestic and foreign affairs.

The political highlight of 1976 came in April,

when the Communist Party held its 15th Congress in the nation's capital. The congress confirmed the leadership of General Secretary Gustáv Husák, who indicated there would be no return to the preinvasion reforms of 1968. Husák said that certain backers of the ill-fated reform movement might be readmitted to the party if they agreed to "support present party policies"—a formulation which continued to exclude liberal-minded Communists. Because of Husák's stance, the more liberal Communist parties of Italy and Spain declined to send official delegations to the Prague congress.

The influence of the neo-Stalinist wing of the Communist Party, which was led by Vasil Bilak, remained evident. The cultural scene was heavily censored, and the regime refused to let noted playwrights Václav Havel and Pavel Kohout travel to the West for premieres of their works. Political dissidents were harassed, and even seemingly harmless nonconformity came under attack. In July, for example, three young men were convicted for allowing musicians to perform popular music at a youth club.

The regime made a conscious effort to upgrade living standards. In 1976 Czechoslovakia's estimated income per capita was second only to that of East Germany in the Communist world, and one in four households owned a car. There were economic shortcomings, however. Grain and sugar beet harvests were poor, and a rise in 1976–77 agricultural import costs was forecast. At a Communist Party Central Committee meeting in September, two senior deputy premiers—Ján Gregor and Frantisek Hamouz—and Agricultural Minister Bohuslav Vecera were dismissed on account of failures in the fields of farming, engineering, and foreign trade.

United States–Czechoslovak relations remained cool, although talks on cultural and scientific exchanges began in February. That same month, Chancellor Bruno Kreisky made the first official visit to Prague by an Austrian head of government since World War II; improvements in economic and political cooperation were discussed. In September Czechoslovak Foreign Minister Bohuslav Chňoupek held discussions in London with British Foreign Secretary Anthony Crosland. Relations between the two nations had been strained since the 1968 Soviet invasion.

Zdeněk Fierlinger, Czechoslovakia's first premier following World War II, died on May 2 at the age of 85.

See STATISTICS OF THE WORLD.

D

DAHOMEY. *See* STATISTICS OF THE WORLD.

DANCE. In 1976 the dance world was shaken by changes in producing organizations and by financial difficulties. At the same time more ballet was performed than ever before, with special Bicentennial programs abounding.

Organizational Changes. The most far-reaching events in dance concerned changes in producing organizations. The New York City Center of Music and Drama, a longtime sponsor of American and foreign dance troupes, virtually went out of existence. In its place a consortium of four dance companies—the Alvin Ailey City Center Dance Theater, the American Ballet Theatre, the City Center Joffrey Ballet, and the Eliot Feld Ballet—took over management of the City Center theater on a cooperative basis for a year's trial run beginning Sept. 1.

Hurok Concerts Inc., which had presented dance troupes such as the Bolshoi Ballet of Moscow, the British Royal Ballet, and the Stuttgart Ballet of Germany at the Metropolitan Opera House in New York City each spring and summer, declined to renew its leasing option for 1977. This action forced many of the world's major dance companies to find other ways of financing tours of the United States.

Dance companies, especially in New York City, experienced financial pressures during the year. The expansion of the past ten years (139 U.S. companies were performing in 1976) had brought problems of size and market saturation. The Paul Taylor Dance Company, a highly acclaimed modern dance troupe, disbanded because of inadequate funds.

Bicentennial Productions. The Bicentennial was a great stimulus to companies across the nation. The Martha Graham Company toured the U.S. with programs entitled "In the American Grain," reflecting Graham's deep interest in American themes in such dances as *Appalachian Spring, Frontier,* and *Letter to the World* (based on the life of the poet Emily Dickinson). In honor of Graham's achievements as a pioneer in an American art form, she was the first dancer to receive the Presidential Medal of Freedom. Her company was also the first modern dance group to perform at the Covent Garden Theatre in London. A two-week season there in July and an October appearance in Paris were both triumphs.

Other Bicentennial motifs abounded. The Alvin Ailey Company's tribute to Duke Ellington was highlighted by *Pas de Duke,* a duet created by Ailey for Judith Jamison and ballet's new superstar Mikhail Baryshnikov. For its fall season at the City Center, the Joffrey Ballet featured thirty works by American choreographers. The Joffrey produced an outstanding version of Agnes De Mille's *Rodeo* and a much praised new ballet by Twyla Tharp, *Happily Ever After.*

Perhaps the most lavish Bicentennial ballet was George Balanchine's *Union Jack,* presented by the New York City Ballet during its spring season (April 27–June 27) at the New York State Theater. *Union Jack* pays homage to Great Britain's military and music-hall traditions. Beginning with a Scottish tattoo and ending with a cast of seventy-five signaling "God Save the Queen" in semaphore code, *Union Jack* was an extravaganza that surprised and delighted its audiences. A more modest surprise was Balanchine's *Square Dance,*

to music by Antonio Vivaldi and Arcangelo Corelli. Termed a revival, it was actually a new ballet, more an extension of his courtly *Chaconne,* premiered in January, than of the bouncy square-dance patterns that had marked the original *Square Dance* (1957).

American Ballet Theatre. Although the American Ballet Theatre (ABT) presented programs of Americana during a summer season (June 29–Aug. 7) at the New York State Theater, prime interest focused on its productions of the full-length classics. These included Baryshnikov's new production of *The Nutcracker,* first given at the Kennedy Center, Washington, D.C., on Dec. 21, and *The Sleeping Beauty,* unveiled on June 15 at the Metropolitan Opera House. The reception of the latter was mixed; many critics felt, however, that the first performances of such a complex and challenging ballet had to be tentative. The growing roster of guest artists appearing with ABT—Rudolf Nureyev, Marcia Haydee, Lynn Seymour, Alicia Alonso, Natalia Makarova, and Baryshnikov was evident in galas in Los Angeles, San Francisco, Washington, D.C., and New York City. Prima ballerina Cynthia Gregory, who had announced her retirement in 1975, rejoined the company in November.

Martha Graham receives the nation's highest civilian award, the Medal of Freedom, from President Gerald R. Ford at a White House ceremony on Oct. 14. The 82-year-old dancer-choreographer hailed the "new attitude toward the arts and dance."

Opposite page, top: The New York City Ballet observes the Bicentennial unconventionally with Union Jack. *This new work by George Balanchine playfully celebrates and satirizes Great Britain and the British people. Opposite page, bottom: Judith Jamison and Mikhail Baryshnikov provide a striking contrast in* Pas de Duke, *performed on May 11 as part of the Alvin Ailey Company's tribute to composer Duke Ellington.*

Visiting Foreign Companies. After an absence of eleven years, the Royal Danish Ballet visited Washington, D.C., and New York City in May and June. Renowned as the custodians of the Bournonville tradition, the Danes brought only a few ballets by that revered 19th-century choreographer. Much more of the repertory was devoted to works by the company's present director, Flemming Flindt. Boasting no star names and with a largely unfamiliar repertory, the tour was not a great financial success. Nor were many artistic points garnered, since most critics found the quality of the dancing slightly anemic.

The Royal Ballet of Great Britain, on the other hand, impressed everyone with the beauty and discipline of its dancing during a tour of New York City, Washington, D.C., and Philadelphia in April and May. The chief novelty offered by the company was Frederick Ashton's *A Month in the Country,* based on the play by the 19th-century Russian author Ivan Turgenev. Once again the critics agreed that Ashton had a unique ability to realize characterization and to transmit plot in dance.

Other visitors from abroad included the Australian Ballet, which performed *The Merry Widow,* starring Margot Fonteyn; the Dutch National Ballet, which toured Canada before making its American debut in New York City; and Igor Moiseyev's Russian Festival, a potpourri of companies from all over the Soviet Union.

Televised Dance. The educational television station in the New York City area, WNET, produced a series of four programs for national distribution called "Dance in America." Featuring the Pennsylvania Ballet and the Joffrey, Graham, and Tharp troupes, the programs were highly praised for their sensitive treatment of an art form that has usually fared poorly on television. A second season of "Dance in America" began in December with an ABT performance. On June 30 WNET presented the first live telecast of a full-length ballet, the ABT production of *Swan Lake..*

Deaths. Film choreographer Busby Berkeley died on March 14; *see* OBITUARIES. Other deaths included those of Cyril W. Beaumont, dean of dance historians (May 24 at 85), and David Blair, formerly a principal dancer of the Royal Ballet (April 1 at 43). N.T.G.

DELAWARE. *See* STATISTICS OF THE WORLD.

DEMOCRATIC PARTY. For Democrats 1976 was the year of Jimmy Carter's remarkable rise from obscurity to the Presidency; *see* PEOPLE IN THE NEWS. Starting out with little money and a weak political base in Georgia, he progressed to his goal in ten strenuous months of campaigning. Along the way he unified the party. In the United

Twyla Tharp, who had a banner year in 1976, directs as Olympic champion skater John Curry practices a routine she choreographed for him. Curry performed the 7-min. marriage of figure skating and dance on Nov. 15 in the ice show Superskates III *at Madison Square Garden in New York City.*

The Changing of the Guard
As the 94th Congress of the U.S. adjourned, two of the most familiar and influential Democrats in Washington went into retirement. Oklahoma Rep. Carl Albert, 68, a fiery orator, won his first House seat in 1946; in 1971 he was elected Speaker of the House. Patient, thoughtful Montana Sen. Mike Mansfield, 73, served in the House for ten years before moving to the Senate in 1952. He was majority leader there for fifteen years, a Senate longevity record.

Rep. Carl Albert (right) and Sen. Mike Mansfield.

States Congress Democrats complained all year long of being prevented from enacting needed legislation by Presidential vetoes. The party's main themes in 1976 were more jobs, fairer taxes, and stronger leadership. At the year's end the Democrats, about to assume control of the government, sought to translate these themes into a practical national program.

Campaign for the Nomination. As the primary election season approached in January, Jimmy Carter, energetic but underfinanced, was one of a dozen Democratic aspirants. A surprise victory in the Iowa caucuses for selecting convention delegates first brought him national attention. Carter then defeated Rep. Morris K. Udall of Arizona, his chief rival on the party's left wing, in the Feb. 24 New Hampshire primary. On March 2 Carter won in Vermont but in Massachusetts trailed Sen. Henry M. Jackson of Washington and Udall. Sen. Birch Bayh of Indiana withdrew from the race after his

Left: A radiant U.S. Representative, Barbara Jordan of Texas, acknowledges the applause of the Democratic National Convention at New York City. She had just delivered a keynote address at the opening session, July 12.

Opposite page: Democratic Presidential candidates take part in an urban affairs forum on March 29 in New York City: (left to right) Sen. Frank Church, former Gov. Jimmy Carter, Rep. Morris Udall, former Sen. Fred Harris, and Sen. Henry Jackson.

poor showing in Massachusetts. Two earlier drop-outs were former Gov. Terry Sanford of North Carolina and Sen. Lloyd M. Bentsen, Jr., of Texas.

By this time Carter had evolved his main campaign themes: new leadership and vision for the nation, tax reform, tighter fiscal management, and government "as good and honest . . . and filled with love as the American people." He turned his inexperience to advantage by claiming to be a political outsider, uncompromised by the Washington scene. His smiling face and soft, articulate Southern voice became familiar. The other candidates were failing to make much impact on a largely indifferent electorate.

Gov. George C. Wallace of Alabama succumbed to Carter in Florida (March 9) and North Carolina (March 22), defeats that put an end to the Alabamian's well-financed campaign. Gov. Milton J. Shapp of Pennsylvania, 1972 Vice-Presidential candidate R. Sargent Shriver, and former Sen. Fred R. Harris of Oklahoma also dropped out of the race. On April 6 Jackson achieved his high-water mark with a victory in New York while Carter was edging out Udall in Wisconsin. A careless remark about preserving the "ethnic purity" of neighborhoods apparently did not hurt Carter among black voters, who gave him solid support in his victories in Pennsylvania, Texas, and Indiana. The results from Pennsylvania on April 27 persuaded Jackson to end active campaigning and moved Sen. Hubert H. Humphrey of Minnesota to decide against a stop-Carter effort of his own.

May and June brought effective late-starting campaigns by Sen. Frank Church of Idaho (who won primaries in Nebraska, Idaho, Oregon, and Montana) and Gov. Edmund G. Brown, Jr., of California (who won in Maryland, Nevada, Rhode Island, and California). But they failed to slow Carter's mounting delegate count. The Georgian topped Udall in Michigan and South Dakota; Udall's seventh second-place finish without a victory made it clear that the Arizonan could not broaden his liberal constituency.

Carter's June 8 triumph in Ohio settled the matter for most party leaders. The next day, Mayor Richard J. Daley of Chicago and George Wallace endorsed him, and Humphrey and Jackson conceded him the nomination. In succeeding days Sen. Edward M. Kennedy of Massachusetts, Sen. George McGovern of South Dakota, Frank Church, and Morris Udall promised help and called for party unity.

The Convention. The Democratic National Convention was convened July 12 at Madison Square Garden in New York City. Rep. Barbara Jordan of Texas welcomed the delegates with a stirring keynote address that followed a speech by Sen. John Glenn of Ohio. The party platform was adopted with virtually no debate; it gained equal approval from Wallace conservatives and Udall liberals. Incorporating much of Carter's views and language, it urged tax reform, federalized welfare, and national health insurance. It committed the Democrats to seek full employment. A statement of sup-

port for strong national defense was coupled with a proposal to reduce defense spending by $5 to $7 billion.

On July 14 Jimmy Carter was nominated for President on the first ballot with no significant opposition. After lengthy scrutiny of numerous possibilities, he chose the liberal Sen. Walter F. Mondale of Minnesota to be his running mate. The convention ratified his choice and also renamed Robert S. Strauss to the post of national party chairman before adjournment on July 15.

The Presidential Campaign. "My strategy for the fall is to run flat out," said Carter in July, although opinion polls showed him far ahead of President Gerald R. Ford. Carter set up his campaign headquarters in Atlanta, Ga., with his longtime aide Hamilton Jordan in charge. By Sept. 4, when the Democratic campaign officially began, Ford had narrowed the gap considerably.

Many observers believe that three televised debates between the candidates helped the Democrat to convey his grasp of information and his general trustworthiness. Ford's charges of vagueness and fiscal irresponsibility, however, apparently made an impression. The President gained steadily in the opinion polls until a dead heat was predicted by the political pundits and the pollsters the weekend before election day.

Election Results. In winning a narrow majority of the electoral vote (he won states with 297 electoral votes, to Ford's 241), Carter managed to reconstitute the old Democratic coalition of Southerners, Blacks, and blue-collar workers in the solid South and the industrial northeast. The Democrats retained their heavy Congressional majorities: unchanged at 62–38 in the Senate and increased by two to 292–143 in the House of Representatives. The party also had a net gain of one governorship.

Electoral success for the party brought responsibility for governing the nation and many uncertainties as well. Congressional Democrats elected new leaders to replace Speaker of the House Carl Albert (D, Okla.) and Senate majority leader Mike Mansfield (D, Mont.), who retired in 1976. And President-elect Carter, a novice to Washington politics, faced the task of forging a working relationship with an independent-minded Congress. *See* CONGRESS OF THE UNITED STATES. W.M.H.

DENMARK. The country's foreign trade deficit climbed to a record $1.1 billion during the first half of 1976. To help combat this deficit, the government negotiated a fixed-term loan of $292,500,000 from an international consortium headed by Westdeutsche Landesbank Gerozentrale of West Germany. This was the biggest foreign loan in Danish history.

In a further effort to reduce the foreign trade deficit, the *Folketing* (parliament) on Aug. 19 enacted a new austerity program that put a limit of 6 percent on annual wage increases for the next two years. The program included an $850,000,000 cut in public spending in the next eighteen months, price and profit ceilings, a two-year halt in dividends, and many new indirect taxes. Danes had been paying a value-added tax of 9.25 percent since October, 1975. This was increased to 15 percent on March 1, 1976.

More than 15,000 workers had massed before the *Folketing* on Aug. 19 in a futile effort to defeat the wage curbs. Following passage of the bill, wildcat strikes erupted for five days.

The government in 1976 was reportedly stepping up its pressure on purveyors of pornography, prostitution, and drugs. A crackdown on narcotics dealers had begun in the first half of 1975. In November, 1975, live sex shows were banned, and the police had started raiding "massage parlors" that operated as houses of prostitution.

The self-proclaimed "free city" of Christiania, in the center of Copenhagen, was ordered by the *Folketing* to be razed. The 190 buildings, which many citizens said housed militant radicals and drug addicts, had served as barracks until the army evacuated them in 1971.

Europe's Socialist and Social Democratic parties met in Elsinore on Jan. 18 and 19, on the invitation of the Danish Social Democratic Party, to discuss mutual problems. The most controversial issue, which the meeting failed to resolve, was that of cooperation with the Communists.

It was disclosed early in the year that in October, 1975, the Danish government had expelled four Soviet citizens for alleged spying but had kept the matter secret to avoid possible damage to détente.

On Feb. 27 fresh restrictions were imposed on the use of Danish coastal waters by foreign vessels. The government canceled a previous ruling that allowed foreign warships to stay inside the country's 3-mi. territorial limit for two days. The new ruling would require a notice of intent to enter the 3-mi. zone from all vessels except those with "exclusively commercial activities."

It was announced in June that Denmark was one of twelve nations outside the Western Hemisphere to be accepted for membership in the Inter-American Development Bank.

See STATISTICS OF THE WORLD. L.A.S.

DISTRICT OF COLUMBIA. *See* STATISTICS OF THE WORLD.

DOLE, ROBERT. *See* PEOPLE IN THE NEWS.

DOMINICAN REPUBLIC. *See* STATISTICS OF THE WORLD.

EARTH AND PLANETARY SCIENCES

The most publicized scientific accomplishment of 1976 was photography of the surface of Mars. But the most memorable accomplishment may well prove to be the less noticed discovery that the earth's climate is linked to its path through space and to events on the far distant sun.

A radically altered view of Mars was the most triumphant of the many contributions during the year to a changing concept of the planetary system. Processes thought to be unique on earth only a few years before were in 1976 being compared with similar processes on other planets, and the mysterious role of the sun in affecting planetary behavior began to be probed.

The insights gained by the exploration of the planets profoundly affected the direction of studies of the earth. Events on earth were no longer being considered in isolation but were being correlated with the planet's position in space and its links to the sun. This changed view inspired a new approach to the puzzle of species extinctions and a major report on the ultimate cause of the ice ages. Sea floor sediment cores from ocean drilling projects made important contributions to such studies and dramatized the wide-ranging nature of the new investigations, extending from the edge of the solar system to the depths of Antarctica and engaging the talents of specialists from astrophysicists to marine paleobiologists. It would seem that collaborative effort and complex technology had finally crowded out the individual investigator. Yet a lone astronomer, working with old documents and tree rings, linked the earth's climate to solar events with implications that shook one of science's most fundamental assumptions, that the sun's supply of energy does not vary.

PLANETARY EXPLORATION

Results from the Viking mission of 1976 showed that Mars has oxygen, nitrogen, frozen water, and a strange chemistry. Radar images of Venus suggest volcanic activity and movements of the crust, while studies of Mercury revealed that it may once have been a moon of Venus. Jupiter's long-puzzling colored bands and Great Red Spot were explained as slow-moving atmospheric currents.

Mars. The mysterious Mars suddenly became an almost familiar planet after the successful landing of two Viking spacecraft; see SPACE TECHNOLOGY. Television cameras sent back to earth dramatic color landscapes of the red planet; its surface turned out to be really red and its sky a bright pink. The source of the color is iron-rich particles coating the soil and rocks or mingling in the atmospheric dust. Each lander carried a remote-controlled arm that scooped up soil for three onboard laboratory tests designed to detect the presence of life. Excitement was aroused early in the mission when changes in the soil samples indicated the uptake of carbon and the oxidation of nutrients, activities that on earth are characteristic of life. But repeat tests showed that the rates of the changes were unexplainable in biological terms; other analyses found no organic molecules in the soil. By the end of the first test series in November, when Mars passed behind the sun and communications were interrupted, most scientists had concluded that the provocative results were due to a distinctive Martian chemistry, different from the biological or chemical processes known on earth.

While hope for evidence of life on Mars faded, other discoveries stirred great excitement. The rock-strewn landing sites of the two craft bore a remarkable resemblance to certain desert areas on earth. The thin atmosphere of Mars, composed mostly of carbon dioxide, was unexpectedly found to contain oxygen, nitrogen, water vapor, and other components in a mix such as the earth must have had before the changes wrought by living matter. Studies from the Viking II orbiter showed that the ice cap of the Martian north pole is made up of water, not carbon dioxide as most scientists had thought, since the temperature in the summer was found to be too warm to keep carbon dioxide in solid state. Scientists now believe the poles are the exposed tips of a huge layer of frozen water that covers the planet under a blanket of dust, soil, and rock. When this discovery was joined with the strong evidence that the many deep channels and branching tributaries on Mars were formed by floods and the additional discovery of the existence on Mars of the rare gases krypton and xenon, which are associated with dense atmosphere—the conclusion was almost inevitable that Mars once had warm temper-

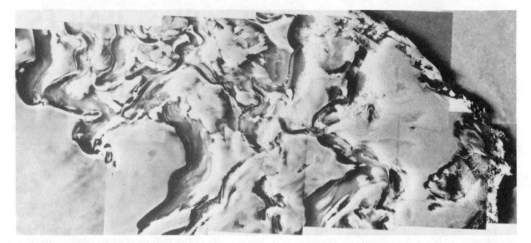

A striking view of ice-draped cliffs near the north pole of Mars, taken by the Viking II orbiter.

atures, an atmosphere heavy enough to screen out ultraviolet rays, and flowing water. Mars therefore may have been able to support the development of life forms. The planet now seems to be in an extreme ice age, probably caused by its shifting orbit (see *Climatology,* below). At some

Radar signals bounced off Venus produced this picture of a large area of the planet. The light section at upper right is about the size of Oklahoma and may be a broad lava field.

future time, when Mars moves closer to the sun, the planet may again warm up, frozen water may thaw, and its potential for supporting life may be renewed.

Venus. A radar map of a large section of the surface of Venus, put together in September from signals gathered by a giant radar telescope at Arecibo, Puerto Rico, revealed an extensive bright area that scientists said was most likely a broad lava field overlaying an older terrain. Earlier in the year a huge trough on Venus, not unlike the East African Rift on earth, was found by scientists of

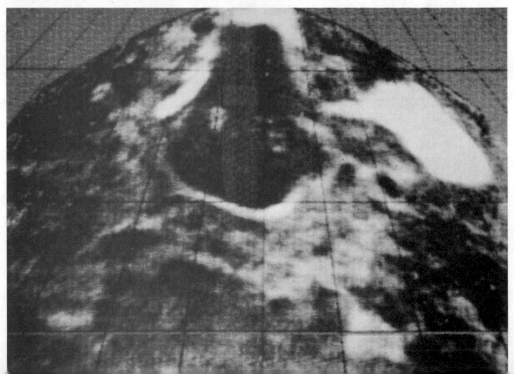

the Jet Propulsion Laboratory at Pasadena, Calif., using a radio telescope at nearby Goldstone. They also saw mountain ranges and peaks shaped like the tops of volcanoes. These signs of crustal movement and volcanism suggest that the surface of Venus has been shaped by the same processes that shape the earth.

Mercury. During the year further analysis of the 1974-75 Mariner X pictures of Mercury was made; the analysis reinforced the view that this planet is more like the earth's moon than any other body in the solar system. One side of Mercury is heavily cratered; the other side is mainly covered in flat "seas" (known as mare), like our moon. The asymmetry of the moon's surface results from one side being shielded from meteoritic bombardment by the presence of the earth. Now, according to a team at the United States Naval Observatory in Washington, D.C., it is possible to explain the asymmetry of Mercury in the same way, if it is assumed that Mercury was once a satellite of Venus. The slow rotation rate of Venus can also be accounted for by this theory. The spin of Venus could have been slowed by the consumption of energy as Mercury escaped its orbit and began to circle the sun as a planet in its own right.

Jupiter. In March Pioneer X returned data showing that Jupiter has an enormous magnetic tail. This tail, almost half a billion miles long, extends into the orbit of Saturn, which the spacecraft entered on its way out of the solar system. Jupiter and the earth are the only two planets known to have magnetic tails; they are caused by the force of "solar winds," energetic particles streaming from the sun, acting on the planets' magnetic fields. The earth's tail, previously found by Pioneer spacecraft, streams 4,000,000 mi. "down solar wind" from the planet. Jupiter's much more powerful tail is also active on the sunward side, sending electrons as far as Mercury, closest planet to the sun. (The study of the effect of the sun's winds and magnetic fields on the planets is an emerging science; see ASTRONOMY.)

In May the National Aeronautics and Space Administration convened a conference to collate data on Jupiter. The planet was described as being mostly atmosphere, containing up to 93 percent hydrogen. Its characteristic bands are produced by slow-moving cloud zones and darker belts between the zones; the earth has one similar cloud zone circling the equator, with clear bands on either side. Jupiter's most famous and most mysterious feature, the Great Red Spot, was described as a very high, centuries-old cloud that is moving slowly in an opposite direction to the cloud layers below. Its redness is believed to be caused by

phosphorus condensing out at the cooler upper layers of the cloud mass. The temperature at the core of Jupiter is six times hotter than the sun's surface; more than half the planet's heat is generated from within, possibly because Jupiter is still contracting in size. At the outer reaches the temperature drops to $-305°$ F ($-187°$ C). One midregion attracting great interest has temperatures and pressures similar to those on earth, with oxygen, water vapor, carbon compounds, and other building blocks of life.

GEOLOGY AND GEOPHYSICS

A rash of earthquakes around the globe in 1976 focused attention on the need to expand reliable prediction techniques. A new theory linking magnetic reversals on earth to species deaths implicated the ozone layer.

Earthquakes. Major earthquakes occurred throughout the year at the boundaries and buffer zones of the earth's major crustal plates, causing extensive damage and loss of life; see ACCIDENTS AND DISASTERS. After the success of the Chinese, in particular, in forecasting some recent earthquakes, this string of disasters created new incentives to expand the embryonic science of earthquake prediction. U.S. researchers claimed that reliable short-term forecasting would become a reality if sufficient funding were provided. Consequently, a bill was proposed to the U.S. Senate by Alan Cranston (D, Calif.). The Cranston bill, introduced in the spring, would authorize the expenditure of $150,000,000 over three years on four distinct areas of research: to predict earthquakes, to find methods to improve the resistance of buildings, to study the social and psychological consequences of large-scale disasters, and to search for the best ways to issue warnings without causing panic. Some version of such a bill seemed assured of passage in 1977. Meanwhile, in October, a five-member Earthquake Prediction Council was established by the U.S. Geological Survey. Headed by Jerry P. Eaton of the Menlo Park, Calif., Earthquake Studies Office, the council was assigned the task of reviewing predictive data and recommending warnings when an earthquake seemed imminent.

But what had set off the spate of earthquake activity in 1976? None of the many theories offered in explanation of this phenomenon received widespread acceptance. Several geophysicists, however, including Charles Richter, inventor of the Richter scale for calculating earthquake magnitude, did draw attention to the number of occasions on which unusual earthquake activity coincided with variations in the rate of the earth's rotation (measured by changes in the length of the daily cycle). Often the occurrences of a series

A soccer field near Gualan in eastern Guatemala shows the effects of the major earthquake that hit on Feb. 4. Ground breakage was continuous for 143 mi. along the boundary between the North American and Caribbean crustal plates.

of large earthquakes coincided with slight changes in the spin and wobble of the earth as it orbited the sun. But whether the earthquake tremors could upset the spin, or whether the rocking of the earth could set off the quakes, was not yet known.

Magnetism and Species Deaths. In 1976, for the second time since 1970, a close correlation was established between a magnetic reversal on earth and the sudden disappearance of species as seen in deep-sea sediment cores. Magnetic reversals, when the north and south poles "swap" charges, have occurred many times in the past, following a weakening of the earth's magnetic field. These reversals, revealed by traces of magnetism in old rocks, have occurred at irregular intervals lasting from a few days to almost half a million years. Toward the end of the Cretaceous Period 70,000,-000 years ago, during a time of renewed magnetic activity following a long quiet spell, one third of all known species abruptly disappeared. Geophysicists have been trying for a decade to find a connection between the magnetic activity and the disappearance of the species.

One plausible explanation was put forward in February by George C. Reid and his colleagues at the National Oceanic and Atmospheric Administration. According to their theory, when the magnetic field weakens, charged particles from solar flares can enter the earth's atmosphere more readily. These particles increase the formation of ni-

trogen oxides, large amounts of which can destroy a significant portion of the ozone layer faster than it can be replaced. Thus the earth's life forms are subjected to damaging amounts of ultraviolet rays. (Earth scientists have estimated that at its present rate of decay the magnetic field will reverse itself again in 2000 to 3000 years.)

CLIMATOLOGY

Two major studies during the year linked the earth's climate to extraterrestrial events.

Origin of the Great Ice Ages. The fundamental cause of the succession of ice ages was identified in December as changes in the earth's orbit, tilt, and rotation as it moves around the sun. This discovery was made by a team of British and American scientists led by James D. Hays of Columbia University. They thereby confirmed a highly controversial theory that had been advanced in the 1920's by the Yugoslav astronomer Milutin Milankovitch and the German geologist Alfred Wegener (who also proposed the long disregarded concept of continental drift). The Hays team constructed an unbroken record of the earth's climate over the past 450,000 years by analyzing climatic effects in fossils found in sediment cores taken from the Indian Ocean. Comparing the large-scale climatic changes with the earth's position in space over the same time span, they found three series of matching patterns.

The first and most important, coming in 100,000-year periods, is a climate pattern that coincides with a cyclic change in the earth's orbit from circular to elliptical and back. When the orbit is elliptical and brings the earth's path closer to the sun for a long period of time, the climate is warm; when the orbit is circular and the time close to the sun is short, the climate is cold. The second climate pattern, recurring every 42,000 years, coincides with a cyclic tilt of the earth's axis. A low degree of tilt brings less summer sunlight to the polar regions, and the ice on the land masses does not melt. The third climate pattern coincides with a third cyclic movement of the earth, affecting the wobble in its rotation (called precession of the equinoxes). This movement occurs every 23,000 years and varies the climatic effects of the two longer cycles by latitude and by season. (The three irregularities in the earth's path around the sun are caused by nonsolar gravitational pulls, especially those of the moon and Jupiter.)

According to Professor Hays, one of the earth's warmest periods is now ending and the next ice age is on its way. Barring human intervention, glaciers will gradually descend over much of the Northern Hemisphere during the next 20,000 years. The Southern Hemisphere, however, has much less landmass, and the oceans will be able to break up encroaching ice sheets.

"Little" Ice Ages. Six lesser periods of cold climate, each lasting from about 50 to 100 years, have been found to coincide with decreased activity of the sun itself. A 5000-year record of the sun's behavior was established by astronomer John A. Eddy of the National Center for Atmospheric Research in Boulder, Colo., by searching through historical accounts of sunspot activity, corona size at eclipses, and northern and southern lights (auroras). Eddy also examined the amount of carbon 14 in tree rings. Carbon 14 is created by cosmic rays, more of which can penetrate to the earth when the sun is quiet. All four indicators correlated and revealed that the sun's behavior has varied to a startling extent in historic times. Thus the widely accepted assumption of a constant solar output of energy may be false.

During the 5000 years that Eddy traced, solar activity fell to low levels six times. Each time a great global cooling occurred. The most recent was during what is known as the Little Ice Age, from 1645 to 1715; in this period almost no sunspots were observed. At six periods of maximum solar activity the climate over much of the earth was benign. A high activity period began in 1900 and should end by the year 2000.

OCEANOGRAPHY

The Deep Sea Drilling Project was completed after seven years; its ocean mapping and sediment core retrieval proved of inestimable value to science. Plans for the next International Phase of Ocean Drilling were being worked out and attention was focused onto a ten-nation study of the Ross Ice Shelf in Antarctica.

Ross Ice Shelf Project. An international team funded by the National Science Foundation was involved in an ambitious study of the nutrient-rich Ross Ice Shelf waters in Antarctica. Flowing north along the floors of the world's oceans, the Antarctic currents of these waters affect the entire ocean food chain. A 12-in. bore hole was to be drilled through the 1400-ft.-thick ice shelf to enable scientists to lower television cameras and other equipment in a search for marine life forms in the totally sunless waters below. On Dec. 14, however, after ten days of drilling and with one day left to reach the bottom of the shelf, the ice closed around the drill assembly. Completion of the project had to be put off a year until the next Antarctic summer; other studies of the shelf and the surrounding ocean currents were, however, continued.

Cayman Trough. The U.S. submersible *Alvin* began its exploration of the Cayman Trough in February. A gigantic fault in the floor of the Caribbean Sea, the trough exposes a 20,000-ft. slice of the earth's crust, making possible observations of the planet's inner structure. During 1976 the *Alvin* repeatedly descended to its diving limit of 12,000 ft. and explored the north wall of the trough. The U.S. Navy bathyscaphe *Trieste*, which is capable of reaching the bottom of the trough, was expected to join the project at a later time. The expedition retrieved the first samples of rock ejected from the earth's mantle layer below the crust. It also recorded undersea earthquake tremors for the first time, from the same Feb. 4 Caribbean plate movement that shook Guatemala (q.v.).

See also Fish and Fisheries.   J.G.

ECOLOGY. *See* Environment.

Sediment core taken from the floor of the Indian Ocean is studied aboard the drilling vessel Glomar Challenger *by an international team of scientists. In the foreground is Roger Hekinian, a French sedimentologist.*

ECUADOR. Turmoil marked Ecuadorian politics in 1976. On Jan. 11 Gen. Guillermo Rodríguez Lara, who had been president since February, 1972, was replaced by a three-man military junta consisting of Vice Adm. Alfredo Poveda Burbano (as president), Col. Luis Guillermo Durán Arcentales, and Gen. Luis Leoro Franco. Their cabinet, like its predecessor, was dominated by military men, but three ministries were assigned to civilians. The coup did not lead to any major change in economic or social policies, however. Lara had pledged a return to civilian government, and the new junta formally reaffirmed that commitment. Nevertheless, after Ecuador's interior minister, Col. Richelieu Levoyer, announced that the return to democracy would be "final and irrevocable" by January, 1978, he was removed from office.

Evidences of popular unrest included violent demonstrations in January and April, and a wave of police, transit, and agricultural strikes in July. The economic outlook was further clouded by the ongoing confrontation between the government and international oil companies. In September a dispute between the government and the Gulf Oil Co. led Gulf to request talks designed to end the company's participation in the Ecuadorian oil industry. Gulf's share amounted to 37 percent of C.E.P.E., the Ecuadorian State Petroleum Corp.

See STATISTICS OF THE WORLD. A.K.M.

EDUCATION. For the nation's educational institutions 1976 was a year of budget cuts and controversy over educational quality. Reflecting demographic changes, elementary school enrollment

Professor Robert E. Schofield impersonates 18th-century chemist Joseph Priestley in a lecture at the University of Delaware in January. Many educators across the U.S. adopted such dramatic visual aids during the Bicentennial year.

fell while high school and college enrollment grew. Colleges and universities braced themselves for severe financial difficulties to come, which they anticipated by charging record-high tuition fees. Teacher strikes were numerous in the school year 1975–76, but fell off in 1976–77. Schoolhouse violence and vandalism were on the increase; conflict over the busing issue, however, waned.

Enrollment Statistics. The National Center for Educational Statistics, a division of the Department of Health, Education, and Welfare (H.E.W.), reported that enrollment in schools and universities in the United States for the school year 1976–77 decreased slightly to about 60,100,000. While the number of elementary school pupils (34,200,000) continued to fall—a continuation of the trend which began in 1970—high school enrollment climbed to a new record high (15,800,000). The U.S. Office of Education also reported a sharp jump for the second consecutive year in the number of students pursuing degree programs in American colleges and universities. It said the combined undergraduate and graduate enrollment rose to 10,100,000 in the fall of 1976, an increase of 4 percent.

H.E.W. also calculated that total expenditures on private and public education in the U.S. during the 1976–77 academic year would exceed $130 billion—up more than $10 billion from the previous year.

Increasing Educational Levels. The proportion of Americans with high school diplomas had more than doubled since 1950, the Census Bureau reported. The proportion of adults who had completed four years of college doubled as well during this period. Only 1 adult in 14 had completed college in 1950; the number had now risen to 1 in 7. The Census Bureau also reported that high

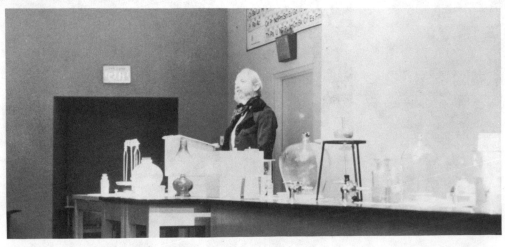

school graduates now made up more than half of the workers in 8 of the 10 major occupational classifications.

Teacher Strikes. The number of teacher strikes in the U.S. reached a record of 203 in the 1975–76 school year, according to the National Education Association (N.E.A.). Sixty percent of the strikes lasted longer than 5 days, and 13 percent lasted longer than 15 days. Pennsylvania had the largest number of strikes with 58, followed by Ohio with 29 and Illinois with 22. The N.E.A. also reported that striking teachers were jailed for refusing to obey court return-to-work orders in a number of localities, among them Elizabeth, N.J., New Haven, Conn., and New Bedford, Mass. While strikes remained illegal in some states, President-elect Jimmy Carter declared his support for the right of teachers to strike. "Although I'd prefer binding arbitration for public-safety employees, under normal circumstances, I would not consider teachers to be in this category and I would not interfere with their right to strike," Carter said during his Presidential campaign.

The N.E.A. reported that the 1976–77 school year started with fewer teacher strikes than in the previous year. It noted, however, that an unusually large number of teachers were working without contracts and warned that this could result in a new wave of strikes in the months ahead. The N.E.A. said the average wage hike for teachers in 1976–77 contracts was running 6 to 8 percent.

Urban Budget Crises and Violence. Financial problems were particularly acute in a number of large urban school systems. Administrators caught

---

---

in a squeeze between rising costs and a shrinking tax base were forced to take drastic steps to pare huge budget deficits. In Chicago officials had to close the nation's second-largest school system for sixteen days early in June when the city ran out of money. Even though Chicago's 26,000 teachers subsequently agreed to a new contract that provided for no salary increases, the new budget for 1976–77 projected a deficit of $147,100,000. This raised fears of massive teacher dismissals or another early closing in 1977.

Budget crises forced a number of other cities to take austerity measures. Detroit cut back its first-grade classes to half a day. Miami saved almost $1,000,000 by cutting down on the amount of paper, materials, and supplies given to pupils. Administrators in Washington, D.C., froze teacher

---

Mapping Out a Solution
How many colors are needed to make a flat map in which no two neighboring countries—excluding those that meet at only one point—are the same color? In July University of Illinois Professors Kenneth Appel and Wolfgang Haken solved the problem that had baffled mathematicians for more than 120 years. The answer (four) took 1200 hr. of computer time to obtain. In effect, Appel and Haken ran 2000 separate map diagrams through the computer, checking up to 200,000 colorings per diagram.

Professors Wolfgang Haken (left) and Kenneth Appel.

positions and warned of a possible payless furlough for the city's 12,000 public school employees. New York City enlarged its public school classes, shortened the school day, and cut back on such services as guidance counseling. Los Angeles canceled some classes because of leaky roofs, and New Orleans issued sheets of plywood to a school with 330 broken windows because the city could not immediately afford to buy vandal-resistant window panes. Cleveland cut costs by assigning some elementary school principals to cover more than one school. Most educators felt that without increased state and federal aid, the plight of big-city school systems would only get worse in the near future.

Violence in U.S. public schools remained a major concern in 1976. A federally financed study prepared by Research for Better Schools, Inc., of Philadelphia, found that assault, mugging, vandalism, and gang warfare were rampant. "It is fair to conclude that school violence and disruption is a serious and costly national problem," the report said. It recommended that the U.S. government spend $12,600,000 on a program to combat crime in the nation's schools.

Educational Quality. Although many educators continued to worry about declining pupil achievement, a federal program for monitoring the achievement of schoolchildren found that reading ability had not deteriorated significantly in the 1970's. The National Assessment of Educational Progress reported that it had administered identical tests to pupils in three age-groups—9, 13, and 17—in both 1971 and 1975. It said the scores of the 9-year-olds had improved markedly, while the scores of the two older groups had remained about the same.

Nevertheless, it was clear that many Americans remained uneasy about the quality of education

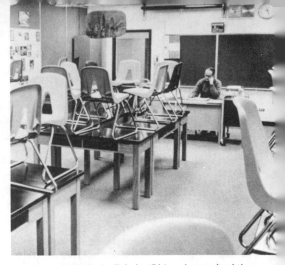

An empty classroom in Toledo, Ohio—the result of the voters' rejection of school tax-increase proposals. The Toledo system, one of many insolvent systems in the U.S., ran out of money on Dec. 3 and closed for the rest of the year.

in U.S. public schools. A Gallup Poll found that 65 percent of those surveyed would like to see all high school students required to pass a standard nationwide examination to get a diploma. The New York State Board of Regents agreed unanimously that the state's high school pupils should have to pass a ninth-grade reading and mathematics examination in order to graduate. The Los Angeles School Board ordered that starting in 1979 pupils would have to pass a reading proficiency test in order to receive a high school diploma.

Desegregation. Court-ordered racial desegregation in the public schools progressed more smoothly in 1976 than in previous years. Most observers agreed that a mood of acceptance and compliance had replaced one of opposition. Bos-

Striking members of the Buffalo Teachers Federation march to city hall on Sept. 21 during their three-week-long strike. School budgets for 1976-77 were cut severely in many U.S. cities as voters and state legislators opposed increased funds for education.

ton, Mass., and Louisville, Ky., where violence marked forced desegregation in 1975, opened their schools in September with no serious incidents.

The courts were unyielding in their insistence on desegregation and on busing as a last-resort means to it, despite the opposition to busing by the administration of President Gerald R. Ford. The U.S. Supreme Court upheld the court-ordered Boston desegregation plan in June and also ruled that private schools may not exclude black students because of race. In August, U.S. District Court Judge John J. Sirica ordered H.E.W. to step up efforts to achieve desegregation in forty-three school districts, including Chicago.

Civil rights groups were enraged in June when President Ford proposed legislation to restrict the power of courts to order busing. The issue was debated in Congress, but no effective limitation on the courts was passed. Large-scale busing programs were begun in September in Dayton, Ohio; Omaha, Nebr.; and Dallas, Texas. For the most part, they were put into effect peacefully. *See also* CIVIL RIGHTS AND CIVIL LIBERTIES.

Colleges and Universities. Increases in enrollment in 1975 and 1976 gave higher education a temporary respite from financial difficulties. Ohio State University stopped taking freshman applications on Feb. 17, 1976—the earliest date in its history—when it had received more than 12,000 applications for the fall semester. The nation's small private liberal-arts colleges, many of which had found themselves in dire financial straits in recent years as a result of soaring operating costs and declining enrollments, also were benefiting from the boom. For example, Lake Erie College in Painesville, Ohio, reported a 65 percent increase in applications.

The breathing spell was welcome, but many colleges realized they might find it hard to survive if enrollment declined as expected in the 1980's. The plight of many institutions was illustrated in a study compiled by the New Jersey Commission on Financing Post-Secondary Education. The panel surveyed 75 percent of all U.S. colleges and universities and then rated them financially. An alarming 49.2 percent were judged to fall in either the relatively unhealthy or unhealthy categories. Church-related colleges were found to be in the biggest trouble, and public community colleges were judged to be in the soundest financial condition.

In the face of these problems, the cost of attending college continued to climb. The average cost of a year of college in 1976–77 was calculated to be $2790 at four-year public institutions and $4568 at four-year private schools.   M.R.B.

EGYPT, ARAB REPUBLIC OF. Despite increasing economic instability and escalating political opposition, President Anwar el-Sadat of Egypt managed to consolidate his power in 1976. He was reelected to a second six-year term by a near-unanimous vote in a referendum that was held on Sept. 16.

Domestic Affairs. In the political sphere the power struggle between civilian and military factions of the Egyptian hierarchy worsened. A number of groups, representing various points of the political spectrum—Social-Democrats, Progressives, Nasserites, Marxists, Conservatives, and the Muslim Brotherhood—supported proposals to develop a multiparty system. A special 150-member committee created to study the issue rejected the proposals in favor of a new system whereby three platforms—left, center, and right—would be instituted within the ruling Arab Socialist Union (A.S.U.). The new system, introduced in March, permitted a broader range of debate within the existing party, under Sadat's leadership, but tended to exclude the radical Marxists and Nasserites and the ultraconservative Muslim Brotherhood. The three platforms presented candidates for local office and for the election of the People's Assembly in October. Sadat himself declined to affiliate with any platform, presenting his services as an arbitrator among factions. After his reelection and the parliamentary election, Sadat announced that the platforms would henceforth be called parties, the first to be recognized in Egypt since 1953.

Prime Minister Mamdouh Muhammad Salem, a centrist, announced formation of a new cabinet on March 19. Eight members of the old cabinet lost their jobs, and four new appointments were made; several portfolios were reassigned. The only politically significant change seemed to be the appointment of a staunch conservative to head the Ministry of Information, a move that was accompanied by more stringent controls on print and broadcast media.

Acting in his capacity as head of the A.S.U., Sadat tightened restrictions on an increasingly critical press by forming a writers union and offering membership by invitation only. New guidelines for the press were handed down regarding acceptable criticisms of the regime, and new appointments to key editorships were made. Several members of the left platform were demoted or dismissed.

The Economy. Most pressing, perhaps, were Egypt's worsening economic woes. Two years of economic liberalization had produced not prosperity but skyrocketing prices and a widening gap between incomes of the middle and upper classes

149

and the lower class. The open-door economic policy had failed to produce the desired results largely because foreign investors had difficulty in converting Egyptian pounds to hard currencies. Inflation rates for 1976 were well above the 25 percent to 30 percent inflation experienced in 1975, and production lagged far below consumption for Egypt's burgeoning population. Complaints were registered repeatedly that the Arab oil-producing states were not contributing enough. Sadat returned from a spring tour of the Arab Gulf states with promises of $700,000,000 in immediate aid for rescheduling of foreign debts and production of essential commodities. Later in the year the Arab oil countries agreed on further aid of some $2 billion to help Egyptian development programs. The trade deficit for 1976, however, was estimated at $3 billion, and the oil-producing countries did not agree to finance the entire foreign debt, as Sadat had hoped. Aid agreements were concluded with the United States, the People's Republic of China, and a number of Western European nations, and some lessening of pressure on the economy was expected, particularly as a result of renewed traffic on the Suez Canal.

Foreign Affairs. In foreign policy too, Sadat

steered his nation toward the moderate right. The May, 1971, Treaty of Friendship and Cooperation with the Soviet Union was abrogated on March 14, to the delight of both the West and China. Severe deterioration of relations with Syria led to a temporary cutoff of diplomatic ties between the former allies, but they were restored after Arab conferences in Saudi Arabia and Egypt in October. Mutual criticisms had been exchanged on domestic issues as well as on Egypt's Sinai accord with Israel and on Syrian intervention in the Lebanese civil war. The bitter exchanges between Sadat and President Muammar el-Qaddafi of Libya modulated somewhat in 1976, but relations continued to be troubled; an Egyptian-Sudanese-Saudi Arabian mutual aid and cooperation agreement announced on July 19 was viewed in Tripoli as aimed primarily against Libyan interests.

The terms of the Sinai accord of September, 1975, were carried out. The Egyptian army took control of the Sinai peninsula buffer zone from United Nations Emergency Forces between Jan. 26 and Feb. 22. Egypt thus assumed control of a line roughly 10 mi. east of and parallel to the Suez Canal, running from north to south, and a 95-sq.mi. strip along the western coast of the Gulf of Suez from Sudr to the Abu Rudeis oil fields. American electronic surveillance posts in the critical Mitla and Gidi passes, also provided for in the Sinai accords, became operational on Feb. 21.

In November Sadat announced that he was in

In an Oct. 6 celebration of its military success in the 1973 war against Israel, Egypt parades Soviet-built missiles past its pyramid memorial to the unknown soldier.

Queen Tiy, grandmother of Egyptian King Tutankhamen and a major figure of the XVIII Dynasty, was found by scientists of the University of Michigan in October. After some eighty years of investigation, a mummy known only as the "elder lady" was identified (by means of X rays and hair samples) as the remains of the powerful queen.

favor of signing a document ending the "state of belligerency" between Israel and Egypt. He subsequently called for the reconvening of the Geneva conference on the Middle East and joined President Hafez al-Assad of Syria and King Khalid of Saudi Arabia in planning for Arab representation at such a meeting.

See STATISTICS OF THE WORLD. *See also* ARAB LEAGUE; MIDDLE EAST; separate articles on countries mentioned above.   S.C.

ELECTIONS. Former Gov. Jimmy Carter of Georgia, a Democrat, won a narrow victory over Republican incumbent Gerald R. Ford in the United States Presidential election. Together with the return of lopsided Democratic majorities in both houses of the U.S. Congress, the executive and legislative branches of the federal government were placed under the control of a single party for the first time in eight years. (For a biography of the President-elect, *see* PEOPLE IN THE NEWS.)

Presidential Election. The election of Jimmy Carter as the thirty-ninth President of the United States,

the first from the Deep South in more than a century, was the tightest contest in the electoral-vote tabulation since Woodrow Wilson defeated Charles Evans Hughes in 1916. However, Carter's popular-vote margin, 50 percent to 48 percent, was clear-cut though not overwhelming. He and his running mate, Sen. Walter F. Mondale of Minnesota (who was elected the forty-second Vice-President of the United States) took 40,827,394 votes to 39,145,977 for the Republican ticket of President Ford and Sen. Robert J. Dole of Kansas. The Carter-Mondale ticket won states with 297 electoral votes—27 more than the minimum needed to win—to 241 for Ford-Dole. Owing to the winner-take-all system of apportioning the electoral votes of each state, a shift of a few thousand votes in two or three key states could have turned the results around. In 13 states the margin of victory was within 2 percent; in 7 of these, less than 1 percent. In Ohio, for example, Carter captured the state's 25 electoral votes with a plurality of only 9330 votes out of more than 4,000,000 cast.

ELECTIONS

(The Electoral College vote for President was tabulated Jan. 6, 1977. The results were: Carter, 297; Ford, 240; one elector voted for former governor Ronald W. Reagan of California.) Most of the remaining 1 percent of the 1976 total vote went to independent candidate Eugene J. McCarthy, former Minnesota Senator and leader of the antiwar Democrats in 1968. McCarthy, hampered by a shortage of funds (and no federal subsidy), managed to get on the ballot in twenty-nine states. He collected 745,042 votes, most of them believed to have come at Carter's expense; he apparently cut into Carter's totals sufficiently in Iowa, Maine, Oklahoma, and Oregon to put these states in the

and the Pacific states, losing in the West only in Hawaii. He also carried his home state of Michigan, plus Illinois and Iowa in the Midwest; Virginia in the South; and Connecticut, New Jersey, and the upper New England states in the East.

Analysis. Whether the Carter victory represented a restoration of Franklin D. Roosevelt's New Deal coalition—primarily a linkage of a "solid South" with the urban industrial North—was debatable. Nonetheless, the results reflected traditional American social and partisan alignments that formed the basis of Democratic victory patterns in the 1930's and 1940's. Generally speaking, Carter did well among younger voters, liberals, the

---

They Also Ran

Lester Maddox beat Jimmy Carter in a Georgia gubernatorial primary in 1966, but as a 1976 Presidential candidate Maddox, 61, won fewer than 171,000 votes. However, the more than 745,000 votes won by the liberal Eugene McCarthy, also 61, in his third Presidential race, spoiled victories for Carter in several states. Had McCarthy—poet, professor, and perennial politician—been listed on the ballot in New York, he might have cost Carter the Presidency.

Former Minnesota Sen. Eugene McCarthy (left) and former Georgia Gov. Lester Maddox.

Republican column. Georgia segregationist Lester Maddox ran in nineteen states as the candidate of the American Independent Party and polled 170,063 votes.

Among the most striking patterns of the 1976 Presidential vote was a sharply defined East-West geographical split. Carter won all the states of the old Confederacy except Virginia and all the border states except Oklahoma. He also carried four of the most heavily populated states of the industrial north (Massachusetts, New York, Ohio, and Pennsylvania); two states in the liberal upper Midwest (Minnesota and Wisconsin); and two smaller constituencies where ethnic minorities make up the majority, Hawaii and the District of Columbia.

Ford, on the other hand, made a near clean sweep of the Great Plains, the Rocky Mountain,

less affluent, and less educated; among union members and other blue-collar workers, and among Blacks and ethnic voters. Ford, on the other hand, won the majority of older voters, suburbanites, the college educated, business people, and professionals. But Carter also made significant inroads into such traditional pillars of Republican strength as white-collar workers and white Protestants.

Three specific factors were crucial to Jimmy Carter's win. First, regional pride in and identity with a native son gave Carter virtually all of the Southern and border states for a total of 158 electoral votes, more than half of the total needed to win. Second, black voters turned out in disproportionately large numbers in many localities and went overwhelmingly for Carter; postelection estimates ranged from a 5-to-1 Carter advantage overall to astounding 9-to-1 advantages in states such as New York and Louisiana. And third, organized labor lent massive support to the Democratic ticket and delivered a 23-point bulge (61 percent to 38 percent) in the votes of households with union members.

For Carter, the successful bid for the White House was the culmination of four years of planning and two years of campaigning. Starting with virtually no national recognition, he adopted a "run everywhere" strategy that saw him entered in every state caucus and in 30 of a record number of 31 state primaries (omitting only West Virginia, where his slate did not qualify). His primary triumphs eliminated rivals one by one, and by June such powerful Democrats as Chicago Mayor Richard J. Daley and George Meany, president of the American Federation of Labor and Congress of Industrial Organizations, had endorsed him. When Sen. Hubert H. Humphrey of Minnesota chose not to lead a stop-Carter movement, nothing further could stop the Georgian's march to a first-ballot nomination in July at the Democratic National Convention in New York City. *See* DEMOCRATIC PARTY.

At the Republican Convention in Kansas City, Mo., in August, Ford also scored a first-ballot victory after turning back a stern challenge from

Two political neophytes: Republican S. I. Hayakawa (right) was elected U.S. Senator from California in November, and Dixy Lee Ray (far right) was named the next Democratic governor of the state of Washington. Three experienced politicians elevated to new posts were (below, left to right) Senator-elect H. John Heinz 3rd (R, Pa.), Governor-elect John D. ("Jay") Rockefeller 4th (D, W.Va.), and Senator-elect Pierre S. DuPont 4th (R, Del.).

Ronald Reagan, the former governor of California; see REPUBLICAN PARTY. At the time, Ford's nomination seemed like an empty win, as some opinion polls found him trailing Carter by a whopping 33 points. But the President staged a remarkable comeback, exploiting the normal advantages of incumbency and a widespread public suspicion that Carter was evading the issues. By election eve, most leading polls termed the contest too close to call. (For a biography of the President, see PRESIDENT OF THE UNITED STATES.)

For the first time since 1960, the Presidential campaign was enlivened by a series of three nationally televised debates (plus a fourth debate— the first ever between Vice-Presidential nominees). Analysts differed on who won, but most agreed that the lesser-known Carter had more to gain from exposure before a national audience that averaged about 87,000,000 viewers for each telecast. The Ford-Carter debates were held Sept. 23 (in Philadelphia), Oct. 6 (in San Francisco), and Oct. 22 (in Williamsburg, Va.).

It seemed as if the Democrats had regained the White House less on the basis of any specific issue and more because of a broadly felt need for a change in the nation's leadership. The President-elect himself spoke of a "new day" and "new spirit" the morning after his victory. Gerald Ford, who served twenty-seven months in the nation's highest office and did much to restore public confidence in an executive branch left in shambles after the Watergate scandals, failed to shed the label of "accidental President."

The 81,681,918 votes cast was the highest total in the history of U.S. Presidential elections. But the percentage of those of voting age participating in the election dropped to 54 percent from 55.4 percent in 1972, marking the fifth straight election in which voter participation had declined. Voter apathy was more alarming in the 1976 primary elections. Only 44 percent of those registered in states holding primaries bothered to vote.

Congressional Elections. Numerically, the makeup of the 95th Congress would be little changed from its predecessor. The party lineup in the Senate— 61 Democrats, 38 Republicans, and 1 Independent—remained exactly as before. In the House of Representatives, Democrats gained 2 seats to swell their majority to 292 to 143. But because of election upsets, plus an unusually large number of retirements of members of the 94th Congress, there was a heavy turnover of personnel on Capitol Hill.

Seventeen new faces were added to the Senate roster, the biggest entering class in nearly two decades. The oldest freshman was California's 70-year-old S. I. Hayakawa (R), the noted semanticist and conservative educator, who defeated incumbent John V. Tunney (D) in a tight race. In New York former United Nations Ambassador Daniel P. Moynihan (D) won handily over incumbent James L. Buckley (C-R). In Montana Rep. John Melcher (D) made a successful bid for the seat of retiring majority leader Mike Mansfield, and in Pennsylvania, millionaire H. John Heinz 3rd (R) won a hard-fought battle over Rep. William J. Green (D) for the seat of retiring minority leader Hugh Scott. Ohio's former Sen. Howard M. Metzenbaum (D), defeated two years ago, returned to the Senate by capturing the seat of incumbent Robert A. Taft, Jr. (R).

Omaha Mayor Edward Zorinsky (D) squeezed past Rep. John Y. McCollister (R) to become Nebraska's first Democratic Senator since 1934. Indianapolis Mayor Richard G. Lugar (R) easily beat Indiana's three-term Sen. Vance Hartke (D), while Michigan Rep. Donald W. Riegle, Jr. (D), topped Rep. Marvin L. Esch (R) to fill the seat held by retiring Sen. Philip A. Hart (D). In Maryland Rep. Paul S. Sarbanes (D) swamped incumbent J. Glenn Beall, Jr. (R). In Wyoming rancher Malcolm Wallop (R) scored a major upset in beating three-term Sen. Gale W. McGee (D).

Others who succeeded in becoming first-term Senators were former astronaut Harrison H. Schmitt (R) of New Mexico, who defeated Democratic incumbent Joseph Montoya; John H. Chafee (R) of Rhode Island, a former Navy secretary; Spark M. Matsunaga (D) of Hawaii, who won the seat to be vacated by Sen. Hiram L. Fong (R); Orin G. Hatch (R) of Utah, who ousted Sen. Frank E. Moss (D); and Missouri's John C. Danforth (R), Arizona's Dennis DeConcini (D), and Tennessee's James R. Sasser (D).

Alice Doesn't Vote Here Any More

One registered voter was unceremoniously disenfranchised in 1976, even before she had a chance to cast her first vote. Alice Grace Toy received her voter's card (she was registered as a Democrat) shortly before the Portland (Oreg.) school elections in the spring. Barbara Toy, a voter residing at the same address, was mystified. She had registered Alice, an 18-month-old schnauzer, with the American Kennel Club. Over-eager election workers, probably convinced that the country is going to the dogs, confirmed Alice's registration.

Familiar names returned for new terms—most of them without any difficulty—included Democrats Edward M. Kennedy of Massachusetts, Hubert H. Humphrey of Minnesota, Edmund S. Muskie of Maine, John C. Stennis of Mississippi, Henry M. Jackson of Washington, and William Proxmire of Wisconsin. Also victorious were Republican Lowell P. Weicker of Connecticut and Virginia's Harry F. Byrd, Jr., the Senate's lone independent (who lined up with the Democrats for organizational purposes). In addition, Minnesota Gov. Wendell R. Anderson, a Democrat, appointed himself to fill the seat vacated by Vice-President-elect Mondale.

The strength of the Democrats was etched most sharply in the races for the House. Democratic candidates generally ran ahead of the party's own Presidential nominee, capturing more than 55 percent of the popular vote nationwide in contested elections.

In the Watergate backlash of 1974 a Democratic surge added forty-three seats to the majority party total. Nearly all of these "Watergate babies" were deemed vulnerable in 1976, but as it turned out, almost all of them were reelected. These included New York's Thomas Downey, 27, the youngest member of Congress.

Indeed, youthfulness characterized the makeup of the new House, with approximately half the 435 seats to be filled by members who have served two terms or less. The number of black members would remain unchanged (at 17), although the number of women would drop by 1 (to 18). Headliners such as Barbara Jordan (D, Texas) and Shirley Chisholm (D, N.Y.) were reelected, but Patsy Mink (D, Hawaii) and Bella Abzug (D, N.Y.) dropped out, both giving up their House seats in unsuccessful bids for Senate nominations. In their stead, Maryland sent another activist Democrat in the person of Barbara Mikulski, who won the seat vacated by Senator-elect Paul S. Sarbanes. Martha E. Keys (D, Kans.) won a close reelection contest in which her marriage to Rep. Andrew Jacobs, Jr. (D, Ind.; also reelected), was an issue.

On the Republican side, Louisiana's Jerry Huckaby scored the biggest upset by downing Otto Passman (D), a fifteen-term veteran. But the most gratifying win from the Republican standpoint was the recapture by Harold S. Sawyer of Michigan's Fifth Congressional District, Gerald Ford's old House seat.

Governors. With 14 statehouses at stake, Democrats won 9 of them to increase their margin over the Republicans by 37 to 12 (a net gain of 1). The fiftieth statehouse was held by James B. Longley of Maine, an independent not up for reelection in 1976.

Victors in 1976 included James R. Thompson (R) of Illinois, a former U.S. attorney who was seen as a potential national Republican leader, and Dixy Lee Ray (D) of Washington, the former chairman of the Atomic Energy Commission, who increased women's representation in the statehouses to two (the other was Gov. Ella T. Grasso of Connecticut). New governors with famous names elected in 1976 included John D. Rockefeller 4th (D) in West Virginia and Pierre S. DuPont 4th (R) in Delaware.

Propositions. Voters in forty-one states were confronted with a total of 330 propositions, and they showed in their choices a general disposition to resist change. Propositions in six states would have put restrictions on nuclear power plants, as by requiring state legislative approval of new plants. All six lost decisively, as did a similar California proposition in the June primary. Proposals to ban nonreturnable bottles and cans won in Maine and Michigan, but were defeated in Massachusetts and Colorado (Oregon and Vermont already had such laws). A Massachusetts proposal to ban the sale of all handguns was defeated by a surprising 3-to-1 margin. Farm laborers' rights failed to get an endorsement from California voters, and New Jerseyites approved legalized gambling in Atlantic City.

See DEMOCRATIC PARTY; REPUBLICAN PARTY.   D.C.

ELECTRONICS. *See* TECHNOLOGY.

EL SALVADOR. In March the military-supported National Conciliation Party (P.C.N.) of El Salvador won all 52 congressional seats and all 261 mayoralties at stake in national elections. The sweeping triumph was made possible by the withdrawal of the opposition parties from the campaign. The withdrawals were prompted by charges of government harassment and fraud stemming from a restrictive election law passed in October, 1975. Armed Forces Chief of Staff Manuel Alfonso Rodríguez was dismissed from his post on May 22; he had been arrested in New York City for smuggling arms. Throughout 1976 the Salvadoran economy benefited from record coffee export prices and increased public investment.

Relations with Honduras, severed in 1969 because of the so-called soccer war between the two countries, showed improvement. In June Salvadoran President Arturo Armando Molina Barraza and Honduran President Juan Alberto Melgar Castro reached a military disengagement agreement. A border flare-up in July, however, required intervention on the part of the Organization of American States. Finally in September the foreign ministers of the two nations agreed to seek a peace treaty by April, 1977.

See STATISTICS OF THE WORLD.   A.K.M.

ENERGY

Energy use in the U.S. began to climb in 1976 toward pre-1973, preembargo levels. Determined attempts to expand the nation's energy sources showed mixed results; dependence on foreign oil increased dramatically.

By the end of 1976 energy use in the United States had risen to just short of 1973 demand levels, which represented an all-time peak. In spite of continued warnings by government and industry that dependence on foreign oil was a danger to national security, the U.S. increased its percentage of oil imported from abroad. In 1976 some 42 percent of U.S. oil was imported, up from 40 percent the previous year and 29 percent in 1973.

The picture for nuclear energy remained cloudy. On June 8, by a 2–1 margin, voters in California rejected a ballot proposition, placed there by popular initiative, that would have severely curtailed the use of nuclear power in that state. Just prior to the vote, the state legislature had passed three resolutions aimed at controlling the use of nuclear power in California, although in effect these resolutions were far less stringent than provisions of the ballot proposition. In the Nov. 2 elections six states had ballot propositions to control the use of nuclear power; all of them were defeated.

On the other hand, the generation of nuclear power failed to increase significantly during the year and accounted for less than 9 percent of electric energy production in 1976 (about 3 percent of all energy use in the U.S.). Fifty-eight nuclear plants were operating in the U.S., with 150 more under construction or planned.

The use of coal continued to increase, although not as rapidly as some had predicted. In 1976 about 46 percent of electrical energy was produced by coal; of that amount, strip mining accounted for 60 to 65 percent and deep mining for the rest. In a related event, federal legislation designed to control the use of strip-mined coal and provide for the reclamation of strip-mined areas died in committee.

Automobile use in the U.S. increased again, following a short decrease after the oil embargo of 1973 and subsequent dramatic price increases in fuel. Although special car-pool lanes were established in cities as diverse as Los Angeles and Boston, their use remained sporadic and did not noticeably reduce automobile miles traveled to and from work. A notable exception to the general failure of car pooling was "van pooling," in which twelve-passenger vans were used to transport workers to and from industrial plants. Such companies as the Minnesota Mining and Manufacturing Co. and General Foods Corp. in Minneapolis and Conoco in Houston successfully established van service for their employees.

FOSSIL FUEL

Coal remained the most abundant energy resource, and considerable attention was paid to utilizing it effectively. Synthetic fuel production made no advances during the year.

Synthetic Fuels. One of the more significant attempts to generate new fossil-fuel supplies is the development of what are called synthetic fuels. These include oil from oil shale, and oil and gas made from coal. If successful, plants producing synthetic fuels could utilize the abundant supply of coal and oil shale in the U.S., and the resultant fuels would burn more cleanly than coal.

Past experience with manufacture of synthetic fuels was disappointing, however. A plant existed in New Jersey for a short time in the 1930's, Germany had plants operating during World War II, and Union Carbide operated a plant in West Virginia in the 1950's, but the production process released carcinogens (cancer-producing substances known as polycyclic aromatic hydrocarbons). The necessity to protect workers and the public from these substances is one of the factors that makes the cost of reviving synthetic fuel production high. In 1976 estimates for synthetic liquid fuel, for example, ranged from $18 to $20 a bbl (42 gal.). Oil was selling at from $11 to $15 a bbl, and natural gas for the equivalent of $2 to $5 a bbl. Congress failed to pass a $4 billion loan-guarantee program in 1976 for the commercialization of facilities to produce synthetic fuels; it had failed in 1975 to pass a similar $6 billion program.

The synthetic fuel program is also controversial because of the large quantity of water that must be used in processing. Most of the oil shale and much of the coal is in the western part of the U.S., where agriculture has a competing need for the

A surveyor, searching for oil or coal, packs seismic recording equipment through the jungles of Ecuador. Signals reflected from rocks deep within the earth indicate the presence of hydrocarbons.

scant water supply. Although several U.S. companies had made plans during the 1970's to develop oil shale operations, by the end of 1976 all had canceled them. Canada, however, with the largest oil shale deposits known (in the Athabascan tar sands) went ahead with plans to produce the oil and began construction on a small pilot plant.

Coal Mining and Combustion. Greater utilization of a promising new method for the deep mining of coal was considered by mine operators and mine equipment manufacturers. Called long-wall mining, it accounted for only about 3 percent of the coal mined in the U.S. in 1976, although 25 percent of the coal extracted in Europe, mostly in Great Britain and Germany, was mined by this method. Designed to cut down both on accidents and on the amount of coal left behind in a mine when it is abandoned, long-wall mining uses large machines to hold up the overburden, or overlying rock, while the coal is being mined. It exposes fewer miners to coal dust and allows for controlled subsidence (collapse of the mine) after the coal has been extracted and the machines removed. Although long-wall mining is much higher in original capital cost because of the machinery, the technique allows for up to 95 percent recovery of coal. This is opposed to 50 to 75 percent recovery in conventional "room-and-pillar" mining, in which some of the coal is left behind to support the overburden. Subsidence of the land above abandoned deep coal mines has been a serious environmental problem in America. Also alleviated by long-wall mining is "black lung" disease, a serious disabling disorder caused by mine dust that is developed by most miners after fifteen to twenty years of exposure.

A promising technique for the burning of coal, called fluidized bed combustion, was being investigated by the U.S. Energy Research and Development Administration (ERDA). Using a moving bed on which the coal is burned, it allows for more complete combustion and easier removal of some pollutants.

In an unsuccessful springtime experiment motorists creep along a Los Angeles freeway while the far-left "diamond" lanes, reserved for buses and car pools in an attempt to reduce traffic, find few takers.

Issues still to be resolved in 1977 included the use of "scrubbers," devices that mechanically, electrostatically, and chemically remove pollutants from smokestack gases and can significantly reduce air pollution from the burning of coal. The U.S. Environmental Protection Agency (E.P.A.) requires the installation of scrubbers by coal-burning utility companies, but many of them objected to the additional costs and were fighting the ruling in the courts. Other utilities, however, were committed to scrubbers, and 1976 saw their increasing installation and use despite the challenge to the E.P.A.

NUCLEAR ENERGY

The nuclear power issues that received greatest attention during 1976 were the reprocessing of plutonium and the disposition of radioactive wastes.

Plutonium Recycling. Plutonium, not found in nature but produced primarily in nuclear power reactors, is extraordinarily volatile and can be used to make atomic bombs. Plutonium, a breakdown product of uranium, is present in the spent fuel rods of every reactor, but it is very difficult to remove and contain separately from spent uranium. Since plutonium can be used as a fuel in nuclear reactors, plans to reprocess the spent fuel, removing and separating the plutonium, have received consideration. While plutonium would thus become available for use in power plants, it could conceivably be obtained by unauthorized persons or organizations to make a bomb.

Ever since India exploded a nuclear device in 1974, the issue of selling reprocessing plants to other countries, so that they may themselves separate plutonium from spent fuel, has been extremely controversial. The U.S., in an attempt to prevent the spread of nuclear weapons, attempted in 1975 and again in 1976 to limit the sale of reprocessing facilities. Although this effort was partly successful, observers predicted that several more nations would soon join the eight that already had nuclear weapons capability.

On Oct. 29 President Ford announced a plan for the evaluation of the commercial recycling of plutonium. The plan, while falling short of a complete moratorium, did mark a decided change in U.S. nuclear policy by stating that plutonium recycling was no longer to be considered an essential part of the nuclear fuel program. Previously, plutonium recycling had been considered necessary to the future of nuclear energy.

Nuclear Waste Disposal. Another key issue was the handling of the radioactive wastes that result from nuclear power plant operations. Although the volume of such wastes is small, there is still no way to deactivate them, that is, remove their radioactivity. They must therefore be contained in such a way that their radiation—which causes cancer, mutations, and in cases of extreme exposure a potentially fatal disease called radiation sickness—does not come in contact with humans or leak into the environment. Steel, lead, and concrete are the most effective containment materials.

Since radioactive decay also produces heat, and the half-lives of some of the radioactive elements are quite long (that of plutonium is 24,000 years), containment is not a simple problem, although it is well within the realm of existing technology and engineering experience. The basic issues remained cost and the longevity of the wastes, which far exceeds the length of existence of any political institutions that humans can devise.

On July 21 the Court of Appeals for the District of Columbia halted all nuclear power licensing until the waste management situation could be further resolved. The orders grew out of suits charging that some plants had been given permits without adequate consideration of the processing of spent fuel and the disposal of waste. Although the National Environmental Policy Act requires consideration of the environmental impacts of nuclear waste disposal, the Nuclear Regulatory Commission (N.R.C.) did not issue a separate environmental impact statement for each plant but instead published one rule covering all instances. The court found this inadequate; the N.R.C. suspended licensing, except on an interim basis, until the matter was resolved.

In a report commissioned by ERDA, Mason Willrich, formerly of the Massachusetts Institute of Technology Energy Research Laboratory, was sharply critical of current regulatory practices. Willrich, backed by other leading experts, proposed that a new institution, federally chartered but free of existing agencies, be established to oversee the problems of nuclear waste management and fuel reprocessing. The new Radioactive Waste Authority, as the report conceived it, would manage all contaminated wastes that were in the U.S. or under its jurisdiction or control.

SOLAR ENERGY

Many people think of solar energy as obtained directly from the sun and used either to heat and cool buildings or to produce electricity by direct conversion or by the heating of water into steam that then drives a turbine. Solar energy also has other manifestations. Wind, bioconversion (the burning of photosynthetic materials), and ocean thermal-electrical conversion (the use of temperature differences in the water levels of the ocean to drive a turbine) are all examples of energy derived from the sun's rays. Although no dramatic progress was made in 1976 in harnessing this energy, substantive work continued in all areas.

Fuel from Wastes. At a major conference held in March, significant progress was announced in two areas: the treatment of municipal wastes to produce gases and liquid fuels and the development of devices to convert organic farm wastes to methane gas, which can be used both as a fuel and as a feedstock for chemical processes.

The Green Mountain Power Corp. in Vermont announced plans for a 50,000-kw plant to be fueled by the waste left behind by logging operations in the state. (Modern nuclear and coal plants average 1000 megawatts, or 1,000,000 kw.) The plant was to consume 400,000 tons of wood chips per year.

Among the most promising conversion methods is burning municipal trash directly in steam-generating units to produce electricity. The first such operation was in Saint Louis, Mo., where a joint project between the Union Electric Co. and the E.P.A., started in 1970, has produced a plant where up to 14 percent of the fuel comes from the municipal waste stream. The ferrous metals are first separated by magnet, then nonferrous materials, such as glass and copper, are taken from the stream mechanically; the remaining organic material is shredded and fed into a furnace along with coal, which is the main fuel. Although the plant has had some operating problems (pri-

A solar pond provides hot water for a new uranium-mining plant near Albuquerque, N.Mex. The collectors are simple plastic tubs, with transparent tops and black bottoms, containing sun-heated water 4 in. deep.

ENVIRONMENT

marily from erosion in the bends of the pipes that transport the abrasive shredded material), it has proved successful. In 1976 the state of Connecticut announced a $250,000,000 project to build ten such plants, which could convert 84 percent of the state's solid waste to furnish 10 percent of its electricity.

CONSERVATION

Conservation is the cheapest and most environmentally attractive way to extend our energy supply, and many experts believe that a serious program could have a significant result in a short period of time without adversely affecting our life-style. Conservation could be accomplished largely through improved efficiency, including such measures as the insulation of buildings to prevent heat loss. This was encouraged during the year by legislation providing $2.5 billion in direct grants and loan guarantees to homeowners for that purpose.

Critics of the effectiveness of conservation in solving the energy problem feel that the use of energy must be expanded to ensure a prosperous and growing economy. In a September report entitled "Energy, The Economy, and Jobs," the Chase Manhattan Bank pointed out that the relationship between energy use per capita and the gross national product remained constant for the last twenty years despite large-scale gains in the efficient use of energy during that period. For example, conversion from steam locomotives to diesel produced an approximate threefold increase in the efficiency of rail transportation. Other savings included a one-third drop in the amount of energy required to produce a kilowatt-hour of electricity and a dramatic decrease in the amount of energy needed to make a ton of aluminum or steel.   A.McG.

Energy waste in a typical "well-insulated" house (top) is revealed when it is photographed by infrared light (bottom). The brightest areas show where the heat loss is greatest, and why the owner's fuel bills are high.

ENVIRONMENT. The White House Council on Environment Quality reported in February, 1976, a slight improvement in air and water quality. The council noted that the number of "severe" and "very poor" water-quality areas had been reduced, but that below-standard water was still widespread and most municipalities would not be able to meet the 1977 deadline for installing water-treatment facilities. In September the United States Congress approved legislation that granted $366,000,000 to the states for solid-waste programs, forbade open dumping by 1982, and set up an Office of Solid Waste under the Environmental Protection Agency (E.P.A.).

Air quality reached the levels established by the Clean Air Act of 1970 in only 91 of the 247 designated regions; all were to have complied with the standards by 1975. In November, under a new policy described as a compromise between economic needs and excessive air pollution, the E.P.A. eased the clean air standards: It permitted communities with cleaner air than required by law to raise pollution to the maximum legal level, and, where the air was below standard, permitted new pollution-causing plants to be built provided there was no increase in overall pollution.

The most promising environmental legislation enacted in 1976 was the Toxic Substances Control Act, passed in October after a series of chemical catastrophes involving the pesticides Kepone and Mirex and the chemical PCB (see *Toxic Chemical Pollution in the U.S.,* below). The law requires companies to test new substances for potential health and environmental hazards before they are marketed. It also authorizes the E.P.A. to take action against harmful chemicals already in use. The act drew criticism, however, for not prohibiting toxic chemicals at places where food for humans or animals is handled. Critics pointed to a 1973 catastrophe in Michigan, in which the accidental mixing of the fire-retardant PBB with animal feeds killed or sickened hundreds of thousands of livestock and poisoned a still unknown number of farmers and their families.

Dioxin Disaster in Italy. On July 10 the town of Seveso, 12 mi. north of Milan in the Lombardy region of Italy, suffered one of the worst pollution disasters in history when an explosion in a local factory released a large amount of dioxin, one of

the deadliest poisons known. Not until many days after the explosion, when a drifting cloud of the poison had already contaminated 750 acres of the surrounding countryside and dead birds lay strewn about the roads and fields, did local officials realize the full extent of the crisis. They divided the affected area into zones A, B, and C. All 730 inhabitants of zone A and more than 1300 children from zone B were evacuated. The remaining residents of zones B and C were warned not to sell or eat their produce or farm animals. In the first weeks after the disaster, small animals died and children broke out in severe skin rashes. Symptoms of kidney and liver malfunction began to appear, and some 500 persons eventually became sick. Because dioxin is suspected of causing defects in unborn children, the Italian government gave special permission for therapeutic abortion to the more than 350 pregnant women in the area.

The Swiss-based owners of the Lombardy factory, Givaudan Co. (a subsidiary of the Hoffman-La Roche chemical concern), claimed that the dioxin, also known as TCDD, was normally created in trace amounts as a by-product of trichlorophenol, which they used in the making of bactericidal deodorants, and that an accidental overheating that led to the explosion had caused large amounts of dioxin to be formed.

No one was sure what the long-range effects of dioxin poisoning would be, but victims of previous instances had developed over the first year or two after exposure such symptoms as violent skin rashes and damage to the brain, vision, nervous system, and vital organs. In Vietnam, where American forces had used dioxin in defoliant sprays, a 30 percent mortality rate was claimed.

Toxic Chemical Pollution in the U.S. The Allied

White-clad workmen remove toxic chemicals from a factory in Seveso, Italy, site of a disastrous release of a deadly gas in July.

Silt dredged from the river bottom is being converted to marshland in the Mississippi River delta. The marsh, begun in 1975 by the U.S. Army Corps of Engineers, has provided new breeding grounds for hundreds of species of birds, fish, and shellfish threatened by loss of natural wetlands.

A thriving specimen of Furbish's lousewort. Presumed extinct, the plant was found in the area to be flooded by the proposed Dickey-Lincoln Power Dam in Maine.

Chemical Corp. was fined $13,375,000 in October for polluting the James R. in Virginia for about four years. The pollutant was Kepone, a persistent chlorinated hydrocarbon similar to DDT. The contamination came to light in the late summer of 1975, when it was learned that more than seventy workers in an Allied Chemical pesticide plant on the river at Hopewell, Va., had suffered severe neurological and other damage as a result of handling the Kepone. Approximately twenty-eight of them were hospitalized with such symptoms as paralysis, uncontrollable tremors, and loss of memory. The James R. was closed to fishing, throwing thousands of commercial fishermen out of work, and a ban was instituted on the harvesting of shad and crabs in Chesapeake Bay, the river's outlet. Toxic levels of Kepone were subsequently found in fish and marine organisms along hundreds of miles of Atlantic coastal waters.

Public anxiety about the spread of Kepone was heightened when a U.S. Department of Agriculture study of the pesticide Mirex, sprayed since 1962 over 200,000,000 acres in the South to combat fire ants, showed that the substance breaks down into Kepone. The state of Mississippi, which recently had acquired the nation's only extant Mirex plant from Allied Chemical, planned to shut down operations by June, 1978. Large amounts of Mirex were also found to be reaching into the Niagara R. and Lake Ontario, presumably from a supply once made at the Hooker Chemical plant in Niagara Falls, N.Y. An investigation was under way to determine whether the contamination would force the delay of plans to open a large trout and salmon hatchery for Lake Ontario.

Meanwhile another toxic chemical group, poly-chlorinated biphenyls (PCB's), continued to pollute many rivers and began to appear in the milk of nursing mothers. These chlorine compounds had been implicated in cases of allergy, cancer, and bone deformities. Dangerous amounts were found in the Hudson R. in 1975 from dumping by two General Electric Co. plants north of Albany, N.Y. In September, 1976, General Electric agreed to pay New York State $3,000,000 toward cleansing the river of the materials and another $1,000,-000 for research on remaining problems. It planned to phase out their use by July, 1977.

Yet another pesticide crisis loomed at year's end, when seven employees at a Velsicol Chemical Corp. plant in Bayport, Texas, were found to have suffered serious nerve damage from handling an organophosphate chemical called Phosvel. An E.P.A. official uncovered the cases in December as he was considering the company's request to market the pesticide in the U.S. At least ten companies in six states were making the pesticide for export. While the E.P.A. was instituting a survey of plant and marine life in the Galveston Bay area, the National Institute for Occupational Health and Safety was planning to examine the health records of all plant personnel who worked with the chemical.

New York Bight. A massive washup of garbage and sewage sludge closed 70 mi. of Long Island beaches in late June. Although the heavily used beaches were cleansed by tides and reopened within ten days, experts predicted that the coastal pollution could recur at any time. A large fish kill and a dramatic rise in the mortality levels of surf clams off the New Jersey coast further underlined the severity of pollution in the New York bight. New York City, which was discharging 200,000,000 gal. of sewage into the Hudson R. each day and dumping treated sewage sludge into New York harbor, was only one of the offending communities.

Aerosols and Ozone. In September the National Academy of Sciences (N.A.S.) issued its long-awaited report on the effects of chlorofluorocarbons on the stratospheric ozone layer. The report confirmed the theory first proposed by F. Sherwood Rowland and Mario J. Molina, chemists from the University of California at Irvine, that these chemicals, released from aerosol cans and other sources, rise through the atmosphere to break down ozone, which protects living forms on earth from excessive ultraviolet radiation. The report stressed that further study was needed on the rate of damage but advised that regulatory action commence in no more than two years. The N.A.S. also recommended the immediate labeling of products that contained the chemicals in order to encourage voluntary curtailment of their use. Acting on this suggestion, the Food and Drug Administration announced in December that all aerosol spray cans containing chlorofluorocarbon propellants, except those for prescription drugs, must carry the label: "Warning: Contains a chlorofluorocarbon that may harm the public health and environment by reducing ozone in the upper atmosphere."

Endangered Species. The U.S. Department of the Interior added 159 animals to its list of endangered species in 1976, prohibiting interstate trade in the animals or in products made from them except by special permit. The list included the Asian elephant, all gibbon species, and several species of monkey. Eighty-one other species of ape and monkey were judged to be severely or moderately threatened. The Interior Department also released its first list of endangered plants, which included 1700 species.

See also ENERGY; FISH AND FISHERIES.   M.J.C.

EQUATORIAL GUINEA. See STATISTICS OF THE WORLD.

ETHIOPIA. As the year 1976 began the ruling Provisional Military Council, or Dirgue, of Ethiopia was faced with strong opposition from radical students, conservative forces led by former landowners, urban workers, dissidents in the military, and the secessionist movements of Eritrea. By spring anti-Dirgue demonstrations and calls for revolution were a regular occurrence in Addis Ababa, the Ethiopian capital. The Dirgue responded with new waves of arrests and executions. In January and February as many as 2000 persons were arrested, among them six deposed members of the Dirgue itself and the head of the Ethiopian Orthodox (Coptic) Church, Archbishop Tewoflos, who was deprived of his office on Feb. 18. In July and August a number of military officers, including the military governor of Eritrea and one high-ranking Dirgue member, were executed for alleged reactionary behavior. Charging that Marxist groups were attacking "genuine revolutionaries" and inciting demonstrations, lootings, and bombings, the government executed fifty leftists in November. Although the Dirgue was able to keep its opponents in Addis Ababa off balance, it was less successful in the countryside, where armed conservative resistance was reported in eight provinces.

Eritrea. Seeking to mobilize the support of Ethiopian peasants and crush the Eritrean rebellion, the Dirgue announced plans in May to arm and launch a peasant march against the rebellious province. Viewed as a holy war against Muslims, not to mention an opportunity to seize land, the march attracted an estimated 50,000 Christian peasants. Following international protests against genocide and a number of rebel attacks against staging areas, the march was canceled on June 19. Small-scale fighting continued in the province through the remainder of 1976.

See STATISTICS OF THE WORLD. See also AFRICA.   J.T.S.

EUROPEAN COMMUNITIES, a supranational organization comprising the European Economic Community, the European Atomic Energy Community, and the European Coal and Steel Community. Because the communities share the same institutional framework, they are frequently referred to as the European Community (E.C.), or Common Market. In 1976 the nine member countries were Belgium, Denmark, France, Great Britain, Ireland, Italy, Luxembourg, the Netherlands, and West Germany.

Internal Affairs. A new political impetus was given to the European Community in July when E.C. heads of government agreed on a method of direct elections to the European Parliament. Following elections in the spring of 1978, the parliament was to be enlarged from 198 to 410 seats. Members, who are now appointed by their national assemblies, would be elected for five-year terms and would be allowed to combine seats in their national legislatures with those in the European body.

Inflation and unemployment continued to plague all E.C. member nations in 1976. Italy and Ireland were granted loans of $1 billion and $300,000,000, respectively, from their E.C. partners to help alleviate balance of payments difficulties. France, faced with a depreciating currency, pulled the franc out of the joint E.C. currency float and joined free-floating Britain, Ireland, and Italy.

External Affairs. The E.C. was active in its relations with nonmember nations in 1976. Negotiations opened in July for Greece to become the tenth member state, and Spain and Portugal expressed interest in applying for membership. New trade agreements were concluded with Portugal as well as with Tunisia, Morocco, and Algeria. On July 6 the E.C. and Canada signed an agreement for economic and commercial cooperation. It was the first such agreement between the E.C. and an industrialized country.

The community spoke with one voice not only in internal affairs but in wider political and economic forums as well. The E.C. as a unit was allowed to occupy one of the eight seats allotted for industrialized countries at the twenty-seven nation Conference on International Cooperation held in Paris in February. On a more political level, leaders of E.C. member nations pledged in July that they would prosecute terrorists and hijackers on their own or extradite them for trial elsewhere.

Trade relations between the United States and the E.C. suffered a setback in June, when U.S. President Gerald R. Ford imposed quotas on imports of steel from E.C. member states. The action followed complaints by the U.S. steel industry that these imports were threatening employment and profits. The community also aroused the anger of U.S. soybean exporters when it initiated a plan to use surplus stocks of skimmed milk powder in animal feeds and to require importers of vegetable proteins to pay a duty on these products. At the end of 1976, the possibility loomed of a new trade war between the U.S. and the E.C., this time over a U.S. government proposal to raise duties on imports of European brandies in retaliation for the E.C.'s refusal to open its turkey market to U.S. farmers.

See articles on individual countries mentioned.   C.B.

F

FASHION. Early in 1976 classics were the major fashion influence. The lines were clean-cut, well tailored but less constructed, more feminine in feeling, and less severe. Then in midsummer the French designer Yves St. Laurent overturned the fashion world with his "Fantasy Peasant" look.

Casual Wear and Sportswear. Pants or skirts in combination with blazers, shirts or sweaters, and vests were the important look in casual wear. The gaucho, or split skirt, was accepted by many women as a pleasing compromise between pants and skirts. The "top," whether it was a sweater, T-shirt, or, for the younger customer, the smock or novelty top, became the most important wardrobe addition. From the plain crew-neck skivvy to the many novelty T-shirts decorated with slogans, trims, pictures, and portraits, tops became the "in" things to buy and wear. Sweaters were another boon to the industry. From late summer on, the cowl neck, although introduced a year earlier, was fully accepted and much in demand. The wrapped and hooded sweater to wear outdoors was less expensive and more versatile than a jacket and became the answer to many wardrobe problems.

The sportswear industry was blessed with another bonanza: Exercising was the name of the game in 1976, and the industry was ready for it.

Far left: On July 28 Paris designer Yves St. Laurent introduced his influential fall collection, featuring the "Fantasy Peasant" look. Shown here is an evening ensemble of taffeta skirt, black velvet bodice, embroidered blouse, and wide, billowing cape.

Left: The 1977 spring and summer collection of the designer Halston, shown in New York City on Nov. 11, featured the "nude look." The model wears an evening pants outfit with halter cape.

Sweatshirts and look-alikes were introduced not only as active wear but as day and evening wear. The hooded sweatshirt jacket, with its kangaroo-pocket zipfront, was available in sweatshirt fabric for the beach as well as in gold or silver lamé for evening. Sweatpants were added for jogging, play, or even office wear.

The layered look continued its vogue. Overdone by many designers, it came down to earth and was accepted by the consumer in a more simplified style: pants or skirt with sweater, shirt, vest, and jacket. Boots were a must to complete the outfit.

Juniors and Misses. Another great plus, especially for the junior customer, was the "disco" influence. Sheer tops, wraps, handkerchief waistlines and sleeves, ponchos, and tunics became the uniform, worn with jeans, dress pants, gauchos, and skirts for both day and evening. The handkerchief hemline and sleeve was an important silhouette in the dress market for evening—smart-looking, especially in prints, it was an important influence for fall.

Dresses. Dresses had a more difficult year. The blouson gained in importance and appeared in many versions. New, soft, and feminine, it was well accepted by the consumer. The short cocktail dress became an important silhouette and served also as a special occasion dress. The classic wrap and shirtdress from Diane Von Furstenberg, as well as the many copies it inspired, continued to do well. For 1977 the sundress and the bare look (mainly in the "Big Dress") seemed to be making an important comeback.

The Peasant Look. Then came the fall collections, and Yves St. Laurent pulled the rug out from under everyone when he introduced the "Fantasy Peasant": billowing taffeta and moiré, big dirndl skirts, peasant blouses, and braid-trimmed jackets and boleros. The trend was set; the peasant look was immediately accepted in the United States. Some designers, such as Oscar de la Renta and Gloria Vanderbilt, continued the St. Laurent opulent look; others modified it into easier-to-wear versions for evening. The look was fresh and crisp for both day and evening with a cotton print tiered or flounced skirt, a peasant-type blouse, and smocked or camisole tops. For spring and summer, 1977, manufacturers said it would be available at all price levels.

Coats and Accessories. Little fashion excitement occurred in the coat market. The reefer coat, introduced in 1975, gained in importance, and the wrap coat held its own. The "Big Coat," especially in rain-and-shine looks, created a big stir early in the year but did not see the year's end. Jumpsuits, too, created much excitement early in the year, but only in off-hours looks and in the children's area did they last through the year.

Color interest throughout the industry continued to focus on the bright reds, greens, blues, and yellows. But fashion forecasters were saying that gray, black, and white would make their reappearance for spring, 1977.

Right: Japanese designer Kenzo Jap revived the miniskirt for his 1976 Paris collection. Usually well ahead of fashion trends, he had observers wondering about the accuracy of his latest forecast.

Far right: The contemporary look for the younger man was a three-piece suit in a polyester-cotton blend called "Denim +" (Denim Plus). Retailing for around $50, it was guaranteed to wear longer and to fade, become soft, and resist wrinkling, puckering, and shrinking.

Accessories remained an important fashion influence. Oversized glasses (initialed or with other novelty treatments), reading glasses, and sunglasses all took on individual looks and became status symbols. Scarves emerged from the accessory category into a necessity as a wardrobe coordinato., or "put-together." Interest in handbags was in the natural straws, especially the "pizza" bag, for spring and summer. The Frye bag in leather and the nylon parachute bag made their appearance during the year, and it was felt they would emerge in strength for 1977. Shoulder bags remained the favorite catchall, gaining in size as well as popularity. One of the most important fashion accessories was the boot. The Frye boot, worn with jeans, pants, and skirts, and the peasant boot, worn with late-day peasant dressing, were very strong. For those desiring a more feminine look, the espadrille, pump, and T-strap were usually the favorites.

Jewelry followed the lead with cords and natural elements—wood, cork, uncut stones—for the peasant look. To try to follow up the 1975 Mood Ring, a mood bracelet called Pulsar Pacer made its appearance but failed to stir up much excitement.

Makeup and hair reverted to a more natural look, thanks to Olympic skater Dorothy Hamill. Short, easy-to-take-care-of hair, in combination with a softened but still bright makeup, seemed to be the trend.

Men's Clothing and Jewelry. In men's wear the big news was the unmatched suit, also known in Europe as the "composé look." It was a three-piece suit, in which only two or even none of the pieces matched. Pants, coat, and vest were usually related, however, whether in pattern, texture, or general color. Vests were seeing their greatest popularity in almost forty years, and the single-breasted suit with matching vest was again a favorite among young businessmen. The shirt collar was often worn open and outside the jacket.

In men's jewelry, the trend was toward two or three bracelets and away from neck adornments, such as chains or lockets. Fragrances continued to gain in popularity with men.

Deaths. Mainbocher, the American couturier, died in December; see OBITUARIES. Antoine of Paris, who was born Antek Cierplikowski in a Polish village and became the world's most famous hairdresser, died in July at 91.   M.H.

FIJI. See STATISTICS OF THE WORLD.

FINLAND. The nation began 1976 in serious economic difficulties. The foreign trade deficit in 1975 had been $2 billion, or about 8 percent of the gross national product, the national debt amounted to $5.2 billion, and unemployment was rising. In an effort to alleviate the difficulties, the government submitted a supplementary budget for 1976 of approximately $750,000,000, most of it allotted to aid for the unemployed.

The labor unions won a 3.5 percent increase in the minimum wage in late January, affecting about 1,300,000 workers, or 80 percent of the labor force. Employers also agreed, reluctantly, to a government proposal of a price freeze intended to keep inflation down to a 5 percent rate.

The agreement led to a rash of strikes. In February 6000 policemen struck for a raise of 50 percent, or $260 a month. After seventeen days, the strike was settled for a $28.60 per month increase. A strike of 43,000 food industry workers on March 25 was settled two weeks later with a raise of 15 percent, or 22¢ an hour. Also in late March more than 17,000 merchant seamen went on strike in a dispute over working at night and on Sunday; 4000 dockworkers joined the walkout five days later, demanding higher pay and better working conditions. The two strikes blocked Finland's sealanes and stranded dozens of vessels in the nation's harbors. The dockers returned to work on May 3, after union leaders accepted an offer of a 20 percent wage increase.

Prime Minister Martti J. Miettunen's five-party coalition cabinet submitted its 1976 legislative program early in March. Stronger economic controls were proposed, together with constitutional revisions sought by the leftist parties, calling for parliamentary majorities to be reduced from five sixths to three quarters. The Communist members of the coalition, however, refused to go along with a proposed increase in the national sales tax from 11 to 15 percent, and Miettunen's government resigned the following day. President Urho Kekkonen, however, refused to accept the resignation or Miettunen's proposal that he form a four-party coalition with no Communist participation.

Continued disagreement between the Communists and other coalition members, this time over farm and unemployment subsidies, resulted in a second resignation on Sept. 17; this time Kekkonen accepted it. Twelve days later Miettunen formed a new coalition, representing the Liberal, Center, and Swedish People's parties and excluding the Communists.

See STATISTICS OF THE WORLD.   L.A.S.

FISH AND FISHERIES. United States commercial fishing landings, the amount of fish brought to docks by fishermen, came to 5.3 billion lb. in 1976, the largest in ten years, and had a record value of more than $1 billion. Chemical pollution closed the James R. to fishing and restricted catches in the Hudson R., Chesapeake Bay, Lake Michigan, and Lake Ontario (see ENVIRONMENT). Surf clams suffered most from pollution problems, and harvests were reduced by one third. But Gulf Coast shrimp rose by a third, and Pacific salmon were up 40 percent over the previous year.

Fishing Limit of 200 Mi. Set. In the continuing deadlock over an international Law of the Seas agreement (see UNITED NATIONS), the U.S. took independent action in March to protect its coastal fish from overexploitation by foreign factory fleets, which were seriously depleting twenty species and threatening the reproduction of cod, halibut, yellowtail flounder, and herring in the northeast waters. Foreign fleets harvested about 80 percent of the total offshore catch beyond the 12-mi. zone. The Fisheries Conservation and Management Act, effective March, 1977, extended the nation's exclusive fishing zone to 200 mi. offshore, limiting foreign fishing within the zone to nations that extend reciprocal rights to American fleets. The act also provided for the creation of eight Regional Fisheries Management Councils to recommend species quotas, conservation measures, and other fish resource requirements to the Department of Commerce which, with the Coast Guard, would enforce the law. The Commerce Department at the same time launched a sweeping long-term program in cooperation with other agencies and departments to restore fish stocks and habitats, revive and develop the nation's commercial and recreational fishing, and "ensure adequate consumer supplies of wholesome seafood." The department, which estimated the total 1976 economic value of U.S. fishing activities at $10 billion, expected to add another $1.5 billion with the new program.

Following the American extension of its fishing zone, Canada, most of the European Economic Community nations, and the Soviet Union also adopted a 200-mi. limit; Mexico closed its 600-mi.-long California Gulf and established a 200-mi. restricted zone off its Pacific and Gulf of Mexico coasts. American shrimp fishermen, who made half of their 208,000,000-lb. catch in the Gulf of Mexico in 1975, protested the Mexican move and called for a protective tariff on imported shrimp.

Whale and Dolphin Quotas. The International Whaling Commission, at its annual London meeting in June, set the global quota for the 1976 whaling season at 28,050 whales, down from the previous season's 32,578. Japan and the U.S.S.R., which accounted for 90 percent of the world catch, protested the reduction but filed no formal objections. Environmentalists continued to press for a total ban on the killing of this rapidly disappearing mammal.

Following the killing of an estimated 134,000 dolphins in 1975 by U.S. tuna fishermen in the Pacific Ocean, the Department of Commerce set a dolphin-kill quota of 78,000 for 1976 and moved to protect these friendly, seagoing mammals from further decimation. Starting in 1977, purse-seine netting of 6 species of dolphin and small whale was to be banned entirely, and netting restrictions were set on 11 other species. These huge purse-seine nets are lowered by teams of tuna boats when dolphins are spotted on the waters, for they frequently swim above schools of tuna. The dolphins become fatally tangled when the nets are raised. More than 1,000,000 dolphins and small whales have been drowned since this method came into use in 1961.   F.L.K.

FLORIDA. See STATISTICS OF THE WORLD.

FORD, GERALD R. See PRESIDENT OF THE UNITED STATES.

FRANCE. Political excitement in France in 1976 was heightened by the Communist Party's announcement of its independence from Moscow, and by electoral victories of the United Left (Communist-Socialist), major cabinet changes, and the government's new austerity plan.

Political Tensions. Striking political developments occurred in 1976 or appeared to be imminent. The French Communist Party charted new directions for itself, declaring independence from Moscow and abandonment of the goal of a dictatorship of the proletariat. While some observers debated whether these moves were sincere or merely tactical, the Communists reinforced their links with the Socialists in the United Left coalition.

In March elections in the ninety-five departments, despite lingering suspicions between the two big leftist parties, the United Left gained a majority of both the popular vote and the offices. Despite the fact that these offices were for the most part advisory and without real power, the elections were regarded as significant. With an impressive 68 percent turnout, the voters accorded the Socialists a stronger endorsement (27 percent) than the Communists (22 percent). The Left eyed with mounting optimism the municipal elections of 1977 and the parliamentary campaign of 1978.

The government of President Valéry Giscard d'Estaing was divided over what strategy to adopt to counteract the growing strength of the Left. Gaullist Premier Jacques Chirac wished to call for early elections, whereas the centrist president preferred to adhere to the 1977–78 schedule in the hope that economic improvements would undercut support for the Left. The estrangement of the president and premier on this and other issues finally resulted in Chirac's abrupt resignation in August. Giscard immediately named politically unaffiliated Raymond Barre as the new premier

French students demonstrated throughout France in April to protest government reforms that would tailor university curriculums and enrollments to existing employment opportunities. This demonstration, in Paris on April 14, formed at the Arc de Triomphe and marched across the city to Napoleon's tomb.

and reshuffled the cabinet. A majority of the posts were assigned to the centrists rather than the Gaullists.

In November, however, Chirac easily won back his seat in the National Assembly for his district of Corrèze, a seat he was forced to give up when he became premier in 1974. In early December, Chirac reorganized the Gaullist party as a new anti-Left force, rechristened it the Assembly for the Republic, and was acclaimed the party's head.

Since the large Gaullist bloc (173) was needed to create majorities with the centrists (120) in the 490-member parliament, the alienated Gaullists under a rankled Chirac could spell serious trouble for the president's future programs.

French politics also reflected concern over the nation's worsening economic condition. The new premier, more an expert economist than a traditional politician, drafted recommendations for increased austerity. Barre's plan, approved by parliament in October, was designed to curb inflation and buttress the sagging franc by means of a temporary freeze on prices and wages and a hike in individual, corporate, and certain indirect taxes. By treating the economic malaise, Giscard and Barre hoped to keep the Gaullists in line and fore-

A Nonpolitician Gets the Job

When French Premier Jacques Chirac quit in frustration in August, President Valéry Giscard d'Estaing chose Raymond Barre, 52, to be the new leader of the government. A genial economics expert who had represented France on the Common Market (1967–73) and joined Giscard's cabinet as minister of foreign trade in January, Barre was well qualified for his chief assignment, namely, to fight inflation and support the value of the French franc. A nonpolitician, Barre became the first premier in the eighteen-year history of the Fifth Republic who was not a member of the Gaullist party.

The new premier of France, Raymond Barre.

stall any gains by the Left in forthcoming elections.

The response to Barre's plan was predictable: grudging support from the Gaullists and vociferous attack from the Left against what they termed a "plan for social regression." Fueling the political infighting was a report in August from the Organization for Economic Cooperation and Development to the effect that the disparity between rich and poor in France was greater than in any other Western European country, including Spain.

Economic Woes. Lagging industrial production, accelerating inflation, larger trade deficits, weakness of the franc, and persistent unemployment plagued the French economy in 1976. Although the last quarter of 1975 and the first quarter of 1976 recorded strong recovery from the world recession of 1974–75, the second and third quarters of 1976 revealed a leveling off or even a decline in most French economic sectors. Industrial production advanced by only 1.7 percent during the first six months, and the foreign trade deficit rose from $80,000,000 in the second quarter to $340,000,000 in July. The franc, allowed to free-float in March, plunged between 8 and 20 percent relative to various Western currencies. Price inflation stubbornly advanced to the level of 10 percent by November. Hourly wages, too, rose at the rate of two and one-half times that of West Germany and the United States, and unemployment hovered around the 1,000,000 mark, or about 5 percent of the work force, throughout the year.

Compounding the economic woes, widespread drought hit the country, producing the unlikely phenomenon of the French buying Maine and Long Island potatoes from the U.S. On the brighter side, the grape harvest was excellent, as were the prospects for record wine production. The energy situation had improved, with the French producing 10 percent of their national needs through new nuclear plants, with promises of an increase to two thirds by 1985.

International Affairs. No marked departures were notable in French foreign policy or its implementation. The French presence was still highly visible in presidential state visits to the U.S. in May, to Great Britain in June, and to Iran in October. Closer ties with Common Market nations, especially West Germany, were stressed, although difficulties surfaced over such items as monetary policy and Italy's continued flooding of France with its wine.

France continued to supply arms and technology to the Middle East (including a subway for Tehran) and to African states, including South Africa, but the French share of these markets was down from 1975. Contracts for nuclear development in Pakistan, South Africa, South Korea, and Iran led to bitter controversy between France and its allies over nuclear proliferation and its control.

See STATISTICS OF THE WORLD.   D.J.H.

On Feb. 5 thousands of French winegrowers, angered by the importing of cheaper Italian wines, staged protests in the south of France. The demonstration at Montpellier (below) ended with a mourner's procession to honor the "dead region."

G

GABON. *See* STATISTICS OF THE WORLD.

GAMBIA, THE. *See* STATISTICS OF THE WORLD.

GEOLOGY. *See* EARTH AND PLANETARY SCIENCES.

GEOPHYSICS. *See* EARTH AND PLANETARY SCIENCES.

GEORGIA. *See* STATISTICS OF THE WORLD.

GERMAN DEMOCRATIC REPUBLIC, *or* EAST GERMANY. East Germany remained the most prosperous and most highly industrialized nation in Eastern Europe in 1976. According to World Bank statistics, its per capita income exceeded that of Great Britain. Even so, the year brought an upswing in public discontent that was unprecedented in recent history.

Politics. The ruling Socialist Unity (Communist) Party held its 9th Congress in mid-May. The gathering took place in East Berlin's glittering new Palace of the Republic, a $500,000,000 civic center on the former site of an imperial residence.

At the congress Communist Party leader Erich Honecker delivered a 45,000-word report that laid down national guidelines for the coming five years. In domestic policy Honecker stressed the Communists' intention to raise living standards still further. Honecker assumed a new party title, that of secretary-general, and the party Politburo was enlarged from 16 to 19 members. Late in October Honecker instituted further changes. He added the job of chairman of the Council of State to his portfolio, replacing Willi Stoph. Stoph took over the premiership from Horst Sindermann, who became president of the People's Chamber, for which elections had been held earlier in the month.

Meanwhile, public disenchantment with Communist rule was more evident than at any time in the past two decades. Many East Germans still resented the Berlin Wall and other sophisticated border fortifications that cut them off from relatives and friends in West Germany. They also chafed at restrictions that allowed only some 40,000 East Germans to visit the West. A series of border incidents in August heightened tensions over this issue and drew a formal protest from the Western powers.

Two dissidents attracted widespread public at-

An East German girl congratulates Communist Party chief Erich Honecker (left), who assumed the title of chairman of the Council of State, or head of state, in October. Looking less pleased is Willi Stoph (center), who left the chairmanship to become premier.

tention. In August a Protestant pastor in Zeitz shocked the nation by setting himself afire in order to protest the regime's repressive attitude against religion. Then, in November, when the popular protest singer and poet Wolf Biermann traveled to West Germany to perform, East German officials stripped him of his citizenship and refused to allow him to return home.

Although they ran the risk of official reprisal, ordinary citizens became less hesitant about making their discontent known. By Western estimates, tens of thousands of people, perhaps even more than 100,000, were on record requesting permission to emigrate. In November the government tightened emigration requirements so that only the elderly, those with family ties with the West, and other "hardship cases" were permitted to leave. During 1976 approximately 5000 East Germans managed to move West illegally.

The Economy. East Germany's new five-year plan called for annual industrial growth of 7 percent, about the same rate achieved under the previous five-year plan. The economy as a whole, however, posed problems for the government. The country was poor in natural resources, and the soaring cost of importing raw materials from the Soviet Union was a serious drain on the national budget. At the party congress Premier Sindermann emphasized that economic progress depended on wiping out waste and increasing efficiency, especially in the use of energy. In a November speech before the People's Chamber, incoming Premier Stoph reiterated the call for harder work.

Existing economic difficulties were compounded by a severe drought. Economists estimated that East Germany would need to buy up to 5,000,000 tons of grain from the West during 1976. In November the United States and East Germany announced an agreement under which the East Germans contracted to buy between 1,500,000 and 2,000,000 tons of grain annually until 1980; because of the drought, purchases for 1976 would total 3,500,000 tons. As part of the pact, East German cargo ships were granted permission to call at U.S. ports for the first time.

Foreign Affairs. Political relations between East Germany and the West were marred by controversy during the year. In March West German Economics Minister Hans Friderichs broke off a visit to East Germany to protest that country's refusal to allow three West German reporters to cover an international trade fair in Leipzig. In June the Bonn government protested East Germany's seizure of two West German border guards.

East Germany remained one of the Soviet Union's staunchest allies. In May Honecker criticized Western Communist parties for challenging Moscow's claim of leadership in the Communist camp. At an international Communist summit held in East Berlin in June, the East Germans were Moscow's most faithful supporters.

See STATISTICS OF THE WORLD. *See also* COMMUNISM. F.W.

GERMANY, FEDERAL REPUBLIC OF, *or* **WEST GERMANY.** West Germany held a nationwide parliamentary election in October, 1976, and the ruling Social Democratic-Free Democratic coalition under Chancellor Helmut Schmidt was returned to power. Because of public dissatisfaction

Huge likenesses of two candidates for chancellor of West Germany (Helmut Schmidt, left, and Helmut Kohl) loom over a Frankfurt street just prior to the Oct. 3 election. Schmidt and his Socialist coalition retained power by a slim majority.

New values for the German mark are recorded at the Frankfurt monetary exchange on Oct. 18. West Germany had revalued its currency the previous day, but the mark retained its comparative strength.

with the economy, however, Schmidt and his Social Democrats received a wafer-thin parliamentary majority.

Politics. The year began inauspiciously for Chancellor Schmidt and his coalition. In February the Social Democrats (S.P.D.) and Free Democrats (F.D.P.) were ousted from power in the state of Lower Saxony. By a two-vote majority, the state legislature chose Christian Democrat Ernst Albrecht as governor, and three of the votes for Albrecht came from the S.P.D.-F.D.P. coalition. The vote put the state under Christian Democratic rule for the first time since World War II. It simultaneously widened an existing Christian Democratic majority in the *Bundesrat,* the upper house of the national parliament. That, in turn, gave the Christian Democrats the power to challenge Chancellor Schmidt's legislative program more readily.

In April Schmidt's coalition suffered another blow. In state elections in Baden-Württemberg,

final results gave the Christian Democrats 57 percent of the vote, up from 53 percent, while S.P.D. and F.D.P. support fell sharply. The election was the last big test of voter opinion before the general election, and it marked the tenth time since 1972 that the Christian Democrats had increased their share of the vote in a state election.

Experts attributed Christian Democratic gains to public concern about the economy, as well as to an increasing unwillingness on the part of the public to pay for the government's social programs. Christian Democratic leader Helmut Kohl seized the opportunity to encourage the Free Democrats to dissolve their coalition with the Socialists. The tiny F.D.P., however, refused to be tempted. In June it committed itself to continuing its partnership with Schmidt. That same month the chancellor opened his national electoral campaign with a rousing rally in Dortmund.

From then until the nationwide ballot in the autumn, Schmidt stressed that, despite difficulties, the German economy was improving markedly and the nation had weathered the worldwide economic crisis better than other industrial countries. Both major parties fought a vigorous election campaign. When the German people cast their votes on Oct. 3, they gave Schmidt's coalition a narrow majority of 10 seats in the 496-seat *Bundestag,* or lower house of parliament, and Schmidt was confirmed as chancellor. Nonetheless, the Christian Democrats, with 244 seats, emerged as the nation's single largest parliamentary party. In balloting by members of parliament on Dec. 15, Schmidt won reelection as chancellor of West Germany. The extremely narrow victory gave him only one vote more than the necessary majority.

Terrorism and terrorists received widespread attention in 1976. Ulrike Meinhof, the 41-year-old woman ringleader of the anarchist Baader-Meinhof gang, was found dead in her Stuttgart cell in May. On trial for nearly a year for masterminding five killings and a wave of bombings, Meinhof apparently took her own life, and her death set off noisy demonstrations by her supporters. In July four other women who stood accused of terrorist acts that included the 1975 kidnapping of Berlin politician Peter Lorenz escaped from a Berlin prison; they were recaptured two weeks later. Berlin Deputy Mayor Hermann Oxfort took political responsibility for inadequate security at the prison and tendered his resignation.

The Economy. Compared with other countries, West Germany did not suffer grievously from the international economic crisis in 1976. As the year began, West German unemployment stood at 5.9 percent and inflation at 6.1 percent. Although both figures were lower than in most Western nations, the German people took no comfort from the statistics.

Throughout the year the fiscal policies enacted by the ruling coalition scored notable economic gains. By October unemployment had fallen to 3.9 percent and inflation to 4 percent. The government estimated that the real rate of annual growth would reach at least 6 percent, offsetting a drop during 1975. Reflecting the strength of the economy, the mark in October was revalued upward against six other West European currencies.

Foreign Relations. Despite the pressure of domestic politics, Chancellor Schmidt spent a busy diplomatic year. In July he made a personal visit to the United States. The trip, in honor of the U.S. Bicentennial, was largely ceremonial, but several policy differences between Bonn and Washington were given a place on the schedule. Schmidt announced at this time that his government, along with the U.S., France, and Great Britain, had agreed at a recent economic conference in Puerto Rico to cut off loans to Italy if Communists were permitted to hold cabinet posts in that government. He was widely criticized for this unilateral

Hundreds of West German students demonstrated on May 10 in Frankfurt (below) and in West Berlin. They were motivated by the apparent suicide the previous day of convicted urban guerrilla leader Ulrike Meinhof in a Stuttgart prison.

disclosure. The U.S. and West German governments reached agreement that the formal "offset" arrangement by which Bonn helped defray the cost of stationing U.S. troops in West Germany would be discontinued, as Bonn wished. Several weeks later another bilateral accord settled the question of developing a common gun and engine for new battle tanks. That agreement was a major step toward the goal of standardizing weapons in the North Atlantic Treaty Organization. (q.v.).

Schmidt continued to cultivate close ties with West Germany's partners in the European Economic Community. He visited Britain for talks in February and played host to British Prime Minister James Callaghan in June. Schmidt also held periodic consultations with French President Valéry Giscard d'Estaing.

West German relations with Communist nations hit several snags. In March Christian Democratic members of the West German *Bundesrat* refused to vote to ratify a treaty with Poland until the Polish regime agreed to rewrite certain portions of it. The matter at issue was Polish agreement to allow ethnic Germans living in Poland to emigrate to the West. After a concession by Poland the treaty was ratified and went into operation.

In March West Germany abandoned plans to build a $600,000,000 nuclear power plant in the Soviet Union because Bonn and Moscow were unable to agree on financing. Western experts believed that one factor influencing Moscow was disapproval of the project by East Germany, an ally of the U.S.S.R. In August there was open friction between East and West Germany when East German border officials stopped a dozen buses carrying West Germans to West Berlin for a rally to protest the continued existence of the Berlin Wall.

During March Egyptian President Anwar el-Sadat made a political visit to West Germany. He appealed for official support for the Palestine Liberation Organization. Chancellor Schmidt declined to agree to that and also refused to sell arms to Egypt. Schmidt did agree, however, to grant Egypt a substantial amount of economic aid.

See STATISTICS OF THE WORLD. F.W.

GHANA. Beset by economic stagnation and continued inflation in Ghana, the government of Gen. I. K. Acheampong tried in 1976 to bolster its popular support. Kofi Awoonor, the novelist and poet, was arrested in February; although the government refused to cite charges against him, the arrest was thought to have been prompted by the dedication of his new book, *The Breast of the Earth,* to Kwame Nkrumah, the late Ghanaian president, who had been deposed in 1966. International protests finally won Awoonor his release in October. In March assets valued at $350,000 were seized from former Prime Minister Kofi Busia, after a special government committee declared them improperly acquired. This seizure, together with the cancellation of an April visit by United States Secretary of State Henry A. Kissinger and the withdrawal of Ghanaians from the Summer Olympic Games in a racial protest, won the government the grudging support of students and the political Left. At the same time, the government mounted a publicity campaign in the Volta region against a secessionist movement aimed at joining the region to Togo. Tensions in the region mounted during the summer after the conviction of five secessionist leaders accused of plotting to overthrow Acheampong.

In July the European Economic Community allotted $6,100,000 to Ghana to compensate for the loss of export earnings resulting from price fluctuations. Also during 1976, West Germany loaned the nation more than $134,000,000, and the World Bank made a loan of $21,000,000 for Ghana's agricultural development.

See STATISTICS OF THE WORLD. *See also* AFRICA. J.T.S.

GISCARD D'ESTAING, VALÉRY. *See* PEOPLE IN THE NEWS.

GREAT BRITAIN, officially the UNITED KINGDOM OF GREAT BRITAIN AND NORTHERN IRELAND. The British economy suffered staggering blows in 1976, with the country experiencing the worst drought in 200 years and the pound sinking to the lowest level in history. Perhaps because of such difficulties, Prime Minister Harold Wilson resigned, though his Labour Party remained in power. The opposition Conservatives used the economic crisis as a weapon in their struggle to regain control of the government.

Politics and Domestic Affairs. Sixty-year-old Prime Minister Wilson jolted the nation in March when he announced his retirement (*see* PEOPLE IN THE NEWS). He told Britons that he had made up his mind two years before, but apart from saying that he wanted to give others a chance to lead the country, he gave no convincing explanation of his surprise move.

Following Wilson's decision, the 317 Labour Party members of Parliament balloted for his successor as party leader and thus prime minister. A first round of voting produced no candidate with the required majority, although Michael Foot, a champion of the party's left wing, was the frontrunner, followed by Foreign Secretary James Callaghan, a moderate. Early in April, after the third round of voting, Callaghan emerged as victor. He

immediately assumed the prime ministership and announced a cabinet that was essentially a reshuffling of the Wilson team. In September he made further cabinet changes.

The rest of the year Callaghan, like Wilson, was forced to draft even ailing party members to take part in parliamentary votes, since the ruling Labourites held only a slim margin in the House of Commons. By the end of the year, by-elections had reduced Labour's majority in the House of Commons to a single vote.

The opposition Conservatives in the House pressed the Labour government at every opportunity. Given the country's severe economic problems and the slimness of the Labour majority, Conservative Party leader Margaret Thatcher repeatedly demanded that Labour call for new elections. In October former Prime Minister Edward Heath, the man Margaret Thatcher had replaced as party leader, appeared at the annual Conservative Party conference in Brighton to make peace with his successor after a year of noticeable cool-

Evidence of Great Britain's worst drought in more than 200 years. This picture of the Thames, England's mightiest river, was taken on Aug. 18 at Strand-on-the-Green, near London.

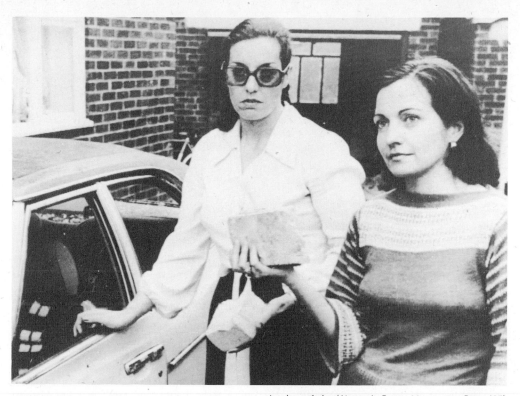

Leaders of the Women's Peace Movement, Betty Williams (left) and Mairead Corrigan, stand beside the car in which they were riding on Oct. 10 on their way to a meeting in Belfast, Northern Ireland. The car was damaged when a mob attacked the two women.

ness. In the view of many political analysts, Heath's move was aimed at strengthening the Conservative hand in the event of new elections. Perhaps such solidarity paid off in the Nov. 4 by-elections, which gave the Conservatives two more House seats and significant gains elsewhere.

The small Liberal Party was rocked by scandal early in the year when its leader of nine years, Jeremy Thorpe, became involved in a widely publicized allegation of sexual misconduct. Under mounting pressure, Thorpe resigned in May and was replaced two months later by David Steel, a 38-year-old Scottish journalist.

The question of "devolution" continued to occupy Britain's politicians. Essentially, devolution was an answer to ethnic nationalist demands for more local autonomy. In 1975 Prime Minister Wilson had announced a plan to give new Scottish and Welsh assemblies authority over local matters such as health and education. In November, 1976, the Labour government introduced legislation in Parliament aimed at making devolution a reality.

Racial tension boiled to the surface during a Caribbean street carnival in London's Notting Hill section on Aug. 30. Hundreds of black youths attacked police in the racially mixed residential area, resulting in 66 arrests and 120 injured police officers.

Northern Ireland. Continued rule over Northern Ireland was a strain on the British political and economic fabric. A constitutional convention charged with devising a new system of government acceptable to both Catholics and Protestants in Northern Ireland failed; it was dissolved in March, and London continued to administer the strife-torn province through its Secretary of State for Northern Ireland. Prime Minister Callaghan made a visit to the province during July to confer with local leaders. A few days later, Christopher Ewart-Biggs, British ambassador to the Irish Republic, was killed by a bomb planted by Irish Catholic extremists. Because of the human and economic cost of administering Northern Ireland, Britons debated the wisdom of maintaining the British presence there.

One notable effort to end the tragic conflict was the Women's Peace Movement, founded during the summer by Betty Williams, an Ulster housewife, and her associate, Mairead Corrigan. Roman Catholic and Protestant members of the growing movement joined in mass demonstra-

London police carry off a black youth, one of dozens charged with attacking the officers during a street carnival in the Notting Hill area on Aug. 30.

tions of public prayers, hymn singing, and extended marches to show their solidarity. Opposition to their efforts was strong and occasionally violent.

Another of the many obstacles to peace occurred late in October when Maire Drumm, former vice-president of the Provisional Sinn Fein, political arm of the Irish Republican Army, was shot to death in a Belfast hospital where she had been recuperating from an eye operation. Although the Roman Catholic activist had been called "Grandma Venom" by British troops and Protestant extremists alike, her murder was strongly condemned by both groups.

The Economy. The economy was the government's prime concern in 1976. Simply put, the British economy was no longer able to meet the requirements of its people for imports or for governmental and social services. The long-range outlook seemed promising; within a few years, North Sea oil would bolster the nation's earnings. In the meantime, however, Britain was financially strapped.

As inflation persisted at an annual rate of 14 percent, Britons continued to lose purchasing power. The pound came under constant pressure, dropping on Oct. 28 to a dollar value of $1.5090, the lowest level in history. Unemployment hit 1,500,000, or 6 percent of the labor force, the highest level since World War II. During the summer a severe drought in southern Britain, said to be the worst in at least 200 years, decimated crops

A New Leader Well-Schooled in Politics
Following Harold Wilson's surprise announcement of his resignation in March, the ruling Labour Party chose James "Sunny Jim" Callaghan, 50, to become Britain's fiftieth prime minister. Highly regarded for his politician's "common touch"—but less well thought of as a problem solver—Callaghan dropped out of school at 15 to support his widowed mother, won his first Parliament seat in 1945 after gaining influence as a trade union official, and went on to fill several top cabinet posts under Wilson. As he moved into 10 Downing Street, Callaghan had two main tasks: to keep inflation down and to keep the falling pound up.

James Callaghan, prime minister of Great Britain.

and added to the country's economic woes. Britain's economic growth rate remained at less than 3 percent annually, about half that of other Western countries. In late September Chancellor Denis Healey announced that Britain would apply for a loan of $3.9 billion from the International Monetary Fund, the third such loan in less than a year.

The Labour government attempted to deal with the crisis by holding down public spending and borrowing abroad to bolster the pound. In December the government announced cuts totaling $4.2 billion over the next two years. Reductions would be made in defense spending, foreign aid, school lunch programs, and housing. New taxes would be added on cigarettes, beer, and whiskey, and the government promised to sell off some $800,000,000 worth of its holdings in British Petroleum. Labour programs at the end of 1976 called for nationalization of the aircraft and shipping industries and the elimination of schools for brighter pupils and beds for private patients in government-subsidized hospitals.

Foreign Relations. Britain celebrated the 200th anniversary of the American Revolution with magnanimity and goodwill. The nation loaned America one of the rare original copies of the Magna Charta, a cornerstone of Western democracy. In July Queen Elizabeth and Prince Philip traveled to the United States for an extensive tour and were warmly received.

Britain moved to integrate its overall trade with that of the European Economic Community (Common Market). In January tariffs between Great Britain and the original six Common Market members were reduced by a further 20 percent, bringing the reduction since British entry into the Common Market to 80 percent. During June a visit to London by French President Valéry Giscard d'Estaing laid the foundation for closer ties between Britain and France.

Africa was another focal point of British diplomacy. In February the Wilson government announced it would recognize the controversial leftist People's Republic of Angola under Agostinho Neto. During July Britain broke relations with Uganda over the matter of Dora Bloch, a British-Israeli national who disappeared and was reportedly murdered during the hijacking of a French plane by Palestinian terrorists at Uganda's main airport.

The status of the former British-administered territory of Rhodesia continued to cause concern. (See AFRICA; COMMONWEALTH OF NATIONS; RHODESIA.) In March James Callaghan, then Britain's foreign secretary, proposed a constitutional settlement that in two years would transfer power to Rhodesia's black majority. The proposal became the basis of U.S. Secretary of State Henry A. Kissinger's negotiations between Rhodesia's Blacks and the ruling Whites. In October, after Rhodesian Prime Minister Ian Smith agreed in principle to majority rule, Britain convened a conference in Geneva to vote on an agreement for the transfer of power. Because of Smith's obstinacy and divisions among the Blacks themselves, progress was slow; the conferees adjourned in December.

See STATISTICS OF THE WORLD. F.W.

GREECE. Labor violence flared briefly in Greece in 1976; educational reforms were decreed. Meanwhile, the strife between Greece and Turkey over the partition of the island of Cyprus continued.

Domestic Affairs. The national minimum wage was raised a total of 17 percent in two steps under an award granted by an official arbitration court on Feb. 19. On July 1 the minimum daily wage for men was increased to $7.35 and that for women to $6.85. Under a government decision the pay of the two sexes would gradually be equalized.

A limited national strike erupted on May 24 in protest against the parliament's approval of a labor bill drastically limiting the right to strike. According to the government, only about 120,000 workers, less than 10 percent of the work force, participated in the walkout. Press reports estimated the number at 150,000. Violence broke out on May 25 when about 10,000 strikers attempted to march on parliament. In clashes with police, one person was killed and more than 100 injured.

A program of sweeping educational reforms was decreed by the government of Premier Constantine Karamanlis in January. The most controversial reform designated the modern, or Demotic, form of the Greek language as the official language of instruction up to the university level. This decision was a defeat for supporters of Katharevusa, the literary form of the language, previously used in all higher school grades. The program also provided for extending compulsory education from six years to nine.

Demetrios Ioannides, former military dictator of Greece, was convicted of conspiracy in the unsuccessful military revolt of February, 1975. Ioannides, already serving a number of prison sentences, including two concurrent life terms, was sentenced by a criminal court in Piraeus to an additional fourteen years in prison.

Foreign Affairs. Greece was reported in January to have bought 500,000 tons of crude oil from the Soviet Union for about $42,000,000. Greece agreed to pay half in convertible currency and half in farm commodities. It was also made known that the Greek Public Power Corp. had contracted with the Soviet trade firm Energomachexport to build two 300-megawatt units

177

for the thermonuclear plant at Ptolemaïs in northern Greece.

On the invitation of Premier Karamanlis, delegates from Turkey, Yugoslavia, Rumania, and Bulgaria met with Greek leaders in Athens from Jan. 26 through Feb. 5. This first conference on Balkan cooperation since World War II was attended by all Balkan nations except Albania, which stated its preference for developing bilateral rather than regional relations.

Greek and United States negotiators in Washington, D.C., agreed "in principle" on April 15 on continued U.S. operation of four military bases in Greece in exchange for $700,000,000 worth of military aid to Greece. Still smarting over Turkey's invasion of Cyprus in 1974 and its continued occupation of 40 percent of the island, Greece first protested a similar U.S.-Turkey agreement signed three weeks earlier. Greece was also contending with Turkey for control of oil reserves under the Aegean Sea.

See STATISTICS OF THE WORLD. L.A.S.

GRENADA. See STATISTICS OF THE WORLD.

GUAM. See STATISTICS OF THE WORLD.

GUATEMALA. On Feb. 4, 1976, an earthquake measuring 7.5 on the Richter scale rocked Guatemala City, the capital of Guatemala, and the surrounding countryside. It left approximately 23,000 people dead, 77,000 injured, and more than 1,000,000 homeless. Material damage was estimated at $750,000,000. Aid programs were mounted by the United States, Venezuela, the United Nations Disaster Relief Office, and the Organization of American States.

Despite the staggering human loss and suffering, the industrial and agricultural sectors of the country's economy came through the quake and subsequent tremors relatively unscathed. The major disruption to the economy was caused by the blockage of roads and rail lines between the ports and the interior.

Overall, the economy registered strong gains, due to favorable world prices for coffee and most of Guatemala's other agricultural export commodities. Some of the economic boost was provided by a 39.4 percent increase in the budget and the inflow of $360,000,000 in foreign aid and grants to pay for the post-earthquake reconstruc-

tion effort. Legislation establishing a 200-mi. exclusive offshore economic zone was approved on June 11.

Politically, an upsurge in violence and terrorist activity occurred in the second half of the year. Several assassination plots against both leftist and rightist politicians were reported, and for the first time in four years a left-wing guerrilla group, known as the Guatemalan Army of the Poor, emerged. In addition, President Kjell Eugenio Laugerud García faced widespread criticism and lack of cooperation from right-wing military elements because he appointed a liberal to head the National Reconstruction Committee.

See STATISTICS OF THE WORLD. A.K.M.

GUINEA-BISSAU. In 1976, the second year of its independence from Portugal, Guinea-Bissau seemed to retire from the world's view to concentrate on economic and social development and on healing the wounds of the long colonial war. During 1976, factions hostile to the ruling African Party for the Independence of Guinea and the Cape Verde Islands continued their attacks against the new government. Using neighboring Senegal as a staging area, the opposition launched armed raids into Guinea-Bissau. Following diplomatic protests, the Senegalese army made a border sweep in March and captured between 150 and 200 Guinean rebels. Some of these were turned over to the Guinean government, and the opposition's attacks temporarily subsided.

Economic development was aided in 1976 by a $9,200,000 loan from Sweden for technical assistance and a $2,000,000 loan from Great Britain. In March a new currency, the peso, was issued in Guinea to replace the escudo. In an effort to support the peso, the government froze the assets of the Guinea-Bissau branch of the National Ultramarine Bank, Portugal's overseas issuing bank. The Portuguese quickly retaliated by suspending all payments to the branch. Despite diplomatic repercussions, however, the peso at year's end appeared safely launched.

See STATISTICS OF THE WORLD. See also AFRICA. J.T.S.

GUINEA, REPUBLIC OF. See STATISTICS OF THE WORLD.

GUYANA. See STATISTICS OF THE WORLD.

H

HEALTH AND MEDICINE

Swine flu, the Legionnaires disease, and controversies over mammographic screening and social drinking for alcoholics—these were the headline subjects. Meanwhile, major gains were quietly made in combating familiar ailments ranging from cancer to tooth decay.

Medical science in 1976 projected a paradoxical image. At a time when its powers and achievements were never more evident, its limitations and uncertainties were also clearly exposed. Signs of continuing medical advance in the United States were abundant in terms of Nobel Prizes, innovative surgical techniques, and new drug therapies. Yet in 1976 a mysterious disease could strike more than 200 people at a convention and not be identified despite intensive months-long analysis by medical scientists employing the most sophisticated tools available to modern science. The same U.S. surgical establishment hailed for such modern miracles as vital-organ transplants and pacemakers was shaken by accusations of unnecessary surgery and unsatisfactory quality, as well as by a record number of malpractice suits. Medical scientists were sharply divided on the need for a vaccination program against swine flu, on the benefits and risk of mammography in cancer detection, and on a variety of issues in medical ethics, including the medical grounds that justify the rights of patients to die and the rights of researchers to undertake genetic engineering experiments.

Many critical reports made it clear that a significant share of the uncertainties in 20th-century medicine derived from the influences of economic, political, legal, and ethical factors on medical practice.

MEDICINE

Significant declines in deaths from cardiovascular diseases and accidents increased life expectancy in the U.S. by half a year. Unusual epidemic threats engaged the efforts of many public health specialists, physicians, and researchers during the year, while some more familiar maladies showed promise of yielding to new drug treatment.

Death Rate Decline. The death rate in the U.S. declined in 1975, the most recent year for which final figures were available. Deaths dropped 2.2 percent to 9 per 1000 persons, the lowest rate since 1900, when record keeping began. Total life expectancy in the nation rose from 71.9 years to 72.4 years.

The major contributors to the declining death rate, according to a 1976 analysis by the National Center for Health Statistics, were lower mortality levels in three of the four leading causes of death: diseases of the heart, cerebral-vascular diseases, and accidents (most notably, fewer automobile fatalities due to the lowered speed limits). Cancer, the second leading cause of death, continued to be the exception; the center anticipated that when the gathering of 1975 data was completed, deaths from cancer would rise to the highest level ever recorded. This rise would occur despite a cure rate of 47 percent of all patients, double that of ten years ago.

Swine Flu. In February, 1976, during what was thought to be a routine outbreak of influenza at Fort Dix, N.J., a soldier died. Subsequent laboratory analyses showed that the infectious organism was similar to the swine strain of influenza virus, the lethal agent of the 1918 pandemic (large-scale epidemic) that took a toll of 548,000 lives in the U.S. alone. This finding sent out an ominous signal to epidemiologic experts. Without vaccination, the population born since 1918 would have little or no protection against the swine flu strain. The director of the Public Health Service's Center for Disease Control (C.D.C.) called a special meeting of its Advisory Committee on Immunization Practices, composed of the country's foremost experts in this field. A recommendation for a national vaccination campaign was subsequently sent forward through governmental channels.

The dilemma that faced public health officials came down to this: If no swine flu epidemic at all occurred, and the Fort Dix incident proved to be an isolated peculiarity, the vaccine and the whole program would have been an embarrassing waste of medical and financial resources. If, on the other hand, a swine flu pandemic hit and the vaccination program had not been undertaken, the potential of providing a national lifesaver of

Disguised as an indigent patient and loaded with drugs for a nonexistent ailment, Sen. Frank Moss (D, Utah) leaves a "Medicaid mill" in the East Harlem section of New York City on Aug. 30. Moss, chairman of the Senate Subcommittee on Long-Term Care, reported on such Medicaid abuses as wrong diagnoses, extensive referrals, and needless batteries of X-ray and blood tests.

unprecedented proportions would have been lost.

On March 24 President Gerald R. Ford announced that he would ask the U.S. Congress for an immediate appropriation of $135,000,000 to buy enough vaccine to inoculate "every man, woman, and child in the United States." Although the appropriation was granted, considerable controversy ensued. Medical scientists debated whether the swine flu would actually return in force and with as much severity as in 1918; some skeptics viewed the proposal in terms of election year politics. Vaccine manufacturers, wary of malpractice claims, demanded protection against liability suits from vaccinated persons before undertaking the massive production effort. The issue was settled when a number of veterans at an American Legion convention in Philadelphia fell victim to a mysterious and deadly disease (see *Legion Disease*, below). Early reports (later proved erroneous) indicated swine flu. Congress acted rapidly to remove the vaccine manufacturing roadblock; it passed a law which, in the absence of proven negligence, made the government responsible for the settlement of malpractice claims in connection with the vaccination program. But problems continued. One manufacturer inadvertently turned out 3,000,000 doses of a variant vaccine. Disputes erupted over the legal and consumer rights aspects of the "implied consent" forms to be signed by those vaccinated. Further scientific controversy arose when results of early field trials indicated that the vaccine provided a lower degree of effectiveness and higher frequency of side effects among children.

Despite the difficulties the program got under way in October with initial vaccine supplies reaching all states. But it was not long before the trouble that had dogged the program from the beginning struck again. Two weeks after vaccination had begun, a report came that three elderly people in Pittsburgh had died within hours of being vaccinated. Pennsylvania halted its program pending investigation. Soon additional deaths in other states were reported, and ten more states announced suspension of the program. However, autopsies and other investigations produced no evidence of connection between vaccination and the deaths. Tests showed nothing wrong with the vaccine. More than 1,000,000 people had been vaccinated and the number of adverse reactions was minimal. Also, as the C.D.C. pointed out, the initial vaccination effort concentrated heavily on those over sixty-five, and the deaths of elderly vaccine recipients were well within the statistical averages for that group. Within a week all of the states that had suspended the program, including Pennsylvania, were back in operation. But public response was poor until other incidents of swine flu were reported in late November in Concordia, Mo., and near Brodhead, Wis. A subsequent outbreak of Guillain-Barré syndrome, a paralyzing disease, with a majority of the 94 cases occurring among those vaccinated, led to a final suspension of the program on Dec. 16.

Legionnaires Disease. The Pennsylvania state convention of the American Legion was held in Philadelphia on July 21-24. A legionnaire from Tonawanda, N.Y., returned home on July 27 suffering from headache, chest pain, lung congestion, and high fever. Admitted to a local hospital, he died soon after. Then a physician in Bloomsburg, Pa., noticed that three of his patients who had similar respiratory symptoms had been to the convention together. Reports began to pour in from various parts of Pennsylvania, and the final toll was 180 cases and 29 deaths. All the victims attended the American Legion convention in Philadelphia or had visited the headquarters hotel, the Bellevue Stratford. The state health agency in collaboration with the Epidemic Intelligence Service of the C.D.C. undertook an intensive effort to identify the cause. Special surveys were made to track patterns of food, drink, room locations, and illness in household contacts of the legionnaire victims. At the C.D.C. in Atlanta a multidisciplinary team of laboratory scientists brought to bear the full technological armament of modern medical science,

from electron microscopic searches for infectious agents to gas chromatographic testing for toxic substances. Swine flu was ruled out early, but the toxicological testing proved ambiguous because of the limited number of experts who specialize in identifying toxic diseases. After months of effort no answer could be found for the cause of the mysterious malady. As the C.D.C. report tersely put it, "The epidemic curve suggests a common source exposure but the source and the agent have not been identified. There is no evidence of person-to-person spread. . . . Surveillance of guests in several hotels has yielded no evidence of a continuing epidemic." The publicity given the Bellevue Stratford, however, caused the public to shun it, and the hotel shut down permanently in November.

Green Monkey Fever. Epidemiologists were faced with a third crisis in October, when Zaire and the Sudan reported 335 deaths from a dangerous new disease that caused high fevers and internal bleeding. Many of the nurses and doctors giving aid in the epidemic became victims themselves. Prompt action by the United Nations World Health Organization, joined by researchers from the U.S., Great Britain, Belgium, and several other countries, led to identification of the disease and its strict containment by late November.

The infectious agent was found to be a variant of the "green monkey" fever virus, first cited in 1967 when it struck thirty laboratory technicians in Marburg, West Germany, who were working with green monkeys imported from Kenya and

On Aug. 5 American Legionnaires of Williamstown, Pa., carry the flag-draped coffin of fellow veteran J. B. Ralph. He was one of twenty-nine persons who died of an unidentified disease apparently contracted at a legion convention held in Philadelphia in July.

Donald Harris, a 23-year-old worker on a Wisconsin pig farm, became in November the first confirmed victim of swine flu after the February outbreak in New Jersey. Harris recovered in a few days.

Uganda. Seven technicians died in the Marburg outbreak. Deeply concerned by the severity of the new epidemic, teams of scientists took up the task of finding out how the infection spreads and how to prevent and treat it.

Levamisole: Next Wonder Drug? In 1976 a number of reports emerged about a therapeutic agent that could be the next candidate for wonder drug status. The drug, known as levamisole, is a thiazole derivative (tetrahydro-phenylimidazo-thiazole-hydrochloride) that is widely used in the worming of pets. When animal studies by French investigators demonstrated that levamisole increased cellular immunity, the discovery aroused great interest, for it suggested a new defense system against many kinds of stubborn diseases. Unlike vaccines, which stimulate the production of antibodies that circulate in the bloodstream to prevent specific diseases, or antibiotics, which destroy bacteria directly, the new drug may arouse from within cells a wide-ranging resistance to foreign invasion. Clinical trials undertaken in Argentina, England, and Belgium reported positive results in the treatment of breast cancer, rheumatoid arthritis, and upper respiratory infections in children. Other current studies indicated that the drug could be useful in treating a wide range of other diseases, including stubborn and recurring infections such as herpes virus sores and staphylococcal abscesses. Levamisole also seems to be effective in restoring the body's defenses after therapy for cancer or transplant surgery have

impaired bone-marrow function and lowered disease resistance.

Not all the clinical trials with the drug reported positive results. No improvement was seen in cancer patients in the U.S., although U.S. researchers had marked success with herpes and stomatitis (mouth) infections. Even in the most promising of studies, investigators emphasized that much more needed to be learned about how levamisole works, how it should be used, and how to overcome the pervasive side effects of loss of appetite, nausea, diarrhea, nervousness, and fatigue. On balance the evidence indicated that levamisole had shown enough promise to justify real hope that it could help ease some of the most distressing disease burdens of our time that have not yielded to other forms of treatment.

New Hope for Cancer Patients. At an American Cancer Society seminar on major developments in the fight against cancer, new hope was raised for treating one of the deadliest lung cancers, known as "oat cell" cancer. Usually affecting heavy smokers, it spreads with great rapidity and has one of the most dismal prognoses. Half the patients live 6 months or less after this disease is diagnosed. Research findings of the National Cancer Institute (N.C.I.) reported unprecedented positive results with a group of 27 patients treated under an extremely intensive regimen combining drugs and radiation. After 3 weeks of intensive radiotherapy, the patients received 3 months of treatment with 3 of the most potent chemotherapeutic agents available: adriamycin, cyclophosphamide, and vincristine. The preliminary results of this therapy were impressive; 21 of 27 patients so treated have remained free of cancer for up to 14 months. This compares with a rate of 1 in 4 oat cell cancer patients who showed good initial response to the conventional treatment regimen.

Another promising report came from Italy, where researchers conducted a controlled study using an N.C.I.-developed combination drug therapy for breast-cancer patients after they had undergone mastectomy (radical breast surgery). A group of patients receiving a three-drug combination (cyclophosphamide, methotrexate, and 5-fluorouracil) for a year following mastectomy had only 5.3 percent recurrence of cancer against 24 percent for a control group receiving surgery alone. Enthusiastic N.C.I. officials were testing this and other chemotherapeutic regimens in their network of cancer centers in the U.S.

Mammography Dispute. A controversy among medical experts in 1976 brought into question a nationwide program of annual mammographic screening for breast cancer in which 270,000 women were participating. The program had been initiated several years earlier by the American Cancer Society and the N.C.I. In July a group of physicians led by an eminent public health expert, Dr. Lester Breslow, dean of the School of Public Health at the University of California at Los Angeles, expressed concern that the exposure to radiation in the screening itself might be increasing the risk of breast cancer among participants. They presented estimates indicating that mammographic screening of 100,000 women could be expected to save 19 lives and cause 3 new cancer cases in the over-50 age-group, but that among younger women only 3 lives would be saved and 15 new cases caused. Other experts immediately protested that the radiation dose received was so low as to present a negligible risk and that the doubts expressed would scare off women who had a special need for such surveillance. The policymakers for the screening project responded to the debate with a commonsense approach: Pending further study, the mammogram was to be given routinely only to women over 50 and to those under 50 who were estimated to be of greater than average risk (for example, those with a family history of breast cancer).

The incident was reminiscent of the mass X-ray program for tuberculosis detection three decades earlier. Originally planned to provide periodic chest X rays for the whole population, the process was phased out after a few years in favor of a more selective approach involving high-risk populations because of the fear of unnecessary radiation exposure.

The Right to Die. The year began with 21-year-old Karen Anne Quinlan still in a respirator, after one full year in a coma. In March the New Jersey Supreme Court ruled favorably on her parents' widely publicized petition that the life-supporting respirator be removed without legal liability to allow her to "die with dignity." Paradoxically, she continued to live after the respirator support was removed. A significant legal precedent had been established, however. By the end of 1976 the nation's first right-to-die law was on the books in California, allowing physicians to shut off life-support equipment where death is imminent and a "living will" authorization has been signed by the patient. *See* STATE LEGISLATIVE REVIEW: *Medicine.* Increasing concern with such ethical issues generated the first encyclopedia in bioethics ever produced. It was scheduled for publication in 1977 by the Kennedy Institute of Georgetown University.   R.R.H. & S.J.A.

DENTISTRY

Encouraging results were reported in 1976 on efforts to find a vaccine against tooth decay. Also of interest to dentists were the application of laser techniques to dental repair work and a study suggesting that adults as well as children could be treated with orthodontic devices.

Tooth Decay Vaccine. A University of Alabama research team reported experimental success with an oral vaccine that induces the production of antibodies against a principal tooth-decaying agent, *Streptococcus mutans.* Earlier studies had shown that a vaccine could be injected into the oral mucosa, salivary glands, or parotid duct to stimulate antibody production, but these inoculations proved to be painful and therefore not likely to be useful. In the Alabama tests the vaccine was made up of killed cells of *S. mutans* and was administered in the drinking water of germ-free rats. The scientists were hopeful that their research would lead in a few years' time to an oral medication that can boost the protection level of antibodies in humans and thereby significantly reduce tooth decay.

New Laser Application. A State University of New York dental scientist, A. M. Patrignani, reported during the year that the laser may replace etching by acid, now used to prepare tooth surfaces for holding resin fillings. Although in preliminary studies the laser-etched surfaces did not yet produce as durable a bond as those that were acid etched, the advantages of laser etching were clear. The adherence of resin fillings when appearance is important depends on the tooth surface being "pebbled," or roughened, as no cement or additional material is used to hold the filling in place. With the laser dentists can accurately target the area to be etched, whereas the application of acid is less precise and the substance may trickle onto the surrounding soft tissues of the mouth. The laser technique also saves time, since only 2 millisec. are required to create the pebbling, compared with 60 to 90 sec. for acid etching.

The Liveliest Flavor Is Lime

At McMaster University, Hamilton, Ontario, a somewhat grisly but definitely thought-provoking experiment was conducted in March. Electrodes were introduced into a bowl of flavored gelatin; an electroencephalogram (EEG) was taken. (An EEG is often the final test made on a patient near death.) The needle moved; the resultant graph showed what would usually be read as evidence of life. The explanation: stray impulses caused by movement of people and by nearby equipment had been picked up and recorded.

Adult Orthodontic Treatment. University of Washington dental scientists discovered new evidence for applying orthodontic treatment to adults as well as children. Studies indicated that although skeletal development is generally completed by one's early twenties, the upper jaw does not completely unite with the frontal bone of the skull until persons are over 70 years of age. Thus it is possible to treat adult patients who have protrusion of the upper jaw or similar facial disfigurement. Henceforth orthodontists will be more encouraged to use the traditional orthodontic appliances instead of, or in addition to, corrective surgery for mid-face problems in adult patients.   J.A.B.

REHABILITATION

Growing world attention to the problems of disability was demonstrated during 1976 in major international forums. Gains were made by the disabled through improved devices and more responsive programs.

United Nations Developments. The U.N. General Assembly, for the second consecutive year, enacted resolutions on the subject of disability. One was designed to bring about implementation of the rights of disabled persons, as set forth in a 1975 declaration. A second resolution named 1981 the International Year for Disabled Persons.

Among the agencies and affiliates of the U.N.,

A panel tests the taste of the less hazardous 1976-style cigarettes developed by the National Cancer Institute. By artificially putting back flavor components, the institute hopes to win acceptance for the cigarettes from the 55,000,000 Americans who still smoke despite cancer warnings.

the annual assembly of the World Health Organization established a new policy placing emphasis on the prevention of all forms of disability and on the integration of rehabilitation into all community services. The General Conference of the U.N. Educational, Scientific, and Cultural Organization (UNESCO) approved a protocol to the "Florence Agreement" on the importation of educational, scientific, and cultural materials that provides for the duty-free entry of items needed by physically or mentally handicapped persons into countries acceding to the agreement. HABITAT, the U.N. Conference on Human Settlements, which was held in Vancouver, Canada, in May, included special design features for increasing the independence and mobility of the disabled and the elderly in each of its major action recommendations.

U.S. Programs. In the U.S. the emphasis placed on services for the severely disabled by the Vocational Rehabilitation Act of 1973 began to show significant results. Of all persons successfully rehabilitated in the federal-state programs, 41 percent were derived from the severely disabled categories, an increase of more than 7 percent over 1975.

Throughout the country the disabled persons themselves and their organizations played a more important role in 1976 in the definition and the management of the programs that were designed to aid them. A significant action in this regard was a grant by the Rehabilitation Services Administration of the U.S. Department of Health, Education, and Welfare to foster such developments. An allocation of $59,400 was made for this purpose to the

A blind student at the University of Utah is enabled to see changing patterns of light through electric stimulation of his brain's visual center. A portable computer-and-camera system that will permit the blind to distinguish people and objects and even read is also being developed.

American Coalition of Citizens with Disabilities, the first organization to speak for most of the nation's physically disabled population.

In the area of education Congress passed the Education of All Handicapped Children Act. It required all states to provide "free, appropriate education" for all handicapped students by 1978. This legislation reinforced a trend to educate severely handicapped children in regular classrooms or in special classes of normal schools rather than in separate institutions.

Improved Devices. Applications of modern technology brought increasing benefits to persons with serious limitations in mobility or communication functions. New electronic devices that could be controlled by breath or pressure made possible an increased range of activity in daily life and work for those with upper-body paralysis; progress toward voice-controlled computers promised added advantages. Electrically operated artificial hands and arms were being used much more extensively than in the past, and the U.S. Veterans Administration was routinely fitting most arm amputees with hands that operate on electric impulses picked up and amplified directly from the muscles. Recently improved plastics made possible the fabrication of much lighter artificial limbs and braces, more comfortable to wear and less forbidding in appearance.   N.A.

MENTAL HEALTH
Mental health issues received wide-ranging pub-

lic attention during the year. A major report released by Congress emphasized the emotional effects of joblessness. Several studies on social drinking by cured alcoholics provoked heated public debate. And the mass media took up such difficult subjects as the treatment of the emotionally disturbed, the dying, and the severely disabled.

Effects of Unemployment. In the midst of continuing high levels of national unemployment, a study released by the Joint Economic Committee of Congress linked a 1.4 percent increase in joblessness in 1970 to a rise in mental illness, crime, and deaths over the following five years. The findings were based on methods, developed by M. Harvey Brenner and fellow researchers at Johns Hopkins University, that made it possible to trace the relationship between economic conditions and measures of national well-being. The study, expanded by Brenner from his previous work, attributed to the effects of unemployment in the U.S. over the five-year period 4.7 percent of the total number of mental hospital admissions, 5.7 percent of suicides, 5.6 percent of state prison admissions, 8 percent of murders, and 2.7 percent

185

of deaths from stress-related diseases of the heart and kidneys. The effects were significant for "all ages . . . for whites and nonwhites." The report also examined stress indications for England, Wales, and Sweden and found the same consistent relationship to the unemployment rate.

Alcoholism Controversy. A heated controversy within the nation's alcoholism treatment establishment erupted during the year when a study conducted by the Rand Corp., an independent research and development organization, suggested that, following treatment, a sizable number of alcoholics could return to moderate drinking without reverting to alcohol abuse. The Rand scientists maintained that the relapse rate among the 1340 alcoholics studied was no higher for those who abstained completely than for those who engaged in moderate drinking. Two related studies released later, one by researchers at the Addiction Research Foundation of Ontario, Canada, and the other at the University of Pennsylvania, gave support to the Rand findings.

Prominent alcohol treatment organizations vociferously refuted the reports. Officials of both the National Council on Alcoholism and of Alcoholics Anonymous, whose treatment approach has always been based on total abstinence for the recovered alcoholic, questioned the scientific validity of the Rand study and pointed to previous studies that drew the opposite conclusions. Dr. Nicholas Pace, president of the New York City affiliate of the National Council on Alcoholism, said, "A person cannot go back to controlled drinking when he has the disease of alcoholism. It's just not possible." Dr. Mary Pendry, head of the California State Alcoholism Advisory Board, also criticized the report, citing the "tragedy" that would result if any alcoholic "should be deterred in his recovery by experimenting with the return to alcohol."

Dr. David J. Armor, who prepared the Rand study, granted that alcoholics who fail in moderating their drinking or those who suffer "physical complications of alcohol" should not drink. He contended, however, that total abstinence "is a tenet that approaches the order of a religious belief," based on an emotional argument rather than scientific proof. Dr. Morris Chafetz, director of the National Institute of Alcohol Abuse and Alcoholism at the time it funded the Rand study, defended the findings: "As long as alcoholism treatment programs insist on abstinence, people who feel that alcohol must remain part of their lives will be discouraged from seeking treatment early in the disease. The alcoholic in remission who takes his first drink is also likely to label himself a failure, and this in itself may cause him to go on a binge."

Mental Health Themes in Mass Media. Motion pictures, television, and popular music contributed to the frank exploration of mental health issues during 1976. The highly popular motion picture *One Flew Over the Cuckoo's Nest*, which was honored with an Academy Award as the best motion picture of 1975, dealt with the institutional treatment of the mentally ill and with the

A scene from "Dying," a moving and highly acclaimed documentary presented on public television during the year. It showed how people, including "Bill" (left), faced their own approaching deaths.

definition of mental illness itself. On the home screen such popular television series as "Maude" and the satiric soap opera "Mary Hartman, Mary Hartman" featured episodes dealing with depression, anxiety, and mental breakdown. Television producer Norman Lear became the center of a considerable controversy when Maude took lithium, a drug prescribed by some practitioners for persons suffering with severe depression. Many mental health experts criticized this episode as oversimplifying both the treatment of depression and the use of a drug that should be administered with great caution and only under the most controlled and supervised conditions.

Mental health reached even into the field of popular music. Barry Manilow's recording of "Feelings," a soulful lament on the need to share emotional experiences openly, became one of the year's best-selling records.

Two special programs shown on public television stations explored difficult themes involving mental health. "Joey" was a dramatization of the life of a severe spastic who was institutionalized as a child when he was thought to be profoundly retarded and uneducable. The documentary portrayed Joey's personal efforts and eventual success in communicating with the outside world. The program graphically illustrated the untapped abilities and will to live of those who are often regarded as hopeless or useless.

"Dying," a documentary made by director Michael Roemer, presented three terminally ill cancer patients as they confronted death. Using *cinéma vérité* techniques, the camera sensitively recorded the experiences of these three persons in coping with their families, friends, and medical practitioners. Touching and often brutal, the widely acclaimed program took a significant step in promoting public discussion of attitudes toward death and how they affect the dying.

Benefits of Planned Relaxation. The physiological benefits of various antistress techniques, such as the relaxation method known as transcendental meditation (T.M.), were documented in several studies during the year. Dr. Herbert Benson, associate professor of medicine at Harvard Medical School, reported that the beneficial effects of T.M. include decreases in blood pressure and heart and respiratory rates and an increase in alpha brain wave activity, all of which are associated with relieving stress. T.M. continued to gain in popularity during the year. It was introduced in the U.S. by Maharishi Mahesh Yogi in the 1960's; its adherents can now be found even in the business community, where a number of companies were reported to have incorporated meditation breaks into the workday. Comparative studies during the year suggested, however, that the T.M. state was physiologically indistinguishable from quiet rest or a nap. P.D.B.

HEARST, PATRICIA. *See* PEOPLE IN THE NEWS.

HONDURAS. Keeping to its 1975 promise to return the government of Honduras to civilian rule, the military government of President Juan Alberto Melgar Castro issued a decree early in 1976 establishing a State Advisory Council, to be made up of seventy-eight members from all walks of political, economic, and social life. In addition to advising the president on economic and social matters, the council was charged with drafting a statute that would lead to the election of a constituent assembly. Despite this step toward civilian rule, the government postponed the date for national elections from September, 1977, to September, 1979.

The country's long-range economic prospects were substantially improved by the establishment of a program for the investment of $400,000,000 to develop its huge, untapped forestry resources. The project was to be funded by the Inter-American Development Bank, the Venezuelan Investment Fund, the Honduran government, and private Latin American sources.

A Feb. 4 earthquake damaged several towns and disrupted power supplies and some factories, but the damage was minor compared with that sustained in neighboring Guatemala (q.v.).

Relations with El Salvador (q.v.), strained since 1969, improved markedly toward the end of 1976. A peace treaty appeared possible by the April, 1977, annual meeting of the General Assembly of the Organization of American States.

See STATISTICS OF THE WORLD. A.K.M.

HONG KONG. *See* STATISTICS OF THE WORLD.

HUA KUO-FENG. *See* PEOPLE IN THE NEWS.

HUNGARY. No formal ceremonies were held in 1976 to mark the 20th anniversary of the Hungarian revolt. Its suppression by the Soviet Union in October, 1956, led to the installation of a government headed by Communist Party First Secretary János Kádár. Despite the brutal origins of his regime, Kádár had transformed Hungary into one of the most prosperous nations in the Soviet bloc. Kádár himself appeared to enjoy considerable public backing.

Concern for the consumer was one basis of Kádár's success. By 1976 two in three households had a refrigerator, a washing machine, and a television set, and the number of cars had doubled in five years. Nevertheless, because of inflation in the West and the mounting cost of oil imports from the Soviet Union, the Hungarian economy experienced some strain. To cut costs and stimulate food production, the government decided that subsidized food prices must be realigned. Kádár was careful to prepare the public for that move; an announcement was made seven months in advance, and the official press took pains to explain why the price hike was necessary. In July Hungarians quietly accepted increases in meat and fish prices averaging 30 percent. These were partially offset by increases in wages and social benefits.

The Kádár regime and the Roman Catholic Church took a major step toward reconciliation in February when, by mutual agreement, Mgr. Lászlo Lékai was installed as Roman Catholic archbishop of Esztergom and primate of Hungary. It was the first time those posts had been filled by a functioning prelate since 1948. Lékai became a cardinal in April.

Kádár continued to expand Hungary's economic ties with the West. Deputy Premier Gyula Szekér led a high-level economic delegation to the United States in May and to Great Britain in July. Premier György Lázár visited France during June. Lázár also exchanged formal visits with Chancellor Bruno Kreisky of Austria.

See STATISTICS OF THE WORLD.   F.W.

I

ICELAND. The long-standing disagreement between Iceland and Great Britain known as the cod war had heated up again in 1975; in 1976 it caused a three and one-half month break in diplomatic relations between the two countries.

In October, 1975, Iceland had barred foreign vessels from fishing in waters within 200 mi. of its coasts, and it reinforced this edict by challenging non-Icelandic trawlers that entered the disputed zone. When British fishing vessels inside the territorial waters were harassed in January, 1976, British warships promptly came to their rescue.

Iceland threatened at least three times during the month of January to cut diplomatic ties with Britain unless the British removed their warships, as well as the reconnaissance planes that made precautionary flights over the waters in which British fishermen were operating.

Various incidents of damaged nets and alleged ramming by Icelandic patrol craft took place at this time, and Iceland called a special session of the North Atlantic Treaty Organization (NATO) Council. At the meeting, held on Jan. 12, Iceland threatened to reassess its NATO commitments if the British ships did not leave at once. NATO Secretary-General Joseph M. A. H. Luns met separately with both parties. On Jan. 19 the British government announced that it was ordering its warships out of the disputed waters.

British-Icelandic talks were held from Jan. 24 to Jan. 27 in a vain attempt to agree on the amount of cod British fishermen could take in the Icelandic zone; on Feb. 12 Luns made a hurried trip to Reykjavík in an unsuccessful effort to explain Britain's position. Confrontation continued between Icelandic gunboats and British trawlers while the meetings went on.

The talks ended in disagreement, and on Feb. 19 Iceland cut off diplomatic relations with Great Britain. British frigates reentered the disputed area to protect the British trawlers; they remained there until May 30. An interim agreement ending the "cod war" was finally signed on June 1, and the two countries resumed diplomatic ties on June 3. The agreement set limits on the number of British trawlers permitted within the 200-mi. limit, and stated that they were to fish no closer than 20 mi. from the Icelandic coast.

In domestic matters more than 40,000 union workers had walked out on Feb. 17 in a general strike for higher pay and other benefits. The strike, which affected fishing and rail operations and communications facilities, was settled on Feb. 29.

See STATISTICS OF THE WORLD.   L.A.S.

IDAHO. *See* STATISTICS OF THE WORLD.

ILLINOIS. *See* STATISTICS OF THE WORLD.

INDIANA. *See* STATISTICS OF THE WORLD.

INDIANS, AMERICAN. The original inhabitants of the United States generally looked on the 1976 Bicentennial celebration with a skeptical eye. In fact over the Fourth of July holiday the Federal Bureau of Investigation issued a nationwide alert against possible Indian violence; it did not materialize. The Bicentennial year did bring legal efforts by various tribes to regain lands and rights lost years ago to white settlers. Dissidents among the nation's largest tribe, the Navaho, challenged the honesty and competence of the ruling coun-

Oglala Sioux tribal chairman Albert Trimble (right) is sworn in on April 12 by tribal elder Moses Two Bulls. Trimble, a reformer who promised to bring honesty and order to the troubled Pine Ridge, S.Dak., reservation, defeated incumbent President Richard Wilson in a federally supervised election.

cil. There was also a new recognition of the vast mineral resources lying beneath western reservation lands.

Land Claims. In Maine real estate transactions were virtually halted in the northern part of the state, pending hearings on the claims of the Passamaquoddy and Penobscot tribes to land amounting to nearly two thirds of the state. Tribal lawyers argued that the land had been acquired from the Indians by state governments without Congressional approval; such acquisition was outlawed by the Indian Intercourse Act of 1790. A similar suit to recover 16,000 acres was filed at Mashpee, Mass., on behalf of the Wampanoag tribe. These suits were at first not taken seriously, but as the strength of the Indians' cases became evident toward the end of the year, concern among white property owners grew. First hearings on the suits were scheduled for early 1977.

In Alaska, where native peoples are still in full possession of their land, further steps were taken to safeguard their rights and benefits. In January Congress passed a bill amending the 1971 Alaska Native Land Claims Settlement Act, authorizing additional benefits and exemptions for native corporations. The Roll of Alaskan Natives conditionally approved in December, 1974, was reopened for another year. Alaskan natives who were enrolled in their regional and village corporations were entitled to share in 40,000,000 acres of land as well as cash distributions of nearly $1 billion to

be made over a period of years. The Bureau of Indian Affairs publicized this settlement in the national media throughout the year in an effort to locate all Alaskan natives, wherever they might be living, and inform them of their settlement.

Other Legal Issues. A victory for tribal sovereignty was won in June. The U.S. Supreme Court ruled that states could not impose taxes on reservation Indians without prior Congressional approval. The case was that of a Minnesota Chippewa, Russell Bryan, who had contested a tax on his mobile home. Another court decision confirmed an 1890 award to the Yurok tribe in northern California of property rights to a 30 mi. corridor along the Klamath R. Legal conflicts had arisen over timber operations and the use of the river for traditional Indian net fishing, which interfered with recreation boating by Whites. In several states disputes continued over the rights of tribes to permit and control fishing on tribal lands.

In October a dispute arose over salmon fishing in Puget Sound. A 1974 U.S. district court decision had confirmed treaty provisions giving local tribes the right to one half of the dwindling fish harvest

A new arts and crafts center built, owned, and operated by the Tigua (or Tiwa) Indians of El Paso, Texas, was opened in July. Contrasting with the authentically reconstructed adobe walls of the pueblo is the bell tower of the Ysleta Mission, completed by Tigua labor in 1682.

each year. Since that time the portion actually taken by Indians had risen from 3 percent to 18 percent. Commercial and sport fishermen, resenting restrictions placed on them, demanded that the state of Washington buy out fishing rights from the tribes. The state refused.

Twenty-two western tribes, which joined in a loosely organized Council of Energy Resources Tribes, sent representatives to meet with Frank Zarb, federal energy administrator. The group's aim was to coordinate leasing policies among major land-holding tribes, which control 53,000,000 acres containing much of America's known uranium and low-sulfur coal resources. As a result of the meeting, some leases were being renegotiated.

Navaho Dissension. Over 600 Navahos gathered peaceably at Window Rock, Ariz., on May 18 to protest alleged corruption in tribal government and the dwindling of the tribe's reserve bank account. A delegation called for an investigatory committee, a reorganization of tribal government, and a moratorium on leasing of the tribe's natural resources. During the year a federal grand jury indicted at least eight Navaho officials in the mishandling of $13,000,000 in housing and urban development money. Navaho tribal chairman Peter MacDonald came under fire from the protesters, who accused him of making decisions without consulting the tribe's 150,000 members.   C.C.

INDIA, REPUBLIC OF. During 1976 the state of emergency that was proclaimed throughout India by President Fakhruddin Ali Ahmed on June 26, 1975, took on a look of permanence, as Prime Minister Indira Gandhi extended and consolidated the extraordinary powers conferred upon her. Opposition efforts were blunted through censorship of the news media and the detention of tens of thousands of persons.

Politics. By presidential decree on Jan. 8 the government suspended freedom of speech and six other basic rights guaranteed by the constitution. At the end of January the *Lok Sabha,* or lower house of parliament, voted to make government censorship of newspapers permanent by exempting it from judicial review even after the end of the emergency. This measure was followed, on Feb. 4, by a vote to delay national elections to the *Lok Sabha* for a year beyond March, 1976.

With twenty state governments already controlled by Indira Gandhi's Congress Party and its allies, the central government on Jan. 31 dismissed the Dravidian Progressive Federation government of Tamil Nadu State and imposed presidential rule. Gujarat, the last opposition stronghold, was taken over on March 12 when its coalition government collapsed.

On March 27, in elections held in the state legislatures for seats in the *Rajya Sabha,* or upper house of parliament, the Congress Party gained eighteen seats, thus achieving a two-thirds majority in that body. Since the party already commanded a two-thirds majority in the *Lok Sabha,* there seemed to be few constraints on its power. A supreme court decision on April 28 upheld the government's right to imprison political opponents without trial during the emergency, and on June 16 the Internal Security Act was amended by presidential ordinance to extend the permissible detention period from 12 to 24 months.

On Sept. 1 the government introduced a sweeping constitutional amendment bill in parliament. After an adjournment period, the *Lok Sabha*—with opposition members boycotting—passed the bill on Nov. 2 by a 366-4 vote. The *Rajya Sabha* approved it by 191-0 on Nov. 11. With only the approval of half the state legislatures and the signature of the president still required, ratification was a foregone conclusion. Meanwhile, parliament voted to postpone national elections for another year.

The constitution bill, in addition to rewriting the preamble, contained fifty-nine amendments, some of them critically important. The supreme court would still be permitted, by a two-thirds majority, to declare a federal law unconstitutional, but the lower courts were denied this power. Parliament would be permitted to ban antinational activities and associations. Most important of all, the president, acting at the prime minister's request, would have practically unlimited power to amend the constitution still further over the next two years. Indira Gandhi's victory appeared complete.

The Economy. The economy continued to do relatively well as a result of favorable weather conditions and more effective execution of government measures. In the agricultural year ending June 30, grain production reached a record 116,000,000 to 120,000,000 tons. With increased hydroelectric power production, a strike ban, and improved operation of the transport system, industrial output improved considerably. Inflation was curbed, and the prices of many essential commodities remained almost stationary. On Sept. 25 the government formally adopted a revised version of India's fifth five-year plan, envisioning total investments of $77 billion and emphasizing food, irrigation, and energy.

Population Control. India's family planning program finally moved into high gear. In February the central government announced that it would withhold various forms of assistance from government employees and New Delhi residents who failed to limit their families to two children. The program was later extended to include additional incentives, but it stopped short of direct coercion. In July, however, the Legislative Assembly of Maharashtra State (Bombay) passed a forced sterilization law, applicable to most couples after the third child. Other states enacted laws of varying severity. These programs encountered strong resistance, and at least fifty persons were reported killed in one clash in Uttar Pradesh. By late December, approximately 7,000,000 persons were sterilized. The government hoped to reduce the annual birthrate from 35 to 25 per 1000 population by 1986.

Foreign Relations. In April India and the People's Republic of China agreed to exchange ambassadors, thus opening the way to discussion of their border dispute. On May 14 India and Pakistan agreed to resume normal diplomatic relations in July and to restore rail, road, and air communications. Prime Minister Gandhi paid a five-day visit to the Soviet Union in June, to reaffirm ties with

A Dynasty in the Making?
Sanjay Gandhi is only 30, and he has never held a formal government job. But during the past year he has emerged as the second most powerful person in India next to his mother, Prime Minister Indira Gandhi. An auto designer by trade, Sanjay became an increasingly close adviser to his mother after she declared a state of emergency in 1975 and suspended civil liberties. As he travels politician-style around the country, he is now officially acknowledged as leader of the ruling Congress Party's youth wing; unofficially, "crown prince" Sanjay, whose grandfather Jawaharlal Nehru was India's first prime minister, is seen as his mother's logical successor.

Spokesman Sanjay Gandhi

that country. Meanwhile, relations with Bangladesh deteriorated, as Bangladesh accused India of assisting guerrillas within its borders and of diverting too much water from the Ganges R. Relations with the United States remained strained, and the U.S. government postponed a plan to resume economic assistance.

See STATISTICS OF THE WORLD.   W.J.G.

INDONESIA. A decade after he came to power, President Suharto appeared to be in firm control of Indonesia. In preparation for the parliamentary elections scheduled for May, 1977, the Suharto government continued to weed out and consolidate the dozens of political parties left over from the era of the late President Sukarno. As a result, this time Suharto's governing Sekber Golkar movement was to face only two opponents—the Indonesian Democratic Party, made up of the old Nationalist Party and various Christian parties, and the United Development Party, an alliance of Islamic groups.

In September the government announced that a plot to overthrow Suharto had been put down. Independent sources, however, said that the "plot" was nothing more than a call by a former government functionary and mystic, Sawito Kartowi Bowo, for the president to resign. The alleged plotter also had written a letter denouncing the "moral decay" in Indonesia—a deep embarrassment to the government, since the letter was signed by Muslim, Catholic, and Protestant leaders as well as by the elder statesman Muhammad Hatta.

After heavy fighting and an estimated total death toll of 60,000, Indonesia had gained control over almost all of East Timor by the end of 1976. Remnants of left-wing, pro-independence East Timorese were still fighting on in the jungles, but on July 17 President Suharto signed a bill incorporating the former Portuguese territory into Indonesia as its twenty-seventh province.

In March President Suharto took steps to deal with Indonesia's chief economic problem—mismanagement of the giant state-owned oil company, Pertamina. The president fired the free-wheeling top man at Pertamina, Lt. Gen. Ibnu Sutowo, and appointed a task force of Western-trained technocrats and trusted generals under Maj. Gen. Piet Haryono to oversee the oil giant. The new team promptly halted expensive development projects, renegotiated contracts, and acquired about $1 billion in fresh working capital from consortia led by United States and Japanese bankers. During the summer Pertamina renegotiated contracts with major U.S. oil producers, increasing the government's share of oil revenues.

Indonesia's major thrust in foreign policy was to strengthen ties with other non-Communist governments in Southeast Asia. In February Indonesia played host to the first summit meeting of the Association of Southeast Asian Nations (ASEAN). The emphasis at the conference was on economic cooperation, but the five ASEAN countries—Indonesia, Malaysia, the Philippines, Singapore, and Thailand—did ask the Communist states of Indochina to join them in building a peaceful neutral zone in the area.

See STATISTICS OF THE WORLD.   R.J.C.

INSURANCE. Although 1976 was a successful year for most insurers, several of the year's events led them to believe that the government would play a much larger role in their industry in the near future. These events included the near failure of one of the country's largest liability-insurance firms, massive rate increases throughout the industry, and the difficulties consumers had in obtaining some vital types of coverage.

Liability Insurance. During 1976 liability insurers continued to increase premiums to offset the skyrocketing costs of claims. Also, numerous firms withdrew from offering unprofitable types of coverage, notably medical malpractice insurance. As in 1975 physicians in several states countered by forming mutual malpractice-insurance companies or by setting up reciprocal exchanges. In December New Jersey became the seventh state to establish a physician-owned malpractice-insurance firm. Professionals other than doctors, such as architects and lawyers, in many cases also were faced with extremely high insurance rates, as were some government bodies. A few hospital administrators decided against purchasing liability insurance, reasoning that eventual claims would amount to less than policy costs.

In a case that drew national attention, manufacturers of swine flu vaccine threatened at midyear to halt production because they had been unable to purchase reasonably priced product-liability insurance for the vaccine. The pharmaceutical companies thereby imperiled the massive federal immunization program against swine flu, which had been established after public health experts had predicted a possible epidemic of the disease in the United States in 1976. The manufacturing impasse was resolved in August when President Gerald R. Ford signed a bill making the U.S. government liable in damage suits arising out of the vaccination program, except where negligence by companies or by individuals could be proved. See also HEALTH AND MEDICINE.

Company Earnings. For most property and casualty (nonlife) insurers 1976 was an encouraging year, especially after the record underwriting losses ($4.5 billion) they had incurred as a group in 1975. Although underwriting losses in the first quarter of 1976 continued to outpace gains on investment, the situation turned around in the third and fourth quarters, allowing companies to replenish their badly depleted surplus funds. (Such funds are tapped when actual claims outpace anticipated settlements, which are covered by loss reserves.)

The trend toward profitability began in the nick of time for one of the giants of the industry. This firm, the Government Employees Insurance Co. (GEICO), which had suffered underwriting losses of $141,000,000 in 1975, announced in February that it had added $50,000,000 from its surplus fund to 1975 loss reserves. GEICO thus allowed its surplus to fall below the minimum level required by the District of Columbia, where it was chartered, and the insurer was rendered technically insolvent. As a temporary remedy, GEICO reduced the par value of its stock, thereby transferring funds from its capital account to its surplus fund. GEICO also substantially raised premiums and divested itself of some unprofitable business.

In a major move designed to repair the damage caused by its relatively unrestrained expansion in recent years, GEICO obtained commitments in July from twenty-seven other firms to reinsure about 25 percent of its business. These promises hinged on GEICO's ability to obtain $50,000,000 in additional capital by year-end. To raise the funds GEICO made a public offering of new preferred stock, which was fully subscribed. Optimism over the company's future was buoyed also when the firm achieved a small net profit in the third quarter of the year.

Other Developments. In December the Federal Trade Commission announced it would investigate the life insurance industry to determine whether consumers were being properly informed about the costs of coverage. The agency noted that different companies charged widely varying rates for essentially the same policies. About $2.1 trillion in life insurance, spread over approximately 380,000,000 policies, was in force in early 1976.

In a controversial decision the U.S. Supreme Court ruled on Dec. 7 that disability insurance plans of private firms were not required to cover pregnant women. *See* WOMEN.   J.F.M.

IOWA. *See* STATISTICS OF THE WORLD.

IRAN. Still exercising his imperial powers with great pomp and ceremony, in 1976 Shah Mohammed Riza Pahlavi focused his attentions on building up the Iranian military arsenal and strengthening internal and regional security.

Political and Economic Affairs. Having restricted political activity through the institution of a single-party system in 1975, the shah's government in 1976 resorted to force to control dissidents. Two radical groups—the Muslim People's Fighters and the Marxist People's Fedayeen—were the chief internal opponents, and hence the chief targets of police repression. A report from the International Commission of Jurists published on May 28 censured Iran for failure to guarantee its citizens "basic human rights." The report charged that Savak, the security force trained by the United States Central Intelligence Agency and Israeli secret police, operated as a "law unto itself." No fewer than fifty-one "terrorists" were killed or executed in Iran during the first five months of 1976, it said, and countless more political prisoners were in Ira-

Two American-built Grumman F-14 Tomcats on the ground at Katami Air Base, Isfahan, Iran. Dozens of the swift fighters were delivered to the Imperial Iranian Air Force during 1976.

nian jails. In November Amnesty International reported the number of such prisoners to be up to 100,000.

The first elections under the new party, the *Rastakhiz* (National Resurrection), were held on Oct. 15. An unprecedented electorate representing one sixth of the population turned out to vote for 5700 new members of city, provincial, and educational councils. The first *Rastakhiz* Grand Party Congress was held in November.

The country suffered a deficit of more than $1 billion in its balance of payments during the fiscal year ending March 20. The Central Bank of Iran attributed the failure to balance the accounts to a drop in oil exports at a time when the cost of imports was inflated by 8 to 16 percent. The non-oil sector of the economy, however, experienced growth of more than 15 percent during the same period, particularly in construction and industry.

At a meeting of the Organization of Petroleum Exporting Countries (q.v.), or OPEC, in Bali, Indonesia, May 27–28, Iran joined Iraq in pressing for raised oil prices, but they were opposed by Algeria, Kuwait, Saudi Arabia, and the Union of Arab Emirates. Thus the price freeze scheduled to end on July 1 was retained until December. (Iran more successfully urged price increases on OPEC members at their December meeting in Qatar.) In June Iranian crude production rose by 9 percent, and by September a record 6,400,000 hbl of oil were being produced daily. Operating at 99 percent of capacity, the oil industry made stockpiling in the West possible before the higher prices due in January, 1977, were to go into effect. As a result of this increased output, Iran might expect to erase its budget deficit and perhaps provide a surplus for the 1976–77 fiscal year.

Military and Foreign Affairs. A large proportion of Iranian oil revenues was being spent on military hardware. Oil-for-arms barter arrangements were concluded with both American and British firms. A protocol signed with the U.S. on Aug. 7 in Tehran provided for the purchase of $10 billion in arms during the period 1976–80, in exchange for a roughly equivalent amount of oil. Despite the protests of the U.S. Senate Foreign Relations Committee that arms sales to Iran were "out of control," Secretary of State Henry A. Kissinger maintained that Iranian strength was crucial to U.S. security interests. The arms sales were complicated by the necessity of training the Iranians to use the complex weapons they were ordering. In November a contract was signed by the two governments to provide American civilian experts to teach some 10,000 Iranians how to set up supply management and inventory controls for their country's air force. Americans already in Iran were

to be joined by about 450 more experts in March, 1977. The possibility that the U.S. might be drawn into any conflict that Iran took part in was noted during the debate in the U.S. Senate. The murder of three Americans by Iranian guerrillas in August reinforced U.S. doubts.

See STATISTICS OF THE WORLD. See also MIDDLE EAST. S.C.

IRAQ. In spite of the year-old pact with Iran to end the border dispute, the rebellion of the Kurds in the north continued to plague Iraq in 1976. Intermittent clashes between Iraqi troops and Kurdish guerrillas were reported throughout the spring. On March 24 the Kurdish Democratic Party vowed to renew the struggle and assailed the shah of Iran and the United States Central Intelligence Agency for false promises of assistance. On July 5 the army was ordered to discontinue forcible dispersion of the Kurdistan population to other parts of Iraq.

Relations with neighboring Syria were strained almost to the breaking point, and on July 8 Iraqi troops were positioned at the Syrian border. Baghdad declared that the move was designed to bolster the Arab front against Israel, but the climate of hostility between Iraq and Syria suggested that it was intended to draw Syrian fighters away from Lebanon. Acts of violence, related or not, continued throughout the year on both sides of the border. On Dec. 14 a bomb exploded at the Baghdad airport, killing or injuring at least forty persons.

As a member of the Organization of Petroleum Exporting Countries (q.v.), Iraq continued to press for higher oil prices, to be pegged to inflation in the West. Although oil production in the Middle East was down 10.5 percent in 1975, oil production in Iraq rose by 17.1 percent. But despite high oil revenues, the Iraqi economy remained unstable, with industrial establishments running a deficit of $360,000,000. Observers agreed that still higher oil receipts would be necessary to meet ambitious industrial and development plans.

See STATISTICS OF THE WORLD. See also ARAB LEAGUE; MIDDLE EAST. S.C.

IRELAND, NORTHERN. See GREAT BRITAIN.

IRELAND, REPUBLIC OF. Government policy against terrorism by the Irish Republican Army (I.R.A.) provoked sharp controversy within the Republic of Ireland during 1976 and led to the resignation of President Cearbhall O'Dalaigh. And although government efforts to attract industry to Ireland were showing signs of success, unemployment continued to increase.

Action Against Terrorism. The Irish parliament on June 1 approved the Criminal Law (Jurisdiction) Acts, designed to permit greater cooperation with

Great Britain in the war on terrorism; the British Parliament had passed these accords in August, 1975. The measures, which took effect at once, closed loopholes in the extradition treaty between Northern Ireland and the Irish Republic. They specified that charges of murder, kidnapping, arson, and other terrorist acts could be tried on either side of the border, and they required officials to cross the border to testify or otherwise assist in such prosecutions.

The new laws were denounced by the Provisional wing of the outlawed I.R.A., which warned that any official crossing the border to testify or act against I.R.A. suspects "will be struck down ruthlessly."

The British ambassador to Dublin, Christopher T. E. Ewart-Biggs, was killed in Sandyford, a Dublin suburb, on July 21 when a land mine exploded under the car in which he was riding. His secretary was also killed; the chauffeur and another occupant of the car were injured.

The Irish parliament, acting Sept. 1 on Prime Minister Liam Cosgrave's request, declared a state of emergency in Ireland. Emergency powers legislation, introduced immediately thereafter, was passed by parliament on Sept. 17. Among its provisions was a measure calling for police authority to detain I.R.A. suspects for up to one week without charge. President Cearbhall O'Dalaigh did not sign the bill immediately. On Sept. 24 he asked the supreme court to decide whether some sections of the bill might be "repugnant" to the Irish constitution. On Oct. 15 the supreme court found the bill valid.

O'Dalaigh's action, however, drew sharp criticism from Defense Minister Patrick Donegan, and in an Oct. 18 speech he denounced O'Dalaigh as "a thundering disgrace." Prime Minister Cosgrave ordered Donegan to apologize at once. Donegan did so, in a letter written after Oct. 19, when O'Dalaigh had refused to receive him. A motion by the opposition, introduced on Oct. 21, called for Donegan's resignation; the motion was voted down. The following day O'Dalaigh resigned. On Nov. 9 Patrick J. Hillery, social affairs commissioner for the European Community, was declared president-elect by parliament. He assumed the office on Dec. 3.

The Economy. Ireland finally began to show signs of reversing its thirty-year-old balance-of-trade problem. Figures made public in January showed that in October, 1975, the country had registered a trade surplus for the first time since November, 1945. Balance-of-payments deficits continued, however, and the finance ministers of the European Community agreed on Feb. 16 to help Ireland with a $300,000,000 five-year loan.

Unemployment continued to mount despite the success of the Industrial Development Authority (I.D.A.) in attracting job-producing industry to the country during a three-year campaign. In its annual report, issued July 28, the I.D.A. said that its efforts had created 14,500 new jobs in 1975—but 28,600 jobs had been lost by layoffs and factory closings. High school dropouts, who had recently entered the work force in large numbers, also added to the growing unemployment problem. The Irish birth rate, an additional problem, was the highest in the European Community.

Underseas oil and gas deposits were discovered early in the year off the County Cork coast south of Kinsale. Industry and Commerce Minister Justin Keating announced on Feb. 1 that the finds had been made in wells drilled by the Exxon Corp. of the United States.

See STATISTICS OF THE WORLD.   L.A.S.

ISRAEL. Political uncertainty faced Israel at home and abroad throughout 1976. Israelis were apprehensive about the outcome of the civil war in Lebanon and its effect on their own country, the American Presidential election and the resulting shape of relations with the United States, growing restiveness in the occupied West Bank, and the

At Tel Aviv airport on July 4, relatives rejoice as they welcome hostages rescued from Entebbe, Uganda.

At Gidi Pass in February, Israeli leaders confer on their military withdrawal from the Sinai buffer zone, set up in 1975. From left, they are Maj. Gen. Yekutiel Adam, Prime Minister Itzhak Rabin, and Defense Minister Shimon Peres; in the right foreground is Maj. Gen. Ariel Sharon, then military adviser to the prime minister.

rising spirit of nationalism in the community of Arab citizens in Israel. The Middle East arms race took its toll, and Israel was forced into ever-higher military expenditures to compete with its Arab neighbors.

The Lebanese War. Although Israel did not become directly involved in military operations, its armed forces frequently patrolled villages along its border with Lebanon. During the year the Israelis opened several frontier posts to Lebanese who were isolated from the rest of Lebanon by the war, unable to find food or to reach their work places. Temporarily, they received medical treatment from Israeli physicians and found employment in Jewish settlements. This "good fence" policy attracted attention after it was reported that Defense Minister Shimon Peres and Prime Minister Itzhak Rabin had conducted informal talks inside Lebanon, although they denied the allegations. By the end of 1976 it was clear that Lebanese Christian forces fighting in the south were receiving substantial amounts of military equipment from Israel and that the Rabin government was determined to prevent establishment of hostile bases in the area along Israel's northern border.

Arab Unrest. Early in 1976 Israel sent troops into the occupied areas of the Jordan River's West Bank and into Arab Jerusalem. They were responding to demonstrations against an Israeli court decision permitting Jews to pray on the Temple Mount in Jerusalem, adjoining the al-Aqsa Mosque, which is considered the most holy Muslim place after Mecca and Medina. Later a higher court reversed the decision. The demonstrations were symptomatic of growing support among West Bank Arabs for the Palestine Liberation Organization (P.L.O.) and resolutions in the United Nations (q.v.) supporting the "inalienable national rights" of the Palestinian people. Several mayors of West Bank towns resigned in protest against Israeli actions aimed at restoring order, and students at the only Arab higher educational institution, Bir Zeit College, boycotted classes. Confrontations between the students and Israeli troops led to several Arab deaths.

In October confrontations of Israelis and Arabs in the West Bank town of Hebron centered on religious observances at Abraham's tomb, a holy site for both Muslims and Jews. Again curfews were imposed, and members of the cabinet clashed over the affair. Prime Minister Rabin and Defense Minister Peres, the two major contenders for leadership of the Labor Party in the national elections scheduled for 1977, hotly criticized one another. Both focused public attention on the

The flag of the Palestine Liberation Organization flies over al-Aqsa Mosque in Jerusalem in May. Young Arabs hoisted the banner to emphasize their defiance of Israeli authority, responsible for the death of one of their friends during a demonstration at the mosque.

problems of Israel's relations with Arab populations under its jurisdiction.

A major issue in the 1977 election was expected to be government policy toward Jewish settlement in the occupied territories. One large group of religious zealots, Gush Emunim (Bloc of the Faithful), attempted to force a change in the government policy against unauthorized new Jewish communities by preemptive settlement in such West Bank areas as Hebron. When Gush Emunim followers attempted to set up another settlement nearby at Kaddum, they were persuaded to move to an Israeli army encampment in the area. Throughout the year the settlement issue stimulated debate over administration of the occupied areas, affecting relations among the various Israeli political parties and arousing anxiety in the Arab population.

The growing restiveness of the Arabs was demonstrated again in the West Bank municipal elections held under Israeli supervision during April. For the first time women and men without property were included in an election that was probably as free as any held in the Arab world. The winners were primarily young radicals running on nationalist slogans, generally supporting the P.L.O. In such larger Arab centers as Nablus, Hebron, and Ramallah, they won a surprising victory over traditional leaders, who by and large had cooperated with the Israeli occupation authorities.

The most serious and unexpected Arab unrest occurred in Israel during March. A general strike protesting government expropriation of Arab land in Galilee led to violent altercations between demonstrators and police, and 6 Israeli Arab citizens were killed and more than 70 wounded. Soldiers also attacked the home of the recently elected Communist mayor of Nazareth, Israel's largest Arab town. Although Prime Minister Rabin accused the New Communist (Rakkah) Party of instigating the unrest, he announced that his government would reexamine its policy toward Arab citizens and appointed a new advisory body to look into the situation.

Entebbe. The tension was temporarily dispelled by the extraordinary escapade of Israeli security forces at Entebbe, Uganda, July 3–4. More than 100 hostages, most of them Israeli Jews who had been hijacked to Uganda on an Air France flight a week before, were rescued and brought back to Tel Aviv in Israeli planes following a spectacular night commando raid at Entebbe airport. Three civilian hostages and an Israeli commando officer were killed. The 7 terrorists, representing a militant Palestinian organization, and 20 Ugandan soldiers were also killed. All political factions in Israel (except the Communists) and Israel's

friends abroad gave unqualified approval to the raid, congratulating the prime minister on the rescue. *See also* MILITARY AND NAVAL AFFAIRS; UGANDA.

The Economy. The cost of security and of competition in the Middle Eastern arms race continued to drain Israel's economy, cutting into all aspects of national life. Despite massive American assistance, totaling about a third of all U.S. foreign aid for 1976–77, Israelis themselves carried a larger burden than ever for defense. During 1976 the U.S. passed legislation providing Israel with a total of $4.3 billion in military aid and additional economic assistance for the period from July, 1976, to the end of September, 1977. But the costs of doubling the army since 1971 reached 35 percent of the annual budget in 1976, stimulated an inflation rate of over 30 percent in 1976, increased the state budget for 1977–78 by some 40 percent, caused an annual trade deficit of nearly $4 billion, and necessitated a series of devaluations of the Israeli pound in 1976, from 6.24 (16¢) to 8.61 (11.6¢) per dollar. The resulting increase of 20 percent in prices of commodities such as milk, bread, butter, eggs, and cooking oil, higher interest rates, and loss of government services caused further labor unrest. Improvement depended by and large on diminishing the level of military expenditures, which in turn was contingent on a settlement with the neighboring Arab states.

Prospects for 1977. By the end of the year progress toward peace was still uncertain. A rapprochement between Egypt and Syria and Rabin's proposals for reconvening the Geneva conference on the model of the Helsinki conference of 1975 had led to no concrete action. The surprising resignation of the Rabin government late in December seemed to make such action unlikely in the immediate future; the 1977 elections were not scheduled to take place before May.

See STATISTICS OF THE WORLD. *See also* MIDDLE EAST. D.P.

ITALY. As a result of 1976 elections, the Italian Communist Party became a decisive force for the first time. The ruling coalition discovered that the Italian parliament could not conduct the nation's business without the cooperation of the Communists.

Domestic Politics. The coalition of Christian Democrats and Republicans resigned on Jan. 7, when the Socialist Party withdrew its parliamentary support on the ground that the Christian Democrats, headed by Premier Aldo Moro, ignored the Socialist views in favor of those of the Communists. A few days earlier it was disclosed that the Christian Democrats and the Communists had reached a tacit agreement on the controversial abortion legislation. (The Christian Democrats conceded that abortion should no longer be regarded as criminal; the Communists agreed that a physician rather than a pregnant woman should make the final decision.) Also, the Communists had gone along with the government in condemning wildcat strikes. The Socialists objected to Moro's policies on tight credit, which had reduced inflation but at the expense of mounting unemployment. Just before the coalition resigned, reports were published that the United States Central Intelligence Agency had secretly paid $6,000,000 to support non-Communist leaders. The headquarters of the coalition parties quickly denied this.

After five weeks of frantic effort, Moro formed a new government (his fifth) on Feb. 11. It consisted mostly of Christian Democrats. The Chamber of Deputies approved the government on Feb. 21 by a vote of 287 to 220, with 60 abstentions. On March 18 the government announced an austerity program to raise gasoline prices as well as taxes on autos, alcohol, motion picture tickets, and other luxury items. The bank lending rate was to be increased from 8 to 12 percent. Experts considered these steps inadequate, however.

On March 20 Moro warned his deeply divided party at its Rome congress against accepting a coalition with the Communists. U.S. officials had advised Italy that relations with Washington would have to be reappraised if such an alignment developed. But party secretary Benigno Zaccagnini, who was reelected by the Christian Democrats, said he was counting on Communist cooperation to deal with the economic crisis. In mid-April the Socialists withdrew their pledge of parliamentary abstention from the faltering government; they had originally decided to abstain because of the government stand on abortion and the economy.

On April 30 Moro resigned; on May 1, President Giovanni Leone dissolved parliament a year ahead of the scheduled time for national elections. New elections were set for June 20 and 21. A referendum on legalizing abortion was delayed for two years. Conditions had worsened for the government: Inflation and unemployment had increased, the lira was on the verge of collapse, and the newspapers were printing stories of Lockheed Aircraft Corp. payoffs to top government officials. Political violence had become rampant, with police reporting 300 acts of terrorism.

In the June elections the Christian Democrats barely managed to keep the Communists from winning a majority by arousing fears of the damage that a Communist victory could do to the North Atlantic Treaty Organization (NATO) alliance. The Christian Democrats garnered 14,200,-

In Rome on June 21 Italian Communist Party leader Enrico Berlinguer displays a copy of the party newspaper Unita. It proclaims that the P.C.I. (Italian Communist Party) has made a "new, impetuous advance" by means of the national elections.

000 ballots out of 37,000,000 cast, or 38.7 percent of the total. This meant that they retained 263 of the 630 seats in the Chamber of Deputies, a loss of 3. In the Senate they held onto 135 seats out of 315. The Communists won 49 more seats in the Chamber of Deputies for a total of 228, and they gained 22 more seats in the Senate for a total of 116. The smaller parties suffered serious losses, suggesting a polarization of politics between the two major parties. The Socialists, who had precipitated the elections, were penalized by losing 4 seats in each house, while retaining 57 in the Chamber of Deputies and 28 in the Senate.

It was not until July 29 that the new premier-designate, the veteran minister Giulio Andreotti, could organize a minority cabinet of Christian Democrats. To survive a vote of confidence, he had to count on Communist abstentions in return for policy consultations. For the first time, a Communist, Pietro Ingrao, became president of the Chamber of Deputies, as seven other Communists became chairmen of key parliamentary committees.

Lockheed Scandals. Late in April Italian newspapers cast suspicion on President Leone, Premier Moro, and Foreign Minister Mariano Rumor for accepting bribes from the Lockheed Aircraft Corp. in the 1960's. All denied the charges. On Dec. 2 a committee of parliament members accused Rumor and two former ministers, Luigi Gui and Mario Tanassi, of corruption and fraud in the Lockheed matter. All three denied the charges. They were scheduled to appear before parliament to offer their defense and, if stripped of their immunity, could be ordered to stand trial.

The Economy. Andreotti received his vote of confidence early in August and immediately announced austerity measures, including specific proposals and deadlines, to forestall a collapse of the economy. The inflation rate had climbed to 20 percent, the foreign debt was $17 billion, the value of the lira was falling, and imports were climbing. Italy was seeking a $530,000,000 loan from the International Monetary Fund, not to mention other loans. The Andreotti plan called for prevention of tax evasion, an increase in public service rates, cuts in public spending, a decrease in imports, a new increase in the bank lending rate (from 12 to 15 percent), and efforts to curb pay raises. On Nov. 30 more than 7,000,000

workers went on strike to protest these measures.

The economy was further damaged by several disasters. An earthquake on May 6 set off a series of shocks in the Friuli Region; more than 900 people died and 100,000 were left homeless. On July 10 an explosion in a chemical plant at Seveso released the deadly poison dioxin, causing the evacuation of hundreds in this immensely productive region (*see* ENVIRONMENT).

Foreign Affairs. On July 19 Premier Moro charged fellow NATO members West Germany, Great Britain, France, and the U.S. with impropriety because of their reported agreement to withhold aid to any Italian ministry that included Communists. In mid-December, however, Premier Andreotti visited the U.S. Following talks between Andreotti and U.S. President Gerald R. Ford at the White House, the two heads of state reaffirmed the close ties between their countries.

Late in November Italy and the Vatican agreed on revisions in their 1929 Concordat. The new accord would abolish Roman Catholicism as the state religion, annul the prohibition of divorce, and end compulsory religious education. *See* RELIGION.

See STATISTICS OF THE WORLD.   J.N.

IVORY COAST. *See* STATISTICS OF THE WORLD.

J

JAMAICA. In the face of growing violence and increasing economic difficulties, Jamaican Prime Minister Michael Manley won an overwhelming electoral mandate in December.

On Nov. 21, the prime minister told a rally of his People's National Party (P.N.P.) that elections would be held on Dec. 15, five and a half weeks ahead of the constitutionally required date but before the onset of the main tourist season. The election offered Jamaican voters a clear choice between Prime Minister Manley's brand of democratic socialism, featuring stronger ties with developing countries, including Cuba; and the opposition Jamaica Labor Party, led by Edward Seaga, who was committed to private ownership and "balanced" relations with all countries, including the United States. The campaign was marked by sporadic violence, including an apparent attempt to assassinate *reggae* musician Bob Marley, who later shared a stage with Manley at a "Smile Jamaican" festival. The final result was a decisive victory for the P.N.P., which won more than a two-

thirds majority in the House of Representatives.

The election took place while the country was still under a state of emergency, declared on June 19 to allow security forces to combat a wave of organized crime and terrorism which claimed 163 lives during the first six months of the year. While the outbreak of violence was primarily attributed to political infighting, it was compounded by the difficult economic conditions. Unemployment, normally in the 20 percent range, was at least 27 percent by November, and the inflation rate for 1976 was nearly 15 percent. Jamaica's export performance was hurt by the fall in sugar prices and by sluggish bauxite demand, and the government was forced to introduce a restrictive import control program.

Despite the economic difficulties, the government pressed ahead with its goal of achieving a stake in the all-important bauxite-alumina industry, winning participation in the alumina sector for the first time.

See STATISTICS OF THE WORLD.   A.K.M.

JAPAN. Throughout 1976 the scandal-ridden Liberal-Democratic government of Japan struggled frantically for political survival, barely managing to hold its effective majority in December legislative elections. Meanwhile, a general calm in international relations was marred by an imbroglio with the Soviet Union over a military defector and the jet aircraft he brought with him.

Politics. Despite sensational revelations of financial corruption at the highest levels of the ruling Liberal-Democratic Party, Prime Minister Takeo Miki managed to maintain his political leadership throughout 1976. Early in the year the nation was rocked by the disclosure, in testimony before the United States Senate Subcommittee on Multinational Corporations, that Yoshio Kodama, a founder of the Liberal-Democratic Party, had accepted more than $7,000,000 from officials of the Lockheed Aircraft Corp. to influence the government to purchase Lockheed Tristar jet aircraft. Another $2,000,000 was reportedly funneled to government officials for the same purpose. Kodama was arrested and charged with tax evasion and violation of foreign exchange control laws.

Pressed by the opposition parties, the Liberal-Democratic government, with the cooperation of U.S. authorities, launched an investigation to uncover further payoffs. In July former Prime Minister Kakuei Tanaka was arrested, jailed, and charged with violation of foreign exchange control regulations in connection with $1,670,000 he allegedly received to ensure that Japan's largest domestic airline, All-Nippon Airways, purchased Lockheed Tristars instead of McDonnell Douglas DC-10's.

Since Tanaka was the leader of an important faction of the Liberal-Democrats, his involvement in the widening scandal split the party leadership. Deputy Prime Minister Takeo Fukuda and other factional leaders called on Prime Minister Miki to resign, charging that his conduct of the investigation was dividing the party and endangering its electoral prospects. In September Miki reached a compromise with the factional leaders—a reshuffle of the cabinet to include representatives of opposing factions—but this failed to heal the split in the party. Fukuda quit the cabinet on Nov. 5, and the Liberal-Democrats suffered sharp losses in Dec. 5 parliamentary elections. The party's representation in the 511-seat House of Representatives (the lower house of the diet) dropped from 265 to 249, just enough to enable the Liberal-Democrats to piece together a working majority of 260 with the aid of independents who subsequently joined the party. The biggest gainers were the Socialists, Democratic Socialists, the Komeito (Clean Government) Party, and the New Liberal Club. The Communists also suffered a setback, losing 20 seats.

Miki announced his decision to resign his office on Dec. 17, and Fukuda was elected by the diet as prime minister a week later.

Japanese officials place under wraps a supersecret Soviet MIG-25 jet fighter flown to Hakodate Airport in Hokkaido on Sept. 6 by a defecting pilot. The jet fighter was meticulously examined by U.S. and Japanese experts before being returned to its irate owners in November.

Another Scandal for the Prime Minister
Japan was rocked in July by the arrest and brief incarceration of a parliament member and former prime minister, Kakuei Tanaka, in connection with a wide-reaching bribe scandal involving the Lockheed Aircraft Corp. For Tanaka, who rose to power from poverty-stricken beginnings, the disgrace was not his first: In 1974, after two years as prime minister, he was forced to resign under suspicion of improper financial dealings. If found guilty of taking Lockheed money—$2,000,000 according to some estimates—he would face three years in prison. But his career seemed to be intact: In December's national elections, he was returned to parliament by his trusting rural constituents.

Former Prime Minister Kakuei Tanaka.

The Economy. Despite the political unrest generated by the Lockheed scandal, economic recovery proceeded throughout the year, but at a decelerating pace. Spurred by the government's antirecession measures (including extensive public works programs and a 15 percent growth in the money supply), the gross national product for fiscal year 1975 (April, 1975–March, 1976) increased by 2.6 percent after adjustments for inflation, up from a loss of 0.6 percent in 1974. Industrial production, which bottomed out in 1975, was growing at the annual rate of 8 percent by early 1976. Although foreign trade fell off in volume, a record surplus of $5.9 billion was achieved, owing to the particularly strong showing of Japanese automobiles and color television sets on the export market.

The Economic Planning Agency forecast a growth rate of 5.6 percent in the economy (after adjustments for inflation) in fiscal year 1976. But recovery slowed in the spring and summer. Sluggish performance in basic industries such as steel, chemicals, and shipbuilding resulted in a growth rate of just over 4 percent, and industrial capacity remained at about 80 percent. Meanwhile, the annual inflation rate surged above 9 percent, exceeding the 8.8 percent in average annual wage increases won by Japanese workers earlier in the year. Partly for this reason, personal spending, which the government hoped would lead the recovery, remained weak. Although some politicians pressed for a 10 percent tax cut to stimulate spending, the Finance Ministry resolutely rejected such an idea, warning that it could result in a return to the double-digit inflation of previous years. The continuing scandal and the upcoming elections left the government little room for decisive action.

Foreign Affairs. In the international arena negotiations for a peace treaty with the Soviet Union were stalled by the Soviets' refusal to return to Japan the strategic islands off the northwest coast of Hokkaido which the U.S.S.R. has occupied since the close of World War II. Relations were further complicated after a Russian pilot, on Sept. 6, flew one of the Soviet Union's super-secret MIG-25 jet fighters into Hakodate Airport, Hokkaido. Despite Soviet demands for return of the jet and its pilot, Air Force Lt. Viktor Belenko, he was granted political asylum in the U.S. and the aircraft was dismantled and examined by Japanese and U.S. authorities. It was returned in November.

Negotiations for a peace treaty with the People's Republic of China also came to a standstill when Tokyo objected that China's insistence on a statement of mutual opposition to "big-power hegemony" was too pointedly anti-Soviet and likely to upset Japan's delicate relationship with Moscow. During the summer relations with Peking were further complicated when Foreign Minister Kiichi Miyazawa cautioned against rapid normalization of Washington-Peking relations, since this would mean an end to the U.S.-Taiwan security pact and would force other Asian nations, including Japan and South Korea, to reassess their security ties with the U.S. The impasse which Miyazawa's remarks created in Sino-Japanese relations was relieved in September when Miyazawa was replaced by Zentaro Kosaka, who had served as foreign minister from 1960 to 1962. Late in the year, when the official Soviet press charged that the defection of the MIG-25 pilot was an act of conspiracy by Japan and the U.S., Japan seemed more willing to accept the Chinese position against big-power hegemony, and the prospects for a Sino-Japanese treaty seemed somewhat improved.

After a six-year delay, Japan ratified the Treaty on the Non-Proliferation of Nuclear Weapons on May 24. The agreement had been signed by the Japanese with reservations on Feb. 3, 1970.

Foreign diplomats joined Japanese government officials on Nov. 10 in honoring the 50th anniversary of Emperor Hirohito's reign, the longest in Japan's recorded history.

See STATISTICS OF THE WORLD.   T.L.K.

JENNER, BRUCE. *See* PEOPLE IN THE NEWS.

JORDAN, HASHEMITE KINGDOM OF. In a move that was seen by many Arabs as contrary to the resolutions of the 1974 Arab summit conference at Rabat, Morocco, the Jordanian parliament, meeting in extraordinary session Feb. 5–7, 1976, amended the constitution to allow indefinite postponement of elections. At issue was the future of the West Bank—a portion of the Palestine region that was occupied by Jordan in 1948 and captured by Israel in 1967. Even after 1967 one half of the Jordanian parliament have been representatives of the West Bank. Following the 1974 Rabat resolution that the Palestine Liberation Organization (P.L.O.) was the only legitimate representative of the Palestinian people, the Jordanian parliament was dissolved, ostensibly until it could be reconstituted by elected members from the East Bank (Jordan proper) alone. While the Hashemites maintained that to reconstitute the parliament without West Bank representation would only allow Israel to consolidate its political hold over the disputed region, Palestinian and other Arab leaders charged that King Hussein I was reneging on his promise at Rabat to relinquish claims to sovereignty over the West Bank. Following the dissolution of parliament on Feb. 7, a consultative committee, including representatives of the West Bank, was formed under the king's chairmanship.

A new cabinet was formed July 13 after the resignation of Prime Minister Zaid al-Rifai, who had been the king's right-hand man for several years. He was replaced by former Intelligence Chief Mudar Badran, who formed a new eighteen-member cabinet.

In a series of press releases early in January, extensive plans for the reorganization of the military were disclosed. Conscription was introduced Jan. 1 with a special mandate for the induction of "skilled city dwellers" to man sophisticated new weapons. Plans were also announced for doubling the air force and for completely mechanizing the ground force. On Jan. 11 a new commander in chief took charge. An arms agreement with the United States was signed Sept. 5 for the purchase of Hawk missiles and Vulcan antiaircraft guns. The agreement had taken more than a year to negotiate. Saudi Arabia, which was to share the defense system, agreed to pay the bill.

A new five-year plan costing $2.2 billion was launched May 31. The ambitious plan envisioned a total economic growth of 12 percent. Although some $1 billion in foreign loans would be required initially, it was hoped that greater self-sufficiency would be attained through development of transport routes throughout Jordan and by the exploitation of natural resources, especially phosphate.

See STATISTICS OF THE WORLD; *see also* ARAB LEAGUE.   S.C.

K

KANSAS. *See* STATISTICS OF THE WORLD.
KENTUCKY. *See* STATISTICS OF THE WORLD.
KENYA. The threat of war with neighboring Uganda hung over Kenya in 1976. Resentment in Kenya simmered over the mistreatment of Kenyan nationals in Uganda, over Ugandan claims to large portions of Kenyan territory, and over Uganda's nonpayment of money owed the East African Community (comprising Kenya, Tanzania, and Uganda). Delays multiplied on the Kenya-Uganda railway as Kenyan tanker drivers, fearing arrest, refused to enter Uganda.

On July 3 Israeli commandos raided the airfield at Entebbe in Uganda (*see* ISRAEL); Kenya was alleged to have granted logistic support for this raid. On July 8 announcement was made that Uganda would be required to pay in Kenyan currency to ship goods through Kenya; Idi Amin, the president of Uganda, threatened military retaliation. At the same time Kenyan newspapers reported that about 245 Kenyan nationals had been killed in reprisal for the Entebbe raid, and on July 12–13 the United States sent a frigate and two naval aircraft to Kenya as a display of support. The crisis abated when, on Aug. 7, Amin met with the president of Kenya, Jomo Kenyatta, and agreed to remove troops massed at the Kenya-Uganda border. Amin further agreed to end threats to invade Kenya and to provide full back payment for goods and services. A six-nation commission was to be organized to help formalize relations. Although ninety-nine Kenyans were quickly released from protective custody in Uganda, Kenyan officials moved ahead with plans to purchase some $5,000,000 in military equipment from the U.S., including twelve F-5 jet fighters. These, it was hoped, would offset military buildups in Uganda and Somalia.

See STATISTICS OF THE WORLD. See also AFRICA.   J.T.S.

KHMER REPUBLIC. See STATISTICS OF THE WORLD.
KISSINGER, HENRY A. See PEOPLE IN THE NEWS.
KOREA, DEMOCRATIC PEOPLE'S REPUBLIC OF, or **NORTH KOREA.** For rigidly controlled North Korea, 1976 was a year of barely concealed political turmoil, evident economic problems, and a serious loss of face in the international community.
Politics. President Kim Il Sung continued to be the subject of a personality cult unrivaled anywhere in the Communist world. Shortly after the New Year, rumors spread that the 63-year-old strongman might be suffering from cancer, but in February he appeared in public and seemed in good health. Departing from usual Marxist practice, Kim quietly promoted his son, Kim Jong Il, to the number-two post in the Communist Party and named him as his heir apparent. Although opposition to Kim's dictates has been almost unheard of, Western analysts detected signs of strong resistance within the party to Kim Jong Il's elevation. In other leadership changes Pak Sung Chul in April replaced Premier Kim Il, who became first vice-president.
The P'anmunjŏm Incident. On Aug. 18, while supervising the trimming of a tree in the demilitarized zone at the truce site of P'anmunjŏm, two United States officers were murdered by ax-wielding North Korean soldiers. The brutal incident caused the U.S. and North Korea to place their armed forces in the area on alert and prompted President Gerald R. Ford to dispatch the U.S.S. *Midway* and a naval task force to Korean waters. As a further show of force, a South Korean work gang protected by U.S. troops cut down the tree. Tensions mounted, but President Kim made an unprecedented statement of regret, and the situation was defused. The two sides then agreed to

separate their forces in the demilitarized zone, in effect dividing what had been a jointly held area.
The Economy. Because of a combination of bad luck and apparent mismanagement, North Korea's economy tottered under the strain of foreign aid and trade debts. The crisis began three years earlier, when oil prices zoomed upward just as demand for North Korea's major export, nonferrous metals, all but collapsed. Consequently, North Korea was unable to pay for the heavy machinery and advanced technology it had purchased from Japan and the West. By April, 1976, North Korea, the first Communist country not to pay its foreign debts on time, owed the Communist world an estimated $700,000,000; Japan, $250,000,000; and Western Europe, $250,000,000. The Japanese and Western Europeans rescheduled the debts in 1975, but early in 1976 the North Koreans began to default on the rescheduled obligations and exporters shipped goods to them only for cash.
Foreign Affairs. Its unpredictable, sometimes even bizarre, behavior cost North Korea support among Third World countries and even in the Communist world. In September North Korea's friends at the United Nations withdrew their usual pro-P'yŏngyang resolution—calling for a withdrawal of U.S. troops from South Korea and an end to the U.N. command there—because sufficient votes for passage were lacking.

So hard-pressed was North Korea for foreign exchange that its diplomats abroad were under instructions to use every means, legal or not, to raise funds. In May Egyptian authorities accused two North Korean diplomats of smuggling narcotics into Egypt. In October Denmark, Norway, and Finland each ousted high-ranking North Korean diplomats for dealing in narcotics and black market liquor and cigarettes. On similar grounds, the Swedish government declared the North Korean ambassador non grata, forcing P'yŏngyang to recall him and several other diplomats.

See STATISTICS OF THE WORLD.   R.J.C.
KOREA, REPUBLIC OF, or **SOUTH KOREA.** During 1976 the one-man rule of President Park Chung Hee became increasingly repressive; at the same time, South Korea made impressive economic gains and its lobbying methods attracted worldwide attention.
Politics. For the most part, South Koreans seemed to accept President Park's tough, no-nonsense brand of government. But in March a group of dissidents issued a manifesto calling for the president's resignation and a return to democratic freedoms. In response, the government tried eighteen South Koreans—including former President Yun Po Sun and former presidential candidate Kim Dae Jung, a longtime critic of the Park re-

203

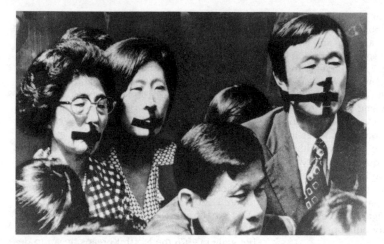

In May demonstrators in Seoul tape their mouths to protest suppression of freedom of speech by President Park Chung Hee of South Korea. At left is the wife of Kim Dae Jung, a former presidential candidate who was later convicted on charges of treason.

gime—on charges of seeking to overthrow the government. After a lengthy trial, the defendants were found guilty on Aug. 28 and sentenced to terms ranging from two to eight years in prison. After an appeal, a retrial began in Seoul in November.

The Economy. Over the year South Koreans were better fed, better clothed—in fact, better off in most material ways—than ever before. South Korea rebounded from the 1974–75 recession so strongly that the government's original economic growth rate target of 8 percent for 1976 was revised upward to 11 percent during the summer. Exports soared, inflation decreased sharply, and the country's industrial growth was such that world banking circles began to talk of South Korea's becoming a "New Japan" in the year ahead. Optimism cooled somewhat in October, when industrial output and export figures showed a downturn.

With little fanfare, South Korea strengthened its position as one of the world's major overseas builders, particularly in the Middle East. It was estimated that during 1976 about 20,000 South Koreans were employed abroad, building roads, bridges, factories, refineries, tanker terminals, and hospitals in more than twenty countries. Overseas construction contracts for the year exceeded $2 billion.

Foreign Affairs. In 1976 South Korea again offered to resume negotiations with North Korea on a wide range of topics but was firmly rebuffed. The United States remained South Korea's chief ally in the world community, but in April President Park told confidants that he did not expect strong American support to last more than a few more years. (A phased withdrawal of U.S. ground troops from Korea had been one of President-elect Jimmy Carter's campaign pledges.) To make up for the expected slackening in U.S. support, Park stepped up plans to make South Korea militarily self-sufficient by 1980.

In the meantime, South Korean lobbyists were extremely active in Washington in their efforts—some of dubious legality—to influence American Congressmen and government officials. One federal inquiry focused on charges that South Korean lobbyists, led by Park Tong Sun, had handed out from $500,000 to $1,000,000 a year to U.S. citizens in campaign contributions, bribes, travel gifts, and entertainment. Another investigation sifted charges that agents of South Korea's Central Intelligence Agency, known as the K.C.I.A., had harassed Korean-Americans and Korean residents of the U.S. who did not support the regime of President Park. In December, as the U.S. investigations proceeded, the head of the K.C.I.A. was ousted as part of a general cabinet shake-up conducted by President Park.

See STATISTICS OF THE WORLD.   R.J.C.

The More It Remains the Same

In 1894 the Yi dynasty issued an edict: Korean men must chop off their pigtails. In 1976 the Park Chung Hee government pronounced a warning: South Korean men must not allow their hair to reach their collars or wave it so that it resembles the hair of women. Other Park proscriptions were against T-shirts bearing words or designs deemed obscene, open signs of affection in public, and 260 "decadent" songs, including "Tom Dooley" and "Never on Sunday."

KUWAIT. The last remaining elected assembly in the Arab Gulf, the sixty-four-member National Assembly of Kuwait, was dissolved by the head of government, the emir Sheikh Sabah al-Salem al-Sabah, on Aug. 29, 1976. The cabinet also was dismissed, and several articles of the 1968 constitution suspended. New stringent restrictions were imposed on the press in reporting both national and international affairs, and a number of newspaper offices closed. The prime minister, Crown Prince Jaber al-Ahmad al-Sabah, formed a new cabinet on Sept. 6.

The emir charged that both the assembly and the press had acted against the national interests of Kuwait. The assembly had been elected for a four-year term by literate Kuwaiti males over 21, and included both young radicals and members of older established families opposed to the ruling Sabah family. It had been noted for its independent stand on both foreign and domestic issues. The press had been outspokenly critical of a number of government policies, notably the emir's support of the right wing in the Lebanese civil war. A related source of political tension was the residence of 270,000 Palestinians in Kuwait—27 percent of the total population—and their support for the Left in the Lebanese civil war. Some observers felt that the drastic moves by the government were an attempt to control the Palestinian population. In lieu of the National Assembly, powers were invested in the emir and his Council of Ministers pending proposals from a committee directed to rewrite the constitution.

As Finance Minister Abd el-Rahman Salem Atigi reported Feb. 7, Kuwait's foremost economic problem continued to be the allocation of its oil revenues. Oil income alone for 1976 was projected at $7.2 billion, a 25 percent increase over 1975. With the small domestic market incapable of absorbing such huge revenues without tremendous inflation, planners determined to concentrate on capitalizing light and medium industries which require neither a large work force nor intricate organization. Still inhibiting the growth of industry were a severe manpower shortage and a lack of housing.

On April 1 the cabinet approved an enlarged budget of $3.5 billion for domestic investments and expenditures. The largest single allocation, $1.1 billion, was earmarked for development programs. Even with this 25 percent increase in the national budget, a surplus of $2.9 billion (39 percent of total revenues) remained for investment outside Kuwait, either in the international market or in development funds for Arab and other Third World countries. To assure the maximum in future revenues, an Oil Conservation Council was established Feb. 2 to develop programs for exploration, production, processing, utilization, and distribution of petroleum products.

See STATISTICS OF THE WORLD. *See also* ARAB LEAGUE; MIDDLE EAST. S.C.

L

LABOR. Contracts covering nearly 4,500,000 workers were negotiated in the United States in 1976, making it the heaviest year for collective bargaining since 1973. As the year began union members were in a militant mood—inflation had so eroded their paychecks that the adjusted aftertax earnings of a worker with three dependents were at their lowest level since 1965. Therefore contract negotiations were marked by intense bargaining and long strikes. Inflation did taper off during the year, but the unemployment rate, another indicator of the economic well-being of labor, remained high through December.

Unemployment. Joblessness was labor's most intransigent problem in 1976, just as it had been in the previous year. According to the U.S. Bureau of Labor Statistics (B.L.S.), the unemployment rate fell from 7.8 percent of the labor force in January to 7.3 percent in May. But it edged upward in the following months, and in December it stood at 7.9 percent (compared to 8.3 percent in December, 1975). The average for the year was 7.7 percent. In December 88,352,000 persons were employed (compared to 85,511,000 in December, 1975), and 7,558,000 workers were unemployed (compared to 7,768,000 in December, 1975).

U.S. President Gerald R. Ford decided against taking any bold measures to alleviate the unemployment problem, because he felt that broad new programs would bring back a high rate of inflation. Organized labor, on the other hand, clamored loudly for federal programs to improve the dismal job picture. George Meany, head of the 14,200,000-member American Federation of Labor and Congress of Industrial Organizations (A.F.L.-C.I.O.), charged that the unemployment problem was far worse than the B.L.S. figures indicated. Meany said that if people who had given up looking for work and people who were able to find only part-time positions were included among the unemployed, the rate would exceed 10 percent. (The B.L.S. classifies people as unemployed only if they are actively seeking work; part-time employees are considered fully employed even if they had accepted their jobs only after failing to find full-time positions.)

The U.S. Congress continued a program of extended jobless benefits and enacted some new, although relatively minor, measures over President Ford's vetoes. Labor leaders were far from satisfied. The A.F.L.-C.I.O. and its allies in Congress had hoped for at least $6 billion in public works programs to create new jobs. Indeed, a bill providing $6.1 billion was passed by both houses of Congress, but it was vetoed in February by the President. He called it "little more than an election-year pork barrel." Congress sustained the veto. Once again, in midsummer, another version of the public works bill, this time authorizing expenditures of only $3.95 billion, was rejected by the President. But this time Congress overrode his veto, with many Republicans voting against the President's position in an effort to bolster their chances with the electorate back home.

Collective Bargaining. With the country still trying to recover from the worst recession since the Great Depression of the 1930's, major strikes oc-

On Oct. 22 in Los Angeles, Cesar Chavez, head of the United Farm Workers, leads a demonstration backing Proposition 14. The initiative, designed to safeguard agricultural workers' right to organize, was rejected by California voters on Nov. 2.

curred in several big American industries. On April 21 the United Rubber Workers (U.R.W.) began strikes against the nation's four largest tire and rubber manufacturers. The walkouts lasted more than 4 months and idled some 68,000 workers in 21 states. The first company to settle with the U.R.W. was Goodyear Tire and Rubber. Late in August the company agreed to a new 3-year pact, including an hourly wage increase of $1.35 by 1978, plus cost-of-living adjustments based on the consumer price index and increased company payments for employee pension plans. The other manufacturers, Firestone Tire and Rubber Co., B. F. Goodrich Co., and Uniroyal Inc., settled with the U.R.W. soon after Goodyear, and by mid-September almost all the plants were functioning again. American consumers, meanwhile, were little affected by the walkouts.

On Oct. 12 members of the United Automobile Workers ratified a new 3-year contract with the Ford Motor Co., thus ending a 28-day strike of about 170,000 Ford workers at 102 plants in 22 states. Among the provisions of the Ford settlement were annual wage increases of 3 percent, automatic cost-of-living increases, and thirteen extra paid holidays over the final two years of the contract. Some experts viewed the additional days off as a step toward a four-day workweek in the industry.

At a Washington news conference on Jan. 14, John T. Dunlop announces his resignation as U.S. secretary of labor. The move came after President Gerald R. Ford vetoed a construction-site picketing bill that Dunlop had helped draft.

Other serious labor disputes affected a variety of industries. A marathon walkout concluded Jan. 4 when flight attendants employed by National Airlines ratified a new multiyear agreement. The workers had been on strike for 127 days. A 2-day strike by 400,000 truck drivers belonging to the giant International Brotherhood of Teamsters (I.B.T.) ended April 3 after bargainers agreed to a new 3-year contract. Among other things, the pact provided for an immediate 9-percent wage hike, cost-of-living pay increases, higher company contributions to employee pension funds, and better working conditions for long-haul drivers. An 11-day strike by 30,000 cannery workers disrupted the processing of the summer fruit and vegetable harvest in California. Another work stoppage, a wildcat walkout that began in the West Virginia coalfields on July 19 and eventually idled nearly 100,000 miners in 9 eastern states, ended by mid-August.

Although many millions of man-hours were lost by these and other strikes, U.S. Labor Department officials expressed relief that the large number of major labor agreements up for renegotiation in 1976 had not led to far more lost work time. A department report issued in January stated that in 1975, a relatively light year for collective bargaining, approximately 1,800,000 workers had taken

Former Teamsters head Dave Beck addresses 2300 delegates at the union's convention in Las Vegas in June. Current head Frank E. Fitzsimmons (below, left), elected to another five-year term at the meeting, had stated earlier that he bitterly resented talk of reforming the scandal-ridden organization.

part in some 5200 strikes that had resulted in roughly 35,000,000 lost workdays.

Dunlop Resigns. John T. Dunlop resigned as U.S. secretary of labor on Feb. 1, less than a year after he had taken the post. The resignation came as a result of President Ford's veto of a bill which Dunlop had helped draft. The bill would have given a union that had a grievance against a single subcontractor on a construction job the right to picket the entire building site. Earlier, during the legislative process, Ford had given Dunlop a pledge that he would sign the measure into law. But the President reversed himself in the face of pressure by advisers who claimed that the legislation would lead to serious disruptions in the building industry.

Dunlop was replaced as secretary of labor by W. J. Usery, Jr., previously the Ford administration's chief labor mediator. Usery, a former official of the International Association of Machinists, came under fire in June after he lavishly praised the I.B.T., then under investigation by the Labor and Justice departments for alleged mismanagement of its $1.4 billion fund, known as the Central States Pension Fund. Usery was called before the Senate labor committee, where he testified that his praise of the I.B.T. "may have been a little more enthusiastic than [it] should have been."

U.S. Supreme Court Decisions. In late June and early July the Supreme Court dealt with several issues affecting labor. On June 24 it ruled that federal minimum-wage laws were not binding on state and local governments because such entities were not engaged in interstate commerce. The next day the Court held that an employee may refuse to work overtime in order to exert pressure on his employer during new contract negotiations. On June 28 the High Court maintained that states were liable for compensatory damages in cases in which they had violated federal bans on discrimination in employment. And finally on July 6 the Court decided that workers may strike in support of another union's legal walkout even if they had a no-strike pledge in their contracts.

In March the National Labor Relations Board ruled that hospital interns and resident physicians were not covered by federal labor laws because they were students pursuing advanced medical education, and therefore could not be classified as employees of the institutions to which they were attached.

Other Developments. National politics dominated much of organized labor's attention during 1976. In July the A.F.L.-C.I.O. executive council endorsed the candidacy of Jimmy Carter, the Democratic Party nominee for President. Most independent labor organizations (except the I.B.T., which did not endorse a candidate) followed suit. Speaking of Carter, Meany said, "His overall purpose is our overall purpose: To put Americans back to work." During the campaign organized labor spent about $5,000,000 to promote Carter's successful quest for office. In December virtually all of the labor leaders voiced their approval of Carter's decision to nominate Texas economist F. Ray Marshall as his secretary of labor.

An important merger of labor organizations took place in June, when the Amalgamated Clothing Workers of America joined with the Textile Workers Union of America to form the 524,000-member Amalgamated Clothing and Textile Workers Union. The new grouping immediately began a drive to organize workers of J. P. Stevens and Co., the nation's second-largest textile manufacturer. This move was part of a plan to enroll approximately 630,000 nonunion textile workers in eight southeastern states, where manufacturers have strongly opposed unionizing efforts. By year-end the organizing effort at Stevens had received much outside support, and a nationwide boycott of the firm's products was gathering momentum.   T.H.J.

LABRADOR. *See* STATISTICS OF THE WORLD.

LAOS. Intent on turning their tiny landlocked country into a self-sufficient socialist state, the Communist rulers of Laos experienced a rocky first year of power in 1976.

So far as outsiders could tell, Kaysone Phoumvihan, prime minister and secretary-general of the Lao People's Revolutionary Party, was top man in the regime. But there were signs that his hold on power was not secure. At a secret meeting of the party's central committee in July, a majority reportedly backed the criticisms of Kaysone's inflexibility that were voiced by President Souphanouvong.

Although not as brutal as the Communist regime in Cambodia, the Laotian government was nonetheless harsh and repressive. No criticism was tolerated, and by conservative estimates some 20,000 Laotians were arrested and sentenced—usually without trial—to indefinite terms in so-called reeducation centers deep in the mountains and jungles.

In June Kaysone admitted that his Pathet Lao army had not yet wiped out resistance to the government. In wide areas of the countryside anti-Communist insurgents made it dangerous for Pathet Lao troops or government officials to venture abroad after dark. Antigovernment leaflets were distributed in schools and factories, and in the capital of Vientiane, grenades were thrown into the Soviet and Cuban embassies.

Economic prospects for the new Laos were not auspicious. Soviet and other Communist aid did not compensate for the loss of assistance from the United States, and in the towns the standard of living fell dramatically. Prices soared, black markets flourished, and the new leaders seemed at a loss to cope with the economic disarray. Most of the country's skilled technocrats, agronomists, economists, and businessmen had fled. Estimates were that 200,000 Laotians had crossed the Mekong R. to find refuge in Thailand. In an effort to build up the population of Laos, the government banned all forms of birth control.

The two chief allies of the Laotian government were Vietnam, which retained 30,000 troops in the country, and the Soviet Union, which provided hundreds of technicians and advisers. Kaysone, however, did not want to alienate China; in March he visited Peking, where he got a promise of economic aid. Relations with Thailand, strained by a series of border incidents involving the activities of Laotian refugees, improved after Aug. 3, when the two nations signed a border agreement. But border tensions resumed in October, after the ouster of Thai Prime Minister Seni Pramoj and the formation of a left-wing Thai government-in-exile in Laos.

See STATISTICS OF THE WORLD.   R.J.C.

LEBANON. War raged in Lebanon throughout 1976 despite many announced cease-fires, but at year's end the possibility of peace seemed within reach. The new president, Elias Sarkis, in his first public address on Nov. 7, issued a cautiously optimistic plea for a permanent end to the nineteen-month-old war, which had shattered the political, economic, and social life of the country and left countless thousands dead.

Background of the War. Fighting had erupted in April, 1975, between Christian and Muslim forces in Beirut as an internecine dispute over the formal distribution of political power, which favored the Christians. It continued to accelerate throughout 1975, and by the end of that year had assumed the character of a civil war.

Early in 1976 the Christians mounted a propaganda campaign and military offensive against the Palestinian presence in Lebanon, thereby drawing the sizable Palestinian militia into the thick of the fighting. The principal factions and their leaders included the moderate Muslims, led by Premier Rashid Karami, who urged political reforms; Lebanese leftists, represented by the Druze leader of the Progressive Socialist Party, Kamal Jumblat, demanding a more radical redistribution of power; conservatives (mostly Christian), led by former president Camille Chamoun and Phalangist Party head Pierre Gemayel, fighting in defense of the status quo; and Palestinians, led by Yasir Arafat,

The Arab League's peacekeeping force moves into Beirut on Nov. 15, completing its takeover of the Lebanese capital. Nineteen months of war had reduced the ancient Middle Eastern financial center to rubble; barricades marked the Muslim-Christian battle lines.

anxious to ensure the security of their presence in Lebanon and espousing the radical position. Within the Palestinian ranks were many small groups, some backed by individual Middle Eastern countries, vying for the leadership held by Arafat in the Palestine Liberation Organization (P.L.O.), which had been recognized by the Arab League as the legitimate representative of all Palestinians displaced by Israel.

The Conflict Heightens. In January President Suleiman Franjieh attempted several times to obtain a cease-fire, and on Feb. 14 he proposed a series of political reforms designed to allow Muslims a greater share of political power within the existing division of offices. The plan was supported by Christians and a few Muslims but was rejected by the Left as offering petty reforms in lieu of substantive changes. Fighting continued amid demands from the Left for Franjieh to step down.

On March 11 a moderate Muslim general declared a state of emergency and challenged Franjieh to resign or be removed from office by force. Muslim army rebels marched on the presidential palace demanding Franjieh's deposition and might have succeeded had it not been for Syrian intervention on behalf of the president to prevent a total collapse of political authority. The intervention contributed to a breach in Syrian relations with the Lebanese Left under Jumblat.

Major Muslim-leftist military advances in March strengthened the right-wing Phalangist appeals to Christians, further polarizing the political configurations. President Hafez al-Assad of Syria called repeatedly for a cease-fire and threatened to suspend arms shipments to the Left, but Jumblat was adamant in his refusal to accept a cease-fire in advance of Franjieh's resignation. Syrian regular troops intervened directly again on April 9. Within two days the Lebanese parliament voted to amend the constitution to permit selection of a new president.

On May 8 Elias Sarkis, a moderate Christian who had opposed Franjieh in the 1970 presidential elections, became president-elect. The Left, accusing Syria of imposing a "designated president" on Lebanon, had boycotted the parliamentary election meeting. The election was followed by some of the fiercest battles of the war, and more Syrian troops crossed the border. Finally, on May 31, a three-pronged Syrian attack was launched to relieve pressure on besieged Christian villages and towns.

This was a turning point in the war. Many of the remaining foreigners left the country. The United States Navy evacuated more than 275 persons from Beirut on June 20, and the Beirut airport was closed. Another 460 persons left the country in four overland convoys to Damascus in the third week in June, and a second U.S. amphibious

Elias Sarkis, seated left, takes office as president of Lebanon on Sept. 23. He replaced Suleiman Franjieh after months of wrangling over the nature of the Lebanese government.

evacuation of 208 persons was carried out on July 27. Meanwhile, on June 21, the first troops of an Arab League peacekeeping force had entered Lebanon. By late June large-scale battles were being fought throughout the country. The Tel Zaatar Palestinian refugee camp fell to rightist forces after a bloody fifty-two-day siege on Aug. 12. Syrian and Christian-rightist forces launched a major offensive on Sept. 28 that ended about Oct. 2 with the elimination of Palestinian-leftist strategic positions on the Beirut-Damascus highway.

The Winding Down. Sarkis finally became president at an inauguration ceremony on Sept. 23 that was boycotted by Karami and Jumblat. Leftist conditions for a cease-fire were satisfied, however, and serious negotiations were engaged, although fighting continued. At a meeting in Riyadh, Saudi Arabia, of Sarkis, Assad, Arafat, Egyptian President Anwar el-Sadat, Kuwaiti Sheikh Sabah al-Salem al-Sabah, and Saudi King Khalid, a truce plan was hammered out and signed on Oct. 18. It called for a 30,000-man peacekeeping force made up of some 20,000 Syrian troops and token forces from Saudi Arabia, North and South Yemen, Libya, and the Union of Arab Emirates, to divide the warring factions and confiscate heavy weapons. A cease-fire went into effect on Oct. 21 and the sporadic fighting began to subside. The mediation forces moved into Beirut on Nov. 10, completing their takeover on Nov. 15, but the most critical clause of the agreement— requiring all parties to retreat to 1975 positions— remained to be implemented.

On Dec. 9 an interim cabinet was formed under Premier Selim al-Hoss. The premier and his cabinet were supposed to attempt to rebuild the police force and the army and to start the reconstruction of the Lebanese economy. Later in the month, parliament voted them emergency powers for six months to carry out their mandate.

Meanwhile, the P.L.O. was relocating its forces

under pressure from the peacekeeping troops. By the end of the year, some slight progress had been made in removing heavy weapons from belligerent hands, and the cease-fire was holding with only minor exceptions.

See STATISTICS OF THE WORLD. See also ARAB LEAGUE; MIDDLE EAST; UNITED NATIONS.   S.C.

LESOTHO. See STATISTICS OF THE WORLD.

LIBERIA. See STATISTICS OF THE WORLD.

LIBRARIES. In 1976 drastic cutbacks in funding and consequent reductions in service continued to plague libraries for the second straight year in the United States and Canada. Among the hardest hit were the San Francisco Public Library and New York City's Queens Borough Public Library. The latter was forced not only to discontinue its bookmobile program but also to cancel its building program and to curtail service at its branch libraries. In California the Riverside Public Library was forced to reduce its staff and service along with expenditures for book buying, due to a cutback in city aid. The National Library of Canada found it necessary to eliminate reference services on weekends and holidays.

New Grants. On the brighter side, another besieged institution, the Detroit Public Library, received a $5,500,000 grant from the state of Michigan. In return, the Detroit Library Commission gave director Clara Stanton Jones permission to declare free statewide access to the main library. Grants to libraries totaling $4,250,000 were made by the W. K. Kellogg Foundation of Battle Creek, Mich. The bulk of these grants (over $2,500,000) went in $8000 units to 316 small, private, liberal arts colleges across the country. The sum of $1,500,000 was slated for the development within Michigan of a computerized network of library information services.

Library of Congress. Daniel J. Boorstin faced his first crisis as the new Librarian of Congress when the House of Representatives, led by Rep. Teno

Roncalio (D, Wyo.), petitioned to take over most of the new Madison annex of the Library of Congress for use as a House office building. Aroused librarians throughout the country were able to enlist public as well as Congressional support, forcing the House to abandon its takeover plan. A compromise plan was worked out which would allow the House to use a small portion of the building (between 6 and 7 percent) for temporary office space. A bill was then passed authorizing $30,000,000 to complete the building for library use. The additional money was required because bids on the final phase pushed the total beyond the $90,000,000 originally appropriated for the marble building.

In May Boorstin announced that James Parton, former president and a cofounder of American Heritage Publishing Co., would join the Library of Congress as assistant librarian for public education.

Library Conferences. In July the ninety-fifth annual conference of the American Library Association was held in Chicago. More than 9000 members attended the week-long conference, which celebrated the organization's one-hundredth year. The thirty-first annual conference of the Canadian Library Association was held in Halifax, Nova Scotia, in June, with more than 1000 delegates attending. "Libraries in the Canadian Mosaic" was the conference theme. The membership voted to encourage government payments to writers, possibly based on library circulation of their books, but only "in recognition of the cultural contribution of Canadian writers and not . . . any legal entitlement to recompense for the library use."

New Libraries. Final plans were drawn up by the John F. Kennedy Library Corp. to begin construction of a $12,000,000 library complex on a 9.5-acre site overlooking Boston harbor. The eight-story building was to have a museum and visitor facilities on the lower two floors and archives and research facilities on the upper six levels. The site, Columbia Point in Dorchester, was also the location of a day campus of the University of Massachusetts. The Rensselaer Polytechnic Institute in Troy, N.Y., dedicated its new Richard Gilman Folsom Library. The $6,900,000 building was to house some 500,000 volumes and provide study facilities for 800 students. R.J.S.

LIBYA. In 1976 Libya's outspoken President Muammar el-Qaddafi remained one of the most controversial leaders of the Third World. He was highly visible internationally as a fanatic supporter of the Arab hard line against Israel, as an unfailing advocate in the Organization of Petroleum Exporting Countries (q.v.) of ever-higher oil prices, and as the leader most likely to grant landing privileges to air hijackers. His own political philosophy, published in 1976, appeared to be a combination of Islam and Marxist Leninism.

The first General National Congress of the Libyan Arab Socialist Union convened in Tripoli, Jan. 5–18, with Qaddafi presiding. Premier Abdul Salam Jalloud was elected secretary-general. Following budgetary debates, Qaddafi reportedly recommended that the congress assume lawmaking responsibilities from the Revolutionary Command Council (R.C.C.), but the motion was tabled until 1977, pending a constitutional amendment.

The R.C.C. on Jan. 22 approved a five-year plan drafted at the congress. The $24.3 billion budget allocated $1.7 billion for 1976, with the largest expenditure going for agriculture, followed by education, housing, and industry. To utilize the new weapons imports provided for in the five-year plan, the national congress in its closing session voted to introduce military conscription. Many of the weapons were to be purchased from the Soviet Union.

The countless stories of student protests and other civil disturbances that appeared in the Egyptian press during the year were considered by knowledgeable observers to have been considerably exaggerated. R.C.C. member Omar Muhaishi, who had allegedly plotted to overthrow Qaddafi in August, 1975, and fled to Tunisia when the coup failed, was later granted asylum in Egypt. From Cairo, observers said, he has conducted an anti-Qaddafi campaign, as much personal as political, which aggravated the already tense relations between Cairo and Tripoli. On Sept. 1, in a speech commemorating the 7th anniversary of his overthrow of King Idris, Qaddafi adopted a surprisingly conciliatory tone. He said that although he and President Anwar el-Sadat of Egypt had their personal differences, the Libyan people had feelings of friendship for the Egyptian people. Qaddafi's speech followed several unsuccessful attempts by Premier Jalloud to mediate the Lebanese civil war; it may be that their shared opposition to the Syrian intervention in Lebanon provided a basis for the attempts at resolution of Egyptian-Libyan differences.

Maps released by Libya in September indicated a 52,000-sq.-mi. expansion of Libyan borders into territory previously claimed by Algeria, Chad, and Niger. Although the desert territory is thought to be rich in phosphates, iron ore, and uranium, no protest was lodged by any of the three countries whose land Libya had apparently appropriated.

See STATISTICS OF THE WORLD. *See also* ARAB LEAGUE; MIDDLE EAST. S.C.

LIECHTENSTEIN. *See* STATISTICS OF THE WORLD.

LIFE SCIENCES

What were they up to, the scientists who study life? Biologists created a working artificial gene. Botanists discovered that a common carbohydrate induces immunity in plants. And zoologists found that migratory birds can navigate by using the earth's magnetic field.

Those scientists whose specialties are the life sciences concentrated in 1976 on uncovering the fundamental processes that govern the immense variety of living forms. They made startling discoveries in such new areas of study as the evolutionary relationships of all living creatures and the similarities in behavior that exist in entirely different orders of animals. Zoologists were finding on the highest levels of biological organization what geneticists were finding in the tiniest bits of a cell: universal mechanisms of adaptation that increase success in the environment.

BIOLOGY

Recombinant genetics, the recently developed technique of transferring genetic material from one cell into another, usually creating a hybrid cell of two alien species, proceeded during 1976 under new National Institutes of Health regulations. These rules were worked out by scientists themselves to prevent the escape into nature of new life forms against which existing creatures might be defenseless. But some scientists still objected to the use in these experiments of a bacterium that normally lives in the intestines of humans and many animals.

Other cell biologists reached the culmination of many years of work with a yellow-pigment protein, cytochrome c, when the substance was traced through almost all living species and provided a means of following evolutionary branching through the three billion years of life on earth. And a bacterial survivor of an unusual form of photosynthesis offered clues to the development of vision.

Gene Transfer Research. A historic milestone in biology was passed in August when 1968 Nobel laureate Har Gobind Khorana and his coworkers at the Massachusetts Institute of Technology (M.I.T.) announced that they had made an artificial gene that functioned normally within a living cell. The group had spent nine years constructing from "off the shelf" chemicals the sequence of 207 pairs of nucleotides that make up the gene of *Escherichia coli,* a common intestinal bacterium.

Nucleotides are the subunits that link the rungs of the DNA (deoxyribonuclease) spiral ladder that constitutes the gene. There are only four types of nucleotides, but by their arrangement in pairs and sequences, as in a four-letter alphabet system that can create words and sentences, they issue an enormous variety of instructions for the genes to carry out, resulting in a vast diversity of cells within and among living things.

Of the 207 paired nucleotides painstakingly strung together by the M.I.T. scientists, the first 56 tell the *E. coli* gene to go into action; taken together, they are called the promoter. The next 126 pairs govern the production of a chemical that delivers a special "building block" of protein to the cell's protein assembly line; the cell cannot make normal proteins if any of these pairs are missing or out of place. The final 21 nucleotide pairs in the sequence tell the gene to stop working; they are collectively called the terminator. When Khorana and his team inserted the correctly sequenced gene into a genetically defective strain of *E. coli,* the "sick" bacteria began to function normally.

The construction of the promoter and terminator sections of the gene held particular promise for medical and various other applications. By learning the correct sequences of these gene segments in humans, for example, scientists could "turn on" helpful genes that are dormant and "turn off" active harmful genes, thus preventing or curing many devastating genetic diseases.

In the Khorana method of combining outside genetic material with naturally occurring genes within a cell, no foreign species were being brought together. The formerly defective bacteria were simply restored to a state that was normal for the species. Other researchers, however, experimented with the introduction of gene fragments from one species into the cell of a totally alien species. One of the potential benefits of this work is that it may expose the nucleotide sequences in the genes of different types of cells, making it possible to understand, imitate, or even

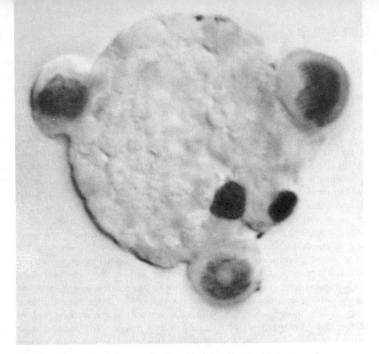

This hybrid cell contains nuclei from the plant kingdom and the animal kingdom. Tobacco plant cells and human tumor cells (the large black spots) were joined in a single biological unit by scientists working at Brookhaven National Laboratory.

change a "message." Four groups of scientists spliced into bacterial cells some genetic material from rabbits that directs the production of the protein portion of hemoglobin, which transports oxygen in red blood cells. Other groups fused human cervical cancer cells with tobacco cells and with carrot cells. The human genetic material disappeared as the hybrid cells subdivided, offering a means of tracing the functions of the human genetic segments by their exclusion at different stages of cell division. Should human proteins be able to grow in plant or bacterial cells, cell "factories" could be established for the production of now-scarce enzymes that are needed for many human ailments.

Universal Genealogy. During the year continuing work by several groups of scientists established a chemical method for tracing the branches of the evolutionary tree.

More than 3,000,000 species of animals and plants inhabit the earth today. Yet fossil records reveal that as recently as 600,000,000 years ago only a few species of life struggled for survival on our planet. Did the 3,000,000 species now on earth evolve from the few? Can all the living forms we know today be related to one another? With very few exceptions in simple organisms, animal species from humans to fish down to yeasts and bacteria are alike in a fundamental way. All are oxygen-dependent, or aerobic; they have a built-in system for producing energy through the burning of food with oxygen.

Scientists examining living cells, where energy is produced and stored, found a chemical substance common to all the aerobic species, cytochrome c. Cytochrome c is a yellow-pigment protein that triggers cell respiration. Without it, aerobic cells would "suffocate." Its structure in horse heart cells was uncovered in 1961 by Emil L. Smith and Emanuel Margoliash, then working at the University of Utah College of Medicine, and Gunther Kreil and Hans Tuppy of the University of Vienna. As in many other proteins, the cytochrome c molecule is made up of a central coiled "rope" (a peptide chain) consisting of connected "bristles" (amino acids). In nature there are 20 different amino acids, made up of atoms of carbon, hydrogen, oxygen, nitrogen, and, in a few cases, sulfur. The peptide chain of horse-heart cytochrome c contains 104 amino acid "bristles." Each amino acid is found in the same place in every molecule of horse-heart cytochrome c.

In 1962 and 1963 Smith and Margoliash and other researchers analyzed the structure of cytochrome c obtained from human beings, other animals, and yeasts. Their results were startling. The organisms studied had many differences in form and function, but 58 specific positions on the peptide chain of each cytochrome c molecule contained identical amino acids. Could this result from chance? The probability of any 2 amino acids being in identical positions is 20 times 20, or 1 in 400. For 58 amino acid matches, the chances are equal to 20 multiplied by itself 58 times, an astronomical number. As the scientists studied the similarities and differences among species in the rest of the cytochrome c molecule, a certain pattern emerged. The cytochrome c of human beings and that of rhesus monkeys differ in the position of only 2 amino acids. There are 12 such differences between human beings and horses, 21 between human beings and fish, 30 between human beings and the moth, and 45 between human beings and yeasts. The more primitive the form of life, the larger the number of differences between it and the human in the amino acid positions. Smith and Margoliash ascribed this pattern to the branching of the evolutionary tree. Yeasts are near the bottom of the tree. They evolved from 1 to 2 billion years ago. Insectlike animals are believed to have evolved about 600,000,000 years ago; fishes, 400,000,000; horses, 70,000,000; and monkeys at about the same time as the early ancestors of present-day human beings, 50,000,000 to 60,000,000 years ago. Thus, one might expect animals that evolved at about the same time to have very similar cytochrome c molecules. It was found that, in fact, the cytochrome c of pigs, cows, and sheep, all of which evolved during much the same period, is identical. This evidence strongly suggests that the gene controlling the design and production of cytochrome c in yeasts and in human beings is essentially the same; thus it points to a genetic link between all oxygen-dependent life.

In 1976 this evolutionary link was traced even further back in the history of our planet. Richard E. Dickerson of the California Institute of Technology and other scientists followed the evolutionary trail of cytochrome c back three billion years and found evidence that sulfur bacteria, which evolved at about that time, produced the first cytochrome c proteins. These bacteria relied on photosynthesis, on the hydrogen sulfide then present in the earth's atmosphere, and on their primitive cytochrome c to produce and store the energy required for them to carry on life processes. The next "generation" of photosynthetic bacteria to evolve was able to tap the richer energy supply locked in the chemical bonds of minerals called sulfates. (Today, the descendants of these organisms help digest sewage.) Other living things then developed, among them early green plants that used water instead of sulfur compounds in the process of photosynthesis. Slowly through the years the green plants began to release into the earth's atmosphere the oxygen that had been bound in the water, and oxygen-dependent forms of life began to evolve. Dickerson's studies of cytochrome c suggest that this vital chemical was a basic part of both aerobic and photosynthetic processes, thus linking almost all living things in a three-billion-year evolutionary chain.

Photosynthesis in Bacteria. A purple pigment similar to the pigment rhodopsin in the eyes of animals enables a species of bacteria to convert sunlight to chemical energy, much as a green plant uses chlorophyll for the same process. The pigment, a cell membrane material called bacteriorhodopsin, was found in 1971 by Walter Stoeckenius of the University of California at San Francisco, in the halobacteria (*Halobacterium halobium*) that live in calm, very salty waters such as the Dead Sea or the stagnant salt flats at the edge of ocean bays. At times when the habitat becomes devoid of oxygen and nutrients, the purple membranes, under the influence of sunlight, remove hydrogen nuclei from the bacteria and eject them into the surrounding water (changing its color to red); the negative electric charge of the hydrogen electrons left in the bacteria creates the energetic conditions for the manufacture of adenosine triphosphate (ATP), the molecule in all life systems that stores energy.

In March a team of cell biologists headed by Stoeckenius announced that they had discovered

A maple tree stricken with maple dieback. In 1976 botanists decided that the rapidly spreading disease could be caused by environmental conditions.

the structure of bacteriorhodopsin and had duplicated in the laboratory the energy-producing process of the halobacterium. The very stable pigment was considered to be potentially useful in solar-energy conversion systems.

Stoeckenius pointed out that in the two major systems of utilizing the energy of light, plants use chlorophyll to convert light to chemical energy and animals use rhodopsin to convert light to nerve impulses. The halobacteria's intermediate system may represent an ancient form of light conversion along the evolutionary pathway to vision.

Deaths. Two Nobel laureates, Jacques Monod and George H. Whipple, died during the year; *see* OBITUARIES. C.P.

BOTANY

Events of botanical importance in 1976 included the identification of a natural chemical that triggers plant immunity, new methods for controlling Dutch elm and fruit tree diseases, and the passage of legislation to protect endangered plants.

Elicitors of Plant Immunity. A chemical substance that helps plants to resist infection was isolated from the surface of a fungus that attacks soybeans. Peter Albersheim and his colleagues at the University of Colorado found that the substance, a harmless polysaccharide (a carbohydrate formed of a chain of simple sugars) elicited a basic immune response in a wide variety of plants from garden vegetables to shade trees. That response was the production of phytoaxelins, chemicals that are toxic to invading bacteria and fungi. Further research showed that very similar elicitors of plant immunity were present on the surfaces of many bacteria and fungi, and even on brewer's yeast. This raised hope for the commercial production of an almost perfect bacteriofungicide to work against many types of blight. Such a fungicide could be produced cheaply, would protect plants without killing beneficial organisms, and would break down naturally into the soil. But first—and this was possibly a major stumbling block—ways had to be found to make the plants absorb enough of the elicitor to be able to produce effective quantities of phytoaxelins.

Battle Against Tree Diseases. Hopes were raised for a treatment to prevent the spread of Dutch elm disease. The condition, often fatal to the American elm, is caused by a fungus spread by elm bark beetles. Researchers created effective resistance to the fungus by injecting a common fungicide (nystatin) diluted with water and dextrose into a hole drilled at the base of the tree. Widespread Dutch elm vaccination programs were being planned for the spring of 1977. Also during 1976 peach X disease, a serious problem

with fruit growers in the Northeast, was successfully controlled by injecting peach trees with a common antibiotic, tetracycline. However, a rapidly spreading disease of maple trees, called maple dieback, resisted the efforts of researchers to determine its cause. This failure suggested to botanists that dieback resulted from a variety of causes that might be related to adverse environmental conditions. Finally, fireblight, a highly infectious bacterial disease of pear and apple trees, was found to produce its fatal results through blockage by bacterial toxin of the vessels that convey water through the tree's trunk. Identification of the problem made it easier to work toward a cure.

Endangered Plants Legislation. In 1973 the United States Congress joined legislative bodies in other countries in beginning to formulate laws for the preservation of natural habitats of plants and animals. Three documents emerged from these activities: the 1973 Endangered Species Act, the 1973 Convention on International Trade in Endangered Species of Wild Fauna and Flora, and the 1975 Smithsonian Report on Endangered and Threatened Plant Species of the United States. Recommendations for land acquisition, for punishment of violators, and for international cooperation were stressed. Many countries agreed to the terms of the convention, and on April 13, 1976, President Gerald R. Ford signed an executive order that made its legal provisions binding in the U.S. For botanists, the law made the gathering of many field-collected plants more difficult. At the same time it gave them some assurance that endangered plants and their environments would be around for them to study in the future.

New Dictionary and a Botanic Gardens Inventory. An important new reference book, *Hortus III*, appeared in 1976. This dictionary of plants cultivated in the U.S. and Canada was compiled by the staff of the Liberty Hyde Bailey Hortorium at Cornell University. Coverage includes 34,305 families, genera, and species as well as an uncounted number of subspecies, varieties, forms, and cultivars. Each botanical name appears with its botanical synonyms, common names, country of origin, and cultural notes.

The Plant Sciences Data Center of the American Horticultural Society in Mount Vernon, Va., compiled a master inventory of plant records from the North American botanical gardens and arboretums. This list covers 139,162 records, which include the plant names, location, original source, and year of acquisition. The list was to be updated annually. R.P.P.

ZOOLOGY

Reports of intraspecies slavery, display tournaments, and tool use in ants attracted wide attention during the year. Migratory aids in birds and lobsters were revealed and a large collection of strange fossil sharks was uncovered in Montana.

Ant Slavery. Interspecies slavery among ants has long been documented, but the enslavement of one's own species seemed to have been confined to humans. But in May Bert Holldobler of Harvard University reported several observations of the capture by invading desert honeypot ants of an entire colony of defeated opponents of the same species. (The invaders had first to kill or drive off their opponents' queen.) Such conquests occurred only if one of the contesting colonies had overwhelming numbers, rather than greater strength in one-to-one combat. Unlike the deadly battles between opposing ant species, however, these wars within one species were mainly display tournaments and resulted in very few injuries or deaths, and only occasional enslavement. These desert honeypot ants, which are abundant in the southwestern U.S., thus demonstrated behavior that occurs in most animal orders—a threatening, relatively harmless display of strength within a species.

In other ant studies during the year, four species of ants were observed to employ tools—leaves, pine needles, bits of wood, dried mud, or even sand grains—to carry much greater loads of

This 4½-in.-long crustacean, recently discovered alive in the South China Sea, is a member of the Glypheidae family. The living fossil was previously thought to have been entirely extinct for 50,000,000 years.

food than they could have carried without the tools. The observers saw the ants search the ground and test various objects before selecting a suitable one, which they then carried off to the food supply.

Magnetic Compass in Birds. In the early 1960's F. W. Merkel of the University of Frankfurt in Germany discovered the ability of many birds to detect and use the earth's magnetic field as a compass. His research opened a new era in work on avian orientation and migration. Recent studies by W. Wiltschko, a student of Merkel, showed that the birds use the magnetic field as an "inclined compass," not to detect north, but to guide their flights by the angle between the inclination of the magnetic field and the pull of gravity. The system is not useful when migrating birds cross the magnetic equator, for there they would be led in the wrong direction. And it is not available during those periods in the earth's history when the magnetic field intensity is reduced to zero during the course of a reversal. The birds would then seem to need secondary orientation clues, such as the stars and the sun, to find their way.

Queuing Behavior in the Lobster. During their autumnal mass migration, spiny lobsters *(Parulirus argus)* move in long, single files (queues) of up to sixty-five individuals. Ordinarily, solitary and combative migrating lobsters may remain in queues for well over half of the day, each maintaining bodily contact with the one in front of it by means of its antennae, mouth parts, or anterior legs. Such queuing migrations are analogous to

A cirrate octopus, rarely seen alive, was photographed by an automatic camera aboard the Alvin, a deep-water submersible craft, during its exploration of the Cayman Trough in the Gulf of Mexico. The "ears" on the mysterious yard-long creature are actually fins.

the V formations of geese and other birds, suggesting that the advantage of these single line formations lies in drag reduction, making for a smoother, and therefore speedier, flow of air or water past a moving body. William Herrnkind of Florida State University tested this idea by measuring lobster movement with motion pictures and comparing drag resistance in solitary and queue-linked lobsters. He found that in a queue of nineteen lobsters, the drag was reduced by 65 percent. Reduction in drag increased with the length of the line and the speed at which it traveled. The characteristics of lobster mass movement are unique among bottom-dwelling marine crustaceans and are of special interest in comparison with migrations of army ants, as well as of birds

Fossil Sharks. Recent excavations at Bear Gulch in Montana by Richard Lund of Adelphi University, in Garden City, N.Y., have led to the discovery of a number of new species of fossil sharks. Working in soft limestone laid down in a shallow sea during the late Carboniferous age, Lund found many complete skeletons of sharks, some only an inch and a quarter long, that are so well preserved that the outline of the soft parts of the body and the pattern of surface scales can be seen in addition to the skeleton. These sharks possess many peculiar features. Some have spines protruding from the top of their skulls; others have flounderlike bodies or greatly enlarged fins. Some bizarre fossils have crablike claws on their snouts. Perhaps the most remarkable species is a 4-ft. shark whose dorsal fin is hinged like an airplane rudder. This fin would have enabled the fish to make rapid changes of direction. The quarry at Bear Gulch has yielded other species of fish as well as many shrimps and worms, and some unidentified forms that were being investigated.

Insect Zoo. The first insect zoo in the U.S. was opened to the public by the Smithsonian Institution's Natural History Museum in August and immediately became one of the most popular exhibits in Washington, D.C. The living collection, beautifully displayed in clear plastic cages, is arranged to explain and demonstrate the variety of behaviors and special adaptations in each representative group. The zoo actually houses more than a hundred species of arthropods, animals with jointed legs, segmented bodies, and external skeletons, and it includes centipedes, arachnids (spiders, scorpions, and mites), and crustaceans (crayfish, crabs, lobsters, and barnacles), as well as insects.   W.J.B.

LITERATURES OF THE WORLD. The 1976 Nobel Prize for literature went to American novelist Saul Bellow, who warned in his acceptance speech that contemporary writers were avoiding important human issues in favor of trivia. His criticism was leveled chiefly at American, British, and French literature, in which the novel was clearly ailing and a spirit of novelty and escapism prevailed. But elsewhere literature was demonstrating vigor, force, and relevance to the lives of readers. This was especially so where authoritarian regimes threatened and persecuted it. From Latin America, Eastern Europe, and Africa came many interesting new works, often published in exile and quickly made accessible in English translation.

LITERATURES OF THE WORLD

AFRICAN

The year proved rich in new fiction and critical writing, especially from southern Africa, where political eruptions were mirrored in an outpouring of translations and new poetry and prose.

Southern Africa. The roots of contemporary Rhodesian writing were partly revealed in an English-language translation of the first black Rhodesian novel, *Feso,* by Solomon M. Mutswairo. This important work was included in *Zimbabwe: Prose and Poetry,* along with twenty-five of Mutswairo's poems. The long-silent Zulu novelist Jordan Kush Ngubame published his umlando (novel-epic) *Ushaba,* which again dramatized the effects of apartheid on Zulu folk life. J. M. Coetzee's *Dusklands* provided a two-part novel of men obsessed and corrupted by the power of technology in Vietnam and South Africa. A retrospective look at Nathaniel Ndzivane Nakasa, the first black South African to write a column in a "white" newspaper, was provided in *The World of Nat Nakasa.* One of South Africa's leading black poets, Mongane Wally Serote, issued a new collection called *Yakhal' Inkomo* ("The Cry of the Cattle at the Slaughterhouse"), while the rebel poet Wopko Jensma published his new collection *Sing for Our Execution.* Certainly the best-known work to emerge from southern Africa in 1976 was a new edition of *Sizwe Banzi Is Dead and The Island.* Written by Athol Fugard and the two black actors John Kani and Winston Ntshona, both plays had appeared on Broadway in 1974 and both voice powerful denunciations of the repression of black identity and self-respect.

Arab and West Africa. Writing from the rest of the continent was scattered, but it provided the same basic mixture of retrospective collections and new writing. *Modern Arab Poets: 1950–1975* brought together writings of twenty-two poets of the Arab world, including poets from Sudan. In an impressionistic story of the pilgrimage of a dying nobleman, *The Thirteenth Sun,* Ethiopian novelist Worku Daniachew shows a people and a country torn between African and European tradition. In *Xala,* Sembene Ousmane returned again to his roots and wove traditional African narrative forms together with the realities of modern Senegalese life. Nigeria's Cyprian Ekwensi set his latest novel, *Survive the Peace,* in the Biafran war (1967–70). Two of West Africa's most exciting women writers produced major new works in 1976. Ama Ata Aidoo, the prizewinning Ghanaian poet, playwright, and short-story writer, published her first full-length novel. *Our Sister Killjoy* describes the thoughts, encounters, and actions of a girl traveling through Europe on her way back to her African homeland. Buchi Emecheta, a Nigerian sociologist and novelist, reexamined the clash of cultures and its impact on matrimony in her *The Bride Price.*   J.T.S.

AMERICAN

In America's Bicentennial year of 1976 its writers took a long look back at the road so far traveled, with only an occasional glance at the present or glimpse into the future. Recent historical events such as the Watergate scandal and the Vietnam war continued to engage both fiction and nonfiction writers, while such contemporary issues as the women's movement seemed to draw a deeper and less frenetic attention.

Fiction. More than other American novelists, Gore Vidal capitalized on the Bicentennial with *1876,* regarded by the critics as an inferior sequel to his popular *Burr* (1973). The new novel continues the

John Kani (left) and Winston Ntshona won prizes for their performances in New York City in Sizwe Banzi Is Dead, a play they had written with Athol Fugard. In 1976 the two were briefly imprisoned for performing the same play in Transkei, near their South African homes.

story of Aaron Burr's illegitimate son through the year of the nation's Centennial celebration. American history takes on a more bizarre and telling shape in Ishmael Reed's *Flight to Canada,* the fifth novel of this innovative black novelist. By mixing past and present into a humorous montage, Reed convinces us that the issue of slavery cannot be forgotten. James Purdy's *In a Shallow Grave* combines comedy with pathos in the story of a horribly disfigured veteran of the Vietnam war.

John Updike, chronicler of midcentury suburban America, continued exploring the same turf that produced his earlier novels with *Marry Me,* a tale of neighborly adultery. Other works by bestselling novelists included Leon Uris's *Trinity,* a historical narrative about the troubled times in Ireland from the late 19th to early 20th centuries; Kurt Vonnegut's *Slapstick,* detailing the unusual story of a brother and sister who individually are perceived as idiotic but who in combination form a kind of bizarre genius; and Peter Benchley's *The Deep,* in which the author of *Jaws* (1974) switches from sharks to treasure hunting off Bermuda for another thrilling plot.

Another well-known writer, Vance Bourjaily, produced his best novel to date, *Now Playing at Canterbury,* an analysis of American society as represented in the microcosm of the production of an opera in the Midwest. James T. Farrell, author of the famous *Studs Lonigan* trilogy (1932–35), published his fiftieth book in 1976: *The Dunne Family,* set in Chicago during the Depression.

Two members of the administration of President Richard M. Nixon became first novelists in 1976. Former Vice-President Spiro T. Agnew exploited his insider's knowledge of government in *The Canfield Decision* with much energy but little artistic success. And John D. Ehrlichman, former assistant to the President for domestic affairs, presented *The Company,* a well-plotted and entertaining roman à clef.

Poetry. Volumes by established and new American poets marked the Bicentennial year. Karl Shapiro's *Adult Bookstore* includes thirty-two new poems all carrying his usual blend of irony and sharp realism. The *Selected Poems* of Robert Lowell showcases the work of an acknowledged contemporary master. Elizabeth Bishop was widely acclaimed for *Geography III.* Richard Wilbur, one of the few prominent poets who still regularly employ rhyme, offered *The Mind-Reader,* a collection of graceful and witty verse. In *Searching for the Ox,* his seventh volume, Louis Simpson defines issues of body and soul in terms that are addressed to the reader, avoiding the all too fre-

Alex Haley began his unusual twelve-year research for his 1976 best-seller Roots *among the African delegates to the United Nations (background).*

quent poet's recourse to private monologue. Another eminent bard, Archibald MacLeish, combines lyrical expression with deep emotion in *New & Collected Poems, 1917–1976.* The narrative poetry of James Merrill's *Divine Comedies* continued to establish his place as one of America's ranking makers of verse.

Among the new poets, Marilyn Hacker, who won a National Book Award in 1975 for *Presentation Pieces,* produced *Separations,* a collection of technically proficient poems ranging in form from sonnets to villanelles. Robert Hayden offered his sixth volume, *Angle of Ascent,* which includes portraits of famous black Americans ranging from Frederick Douglass to Bessie Smith.

First volumes of note included Bryan Alec Floyd's *The Long War Dead,* a collection of monologues in the tradition of Edgar Lee Masters' *A Spoon River Anthology.* The monologues in Floyd's book are delivered by a variety of soldiers fighting in the Vietnam war. In *First Selected Poems,* Leo Connellon strikes a pessimistic tone in his tough and biting examinations of death, poverty, insanity, and despair.

History and Biography. The Bicentennial produced a major popular history in Page Smith's *A People's History of the American Revolution,* a mammoth work articulating the author's thesis that the revolution can best be described as a populist uprising. The continuing examination of

219

slavery by American historians took a significant new turn with Herbert G. Gutman's *The Black Family in Slavery and Freedom*. Gutman maintains that during slavery and afterward the black family was a viable and creative social unit.

In *Roots* Alex Haley (who helped write *The Autobiography of Malcolm X* in 1964) personalizes the discussion of slavery by tracing his lineage back in fictionalized form to the 18th-century African village from which his ancestor was forcibly taken and brought to America as a slave.

Terrence Des Pres examines 20th-century oppression in *The Survivor,* a study of those who lived through the death camps of Adolf Hitler and Joseph Stalin. Des Pres finds a tremendous will for life combined with a persistent sense of humanity in those who survived.

The fear-ridden era of the early 1950's is brought into focus by Lillian Hellman in *Scoundrel Time,* which describes her refusal to serve as a "friendly" witness before a Congressional committee investigating Communist influence among writers and artists. The book takes an unsparing look at those intellectuals who did cooperate in the harassment of their colleagues.

Doris Kearns used her service as a White House Fellow and her subsequent friendship with Lyndon B. Johnson as sources for an unusually personal perspective on the former President in *Lyndon Johnson and the American Dream*.

Literary biographies included Geoffrey Wolff's *Black Sun,* the story of Harry Crosby, an eccentric, rich, and morbid literary man of the 1920's whose personal life was more memorable than his writing. Joseph Frank tackled another troubled, but infinitely more talented, man in his *Dostoevsky,* the first of a projected four volumes on the Russian novelist. Ernest Hemingway's warmer human side was presented in two works by people who knew him intimately. In *Papa* Hemingway's son Gregory portrays the writer as a gentle and loving but difficult father. Mary Welsh Hemingway, the novelist's fourth and final wife, indicates in *How It Was* that Hemingway's public bravura was counterbalanced by an increasing private gloom.

Contemporary Affairs. In another runaway best-seller, Bob Woodward and Carl Bernstein, the Washington (D.C.) *Post* reporters who broke the Watergate case, document the end of the Nixon Presidency in *The Final Days*. Watergate also provided an opportunity for one of the main actors in the drama to profit from his role by writing an insider's book. John W. Dean 3rd's *Blind Ambition* was hailed as a brutally honest and detailed account of how his career responded only to the demands of his own ambition.

C. D. B. Byran's *Friendly Fire* presents the an-

American author Lillian Hellman appears as a legend in a 1976 Blackglama fur ad. Her 1976 book was Scoundrel Time, *an account of her role in the loyalty investigations of the early 1950's.*

guish of Iowans Gene and Peg Mullen as they attempted to learn the circumstances of their GI son's death during the Vietnam war. Betty Friedan, one of the main architects of the women's movement, describes the political infighting of the last twelve years in *It Changed My Life*. Adrienne Rich, a well-reputed poet, published *Of Woman Born,* a bitter investigation of motherhood and marriage. In *Words and Women* Casey Miller and Kate Swift examine language from a feminist perspective. Gail Sheehy's *Passages* was the year's pop-psychology winner; its thesis is that personal crises, such as those of adolescence, occur at predictable ages throughout adult life.

The problems of modern industrialized American society are explored from different perspectives in *Medical Nemesis* by Ivan Illich and *Schooling in Capitalist America* by Samuel Bowles and Herbert Gintis. Illich claims that prescribed medicines and treatments can actually cause and prolong diseases for the benefit of the medical profession. Bowles and Gintis attack American education from a Marxist point of view. From still another perspective, modern American society is examined in Irving Howe's *World of Our Fathers,* which establishes links between contemporary

Novelist and playwright David Storey returned to the northern English setting of his childhood for his novel Saville. *Storey was awarded the 1976 Booker Prize for the absorbing work.*

American Jews and their immigrant beginnings. One American Jew, Nobel laureate Saul Bellow, observes and briefly participates in the turbulence of Israeli life in *Jerusalem and Back.*

Deaths. Patrick Dennis, Paul Gallico, Samuel Eliot Morison, William Red Fox, H. Allen Smith, and Frank Sullivan died during the year; see OBITUARIES. Other deaths included those of novelist and screenwriter James Warner Bellah (Sept. 22 at 77), novelist and journalist Joe David Brown (April 22 at 60), New York State historian Carl Carmer (Sept. 11 at 82), poet Louis Ginsberg (Aug. 8 at 80), Russian literature critic Marc Slonim (May 8 at 82), and the author of *Father of the Bride,* Edward Streeter (March 31 at 84). S.C.L.

AUSTRALIAN

Most of the better-known Australian novelists published new works during the year, which also saw important contributions by writers of nonfiction.

Fiction. Patrick White's tenth novel, *A Fringe of Leaves,* was generally acclaimed for its directness and readability. Based on the 19th-century story of Eliza Fraser, who was shipwrecked among aborigines on an island off the Queensland coast, it offered White the opportunity to investigate his

favorite theme, that of an individual enduring a term of trial. Christina Stead's *Miss Herbert (The Suburban Wife)* was a significant addition to her large body of work. It is an English beauty's life story, in which private and social anguish mesh perfectly. Thomas Keneally, now living in the United States, continued his exploration of European history in *Season in Purgatory,* a straightforward narrative about a young English surgeon tending wounded Yugoslav partisans on an Adriatic island during World War II. Robert Drew's first novel, *The Savage Crows,* astonished critics with its maturity and tremendous potential. The book successfully intertwines an assessment of present-day Australian society with an account of the genocide of the Tasmanian natives by Whites.

Nonfiction. Volume six of the *Australian Dictionary of Biography* brought the nation's costliest and most elaborate publishing project to the halfway mark. The first volume appeared in 1966; a total of twelve volumes comprising 7000 biographies was projected.

Donald Horne, whose *The Lucky Country* (1964) established his reputation as a highly original social critic, investigates how economic values have shaped Australian society in his 1976 work *Money Made Us.* It is vintage Horne—witty, incisive, and certain to cause controversy. Journalist and social historian Gavin Souter wrote a literate and dramatic account of Australia's first years of nationhood, *Lion and Kangaroo; The Initiation of Australia, 1901–1919.* It examines the special relationship between Australian nationalism and imperial sentiment.

Awards. The irascible old man of Australian letters, Xavier Herbert, reluctantly accepted the Miles Franklin award for his mammoth novel *Poor Fellah My Country.* A. D. Hope received the Robert Frost award, made by the Californian Friends of Robert Frost through the Fellowship of Australian Writers. The F. A. W. Barbara Ramsden award was shared by three authors: Geoffrey Blainey for his history of ancient Australia, *Triumph of the Nomads;* Thomas Keneally for *Gossip from the Forest,* a fictional recreation of the signing of the armistice in 1918; and Mary Liverani for *The Winter Sparrows,* describing her childhood in the slums of Glasgow. The National Book Council prize went to *Cape Solitary,* Ray Ericksen's account of his experiences as a dropout. Les Murray won the C. J. Dennis Memorial Poetry Competition for his *Selected Poems: The Vernacular Republic.* I.K.

CANADIAN

A prosperous year for Canadian publishing was highlighted by novels in English and French that mixed realism and fantasy.

Fiction. In *Bear* by Marian Engel a Toronto girl working in the cottage country meets a bear and falls in love. Her love is not that of a zoologist or conservationist, but love rooted in sexuality. The novel has a good deal to say about the synthesis of two cultures and the possibilities of human survival, and one learns a lot about bears. With an incisive wit, Margaret Atwood's *Lady Oracle* cuts into one fat girl's inability to shed her layers of personality (and fatuous lovers) and get down to the real "her." The novel has energy and flair, but somehow lacks warmth.

French-speaking writers in Canada were now talking less of the Québec condition and more of *la condition humaine:* a philosophic, if not necessarily aesthetic, progression. André Langevin's novel, *Une Chaîne dans le Parc* (translated by Alan Brown as *Orphan Street*) portrays an urban slum childhood in Québec a generation ago. Pierrot, the child hero, enters a world where death by tuberculosis is expected and where the survivors need a vast amount of goodness if they are not to become bitter and dessicated pietists. Yet there are free spirits who teach that, despite all, human relationships are better than the companionship of dreams. Roch Carrier's *Le Jardin des Délices* ("The Garden of Delights") is a robust novel of Rabelaisian gusto, macabre Gothic humor, and Québec burlesque. The author's fifth novel in ten years, it is more ambitious and assured than any to date, yet as fresh as his first.

Biography. The year's most popular biography was Peter Desbarat's timely portrait of René Lévesque, the French-Canadian separatist who was elected premier of Québec in November. *René: A Canadian in Search of a Country* traces Lévesque's career from his birth in primarily English-speaking New Carlisle on the Gaspé Peninsula, through his remarkable journalistic career (including a stint as an American war correspondent), to his entry into politics and, finally, to his leadership of the separatist Parti Québécois.

A Death. Roderick Haig-Brown, environmentalist and author of books on fishing and the outdoors, died Oct. 9 at 68.   B.M.P.

ENGLISH

English fiction and poetry in 1976 were dominated by established writers in mid-career. The outstanding nonfiction was mainly memoirs and reminiscences of colorful figures of the first half of the 20th century.

Fiction. The £5000 ($8500) Booker Prize was won by David Storey's *Saville,* which tells of two brothers from a northern English mining family and the different courses their lives take. Other impressive novels were Kingsley Amis's *The Alteration,* a witty and inventive fantasy of life in the 20th century if English history had taken a different path at various turning points; William Trevor's study of an emotionally deprived boy, *The Children of Dynmouth;* and Brian Moore's account in *The Doctor's Wife* of how a Belfast woman makes a complete break with her married life. Iris Murdoch drew contrasting portraits of two men, one worldly and one religious, in *Henry and Cato.* Muriel Spark published a witty book about the rich in Italy, *The Takeover,* and Beryl Bainbridge offered *A Quiet Life,* her study of a wartime childhood in a lower-middle-class home. A racy novel sequence, Simon Raven's *Alms for Oblivion,* came to a satisfying end with its tenth and final book, *The Survivors.*

Nonfiction. Historian Hugh Trevor-Roper uncovered a remarkable tale in his book *A Hidden Life: The Enigma of Sir Edmund Backhouse.* Backhouse was an Englishman who lived as a scholar and secret agent in China in the years before the fall of the Chinese Empire, and wove into his diaries an amazing blend of fact and erotic fantasy. The life of another pre-World War I figure, a young

Part of a letter by Lord Byron to his friend Scrope Berdmore Davies, dated June 22, 1809. The letter was found at a London bank in December, along with other important literary manuscripts.

poet, is sensitively retold in *Julian Grenfell* by Nicholas Mosley. David Pryce-Jones's *Unity Mitford* is about an aristocratic young woman, sister of the writer Nancy Mitford, who became a close friend of Adolf Hitler and shot herself when war broke out between Great Britain and Germany in 1939. A lighter-hearted biography of a man who first became famous between the two World Wars, the playwright Noel Coward, was written by his friend of many years, Cole Lesley, under the title *The Life of Noel Coward*. The novelist Anthony Powell published the first volume of his memoirs, *Infants of the Spring*, in which readers met some factual details of the life that had been transmuted into his novel sequence, *A Dance to the Music of Time*, completed in 1975 with the publication of the twelfth volume.

A second volume of letters of Virginia Woolf's, covering the years 1912 to 1922, was entitled *The Question of Things Happening*; the editors once again were Nigel Nicolson and Joanne Trautmann. *The Diaries of Evelyn Waugh*, edited by Michael Davie, evoked a great deal of interest. Full of wit and insult, they gave a vivacious account of one swath of English life from the 1920's to the 1960's, and they also showed how a sensitive boy remained behind the facade of the savagely satirical novelist.

In other fields the second volume of Richard Crossman's *Diaries of a Cabinet Minister* continued to shed light on the process of government in recent years; and Sir Isaiah Berlin's *Vico and Herder* was an elegant and eloquent pair of philosophical essays on two underestimated thinkers. The most praised volume of literary criticism was probably *The Uses of Diversity*, a spirited study of the nature of the novel by John Bayley, the husband of Iris Murdoch.

Poetry and Drama. Two volumes of English poetry stood out in 1976: *Season Songs* by Ted Hughes, a tender evocation of nature, and *Jack Straw's Castle* by Thom Gunn, set largely in California.

A major literary discovery was made in December when a chest of 19th-century papers turned up in a London bank vault. The chest contained two unpublished poems by Percy Bysshe Shelley, fourteen unpublished letters by Lord Byron, and several other manuscripts by the two poets.

Although 1976 saw the long-awaited opening of the National Theatre, it was not notable for English plays. Among those which received the most critical praise were two by Michael Frayn, *Donkeys' Years* and *Clouds*. Tom Stoppard's political comedy *Dirty Linen* was also well received.

Deaths. Agatha Christie died on Jan. 12; *see* OBITUARIES. Others who died during the year were novelist Stuart Cloete (March 19 at 78) and Richard Hughes, author of *A High Wind in Jamaica* (April 28 at 76). D.M.

FRENCH

The trend among French writers toward less experimental, more entertaining novels with clear story lines continued in 1976. Nonfiction proved more original and inventive, as several first-rate autobiographies and histories were produced.

Fiction. Best-sellers dealt with such matters as gunrunning, the Mafia, oil, money, and sex. Suspense and high color, presented in traditional fashion, characterized *Monsignore* by Jack-Alain Léger, *Bakchich* by Michel Clerc, and *Le Roi* ("The King") by Jacques Alain. Soviet-born popular author Henry Troyat brought out *Grimbosq*, a tragic story of love and adventure set in the Russia of Peter the Great. Another mixture of love, adventure, and local color was Yves Berger's *Le Fou d'Amérique* ("The Man Mad About America"). Robert Merle again utilized fantasy in a "no exit" kind of tale, *Madrapour*, about people in a plane which will never land. François Régis Bastide's *La Fantaisie du Voyageur* ("The Traveler's Fantasy")

Prolific French author Françoise Sagan's new book is Les Yeux de Soie *("Silken Eyes"), a characteristic volume of lucidly written tales about sad little love affairs.*

A reflective Simone Signoret, photographed during a 1968 New York City interview. The memoirs of the glamorous French actress were published in 1976.

takes place in Germany immediately after World War II.

Allegra by Françoise Mallet-Joris was notable for its almost exclusively female cast of characters and for its sharp psychological insight into personal relations and conflicts. Other feminist novels were Michèle Perrein's *Gemme Lapidaire,* centered on a group of strong-minded women; and Françoise Dorin's book with the revealing title *Va Voir Maman, Papa Travaille* ("Go See Mommy, Daddy's Working"). On the other hand, Frédérique Hébrard's *Un Mari C'est un Mari* ("A Husband Is a Husband") is a novel written by a decidedly nonfeminist woman.

Regionalism remained a factor in current French literature. In *Le Créa* ("The Sturgeon") Jean-Marc Soyez, a motion picture and television director, brings to a fable about the danger of sudden wealth and modernization his knowledge of the Charente-Maritime district and a photographer's sensitivity to images.

Two books that showed technical originality belonged to the avant-garde movement: *Louve Basse* ("Base She-wolf") by Denise Roche, a spirited challenge to death, and *Histoire du Gouffre et de la Lunette* ("The Tale of the Chasm and the Telescope") by Pierrette Fleutiaux, a young writer of great promise.

Nonfiction. The Bicentennial of the U.S. inspired many books. The most important were Robert Lacour-Gayet's *Histoire des États-Unis;* Claude Julien's *Le Rêve et l'Histoire,* an account of the "American dream"; and André Castelot's publication of an exchange of letters that he called *My Friend La Fayette, Mon Ami Washington.*

First-rate autobiographies included *Somme Toute* ("On the Whole") by Claude Roy, a former Communist, and *Histoire Égoïste* by Jacques Laurent, a right-wing individualist. The most interesting was the *Journal* of international statesman Jean Monnet, who had helped found the European Common Market. French bibliophiles agreed that actress Simone Signoret's life story *La Nostalgie N'est Plus Ce Qu'elle Était* ("Nostalgia Isn't What It Used To Be") makes for good reading. But by far the most popular first person narrative was *La Dérobade* ("The Cop-out") by Jeanne Cordelier, a former prostitute whose realistic account of her experiences made the best-seller lists.

Biographies included *La Fontaine ou la Vie Est un Conte* ("La Fontaine, or Life Is a Story") by Jean Orieux; *Gilles de Rais* by Michel Babille, about the prototype of Bluebeard; *Diane de Poitiers,* a life of the 16th-century courtesan by Philippe Erlanger; and *Portrait d'une Séductrice* by Jean Chalon, about Nathalie Barney, an American-born woman who inspired the turn-of-the-century French critic Remy de Gourmont.

Le Bon Plaisir ("The King's Good Pleasure"), third volume of *Les Hommes de la Liberté,* Claude Manceron's fine historical fresco, relates with consistent effectiveness the events of the late 18th century. But several other important essays treated of current trends and problems. Jean-François Revel published *La Tentation Totalitaire* ("The Totalitarian Temptation") and Bertrand de Jouvenel brought out *La Civilisation de Puissance* ("Power Civilization"). Jean Bernard discussed similar themes in *L'Homme Changé par l'Homme* ("Man Transformed by Man"). Maurice Clavel's *Dieu Est Dieu, Nom de Dieu* ("Damn It, God Is God") was a strong statement on today's church. And late in the year there appeared President Valéry Giscard d'Estaing's *Démocratie Française* ("French Democracy"), interesting in itself but especially so because of its author's position and political background. Another provocative critique of French society, *Le Mal Français* ("The French Disease"), was published by former Gaullist minister Alain Peyrefitte.

Poetry. In verse, too, feminism was represented: *Me Sentir une Femme* ("To Feel Myself a Woman") is a sincere poetic appraisal of the women's movement by Danielle Jaeggi. Two young male poets, Jean-Pierre Amée and Jean Maxence, published collections of vivid imaginative pieces, the former in a book entitled *Hébuternes* (a coined word), the latter, an angry young Christian leftist, in a work called *Croix sur Table* ("The Cross Laid on the Table").

Prizes. *Les Flamboyants* ("Tropical Trees") by Patrick Grainville, a novel set in Africa and characterized by a self-conscious, arty emphasis on the exotic, was awarded the Goncourt Prize amid considerable controversy. The Renaudot Prize went (also amid controversy) to *L'Amour les Yeux Fermés* ("Love with Closed Eyes"), a fable of modern times set in an imaginary town. Its author, Michel Henry, is a philosopher interested in Marxism and its interpreters. A difficult and interesting work in which a detective story is integrated into an analytical novel of love, Marc Chodolenko's *Les États du Désert* ("The States of the Desert") won the Médicis Prize. *Le Trajet* ("The Journey") by Marie-Louise Haumont, telling of an obsessively organized woman's mental breakdown, received the Prix Femina.

Deaths. Perhaps the most important event of the French literary year was the death of André Mal-

raux; *see* OBITUARIES. Other deaths included those of novelists Paul Morand (July 23 at 88) and Raymond Queneau (Oct. 25 at 73); the last named was the author of the popular novel *Zazie dans le Métro.*   D.R.B.

GERMAN

A trend toward subjectivity and inwardness was evident in the year's literary output from the German-speaking world. The preoccupation with political issues diminished in favor of a discussion of private topics.

Fiction. Heinz Piontek in his *Dichterleben* ("Life of a Poet") describes the sufferings and final failure of a contemporary writer who cannot cope with the demands made on him by society. This second novel of Piontek, who had been noted more for his short prose and poetry, attracted great attention since he received the 1976 Georg Büchner Prize, West Germany's highest literary award. Another "life of a poet" is Peter Härtling's *Hölderlin,* at once novel, biography, and report on the 19th-century poet. The voluminous work is an attempt to recreate the various stages of J. C. F. Hölderlin's eventful life by going beyond a purely biographical approach. A generally acclaimed first novel was Elisabeth Plessen's *Mitteilung an den Adel* ("Message to the Aristocracy"). This autobiographical work examines the author's aristocratic background and contrasts it with her present independence and social awareness. Probably the most provocative of 1976's novels from West Germany was Nicolas Born's *Die erdabgewandte Seite der Geschichte* ("The Side of History Turned Away from the Earth"). Set in West Berlin, Born's novel depicts a writer's inner isolation.

In East German prose a direct and challenging grasp of reality found expression. Yet some of the important writers were still not allowed to be

The 34-year-old Austrian novelist Peter Handke, better known in the U.S. as a playwright, wrote Die linkshändige Frau *("The Left-handed Woman"), a best-seller in 1976 German fiction.*

The first novel of young Ryu Murakami (left) won an important Japanese literary award in 1976; thirty novels by veteran Seishi Yokomizo were available in paperback at the end of the year.

published in their own country. This was the case with Rainer Kunze, who, in his *Die wunderbaren Jahre* ("The Wonderful Years"), portrays life in East Germany with subtlety and poignancy.

The Austrian Peter Handke, as expected, again reached best-seller lists with his story *Die linkshändige Frau* ("The Left-handed Woman"). He rated among the most original and talented contemporary German-speaking authors. Striking in his latest work was an unfamiliar stylistic simplicity, which he uses to tell about the most startling happenings in the life of a woman who separates from her husband. The widely discussed Austrian dramatist Thomas Bernhard also came out with a new work of prose, *Der Keller* ("The Cellar")—his second book about his youth in Salzburg. It expresses extreme emptiness and a complete negation of the values and meaning of life. Michael Scharang is a new name on the Austrian literary scene. His *Sohn eines Landarbeiters* ("The Son of an Agricultural Laborer") recounts the struggle for happiness of a young blue collar couple who find themselves hopelessly exploited.

The only new novel in which humor plays a part—although mainly in the form of the grotesque—is the Swiss author Urs Widmer's science-fiction story *Die gelben Männer* ("The Yellow Men").

Nonfiction and Poetry. The 100th anniversary of the Richard Wagner music festival in Bayreuth was the occasion for the publication of a number of successful books. Noteworthy among these were Hans Mayer's *Wagner in Bayreuth 1876–1976*, Hartmut Zelinsky's *Richard Wagner, ein deutsches Thema* ("Wagner: A German

Theme"), and Michael Karbaum's *Studien zur Geschichte der Bayreuther Festspiele* ("Studies in the History of the Bayreuth Festival"). A sensation was caused by the publication of Cosima Wagner's diaries, which were acclaimed as an essential 19th-century document.

In the field of biography the Swiss writer Klaus Völker made a remarkable contribution with his comprehensive study of Bertolt Brecht. A bestseller for many months was Klaus Mehnert's *Jugend im Zeitbruch* ("Youth in Transition"). The renowned political scientist and journalist offers a worldwide analysis of youth movements during the last decade.

In East Germany poetry continued to be a useful form in which to express private feelings that might not find a publisher if stated in prose. Poets like Peter Huchel, Gunter Kunert, Eva Strittmater, and Volker Braun were concerned mostly with the individual and his feelings of loneliness, fear, and futility. F.U.J.

IRISH

In 1976 there was a greater emphasis placed by Irish writers on critical work than on creative writing, and there was greater richness in their poetry than in their drama or fiction.

Fiction and Nonfiction. A new young writer named Des Hogan met success with his first novel, *The Ikon-Maker*. Also winning praise were *Proud Island* by Peadar O'Donnell, dealing with the theme of emigration in Ireland, and *Victims* by Eugene McCabe, the story of an Irish Republican Army hostage-seizing operation. Brian Moore's *The Doctor's Wife* deals with middle-class life in Northern Ireland.

Works on the playwright Sean O'Casey, who died in 1964, were abundant. The best of these included *Paycocks and Others: Sean O'Casey's World* by Bernard Benstock, exploring character types in the playwright's work; *Sean O'Casey and His World* by the definitive O'Casey biographer David Krause; and *Continuity and Innovation in Sean O'Casey's Drama* by Ronald Ayling, a monograph which carefully treats the later O'Casey plays. Books on the poet William Butler Yeats were also plentiful. Frank Tuohy's visually magnificent biography is entitled *Yeats. The Drama of W. B. Yeats: Irish Myth and the Japanese Nó* by Richard Taylor explores the Irish writer's use of Japanese theater. Two volumes of a series on modern Irish drama were published by Dolmen Press. These were *The Irish Literary Theatre, 1899–1901* and *Laying the Foundations, 1902–1904* by Robert Hogan and James Kilroy. *The Anglo-Irish Tradition* was explored historically by J. C. Beckett; W. B. Stanford considered *Ireland and the Classical Tradition*.

Poetry and Drama. Several collections by well-known Irish poets were published during the year, including *New and Selected Poems* by Brendan Kennelly, rich in Irish landscape; *Site of Ambush* by Eiléan Ní Chuilleanáin, difficult and beautiful in its strong imagery; *A Slow Dance*, love poems by John Montague; and *The Retreat of Ita Cagney: Culee Ide* by Michael Hartnett, about the writer's decision to give up writing in English. John Ennis received the Patrick Kavanagh award for his *Night on Hibernia*. *The Wolfhound Book of Irish Poems for Young People* was excellently edited by Bridie Quinn and Seamus Cashman.

Playwright Tom Murphy received great attention for two plays published and produced in 1976: *On the Outside/On the Inside* and *Sanctuary Lamp*. Desmond Forristal had a successful first production of *The True Story of the Horrid Popish Plot*, a historical drama. Kevin O'Connor saw his play *Friends* produced at the Peacock Theatre, and Maeve Binchy, an *Irish Times* writer, had a first production of her *End of Term*, which is based on her teaching career.   B.K.C.

JAPANESE

An appetite for factual information was apparent in the year's nonfiction from Japan, and in fiction several interesting young first novelists entered the literary scene.

Fiction. At a time when radical student activity was down, a surprising winner in Japan's fierce annual competition for reader attention was a kind of slap at the presence of American military bases. Awarded the prestigious Akutagawa Prize for the first half of 1976, *Kagirinaku Tomei ni Chikai Buru* ("An Almost Transparent Blue"), by first novelist Ryu Murakami, takes an impressionistic look at young people living in the area around Fussa Air Force Base outside Tokyo. It was a big year for young first-novel writers, with 22-year-old Hidetoshi Fotooka, a University of Tokyo senior, winning the Bungei Prize for his novel *Hokkiko* ("Going North"), the description of a youth's return to his home prefecture, Tohoku.

A perennial bestselling author, Hiroyuki Itsuki, scored again with the sixth in his award-winning sequence of novels about youth, *Seishun no Mon* ("The Gates of Youth"). The 1975 work was quickly made into a successful television drama and a film. Mystery writer Seishi Yokomizo, popular in the immediate postwar years, was at the top of the mystery novel revival that began several years ago. Thirty of his works had been reprinted in paperback by the end of 1976. As with many Japanese novels, Yokomizo's works were first revived in Japan's famous *manga* (comic books).

An important book of 1976 was *Mazagusu no Uta*. This illustrated version of the well-known tales of Mother Goose was by Shuntaro Tanigawa.

Nonfiction. Books on pollution, health and medicine, science, and philosophy continued to dominate the nonfiction lists. The year's top book was *Tensei Jingo* (literally "Words from Heaven," but popularly translated as "Vox Populi, Vox Dei"). This is a collection of essays from a newspaper column of the same name by *Asahi Shimbun* ("Asahi News") columnist Junro Fukashiro, who died early in the year. Sawako Ariyoshi's documentary narrative *Fukugo Osen* ("Compound Pollution, Vol. 2") treats pollution resulting from food additives and farm chemicals, and *Matsuri no Ba* ("A Festival Site") by Kyoko Hayashi is a look at the atomic bombing of Nagasaki and its aftermath by one who lived through it all. Ryotaro Shiba's serial work, *Harimada Monogatari* ("Tale of the Harima Sea, Vol. 2"), portrays the civil war in Japan that preceded the 1603 Tokugawa takeover. *Miraieno Isan III* ("A Legacy for the Future"), derived from a well-known Japan Broadcasting Co. television series, discusses the contacts between East and West over 1000 years ago. Two other notable titles were *Buraku Horu* ("Black Hole,") by John Taylor and *Uchu to Hoshi to 99 no Nazo* ("The Universe, Stars and 99 Mysteries,") by Genichiro Hori.   A.A.A.

LATIN AMERICAN

An International Theater Festival, new English translations, and a monumental new work by Carlos Fuentes, one of the foremost exponents of the "New Spanish American Novel," highlighted the literary year in Latin America.

Publications. Carlos Fuentes of Mexico published his monumental novel *Terra Nostra* (in Spanish late 1975; in English translation by Margaret Sayers Peden, 1976). Fuentes' probing of the roots of Mexican identity is centered in the Spain of Philip II but ranges forward in time to 1999. Juan Goytisolo, Spanish novelist, aptly observes, "*Terra Nostra* leads us into a fascinating gallery of mirrors, into which the reader must penetrate as if in his dreams, immersed in a fantastic world (the mortuary of the Hapsburgs, the Aztec sacrifices) which disintegrates and is recreated incessantly before his eyes." Fuentes, a diplomat as well as an author, continued to serve as Mexico's ambassador to France during the year.

The major literary event of 1976 in Brazil was the publication of the second volume of the memoirs of Brazilian novelist Erico Verissimo, who died in 1975. The work is entitled *Solo de Clarineta* ("Clarinet Solo"). The Tenth Brazilian National Literary Contest was held, and first prize went to Clarice Lispector, known for such strangely introspective novels as *A Paixão Segundo G. H.* ("The Passion According to G. H.").

Two notable Latin American novels appeared in English translations in 1976. They were Uruguayan Juan Carlos Onetti's 1950 novel *A Brief Life,* translated by Hortense Carpentier; and Argentine novelist Manuel Puig's *The Buenos Aires Affair,* translated by Suzanne Jill Levine. The latter combines satire on sexism with a detective story and a psychological case study.

Cultural Events. In April, Caracas, Venezuela, was the scene of the Third International Theater Festival (with the fourth Third World Theater Conference), sponsored by the Ateneo de Caracas and

Mexican author-diplomat Carlos Fuentes was once denied a visa to visit the U.S. because of his leftist opinions. He received a warmer welcome in 1976, as did Terra Nostra, *his most ambitious novel to date.*

the United Nations Educational, Scientific, and Cultural Organization. Forty-three nations, including 12 Latin American countries, sent performing stage groups and conferees. "La Candelaria," a Colombian theatrical company, presented the sociohistorical drama *Guadalupe, Años sin Cuenta* ("Guadalupe, Numberless Years"), on a guerrilla warfare theme. The Puerto Rican troupe "La Rueda Roja" ("The Red Wheel") staged *La Pulga* ("The Flea"), a play with political overtones. Host country Venezuela presented fifteen performing groups, including "Teatro Negro de Barlovento," which dramatized Afro-American rites.

Also in April, at San Jose, Calif., a First Interamerican Congress of Women Writers was held, presided over by Argentine poet Celia Correas de Zapata and keynoted by Argentine critic Enriqué Anderson Imbert. Mario Vargas Llosa of Peru was elected president of the International P.E.N., the organization of writers, at its congress in London. The International Book Fair held in Frankfurt, West Germany, in September had the theme "Latin America—An Unknown Literary Continent." Present at the fair were Vargas Llosa, Argentine exiles Julio Cortázar and Manuel Puig, Chilean José Donoso, Brazilians Jorge Amado and Thiago de Mello, and Uruguayan Eduardo Galeano.

Deaths. Deaths during the year included those of Mexican historian and essayist Daniel Cosio Villegas (March 10 at 77), Colombian poet León de Greiff (July 10 at 80), and Cuban poet and novelist José Lezama Lima (Aug. 9 at 65).   J.W.R.

PORTUGUESE

The Portuguese publishing world was still reflecting the turmoils and frustrations of the revolution that began in April, 1974. Political writing—revolutionary classics, works on the Portuguese revolution, pamphlets—continued to gush forth, inundating the more reflective and private forms of literature. But literature brilliantly went on, even if outshouted by a press hysterically devoted to politics.

Poetry. The first volume of the second revised and augmented edition of *Líricas Portuguesas* ("Portuguese Lyrics"), edited by Jorge de Sena, appeared in Portugal. The first edition, long out of print, had since 1958 been a fundamental reference work and anthology of 20th-century Portuguese poetry. Eugénio de Andrade published a new book of poems, *Limiar dos Pássaros* ("The Threshold of the Birds"). Another of the older Portuguese poets, José Gomes Ferreira, launched his *Poesia-VI* (sixth volume of collected poems). António Ramos Rosa offered two books: *Respirar a Sombra Viva* ("To Breathe the Living Shadow") and *Ciclo do Cavalo* ("Cycle of the Horse"). Other works by established names were Luis Amaro's

Bellow's Prize

For fiction that combined, in the words of the Swedish Academy, "human understanding and subtle analysis of contemporary culture," 61-year-old Saul Bellow became the seventh American to win the Nobel Prize in literature, which in 1976 was worth about $150,000. The son of Russian immigrants, Bellow was born in Canada and raised in Chicago, where much of his fiction takes place. His first novel, *Dangling Man,* was published in 1944; his eighth and latest, *Humboldt's Gift,* appeared in 1975 and won the 1976 Pulitzer Prize in fiction. In his Nobel speech Bellow asserted that modern novelists dealt too much with peripheral aspects of life rather than with its central struggles. "We do not, we writers, represent mankind adequately," he said.

Saul Bellow, the first American to win the Nobel Prize in literature since John Steinbeck (1962).

Diário Intimo ("Private Diary"), J. J. Cochofel's *Bispo de Pedra* ("The Stone Bishop"), Pedro Tamen's *Agora, Estar* ("Now, Being"), and Ruy Belo's *Toda a Terra* ("All the Earth"). On the experimental side, António Aragão's *Os Bancos Antes da Nacionalização* ("The Banks before Nationalization") is a spoof that includes photomontage. From London came *Camões, Some Poems,* an English translation by Jonathan Griffin of some of the lesser known lyric poems of Luís Vaz de Camões, generally regarded as Portugal's greatest poet.

Fiction. Rodrigues Miguéis published the second and last volume of *O Milagre segundo Salomé* ("The Miracle According to Salome"); it crowns a seriocomic portrait of the years preceding the Portuguese dictatorship of 1926–74. Another book that had to wait until after the 1974 revolution to be published was Jorge de Sena's *Os Grão Capitães* ("The Illustrious Captains"), a collection of short stories attacking life and the military establishment under the long dictatorship. Augustina Bessa-Luís added another novel to her vast output: *Crónica do Cruzado Osbe* ("Chronicle of Osbe, the Crusader"). Armando Silva Carvalho published *O Uso e o Abuso* ("Use and Abuse"). A scandalous novel by a woman was Margarida Victoria's *Amores da cadela "Pura"* ("Loves of 'Pure,' the Bitch").

Criticism. From the mountains of political writing one book should be mentioned: *O Fascismo Nunca Existiu* ("Fascism Never Existed"), by Eduardo Lourenço, a literary critic and outspoken political columnist. The internationally known art critic José-Augusto França published two vast works: the last volume of *O Romantismo em Por-*

tugal ("Romanticism In Portugal") and a study of the early-20th-century avant-garde writer and painter Almada-Negreiros, *Almada, o Portugues Sem Mestre* ("Almada, a Portuguese on His Own"). Jacinto do Prado-Coelho published *Ao Contrário de Penélope* ("Against Penelope's Example"), a collection of critical essays, and Eugenio Lisboa, the foremost critic from Mozambique, issued the second volume of *Crónica dos Años da Peste* ("Chronicle of the Plague Years").   J. de S.

SLAVIC

Soviet émigrés appeared increasingly on publishers' lists in 1976, although two poets did contribute major works within the Soviet Union. Elsewhere, there appeared an impressive new Bulgarian novelist, evidence of a literary thaw in Czechoslovakia, English translations of Polish novels, and a curious Yugoslav narrative about the Eastern European underworld.

Union of Soviet Socialist Republics. While some of the younger Russian émigré writers—the newly departed Andrei Amalrik, for instance—were still hoping that the Helsinki agreement and the politics of détente would result in greater artistic freedom for Soviet writers, Aleksandr I. Solzhenitsyn, the doyen of Russian exiles, remained opposed to any cooperation with the Soviet regime. In his latest polemical work, *Warning to the West,* Solzhenitsyn resorts to intellectual simplifications and raises questions about the efficacy of democratic institutions.

Joining the ranks of the established literary émigrés, some of those who emigrated more recently began to publish their works in the West. For example, Grigori Gerenstain made his literary

With his 1976 novel The Farewell Party, *Milan Kundera secured his place at the forefront of contemporary Czech writers.*

debut with *The Fall,* a witty and whimsical collection of stories about the typical absurdities of Soviet life. Vladimir Voinovich's *The Life and Extraordinary Adventures of Private Ivan Chonkin* finally appeared in print in the West. The chronicle of a bungling Russian soldier, it circulated inside the Soviet Union in *samizdat* (illegal, underground editions) for a number of years. A new novel by Lydia Chukovskaya, the grand old lady of Russian literature, also appeared in translation during the year. The novel *Going Under* was judged by American critics as an earnest but conventional study of Soviet artists trapped by the system.

Published inside the Soviet Union, a new volume of poetry by Andrei Voznesensky, *Vypusti ptitsu!* ("Set the Birds Free!"), contains a number of satiric and farcical poems. The title itself suggests political overtones, though as a satirist Voznesensky cleverly dodges serious political issues. Another Soviet poet, Olga Bergholz, published a haunting memoir, *Dnevnye zvezdy,* ("Day Stars"), in which she describes, among other experiences, her childhood in wartime Leningrad.

Bulgaria. The prolific Jordan Radichkov, probably the best-known Bulgarian writer today, published a new novel entitled *Vsichky i nikoy* ("All and None"). The stark story of a tragic friendship, *Vsichky i nikoy* is especially notable for its simple though resonant style. Another new Bulgarian

novel—Pavel Vezhinov's *Noshtem s belite kone* ("With the White Horse at Night")—created an even greater stir. Vezhinov's novel deals with the innermost torments of a Bulgarian scientist, and it was hailed as a major achievement of contemporary Bulgarian literature.

Czechoslovakia. The most important Czech work to be published during the year was Milan Kundera's *The Farewell Party* which, like Kundera's previous novel *Life Is Elsewhere* (1974), appeared outside his native country. *The Farewell Party* is about the zany goings-on in a Czech fertility spa; it is also replete with less amusing political allusions. An eminent Czech economist, Eugen Loebl, wrote his memoirs under the title *My Mind on Trial.* In his book Loebl describes his imprisonment in Czechoslovakia in the early 1950's and his captors' temporarily successful attempts to brainwash him.

In Prague the literary sensation of the year was the appearance of Bohumil Hrabal's deceptively simple novel *The Haircut,* about a young girl who eagerly conforms to the prevailing style in hairdos. Hrabal fell silent after the 1968 invasion of Czechoslovakia by Soviet troops, and the publication of his new novel was seen by some observers as the beginnings of a cultural thaw in that Eastern European country. Another subtle and low-key Czech novel—Marta Staňková's *Prázdný byt* ("The Empty Flat")—eschews politics altogether; instead, it movingly recounts the aftermath of the death of an unloved spinster.

Poland. Stylistically interesting works were published by two lesser-known Polish writers in 1976. Jerzy Harasymowicz's *Barokwe czasy* ("Baroque Times") is a collection of surrealistic poems about the glories of Poland's past, and Jarosław Iwaszkiewicz's *Ogrody* ("Gardens") is a series of reflective autobiographical fragments narrated by an old man who, because he is close to death, feels he has nothing more to hide.

The latest work by Stanisław Lem, the celebrated Polish science-fiction writer, to be translated (by Michael Kandel) was *The Star Diaries,* a group of hilarious and thought-provoking stories about a space voyage. Two more Polish prose works became available in English during the year: Tadeusz Konwicki's *A Dreambook for Our Time* (translated by David Welsh), a semiautobiographical account of the author's harrowing wartime experiences; and Tadeusz Borowski's chilling *This Way for the Gas, Ladies and Gentlemen,* a collection of narratives about the Nazi death camps.

Yugoslavia. The eminent Yugoslav novelist Miodrag Bulatović produced a fascinating work about criminal subcultures in major European societies.

The Russian film Solaris, based on a science-fiction novel by the popular Polish author Stanisław Lem, was widely distributed in the U.S. in 1976. In this scene Donatis Banionis, in the leading role, carries Natalya Bondarchuk.

Entitled Ljudi s četiri prsta ("Men with Four Fingers"), the novel focuses on Eastern European families that flee political persecution only to become outlaws in foreign lands. Dragi Bugarčić, only 27 years old, had already published several works of fiction. In his new novel, Pustolovine Želimira Besničkog ("The Adventures of Želimir Besnički"), Bugarčić successfully depicts the aimlessness of the generation that reached adulthood in the late 1960's. A work by the veteran Lojze Kovačič, a leading figure in Slovenian literature, is Preseljevanja ("Migrations"), a compelling narrative in which the author tries to recapture his crucial formative experiences. On the Edge of Reason, one of Miroslav Krleža's many social novels, was translated into English in 1976, as was Borislav Pekić's The Time of Miracles, a humanized though not completely despiritualized rewriting of the New Testament.

A Death. Polish poet and civil libertarian Antoni Słonimski died on July 4 at 81.   I.S.

SPANISH

The year 1976 was marked by an unusual number of new writers entering the Spanish literary scene, an indication of the livelier social and political status of Spain in the post-Franco era.

Fiction. A trend toward the autobiographical narrative was evident. Francisco García Pavón's Ya No Es Ayer ("It Is No Longer Yesterday") focuses on the author's early life and depicts Spanish society prior to 1936. García Pavón also brought out a short story, "Confidencias 1916" ("Confidences 1916"), that won for its author the Hucha de Oro prize. The prestigious Nadal prize was awarded in 1976 to the well-known Francisco Umbral for his novel Las Ninfas ("The Nymphs"), which completes a cycle of four autobiographical works. With Barrio de Maravillas ("City of Wonders")

Rosa Chacel initiates a trilogy of novels about her childhood and adolescence. This novel, remarkable for its freshness and ingenuity, provides an intimate view of the problems that women faced in Spanish society at the beginning of the century. José María Guelbenzu's El Pasajero de Ultramar ("The Traveler from Overseas") reveals a promising young writer praised by critics both for his originality and his genuine search for a personal style. Guelbenzu carefully utilizes avant-garde novelistic techniques, weaving the plot into a complex structure in which dialogue and stream of consciousness are intertwined.

Poetry and Drama. As in the preceding year, significant new works of poetry appeared in 1976. Francisco Toledano Serrano was the recipient of the Leopoldo Panero prize for his book Trilogía Interrogante ("Questioning Trilogy"), a work consisting of three books devoted to the themes of love, death, and man's most intimate beliefs. The poet's language shows increasing sophistication and enrichment by elaborated images and metaphors. Antonio Colinas received the Critics' prize for his book Sepulcro en Tarquinia ("Grave in Tarquinia"). Strongly influenced by Italian poetry, Colinas uses two distinct styles. The book starts off with a luxurious and almost baroque exuberance, then becomes more refined and sober. The important Adonais prize was awarded to Angel Sánchez Pascual, a student at the University of Madrid and the author of Ceremonia de la Inocencia ("The Course of Innocence"). The poet views innocence as a dynamic phenomenon, a virtue that man first possesses, then contemplates, and finally loses because life destroys it. Sánchez Pascual uses the classical Spanish verse form, the endecasyllable, progressively altering it to fit his meaning. Los Círculos del Infierno ("Circling In-

231

The Ambassador

It was unveiled in June, 1976, sixty years after his death, a marble plaque in the floor of the Poets' Corner in Westminster Abbey, London, hard by those of Longfellow, Eliot, and Auden. Born in America, he settled permanently in England at the age of 32, and he became a British citizen one year before his death. The simple inscription: "Henry James/O.M./for Order of Merit/Novelist New York 1863 London 1916."

ferno") by Jorge Justo Padrón offers a cosmic vision of human life and depicts a world of darkness, desperation, and anguish.

Only one play of significance appeared in 1976, Jorge Díaz's *Mata a tu Prójimo Como a ti Mismo* ("Kill Thy Neighbour as Thyself"). It won for its author the Tirso de Molina prize.   O.A.L.

LOUISIANA. See STATISTICS OF THE WORLD.

LUXEMBOURG. The Luxembourg economy was severely troubled during 1976 by the decline in steel output and the resulting increase in unemployment. In the face of decreasing markets, Luxembourg had been forced to cut steel production by 27 percent in 1975 to an annual total of 4,100,-000 tons. This cut was at least partly in response to a European Community decision to coordinate steel supply and avert destructive competition (Luxembourg is a member of the community). The cutbacks in steel production caused a rise in unemployment. By early 1976, Luxembourg's 50,000-man work force, which included 20,000 steelworkers, had 600 hard-core unemployed and between 1000 and 1500 others working only part-time. To help pay for unemployment benefits, Luxembourg imposed a special 2.5 percent levy on taxpayers.

The country's efforts to utilize foreign investment and expand its industrial activities into such products as chemicals were repaid in 1976. The twelve-year activities of the United States-based DuPont and Monsanto organizations were reportedly already accounting for 20 percent of the nation's gross national product (G.N.P.). This was already equal to the percentage of the G.N.P. represented by steel. The number of the nation's banks had also risen rapidly, from 13 in 1955 to 75 in 1976.

Luxembourg and its prime minister, Gaston Thorn, were heavily involved during 1976 in a variety of efforts at international cooperation. Thorn, president of the European Community's Council of Ministers, presided over its fourth "summit conference," held in Luxembourg on April 1 and 2. But he complained at the conclusion of the meetings that the conference had accomplished little. Thorn was also the European Community's spokesman at the fourth United Nations Conference on Trade and Development in Nairobi, Kenya, in May. Thorn, who had been serving for the past year as the U.N. General Assembly's president, completed his term and was replaced on Sept. 21 by Hamilton Shirley Amerasinghe of Ceylon.

See STATISTICS OF THE WORLD.   L.A.S.

M

MAINE. See STATISTICS OF THE WORLD.

MALAGASY REPUBLIC. See STATISTICS OF THE WORLD.

MALAWI. See STATISTICS OF THE WORLD.

MALAYSIA. In 1976 Malaysia remained one of the most politically stable and economically prosperous countries of Asia.

After the sudden death of Prime Minister Tun Abdul Razak on Jan. 14 (*see* OBITUARIES), Deputy Prime Minister Datuk Hussein bin Onn—a brother-in-law to Razak and a man little known outside Malaysia—was named as his successor. Hussein proved to be a decisive leader. In one of his first acts he postponed the new five-year plan

(1976–80) that had been devised by Razak. In July Hussein launched a strong, revised plan calling for an all-out attack on poverty, improved rural development schemes, and a commitment to help all Malaysians, whether of Malay, Chinese, or Indian ancestry. The plan envisaged an annual economic growth rate of 8.5 percent, creation of 743,000 jobs, and a total expenditure of $44 billion, of which $26.8 billion would come from the private sector.

Hussein also served notice that he would crack down hard on Communist insurgents, announcing plans to strengthen the armed forces and police by 30,000 men. The prime minister named his

The 53-year-old statesman was prime minister of Malaysia from 1970 until his death from leukemia on Jan. 14. The body of Tun Abdul Razak is returned from London to Kuala Lumpur for burial.

brother, Brig. Jaafar Datuk bin Onn, to command the troops attempting to root out Communist guerrillas in the northern areas near the Thai border. Moreover, Hussein cracked down on high-level corruption, in one case successfully pushing for the ouster and trial of a state official who had been a power in the prime minister's own party, the United Malays National Organization.

Under the guidance of Finance Minister Tengku Tan Sri Razaleigh Hamzah, Malaysia rebounded strongly from the recession of 1974–75. The inflation rate fell from 18 percent to around 8 percent, and government estimates of real economic growth for 1976 were a substantial 7.5 percent. Over the year the Malaysian government put heavy pressure on Shell and Exxon, the two principal oil companies operating in the country, to increase the share of profits going to Petronas, the state-run oil company. A compromise settlement was finally reached in November: The companies, granted new tax benefits, agreed to increase Petronas's share of the profits to approximately 83.5 percent.

Immersed in domestic matters, Hussein had little time for external affairs. However, to show his solidarity with the other non-Communist states of the area, he did travel to Indonesia in February for a summit meeting of the Association of Southeast Asian Nations. And on May 19, while Hussein was visiting Riyadh, Malaysia and Saudi Arabia signed an agreement on cultural and scientific cooperation.

See STATISTICS OF THE WORLD. R.J.C.

MALDIVES. *See* STATISTICS OF THE WORLD.

MALI. *See* STATISTICS OF THE WORLD.

MALTA. The year 1976 was one of hard-fought decision for Malta. In September the more than 200,000 voters of this strategic Mediterranean island went to the polls. At issue was the five-year rule of Prime Minister Dominic Mintoff and his policies of limited socialism at home and nonalignment in world affairs. The election was close, but Mintoff and his Labour Party emerged with a narrow victory of 51 percent of the vote. The party also won a three-seat margin over the opposition Nationalists in the House of Representatives.

The campaign was fought in an atmosphere of extreme tension. The Nationalists charged that Mintoff's stress on socialism frightened away potential foreign investors and contributed to a rise in unemployment. But Mintoff won support for a number of social reforms, including a higher minimum wage and increased benefits for the aged and the poor. The Labour Party also pointed out, with some justification, that the continued boom in industry, tourism, and shipping had enabled the island to escape most of the ill effects of the worldwide recession of 1974–75.

In foreign policy Mintoff continued to loosen the onetime British colony's ties with the West and court friends in the Arab and Communist worlds. Relations were especially close with both Libya, which had helped Malta with loans and investment funds, and the People's Republic of China, which had built docks and factories on the island.

See STATISTICS OF THE WORLD. R.J.C.

MANITOBA. *See* STATISTICS OF THE WORLD.

MANUFACTURING INDUSTRIES. In 1976 industry in the United States made a generally good recov

Workers and sympathizers demonstrate in downtown Akron, Ohio, in June. The record-long strike against the "Big Four" rubber companies (Goodyear, Firestone, Goodrich, and Uniroyal) lasted more than four months.

ery from the 1974–75 recession. Strong consumer buying at the beginning of the year petered out by late spring, however, and expectations of a surge in inventory buildups and new plant investments were not realized. Most manufacturers looked for new markets and new ways to cut costs; all of them worried about the price of oil and the threat of fuel shortages.

STEEL

The domestic steel industry benefited as the U.S. recovered from its worst recession in a generation, but long-standing problems remained.

Production. During 1976 domestic steelmakers produced about 128,000,000 tons of raw steel and shipped more than 90,000,000 tons of· finished steel products. This compared favorably with the 117,000,000 tons of raw steel and 80,000,000 tons of finished steel produced and shipped during the previous year, which was the lowest in a decade. At the end of 1976 about 454,000 persons were employed in the steel industry, in comparison to about 432,000 the year before.

Steel's recovery was not even, however. Flat-rolled steel picked up strongly with renewed demands from the automobile industry, but the heavier weight steels suffered with the continuing slump in capital goods. Specialty steels were hit by foreign competition, and after a finding by the International Trade Commission that imports of stainless and tool steels were injuring domestic producers, President Gerald R. Ford imposed import quotas on these commodities. A complaint seeking relief from allegedly similar injury was subsequently filed by producers of specialty steel tubing. In addition, the domestic steel industry sought action against an agreement between the European Common Market and Japan that placed limits on Japanese steel exports to Europe, alleging that the agreement was deflecting an extra 1,500,000 tons of Japanese steel to the U.S. market at artificially low prices.

Price Increase. In late November, National Steel Co. announced a 6 percent price increase in flat-rolled steel. The other major steel companies followed, citing rising costs, shrinking orders in specialty steels, mounting imports, pollution control requirements, and the need for additional profits to finance the modernization and expansion of obsolescent plants. Some argued that, considering the industry's problems, the increase should have been higher. But most companies hoped for an improvement in 1977. "The longer the delay in capital-goods spending," said Bethlehem Steel's chairman Lewis Foy, "the longer the period of economic catch-up."

PLASTICS

Rebounding from the economic doldrums, the consumption of plastic resins hit an all-time record of roughly 29.3 billion pounds in 1976, up 25 percent over the year before. The driving force behind these gains came primarily from three of plastics' major markets: packaging, construction, and the automobile industry.

In packaging the production of industrial containers and wrapping materials climbed to record levels, despite sluggish sales of some consumer goods. In building construction the key factors in higher sales were the growing use of foam insulation to reduce heating and cooling costs, and increasing acceptance of plastic plumbing and bath fixtures, vinyl siding, "unbreakable" window glazing, and carefree wall and floor surfacing. Among automakers, efforts to reduce the weight of cars and thereby improve mileage performance prompted the substitution of more plastic parts for metal. In the 1977 model cars the average plastics content amounted to 180 lb., up about 10 lb. from the previous year.

Raw Materials Research. Faced with the inevitable long-range scarcity of oil and natural gas (two of the principal sources of plastics—coal is the third), the plastics industry began to look for alternative sources of raw materials. Among the promising developments was a report by 1961 Nobel laureate Melvin Calvin of the University of California at Berkeley. He had found that the sap from two shrubs, *Euphorbia lathyrus* and *E. tirucalli*, could be used in present oil refineries. And he estimated that cultivated fields of these plants could yield an annual average of 10 to 50 bbl of sulfur-free oil per acre. This meant that an area the size of Arizona could produce as much oil as is now imported. Another alternative, long known but ignored until the cost of petroleum began to escalate, was to derive the plastics from inorganic substances, such as silica or sulfur. Soviet scientists were pursuing this research with particular vigor. Spokesmen for companies in the U.S. complained that pollution and industrial health regulations in plastics-related industries were diverting funds from research projects, but many of them conceded that better standards were desirable and in many instances would benefit industry in the long run.   C.O.P.

RUBBER

Worldwide consumption of rubber in 1976 amounted to 11,550,000 metric tons, almost two thirds of which was synthetic rubber. The U.S. tire industry, the major consumer of synthetic rubber, was hit with a record-long labor strike (April 21 to early September), but during the last half of the year, rubber and tire plants were running at near capacity in an attempt to rebuild depleted inventories. With energy conservation a serious matter, greater attention was given to the search for easier and cheaper processing methods.

A rising demand for quilted goose-down jackets, vests, and comforters led to a doubling of down prices within a year.

Synthetic Rubber. Approximately 7,875,000 metric tons of synthetic rubber were used in 1976. Since synthetic rubber is derived from petroleum or natural gas, prices remained high because of the crude-oil pricing policies of the Organization of Petroleum Exporting Countries. The improvement in the U.S. economy benefited Japanese and European synthetic rubber producers as well as domestic producers and consumers. Industry spokesmen stressed the need for long-range research to seek out new or improved uses of synthetic rubber in order to create new markets in such areas as high technology industries and the expanding trucking industry.

Natural Rubber. About 3,675,000 metric tons of natural rubber were consumed in 1976. Increasing yields continued to flow from rubber plantations through the use of chemicals that prevent the raw rubber (latex) from coagulating as it pours from the tree. Yields of 3000 lb. per acre per year were achieved, double the average in 1973.

Tires represented the largest single increase in the use of natural rubber. Most of this gain resulted from the growing production of radial tires, which require twice as much natural rubber as standard bias-ply tires.   J.Gr.

TEXTILES

The textile industry in 1976 recovered from the recession at a slow pace. Estimates by the American Textile Manufacturers Institute of overall fiber consumption in the U.S. were 11.8 billion lb., compared with 10.6 billion lb. the previous year. Third-quarter earnings for some of the major textile mills were up over the previous year, with profits slightly ahead.

Cotton. The cotton industry was on the upswing for the first time in ten years. Prices were rising, reflecting a greater worldwide demand, and shortages abroad produced commitments for the 1976–77 season of a near-record 3,340,000 bales. Some industry spokesmen estimated that advance orders would add up to 4,600,000 bales by the end of year. Fortunately, a U.S. cotton crop of 10,200,-000 bales, up 23 percent from 1975, was predicted.

Demand for denim and corduroy (both sometimes blended with polyester fibers) remained strong throughout the year. Despite annual warnings that the "blue jeans boom" would soon fade, the popularity of denim clothing showed no sign of waning. Corduroy was not only heavily used in men's suits and jackets, it began to be seen in women's apparel as well. Some producers were worried about a possible shortage of the fabric in 1977.

Man-Made Fibers. The demand for artificial fibers, which are produced in large quantities in the U.S., was weakened by a drop in overseas buying and

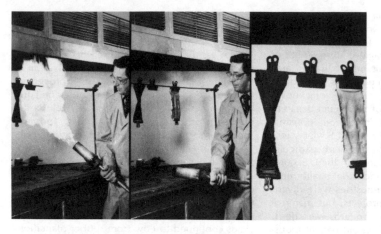

"Nomex 3," a new fire fighter's fabric by Du Pont Co., remains intact after an intense flame test (left panel). It is compared with rubber and cotton shell fabrics (right panel) that were put to the same test.

by an oversupply of some fibers, such as polyester staple. A sudden decline in retail purchases in the spring piled up inventories all along the line and put off further orders.

In November Monsanto, a major producer of man-made fibers, introduced its "Fina," a fine-denier acrylic, claimed to be the finest ever spun in the U.S. It was designed to be used in apparel such as sleepwear and blouses.

Many American producers were still demanding that the government set controls over imported fabrics, which they felt hurt U.S. manufacturers and kept profits down. But Joan Braden, consumer affairs coordinator for the State Department, told a meeting of the American Apparel Manufacturers Association that imports helped poorer nations and kept down costs to the American consumer; she urged the textile industry to "look to its own resources rather than protection as the prime generator of its profits."

Textile Union Drive. The Clothing and Textile Workers Union continued its push to unionize southern mills. At a J. P. Stevens plant in Roanoke Rapids, N.C., however, an anti-union movement emerged even though the mill had voted for union representation two years before. The union accused Stevens of intimidating its employees and of not bargaining in good faith. Plans were being developed for a boycott of all Stevens products.

See also LABOR; UNITED STATES OF AMERICA: THE ECONOMY.   D.G.S.

MARYLAND. *See* STATISTICS OF THE WORLD.

MASSACHUSETTS. *See* STATISTICS OF THE WORLD.

MAURITANIA. *See* STATISTICS OF THE WORLD.

MAURITIUS. *See* STATISTICS OF THE WORLD.

METEOROLOGY. *See* EARTH AND PLANETARY SCIENCES.

MEXICO. On Dec. 1, 1976, José López Portillo became president of Mexico in the midst of the worst political and economic crisis since the 1910 revolution.

Politics. Although former Finance Minister López Portillo, the officially supported candidate of the Institutional Revolutionary Party, won the July 4 presidential election as expected, the transfer of power from Luis Echeverría Alvarez, an unusually strong president, to his relatively unknown successor was accompanied by a surprising amount of tension and uncertainty. During the campaign there was an upsurge of violence and student demonstrations. The already tense atmosphere was further charged by the surprise floating of the Mexican peso from Aug. 31 to Sept. 12 and by the massive expropriation of nearly 250,000 acres of agricultural land in the state of Sonora less than three weeks before President Echeverría turned over the presidency. Almost overnight, peasants occupied the farmlands. These moves set off seizures and blockades of private lands in the neighboring state of Sinaloa, a major protest by affected landowners and private organizations and businesses throughout the nation, and widespread rumors of an impending coup.

In his inaugural address López Portillo responded to the critical political and economic situation. He outlined an economic austerity program and urged a national effort to increase production. Calling for a cut in taxes and government spending, López Portillo also promised to curb overseas borrowing and imports and to attack inflation. His speech and the announcement of his nineteen-member cabinet, made up of close associates with strong administrative records, restored some confidence among the business community. However, a court decision reversing Echeverría's land expropriation order was issued quietly on Dec. 7 and announced four days later. This reversal set the stage for a possible open confrontation between the new government and the peasants.

In his decision, Mexico City Federal Judge Carlos da Silva y Nava held that the decree violated a restraining order previously issued on behalf of the landowners; the judge ordered that the land be returned to private hands. If the ruling were upheld, peasants would have to be forcibly removed from the land.

The Economy. The political crisis was compounded by the sharp erosion in the value of the Mexican currency. On Aug. 31, the day before the annual state of the union message was due to be delivered, Finance Minister Mario Ramón Beteta announced that the peso would be allowed to float freely against the United States dollar, after twenty-two years at a fixed rate of 12.50 pesos per dollar. This step was taken to arrest the increasing balance of payments deficit caused by a decline in export competitiveness and by capital outflows in anticipation of a peso devaluation. Between 1970 and 1975 current accounts deficits of more than $11 billion had been recorded; the foreign debt totaled $24 billion at the end of 1976.

When the banks reopened on Sept. 2, the peso moved down to 20.60 per dollar, representing an effective devaluation of 39 percent. In conjunction with the float, the government also imposed price controls, increased wages by 10 to 23 percent, introduced an excess profits tax, promised to provide financial assistance to firms adversely affected by the depreciation of the peso, reduced import duties on some products, and introduced a new tax on certain exports.

Although the Bank of Mexico announced on Sept. 12 that a new rate of 19.90 pesos per dollar would be set and that the bank would maintain this rate as long as possible, the peso was allowed to float once again on Oct. 27. Following the second float, the peso fell to 26.50 per dollar, representing an overall effective depreciation of 52.8 percent since the beginning of September. The Bank of Mexico was unable to hold the 19.90 rate, despite a $600,000,000 loan from the U.S. Federal Reserve System, because of a steady outflow of capital inspired by continued political uncertainties and the government's failure to follow through with its economic program. Capital outflows reached staggering proportions after President Echeverría announced his massive land reform program. The central bank was forced to prohibit banks and credit institutions from dealing in foreign exchange and to transfer this function to stock and exchange brokers. This move, and the fact that the transfer of power was apparently going to occur on Dec. 1 as scheduled, brought positive results: The peso firmed to around 19–20 per dollar.

The restoration of monetary stability, though welcome, still left a host of other economic problems unsolved. These included high inflation, unemployment approaching 25 percent, enormous population growth, and rapid urbanization.

Foreign Affairs. During his last months in office President Echeverría continued to press for a new world economic order and to criticize the U.S. for opposing this effort. Despite strained U.S.-Mexican relations, Echeverría and U.S. President Gerald R. Ford signed an agreement calling for the mutual exchange of U.S. prisoners in Mexican jails and Mexican prisoners in U.S. jails. In December Echeverría failed in a bid to unseat Kurt Waldheim of Austria as United Nations secretary-general.

With his attention concentrated on domestic problems, President López Portillo made no major foreign policy statements. Although observers felt it was likely that he would maintain a firm attitude toward trade and economic negotiations with the U.S., they also expected him to avoid the careless rhetoric that had caused strained relations between the two countries.

See STATISTICS OF THE WORLD.　　　　A.K.M.

MICHIGAN. *See* STATISTICS OF THE WORLD.

The Mexican peso dropped nearly 53 percent in value against the U.S. dollar between Aug. 31 and the end of October.

MIDDLE EAST

Conflict was everywhere in the Middle East—war in Lebanon, skirmishes in the Western Sahara, power struggles among Palestinian factions, demonstrations by Jews against Muslims and by Arabs against Israelis. Petrodollars flowed into the oil-exporting countries and back to the West for arms. Yet in December, peace actually seemed closer.

The nearly two-year-old civil war in Lebanon dominated events in the Middle East during 1976. It became the focal point of nearly every contentious dispute among the Arab states and threatened the tenuous disengagement agreements signed in 1975 by Israel with Syria and Egypt. By the end of 1976 the war had claimed between 40,000 and 50,000 lives, several times that number of wounded, and had made refugees of nearly one in three inhabitants of the country. After more than fifty-five attempts to negotiate a series of cease-fires or truces, fighting was halted through an agreement signed at Riyadh in October under Saudi Arabia's auspices. A few days later the agreement was confirmed at an Arab summit conference in Cairo.

Lebanon. Massive intervention by Syrian forces in Lebanon during 1976 provoked angry quarrels with other Arab states and aroused apprehensions in Israel. Kamal Jumblat, the Lebanese Druze leftist leader, proclaimed his intention to press for "full military victory" against the Christian-rightist coalition in April. Until then Syria had been a neutral intermediary, seeking to mediate among the diverse Lebanese and Palestinian factions. But fear that an all-out victory by Lebanese leftists and Palestinians would upset the power balance in the whole Middle East impelled Syria's president, Hafez al-Assad, to send several thousand of his troops into Lebanon in April. Their purpose, he claimed, was to prevent either side from destroying the other, and to restore peace.

Syria's intervention was advantageous to the Christian forces. The Muslim-leftist-Palestinian coalition was driven into defense positions. When the fighting stopped, the country was divided into several enclaves. The Syrian forces held about two thirds of Lebanon, and the rest was divided among the various Lebanese Christian, Muslim, and Palestinian forces. In the south, Christian forces, supported and supplied with Israeli armament, held the upper hand.

The Lebanon upheaval reverberated throughout the Arab world. Syria and its neighbor Iraq were both controlled by Ba'athist Arab socialist regimes, but relations between them deteriorated. Iraq accused Syria of attempting to seize Lebanon and mobilized a substantial part of its army along the Syrian frontier. Iraqi troops were sent into southern Lebanon to assist the Muslim leftist forces there. Relations between Egypt and Syria worsened as Cairo retaliated in the propaganda war waged by Damascus against the Sinai disengagement agreement signed by Israel and Egypt during 1975. Hostilities between Libya and Sudan also threatened to break out among their contingents in the small Arab peacekeeping force stationed in Lebanon.

Israel played a more active role than previously during 1976. It opened its northern frontier to Lebanese wounded and others seeking assistance or employment and supplied substantial amounts of military supplies, including tanks, to Christian forces in southern Lebanon.

The growing dangers of inter-Arab conflict and of Israeli intervention aroused Saudi Arabia. Its massive oil income had transformed Saudi Arabia into a new, and perhaps the most influential, power among the Arab states. In June Crown Prince Fahd summoned the prime ministers of Egypt and Syria to Riyadh for "friendly, frank" talks. By October the civil war in Lebanon was still

---

The Bill Came to $1,500,000

On Oct. 4 a cargo jet left Chicago. Chartered by Qabus Bin Said, the sultan of Oman, it was bringing him a few items from his most recent shopping list: 6 Cadillac Sevilles, 6 Mercedes-Benz sedans, one 25-ft. speedboat, 1 Chevrolet Blazer, 1 Targa Porsche, one 911-S Porsche, 1225 pieces of luggage, 8 refrigerators, a gas range, 20,000 lb. of automotive tools, two 5-ft. grapefruit trees, and 2 La-Z-Boy reclining chairs.

Reconciliation was in the air among Arabs late in the fall of 1976. In Cairo, during an Arab League summit conference that approved the Riyadh agreement ending the Lebanese conflict, President Anwar el-Sadat of Egypt greets Yasir Arafat, head of the Palestine Liberation Organization, while President Hafez al-Assad of Syria (right) looks on.

raging, and Damascus and Cairo were still feuding. Again Saudi Arabia took the initiative, summoning the presidents of Egypt, Syria, Lebanon, and the head of the Palestine Liberation Organization (P.L.O.) to a mini-summit. Kuwait, influential because of its oil wealth, also attended.

At Riyadh the six Arab leaders signed a peace plan that established a cease-fire, created a 30,000-member Arab "deterrent" force to supervise the truce, reactivated the 1969 Cairo agreement restricting movements of Palestinian guerrilla forces in Lebanon, and temporarily healed the rift between President Anwar el-Sadat of Egypt and President Assad. These arrangements were confirmed at the eighth Arab summit conference a few days later in Cairo.

Although the newly elected president of Lebanon, Elias Sarkis, was the official chief of the new "deterrent" force, some two thirds of its members were Syrian troops, now functioning under a "joint" command. By the end of November the Syrians had extended their control to nearly all of Lebanon except the sensitive region south of the Litani R., which Israel considered vital to its security.

In the rest of Lebanon, hostilities were greatly diminished. Curfews were lifted, road blocks were removed, the Beirut airport was reopened, and attempts to move toward normal life were speeded up.

Israel. Within Israel, too, tensions between Arabs and Israelis took their toll. Restiveness among the Arab citizens of Israel and those who lived in the occupied territories caused major clashes with Israeli security forces. Troops were sent into the oc-

cupied area of Jerusalem early in 1976 to put down Arab demonstrations against a court order permitting Jews to pray on the Temple Mount, adjoining the al-Aqsa Mosque, considered by Muslims to be their third most holy place, after Mecca and Medina. (Later a higher court reversed this decision.) Later in the year, another dispute between Jews and Arabs erupted in Hebron, on the West Bank of the Jordan R., over Abraham's tomb, also a site considered holy by both Muslims and Jews. These disputes provoked controversy within the Israeli cabinet, especially between Prime Minister Itzhak Rabin and Defense Minister Shimon Peres over policy in the occupied areas.

Inside Israel, Israeli Arab citizens clashed violently with security forces as nationalist sentiment and support for the P.L.O. increased among the minority Arabs. The violence was precipitated by a general strike in March protesting government expropriation of Arab land for Jewish settlement in Galilee. During the demonstrations Israeli soldiers attacked the home of the recently elected Communist mayor of Nazareth, Israel's largest Arab town. Prime Minister Rabin accused the New Communist (Rakkah) Party of instigating the unrest, but he appointed an advisory group to reexamine the position of the Arabs.

Oil, Arms, and Influence. The repercussions of unrest in Lebanon throughout the Arab world drew attention to dramatic shifts of power and new regional alignments taking shape in the Middle East. It was apparent that the major oil-producing states, especially Saudi Arabia, Kuwait, and Iran, were rapidly replacing other Arab states and Israel as the predominant regional powers. Through their massive oil revenues they were acquiring larger supplies of, and more sophisticated, weapons than had previously been introduced into the area. Arms sales, especially to Saudi Arabia and Iran, were far larger than the United States made to any of its allies in the North Atlantic Treaty Organization (NATO), and the quantities of advanced air, tank, and ground systems acquired by Iran exceeded those of most NATO countries except the U.S. itself.

Saudi Arabia and Kuwait increased their relative power during the year, less through military might than through generous financial aid to various other Arab countries. Ever since its defeat in the 1967 June war with Israel, Egypt's economy had continued to deteriorate, forcing President Sadat to seek large-scale financial assistance abroad. During 1976 he persuaded the leaders of Kuwait, Qatar, Saudi Arabia, and the Union of Arab Emirates to help pay for agricultural, industrial, and housing projects in his four-year, $20 billion economic development plan. Their consortium, called the Gulf Organization for Development of Egypt, was the foundation for more extensive loans from a larger European group, including West Germany and France.

With Egypt and Syria relying economically on Saudi Arabia, Riyadh replaced Cairo as the most politically influential Arab capital. The Saudi leaders were assuming a role that, only a few years earlier, Egypt's President Gamal Abdel Nasser had played: conciliator and mediator among contending ideological and nationalist Arab factions. Saudi Arabia's support was also believed to be a major factor in moderating Syrian demands on Israel. Damascus, once leader of the "Rejection Front" opposed to any settlement with Israel, now joined Cairo and Riyadh in calling for renewal of peace negotiations. Syrian defection from the "Rejec-

tion Front" left Iraq isolated in the Arab east. Only other nonconfrontation states, such as Libya and the Democratic People's Republic of Yemen, and the most militant of the Palestinian factions, such as the Popular Front for the Liberation of Palestine, joined Iraq in opposition to a renewed peace effort.

Egypt. Egypt's growing economic dependence on the conservative Arab regimes and the West influenced both its foreign and domestic policies. Not only did Cairo continue its moderate role in the Arab-Israeli dispute, it also shifted its orientation away from the Soviet Union. When Moscow declined to provide the economic and military assistance requested by President Sadat, he persuaded the Egyptian People's Assembly to abrogate the country's friendship treaty with the U.S.S.R. To encourage increased Western investment in Egypt, restrictions on trade and commerce were modified, favoring greater free enterprise. Political life was also liberalized in October when the first relatively free balloting since 1953 was permitted. After the election Sadat sanctioned the formation of three political parties from the left, center, and right factions formerly associated with the single-party Arab Socialist Union.

Kuwait. Despite Kuwait's emergence as an influential Arab League member, the situation in Lebanon sparked internal unrest, which led to suspension of the elected National Assembly and imposition of press controls during the summer. These measures were taken in response to dissension among the nearly 300,000 Palestinians living in Kuwait, who constituted almost a third of the sheikhdom's population. The Palestinians were rallying increasing support among the indigenous Kuwaitis for their opposition to Syria's intervention in Lebanon. Some observers believed that the

Although Egypt invalidated its treaty with the Soviet Union in March, Col. Muammar el-Qaddafi of Libya continued to court friendship with Moscow. Here President Nikolai V. Podgorny (left) welcomes Qaddafi to the U.S.S.R. in June.

Syria's expanded intervention in Lebanon brought a sharp reaction from other Arabs in 1976. Students who occupied the Syrian Embassy in Cairo for a brief period in June upended President Hafez al-Assad's photograph to indicate their scorn for his Syrian government.

strict new government controls were taken to prevent pretexts for outside intervention in Kuwait's internal affairs, thus turning it into another Lebanon.

North Africa, Cyprus, and Turkey. Political instability and the local unrest of previous years continued elsewhere in the Middle East during 1976. A year after Morocco's "march of conquest" into Spanish (later Western) Sahara, integration of the former colony seemed irreversible. But guerrilla war by the Algerian-backed Polisario forces caused periodic clashes between the two countries. Libya continued its war of words against both Sudan and Egypt, causing Sadat to call Libyan President Muammar el-Qaddafi a "madman."

In Cyprus, the Turkish Cypriot government accelerated its expulsion of ethnic Greeks from the northern part of the island. The object seemed to be total separation of Turks and Greeks and an eventual division of Cyprus into two states.

In Turkey, student demonstrations against the government and violent altercations with the police disrupted the country's universities throughout the year. The worsening economic situation, intensified by the return of large numbers of Turkish laborers from recession-plagued Western Europe, threatened the already unstable Ankara government.

Peace. The last months of the year brought renewed attention to the major problem of the Middle East. The Sinai agreement had been implemented in February, Syria had agreed to an extended term for the United Nations peacekeeping force on the Golan Heights in November, and the war in Lebanon was, at least for a time, over. But progress toward overall peace was little closer than at the beginning of the year.

The Palestinians, who had been deeply involved in Lebanon, met in November to consider the effect of that involvement. In Damascus in December P.L.O. leaders publicly called for an independent Palestinian state as one of their "legitimate rights" but did not renew their demands for the abolition of Israel.

Arab solidarity had been established at the Riyadh conference in October. Egypt and Syria composed their differences and announced plans for "united political leadership" of the two countries in December. The Egyptian foreign minister, Ismail Fahmy, indicated that the purpose of the union was to provide better Arab representation at a renewed Geneva conference on peace in the Middle East. Syria had made overtures to Jordan early in the year, and Libya and Egypt had been reconciled at Riyadh; it seemed that the Arabs had achieved substantial unity. Israel was apparently also moving to decrease tension. Prime Minister Rabin dismissed extreme religionists from his cabinet in December and thus repudiated pressure for unrestricted Jewish settlement in the occupied territories. He nevertheless still refused to go to Geneva if P.L.O. representatives were seated.

How long Arab unity would last, how long extreme Palestinians would refrain from terrorism, and whether Israel would join in direct negotiations for peace remained to be seen.

See also AFRICA; ARAB LEAGUE; ORGANIZATION OF PETROLEUM EXPORTING COUNTRIES; and articles on most of the countries mentioned. D.P.

On June 28 thirteen mercenaries who had hired themselves out to fight in the Angolan civil war listen to a Revolutionary Tribunal in Luanda sentence them for crimes against the Angolan "people's revolution." Three Britons and one American were condemned to death; they were executed on July 10.

MILITARY AND NAVAL AFFAIRS. Civil wars in Africa and Lebanon and a daring Israeli commando rescue operation were the leading military events of 1976. In the United States defense expenditures were increased to meet what was considered a growing Soviet threat, and the military establishment was disturbed by improprieties committed by some of its leaders and by a West Point cheating scandal.

Wars and Near Wars. The civil war in Angola (q.v.) involved three factions supplied by rival foreign nations early in 1976. By the end of March the Soviet-backed Popular Movement for the Liberation of Angola (M.P.L.A.) was in effective control of all main cities and roads. Cuban troops numbering from 15,000 to 18,000 remained throughout the year to help the M.P.L.A. maintain order and mop up resistance. The U.S. Congress voted against further aid to the losing factions in January, and several thousand South African troops were withdrawn by March.

The guerrilla war in Rhodesia (q.v.) continued between black nationalists and the forces of the white-minority government of Prime Minister Ian D. Smith. Government troops began a counteroffensive against guerrilla bases along the Mozambique border in February. In April the guerrillas severed Rhodesia's only rail link to South Africa. Terrorist incidents were numerous from May through September; a surprise attack on Sept. 14 killed five government security officers. Thereafter, no major incidents occurred as nationalist leaders conferred with government representatives in Geneva on a British–U.S. peace plan.

Last Ride for the Riderless Horse

His official Army designation was "2V56," but he was better known as Black Jack, the stately horse that walked riderless, carrying boots reversed in the stirrups, behind the coffin of President John F. Kennedy in 1963. In February, at the age of 29 (over 100 in human terms), Black Jack died at his stable near the Pentagon and was buried without ceremony. In twenty-two years of Army duty, the horse walked in thousands of funerals, including those of former Presidents Herbert Hoover and Lyndon Johnson. Black Jack lived to be the last of the Army's quartermaster-issued cavalry horses, and the last to bear the military "U.S." brand on his hide.

Black Jack marches in the 1963 funeral procession of John F. Kennedy.

Civil war also raged in Lebanon (q.v.) until an Arab League force imposed a shaky peace agreement in October. Syrian troops and Lebanese Christians appeared to have the upper hand over Lebanese Muslims and their Palestinian allies.

War nearly broke out between Great Britain and Iceland (qq.v.) over fishing rights within 200 mi. of the Icelandic coasts. British warships were assigned to escort British fishing trawlers within the disputed zone; in protest, Iceland threatened to withdraw from the North Atlantic Treaty Organization. A temporary agreement in June, however, prevented a "cod war."

The Entebbe Raid. In one of the most daring and dramatic military operations in years, Israeli commandos assaulted the airport at Kampala, Uganda, on July 3, and in a bloody battle rescued 91 passengers and 12 crew members of an Air France jet which had been hijacked a week earlier by Palestinian terrorists. Landing in three C-130 transport planes under cover of darkness, the commando force stormed the passenger terminal at Entebbe airport, killing all 7 hijackers and 20 Ugandan troops. Also killed in the assault were 3 Israeli hostages and the leader of the assault force. Several Soviet-made MIG aircraft were destroyed by the Israelis, and the terminal was heavily damaged from the fighting. The commandos and their rescued hostages flew back to Israel to an emotional welcome after a refueling stop in Kenya. Ugandan President Idi Amin condemned the raid but Israeli officials defended it as a deterrent to future terrorist attacks against Israeli citizens. World reaction was mixed but predominantly favorable; U.S. President Gerald R. Ford sent a message to Israeli Prime Minister Itzhak Rabin expressing "great satisfaction" in the successful completion of the operation.

Korean Clash. Two U.S. Army officers were killed by ax-wielding North Korean soldiers during a clash at P'anmunjŏm on Aug. 18 in the demilitarized zone (DMZ) separating North and South Korea. The U.S.-South Korean work party was trimming a large tree when the attack occurred. President Ford promptly labeled the killings "vicious and unprovoked murder" and ordered a buildup of American forces in South Korea. Several squadrons of jet fighters were flown in from Okinawa, twenty F-111 fighter-bombers were dispatched from the U.S., and B-52 bombers began practice bombing runs in the skies near the DMZ. After several days of negotiations, the United Nations Command and North Korean representatives signed an agreement on Sept. 6 for separating the security forces at the sensitive P'anmunjŏm site, and U.S. forces in South Korea returned to normal duty status.

Soviet Pilot Defects. In what was described by Western analysts as the greatest intelligence coup in years, a defecting Soviet pilot flew his MIG-25 Foxbat swing-wing jet fighter to the Japanese island of Hokkaido on Sept. 6. Lt. Viktor I. Belenko received political asylum in the U.S. while the Japanese, reportedly with "unofficial" help from U.S. aviation specialists, began dismantling the plane to decipher its secrets. The MIG-25 was confirmed to be the world's fastest jet fighter, but its radar and other equipment were judged inferior to U.S. counterparts. After a thorough examination, the plane was returned to the Russians in November in a series of crates.

Arms Race. The U.S. and the Soviet Union continued efforts in 1976 to reach further agreement in the strategic arms limitation talks (SALT), but little progress was apparently achieved, and some defense experts feared that an extension of SALT agreements expiring in October, 1977, might not be possible. The European force-reduction talks in Vienna were also deadlocked. In the absence of significant breakthroughs, both sides proceeded with development of a variety of new strategic programs. The keel was laid for the U.S.S. *Ohio,* first of the Navy's *Trident* ballistic missile submarines. Both air-launched and submarine-launched cruise missiles completed their first test flights during 1976, and development continued on a new warhead for the *Minuteman III* ballistic missile and a new strategic missile, the *M-X.* Research and development were completed on the

A small boy from Beirut shows off his collection of spent shells—souvenirs of the Lebanese civil war—aboard the U.S.S. Spiegel Grove. The ship carried 276 evacuees across the Mediterranean Sea to Greece in June.

Switzerland: 0, Liechtenstein: 0

One August midnight the residents of Iradug awoke to a startling sight: an invading army of seventy-five soldiers and fifty horses. The "invaders" were even more startled. Swiss militiamen on maneuvers, they had taken a wrong turn in the dark and marched 1600 ft. into Liechtenstein. A few days later the Swiss Defense Ministry issued an official apology and a request for understanding from the government of the tiny principality. No war was declared; no reparations were demanded. It was even rumored that the villagers had served coffee to the invaders.

U.S. Military Strength. Continuing a trend of increasing expenditures that military experts insisted were necessary to maintain a credible level of deterrence, the U.S. Congress approved a fiscal 1977 budget for the Department of Defense of $104.3 billion, roughly $3.6 billion less than the Pentagon had requested but nearly $14 billion more than the appropriation for fiscal 1976. More than $28 billion was approved for military procurement and $10.4 billion for research and development. The Navy received the largest share of the budget, $35.9 billion; the Air Force received $30.8 billion and the Army $25.5 billion. The budget supported a military establishment of 16 Army and 3 Marine divisions, 26 Air Force tactical wings, 16 Navy and Marine air wings, and a Navy fleet of 470 vessels. A force level was authorized of 2,092,600, including 789,000 Army, 540,600 Navy, 571,000 Air Force, and 192,000 Marine troops.

West Point Cheating Scandal. The admission of women for the first time to the U.S. service academies in 1976 was overshadowed in the news media by a cheating scandal at the United States Military Academy that forced a review of the academy's honor code. The scandal was triggered in April when fifty West Point cadets were found guilty by cadet honor boards of cheating on a take-home examination. The accused cadets alleged that several hundred classmates were equally guilty and that as many as 700 had cheated on examinations and engaged in other honor-code violations. Some of the 130 cadets expelled for cheating charged that the Army was deliberately narrowing the scope of the inquiry to avoid unfavorable publicity. The charges touched off a Congressional inquiry and prompted Secretary of the Army Martin Hoffmann to appoint a special review panel (headed by former astronaut Frank Borman, president of Eastern Airlines) to assess the validity of the honor code and consider appropriate changes. The West Point cadet corps voted on Nov. 9 to change several provisions in the code, including abolishing boards of military officers to handle violations and placing such authority solely in the hands of cadets themselves. But no change was made in the penalty of expulsion for all honor-code violations, a provision critics claimed was arbitrary and excessive.

Improprieties. Two senior Pentagon officials were reprimanded in March for accepting expense-paid trips to lodges operated by Rockwell International, a major defense contractor and builder of the controversial B-1 bomber. Secretary of Defense Rumsfeld reprimanded Malcolm R. Currie, director of defense research and engineering, ordering a forfeiture of four weeks' pay and reim-

controversial B-1 supersonic bomber. The Pentagon planned to build a fleet of 244 B-1's at a cost of $22.8 billion to replace the aging B-52's. Actual production of the plane was delayed, however, until the administration of President-elect Jimmy Carter could make the final decision. Carter and others had criticized the B-1 program as wasteful and unnecessary during the campaign.

Despite Carter's claim that the defense budget could be cut by several billion dollars, Pentagon officials revealed that the defense budget request for fiscal 1978 would rise considerably to keep pace with Soviet military advancement, possibly to the $125 to $130 billion range.

At a Pentagon news conference on Sept. 27, Secretary of Defense Donald H. Rumsfeld noted that "the Soviet Union today is clearly militarily stronger and busier than in any other period of its history." Rumsfeld reported that the Russians were continuing to deploy three new intercontinental ballistic missiles (ICBM's) with multiple warheads and testing was nearing completion for two other ICBM's, the *SS-X-16* and *SS-X-20.* A new type of Soviet weaponry, disclosed in November, raised the possibility of warfare in outer space. The Defense Department announced that the U.S.S.R. was developing "hunter-killer" satellites to intercept and destroy enemy satellites.

The global arms race accelerated to record levels in 1976. According to studies published during the year, annual world military outlays were approaching $300 billion, 45 percent higher, measured in constant dollars, than in 1960. The U.S. and the U.S.S.R. accounted for 60 percent of total arms expenditures, but the sharpest increases were in the Middle East and in developing nations generally.

North Koreans attack white-helmeted United Nations Command personnel with axes and pikes near P'anmun-jŏm on Aug. 18. Two U.S. Army officers were killed during the incident.

bursement of Rockwell for his expenses during a trip to a fishing lodge in the Bahamas. Secretary of the Navy J. William Middendorf II was given a letter of admonition for visiting a Maryland hunting lodge at the invitation of the Iranian ambassador to the U.S. A number of lesser military and civilian officials received varying forms of reprimand for accepting free trips to the lodges.

Gen. George S. Brown, chairman of the Joint Chiefs of Staff, had to apologize in October for indiscreet remarks made during an April interview with an Israeli journalist. Brown had said that Israel was more of a burden than a blessing militarily to the U.S., that the British armed forces were "pathetic," and that Iranian armament programs "make you wonder whether [the shah] doesn't some day have visions of the Persian Empire." In July the Senate confirmed Brown's reappointment to another two-year term as chairman of the Joint Chiefs.

Vietnam Arms. The Pentagon revealed in November that an estimated $5 billion in American military weapons and matériel had been captured by the North Vietnamese in the aftermath of their 1975 victory in the Vietnamese war. Almost overnight these captured arms converted Hanoi's military establishment into one of the most formidable in Asia. Among the American equipment captured from the South Vietnamese were 300 light and 250 medium tanks, 1200 armored personnel carriers, 80 self-propelled 175-mm cannons, 1250 howitzers, 63,000 antitank weapons, 791,000 sophisticated M-16 automatic rifles, 130,000 tons of ammunition, 50,000 machine guns, 47,000 grenade launchers, 12,000 mortars, and nearly 1,000,000 pistols and rifles. Also captured were more than 70 Tiger F-5 jet fighters, approximately 350 other planes, 465 helicopters, and 940 ships and small naval vessels.

Naval Affairs. The two naval superpowers, the U.S. and the U.S.S.R., continued their duel for world-wide naval supremacy in 1976. Soviet fleet strength dropped slightly with the retirement of large numbers of antiquated diesel submarines, but the Soviet navy maintained a significant lead over the U.S. in attack submarines and major surface combatants. The authoritative International Institute for Strategic Studies in London placed Soviet fleet strength in mid-1976 at 58 nuclear-powered and 20 diesel-powered ballistic missile submarines, 162 attack and 65 cruise missile submarines, 1 aircraft carrier, 2 helicopter cruisers, 34 cruisers, 80 destroyers, and 97 oceangoing escort ships. By contrast, U.S. Navy fleet strength dropped from 496 to 479 ships by mid-1976 and was expected to drop to 470 ships by 1977. The fleet included 41 nuclear ballistic missile submarines, 75 attack submarines, 13 aircraft carriers, 26 guided-missile cruisers, 38 guided-missile destroyers, 24 other destroyers, 58 guided-missile frigates, 6 gun frigates, 8 patrol gunboats, and 62 amphibious warfare ships, including 7 helicopter carriers. Construction continued during the year on major combatants. Ships joining the fleet or being commissioned during 1976 included the first of the 688-class nuclear attack submarines, the U.S.S. *Los Angeles.*

On Nov. 11 the U.S. Navy finally retrieved an F-14 Tomcat swing-wing jet fighter from a depth of nearly 2000 ft. in the North Atlantic. The sophisticated plane was lost Sept. 14 when one of its throttles jammed and it rolled off the deck of the carrier U.S.S. *John F. Kennedy* about 75 mi. northwest of Scapa Flow, Scotland. Extraordinary importance was attached to the salvage operation because the F-14, with its Phoenix air-to-air missile, was probably the most sophisticated airborne weapons system in the world and incorporated highly secret technology. The plane went overboard within view of several Soviet ships, and there was fear that the Russians would attempt to recover the plane. The F-14 was located with the aid of sonar devices and the NR-1 nuclear-powered minisubmarine.   T.D.

MINERALS AND METALS. During 1976 Congressional actions pertaining to energy-related subjects played a major role in many mining and metallurgical activities and plans.

Strip-Mine Coal and Oil Shale Programs. A third attempt by the United States Congress in as many years to obtain a strip-mining bill to oversee and limit the surface mining of coal never even got past committee consideration; as a result, the industry went ahead with plans to strip-mine extensive deposits of coal found in many sections of the U.S. Recent estimates showed that, unlike oil and natural gas reserves, the nation's coal resources are sufficient to supply its needs for several hundred years; the biggest problem will be to extract and process the coal without major deterioration to the environment or disruption to local communities.

Congressional activities also had a major effect upon oil shale minerals. The House of Representatives struck out two segments of the funding bill for the Energy Research and Development Administration (ERDA). These would have made additional public lands available for the commercial exploitation of oil shale and would have provided $6 billion in loans to encourage the development of synthetic fuel, mainly from coal and oil shale. In addition, with the passage of the Energy Policy and Conservation Act, which rolled back the price of domestic crude oil to an average of $7.66 a barrel, the likelihood dimmed of commercial development of oil shale deposits in the immediate future, since it was estimated that a price of $20 a barrel was needed to make shale extraction profitable (the world price for oil was about $12). Because of this problem, several companies petitioned the Department of the Interior for two-year suspensions of operations on mineral tracts they had previously leased on public lands; the suspensions were granted. There were other reasons for the suspensions, namely, mounting technical and environmental problems. For example, studies had shown that in some oil shale areas, for intermittent periods, the natural levels of dust particles and other air pollutants exceeded federal clean air standards.

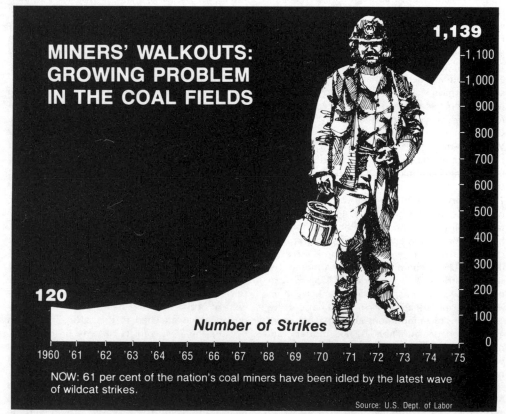

MINERS' WALKOUTS: GROWING PROBLEM IN THE COAL FIELDS

1,139

120

Number of Strikes

1960 '61 '62 '63 '64 '65 '66 '67 '68 '69 '70 '71 '72 '73 '74 '75

NOW: 61 per cent of the nation's coal miners have been idled by the latest wave of wildcat strikes.

Source: U.S. Dept. of Labor

Hearses leaving the gate of the Scotia Mine in Kentucky in November carry the bodies of eleven coal miners who had been trapped in an explosion eight months earlier. Coal mining is still the most hazardous major occupation in the U.S.

Mineral Recovery from Wastes. After two years of hearings, Congress passed the Resource Conservation and Recovery Act of 1976, which fostered programs for the recovery of valuable minerals and energy from solid wastes, including urban refuse. In addition to providing assistance to communities to develop plans for recovering energy and mineral materials from municipal wastes, the law directed the Environmental Protection Agency (E.P.A.) to study and publish a report on discarded mineral materials resulting from mining. The study was to include an analysis of present disposal practices and recommended alternatives, an analysis of the potential dangers to human health and the environment from surface runoff and from air pollution, and estimates of the impact on mine-product costs.

Mineral Production. Domestic mineral production in 1976 set a record high for the eighteenth straight year and was estimated to be worth $67.7 billion, up 9 percent from 1975. Fuels showed the highest value gain.

Total value of the fuels produced amounted to $52.1 billion, up about 9 percent from 1975. Bituminous coal and lignite production reached a record high of 665,000,000 tons, valued at $13.3 billion. The average freight-on-board mine price was estimated at $20 per ton. Increased direct use of coal from the Western states, plus an increase in coal-fired electric power generation in the Western and Gulf states, accounted for much of the increase. Anthracite production was 6,200,000 tons, about the same level as 1975. Crude petroleum production was valued at $24 billion. The average price for all domestic oil was estimated at $8.13 per barrel.

The total value of metals produced in 1976 increased by 14 percent to $5.6 billion. The increase reflected the general improvement in economic conditions and higher prices for most commodities. Aluminum production rose to 4,200,000 tons; several plants that had cut down production in 1975 by as much as 20 percent were at full capacity. Domestic mine production of recoverable copper was 1,600,000 tons, valued at $2.3 billion. Gold production declined to 1,030,000 troy oz., worth $126,000,000; the drop was mainly attributable to the close of a major Nevada mine (the Cortez) because of general depletion of ore. The average price of gold was about $123 per ounce. Domestic mine production of silver amounted to 34,000,000 troy oz., valued at $149,000,000. Iron ore shipments amounted to 76,700,000 tons, about the same as in 1975; the total value of mine shipments was about $1.8 billion.

The value of nonmetallic mineral production was $10 billion, an increase of about 5 percent. The demand for phosphate rock remained at about the same level as in 1975, 49,000,000 short tons. The production of fluorspar increased by 29 percent over 1975 to 182,600 tons, valued at $18,800,000. Cement production was up 8 percent to 74,000,000 tons, worth over $2.4 billion, and sand and gravel production declined 2 percent to 770,000,000 short tons, valued at $1.5 billion.

See also ENERGY. K.B.H.

MINNESOTA. *See* STATISTICS OF THE WORLD.
MISSISSIPPI. *See* STATISTICS OF THE WORLD.
MISSOURI. *See* STATISTICS OF THE WORLD.
MONACO. *See* STATISTICS OF THE WORLD.
MONDALE, WALTER F. *See* PEOPLE IN THE NEWS.
MONGOLIAN PEOPLE'S REPUBLIC. *See* STATISTICS OF THE WORLD.
MONTANA. *See* STATISTICS OF THE WORLD.

MOROCCO. Throughout 1976 the question of the political status of the former Spanish Sahara, later known as Western Sahara, virtually monopolized the attention of the government of King Hassan II in Morocco. Under the terms of a tripartite agreement concluded late in 1975, Morocco and Mauritania were to divide the territory following Spanish withdrawal, scheduled for Feb. 28. The agreement was rejected, however, by the Saharan independence movement, known as the Polisario, and by Algeria.

The first battle of the year, fought at the Saharan town of Amgalla on Jan. 27, left the town in Moroccan hands. By early February, Morocco held the four major Saharan towns, but outlying regions were under Polisario control. Fierce fighting continued, with the worst battles being fought at Amgalla between Moroccan forces on one side and Polisario and Algerian forces on the other.

As the fighting continued, Morocco prepared for the economic takeover of the mineral-rich Western Sahara. On Feb. 7 it bought 65 percent of the Bou Crace phosphate mining company from a Spanish government-owned holding company. In return, Spain was granted continued fishing rights in Saharan waters. On Jan. 24 the Société Marocaine pour le Développement du Sahara was set up to exploit Saharan mineral deposits and to begin the economic development of the region. On March 4 an operating budget of about $150,000,000 was allocated for Saharan investment.

Hoping to avoid further involvement in the sovereignty dispute, Spain withdrew its troops two days early, on Feb. 26. The following day the Polisario proclaimed the Saharan Arab Democratic Republic (S.A.D.R.) in the name of the Saharan people. On March 4 the S.A.D.R. formed an eight-member government with Muhammad Lamin Ould Ahmad as premier. Six African nations, including Algeria, extended recognition.

There were conflicting reports on the desires of the Saharan people themselves. It had been reported in November, 1975, that the 102 members of the *Jemaa* (Spanish Saharan assembly) had voted to disband in favor of a provisional council and that they supported Saharan independence. Other reports maintained that a majority of the *Jemaa* favored the conditions of the tripartite agreement. Morocco claimed that sixty-one assemblymen voted Feb. 26, 1976, to acknowledge Moroccan and Mauritanian authority, but the United Nations refused to accept the vote as a popular referendum.

Fighting intensified in the summer. On May 20 the Polisario celebrated the 3rd anniversary of its armed struggle by launching new offensive strikes in Morocco and Mauritania as well as in the Western Sahara area. In the course of the year the Polisario was supported by Algeria, Libya, and some of the radical African regimes, as well as by Cuba and Vietnam. Morocco was backed by the United States, France, and Iran. Mediation efforts by members of the Arab League and the Organization of African Unity were to no avail. Morocco at year's end found itself still confronting guerrilla fighters in a vast, sparsely populated desert.

Although the Western Sahara conflict helped unify diverse factions within Morocco, there were repeated wage strikes and a number of political arrests. In July more than 300 people were tried for allegedly having participated in a 1973 coup attempt. Long-promised national elections were again postponed, and King Hassan issued his annual promise to hold them within a year. The economy suffered from the war and from a drop in phosphate production that was partially attributable to Polisario sabotage of transport lines.

See STATISTICS OF THE WORLD. *See also* AFRICA; ARAB LEAGUE.   S.C.

MOTION PICTURES. The cost of producing motion pictures, along with admission prices, rose

Beloved actress Mary Pickford is filmed at her home on March 23 as she receives a special Oscar from Walter Mirisch, president of the Academy of Motion Picture Arts and Sciences.

A broken King Kong lies in the rubble at the base of the World Trade Center in New York City. Thousands of New Yorkers took part in his death scene, climax of the 1976 remake of the 1933 classic film King Kong.

steadily during 1976. Nevertheless, the most popular films were bringing in record receipts, and the big-budget movie of the 1960's seemed to be making a comeback.

Slow Beginning. Attendance figures for the approximately 10,500 theaters and 3500 drive-ins in the United States slipped 13½ percent in January to a two-year low. With the *Jaws* phenomenon of 1975 waning and no strong releases at the beginning of the year, the first four months were nearly disastrous for the motion picture industry. A slow recovery followed during the next few months with the fall and winter bringing several important films. Total box office receipts for the year were slightly lower than the $1 billion reported in 1975. Of the 300 motion pictures in production in 1976, only 60 were being produced by the major studios; the remainder were being made by "independents," whose strength was continuing to encroach on that of the big studios. Of the films produced in 1976, some 80 percent were action adventure pictures that would seek PG or R (restricted) ratings, 12 percent were family-theme with G ratings, and 9 percent were X-rated (adults only).

Popular Violence. Action-adventure films continued to draw the largest audiences, and most of the successful films made during 1976 stressed violence. One of the movies in this mold was *The Enforcer,* the third in the popular Dirty Harry series. It stars Clint Eastwood as the policeman with unorthodox methods, ready to do whatever is necessary to bring in the "bad guys." *Taxi Driver,* director Martin Scorsese's frighteningly believable case history of a modern vigilante-assassin, stars Robert De Niro. Another type of film popular in 1976 was the car-crash movie, produced mainly by Roger Corman's New World Pictures: *Death Race 2000, Eat My Dust,* and *Cannonball.*

Made with a large budget and a long list of stars, *Two-Minute Warning* is a mixture of two genres—the disaster movie and the police drama. In it masses of people are brought together and imperiled by a sniper in a football stadium. The film ends with a screaming stampede of fleeing spectators. *Marathon Man,* another big-budget film, was taken from a successful novel by William Goldman and stars Dustin Hoffman and Sir Laurence Olivier. John Schlesinger directed this spy-counterspy thriller, which deals explicitly with the savagery that in past years would have been only suggested. Several brutal slayings are topped by a scene of dental torture, sure to be recorded as one of the most terrifying in screen history.

Supernatural and Political Films. The most successful of the supernatural horror stories was *The Omen,* similar in theme and treatment to the 1973–74 blockbuster, *The Exorcist.* This big-budget film, starring Gregory Peck and Lee Remick, deals with a little boy who is the incarnation of the devil. Other 1976 films in this genre were *Burnt Offerings, J.D.'s Revenge, To the Devil a Daughter, The Devil within Her,* and *Carrie.*

American politics was the subject of two important films released during the year. *All the President's Men* was adapted by screenwriter William Goldman from the book by Bob Woodward and Carl Bernstein about their reporting of the Watergate scandal. The two reporters were played by Robert Redford and Dustin Hoffman, and the film was directed by Alan J. Pakula. It brought in $20,000,000 in box office receipts during its first

Lee Remick (left) and Harvey Stephens are confronted by a malevolent baboon in a scene from the 20th Century-Fox chiller, The Omen. Young Stephens plays a child possessed of evil powers.

twenty-four days of distribution. *The Front,* an absorbing chronicle of show business in the 1950's, was written by Walter Bernstein and directed by Martin Ritt, both of whom had been blacklisted and kept from working at that time. The film stars comic Woody Allen in his most serious role to date. Other films about an earlier America were *Bound for Glory* and *Leadbelly.* Both of these are biographies of American folksingers—in the first David Carradine portrays Woody Guthrie; in the second Roger E. Mosley is Huddie Ledbetter.

Successes and Failures. Among the few films suitable for all ages, *The Bad News Bears,* an antic look at Little League baseball, stars Walter Matthau and Tatum O'Neal. *The Slipper and the Rose,* a modernization of the Cinderella story, stars Richard Chamberlain and Gemma Craven. Possibly the most unusual film of the year is *Bugsy Malone,* a musical-comedy spoof of 1930's gangster films, played entirely by juveniles. And *The Bingo Long Traveling All-Stars and Motor Kings* casts Billy Dee Williams, James Earl Jones, and Richard Pryor as a depression period band of black baseball players and con men.

Other notable films of the year include *The Seven-Per-Cent Solution,* in which Sherlock Holmes (Nicol Williamson) teams with Sigmund Freud (Alan Arkin) and Robert Duvall plays Dr. Watson. *Rocky,* the story of a down at the heels boxer, was written by Sylvester Stallone, who also plays the title role. *Network,* starring Faye Dunaway, William Holden, Peter Finch, and Robert Duvall, is a strong, satiric look at the power of television; it was written by Paddy Chayefsky and directed by Sidney Lumet.

The year also brought its disappointments. *The*

Missouri Breaks, directed by Arthur Penn, is a beautifully photographed Western starring Jack Nicholson and Marlon Brando; the two stars were paid near-record salaries for their work in the film; it was a critical and box office failure. Another disappointment at the box office was *The Blue Bird,* a fairy tale of two children searching for the bluebird of happiness. The movie, starring Elizabeth Taylor, Jane Fonda, Cicely Tyson, and other international names, was filmed in the Soviet Union and coproduced, cofinanced, and codistributed by Soviet and American groups. One of the year's most expensive mistakes was 20th Century-Fox's $12,000,000 *Lucky Lady,* starring Liza Minnelli, Burt Reynolds, and Gene Hackman. Paul Newman created little interest with his *Buffalo Bill and the Indians,* directed by Robert Altman, and Barbra Streisand's musical remake of *A Star Is Born* opened at year's end to generally unfavorable reviews—and huge audiences.

King Kong. Dino de Laurentiis, an accomplished producer in Italy and in America, took two film ideas which had been successful in the past and combined them to make a film that may prove to be the most successful of all time. In 1933 a pioneer filmmaker named Merian C. Cooper, intrigued by the legend of Beauty and the Beast, transformed it into a film he called *King Kong.* It was de Laurentiis's idea to produce a contemporary version of *Kong* and apply the exploitation techniques that had worked so well for *Jaws.* The publicity campaign began long before the first day of production. Throughout the year bulletins were issued—on the money being spent on the many special effects needed; on the 40-ft. version of Kong (this alone cost $1,700,000); on the legal battles de Laurentiis went through to gain the rights for a remake; and on the search for the appropriate actress to reenact the role of Kong's nemesis, played by Fay Wray in the 1933 version. With much fanfare, it was announced that Jessica Lange, a former dancer and model, had finally been selected to play Beauty. British director John Guillermin, screenwriter Lorenzo Semple, Jr., and a large technical crew completed the production for about $24,000,000. Then an additional $15,000,000 was spent on preopening publicity. On Dec. 17 the film opened in 1200 theaters across the U.S. In its first three days of distribution, *Kong* grossed nearly $7,000,000, and de Laurentiis was clearly in the running for the top receipts's film record now held by *Jaws,* which has grossed nearly $200,000,000.

Foreign Language Films. A number of intriguing imports were seen in the U.S. in 1976. *Small Change* is François Truffaut's bright and funny film about children. *Lumière,* which was directed by and stars Jeanne Moreau, is the story of four actresses and the ways in which they deal with

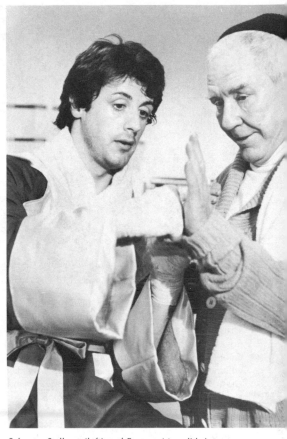

Sylvester Stallone (left) and Burgess Meredith in a scene from Rocky, the story of the triumph of a small-time boxer. Stallone wrote the screenplay and played the title role in this low-budget hit.

Barbra Streisand sings to an enthusiastic crowd in a key scene from her new musical, A Star Is Born. *The sentimental story was filmed twice before—with Janet Gaynor and with Judy Garland—but the Streisand version packed them in after its December opening.*

life and each other. Eric Rohmer's *The Marquise Of O . . .* tells a poignant tale of a clash of morals and manners in the early 19th century. *Cousin, Cousine* by Jean-Charles Tacchella is a touching romantic comedy. And *The Memory of Justice* is a documentary by Marcel Ophuls that examines moral responsibility. All of these French films received wide acclaim.

Academy Awards for 1975. The Academy of Motion Picture Arts and Sciences presented its awards for the previous year's work in Los Angeles on March 29. For the first time since 1934 and *It Happened One Night* a single film, *One Flew Over the Cuckoo's Nest,* swept the four major awards, winning in the categories of Best Picture, Best Director, Best Actor, and Best Actress. Set in a mental ward, it was produced by Michael Douglas and Saul Zentz and directed by Milos Forman. The film starred Jack Nicholson as McMurphy, the perhaps sane hero, and Louise Fletcher as the evil

Chris Chandler of Seattle (second from right) celebrates with other members of the American Bicentennial Everest Expedition. He was one of two climbers to reach the summit of the world's highest peak on Oct. 8.

Nurse Kratchit. *Cuckoo* also won Oscars for authors Bo Goldman and Lawrence Hauben, whose screenplay had been adapted from Ken Kesey's novel. The Best Supporting Actor award went to George Burns for his portrayal of an aging vaudevillian in Neil Simon's *The Sunshine Boys.* Lee Grant was named Best Supporting Actress for her appearance as a bored wife in *Shampoo.* The financially successful *Jaws* picked up Oscars for Best Film Editing, Best Original Music Score, and Best Sound.

A highlight of the ceremonies was a filmed interview with Mary Pickford and a tour through her fabled mansion, Pickfair. The 82-year-old actress was given an honorary Oscar for her contribution to the motion picture arts. A major force in the medium from 1913 to 1933, she was one of the original thirty-six founders of the academy.

Deaths. Richard Arlen, Busby Berkeley, Jean Gabin, James Wong Howe, Fritz Lang, Sal Mineo, Sir Carol Reed, Rosalind Russell, Alastair Sim, Dalton Trumbo, Luchino Visconti, and Adolph Zukor died during the year; *see* OBITUARIES. Other deaths included those of British actors Sir Stanley Baker (June 28 at 48) and Roger Livesey (Feb. 5 at 69), former Dead End Kid Billy Halop (Nov. 9 at 56), producer Arthur Hornblow, Jr. (July 17 at 83), and Production Code head Geoffrey M. Shurlock (April 26 at 81).   R.W.B.

MOUNTAINEERING. The popularity of mountaineering as a sport continued to increase in 1976, but with that popularity came problems. Especially noteworthy were the accidents that occurred; during the year numerous groups had to be rescued. In Yosemite National Park, on Mt. Hood in Oregon, and on Mt. McKinley in Alaska several groups went out with inadequate equipment, disregarded weather advisories, or went unroped on crevassed glaciers, requiring expensive rescue operations. Such misadventures led to much discussion of new regulations and even to stiff fines for groups requiring expensive rescues. The American Alpine Club maintained a file to which persons involved in accidents were urged to report, in the hope that better statistics might permit more detailed analysis of these mishaps and prevent others. Indignation was also expressed concerning the "amount of trash on Mt. McKinley" and elsewhere, left by thoughtless climbers.

The season saw climbs of a few new peaks, but mostly of old and familiar ones by new routes. On Feb. 22 a team consisting of John Bragg, Jim Donini, and Jay Wilson climbed Cerro de la Torre and Torre Egger in the Patagonia region of South America. This involved 4500 ft. of hard technical climbing; the climbers also had to cope with the usual extremely bad weather. In California, Split Mountain was climbed by Galen Rowell and David Belden; their accomplishment included ascents of sixteen pitches on Split's east ridge. In Nevada, Dennis Hennek, Mike Graber, and Rowell ascended the west face of Mt. Conness.

The north face of Mt. Athabasca in the Canadian Rockies was climbed by John Roskelly and Chris Jones; Roskelly and Jim States climbed Bourgeau. Meanwhile Naomi Uemura, a Japanese woman who had earlier climbed Mt. Everest (29,028 ft.) on the Nepal-Tibet border, completed an 8000-mi. solo dogsled journey from Greenland to northwestern Alaska.

In the Himalayas a party consisting of Willy Unsoeld and his daughter Nanda Devi Unsoeld, Martin Hoey, and Pete Lev climbed Nanda Devi in India (25,645 ft.). Unsoeld's daughter died of acute high-altitude sickness during the climb; by tradition, she was buried on the mountain.

The American Bicentennial Everest Expedition, led by Phillip Trimble and including Barbara and Gerard Roach, Arlene Blum, Dee Crouch, and others, attacked Everest, the world's highest peak, in the autumn. On Oct. 8 expedition members Chris Chandler of Seattle and Bob Cormack of Boulder, Colo., reached the top. They thus became the fifty-fourth and fifty-fifth persons to stand on the summit. Winds of over 100 m.p.h. were encountered, forcing the remainder of the party to stop short of their goal.

In the Karakoram range of northern India a Pakistani group reached the top of Paiju Peak. In Alaska on July 6 a Bicentennial surge of eighty climbers reached the summit of 20,320-ft. Mt. McKinley. Fritz Stammberger disappeared on a solo climb of the 25,230-ft. Tirich Mir in the Pakistan section of the Hindu Kush. S.A.K.

MOYNIHAN, DANIEL P. *See* PEOPLE IN THE NEWS.
MOZAMBIQUE. In 1976, its second year of independence, Mozambique faced severe hardships, primarily because of its determination to support black nationalists fighting the white-dominated government of neighboring Rhodesia. By permitting the Rhodesian nationalists to maintain guerrilla camps on its soil, Mozambique opened itself to retaliation. Following their policy of "hot pursuit" against guerrillas, white Rhodesian forces repeatedly launched large-scale attacks against Mozambique border villages and military camps. Hundreds of guerrillas, as well as Mozambique soldiers and citizens, were reported to have been killed in these attacks.

Following an attack on Feb. 24, President Samora Machel put Mozambique on a war footing and closed the border with Rhodesia. Although this affected some 20 to 30 percent of Rhodesia's foreign trade, it had an even graver impact upon the Mozambique economy, heavily dependent upon foreign-exchange earnings from transit fees collected when goods were shipped across the country. In addition, some 10,000 workers normally employed on plantations in Rhodesia were left without jobs. It was estimated that during 1976 Mozambique would lose about $165,000,000 in revenues due to the closing of the border. Pledges of aid totaling $60,000,000 were received from the United States, Great Britain, Sweden, Finland, Denmark, the Netherlands, the Arab League, and Nigeria. The Soviet Union agreed to supply Mozambique forces with a variety of weapons, including ground-to-air missiles.

See STATISTICS OF THE WORLD. *See also* AFRICA. J.T.S.

MUSIC. Inevitably, the celebration of the Bicentennial of the United States of America in 1976 was reflected in the music heard across the land during the year. Long forgotten compositions were resurrected and performed in a burst of patriotic euphoria.

New Works and Revivals. New works by native composers found audiences in opera houses and

Early in September the famed La Scala opera company of Milan, Italy, paid its first visit to the U.S. Seen here is a performance of La Cenerentola, Gioacchino Rossini's early 19th-century version of the tale of Cinderella, at the Kennedy Center in Washington, D.C.

They Also Laid More Eggs

An experiment conducted at Rockefeller University revealed an interesting fact: The more the male canary sings, the faster the female builds her nest. Dr. Donald E. Kroodsma played tapes of the varying repertories of several male canaries and counted the pieces of string the listening females gathered. The shorter the arias, the doctor discovered, the skimpier the nests.

---

concert halls across the country. There were world operatic premieres of Carlisle Floyd's *Bilby's Doll* in Houston, Thomas Pasatieri's *Ines de Castro* in Baltimore, and his *Washington Square* in Detroit. Gian-Carlo Menotti's *The Hero* was done in Philadelphia, and his *Egg* premiered in Washington, D.C. *Voyage of Edgar Allen Poe,* by Dominick Argento, was seen in Saint Paul, and *Angle of Repose* by Andrew Imbrie received a production in San Francisco. Roger Sessions's monumental *Montezuma,* first staged in Berlin in 1964, found its way home to Boston in a well-received production under the aegis of Sarah Caldwell. Even a ballad opera by Andrew Barton, *The Disappointment,* which had rarely been performed since its premiere in Philadelphia in 1767, came to light again in August at Washington Crossing Park in New Jersey. Douglas Moore's durable *Ballad of*

A completely remodeled Avery Fisher Hall reopens in New York City on Oct. 19, as the New York Philharmonic waits for Pierre Boulez to raise his baton.

Baby Doe (1956) and Robert Ward's *Crucible* (1961) had many revivals.

Governmental and Other Organizations. The National Endowment for the Arts and the Humanities had commissioned works by six American composers for performance by six major orchestras. The first of these was John Cage's *Renga with Apartment House 1776,* played in October by the Boston Symphony Orchestra and in November by the New York Philharmonic. Constructed in the radical style of Charles Ives, it was politely received in Boston but reportedly caused a massive exodus in New York City. John La Montaine's musico-historical pageant *Be Glad, Then, America,* commissioned by Pennsylvania State University and staged by the ubiquitous Sarah Caldwell, was cordially greeted but was not performed again. Great Britain's Bicentennial Commission sent such organizations as the Grimethorpe Colliery Band and the King's College, Cambridge, Choir on a successful tour of England's former American colonies. In Boston in March, the New England Conservatory of Music launched a $2,000,000 fund drive to name a course of studies in American music for its retiring president, Gunther Schuller. At the same time New Yorkers were protesting a $4,000,000 cut in the budget of their State Council on the Arts.

Visitors. Thanks to last-minute funding by its hosts, the Kennedy Center for the Performing Arts in Washington, D.C., the famed La Scala opera company of Milan, Italy, finally made its first visit to the U.S. in September. In its repertoire, seen only at the center, were works by Verdi, Rossini, and Puccini. The Paris Opéra, also appearing in

A Giant Force in Opera
When Sarah Caldwell, 49, raised her baton on the 13th of January, the orchestra began the overture to Giuseppe Verdi's opera *La Traviata* and Caldwell became the first woman ever to conduct New York City's fabled 93-year-old Metropolitan Opera. (A few weeks earlier she had become the second woman ever to lead the New York Philharmonic.) The first lady of American opera had been breaking new ground for decades. As founder, stage director, and chief conductor of the Boston Opera Company, Caldwell, a stagecraft genius, routinely gave old operas an exciting new look, all in a converted vaudeville theater with a postage-stamp stage.

Sarah Caldwell conducts.

the U.S. for the first time, prefaced its own Kennedy Center engagement with performances in September at New York City's Metropolitan Opera House. Its repertory consisted of Mozart's *Le Nozze di Figaro,* Gounod's *Faust,* and Verdi's *Otello,* with Georg Solti conducting the Mozart and Verdi works to considerable acclaim. Soviet pianist Lazar Berman, making his U.S. debut in January, impressed the critics with his extraordinary virtuosity and was brought back in October for more concerts. In November the London Philharmonic Orchestra under Bernard Haitink made a short goodwill tour of the northeastern U.S., while conductor Herbert von Karajan with the Berlin Philharmonic Orchestra and the Vienna Singverein filled Carnegie Hall for a series of orchestral and choral concerts at more than double the usual prices. In a reverse movement, the New York Philharmonic under Leonard Bernstein paid a Bicentennial visit to Vienna in June and created a sensation among Austrian critics and concertgoers.

New and Old Homes. Fourteen years after its opening, Avery Fisher Hall in New York City's Lincoln Center was closed down for five months and $6,400,000 worth of reconstruction. The hall (formerly known as Philharmonic Hall) was entirely gutted and rebuilt in an all-out effort to remedy its faulty acoustics. Under the direction of the experienced acoustician Cyril M. Harris, the task was generally agreed to have been successfully completed. The gala reopening on Oct. 19, with Pierre Boulez conducting the New York Philharmonic, was an unqualified critical success. Meanwhile, on March 18, Carnegie Hall in New York

City announced a $6,500,000 fund drive, to make structural changes in its auditorium and to form a youth orchestra. A gala concert on May 18 marked the hall's 85th year and enlisted the talents of such luminaries as Leonard Bernstein, Dietrich Fischer-Dieskau, Vladimir Horowitz, Yehudi Menuhin, Mstislav Rostropovich, and Isaac Stern. Widely proclaimed the "Concert of the Century," the gala event raised $1,200,000 for the cause. On June 16 the Philadelphia Orchestra christened its new outdoor home at Robin Hood Dell. Led by Eugene

The remarkable Soviet pianist Lazar Berman prepares for his American debut. The 46-year-old virtuoso was so enthusiastically acclaimed in January that he was brought back for another series of concerts in October and November.

Ormandy, the inaugural concert featured Gregor Piatigorsky in what proved to be the famed cellist's last public appearance. He died Aug. 6 at the age of 73; see OBITUARIES.

New Posts and Awards. Conductor Max Rudolf's appointment as music adviser of the New Jersey Symphony was announced on April 20. It was hoped that this move would resolve several years of unrest within the orchestra. Two months earlier it was announced that Zubin Mehta would succeed Pierre Boulez as principal conductor of the New York Philharmonic, effective September, 1978. And Dutch Conductor Edo de Waart was scheduled to follow Seiji Ozawa as director of the San Francisco Symphony in the fall of 1977.

The first noncompetitive Avery Fisher Prizes, announced in February, went to pianists Ursula Oppens and Paul Shenly, violinist Anni Kavafian, and harpist Heidi Lehwalder. Established as an aid to young artists, each prize consisted of $1000

cash and several appearances with orchestra. The Metropolitan Opera National Council Auditions were won on March 29 by tenor John Carpenter and soprano Ashley Putnam. On May 4 Ned Rorem's *Air Music,* a work for orchestra, won the Pulitzer Prize; also honored, posthumously, was composer Scott Joplin. In a White House ceremony on April 1, U.S. President Gerald R. Ford presented veteran pianist Arthur Rubinstein with the Presidential Medal of Freedom, the highest U.S. civilian award.

Deaths. Benjamin Britten, Lotte Lehmann, Lily Pons, and Paul Robeson were among the musical celebrities who died during the year; see OBITUARIES. Other deaths in the music world included those of Austrian pianist Geza Anda (June 13 at 54), American conductor Dean Dixon (Nov. 3 at 61), German conductor Rudolf Kempe (May 11 at 65), and Italian tenor Nino Martini (Dec. 9 at 72).   L.S.

N

NAURU. *See* STATISTICS OF THE WORLD.
NEBRASKA. *See* STATISTICS OF THE WORLD.
NEGROES IN THE UNITED STATES. The 200th birthday of the United States was observed soberly, rather than exuberantly, by black Americans. To them the Bicentennial was another reminder that the "created equal" ideal of the Declaration of Independence was still to be achieved. To that end, they exerted a more concerted effort in attacking the obstacles to equality. Seeking safer neighborhoods, they launched communitywide anticrime programs in many cities. On a broader scale, forty-five black organizations throughout the country worked together in May to get out the vote in the 1976 elections; black support was crucial to Jimmy Carter's election to the Presidency in November.

Political Activity. In 1976 a larger proportion of Blacks began to view participation in politics as the new cutting edge of the civil rights movement. It became more evident that black elected officials, although still less than 1 percent of the total number, were here to stay. In September Joseph W. Hatchett, named a judge of the Florida Supreme Court in 1975, became the first Black elected to statewide office in the South since Reconstruction. At the U.S. Conference of Mayors, held in Milwaukee in July, Kenneth A. Gibson of Newark was elected president.

Headed by Yvonne B. Burke (D, Calif.), the Congressional Black Caucus, made up of the black members of the U.S. House of Representa-

Benjamin L. Hooks, member of the Federal Communications Commission, reacts to his selection in November as the new executive director of the N.A.A.C.P. "This is one of the most important jobs in the country," he said.

tives, was particularly active in 1976. Among its many undertakings was the formulation of a legislative agenda of ten major "issue concerns" for consideration by Congress. The caucus also presented these issues to the platform committees at the Democratic and Republican national conventions, having considerable success in influencing the text of the Democratic Party platform.

For Blacks the political high point of the year was the election of Jimmy Carter as President. Carter first demonstrated his appeal to black voters in the primaries, especially those in Florida, Texas, and Pennsylvania. He enjoyed strong endorsements from Rep. Andrew Young (D, Ga.; *see* PEOPLE IN THE NEWS) and Martin Luther King, Sr., father of the slain civil rights leader. These and other black spokesmen stood by him in April when he said that he saw "nothing wrong with ethnic purity" in urban neighborhoods. Carter later apologized for the remark and reaffirmed his opposition to racial discrimination in housing. Blacks voted overwhelmingly for Carter in November; some estimates put the proportion at 90 percent of a total 6,600,000 votes. All seventeen black members of the House of Representatives

were reelected, but most Blacks who attempted to gain new elective offices were unsuccessful.

Economic Plight. Among the measures pushed by the Black Caucus, full employment ranked first. According to a report issued in June by the Bureau of Labor Statistics, the unemployment figure for black teenagers reached 40.3 percent, as compared with 16.1 percent for Whites of the same age. Total black unemployment stood close to 14 percent. The U.S. Census Bureau reported in October that 31 percent of the black population lived below the poverty level ($5500 annual income for an urban family of four).

The N.A.A.C.P. For allegedly having encouraged a boycott in Port Gibson, Miss., of white businesses that did not employ Blacks, the National Association for the Advancement of Colored People (N.A.A.C.P.) faced a financial crisis when a Mississippi judge awarded damages of $1,250,000 to twelve white merchants. The N.A.A.C.P. was put to the ordeal of hastily raising the huge sum necessary for an appeal. In November the N.A.A.C.P. announced that as of Jan. 1, 1977, its new executive director would be Benjamin L. Hooks, the first Black to serve on the Federal Communications Commission. Hooks would succeed the 75-year-old Roy Wilkins.

Other Events and Appointments. The U.S. Civil Rights Commission reported that desegregation of the nation's public schools had for the most part been successfully accomplished. For every scene of racial strife over busing, said the commission, there were "dozens of communities where desegregation is proceeding without major incident." *See* EDUCATION.

The Rainbow Girls, an international Masonic-sponsored fraternal and charitable order of young women, voted in December to drop an unwritten rule denying membership to Blacks. The vote settled a dispute arising from the cancellation of the charter of an Iowa chapter that admitted a black woman in October.

Joseph H. Evans of New York City became the first Black to be elected president of the United Church of Christ, and Thelma D. Adair was elected as moderator of the General Assembly of the United Presbyterian Church in the U.S.A., a breakthrough for black women. Pulitzer Prize-winning poet Gwendolyn Brooks became the first black woman elected to the National Institute of Arts and Letters, and Robert E. Hayden was appointed Library of Congress Consultant in Poetry for 1976–77. Rear Adm. Samuel L. Gravely, Jr., was promoted to vice admiral and assigned as commander of the U.S. Third Fleet.

Deaths. Paul Robeson, concert singer, athlete, scholar, and civil rights activist, died in 1976, as

Clarence Norris (right) receives his pardon from Alabama parole-board chairman Norman Ussery in Montgomery on Nov. 29. Norris was the last known survivor of the so-called Scottsboro boys, nine black youths unjustly convicted of rape in a famous 1931 case.

did concert singer Roland Hayes and entertainers Godfrey Cambridge and Howlin' Wolf; see OBITUARIES. Other deaths included those of Florence Ballard, former member of the rock-music group the Supremes (Feb. 22 at 32); Dean Dixon, symphony orchestra conductor (Nov. 3 at 61); William H. Hastie, the first Black to be appointed to a fed-

eral appeals court (April 14 at 71); De Hart Hubbard, former athlete who in 1924 became the first black American to win an Olympic gold medal (June 23 at 72); and Lewis H. Michaux, Harlem bookstore owner and literary figure (Aug. 25 at 92).

See also CIVIL RIGHTS AND CIVIL LIBERTIES.   B.Q.

NEPAL. See STATISTICS OF THE WORLD.

NETHERLANDS, THE. The political scene in the Netherlands during 1976 was largely monopolized by a bribery scandal that reached into the royal family and threatened to bring disgrace to the queen's husband.

The cabinet confirmed on Feb. 8 that Prince Bernhard, husband of Queen Juliana, was the "high Dutch government official" who had been cited by a top official of the Lockheed Aircraft Corp., an American firm, as having taken $1,100,-000 for his help in getting the Netherlands to buy Lockheed planes. The story came out in testimony before a United States Senate subcommittee.

The prince denied the accusation, but Prime Minister Joop den Uyl told the nation on television that private discussions had led him to conclude that Bernhard was implicated. The newspaper De Telegraaf reported on March 12 that Bernhard had helped the Werkspoor company, a Dutch rail-engineering firm, in a 1951 arrangement whereby Werkspoor had paid nearly $12,000,000 in bribes to the late President Juan D. Perón and other Argentine officials to obtain a rail-equipment contract. The prince forthwith resigned almost all his military and business positions.

A motion from left-wing members for criminal

The Merchant Prince

It could not be proved that he had accepted gifts of $1,100,000 for helping the Lockheed Aircraft Corp. sell planes to the Dutch, but investigators concluded that Prince Bernhard, the widely admired husband of Queen Juliana of the Netherlands, had nevertheless shown himself "open to dishonorable requests and offers" in his dealings with the bribe-prone aircraft manufacturer. The Queen survived the scandal with her throne intact, but Bernhard was forced to step down as inspector general of the Dutch Armed Forces and resign from the boards of nearly 300 corporations and organizations, ranging from Royal Dutch Airlines (KLM) to the World Wildlife Fund.

Prince Bernhard of the Netherlands.

prosecution of Bernhard was rejected by a vote of 146–2 in parliament on Aug. 30, although leaders of all five major parties criticized the prince's imprudent behavior in the Lockheed situation.

Figures released during the year showed that exports from the Netherlands were down $1.5 billion from 1974 to a total of $31.3 billion in 1975. The unemployment situation, which had shown signs of improving during the last two months of 1975, worsened again in 1976. The cost of living in the Netherlands had risen by 10.2 percent during 1975, according to government data released on Jan. 20, but inflation declined to a rate of about 8 percent during 1976.

Industrial output had dropped by 4 percent to a total of $108 billion. Food and luxury goods were the only products not affected by the decline. The drop was especially severe in paper products, down 20 percent, and textiles, ready-made clothing, and chemicals, each of which declined by 15 percent.

Bad weather throughout Western Europe had caused a serious shortfall in the 1975 potato crop, and in many parts of the area retail potato prices more than tripled in the final two months of 1975. On Feb. 12, 1976, the Netherlands Potato Board banned all potato exports to countries outside the European Community. Such exports had normally accounted for around 10 percent of the total Dutch potato business.

Queen Juliana, addressing parliament on Sept. 21, said that price and wage controls, first instituted in January, 1974, would continue through fiscal 1977. The $33.2 billion budget for 1977, presented to parliament after the queen's speech, assumed a deficit of about $5.6 billion.

See STATISTICS OF THE WORLD.　　　　L.A.S.

NEVADA. See STATISTICS OF THE WORLD.

NEW BRUNSWICK. See STATISTICS OF THE WORLD.

NEWFOUNDLAND. See STATISTICS OF THE WORLD.

NEW HAMPSHIRE. See STATISTICS OF THE WORLD.

NEW JERSEY. See STATISTICS OF THE WORLD.

NEW MEXICO. See STATISTICS OF THE WORLD.

NEW YORK. See STATISTICS OF THE WORLD.

NEW ZEALAND. The National Party Government of New Zealand's Prime Minister Robert Muldoon, which took office in December, 1975, faced massive economic problems as 1976 began. For years New Zealand had been living beyond its means. By his own admission Muldoon had to deal simultaneously with inflation running at 18 percent, all-time high unemployment, a serious balance-of-payments deficit, and an equally troubling domestic budget deficit.

The prime minister began the year by slashing subsidies that had kept prices for essential goods and services at an artificially low level. Although his move caused an immediate drop in the standard of living, Muldoon said the government's first priority was to balance its books. In a further move Muldoon announced in May a twelve-month pay freeze, and his first budget, delivered to parliament in July, introduced controls aimed at drastically reducing imports.

A police launch at Wellington, New Zealand, warns a protest boat away from the U.S.S. Truxton. The nuclear-powered U.S. warship arrived Aug. 30 for a six-day visit; a nationwide shipping strike was also staged to protest the Truxton's layover.

Muldoon encountered difficulties with the nation's labor unions. Workers resented the wage freeze, and the government attempted to mollify them by enacting a control on rents. In August, however, Muldoon took a firm stance against strikes. He introduced legislation to halt "rolling" strikes, in which one group of workers refuses to work one day and another the next, thus stopping an industry for several days at a time with a minimum pay loss to each worker. In addition Muldoon restricted the right of unions to call political strikes. One purpose was to put an end to work stoppages protesting visits to New Zealand by nuclear-powered warships from the United States. The vessel U.S.S. *Truxton* made the first such visit in many years during August.

In further efforts to ease New Zealand's economic crisis, Prime Minister Muldoon worked to stimulate exports. In April plans of the administration of U.S. President Gerald R. Ford to limit U.S. purchases of New Zealand beef were the topic of discussions between Muldoon and visiting U.S. Vice-President Nelson A. Rockefeller. That same month Muldoon held official talks in Great Britain, France, South Korea, Japan, and China. In each case the New Zealand leader emphasized the importance his nation placed on continuing its access to world markets. A major boost to exports came in November when New Zealand devalued its currency by 12.7 percent against the Australian dollar and 7 percent against other world currencies.

In midsummer New Zealand found itself a target of international controversy on account of its sports policies. The Muldoon government refused to cut sports ties with the white-dominated government of South Africa. As a result more than thirty-one countries, most of them African, withdrew from the 1976 Summer Olympic Games to protest New Zealand's participation. New Zealand Foreign Minister B. E. Talboys circulated a letter to foreign governments stressing the nation's abhorrence of South Africa's racial policies. Nonetheless, the New Zealand government, with wide public approval, refused to ban the scheduling of sports events against South African teams.

See STATISTICS OF THE WORLD. F.W.

NICARAGUA. In 1976, despite the improving economic outlook, President Anastasio Somoza Debayle continued to govern under the state of siege that was imposed at the end of 1974, following the kidnapping and ransoming of a number of prominent political and business leaders. The influence of the president, who was nearing the end of a decade in office, appeared to most observers to have increased during the year.

Economic prospects brightened in 1976 because of improved world prices for cotton and coffee, the country's two major export commodities. After growing by only 2 percent in 1975, the real gross domestic product increased by an estimated 5 percent in 1976. With the economy expanding, the money supply was growing at an annual rate of 30 percent by July, and foreign exchange reserves were 36 percent higher than at the close of 1975. One cloud arose on the economic horizon in September, when the United States tripled sugar import duties.

Economic activity was also spurred by the ongoing reconstruction of Managua, the capital city, which was destroyed in a devastating earthquake in 1973. Residential construction began as a result of borrowings undertaken in 1975. And in February it was reported that President Somoza flew to Guatemala to offer his country's aid to that earthquake-stricken nation.

See STATISTICS OF THE WORLD. A.K.M.

NIGER. See STATISTICS OF THE WORLD.

NIGERIA, FEDERATION OF. Murtala Ramat Muhammed, head of state of Nigeria and commander in chief of the armed forces, was ambushed and assassinated on Feb. 13, 1976. But the coup, organized by a small group of "young revolutionaries," failed when the army rallied to support the government. The following day the Supreme Military Council appointed Lt. Gen. Olusegun Obasanjo, chief of staff of the armed forces, as the new head of state. By May 16 at least thirty-seven persons, including the leader of the abortive coup, Lt. Col. Bukar Dimka, had been captured, tried, and executed. The former head of state, Gen. Yakubu Gowon, who had been overthrown in July, 1975, was implicated in the plot. Gowon, an exile in England, denied the charge, and Great Britain refused to extradite him.

The new government continued Muhammed's programs to weed out government corruption, to give Nigerians control of the economy through majority ownership of firms, and to implement a nationalistic and neutral foreign policy. Nigeria remained the richest, most powerful, and most populous of the black nations, as well as sixth among the world's oil producers. Following a planned cut in oil production, the government on April 1 announced an austerity budget of $8.9 billion, down 20 percent from 1975. Revenues for the year were projected at a record $9.3 billion. Cutting back on most nonessential projects, the government concentrated on new programs for housing, health, and agriculture. In an effort to relieve port congestion and stimulate domestic production, a six-month ban on certain consumer imports was imposed. In the fall a new five-year plan was implemented to achieve free and compulsory primary education by 1980. Despite shortages of teachers and classrooms, the plan received enthusiastic public support.

The shift from a pro-Western foreign policy continued through 1976, with Nigeria taking the lead in supporting the new Marxist-oriented government of Angola. In addition, it stepped up supplies of money and arms to nationalist movements in southern Africa. A new constitution was drafted in October; it promised to restore power to civilians by October, 1979.

See STATISTICS OF THE WORLD. See also AFRICA.   J.T.S.

NIXON, RICHARD M. See PEOPLE IN THE NEWS.

NORTH ATLANTIC TREATY ORGANIZATION, abbreviated NATO. The year 1976 saw the first breach between two NATO members, when Iceland broke off diplomatic relations with Great Britain over cod-fishing rights within Icelandic waters. Gen. Alexander M. Haig, Jr., continued as supreme commander of NATO forces and was reappointed in November as commander in chief of American forces in Europe.

Italian Crisis. The crisis over Portugal's internal stability in 1975 gave way to a new and potentially more serious threat in Italy in 1976. In the spring there appeared a strong chance that the Italian Communist Party might win the June elections, a prospect which greatly disturbed other NATO members. Officials from several member nations talked openly of the possibility of having to expel Italy from the alliance in the event of a Communist takeover, although Italian Communists insisted they would honor Italy's commitments to NATO. United States officials repeatedly stressed that a Communist victory in Italy would grievously impair the alliance and conceivably lead to its disintegration. The eventual victory of the Christian Democrats in Italy only partially allayed the fears. In a speech in Paris on June 22, U.S. Secretary of State Henry A. Kissinger warned that the threat of Communist participation in the Italian government continued to be a future possibility.

Ministerial Meeting. NATO ministers met May 20–21 in Oslo, Norway, and in a communiqué released at the conclusion of the session expressed great concern over what was described as a major and troublesome buildup of Soviet bloc power in Eastern Europe. The ministers worried over "the sustained growth in the Warsaw Pact countries' military power . . . beyond levels apparently justified for defensive purposes." They were also concerned that if the trend continued it could lead to "an arms race of dangerous dimension." The ministers vowed that NATO would reduce its military strength only in the context of mutual and balanced force reductions by the Warsaw Pact. In a speech on May 20 Kissinger sought to reassure America's allies in the wake of the U.S. policy setback in Angola, pledging that American foreign policy would continue to support a hard line against the Soviet Union regardless of who won the Presidential election in November.

Air Power Buildup. On Oct. 27 the U.S. Defense Department announced a major increase in

Some 200 warships participated in the largest exercises ever held by the Northern command of NATO. Near the coast of Norway on Sept. 20 are, left to right, the Stavanger (Norway), Bigellow (U.S.), Norfolk (U.K.), Amsterdam (Netherlands), and Oslo (Norway).

The wreckage of an F-14 Tomcat fighter plane arrives at the naval dockyard in Edinburgh, Scotland, on Nov. 13. The highly advanced plane, which had toppled from the deck of the carrier John F. Kennedy during a NATO exercise in September, was salvaged from a depth of 1800 ft.

American tactical air power in Europe in a move to underscore the extent of the U.S. commitment to NATO, as well as in reaction to what the Pentagon described as an increasing buildup of Soviet air power in Eastern Europe. Beginning in the spring of 1977, the U.S. Air Force planned to deploy 72 new F-15 jet fighters to West Germany. A second wing of 84 F-111 fighter-bombers was to be assigned to England, replacing several squadrons of F-4 Phantom jets. The new deployments would bring American tactical air strength in Europe to approximately 550 planes. Even with the added strength, Pentagon sources said NATO tactical air power was still far below the estimated 5000 Soviet and Warsaw Pact planes stationed in Eastern Europe. In a related move, reportedly designed to bolster NATO's ability to conduct limited nuclear war in Europe, the Pentagon decided to incorporate a nuclear capability in the new F-16 jet fighter under development.

Military Developments. The military preparedness of NATO came under criticism from several sources during the year. A study written by a Belgian general, vigorously disavowed by NATO headquarters, maintained that Warsaw Pact forces could successfully launch a surprise attack against Western Europe as a result of NATO's "chronic unpreparedness." In October NATO commander U.S. Gen. Alexander M. Haig, Jr., warned of the "relentless growth in sheer Soviet military power," and advised NATO forces to "break the grip of the long-standing complacency." A U.S. General Accounting Office classified survey was reportedly sharply critical of the combat readiness of U.S. units stationed in Europe. And the annual report of the prestigious International Institute for Strategic Studies in London predicted that NATO was losing ground to the Warsaw Pact, and that its superiority would continue to diminish unless Western military expenditures were increased.

Responding to past criticism of a lack of standardization in equipment, the U.S. and West Germany agreed to standardize several components of each nation's new main battle tank. Under the plan, announced Aug. 4, the U.S. would adopt the German tank's gun and the Germans would incorporate a U.S. turbine engine.

NATO held several major military exercises during 1976, including the largest ever held in its northern command. This was conducted Sept. 20 on the central coast of Norway and involved 200 ships and submarines, 900 aircraft, and 80,000 personnel, including U.S. Marines, American reserve troops, and civilians.

Meeting in Brussels on Dec. 9, the foreign ministers of NATO rejected a Warsaw Pact proposal for a mutual ban on the first use of nuclear weapons, and also for a freeze on member nations in the opposing organizations.

See articles on individual countries.   T.D.

NORTH CAROLINA. *See* Statistics of the World.
NORTH DAKOTA. *See* Statistics of the World.
NORTHWEST TERRITORIES. *See* Statistics of the World.

NORWAY. Prime Minister Trygve Bratteli of Norway, who had told the ruling Labor Party in 1975 that he would soon leave the government, resigned on Jan. 9, 1976. He was succeeded as prime minister by Odvar Nordli, who had been chosen by the Labor Party for the post in 1975. The Nordli cabinet assumed office on Jan. 12.

On Jan. 5 the government-operated Statoil Co. made public its plans for exploiting the promising North Sea oil discovery in the Statfjord Field. It was anticipated that an investment of more than $2.5 billion would be required for production facilities. Two days later parliament approved a government plan to set up an additional national petroleum company with the provisional title of Norsk Braendselsolje II to refine and distribute petroleum products. Under the new proposal the government was to take over all or parts of three petroleum marketing companies, including 95 percent of Norsk Braendselsolje A/S, a subsidiary of British Petroleum Co. Ltd.

In London on Sept. 10 Norway and Great Britain

agreed to cooperate more closely on the development of North Sea oil and natural gas reserves. Representatives of the two countries adopted a plan to set up a joint cabinet-level coordinating committee on offshore matters, specifically those relating to these resources.

Norway participated in the search for a peaceful resolution of the "cod war" between Iceland and Great Britain (see ICELAND). Norwegian spokesmen offered Oslo as the site for British-Icelandic negotiations, and an interim agreement was signed there on June 1.

During 1976 Norway enjoyed almost full employment. Its economy was growing annually at an impressive rate of 6 percent. The nation's oil production was expected to increase fourfold by 1980. With oil revenues then at around $3.6 billion, Norway would become the most affluent country in Europe. Minor flaws in 1976 were the country's inflation rate, still above 10 percent a year, and taxes that were among the world's highest. But the Norwegian economy showed no signs of flagging, and most Norwegians were participating in the new prosperity.

See STATISTICS OF THE WORLD.   L.A.S.

NOVA SCOTIA. See STATISTICS OF THE WORLD.

O

OBITUARIES. Each entry below contains the name and, wherever possible, date and place of birth and death of a notable person who died in 1976. It also contains a brief description of the accomplishments and the events that contributed to making each person notable.

AALTO, (Hugo) Alvar Henrik. Finnish architect, b. Kuortane, Feb. 3, 1898, d. Helsinki, May 11. His works, including the famous Baker House at the Massachusetts Institute of Technology, show this master's deep feeling for the humanistic and nature-related aspects of architecture, as well as his concern with lighting and acoustics.

ALBERS, Josef. German-born American painter, b. Bottrop, March 19, 1888, d. New Haven, Conn., March 25. Important also as a teacher and color theorist, he shunned self-expression in his vastly influential geometric paintings. He taught for fifty years: at the Bauhaus in Germany, at Black Mountain College in North Carolina, and at Yale University.

ARLEN, Richard. American actor, b. Van Mattimore in Charlottesville, Va., Sept. 1, 1900, d. North Hollywood, Calif., March 28. He appeared in approximately 250 films in his fifty-year career. His first starring role was in *Wings* (1927), the first motion picture to win an Academy Award.

BACHAUER, Gina. Greek-born British pianist, b. Athens, May 21, 1913, d. there Aug. 22. Her New York City debut in 1950 caused a sensation; thereafter she was acclaimed for her performances with all the world's major symphony orchestras, in recital, and in recordings.

BERKELEY, Busby. American motion picture director, b. William Berkeley Enos in Los Angeles, Nov. 29, 1895, d. Palm Desert, Calif., March 14. He devised and directed the spectacularly gaudy dance numbers for the classical Warner Brothers musical films of the 1930's, such as *Gold Diggers of 1933* and *Footlight Parade* (1933).

BLOOMGARDEN, Kermit. American theatrical producer, b. New York City, Dec. 15, 1904, d. there Sept. 20. A producer for thirty-five years, he introduced such important plays as *Death of a Salesman* (1949), *The Music Man* (1957), and *Equus* (1974).

BONAVENA, Oscar. Argentine boxer, b. Buenos Aires, Sept. 25, 1942, d. near Reno, Nev., May 22. The seventh-ranked heavyweight contender at the time of his death by rifle fire, he won 56 of his 65 professional fights. He was knocked out only once, by Muhammad Ali (Dec. 7, 1970).

BOSWELL, Connee. American singer, b. New Orleans, Dec. 3, 1907, d. New York City, Oct. 11. With her sisters, Martha and Vet, she formed the Boswell Sisters, a popular singing trio of the 1930's. After 1936 she sang alone, a sultry-voiced star performer on stage, screen, and especially radio. Partly paralyzed from the age of 4, she performed in a wheelchair.

BRAILOWSKY, Alexander. Russian-born pianist, b. Kiev, Feb. 16, 1896, d. New York City, April 25. Noted for his enormous repertory, he was the first pianist to perform all 169 piano works of Chopin in a cyclic format, requiring six separate recitals.

BRITTEN, (Edward) Benjamin, 1st Baron Britten of Aldeburgh. British composer, b. Lowestoft, England, Nov. 22, 1913, d. Aldeburgh, Dec. 4. One o͏ the leading composers of the 20th century, he w͏ noted for his operas, including *Peter Grim͏*

In 1963 Benjamin Britten rehearses for a performance of his opera Gloriana.

CAMBRIDGE, Godfrey MacArthur. American actor, b. New York City, Feb. 26, 1933, d. Los Angeles, Nov. 29. Known primarily as a comedian, he also played serious roles on stage, screen, and television. He died while acting in a film, *Victory at Entebbe.*

CAREY, Max. American baseball player, b. Maximilian Carnarius in Terre Haute, Ind., Jan. 11, 1890, d. Miami Beach, Fla., May 30. An outfielder with the Pittsburgh Pirates (for 16½ seasons) and the Brooklyn Dodgers, he held the National League career record for stolen bases (738) for many years. He was elected to the National Baseball Hall of Fame in 1961.

CASSIDY, Jack. American actor, b. John Cassidy in New York City, March 5, 1927, d. Los Angeles, Dec. 12. He began his career as a singer in Broadway musicals. Later he appeared in films and became popular on television, especially on talk and game shows.

(1945) and *The Turn of the Screw* (1954), his songs, and other works such as *A Ceremony of Carols* (1942) and *War Requiem* (1962).

BULTMANN, Rudolf Karl. German theologian, b. Wiefelstede, Aug. 20, 1884, d. Marburg, July 30. His controversial philosophy urged a reinterpretation in existential terms of the Bible, especially of the doctrines of the Resurrection and the Virgin birth.

CALDER, Alexander. American sculptor, b. Philadelphia, July 22, 1898, d. New York City, Nov. 11. One of the most beloved artists of the 20th century, he is best known for his mobiles and stabiles, made from sheet metal, rods, and wire. Many are prominently displayed in public places throughout the world. Calder also created paintings, prints, murals, tapestries, and commercial decorations in a decorative abstract style.

Actor Godfrey Cambridge in 1975.

Alexander Calder, with an airplane that he was decorating in Dallas, Texas, in 1975.

Base stealer Max Carey in his playing days with the Pittsburgh Pirates.

CASSIN, René. French jurist, b. Bayonne, Oct. 5, 1887, d. Paris, Feb. 20. He was awarded the 1968 Nobel Peace Prize for his role as principal author of the Universal Declaration of Human Rights for the United Nations. A World War I veteran, he was active in the League of Nations and was a leader of the French resistance during World War II, a founder of the U.N. Educational, Scientific, and Cultural Organization, and a president of the European Court of Human Rights.

CHOU EN-LAI. Chinese statesman, b. Huaiyin, Kiangsu Province, 1898, d. Peking, Jan. 8. In 1949 he was named premier and foreign minister of the newly established People's Republic of China. For a quarter of a century he remained one of the two or three most powerful men in China, although he relinquished the post of foreign minister in 1958. Regarded as one of the world's master diplomats, he brought China into the ranks of the Great Powers, always remaining fiercely loyal to his party.

CHRISTIE, Dame Agatha. British novelist and playwright, b. Agatha Mary Clarissa Miller in Torquay, England, Sept. 15, 1890, d. Wallingford, Jan. 12. Author of more than one hundred books, she created the detectives Hercule Poirot and Miss Marple. One of her plays, *The Mousetrap,* opened in London in 1952 and has run continuously ever since.

CHU TEH, Chinese Communist leader, b. Szechwan Province, Dec. 18?, 1886, d. Peking, July

Chou En-lai, a year before his death.

Dame Agatha Christie at 83 (1974).

6. He was commander in chief of the Communist army from the late 1920's, and architect of the Long March, the resistance to Japanese occupation, and the defeat of the nationalist armies. As chairman of the Standing Committee of the Na-

Lee J. Cobb, starring in the television series "The Virginian" (1962).

tional People's Congress after 1959, he was ceremonial head of state.

COBB, Lee J. American actor, b. Lee Jacob in New York City, Dec. 9, 1911, d. Woodland Hills, Calif., Feb. 11. Although he was a star in the legitimate theater, the creator of the title role in *Death of a Salesman* (1949), and a member of the prestigious Group Theater, he achieved his greatest fame as Judge Garth in "The Virginian" series on television.

COHEN, Meyer Harris ("Mickey"). American underworld leader, b. New York City, 1914?, d. Los Angeles, July 29. A former bantamweight boxer, he reputedly led the gambling rackets on the West Coast in the 1940's and 1950's, before serving ten years in prison for tax evasion.

COMBS, Earle. American baseball player, b. Pebworth, Ky., May 14, 1899, d. Richmond, Ky., July 21. An outfielder with the New York Yankees (1924–35), he was elected to the National Baseball Hall of Fame in 1970.

COSTELLO, John Aloysius. Irish statesman, b. Dublin, June 20, 1891, d. there Jan. 5. Leader of the moderate Fine Gael (United Ireland Party), he served as prime minister of the Irish Republic (1948–51; 1954–57).

COWAN, Louis G. American broadcasting executive, b. Chicago, Dec. 12, 1909, d. New York City, Nov. 18. Creator of the "Quiz Kids" radio program (1940) and "The $64,000 Question" on television (1955), he was president of CBS in 1958

and 1959. He and his wife died in an apartment fire.

CUNNINGHAM, Imogen. American photographer, b. Portland, Oreg., April 12, 1883, d. San Francisco, June 24. In a seventy-five-year career, she brought her individuality and fresh wit to a widely varied list of subjects.

DALEY, Richard Joseph. American political leader, b. Chicago, May 15, 1902, d. there Dec. 20. Mayor of Chicago from 1955 until his death, he was the last of the big-city bosses, an old-style politician who not only ran his own city but wielded vast influence on the Democratic Party. His role in the 1968 national party convention, at which antiwar demonstrators clashed with Chicago police, brought him international attention.

DAM, (Carl Peter) Henrik. Danish nutritionist, b. Copenhagen, Feb. 21, 1895, d. there April 17. He discovered vitamin K, a blood coagulant, in 1939; for this discovery he shared the 1943 Nobel Prize in medicine and physiology with the American biochemist E. A. Doisy.

DAVIS, Meyer. American orchestra leader, b. Ellicott City, Md., Jan. 10, 1899, d. New York City, April 5. For half a century he was the preeminent leader of what is known as the society band. His orchestras graced such social functions of the rich and the powerful as debutante balls and White House gatherings.

DENNIS, Patrick. American author, b. Edward Everett Tanner 3rd in Evanston, Ill., May 18, 1921, d. New York City, Nov. 6. His *Auntie Mame* (1955) sold more than 2,000,000 copies. He wrote a sequel, as well as several other best-sellers, some under the pen name of Virginia Rowans.

Mayor Richard J. Daley of Chicago at a 1975 news conference.

DÖPFNER, Cardinal Julius. German Roman Catholic prelate, b. Hausen (Franconia), Aug. 26, 1913, d. Munich, July 24. He was the liberal archbishop of Berlin from 1957 until 1961, when he was named archbishop of Munich and Freising.

DOUGLAS, Paul Howard. American economist and legislator, b. Salem, Mass., March 26, 1892, d. Washington, D.C., Sept. 24. He taught economics at the University of Chicago and the New School for Social Research in New York City, wrote seminal texts on wages and production analysis, and was a crusader for liberal causes. From 1949 to 1967 he was a member (D, Ill.) of the United States Senate.

DOWLING, Eddie. American actor, b. Joseph Nelson Goucher in Woonsocket, R.I., Dec. 9, 1894, d. Smithfield, R.I., Feb. 18. An award-winning producer, a director, playwright, songwriter, and performer, he was a fixture on the Broadway scene for forty years.

DYKES, James Joseph ("Jimmy"). American baseball player and manager, b. Philadelphia, Nov. 10, 1896, d. there June 15. An infielder, he played with the Philadelphia Athletics and the Chicago White Sox. He also managed those teams, as well as the Baltimore Orioles, Detroit Tigers, and Cleveland Indians.

ERNST, Max. German-born French artist, b. Brühl, April 2, 1891, d. Paris, April 1. He was a painter, sculptor, writer, and maker of objects, first a Dadaist and later a surrealist. He was noted for his inventiveness, craftsmanship, and power.

EVANS, Dame Edith Mary. British actress, b. London, Feb. 8, 1888, d. Cranbrook, Oct. 14. She was one of the foremost actresses of the English-speaking stage, appearing in the classics and contemporary drama during a sixty-four-year career. Lady Bracknell in *The Importance of Being Earnest* and the nurse in *Romeo and Juliet* were among

Painter Max Ernst, a founder of the Dadaist and surrealist movements.

her memorable roles. Her films included *Tom Jones* (1963) and *The Chalk Garden* (1964).

FAITH, Percy. Canadian-born conductor, b. Toronto, April 7, 1908, d. Los Angeles, Feb. 9. From 1940 to 1950 he was one of radio's most popular orchestra leaders. Thereafter he retained his popularity through recordings, mostly lush renditions of popular melodies.

FARLEY, James Aloysius. American political leader, b. Grassy Point, N.Y., May 30, 1888, d. New York City, June 9. Known as Mr. Democrat, he was chairman of the Democratic National Committee

Postmaster General James A. Farley with President Franklin D. Roosevelt in 1940.

(1932–40), manager of the first two Presidential campaigns of Franklin D. Roosevelt, and U.S. postmaster general (1933–40).

FISHBEIN, Morris. American physician and editor, b. Saint Louis, July 22, 1889, d. Chicago, Sept. 27. For twenty-five years (1924–49) he was chief spokesman of the medical profession as editor of the *Journal of the American Medical Association.* He was also the author of many books on medicine.

FOLSOM, Marion Bayard. American businessman, b. McRae, Ga., Nov. 23, 1893, d. Rochester, N.Y., Sept. 28. From 1914 until 1969, except for periods of government service, he was associated with the Eastman Kodak Co. He was the chief architect of the Social Security Act of 1935 and was secretary of health, education, and welfare from 1955 to 1958.

FORD, Paul. American actor, b. Paul Ford Weaver in Baltimore, Md., Nov. 2, 1901, d. Mineola, N.Y., April 12. Best known as the irascible Col. Hall in the "Sergeant Bilko" show on television, he also appeared on scores of radio programs and in films and Broadway plays.

FORNI, Cardinal Efrem. Italian Roman Catholic prelate, b. Milan, Jan. 10, 1889, d. Rome, Feb. 26. A member of the diplomatic service of the Vatican for more than forty years, he was named a cardinal in 1962.

FRANKLIN, Sidney. American bullfighter, b. Sidney Frumkin in New York City, July 11, 1903, d. there April 26. From his debut in Mexico City in 1923 until his retirement in the late 1950's, he won both acclaim and notoriety as *The Bullfighter from Brooklyn* (the title of his 1952 autobiography).

GABIN, Jean. French actor, b. Jean-Alexis Moncorgé in Paris, May 17, 1904, d. Neuilly, Nov. 15. He starred in more than one hundred films, most of them in French. The best known of his characterizations, usually a tough but gentle outsider, were in *Pépé le Moko* (1937), *Grand Illusion* (1937), and *Daybreak* (1939).

GALLICO, Paul William. American author, b. New York City, July 26, 1897, d. Monaco, July 15. He was the author of *The Poseidon Adventure* (1969) and *The Snow Goose* (1941), several books about the charlady Mrs. 'Arris, children's books, and animal books. He was also a sports columnist and screenwriter.

GAMBINO, Carlo. Italian-born underworld leader, b. Palermo, Sept. 1, 1902, d. Massapequa, N.Y., Oct. 15. He arrived in the U.S. as a stowaway in 1921. By 1957 he was in command of one of the twenty-six families of the so-called Mafia; at his death he was reputed to be the preeminent figure in organized crime in the U.S. Deportation orders

Carlo Gambino, reputed leader of organized crime, in 1970.

against him were upheld by the Supreme Court in 1970 but were not carried out because of his ill health.

GETTY, J(ean) Paul. American oil executive and financier, b. Minneapolis, Dec. 15, 1892, d. near Guildford, England, June 6. As owner of a major or controlling interest in the Getty Oil Co. and 200 other concerns, he was reputedly worth between $2 billion and $4 billion.

GINGRICH, Arnold. American editor, b. Grand Rapids, Mich., Dec. 5, 1903, d. Ridgewood, N.J., July 9. A founder of *Esquire* magazine, he was its editor (1933–45; 1949–52), publisher (1952–74), editor in chief (1974–76), and founding editor (1976).

GOULART, João Belchior Marques. Brazilian statesman, b. in the state of Rio Grande do Sul, March 1, 1918, d. northern Argentina, Dec. 6. The last civilian president of Brazil (1961–64), he served during a period of political and economic chaos that prompted a military takeover.

GRECHKO, Andrei Antonovich. Soviet military leader, b. Golodayevka (now Kuybyshevo), Oct. 17, 1903, d. Moscow, April 26. A hero of World War II, he was later active in suppressing the East German revolt and in invading Czechoslovakia. He commanded the Warsaw Pact forces and was, after 1967, Soviet defense minister.

HACKETT, Robert Leo ("Bobby"). American musician, b. Providence, R.I., Jan. 31, 1915, d. West

J. Paul Getty, with a wax figure sculpted in 1974 for Madame Tussaud's London wax museum.

German philosopher Martin Heidegger.

Chatham, Mass., June 7. His mellow, graceful cornet style, heard with big-name swing bands as well as small jazz ensembles, made him an audience favorite from the early 1930's until his death.

HART, Philip Aloysius, Jr. U.S. Senator (D, Mich.), b. Bryn Mawr, Pa., Dec. 10, 1912, d. Washington, D.C., Dec. 26. He was elected to the Senate in 1958, 1964, and 1970, but declined to run again in 1976 because of ill health. He actively promoted legislation supporting consumer protection, minority voting rights, gun control, and trust and monopoly busting.

HAYES, Roland. American singer, b. Curryville, Ga., June 3, 1887, d. Boston, Dec. 31. A tenor, he was the first black American to achieve fame as a serious recitalist. He appeared as soloist with symphony orchestras throughout the world.

HEIDEGGER, Martin. German philosopher, b. Messkirch, Sept. 26, 1889, d. there May 26. Regarded as the most influential continental philosopher of the 20th century, he was not identified with a single school. He strongly influenced the existentialists, in philosophy, literature, and psychoanalysis, and his writings on the nature of being had a profound effect on theology.

HEISENBERG, Werner. German physicist, b. Würzburg, Dec. 5, 1901, d. Munich, Feb. 1. He was awarded the 1932 Nobel Prize in physics for his work in charting the structure of the atom. Later he took charge of the atomic research programs of Germany and West Germany.

HOWE, James Wong. Chinese-born American cinematographer, b. Wong Tung Jim in Kwangtung, Aug. 28, 1899, d. Los Angeles, July 12. During his 53 years in Hollywood, he was nominated for 16 Academy Awards and won 2 (*The Rose Tattoo,* 1955; *Hud,* 1962). Perhaps the best known of all motion picture cameramen, his forte was absolute realism.

HOWLIN' WOLF. Professional name of Chester Arthur Burnett, American blues singer, b. West Point, Miss., June 20, 1910, d. Chicago, Jan. 10. Through records and concerts he had an enormous influence on contemporary popular music. His Delta blues were performed with harmonica and guitar in the time-honored oral tradition of Southern Blacks.

HUGHES, Howard Robard. American entrepreneur, b. Houston, Dec. 24, 1905, d. en route there, April 5. He achieved fame as an aviator and motion picture producer in the 1930's and 1940's; he also expanded the Hughes Tool Co., most of which he inherited, into a group of multimillion dollar corporations. He achieved even greater fame in his later years as an eccentric recluse, involved in literary hoaxes (the Clifford Irving affair), Central Intelligence Agency plots (the Glo-

269

Howard Hughes in one of his last public appearances (1952).

mar Explorer), and politics (the 1972 Richard Nixon campaign).

INGERSOLL, Royal Eason. American naval officer, b. Washington, D.C., June 20, 1883, d. Bethesda, Md., May 20. As commander of the U.S. Atlantic Fleet from Jan. 1, 1942, until late in 1944, he supervised the war against German submarines and the transport of men and matériel to Europe at the height of World War II.

JOHNSON, Eyvind. Swedish author, b. Överluleå, July 29, 1900, d. Stockholm, Aug. 25. He shared the 1974 Nobel Prize in literature with another Swedish writer, Harry Martinson. He wrote more than 40 novels and autobiographical works; 3 of them were translated into English and 4 into French.

JONES, (Mary) Anissa. American actress, b. West Lafayette, Ind., March 11, 1958, d. Oceanside, Calif., Aug. 28. During the 1960's she played Buffy in the popular television series "Family Affair."

KERNER, Otto. American public official, b. Chicago, Aug. 15, 1908, d. there May 9. Governor of Illinois (1961–68) and chairman (1967) of U.S. President Lyndon B. Johnson's commission on civil disorders, he was a judge of the U.S. Court of Appeals for the Seventh Circuit when he was indicted (1972) in a racetrack scandal. He was later convicted and served seven months.

KUBITSCHEK, Juscelino. Brazilian statesman, b. Diamantina, Sept. 12, 1902, d. near Rio de Janeiro, Aug. 22. President of Brazil from 1956 to 1961, the former surgeon was most noted for his persis-

tence in creating Brasília, the new inland capital of his country.

KUHLMAN, Kathryn. American evangelist, b. Concordia, Mo., d. Tulsa, Okla., Feb. 20. She began preaching at the age of sixteen (probably around 1930), and she was ordained by the Evangelical Church Alliance two years later. Eventually she reached a vast American audience through her radio and television programs, which featured prayer and healing.

LANG, Fritz. Austrian-born American film director, b. Vienna, Dec. 5, 1890, d. Los Angeles, Aug. 2. A leader of the German expressionist school of the 1920's, he made such seminal films as *Metropolis* (1927) and *M* (1931). His American films included *Fury* (1936), *You Only Live Once* (1937), and *Scarlet Street* (1945).

LEAF, Munro. American author and illustrator, b. Baltimore, Dec. 4, 1905, d. Garrett Park, Md., Dec. 21. He wrote *The Story of Ferdinand* (1936), an immensely popular children's book about a gentle bull, which was illustrated by Robert Lawson. He also wrote and illustrated a long series of "Fun" books that began with *Manners Can Be Fun* (1936).

LEHMANN, Lotte. German-born American singer, b. Perleberg, Feb. 27, 1888, d. Santa Barbara, Calif., Aug. 26. One of the most beloved and highly praised sopranos of the opera and concert stage, she specialized in the operatic works of Richard Strauss and Richard Wagner and in German lieder.

Kathryn Kuhlman invokes the Holy Spirit at a 1974 healing service in Pittsburgh, Pa.

LEIGHTON, Margaret. British actress, b. near Birmingham, England, Feb. 26, 1922, d. Chichester, Jan. 13. A leading performer in the British theater, she also won two Tony awards for her roles on Broadway in *Separate Tables* (1956) and *The Night of the Iguana* (1962). She also appeared in several films, including *The Sound and the Fury* (1959) and *The Go-Between* (1971).

LERCARO, Cardinal Giacomo. Italian Roman Catholic prelate, b. Quinto al Mare, Oct. 28, 1891, d. Bologna, Oct. 18. A successful reformer of the Mass and a less successful fighter against fascism and Communism, he was archbishop of Bologna from 1952 until 1968.

LEVY, Gus(tave Lehmann). American banker, b. New Orleans, May 23, 1910, d. New York City, Nov. 3. As head of the international investment banking firm of Goldman, Sachs & Co., he was one of the most powerful men on Wall Street. He was also a prominent philanthropist.

LHEVINNE, Rosina Bessie. Russian-born American pianist and teacher, b. Kiev, March 28, 1880, d. Glendale, Calif., Nov. 9. She was a successful concert pianist, often in joint recital with her husband Josef. After his death in 1944 she concentrated on her highly influential career as a teacher of piano at the Juilliard School in New York City.

LIN YUTANG, Chinese philosopher, b. Changchow, Oct. 10, 1895, d. Hong Kong, March 26. Poet, novelist, historian, and philologist as well as philosopher, he was for a generation the foremost interpreter of China to the West. Of his twenty books, written in English and Chinese, *My Country and My People* (1935) and *The Importance of Living* (1937) were probably the best known. He lived in the U.S. from 1936 to 1966.

LISAGOR, Peter Irvin. American journalist, b. Keystone, W.Va., Aug. 5, 1915, d. Arlington, Va., Dec. 10. Writer, reporter, commentator, and television personality, he was Washington, D.C., bureau manager of the Chicago *Daily News*, beginning in 1959.

LOWRY, Judith (Ives). American actress, b. Morristown, N.J., July 27, 1890, d. New York City, Nov. 29. At the time of her death she was appearing as Mother Dexter in the "Phyllis" series on television. She had previously acted in scores of films, plays, and television commercials.

LYONS, Leonard. American journalist, b. Leonard Sucher in New York City, Sept. 10, 1906, d. there Oct. 7. His daily column of Broadway gossip, "The Lyons Den," appeared in newspapers across the country from 1934 until 1974.

LYSENKO, Trofim Denisovich. Soviet agriculturist, b. Karlovka, Sept. 29, 1898, d. U.S.S.R., Nov. 20. During the 1930's and 1940's, under the patronage of Joseph Stalin, he was the most influential scien-

Journalist and political commentator Peter Lisagor.

tist of the U.S.S.R. But his Marxist-oriented theories on genetics lost favor after the death of Stalin in 1953.

MACK, Ted. American radio and television host, b. William Edward Maguiness in Greeley, Colo., Feb. 12, 1904, d. North Tarrytown, N.Y., July 12. He was master of ceremonies of "The Original Ama-

"Amateur Hour" host Ted Mack in 1967.

teur Hour" on radio (1946–48) and television (1948–70).

MAINBOCHER. Professional name of Main Rousseau Bocher, American couturier, b. Chicago, Oct. 9, 1891, d. Munich, West Germany, Dec. 27. For forty years, starting in Paris in 1930, he was an influential figure in the world of high fashion. The classic basic-black dress was probably his best-known creation.

MALRAUX, (Georges) André. French author, b. Paris, Nov. 3, 1901, d. near there Nov. 23. He was also an archeologist, aviator, novelist, war hero, orator, philosopher, politician, and cabinet minister. His best-known novel was *Man's Fate* (1934). He was Charles de Gaulle's minister for cultural affairs from 1959 to 1969.

MAO TSE-TUNG. Chairman of the Chinese Communist Party, b. Shaoshan, Hunan Province, Dec. 26, 1893, d. Peking, Sept. 9. As the political and philosophical leader of the People's Republic of China he played a major role in shaping the history of the 20th century. He helped to found the Chinese Communist Party in 1921 and to form the Fourth Chinese Red Army in 1928. He was a leader of the Long March of 1934 to 1936 and of the ensuing civil war against the Nationalist Chinese forces. In 1949 Mao proclaimed the People's Republic of China with its Communist government; he served as chairman of the Chinese Communist Party from 1949 until his death. During this quarter century China experienced the so-called great leap forward of the 1950's, the famine of the early 1960's, the Cultural Revolution and Mao worship of the late 1960's, and the diplomatic, economic, and cultural expansion that marked the 1970's.

MARTINON, Jean. French conductor, b. Lyon, Jan. 10, 1910, d. Paris, March 1. As conductor of the Lamoureux Orchestra of Paris, the London Philharmonic, the Chicago Symphony, and the National Orchestra of French Radio and Television, he won world renown. He specialized in early 20th-century French music.

MAUZÉ, Abby Rockefeller. American philanthropist, b. New York City, Nov. 9, 1903, d. there May 27. The only daughter and the eldest child of John D. Rockefeller, Jr., she was active in philanthropic causes supporting medicine and the arts.

McBRIDE, Mary Margaret. American radio personality, b. Paris, Mo., Nov. 16, 1899, d. West Shokun, N.Y., April 7. For more than twenty years she entertained housewives with her five-times-a-week radio program of recipes, interviews, and chat.

McKELWAY, Benjamin Mosby. American editor, b. Fayetteville, N.C., Oct. 2, 1895, d. Washington, D.C., Aug. 30. Editor of the Washington (D.C.) *Star* from 1946 to 1963 and president of the Associated

British Field Marshal Bernard Law Montgomery (left) shakes hands with Soviet Marshal Georgi K. Zhukov in Berlin (July, 1945).

French writer André Malraux at a 1973 art exhibition.

Press from 1957 to 1963, he was a crusader for freedom of the press.

MERCER, John H. ("Johnny"). American songwriter, b. Savannah, Ga., Nov. 18, 1909, d. Los Angeles, June 25. Primarily a lyricist, he collaborated with most of the best-known popular composers; he also wrote many tunes of his own. He won four best-song Academy Awards for "On the Atchison, Topeka, and Santa Fe," "In the Cool, Cool, Cool of the Evening," "Moon River," and "Days of Wine and Roses."

MIELZINER, Jo. American stage designer, b. Paris, France, March 19, 1901, d. New York City, March 15. From *The Guardsman* (1924) to the Metropolitan Opera production of *Don Giovanni* (1976), he was a preeminent designer of sets for plays, operas, and ballets in the U.S. and in Great Britain. He did famous designs for *Winterset* (1935), *A Streetcar Named Desire* (1947), and *South Pacific* (1948).

MINEO, Sal(vatore). American actor, b. New York City, Jan. 10, 1939, d. Los Angeles, Feb. 12. He was twice nominated for best-supporting-actor Academy Awards: *Rebel Without a Cause* (1955) and *Exodus* (1960). The actor, who appeared on the Broadway stage in *The Rose Tattoo* (1950) and *The King and I* (1951), was murdered.

MITCHELL, Martha Elizabeth Beall. B. Pine Bluff, Ark., Sept. 2, 1918, d. New York City, May 31. One of the most visible and audible personalities on the American scene in the early 1970's, she was a loyal supporter of her second husband, John N. Mitchell, U.S. attorney general under President Richard M. Nixon. The Mitchells separated in 1973.

MONOD, Jacques Lucien. French chemist, b. Paris, Feb. 9, 1910, d. Cannes, May 31. He shared the 1965 Nobel Prize in medicine and physiology with François Jacob and André Lwoff; they were cited for showing how genes regulate other genes. Director of the Pasteur Institute, Paris, he was known for his belief that existence is based on chance.

MONTGOMERY, Bernard Law, 1st Viscount Montgomery of Alamein. British military officer, b. London, Nov. 17, 1887, d. Alton, England, March 24. Called the most famous British soldier of modern times, he was also one of the most controversial. During World War II he led the British North African forces to important victories over the German-Italian armies. Later he was commander in chief of the British armies on the Western (European) front, field marshal and commander of English and Canadian troops, viscount and chief of the imperial general staff, and deputy supreme commander of NATO forces.

MORISON, Samuel Eliot. American historian

Pittsburgh Pirates manager Danny Murtaugh in 1975.

and naval officer, b. Boston, July 9, 1887, d. there May 15. Enormously prolific, he won praise from the critics and the public alike for his scholarly, lively, masterfully styled prose. He won two Pulitzer prizes: for *Admiral of the Ocean Sea* (1942) and *John Paul Jones* (1959).

MOSS, Robert Verelle, Jr. American Protestant leader, b. Wilson, N.C., March 3, 1922, d. Montclair, N.J., Oct. 25. He was president of the United Church of Christ from 1969 until his death. An ardent ecumenicist, he was an official of both the National and World councils of churches.

MURTAUGH, Daniel Edward ("Danny"). American baseball executive, b. Chester, Pa., Oct. 8, 1917, d. there Dec. 2. As manager of the Pittsburgh Pirates (1957–75), he led his team to two World Series titles (1960; 1971).

NEVERS, Ernest Alonzo ("Ernie"). American athlete, b. Willow River, Minn., June 11, 1903, d. San Rafael, Calif., May 3. Twice an All-American fullback at Stanford University (1924, 1925), he established a National Football League record in 1929 for points scored in a game (40).

OCHS, Phil(ip David). American songwriter and performer, b. El Paso, Dec. 19, 1940, d. New York City, April 9. His "I Ain't Marching Anymore" (1963) was the first influential song of the anti-Vietnam war movement. He wrote and performed other successful songs, mostly in the folk idiom. His death was ruled a suicide by hanging.

ODLUM, Floyd Bostwick. American financier, b. Union City, Mich., March 30, 1892, d. Indio, Calif., June 17. Between 1923 and 1970 he reorganized and directed dozens of enterprises, including banks, railroads, department stores, film studios, and aircraft and petroleum companies. He directed the World War II Office of Production Management and was a consultant to three U.S. Presidents.

ONSAGER, Lars. Norwegian-born American chemist, b. Oslo, Nov. 27, 1903, d. Coral Gables, Fla., Oct. 4. He was awarded the 1968 Nobel Prize in chemistry for Onsager's law, a complex theory completed in 1931. It deals with reciprocity, as between temperature and voltage in an electrified wire.

PATMAN, (John William) Wright. U.S. Representative, b. Patman's Switch, Texas, Aug. 6, 1893, d. Bethesda, Md., March 7. A Democrat, he was dean of the House of Representatives, having been Congressman from the First District of Texas since 1929. For twelve years he was the autocratic chairman of the powerful banking and currency committee.

PAYNE, B(en) Iden. British actor, director, and teacher, b. Newcastle upon Tyne, England, Sept. 5, 1881, d. Austin, Texas, April 6. He managed the Abbey Theatre, the Manchester Repertory Theatre, the Shakespeare Memorial Theatre in Stratford-upon-Avon, and the Goodman Theater in Chicago; he taught at Carnegie Institute of Technology and, for nearly thirty years, at the University of Texas.

PENFIELD, Wilder Graves. American-born Canadian neurologist, b. Spokane, Wash., Jan. 26, 1891, d. Montréal, Québec, April 5. He founded the Montréal Neurological Institute in 1934 and was its director until 1960. Meanwhile he did seminal work on the causes and surgical cures of epilepsy and on mapping the regions of the human brain.

PETTY, Mary. American cartoonist, b. Hampton, N.J., April 29, 1899, d. Paramus, N.J., March 6. Her 272 drawings for *The New Yorker* appeared between 1927 and 1966. The cartoons were carefully crafted, highly detailed, mordant but hilarious sketches of the upper (or leisure) class.

PIATIGORSKY, Gregor. Russian-born American cellist, b. Ekaterinoslav (now Dnepropetrovsk), April 17, 1903, d. Los Angeles, Aug. 6. One of the tiny group of cellists to achieve worldwide acclaim, he was a master of the Romantic 19th-century tradition.

PISTON, Walter. American composer, b. Rockland, Maine, Jan. 20, 1894, d. Belmont, Mass., Nov. 12. He won Pulitzer prizes (1948; 1961) for his third and Seventh symphonies. He taught at Harvard University from 1926 until 1960. Several of his books have become standard musicology texts.

POLANYI, Michael. Hungarian-born British chemist and philosopher, b. Budapest, March 12, 1891, d. Northampton, England, Feb. 22. Best known for his work on reaction kinetics, he was a visiting professor at fourteen universities, as well as at the University of Manchester. After the publication of his *Science, Faith and Society* (1946), he taught and wrote primarily as a philosopher.

PONS, Lily. French-born American coloratura soprano, b. Draguignan, April 12, 1904, d. Dallas, Feb. 13. For a quarter of a century she was the undisputed coloratura queen of the Metropolitan Opera Company. She made her Met debut in *Lucia di Lammermoor* in 1931; in 1972 she sang a final recital in Carnegie Hall. Meanwhile the petite, glamorous diva had appeared on concert and opera stages around the world and in three motion pictures.

RAY, Man. American artist, b. Philadelphia, Aug. 27, 1890, d. Paris, Nov. 18. (His original name was reputed to be Emmanuel Rudnitsky.) He helped to popularize Dadaism in the 1920's. He was also in turn a Fauvist, a cubist, and a surrealist, and he was a master of assemblage. Even more, he was a respected photographer and filmmaker.

RAZAK, Tun Abdul. Prime Minister of Malaysia, b. Pekan, March 11, 1922, d. London, Jan. 14. A leader of the movement for the independence of Malaysia, he was the nation's second prime minister (from 1970 until his death). He favored international nonalignment and limited democracy for his nation.

RED FOX, William. Self-styled Sioux Indian chief, b. Dakota Territory, 1870?, d. Corpus Christi, Texas, March 1. His bestselling *The Memoirs of Chief Red Fox* (1971) caused a literary furor when it was revealed that much of the book had been plagiarized from a 1940 history of the Wounded Knee massacre. Red Fox claimed to have witnessed the Battle of the Little Big Horn as a 6-year-old child.

REED, Sir Carol. British motion picture director, b. London, Dec. 30, 1906, d. there April 25. *Odd Man Out* (1947), *The Fallen Idol* (1949), and *The Third Man* (1950) are among his classic films; *Oliver* (1968) won an Academy Award as the best picture of the year.

RETHBERG, Elisabeth. German-born American soprano, b. Lisbeth Sättler in Schwarzenberg, Sept. 22, 1894, d. Yorktown Heights, N.Y., June 6. A mainstay of the Metropolitan Opera for twenty years, she sang lyric-dramatic roles in both the German and Italian repertory.

RICHTER, Hans. German-born American artist and motion picture director, b. Berlin, 1888, d. Lo-

Paul Robeson, American concert singer, actor, and civil rights activist.

Rosalind Russell outside her London hotel during a 1971 film-promotion tour.

carno, Switzerland, Feb. 1. One of the leaders of the Dadaist movement, he produced several abstract, imaginative, and influential films, including *Rhythm 21* (1921), *Dreams that Money Can Buy* (1947), and *8 × 8* (1957).

RITZ, Charles César. French hotelier, b. Niederwald, Switzerland, Aug. 1, 1891, d. Paris, July 11. He was director of the famed Ritz Hotel in Paris, a symbol of elegance founded by his father in 1898, and of the Ritz Hotel Syndicate, Inc.

ROBESON, Paul. American singer, actor, athlete, and civil rights activist, b. Princeton, N.J., April 9, 1898, d. Philadelphia, Jan. 23. He was one of the first black All-American football players, a world-renowned baritone recitalist, an actor on the British and American stage in such roles as the Emperor Jones and Othello, and a performer in eleven films, including *Sanders of the River* (1935) and *Show Boat* (1936). His praise for the Soviet Union (he was awarded the Stalin Peace Prize in 1952), his active opposition to racism, and his refusal to sign a non-Communist loyalty oath caused his career to go into a decline in the 1950's; his U.S. passport was revoked from 1950 to 1958.

ROSENBLOOM, Maxie. American boxer and actor, b. New York City, Sept. 6, 1904, d. South Pasadena, Calif., March 6. As light heavyweight boxing champion of the world from 1932 until 1934 he earned the nickname "Slapsie Maxie." In his subsequent movie career he played dozens of punch-drunk fighters.

RUSSELL, Rosalind. American actress, b. Waterbury, Conn., June 4, 1911, d. Beverly Hills, Calif., Nov. 28. She was a film star for thirty years, remembered for notable appearances in *Craig's Wife* (1936), *The Women* (1939), and *Picnic* (1956). She starred on Broadway in *Wonderful Town* (1953) and *Auntie Mame* (1956); her appearance in the film version (1958) of the last named was perhaps her most memorable success.

RUTH, Claire Merritt. Widow of George Herman ("Babe") Ruth, b. near Athens, Ga., Sept. 11, 1900, d. New York City, Oct. 25. After her husband's death (Aug. 16, 1948), she wrote books and articles, appeared on radio and television, and helped to organize and run the international Babe Ruth baseball league for teenagers.

RUŽIČKA, Leopold. Austro-Hungarian-born Swiss chemist, b. Vukovar (now in Yugoslavia), Sept. 13, 1887, d. Zürich, Sept. 26. For his research into terpenes, a class of hydrocarbons, he shared the 1939 Nobel Prize in chemistry with Adolf Butenandt of Germany. He was also known for his work with the male hormone testosterone.

RYLE, Gilbert. British philosopher, b. Brighton, England, Aug. 19, 1900, d. Yorkshire, Oct. 6. His book *The Concept of Mind* (1949) is a classic of modern philosophy, emphasizing the interrelationship of mind, body, and behavior. He also wrote on logic and linguistics, and he taught at the University of Oxford from 1924 until 1968.

SHEPARD, Ernest Howard. British illustrator, b. London, Dec. 10, 1879, d. Lodsworth, England, March 24. He achieved his greatest celebrity as the illustrator of A. A. Milne's classic stories of Winnie-the-Pooh. He also illustrated forty other books and did dozens of drawings for the magazine *Punch*.

SIM, Alastair. British actor, b. Edinburgh, Oct. 9, 1900, d. London, Aug. 19. With his sad-eyed bloodhound face and his deep, resonant voice, he delighted audiences in more than thirty films. He is probably best remembered for his Scrooge in *A Christmas Carol* (1951).

SMITH, Gerald L(yman) K(enneth). American Protestant clergyman, b. Pardeeville, Wis., Feb. 27, 1898, d. Glendale, Calif., April 15. During the 1930's and 1940's his magazine *(The Cross and the Flag),* his radio broadcasts, and his organizations (The Committee of One Million and the America First Party) spread his extremist philosophy across the country. Smith's goal was "a white Christian America."

SMITH, H(arry) Allen. American humorist, b. McLeansboro, Ill., Dec. 19, 1907, d. San Francisco, Feb. 24. His book *Low Man on a Totem Pole* (1941) was the first of several best-sellers he produced in the 1940's. He wrote a total of thirty-seven books, featuring acerbic anecdotes about pompous and pretentious people.

STRAND, Paul. American photographer, b. New York City, Oct. 16, 1890, d. Oregeval, France, March 31. His great influence was based on his early tradition-breaking devotion to realism in his still photographs and documentary films.

SULLIVAN, Frank. American humorist, b. Saratoga Springs, N.Y., Sept. 22, 1892, d. there Feb. 19. One of the leading wits of pre-World War II America, he contributed to newspapers and magazines and wrote many books. He was perhaps best known for his *New Yorker* magazine interviews with "Mr. Arbuthnot," the cliché expert.

TEYTE, Dame Maggie. British soprano, b. Margaret Tate in Wolverhampton, England, April 17, 1888, d. London, May 26. One of the foremost interpreters of French vocal music, both opera and art songs, she had a remarkable forty-five-year career.

THOMPSON, Danny. American baseball player, b. Wichita, Kans., Feb. 1, 1947, d. Rochester, Minn., Dec. 10. An infielder with the Minnesota Twins from 1970 until June, 1976, he played with the Texas Rangers during his final season. He died of leukemia, first diagnosed in 1973.

THOMSON, Roy Herbert, 1st Baron Thomson of Fleet. Canadian publisher, b. Toronto, June 5, 1894, d. London, Aug. 4. The worldwide Thomson Organization controlled 148 newspapers and 138 magazines and had extensive holdings in radio, television, and book publishing. A self-made millionaire, Thomson purchased *The Scotsman* of Edinburgh in 1952 and *The Times* of London in 1967. He was granted a barony in 1964.

THORNDIKE, Dame Sybil. British actress, b. Gainsborough, England, Oct. 24, 1882, d. London, June 9. During her sixty-five-year career she performed in every theatrical style and in every medium. Also an outspoken social activist, she was made a Dame Commander of the Order of the British Empire in 1931.

Dame Sybil Thorndike, British actress, at home on her ninetieth birthday (1972).

TOBEY, Mark. American abstract painter, b. Centerville, Wis., Dec. 11, 1890, d. Basel, Switzerland, April 24. He was noted for his characteristic "white writing" style, in which he overlaid faint color areas with white brushstrokes resembling Oriental calligraphy.

TRUMBO, Dalton. American writer, b. Montrose, Colo., Dec. 2, 1905, d. Los Angeles, Sept. 10. The best known of the screenwriters blacklisted for refusing to cooperate with the House Un-American Activities Committee, he later won an Academy Award for his screenplay *The Brave One* (1956), written under a pseudonym. His novel *Johnny Got His Gun* won the 1939 National Book Award; a film based on it, written and directed by Trumbo, won the International Critics Award at the 1971 Cannes Film Festival.

VISCONTI, Luchino. Italian motion picture director, b. Milan, Nov. 2, 1906, d. Rome, March 17. His films ranged from the neorealist *Rocco and His Brothers* (1960) to the opulent, almost operatic *The Damned* (1969) and *Death in Venice* (1971). He was also a noted director of plays and operas.

VON CRAMM, Baron Gottfried. German tennis player, b. Berlin, July 7, 1909, d. near Cairo, Egypt, Nov. 8. In the 1930's he was surpassed only by an American, Don Budge, and a Briton, Fred Perry. He held German (1932–35) and French (1934; 1936) singles titles and a Wimbledon (1933) doubles title.

WASHINGTON, Ned. American lyricist, b. Scranton, Pa., 1901?, d. Los Angeles, Dec. 20. He won three Academy Awards: for best score (*Pinocchio*, 1940) and for best song ("When You Wish upon a Star," 1940; the theme from *High Noon*, 1952).

WEIGLE, Luther Allan. American religious educator, b. Littlestown, Pa., Sept. 11, 1880, d. New Haven, Conn., Sept. 2. He directed the writing of the Revised Standard Version of the Bible and served from 1928 to 1949 as dean of the Yale Divinity School.

WHIPPLE, George Hoyt. American pathologist, b. Ashland, N.H., Aug. 28, 1878, d. Rochester, N.Y., Feb. 1. He shared the 1934 Nobel Prize in physiology and medicine with two other Americans, George R. Minot and William P. Murphy, for work on pernicious anemia. Whipple found that the disease could be controlled in animals by means of a liver diet.

WHITE, Minor Martin. American photographer, b. Minneapolis, July 9, 1908, d. Boston, June 24. In addition to being a dedicated photographer whose mystical, philosophical work was highly influential, he was also a teacher and an early and enthusiastic organizer and promoter of exhibitions of photography.

German champion Baron Gottfried Von Cramm at the 1938 Wimbledon, England, tennis tournament.

WIENER, Alexander Solomon. American physician, b. New York City, March 16, 1907, d. there Nov. 6. He was codiscoverer, with Philip Levine and the late Karl Landsteiner, of the Rh factor in human blood. He also taught forensic medicine at New York University.

WRIGHT, Russel. American industrial designer, b. Lebanon, Ohio, April 3, 1904, d. New York City, Dec. 22. His furniture, dinnerware, tableware, and rugs virtually changed the taste of Americans from traditional to modern.

YAWKEY, Thomas A. American industrialist and sports executive, b. Thomas Austin in Detroit, Feb. 21, 1903, d. Boston, July 9. Heir to a mining, oil, and lumber fortune, he bought the Boston Red Sox baseball team in 1933. Under his ownership the Red Sox won three American League pennants (1946, 1967, 1975) but never a World Series.

ZUKOR, Adolph. American motion picture executive, b. Ricse, Hungary, Jan. 7, 1873, d. Los Angeles, June 10. In 1903 he opened a penny arcade in New York City, the beginning of what eventually became his production and distribution empire, Paramount Pictures.

OCEANOGRAPHY. *See* EARTH AND PLANETARY SCIENCES.

OHIO. *See* STATISTICS OF THE WORLD.

OKLAHOMA. *See* STATISTICS OF THE WORLD.

OLYMPIC GAMES. *See* SPORTS: THE OLYMPIC GAMES.

OMAN. *See* STATISTICS OF THE WORLD.

ONTARIO. *See* STATISTICS OF THE WORLD.

OREGON. *See* STATISTICS OF THE WORLD.

ORGANIZATION FOR ECONOMIC COOPERATION AND DEVELOPMENT, abbreviated O.E.C.D. Under the guidance of Secretary-General Emile van Lennep, the twenty-four member O.E.C.D. was active in 1976 in economic forecasting, energy policy, and development aid.

Planning and Forecasting. As the industrialized world struggled to free itself from the specter of recession, the O.E.C.D. sought to formulate policies that would lead to full employment while reducing the inflation rate. Meeting in Paris on June 21–22, under the chairmanship of Greek Coordination and Planning Minister Panayis Papaligouras, the O.E.C.D. Council at Ministerial Level agreed on a strategy whereby member governments would "direct their policies to attaining price stability and full employment through the achievement of an economic expansion which is moderate but sustained." The communiqué following the conference estimated that although nations would have different growth rates, an overall expansion among O.E.C.D. countries of 5 percent in gross national product and 8 percent in world trade was feasible from 1976 to 1980.

The possible limitations of this go-slow consensus emerged at a meeting of top O.E.C.D. economic officials in November. By this time the O.E.C.D. staff was forecasting a growth rate in world trade of 6 percent instead of 8 percent in 1977; economic growth was projected at 5 percent in the United States, 3.5 percent in West Germany, 3 percent in France, and only 2 percent in Great Britain. These modest figures implied a new slowdown in the battle to regain full employment in Western Europe.

Problems of unemployment and underemployment came in for special attention at a ministerial-level meeting of the O.E.C.D. Committee on Manpower and Social Affairs, held March 4–5 in Paris under the chairmanship of French Labor Minister Michel Durafour. The conferees agreed on general guidelines, including assistance to disadvantaged groups and coordination of trade, investment, and labor migration policies.

A new research project designed to foster long-term economic planning was announced by the O.E.C.D. in January. The program, entitled "The Future Development of Advanced Industrial Societies in Harmony with that of Developing Countries," was funded for three years at a total cost of about $4,000,000.

Energy. The International Energy Agency (I.E.A.), established within the O.E.C.D. in November, 1974, welcomed Greece as its nineteenth member country in May, 1976. Even more welcome news appeared in a September I.E.A. report: In 1975 total energy consumption among member countries was 14.3 percent below what it would have been had 1968–73 growth rates in energy consumption been sustained. Actual consumption in 1975 was 4.8 percent less than in 1973. Nevertheless, the report concluded that most countries were "not approaching energy conservation with the same intensity and commitment applied to energy supply expansion."

Other I.E.A. activities during 1976 included the adoption of a long-term energy cooperation program in January and the acceptance of "implementing agreements" on nuclear reactor safety and the development of thermonuclear fusion power in May.

Aid to Developing Countries. Data released in 1976 by the Development Assistance Committee (D.A.C.) of the O.E.C.D. indicated that official development assistance provided by D.A.C. members in 1975 totaled $13.6 billion; this represented a 20 percent increase over 1974 in current dollars and a 10 percent increase in real terms.

A new venture in development cooperation, the Club des Amis du Sahel (Friends of the Sahel Club), held its first meeting on March 29–31 in Dakar, Senegal. The club was established with the assistance of the O.E.C.D. in December, 1975, in an effort to promote long-term economic growth and prevent future drought in the Sahel, the area adjacent to the Sahara that is one of the world's poorest regions and was decimated by drought in the early 1970's.   G.M.H.

ORGANIZATION OF AMERICAN STATES, abbreviated O.A.S. The sixth annual General Assembly of the O.A.S. was held in Santiago, Chile, June 4–18, 1976. Mexico boycotted the conference to protest the selection of Chile as the meeting site. Nevertheless, in his final speech to the assembly, O.A.S. Secretary-General Alejandro Orfila of Argentina asserted that the regional organization had been strengthened as a result of the meeting. More important, observers agreed that the assembly had marked a major step forward in establishing protection of human rights as a major concern in inter-American relations.

For the first time since the O.A.S. was created in 1948, reports of the Inter-American Human Rights Commission were the principal topic of discussion at its General Assembly. In a special report prepared for the meeting, the commission charged the Chilean government with arbitrary arrest, torture, and persecution. The Chilean government reacted by publishing a lengthy rebuttal defending its policies. Finally, by an almost unanimous vote (Jamaica voted against the resolution; Chile and Brazil abstained), the assembly approved a compromise resolution authorizing the commission to continue monitoring and reporting on human rights violations in Chile. In addition, the O.A.S. granted the commission a mandate to extend its surveillance to other countries where serious violation of human rights have occurred. During 1976 the commission also reported on abuses in Cuba and Paraguay.

In addition, the General Assembly received a joint statement from the United States and Panama reporting significant progress in negotiations toward a new canal treaty. In his address to the assembly on June 8, U.S. Secretary of State Henry A. Kissinger responded to pleas for trade preferences for Latin America. He also addressed himself to complaints by Ecuador and Venezuela about their exclusion from tariff advantages under the U.S. Trade Reform Act of 1974 because of their membership in the Organization of Petroleum Exporting Countries. Although the O.A.S. formally expressed "concern and dismay" over the latter issue, hard bargaining on U.S.-Latin American economic relations was deferred until after the U.S. Presidential election in November.   A.K.M.

ORGANIZATION OF PETROLEUM EXPORTING COUNTRIES, abbreviated OPEC. During 1976 OPEC, the cartel that had quintupled world oil prices over a period of four years, continued to wield enormous power over the international economy. But OPEC's ranks were bitterly divided.

Shaken by an attack by Palestinian terrorists on OPEC headquarters in Vienna just before the end of 1975, the thirteen-member group chose Paris for its first important meeting of 1976. In January OPEC finance ministers met there to consider an aid program for developing countries hurt by rising oil prices. After considerable bickering, the ministers set up an $800,000,000 aid fund, less than had been expected. Saudi Arabia and Iran, OPEC's largest producers, agreed to contribute the most: about $200,000,000 apiece.

For much of the year, the question of price-cutting caused bitter animosities among the OPEC states. With world demand for heavy crude oil especially sluggish, some producers—particularly Iraq—sought to capture new markets by cutting prices. In February Algeria refused to take part in a proposed conference unless Iraq rescinded its price cuts. In April at Geneva, and in May on the Indonesian island of Bali, the oil ministers discussed various formulas for pricing the more than forty different types of crude oil produced by OPEC members. But no agreement was reached. In the end only OPEC's so-called bench-mark crude, Saudi Arabian light oil, remained firmly fixed throughout the year, at $11.51 a barrel. OPEC members retained a good deal of latitude in pricing other types of crude.

At the Bali meeting, the ministers also debated the nine-month-long freeze on oil prices that was to end on June 30. Most OPEC members, with Iran

The acknowledged "star" of the meeting of the Organization of Petroleum Exporting Countries at Doha, Qatar, in December was Sheikh Ahmed Zaki al-Yamani, the oil minister of Saudi Arabia. His sudden exit from the meeting, and his later return, dramatized the dissension within the organization.

in the lead, wanted a substantial increase in price at that time. But Saudi Arabia's Oil Minister Sheikh Ahmed Zaki al-Yamani argued that the industrialized world had not recovered sufficiently from the recession to sustain another price increase. After a series of volatile sessions, the ministers bowed to the Saudi position and extended the freeze "for the present."

When the OPEC oil ministers met in the tiny Persian Gulf state of Qatar in December, both the industrialized West and the non-oil-producing

Third World countries feared that a stiff rise in prices would be forthcoming. OPEC surprised them. After days of wrangling, eleven of its members announced a 15 percent price increase—10 percent to take effect on Jan. 1, 1977, and an additional 5 percent at midyear. But Saudi Arabia, backed by the Union of Arab Emirates, held its price increase to 5 percent. For its moderation, Yamani stated, Saudi Arabia would expect the "appreciation" of the West, presumably in the form of pressure on Israel to make concessions in future negotiations with the Arabs.

How world oil prices would be affected by the two-tier price decision was highly uncertain, particularly in light of the Saudi threat to step up its already vast oil production in an effort to keep prices down. Iraq's oil minister, for his part, suggested that other members of OPEC would use political pressure to force Saudi Arabia "to follow the overwhelming majority of the OPEC states." Although some analysts questioned the organization's future effectiveness as the dictator of world oil prices, others expected the group to resolve the dissension and eventually to agree on an adjusted higher price level.

See also ARAB LEAGUE; MIDDLE EAST.   R.J.C.

P

PAKISTAN. Prime Minister Zulfikar Ali Bhutto ruled Pakistan with a firm hand during 1976. The press was strictly controlled, and more than 30,000 political prisoners were reportedly being held. In early 1976 the government suspended parliamentary rule in the province of Baluchistan to combat secessionist activity, and in April Bhutto abruptly abolished the tribal chieftain system there. (Maintenance of the three provincial chieftainships had been made contingent in the late 1960's on the chiefs' pledge to cooperate with the national government.) In September Pakistani government troops crushed a tribal revolt in the Northwest Frontier Province; the revolt was triggered by nationalization of provincial timber forests.

The economy grew by about 6 percent in the fiscal year ending June 30, despite a decline in cotton production, a slump in rice export prices, and a disappointing delay in the inauguration of the huge Tarbela Dam, which needed extensive repairs between April and December to halt erosion. Pakistan continued to receive extensive aid from the United States, other Western countries, and oil-rich Middle Eastern lands. These receipts, together with family remittances from Pakistanis working abroad, largely sufficed to cover a huge trade deficit.

Plans to add twenty-four more medium-sized nuclear power plants by the year 2000 to the one Canadian-built plant already operating in Karachi encountered no major international objections, but an agreement signed with France on March 18 for the purchase of a nuclear reprocessing plant brought protests from Canada and the U.S. After Canada halted all nuclear cooperation with Pakistan in December, the Pakistanis decided to pursue their agreement with the French despite U.S. pressure to cancel the deal.

Important progress was made during the year in restoring normal relations with India. Under an agreement announced on May 14, the two countries exchanged ambassadors in July; during the next few weeks rail, road, and air communications were reestablished. Relations with Afghanistan, traditionally poor, improved slightly. Prime Minister Bhutto made a five-day visit to Kabul in June, and Afghan President Mohammad Daud paid a return visit to Islamabad in August. The two leaders promised there would be further talks in the future.

See STATISTICS OF THE WORLD.   W.J.G.

PANAMA. As negotiations between the United States and Panama concerning the future status of the Panama Canal stalled because of the 1976 U.S. Presidential campaign, Gen. Omar Torrijos Herrera tried to divert attention away from the canal issue toward the nation's economic problems. To prevent a national debate over the negotiations, President Torrijos deported ten prominent businessmen and lawyers, calling them soft on Washington. At the same time, the government also deported the owner of the nation's only independent radio station and sternly warned university students not to agitate over the canal issue. A subsequent protest strike by Panamanian business executives was halted after the government pledged to permit the deportees to return when circumstances permitted.

To shore up his standing with the private sector, Torrijos held out the possibility of revisions in the labor law. In addition, the administration dismissed or shunted aside a number of prominent

Yugoslav President Tito pins the Great Star of Yugoslavia on his Panamanian counterpart, Gen. Omar Torrijos Herrera, during a visit to Panama in March.

leftists in the government. In September violent student demonstrations over high food prices and alleged government repression were harshly suppressed. Panamanian officials charged that the riots were part of a U.S.-backed plan to "destabilize" Panama.

The government continued to pursue its long-range development goals. Despite the uncertain outlook for worldwide copper prices, the government pressed ahead with the development of the vast Cerro Colorado copper deposit, at a total cost of $800,000,000. In January Panama reached agreement with United Brands Co. to purchase its 100,000 acres of banana land; 37,500 acres were to be leased back to the U.S.-based company.

Data released by the Panama Canal Co., a U.S. agency which administers the canal, indicated that canal traffic and revenues had both declined during the 1976 fiscal year.

See STATISTICS OF THE WORLD.   A.K.M.

PAPUA NEW GUINEA. *See* STATISTICS OF THE WORLD.

PARAGUAY. In 1976, midway through his fifth term in office, President Alfredo Stroessner continued to rule Paraguay with an iron hand; the state of siege imposed twenty-two years ago when a military coup brought him to power was still in effect. Although Stroessner was prevented from succeeding himself under the existing constitution, the legislature voted July 16 to authorize the convening in February, 1977, of a constituent assembly which would amend the constitution to permit Stroessner to run again in 1978.

For the second successive year, Paraguay's real gross domestic product grew by more than 8 percent. Although meat exports continued to suffer from the European Economic Community's ban on meat imports, high world prices for the country's forestry and agricultural products fostered economic expansion. At the same time, selective price controls and the requirement that meat producers allocate a certain amount of production for local consumption kept inflation in check.

Paraguay signed bilateral trade, credit, and technology agreements with both Argentina and Brazil during 1976. Meanwhile, work continued on the Itaipú hydroelectric complex on the Paraná R., a project undertaken in partnership with Brazil. Another agreement, between Paraguay and Argentina, provided for acceleration of the Yacreta-Agripe dam project on the Paraná. These projects, as well as other, smaller hydroelectric installations, were designed to make Paraguay a major supplier of energy to the South American continent.

See STATISTICS OF THE WORLD.   A.K.M.

PAUL VI. *See* PEOPLE IN THE NEWS.

PENNSYLVANIA. *See* STATISTICS OF THE WORLD.

PEOPLE IN THE NEWS

The story of 1976 was a tale of kings, presidents, screen and sports stars, murderers, tycoons, dictators, politicians—and of those who were pushed into the spotlight by the strange, unpredictable hand of chance.

A host of interesting faces, young and old, familiar and unfamiliar, peered out of newspaper pages and television screens and became a part of our lives in 1976. The stories behind the faces, including detailed individual biographies of some of the most important of the people of the year, will be found in the pages that follow.

First of all, 1976 was a Presidential election year. **Betty, Susan, Jack,** and other members of **President Gerald R. Ford**'s family were very much in evidence as they went to the hustings and fought gallantly but unsuccessfully to help him win another term in the White House. At the same time Americans made friends with the First-Family-to-be as they came to know **Jimmy Carter**'s wife **Rosalynn;** his stalwart mother **Miss Lillian;** and his sons **Jack** (29), **Chip** (26), and **Jeff** (24), together

with their three wives. All of them worked with the Democratic Party candidate in his strenuous campaign. Helping, too, was his personable 9-year-old daughter **Amy,** purveyor of refreshments and good cheer to the reporters assigned to the Carter home in Plains, Ga. Carter's sister **Ruth Stapleton,** an evangelist, also made appearances on his behalf.

One of the most mysterious figures of recent times was in the news repeatedly in 1976, as he had been in previous years. This was **Howard Robard Hughes,** billionaire industrialist, who ruled an enormous financial empire but had lived a life of such seclusion for the past ten years that the world at large could not even be sure that he was alive. In April it found out: Hughes was rushed from Acapulco to Houston in an ambulance plane, only to die of kidney failure en route. He was 70 years old.

In those seventy years Hughes, starting with the $750,000 Hughes Tool Co. he inherited from his father, had built up a complex of industrial, real estate, and other holdings valued at $2.3 billion.

Sharing a triumphal moment after his acceptance speech at the Democratic National Convention on July 15, Presidential nominee Jimmy Carter holds his daughter Amy. His mother Lillian Carter (left) and his wife Rosalynn (bending at right) flank him while Vice-Presidential nominee Walter F. Mondale and his wife Joan look on.

No sooner was his death confirmed—his finger-prints were matched with Federal Bureau of Investigation (F.B.I.) records—than a multitude of wills attributed to him turned up; one Nevada promoter even published a book of them. All might eventually prove to be hoaxes, but at least one was taken seriously. This purported testament appeared without explanation on a desk in the headquarters of the Church of Jesus Christ of Latter-Day Saints (the Mormon church) in Salt Lake City. The document, handwritten and dated 1968, named as executor **Noah Dietrich,** who was Hughes's chief executive before the billionaire dismissed him in 1957. Dietrich stood to collect 2 percent of the estate. Others named as heirs were four colleges, the Mormon church, the Boy Scouts of America, two former wives, several Hughes employees, and **Melvin Dummar,** operator of an Ogden (Utah) service station. Dummar claimed that he saved Hughes's life once by providing him a ride out of the Nevada desert.

Melvin Dummar reacts to reports that he was left one sixteenth of billionaire Howard Hughes's estate in a purported will found in Salt Lake City in April.

In pretrial investigation of the will it was alleged to be a forgery, and Dummar's fingerprint, according to the F.B.I., was found on the envelope containing it. The document was contested by Hughes's relatives, who stood to inherit part of the estate if no authentic will were found. The relatives included Hughes's elderly aunt and three granddaughters of the late novelist Rupert Hughes, who was his uncle. This will was scheduled to be contested in Las Vegas, Nev., early in 1977.

Trials and the personalities involved in them often dominated the year's news. The long-awaited case of **Patricia Hearst** finally came to judgment, with Patty receiving a seven-year sentence; see below. The appeal of the murder conviction of former Army **Lt. William L. Calley, Jr.,** came before the United States Supreme Court in April. A 1971 court-martial had convicted Calley of the murder of twenty-two South Vietnamese civilians in the hamlet of My Lai in 1968. Calley, considered a scapegoat by some, was first sentenced to life imprisonment. His term was later reduced to ten years. The Supreme Court refused to review the court-martial conviction. But Calley did not have to return to prison, as he had become eligible for parole and was released in late 1974. He then began giving lectures at colleges and took a job as an insurance salesman. Soon after the Supreme Court decision was announced, friends received invitations to Calley's wedding in Columbus, Ga.

Public pressure forced the reexamination of a legal verdict in the case of **Peter Reilly,** 21, of Canaan, Conn. Reilly was convicted in 1974 of the murder of his mother and given a prison sentence. He had made a confession while fright-ened and under pressure, but friends and neighbors doubted his guilt. Their ranks were joined by many prominent figures, including **Arthur Miller,** the playwright. With their support, new evidence was found, and in March a judge threw out the conviction. A new trial was scheduled, but the original prosecutor had died, and another was appointed. Going through the files of the case, he discovered testimony that placed Reilly away from the scene of the murder at the time it occurred. In November the charges against Reilly were dismissed.

A Congressional secretary who could not type, Elizabeth Ray talks with reporters in Washington, D.C., on Aug. 13.

Former Secretary of the Navy John Warner and his new bride Elizabeth Taylor take a stroll in Middleburg, Va. The couple were married in December in a sunset ceremony at Warner's nearby farm. The actress had divorced actor Richard Burton in July.

The U.S. Congress itself was repeatedly touched by scandal in 1976. One particularly well-publicized instance toppled a fourteen-term Congressman, **Wayne L. Hays** (D, Ohio), from a position of power in the House of Representatives. The scandal was revealed in May by the Washington (D.C.) *Post,* which reported that **Elizabeth Ray,** 33, a staff member of the House Administration Committee (headed by Hays) had told newsmen that she had been hired by the 65-year-old legislator to be his mistress and that she spent very little time in the committee office. "I can't type, I can't file, I can't even answer the phone," she said. For her services she was, however, paid $14,000 a year. Just two weeks later Hays was rushed to a hospital in Ohio. He was in a coma brought on by an overdose of sleeping pills. The target of investigations by the Justice Department and a federal grand jury, he resigned from the House in September. Elizabeth Ray, although she had lost her job, found fame and some fortune as the nominal author of a novel, *The Washington Fringe Benefit,* that was said to be based on her experiences in the capital. Readers perused it eagerly to see if they could identify the fictionalized government notables

with whom she and her friends had reportedly had affairs.

Rep. Allan T. Howe (D, Utah), a Mormon and father of five, figured in a scandal in June when he was arrested in Salt Lake City on a charge of "soliciting sex acts for hire." Two part-time policewomen employed as decoy prostitutes appeared as witnesses against him. A jury of four found the Congressman guilty and he was sentenced to thirty days in jail and a $150 fine, the sentence to be suspended on payment of the fine. His appeal of the conviction was rejected in August. Although the Democratic Party withdrew its support and all but one of his paid campaign staff resigned, he persisted in running for reelection in November; he lost.

One of the most sensational court trials of the year came to an end in December with the conviction in White Plains, N.Y., of **Mel Patrick Lynch** and **Dominic P. Byrne** on a charge of extorting $2,300,000 from **Edgar Bronfman,** chairman of the giant Seagram Company Ltd., liquor distillers and distributors. The pair had also been charged with abducting Bronfman's son, **Samuel Bronfman 2nd,** in August, 1975, and holding him for ransom. The defense contended that Bronfman, then 21, had engineered the plot in hope of getting some of the $20,000,000 he would eventually inherit. This argument apparently weighed heavily with the jury, which found Lynch and Byrne innocent of the kidnapping charge. Lynch, a fireman, testified that he had had homosexual relations with the Seagram heir, who had then coerced him into taking part in the plot by threatening to denounce him to the New York City Fire Department as a sex deviant. The verdict did not sway Bronfman's father. "I have nothing but love, trust, and affection for my son," he said.

Racism was reportedly a factor in the closely watched trial of **Rubin "Hurricane" Carter** (once a leading contender for the world middleweight boxing championship) and **John Artis.** Carter and Artis, both black men, had served nine years of a life sentence after being found guilty of the 1966 murder of three white persons in a Paterson, N.J., bar. The state supreme court overturned their conviction, and a new trial began in November, 1976. The prosecution, which in the original trial had offered no motive for the killings, contended that Carter and Artis were motivated by a desire for racial revenge for the shooting of a black man earlier the same day. In spite of some new evidence favorable to the defendants, including a recantation by an eyewitness who had identified them in the first trial, Carter and Artis were again found guilty.

Another black man, awaiting trial, experienced

a spiritual rebirth. **Eldridge Cleaver,** former minister of information of the Black Panther Party, faced charges of assault and attempted murder that resulted from a 1968 shoot-out between police and Black Panthers in Oakland, Calif. He had fled prosecution and spent seven years abroad before returning to the U.S. voluntarily in late 1975 to stand trial. Early in 1976 he was released on $100,000 bail; his trial, several times postponed, was finally set for May, 1977. On Oct. 10 he and his wife were baptized, and thereafter he began testifying at evangelical rallies to the power of Christian faith. Cleaver, 41, was the author of an influential autobiography, *Soul on Ice* (1968).

In March **Claudine Longet,** a French-born entertainer and the former wife of singer **Andy Williams,** was charged with manslaughter after **Vladimir ("Spider") Sabich,** former professional world skiing champion, was shot to death at the mountain chalet the two shared at Aspen, Colo. In December the prosecution said it would go ahead with her trial, although the Colorado Supreme Court had barred the use of her diary and other evidence because they had been obtained without a court order.

The issue of whether capital punishment is a deterrent to murder was reopened during the year when **Gary Mark Gilmore,** 35, convicted for one of two murders he admitted committing in July, asked for and was eventually granted a date of execution by firing squad in Utah. According to some psychologists, the two killings, which were apparently random, were motivated by Gilmore's desire for self-destruction. While Gilmore fumed over the delay, his mother and others mounted appeals as high as the U.S. Supreme Court. The murderer twice attempted suicide in prison, the first time in November as part of an apparent pact with his 20-year-old fiancée, **Nicole Barrett.**

Although the role she played was a completely quiescent one, **Karen Anne Quinlan,** 22, was the center of a precedent-setting case in 1976. The girl, according to witnesses, swallowed some pills and liquor in April, 1975, and slipped into a coma from which she could not be revived. After six months her parents, convinced her condition was irreversible, asked hospital authorities to disconnect the respirator that supported her breathing and thus to let her die "with dignity." The authorities refused. The New Jersey Superior Court rejected a similar request by the Quinlans. In March, however, the New Jersey Supreme Court ruled that Karen's father could transfer her to another hospital and have the life-support system removed if physicians agreed there was no hope for her. In May the respirator was disconnected. But the comatose woman remained alive.

One of the best-publicized weddings in history (some 500,000,000 persons around the world reportedly watched the festivities on television) took place in Stockholm in June. The stars of the event were 30-year-old **King Charles XVI Gustavus** of Sweden and a commoner, **Silvia Sommerlath,** daughter of a West German businessman. Although the royal spectacular was attended by four reigning monarchs and numbers of princes and princesses, the king and his new queen did not wear their crowns of gold; such an act would have been considered unseemly in democratic Sweden. The couple met at the 1972 Olympics in Munich, where she was chief hostess for important visitors.

Echoes of vanished splendor were raised by the announcement of another royal marriage soon to take place. In August **Prince Friedrich Wilhelm of Prussia,** a member of the Hohenzollern family, which formerly ruled Germany, plighted his troth to **Grand Duchess Maria Vladimirovna Romanov,** 23, daughter of the Russian grand duke Vladimir. White Russians had accepted the grand duke as Czar Vladimir II after the death of his father, a cousin of Czar Nicholas II, last royal ruler of pre-Soviet Russia.

Comedian Jerry Lewis (right) and singer Dean Martin—a popular team of the early 1950's—end their twenty-year separation as they meet on the Jerry Lewis Muscular Dystrophy Telethon on Sept. 5. To keep the surprise from Lewis, Martin entered the studio disguised as a waiter.

Another might-have-been monarch, **Dom Duarte Nuno,** the Duke of Braganza, died in Lisbon on Dec. 24 at 69. Dom Duarte was the claimant to the Portuguese throne, which was last occupied in 1834 by his grandfather, King Miguel I.

As always, many people made news in the world of sports. Several of the year's record-makers were women. Fourteen-year-old Rumanian gymnast **Nadia Comaneci** (see below) performed with dazzling grace in the Olympics. American-born **Dorothy Hamill,** only 19, won recognition as the world's foremost woman figure skater. And tennis champion **Chris Evert** was named top athlete of the year by *Sports Illustrated* in December. Evert, winner of the women's singles at both Forest Hills and Wimbledon, was selected by the magazine because of the way she dominated her sport and because she "symbolized in character and performance the ideals of sportsmanship." Said the champion, "In my mind, it was a woman's year. People are starting to appreciate women athletes. . . ."

Another woman tennis player caused a considerable sensation in 1976. This was a physician named **Renee Richards,** who won a minor tennis tournament at La Jolla, Calif., and then competed in a major one at South Orange, N.J. When she applied to the U.S. Open at Forest Hills, N.Y., her participation was strenuously opposed by the Women's Tennis Association. It wasn't just that she stood 6 ft. 2 in. tall and weighed 147 lb.; the main objection was that until recently Renee Richards had been a man.

As Richard Raskind, Richards had been a successful ophthalmological surgeon in New York. Married and a father, he was also a strong amateur tennis player. In 1975 he had a sex-change operation, divorced his wife, and reappeared on California tennis courts as an attractive ash blonde with a strong serve. Before admitting Richards to the U.S. Open at Forest Hills, authorities at the U.S. Tennis Association ordered her to take a chromosome test like that required for women

Renee Richards plays in the Tennis Week Open women's singles tournament in South Orange, N.J., in August.

Princess Margaret, sister of Queen Elizabeth II of Great Britain, leaves her home at Kensington Palace on March 19, accompanied by her son Viscount Linley. She had just announced that her marriage to Lord Snowdon (Antony Armstrong-Jones) was over. After fifteen years, they had agreed to live apart; but they had no plans for divorce.

participants in the Olympics. She refused. When informed she would be barred from the contest, she said she would sue; the chromosome test, in her opinion, was "a very unfair test of a person's sexuality." Richards went on to win $20,000 in a Hawaii tournament in December. The authorities, faced with the prospect of other transsexuals seeking admittance to the women's professional tour, stood by their insistence on the chromosome test.

In October a Japanese baseball star, **Sadaharu Oh,** 36, tied Babe Ruth's career home-run total of 714 after hitting a ball 300 ft. over the fence in Korakuen Stadium in Tokyo. The first baseman of the Yomiuri Giants, he batted around .325 in 1976. The Japanese player was Asia's highest-paid athlete with a salary of $200,000; he earned almost as much again for endorsements. The next mark he set his sights on was Henry Aaron's record total of 755. If he topped it, said the athlete, he would not consider himself the world's Number 1 hitter. "You see, it is only the figures which people compare. Our stadiums are a little smaller. The pitchers are not quite as strong as your American ones, And the competition is perhaps not as good."

Changes occurred in many careers in 1976. In February **Zubin Mehta** was appointed to replace **Pierre Boulez** as conductor of the New York Philharmonic Orchestra. Mehta, born in Bombay, had been leading the Los Angeles Philharmonic for fourteen years, since he was 26. In contrast to Boulez, who specialized in contemporary music, Mehta had a more traditional repertory that was expected to have greater appeal for the Philharmonic's audience. The exotic-looking Mehta was scheduled to take up his East Coast post in September, 1978.

Defections of Soviet citizens to the West continued in 1976. Perhaps the most dramatic case was that of **Viktor Ivanovich Belenko,** a 29-year-old air force lieutenant. In September, flying a MIG-25, Belenko eluded Russian pursuers and landed at the Hakodate airport in Hokkaido, Japan. Experts immediately began to analyze the Soviet airplane. Never before examined by the U.S. or its allies, the MIG-25 was the fastest weapons-carrying aircraft in the world, with a record speed of 1852.6 m.p.h. and a test altitude of 118,000 ft. As for the pilot, Belenko was immediately granted his request for asylum in the U.S. The Soviet Union insisted that he had made a forced landing and was being kept a prisoner against his will; Belenko disagreed and promptly left for Los Angeles. "There is no freedom in the Soviet Union," he told questioners. "Nothing has changed since the czars."

Aleksandr I. Solzhenitsyn, who was expelled

Singer Frank Sinatra and his new wife, the former Barbara Marx, cut the cake after their July 11 wedding in Rancho Mirage, Calif. The bride was the former wife of Zeppo, youngest member of the Marx Brothers comedy team.

from the U.S.S.R. in 1974, also came to the U.S. to live, applying for a permanent resident's visa in June. He bought an estate in Cavendish, Vt., for $150,000 and arranged for $250,000 worth of renovations. According to Solzhenitsyn, Soviet agents had been spying on him at his former home in Switzerland. Curiously enough, his name turned up in the Republican platform of 1976, where he was commended as "that great beacon of human courage and morality." A reference to his "compelling message that we must face the world with no illusions about tyranny" was regarded as an indirect criticism of President Ford's policy of détente.

Vladimir K. Bukovsky, another prominent Soviet human rights activist, had reason to rejoice at the end of the year. In December he was released from prison and allowed to leave the Soviet Union. Bukovsky, who spent more than a third of his life in Soviet prisons and mental institutions, first became known in the West when he smuggled out evidence that sane political dissidents were being confined in psychiatric hospitals in the U.S.S.R. He was traded for **Luis Corvalán Lepe,** the imprisoned head of the Chilean Communist Party, in an exchange arranged by the U.S.

ALI, MUHAMMAD

World heavyweight boxing champion, born Jan. 18, 1942, in Louisville, Ky. The 2-time holder of the world heavyweight title made 5 ring appearances in 1976, earning an estimated $15,500,000. The first was in February against Jean-Pierre Coopman of Belgium, an easy win for Ali. The second was in April, against Jimmy Young in Landover, Md. At 230 lb., the heaviest weight of his career, Ali seemed slower than usual, but won a unanimous decision after 15 rounds. In May the champion scored a technical knockout over British boxer Richard Dunn in the fifth round of a bout held in Munich, Germany. Ali next faced a massive Japanese wrestler, Antonio Inoki, in Tokyo in June; the 15-round boxing-wrestling exhibition ended in a draw. In September, after a close 15-round contest with no knockdowns, he won a unanimous although controversial decision over Ken Norton at Yankee Stadium in New York City. Afterward he announced he was going to retire, but soon was entertaining offers for matches with George Foreman and others. Ali made his next appearance before the cameras in Florida at the end of the year, playing himself in the film version of his bestselling 1975 autobiography, *The Greatest*.

ARMSTRONG, ANNE LEGENDRE

U.S. Ambassador to Great Britain, born Dec. 27, 1927, in New Orleans, La. A prominent Republican politician and an advocate of women's rights, she was nominated as ambassador in December, 1975, by President Ford. The U.S. Senate confirmed her appointment on Jan. 27, 1976, and she became the first American woman to serve as envoy to the Court of Saint James. During the year she was reportedly considered as a possible Republican Vice-Presidential candidate.

The former Anne Legendre earned a B.A. at Vassar (1949). After her marriage in 1950 to a wealthy Texas cattleman, she became active in politics in Kenedy Co., Texas, and in 1968 she was a delegate to the Republican national convention and a member of the platform committee. She was appointed cochairman of the Republican National Committee in 1971 by President Richard M. Nixon. At the national convention in 1972 she became the first woman of either major party to deliver a keynote address. In December, 1972, Nixon named her counselor to the President, a post with cabinet rank. In that capacity she founded the Office of Women's Programs and helped to triple the number of women in policy-making government positions. She stayed on as a counselor under President Ford, resigning on Nov. 28, 1974.

BLACK, SHIRLEY TEMPLE

U.S. diplomat and former actress, born April 23, 1928, in Santa Monica, Calif. As the year began she was U.S. ambassador to Ghana, where she was

Anne Armstrong of Texas, the U.S. ambassador to Great Britain, holds her first news conference in London on March 4.

Shirley Temple Black at her post as chief of protocol in the U.S. State Department. She was the first woman to hold the prestigious post.

a popular figure, promoting American business interests and working to advance the welfare of Ghanaian mothers and children. After Ghana canceled a visit by U.S. Secretary of State Henry A. Kissinger, she was recalled to Washington for "consultations." In July she was sworn in as chief of protocol for the State Department, the first woman to hold the post.

In 1967 Shirley Temple Black ran unsuccessfully for the U.S. House of Representatives in California. President Nixon named her to the U.S. delegation to the United Nations in 1969. In 1974 President Ford appointed her ambassador to Ghana.

BREZHNEV, LEONID I(LYICH)

General Secretary of the Soviet Communist Party Central Committee, born Dec. 19, 1906. Rumors of Brezhnev's declining health faded as he delivered a five-and-a-half-hour address at the party's 25th Congress in Moscow in February. In that speech he reaffirmed his policy of détente. At the congress Brezhnev was lavishly praised and reelected to the post of general secretary. In May his climb above the party's collective leadership continued as he was promoted to field marshal of the army; he was the first party leader since Joseph Stalin to hold that title. Also in May he signed a treaty with the U.S. imposing limits on underground nuclear explosions. In June, at a conference of twenty-nine European Communist Party leaders in East Berlin, he voiced a conciliatory attitude toward European Communist parties opposed to Soviet domination. It marked a sharp break with the Brezhnev doctrine of intervention in Eastern Europe, developed after his suppression of Czechoslovakia in 1968. In November, visiting Yugoslavia, he reiterated vows to honor that country's sovereignty. At year's end he pledged not to contrive an international crisis to test the incoming U.S. administration of Jimmy Carter.

BUSH, GEORGE HERBERT WALKER

Director of the Central Intelligence Agency (C.I.A.), born June 12, 1924, in Milton, Mass. Nominated in November, 1975, by President Ford, he succeeded William E. Colby as chief of the agency on Jan. 30, 1976. In February he was made head of a new committee charged with managing and streamlining the nation's foreign intelligence-gathering system. Among the reforms effected by the agency under his directorship was a prohibition on the hiring of American journalists to serve as C.I.A. agents.

The son of a former U.S. Senator from Connecticut, Bush was educated at Yale University and made a fortune in Texas oil. Twice elected to the U.S. House of Representatives (1966, 1968), he was twice defeated for the Senate (1964, 1970). President Nixon named him U.S. ambassador to

At the center of U.S. intelligence-gathering activities, Central Intelligence Agency Director George Bush poses outside his office in March.

the U.N. in 1970. In 1974 he was made head of the U.S. liaison office in Peking, China.

BUTZ, EARL L(AUER)

U.S. public official, born July 3, 1909, in Albion, Ind. He was secretary of agriculture for five years, serving under Presidents Nixon and Ford. Butz was an outspoken and often controversial cabinet member—his resignation on Oct. 4, 1976, was the result of an obscene and derogatory joke he told about Blacks. The joke was reported in Rolling Stone magazine by author John W. Dean 3rd, former counsel to President Nixon. Butz had been campaigning for the election of President Fo⋯ and was considered his major political asset in t⋯ farm belt. But publication of his joke dre⋯

storm of protest, and Butz, suddenly become a liability, was forced to resign with the admission that he had committed a "gross indiscretion."

The son of a farmer, Butz studied agriculture at Purdue University, where in 1957 he became dean of agriculture. He was named secretary of agriculture by President Nixon in 1971, and was usually credited with having freed U.S. farming from the system of government restraints established during the economic depression of the 1930's.

CARTER, JIMMY

In full JAMES EARL CARTER, JR., President-elect of the U.S., born Oct. 1, 1924, in Plains, Ga. Jimmy Carter, as he preferred to be called, won election in November as the thirty-ninth President after a grueling campaign that lasted almost two years. He had announced his candidacy for the Democratic nomination in December, 1974, just before the expiration of his single term as governor of Georgia. Virtually unknown to the American electorate, he embarked on a journey that took him nearly 500,000 mi. to a thousand American cities, where he tirelessly walked the streets and shook hands with voters, often introducing himself with "Hi, I'm Jimmy Carter and I'm running for President." In his speeches (he delivered some 1500) he emphasized the need to reduce inflation and unemployment, streamline the federal bureaucracy, and reform the tax laws. Above all, he promised strong moral leadership. His ready, open smile and his apparent freedom from ties to the political establishment helped to win him first place in 19 of the 31 Democratic primaries that he entered in 1976. When Carter went to the Democratic Party's National Convention in July he had a wide lead in public opinion polls over both President Ford and former California Gov. Ronald Reagan, the two principal Republican contenders. Carter was nominated on the first ballot. In the following months his lead over Republican candidate Ford fell sharply. Still, on Nov. 2 he won 50 percent of the popular vote, compared to 48 percent for Ford. Carter thus became the first President from the deep South since Zachary Taylor in 1848. By Dec. 25 he had named his cabinet, describing the nominees as "tough, competent managers"; see CABINET, UNITED STATES. Carter's important cabinet-level appointments included those of Zbigniew Brzezinski to be his special assistant for national security affairs, Rep. Andrew Young (D, Ga.) to be ambassador to the U.N., Georgia banker Thomas B. Lance to be director of the Office of Management and Budget, economist Charles L. Schultze to be chief economic adviser, Theodore C. Sorensen (an aide to President John Kennedy) to be head of the C.I.A., and former Secretary of Defense James R. Schlesinger to be

special assistant for energy matters. Meanwhile, his conservative utterances on fiscal policy helped allay the fears of the business community, which had been disturbed by his earlier stands for hiring the unemployed with federal funds and plugging corporate tax loopholes.

The son of the late James Earl Carter, a segregationist peanut farmer, and Lillian Gordy Carter, a nurse of more liberal opinions, Carter graduated in 1946 from the U.S. Naval Academy at Annapolis, Md. He served in the Navy for seven years, seeing duty on submarines and receiving training as a nuclear engineer. In 1953, after his father died, Carter returned to Georgia and took over the family farm, which he managed successfully. Elected to the Georgia State Senate in 1962 and 1964, he was defeated in the Georgia Democratic gubernatorial primary in 1966; it was a hard blow, from which he recovered by a "spiritual rebirth" that made him a devout evangelical Baptist. Elected governor in 1970, he reorganized the state bureaucracy, instituted numerous economies, appointed Blacks to high positions, and won a reputation as a voice of the new, more liberal South. The Georgia constitution forbids a governor to succeed himself, and Carter turned his sights on the Presidency. Through a daring campaign planned by young Georgians, he won it.

See DEMOCRATIC PARTY; ELECTIONS.

COMANECI, NADIA

Rumanian gymnast, born Nov. 12, 1961, in Gheorghe Gheorghiu-Dej, a city in the Carpathian Mts. In July, at the Olympic Games in Montréal, Canada, she won three gold medals (for the uneven parallel bars, the balance beam, and the all-around individual competitions), one silver medal (for team competition), and one bronze medal (for floor exercise). The 14-year-old girl, who weighed 86 lb. and stood 4 ft. 11 in., gave perhaps the most spectacular performance of the 2000 women athletes in the Olympics. The judges awarded her a perfect score in 7 out of 10 events, the highest achieved by any gymnast since the founding of the modern Olympics in 1896.

The daughter of a mechanic, Nadia was discovered at age 6 by a coach, Bela Karolyi, who was scouting kindergartens for promising gymnasts. In 1969 she placed thirteenth in her first meet, the Rumanian Junior National Championships, but she won first place in all subsequent competitions. In 1975, competing as a senior for the first time, she captured the European championship.

DOLE, ROBERT J(OSEPH)

Republican Vice-Presidential candidate and U.S. Senator from Kansas, born July 22, 1923, in Russell, Kans. On Aug. 19 he was nominated to be President Ford's running mate at the Republican National Convention in Kansas City, Mo. Dole carried out much of the day-to-day campaigning for the ticket, stumping his way across the country and attacking Democratic Presidential candidate Jimmy Carter in the North and Vice-Presidential candidate Walter F. Mondale in the South. Dole faced Mondale in a nationally televised debate on Oct. 15. Polls taken at the time of the election (Nov. 2) indicated that in most states Dole was not an asset to the Republican ticket.

Dole's studies at the University of Kansas were interrupted by World War II, in which he served as a U.S. Army platoon commander. After a lengthy recovery from severe shrapnel wounds suffered in Italy, he returned to school at Washburn University in Topeka, Kans.; he earned his law degree there in 1952. He served as a state legislator, county prosecutor, and U.S. Representative before being elected to the U.S. Senate in 1968. In 1971 President Nixon recognized Dole's effective partisan efforts by naming him chairman of the Republican National Committee.

FORD, GERALD R(UDOLPH)
See PRESIDENT OF THE UNITED STATES.

GISCARD D'ESTAING, VALÉRY
President of France, born Feb. 2, 1926, in Koblenz, West Germany, of French parents. Giscard faced many problems in 1976, especially on the economic front. As inflation persisted he introduced a stringent austerity program, and in August he appointed Raymond Barre as premier to carry it out. The program featured a price freeze and tax increases. Giscard paid a Bicentennial visit to Washington, D.C., in May and addressed a joint session of the U.S. Congress, speaking in English. From Chancellor Helmut Schmidt he obtained West German support for the weakened franc. Abandoning his stance of political aloofness, he attacked the French Left in April. But in his book *Démocratie Française* ("French Democracy"), published in October, he advocated a middle road between capitalism and socialism.

Giscard's political career began with his election to the National Assembly in 1956. He later served as minister for economics and finance (1962–66, 1969–74). As leader of the centrist Independent Republican Party, he was elected president of France in 1974.

HEARST, PATRICIA CAMPBELL
American heiress, born Feb. 20, 1954, in San Francisco, Calif. She was found guilty in March on charges of armed robbery and use of a firearm to commit a felony. In September she was sentenced in San Francisco to seven years in prison. Later she was transferred from a jail in Pleasanton, Calif., to San Diego, because of reported threats against her life. On Nov. 19, free on $1,500,000 bail, she re-

On Nov. 19, free on bail after fourteen months in prison, Patricia Hearst grins for the newsmen in San Francisco.

turned to her parents' home in San Francisco. An appeal of the armed robbery conviction was pending, as was an eleven-count indictment in Los Angeles involving charges stemming from a street shooting. In a December interview she said that her 1974 kidnappers "got exactly what they deserved" when they were killed in a gun battle.

The granddaughter of the newspaper publisher William Randolph Hearst, Patricia ("Patty") Hearst was a student in Berkeley, Calif., in February, 1974, when she was kidnapped by members of the self-styled revolutionary Symbionese Liberation Army. Although her father disbursed $2,000,000 to procure her freedom, she stayed with her captors and participated in their activities, including the San Francisco bank robbery for which she was later convicted. In September, 1975, she was captured by the police and was held without bail for fourteen months.

HUA KUO-FENG
Chairman of the Chinese Communist Party and premier of the People's Republic of China. Thought to be in his fifties, he was born in Shansi Province, northern China. After the death in January of the nation's first premier, Chou En-lai (*see* OBITUARIES), Hua, then minister of public security,

Hua Kuo-feng acknowledges the applause of a reported 1,000,000 Chinese in Peking on Oct. 24. He had succeeded Mao Tse-tung as chairman of the Chinese Communist Party.

was named acting premier. In April he became full premier and party first vice chairman. In the struggle for the premiership he apparently edged out Chou En-lai's chosen successor, Teng Hsiao-ping. On Oct. 12 Hua was named to succeed Mao Tse-tung (*see* OBITUARIES) as party chairman. He apparently led the campaign against the "gang of four"; the purged Chinese leaders, he said in a December speech, could have "touched off a major civil war."

Hua emerged as a political leader in Shansi Province in 1947. In 1955 he was party secretary of the home district, in Hunan Province, of Mao Tse-tung. As deputy governor of Hunan (1958–67) he became known as an expert in agriculture. Made a member of the party's Central Committee in 1969, he was called to Peking by Mao in 1971 and put in charge of agricultural affairs. Two years later he became a member of the powerful Politburo. In 1975 Hua was named one of China's twelve vice premiers and given control of public security. Foreign visitors have described him as tall, affable, and a good listener.

JENNER, BRUCE

American athlete, born Oct. 28, 1949, in Mount Kisco, N.Y. A dream came true for Jenner in July when he was awarded a gold medal as winner of the decathlon at the Olympic Games in Montréal, Canada. He scored 8618 points and won recognition as the world's greatest athlete for his outstanding performance in the 10 events, which included a discus throw of 164 ft. 2 in. and a 1500-m run in 4 min. 12.61 sec. The photogenic new

champion realized another ambition in October when he signed a multiyear contract with the American Broadcasting Co. to appear on television programs and in featured roles in television motion pictures.

A 1973 graduate of Graceland College in Iowa, Jenner belonged to the San Jose (Calif.) Stars (an amateur track team) and was an insurance salesman. He rose rapidly to superstardom, winning first place in the 1974 and 1976 Amateur Athletic Union decathlon competitions. In 1975 he established a world record of 8524 points in a U.S.-U.S.S.R.-Poland decathlon meet.

KISSINGER, HENRY A(LFRED)

U.S. Secretary of State, born May 27, 1923, in Fürth, Germany, and naturalized in the U.S. in 1943. Pursuing the energetic personal style of diplomacy recognized as his trademark, Kissinger scored at least a temporary success in September when Ian D. Smith, prime minister of Rhodesia, agreed to discuss Kissinger's plan for yielding power to the Rhodesian black majority. To cement support for his Rhodesian plan, Kissinger visited the surrounding nations of black Africa, as well as the Republic of South Africa, and informed them of developments. Reportedly, his underlying motive in African policy was to prevent the spread of Soviet influence. The U.S.S.R. had scored a considerable success in Angola early in the year.

A design to counter Soviet gains could be discerned in much of Kissinger's program. Early in the year he warned America's Western European

Henry A. Kissinger is greeted by well-wishers at Andrews Air Force Base near Washington, D.C., on Dec. 12. The U.S. secretary of state was returning from his last official overseas mission.

allies not to admit local Communist parties into government. At the same time he criticized the Soviet Union for increasing its military and naval forces and following a policy of "selective détente." When Mao Tse-tung died in September, Kissinger reaffirmed the U.S. commitment to normalizing relations with China and warned that the U.S. would regard any future Soviet attack on China as "a grave matter."

Kissinger generated some controversy in 1976. Information about his practice of approving secret U.S. financial support to anti-Communist leaders abroad, especially in Italy, continued to leak out, bringing him under Congressional fire. Also, Kissinger and his foreign policy were prominent targets in the 1976 Presidential campaign. The Republican platform's foreign policy plank, which abjured "secret agreements, hidden from our people," was viewed as an attack on Kissinger's brand of secret diplomacy. Democratic Party nominee Jimmy Carter also criticized him as a "Lone Ranger" pursuing a "one-man policy of international adventures."

MONDALE, WALTER F(REDERICK)

Vice-President-elect of the U.S., born Jan. 5, 1928, in Ceylon, Minn. While serving his third term as Senator from Minnesota, Mondale was selected by Democratic Presidential nominee Jimmy Carter as his Vice-Presidential running mate. Mondale conducted a vigorous campaign, attacking the Ford administration's record on such subjects as health care, unemployment, inflation, and social security. On Oct. 15 he took part in a televised debate with his Republican counterpart, Sen. Robert J. Dole.

Son of a Methodist minister, Mondale served two years in the Korean War and then obtained a law degree at the University of Minnesota. After only four years of practice, he was appointed state attorney general (1960) to fill an unexpired term. He was twice elected to the same post. A protégé of Minnesota Sen. Hubert H. Humphrey, Mondale was appointed Senator in his place in 1964, after Humphrey was elected Vice-President. He was elected to full terms in 1966 and 1972, and while in the Senate he concerned himself with civil rights and housing problems.

MOYNIHAN, DANIEL P(ATRICK)

U.S. Senator-elect from New York, born March 16, 1927, in Tulsa, Okla. In February he resigned from his post as U.S. ambassador to the U.N. where he had been a flamboyant, outspoken, and often controversial presence. Returning to a teaching job at Harvard University, he soon afterward sought and won the New York Democratic nomination for Senator. In the November general election he defeated the Republican-Conservative incumbent, Sen. James L. Buckley.

After naval service in World War II, Moynihan studied government and urban affairs at Tufts University. In 1955 he went to Albany on the staff of New York Governor W. Averell Harriman. In 1961 he became assistant secretary of labor under President John F. Kennedy; he continued in that post under President Lyndon B. Johnson. Moynihan was summoned from Harvard by President

U.S. Ambassador Daniel P. Moynihan casts a vote in the U.N. Security Council. He resigned in February and was elected U.S. Senator (D, N.Y.) in November.

Nixon in 1969 to serve as an urban affairs adviser. In 1973 Nixon named him ambassador to India, and in 1975 President Ford made him U.N. ambassador.

NIXON, RICHARD M(ILHOUS)

Former President of the U.S., born Jan. 9, 1913, in Yorba Linda, Calif. Nixon spent most of the year quietly on his estate at San Clemente, Calif., writing his memoirs. He enjoyed a brief resurgence of attention in February when Mao Tse-tung, chairman of the Chinese Communist Party, dispatched a Chinese Boeing 707 jetliner to California to bring the former President and his wife to Peking for a visit. On his return to the U.S., Nixon sent a report to the White House that was described as "useful" by President Ford.

Otherwise the year was not a heartening one for the former President. On Jan. 7 three federal judges in Washington, D.C., ruled against his suit to declare unconstitutional the 1974 Congressional law giving custody of his vast collection of documents and tapes to the federal government. On Jan. 15 he made a court deposition that he

had ordered wiretaps of seventeen newsmen and government officials in 1969. In sworn testimony for the Senate Select Committee on Intelligence, released in March, he admitted authorizing secret efforts to undermine the presidency of Salvador Allende in Chile in 1970. The day of July 8 was truly heavy: He was disbarred in New York State, while in California his wife suffered a stroke that left her partially paralyzed.

PAUL VI

Pope of the Roman Catholic Church, born Sept. 26, 1897, in Concesio, Italy. In the fourteenth year of his papacy, Pope Paul worked strenuously to uphold traditional Church doctrines while carrying out the decisions of Vatican Council II. In January, when the Italian parliament considered legalizing abortion, he urged the defense of the rights of the unborn; later in the month he warned that feminism ran the risk of "virilizing women or depersonalizing them." In April, with the Italian Communists making a bid for power in the June elections, he urged a vote against them.

Pope Paul VI, in spite of his arthritis, used a helicopter to reach his summer residence in Castelgandolfo.

Vice-President Nelson A. Rockefeller in the midst of the New York State delegation at the Republican National Convention in August. The telephone he displays replaced one that had been ripped out during the intense struggle over delegate votes for the Presidential nomination.

In May Paul criticized French bishop Marcel Lefebvre, who was fighting the reforms of Vatican Council II; later Paul suspended him while offering reconciliation in a handwritten letter. Via television satellite in August the pope spoke on the theme of Christian solidarity to a million Roman Catholics assembled in Philadelphia for the International Eucharistic Congress.

RICHARDSON, ELLIOT L(EE)

U.S. Secretary of Commerce, born July 20, 1920, in Boston. Nominated as secretary by President Ford late in 1975, he was sworn in in February. In March the President appointed him to head a cabinet-level task force and conduct a policy review of foreign payoffs by U.S. corporations doing business abroad. He and his task force prepared a bill (submitted to Congress in August) requiring all foreign payments to be reported to the commerce secretary. Richardson spoke out in support of President Ford's economic policy and worked for his election throughout the campaign.

After service in World War II, Richardson practiced law in Boston and held various government posts. He was governor of Massachusetts (1967–69), secretary of health, education, and welfare (1970–72), and secretary of defense and attorney general (1973). He resigned the last post rather than obey President Nixon's order to fire Archibald Cox, special Watergate prosecutor. In 1975 he served as U.S. ambassador to Great Britain.

ROCKEFELLER, NELSON A(LDRICH)

Forty-first Vice-President of the U.S., born July 8, 1908, in Bar Harbor, Maine. Having renounced intention of seeking the Vice-Presidency in 1976, Rockefeller spent much of the year campaigning in the northeastern industrial states for the election of President Ford and other Republican candidates.

The Vice-President addressed the National Governors' Conference in Washington in February, proposing a shift of the entire cost of welfare to the federal government. In April he reluctantly apologized for "speculating" that Communists had infiltrated the staff of Democratic Party Presidential hopeful Sen. Henry M. Jackson. In August, to emphasize party harmony, he was chosen to place Sen. Robert J. Dole's name in nomination for the Vice-Presidency at the Republican National Convention.

RUMSFELD, DONALD H(ENRY)

U.S. Secretary of Defense, born July 9, 1932, in Chicago. In January he urged the U.S. House of Representatives armed services committee to approve the Pentagon's increased budget for the fiscal year 1977 to offset rising Soviet military strength. June found him in Brussels, conferring with fellow North Atlantic Treaty Organization (NATO) defense ministers. From Europe he flew to Zaire and Kenya, where he discussed ways of helping those nations to strengthen their military forces against Soviet and Cuban buildups in Africa. He was the first U.S. defense secretary to visit Africa.

A Princeton graduate and ex-Navy jet pilot, Rumsfeld served as a U.S. Representative (R, Il

2

from 1963 to 1969. Later he was an assistant to President Nixon (1969-73), U.S. ambassador to NATO (1973-74), and President Ford's White House chief of staff (1974-75). He was named to the defense post in November, 1975.

SCHMIDT, HELMUT H(EINRICH) W(ALDEMAR)

Chancellor of the Federal Republic of Germany, born Dec. 23, 1918, in Hamburg. In the October parliamentary elections Schmidt led his governing coalition of Social Democrats and Free Democrats to a close victory over the Christian Democratic Union. Parliament reelected him chancellor on Dec. 15 by a majority of two votes. During 1976 he continued his policy of *Ostpolitik* (détente) with Eastern Europe. At the same time he opposed cooperation with Communist parties in Western Europe, and on a visit to the U.S. in July called on it to maintain its troop strength in Europe. In November he underscored his pragmatism when he told the Socialist International in Geneva that bad management, not ideology, was responsible for the world economic crisis.

Schmidt was minister of defense in the cabinet of Chancellor Willy Brandt (1969-72), joint minister of economics and finance (1972), and minister of finance (1972-74). When a spy scandal forced Brandt's resignation in 1974, Schmidt succeeded him as chancellor.

SCRANTON, WILLIAM W(ARREN)

U.S. ambassador to the U.N., born July 19, 1917, in Madison, Conn. He was nominated in February to fill the post at the U.N. that had been vacated by Daniel P. Moynihan. Although he criticized Israel in March, Scranton vetoed a Security Council resolution attacking Israeli policies in the occupied Arab territories. During the summer he declared U.S. support for majority rule in Rhodesia

even if achieved by violence. In November he vetoed Vietnam's application for admission to the U.N. because the country had not accounted satisfactorily for the Americans missing in action in the Vietnamese war.

A descendant of the family that gave its name to Scranton, Pa., the ambassador was educated at Yale University. He was elected to the U.S. House of Representatives in 1960, won the governorship of Pennsylvania in 1962, and campaigned unsuccessfully for the Republican Party Presidential nomination in 1964. After leaving the state capital in 1967, he held posts on various federal commissions and was a special assistant in the U.S. State Department.

TRUDEAU, PIERRE ELLIOTT

Prime Minister of Canada, born Oct. 18, 1919, in Montréal, Québec. The year saw a marked decline in the popularity of the debonair Trudeau and his Liberal Party, in power since 1968. In January business and labor leaders and members of his own party criticized his New Year's pronouncement that "the free market system" was dead. He quickly denied charges that he intended to introduce socialism. His policy of wage and price controls drew fire repeatedly; in October, on its first anniversary, 2,200,000 union workers struck in protest against it.

In September, with polls showing the Liberal Party at its lowest level of popularity in twenty years, Trudeau attempted to restore confidence in his government by reshuffling his cabinet. The effect on voters was minimal, for in the November election in his home province of Québec his party was defeated by the separatist Parti Québécois. With a referendum by Québec on separation from Canada now a possibility, the prime minister

West German Chancellor Helmut Schmidt eloquently emphasizes a point during a speech at Göttingen in August.

Canadian Prime Minister Pierre Elliott Trudeau talks with reporters on Nov. 15. Separatists had just won the Québec provincial elections.

Plains, Ga., is the next stop for world traveler Cyrus R. Vance, President-elect Jimmy Carter's choice for secretary of state.

declared that he would not use force to keep the province in the confederation.

VANCE, CYRUS R(OBERTS)

U.S. Secretary of State-designate, born March 27, 1917, in Clarksburg, W.Va. He was named secretary of state by President-elect Jimmy Carter in December. Vance was an early supporter of Carter and had prepared the candidate's position papers on international affairs.

A 1942 graduate of Yale Law School, Vance served in the U.S. Navy during World War II, then joined a New York City law firm. He became general counsel of the Defense Department in 1961. He next served as secretary of the army (1962–63) and deputy secretary of defense (1964–67). In 1967, as American envoy to Greece and Turkey, he helped prevent a war over Cyprus. In 1968 he was one of a group who advised President Lyndon B. Johnson to negotiate an end to the Vietnam war; he also took part in the early unsuccessful peace negotiations in Paris.

WALDHEIM, KURT

Secretary-General of the U.N., born Dec. 21, 1918, near Vienna, Austria. In December the U.N. Security Council approved Waldheim for a second five-year term as secretary-general; with only to-

ken opposition, the General Assembly reelected him by acclamation.

During his first term Waldheim developed an energetic diplomatic style and a technical command of protocol that won him the approval of the U.N. members. He did often face criticism, however, as in October when the U.S. charged him with yielding to pressure in appointing unqualified candidates to U.N. jobs. During the year the secretary-general shuttled tirelessly among U.N. delegates and across continents as he tried to bring peace to such trouble spots as Angola, Cyprus, the Middle East, the Sahara, and Uganda.

WALLACE, GEORGE C(ORLEY)

Governor of Alabama, born Aug. 25, 1919, in Clio, Ala. In 1976 Wallace conducted his fourth campaign for the U.S. Presidency. As 1975 ended, he was ahead of all the other announced Democratic Party candidates in the public opinion polls. So he optimistically sought to garner delegates in the 1976 Democratic Party primaries across the country. Although paralyzed from the waist down and partly deaf, the Alabamian insisted he was physically able to carry out the duties of the Presidency. His chances were badly hurt by primary defeats in Florida and North Carolina in March,

297

Barbara Walters smiles at Harry Reasoner, who coanchors the ABC "Evening News" with her. She joined the program on Oct. 4.

and by June 8 he had won only 168 delegates and stood fifth among the Democratic Presidential hopefuls. He had spent about $10,000,000 electioneering. On June 9 he released his delegates to Jimmy Carter, the former Georgia governor who seemed to be the inevitable candidate. Wallace was a featured speaker at the Democratic Party convention in July.

WALTERS, BARBARA

American television journalist, born Sept. 25, 1931, in Boston, Mass. On April 22 she accepted a contract that promised her $1,000,000 a year for five years, making her the highest-paid journalist in history as well as the first woman to coanchor a prime time nightly network news program on television. Her contract with the American Broadcasting Co. stipulated that she was to appear on the network's "Evening News" program with Harry Reasoner as the other anchor person, and to serve as host for occasional special interview programs. Her first appearance on the nightly news occurred on Oct. 4 and was a news event in itself. And her first special, in December, was a success in the ratings.

A 1954 graduate of Sarah Lawrence College, Bronxville, N.Y., Barbara Walters worked as a producer and writer for several television networks, including the National Broadcasting Co. She began to appear on NBC's "Today" show in 1961 and became the show's cohost in 1964, earning a reputation for her skillful interviews.

WILSON, (JAMES) HAROLD

British statesman, born March 11, 1916, in Huddersfield, Yorkshire. In March, Wilson, then head of the Labour Party and in his eighth year as prime minister of Great Britain, surprised the public

with the news that he would resign both positions as soon as the party could elect a new leader. On April 5 James Callaghan, Wilson's foreign secretary, was elected to succeed him, and Wilson withdrew to a back seat in the House of Commons. In May he was knighted by Queen Elizabeth II. During the following months he wrote *The Governance of Britain*, published in October.

On March 24 British Prime Minister Harold Wilson greets Queen Elizabeth II as she arrives at 10 Downing Street for a farewell dinner. Wilson had resigned on March 16.

Wilson, who first won a seat in the House of Commons in 1945, headed the Labour Party for thirteen years and served as prime minister for almost eight years (1964–70, 1974–76).

YOUNG, ANDREW J(ACKSON), JR.

U.S. Ambassador-designate to the U.N., born March 12, 1932, in New Orleans, La. He was elected in November to a third term as a U.S. Representative (D, Ga.). But in December he was named by President-elect Jimmy Carter to be chief U.N. delegate. Young had served throughout the year as a Carter campaign adviser, and his work paid off in the number of Blacks who voted for Carter in the November election. When asked during the campaign if he could name one person he would most wish to thank if he won the Presidency, Carter replied immediately, "Yes, just one. Andy Young."

Young attended Howard University and Hartford Theological Seminary. Ordained by the United Church of Christ, he became pastor of a Georgia church. He participated in the 1956 Montgomery, Ala., bus boycott and took a leading role in the 1965 civil rights march from Selma to Montgomery with Martin Luther King, Jr. In 1972 Young became the first Black to be elected to the U.S. Congress from Georgia since the reconstruction era. In Washington the Congressman took a special interest in the problems of black Africa, which he visited six times.   F.D.

Rep. Andrew Young (D, Ga.), appointed in December by President-elect Jimmy Carter to be U.S. ambassador to the United Nations.

PERU. In the face of severe economic setbacks, Peru's eight-year-old economic and social revolution shifted to the center in 1976. Devaluation of the sol on June 28 and the imposition of new economic austerity measures two days later led to a wave of strikes and student disruptions. In response, Peru's military government, headed by Gen. Francisco Morales Bermúdez, proclaimed a state of emergency, took over the nation's newspapers and magazines, and suspended the right to strike. The crisis culminated in the removal of Prime Minister Jorge Fernández Maldonado, the most radical member of the cabinet and the main proponent of an extremist revolutionary philosophy.

The underlying causes of the July political and economic crisis were rising inflation, high unemployment, and a staggering foreign debt to Western bankers who had little sympathy with the aims of the Peruvian revolution. To bring Peru back from the brink of bankruptcy, drastic cuts were made in federal expenditures and new taxes were imposed to increase revenues. (In compensation, a 10–14 percent wage increase was granted.) In addition to the June devaluation of the sol, a minidevaluation system similar to Brazil's was introduced. Between June and December the sol dropped by more than 50 percent against the United States dollar. These monetary adjustments were designed to restore the confidence of international leaders, who by December had extended an estimated $400,000,000 in new loans.

In an abrupt break with past revolutionary practice, the government divided Pescaperú, the state-owned fishing industry, into two entities. While fishmeal production remained in the hands of the state, the government returned the fishing fleet to the private sector to encourage private initiative and reduce unemployment. Many of the boats were bought by cooperatives and small enterprises. The government also played down the idea of worker ownership and control of private enterprises.

Similarly, the administration moved away from intense participation in Third World affairs in favor of improving bilateral relations. Peru agreed to pay the U.S.-owned Marcona Mining Co. for iron ore facilities which had been nationalized without compensation as one of President Juan Velasco Alvarado's last acts before his ouster in August, 1975. In addition to patching up relations with the U.S., Morales Bermúdez met with Brazilian President Ernesto Geisel in November. This meeting marked a major change—relations between the two countries had been frozen since 1968. Meanwhile, Peru found itself in an arms race with neighboring Chile and Ecuador. Peruvian arms purchases in 1976 included thirty-six fighter-bombers from the Soviet Union, at a cost of $250,000,000.

See STATISTICS OF THE WORLD.   A.K.M.

PETROLEUM. *See* ENERGY; ORGANIZATION OF PETROLEUM EXPORTING COUNTRIES.

PETS. Laws restricting owners, shippers, and sellers of pet animals continued to be introduced and implemented in 1976. In addition, existing but seldom-used regulations were employed against keepers and sellers of various classes of pets. In New York City and other densely populated centers, the growing pet population caused problems; agitation grew for the enforcement of laws requiring dogs to be leashed and curbed.

Cats and Dogs. Fanciers of purebred cats showed no dramatic change in their preferences, although some of the newer short-haired cat breeds made sizable gains in registration. Among dog owners the Rottweiler, still a comparatively rare breed, began to find much favor because of its utility as a guard dog. A large, strong dog used as a working animal in its native Germany, the Rottweiler gained recognition because of its allegedly superior stability of temperament over both the German shepherd and the Doberman pinscher, which were the most popular guard dogs.

Left: A peculiar overhung snout characterizes cichlids of the genus Labeotropheus, *like this specimen (approximately 4 in. long) from Lake Tanganyika, central Africa. Cichlids were popular additions to home aquariums in 1976.*

Below: A pair of bearded collies react to the news that their breed qualified in September for listing in the American Kennel Club stud book. The beardie, classified as a working dog, became the 122nd A.K.C.-approved breed.

In February the Westminster Kennel Club held its centennial dog show at Madison Square Garden in New York City. More than 3000 dogs were exhibited. A Lakeland terrier, Champion Jo-Ni's Red Baron, outpointed the favorite, an English springer spaniel, for the Best of Show award.

Other Pets. Tropical-fish hobbyists continued to pay high prices for new species of cichlids from lakes of central Africa, but unsettled political conditions there threatened further importations. The keeping of saltwater fish species continued its recent growth, and numerous first spawnings of marine fish in captivity were recorded.

Keepers of pet birds decided, evidently, that 1976 was to be the year of the cockatiel, a crested parrot native to Australia. Cockatiels became the most sought after of pet birds, and the prices of all varieties soon reached unprecedented levels. As a consequence, the breeding of these birds for profit became attractive to avicultural hobbyists.

Tarantulas and scorpions became more widely available for sale in pet shops than ever before, and another invertebrate pet, the land hermit crab, reached its highest level of popularity. These crustaceans (genus *Coenobita*), inexpensive and easy to care for, promised to be popular for many years to come. They have already outlived the vogue for the strangest "pet" of 1975 or any other year: the pet rock.

Hamsters, guinea pigs, and gerbils remained the most easily available rodent pets, partly because new livestock shipping standards called for by 1976 amendments to the Animal Welfare Act were not to go into effect until 1977. Rats and mice were to be excluded from coverage under the new shipping standards. N.P.

PHILIPPINES, REPUBLIC OF THE. As challenges to his one-man rule receded in 1976, President Ferdinand E. Marcos—with the apparent consent of his countrymen—tightened his grip on power in the Philippines.

Politics. In January, after a series of strikes and demonstrations, Marcos launched the biggest crackdown on dissidents that had occurred during the three-and-one-half years of martial law. Soldiers and police rounded up students, teachers, trade union officials, priests, and known Communists. Most were later released, but the temporary detention put an end to the public protests.

In the spring former President Diosdado Macapagal quietly circulated a book demanding a return to democratic government. After appealing unsuccessfully to the United States embassy for asylum, a fearful Macapagal called the Marcos regime "authoritarian" and went into hiding.

In October Marcos held a referendum on whether to continue martial law. Pro-democratic groups called for a boycott of the vote, but more than 90 percent of the country's 27,000,000 eligible voters, heeding a government warning that failure to vote would bring six months in jail, went to the polls and gave Marcos a landslide victory. Also approved were constitutional amendments empowering Marcos to rule by decree and establishing a 120-member interim constituent assembly. One month earlier, Marcos had announced the creation of a legislative advisory council. One of its more than 120 members was Imelda Marcos, the president's wife, who bolstered her position as governor of Manila and the country's second most powerful political figure.

Insurrections. Over the year the Muslim rebellion in Mindanao subsided considerably, as arms supplies from the neighboring Malaysian province of Sabah apparently dried up. Talks between the Philippine government and the Muslim separatists were held in Libya in December; Marcos claimed that the negotiations had resulted in an agreement in principle and hoped for a final peace pact by April, 1977.

Filipino troops dealt the longtime Communist insurrection in central Luzon a stiff blow in August, when they captured its leader, Bernabé Buscayno, and a number of his top aides. But in November the rebellion came to life again when guerrillas attacked five villages and seized arms from the local civilian militia.

Economic and Foreign Affairs. It was, all told, a good year for the Philippine economy. An oil strike of unknown proportions and several big international sugar deals contributed to a general business boom. Inflation was down to a manageable 10 percent, and the balance-of-payme deficit shrank considerably. There was a subs tial rise in employment. The government mated real growth at 6 percent for the year

In an attempt to expand his country's diplomatic horizons, Marcos visited Moscow from May 31 to June 3, and for the first time formal diplomatic ties were established between the Philippines and the Soviet Union. Diplomatic relations were also established with Jordan, Senegal, Tunisia, Vietnam, and Zaire. Marcos sent representatives to the fifth summit conference of the nonaligned nations of the world, held in Ceylon (Sri Lanka) in August.

In December the U.S. reported that agreement had been reached between Washington and Manila to give the Philippines $1 billion in military and economic aid in exchange for the use of Clark Air Base and Subic Bay Naval Base over the next five years. Marcos, however, denied that any such agreement had been reached, and the year ended on a note of tension between the two nations.

Domestic Developments. Two disasters struck the Philippines in 1976. In May floods caused by Typhoon Olga killed about 215 persons and left some 630,000 homeless in the northern region. Then, on Aug. 17, an earthquake and its resulting tidal wave struck Mindanao and neighboring islands; an estimated 8000 people died.

On May 31 Marcos signed a decree making Manila (instead of nearby Quezon City) the capital of the Philippines. The decree took effect on June 24.

See STATISTICS OF THE WORLD. R.J.C.

PHOTOGRAPHY. In a long-anticipated response to Polaroid Corp.'s challenge for dominance of the consumer photography market, the Eastman Kodak Co. in 1976 introduced its own system of self-developing photographs. The year also saw the United States Congress approve a proposal establishing a multimillion dollar project to document the nation through photographs and film.

Kodak Self-Developing Camera. Kodak's system, including a new type of film and two models of a new camera, was introduced on April 20. The heart of the Kodak process was a so-called instant film that yields fully developed prints in about eight minutes without the necessity of peeling off and discarding material. Each print bears an image $2\frac{5}{8}$ in. by $3\frac{5}{16}$ in. and consists of a complex, multilayered card containing dyes and other chemicals. When a picture is taken with the new film, special dye-releasing chemicals are exposed to light through the back side of the film. As the print is ejected from the camera, it passes between two rollers that break a pod of activator fluid contained in the print. Dyes produced by the interaction of the activator fluid and the dye-releasing chemicals then migrate to an image-receiving layer to form the color image.

Comparison of the Kodak and Polaroid instant-picture systems revealed few significant differences between them. Although the colors provided by Kodak's film were brighter than those of Polaroid's SX-70 film, the Polaroid pictures ap-

.A display case shows the "instant" cameras introduced with great fanfare by the Eastman Kodak Co. in 1976. The new products were promptly challenged by Polaroid Corp., which claimed patent infringements.

Right: A compelling 1888 portrait of the Maharao Raja was one of more than 100 original Victorian photographs of Indian life that toured galleries in 1976 under the title "The Last Empire."

Below, right: A book of photographs by Leni Riefenstahl, The People of Kau, caused controversy in 1976. No one denied the technical excellence of her studies of Sudanese tribesmen, but some critics detected in them a cult of physical beauty that ignored human individuality.

peared sharper. Prices for both new Kodak cameras were competitive with Polaroid's SX-70-type Pronto camera, although the Pronto was significantly lighter than the Kodak models.

Polaroid responded quickly to Kodak's move, filing a series of patent infringement suits less than a week after Kodak introduced its system. Most observers expected the litigation to take years to resolve, leaving the two companies to fight out their battle in the marketplace. At year's end the fierce competition continued, with Kodak reporting unexpectedly brisk sales. It was predicted that both companies would continue to introduce technical refinements of their instant-picture systems in 1977.

Federal Documentation Project. In September Congress approved a measure authorizing $6,000,-000 over a two-year period for the American Bicentennial Photography and Film Project, designed to document the U.S. in the wake of the country's 200th anniversary.

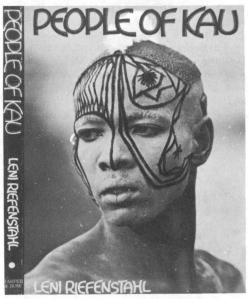

PEOPLE OF KAU

LENI RIEFENSTAHL

A 1961 portrait of Man Ray by Imogen Cunningham. Both beloved photographers died in 1976.

Citing federally funded photography projects of the 1930's as having "created a lasting national historic and artistic resource of priceless value," the project charter called for the creation of "a similar portrait, through photographs and film, of the people and communities of the United States." Administration of the program was assigned to the National Endowment for the Arts, which was also given responsibility for collecting and exhibiting the work produced. Detailed guidelines for spending the authorized funds were to be drawn up by the National Endowment.

Exhibitions and Publications. Major museum shows in 1976 included a retrospective at the Museum of Modern Art, New York City, of 195 photographs by Harry Callahan. Other New York galleries showed works by Alfred Eisenstaedt, Andreas Feininger, and Duane Michals. "The Last Empire: Victorian Photographs of India" premiered at Asia House, New York City, and toured to other U.S. museums. Memorable photographs of the seamy side of Parisian nightlife in the 1930's by the Transylvanian-born Frenchman Brassaï were shown at the Marlborough Gallery in New York City.

Exhibitions were the basis of highly praised publications in the cases of Brassaï (*The Secret Paris of the 30's,* published by Pantheon) and Richard Avedon (*Portraits,* Farrar, Straus & Giroux). Recent interest in the photographic docu-

mentation of the American past continued with *Alice's World* (Chatham Press), which offers pictures taken by a perceptive amateur, Alice Austen, who lived on Staten Island, N.Y., in the decades before World War I. Several books depicting American Indians were published. Most notable was *Crying for a Vision* (Morgan & Morgan), which includes the work of three photographers—John A. Anderson, Eugene Buechel, and Don Doll, S.J.—who lived at different times during the past century among the Brulé Sioux at Rosebud Reservation, S.Dak. Recent pictures by established photographers are collected in Ansel Adams's *Photographs of the Southwest* (New York Graphic Society), André Kertész's *Of New York* (Alfred A. Knopf), and Aaron Siskind's *Places* (Farrar, Straus & Giroux).

Deaths. Imogen Cunningham, Man Ray, Paul Strand, and Minor White died during the year; *see* OBITUARIES.   C.H.

PHYSICS. Details of a new theory of subatomic matter were confirmed by several groups of high-energy physicists in 1976. The reported discovery of a new stable element, however, could not be corroborated.

Naked Charm Exposed. Compelling support came from several sources during the year for the existence of a new ingredient of matter known as "charm," which was postulated as a means of preserving the theory that certain subatomic particles are made up of even more fundamental entities named "quarks." (The name was chosen from a line in *Finnegan's Wake,* an experimental work written by the Irish author James Joyce in 1939: "Three quarks for Muster mark.") The theory, first formulated in 1963, proposed that there were three kinds of "quark," and that any random three quarks or a quark and an antiquark (which would be identical but of opposite electrical properties) could account for the structure and behavior of all the known particles that are subject to the nuclear binding force. These particles, known as hadrons, include the proton, the neutron, and approximately 200 unstable particles that are found in cosmic rays and in high-energy particle collisions created in the laboratory. An additional requirement of the theory is that each species of quark possess three aspects, called "colors," which could explain the way quarks combine to form larger particles. The theory worked perfectly for the known hadrons, but a serious flaw developed when certain predicted decay processes in-

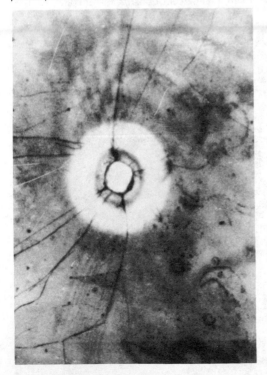

An actual photograph, magnified 100 times, of the piece of mica that was reported in 1976 to contain new elements. The spot in the middle is an impurity embedded in the mica, and the "halo" around the spot is radiation damage caused by the elements within. Because the halo is unusually large, some scientists suspected that superheavy natural elements had been found.

volving unstable particles did not occur. It was then that charm was posited as a fourth type of quark whose existence would prohibit those decays. Since the only purpose for bringing in charm seemed to be to reconcile theory with experiment, the four-quark theory became highly controversial. Yet it also offered an appealing symmetry to the world of subatomic particles, since there were four known leptons—the extranuclear particles that are not subject to the strong binding force. (These extranuclear particles include the electron.)

The rules of charm presupposed an entirely new family of particles, that is, new objects in the universe. These would be made up of either a charmed quark combined with its own antiparticle (in which case charm could be inferred from predictions) or a charmed quark combined with ordinary quarks (in which case charm would be apparent, or "naked"). In November, 1974, came the exciting news that a new type of hadron had been simultaneously discovered by two scientific teams: at the Stanford Linear Accelerator Center (SLAC) in California under the leadership of Burton Richter, who named it "psi," and at the Brookhaven National Laboratory on Long Island, N.Y., under Samuel C. C. Ting, who named it "J." (Richter and Ting shared the 1976 Nobel Prize in physics for this work; *see* PRIZES AND AWARDS). The properties of "psi/J" suggested that it was a charmed quark-antiquark combination, and the hunt was on for a particle that would display naked charm. At least nine more members of the new psi/J family were found. Then, in March, 1975, Brookhaven reported that a new naked-charmed particle had left tracks on a photographic emulsion, and in the summer of 1976 SLAC and the Fermi National Accelerator Laboratory (Fermilab) in Illinois found particles that had precisely the predicted properties for naked charm. But two unexpected particles were also discovered that upset the construct of a four-quark, four-lepton universe. From SLAC in 1975 came the "U" (for unknown), which seemed to be an additional lepton; from Fermilab in 1976 came "upsilon," the heaviest particle ever observed (six times the mass of a proton). The nature of upsilon and other experimental results led physicists to postulate a fifth and even a sixth type of quark.

Element 126 in Nature? In June a team of United States physicists reported the discovery of superheavy element 126 in ancient mica deposits from southern Africa. The heaviest elements known in nature are uranium, with a weight of 92, and some rare traces of plutonium 94. Extremely short-lived elements up to 106 have been created in the laboratory, and scientists believe there may exist an "island of stability" in the vicinity of 114 where the arrangement of protons and neutrons would allow for long-lived elements. These would probably be more fissionable than uranium and therefore capable of producing energy with far less fuel, or even devastating "pocket-size" bombs.

The search for the reported superheavy element began in 1969. At that time Robert Gentry of Oak Ridge National Laboratory found halos of damaged monazite crystal in the mica he was studying. They appeared too large to have been created by radioactive decay of uranium. Together with six other physicists, Gentry directed energetic protons with a small particle accelerator onto the atoms inside the halo. Some of the X-ray emissions of the excited atoms almost perfectly matched the wavelengths predicted for element 126, and others were close to the wavelengths of 116, 124, and 127. But other scientists were skeptical. Some pointed out that the giant halos could have been created by gamma rays or in a series of

decays of known elements. They also postulated that the wavelengths could have been produced in the process of atom smashing, rather than from the original material. The search for convincing evidence continued.

Other Research News. Soviet scientists announced during the year that they had produced a metallic form of hydrogen through the exertion of extremely high pressure; at lower pressures, diamonds and silica had been forced into a metallic state. In the U.S. a new hydrogen ion, with three electrons, was detected in a stream of excited particles. At Fermilab's synchrotron, protons were accelerated to a record 500-bev volts, making possible the detection of new high-energy-state particles.

Death. Werner Heisenberg, a founder of quantum mechanics, died during the year; *see* OBITUARIES.   M.J.C.

PLASTICS. *See* MANUFACTURING INDUSTRIES.

POLAND. Nearly six years had passed since the turbulent period when massive riots by Polish workers forced the ouster of Wladyslaw Gomulka as leader of the Polish Communist Party. In 1976 Edward Gierek, Gomulka's successor, learned that Poland's political climate was as volatile as ever.
Politics and Economics. Since 1970 the policies of the Gierek regime had produced notable improvements in Poland's standard of living, among them a 40 percent boost in real income. As a re-

An atomic clock is readied for a rocket flight in the June 18 Gravitational Redshift Space Probe. At 8700 mi. above the earth, the clock ran .43 billionth of a second faster every second, proving Albert Einstein's principle that time is slowed by the presence of a massive body, a cornerstone of his theory of relativity. Robert Vessot of the Smithsonian Institution directed the test.

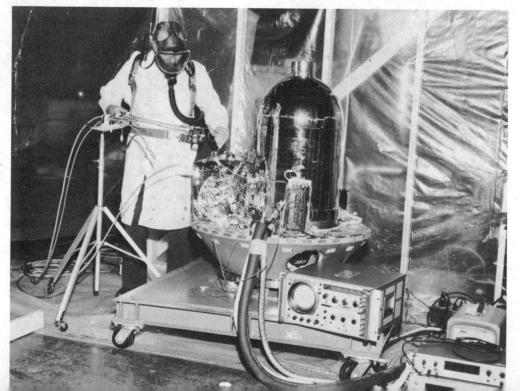

Edward Gierek (left), consulting with miners from Konin. The Polish Communist Party leader talked frequently to workers in an effort to prevent a recurrence of the disturbances that rocked the nation in June.

sult, however, the nation developed a huge balance of payments deficit. The government concluded that one economy it must introduce was a cut in the subsidies that had maintained the stability of food prices. On June 24 Premier Piotr Jaroszewicz announced to the *Sejm* (parliament) that prices would rise 69 percent for meat, 100 percent for sugar, and 40 percent for grain, effective June 28.

Worker reaction to the announcement was immediate and strong. Demonstrations broke out in several cities; workers from one factory ripped up part of the main rail line from Warsaw to the West. On the evening of June 25 Jaroszewicz addressed the nation on television and declared that the proposed price changes had been withdrawn. More gradual price increases were announced in July, along with restrictions on exports of food and other goods. On July 19-20, thirteen workers drew prison sentences for their role in the riots. At a meeting of the Communist Party Central Committee in December Gierek disclosed that the government planned to cut investment for economic development in order to pay for food imports. A revised economic plan released that same month gave a higher priority to production of consumer goods.

The food crisis was not the only example of public discontent. In February the regime was forced to alter several proposed constitutional changes because of public opposition. Intellectuals were particularly incensed by a clause which stated that citizens' rights were contingent on fulfillment of duties to the state. A copy of another protest by Polish citizens became available in the West in May. In it, a group calling itself the Polish League for Independence demanded freedom of association, information, and religion. The modified amendments were adopted by the *Sejm* on Feb. 10.

Cardinal Stefan Wyszynski of the Roman Catholic Church celebrated his 75th birthday in August. Despite his age, Wyszynski remained a vocal critic of many government policies. Antoni Słonimski, 80, a leading poet and outspoken liberal intellectual, died on July 4 after an automobile crash.

Foreign Affairs. The Gierek government maintained close ties with the Soviet Union, and Poland's constitution as amended in 1976 proclaimed that cooperation with the U.S.S.R. was one of the basic principles of Polish foreign policy. Gierek visited Moscow in November to seek financial aid for Poland's economic difficulties. The U.S.S.R. agreed to extend more than $1 billion in additional credits.

A set of treaties marking reconciliation between Poland and West Germany went into effect in 1976 (*see* GERMANY, FEDERAL REPUBLIC OF). Under the terms of these treaties, Warsaw agreed to allow ethnic Germans to emigrate from Poland to the West, and Bonn agreed to supply Poland with $900,000,000 in cash and loans. In June Gierek paid an official visit to West Germany.

See STATISTICS OF THE WORLD.   F.W.

POPULAR MUSIC. The popular music industry had another strong year in 1976, with established

stars like Stevie Wonder, Rod Stewart, and Diana Ross enjoying conspicuous success, and with a promising group of newcomers emerging on the musical scene. Noteworthy among these were Peter Frampton, Donna Summer, Gary Wright, and Natalie Cole.

Trends. With popular music presenting such a broad range of styles and sounds, it was difficult to discern any major trends. Some observers, however, noted an increased interest in returning to the old musical traditions of Tin Pan Alley, with its well-matched melodies and lyrics and its stress on romantic love. Neil Diamond's bestselling album "Beautiful Noise" (Columbia) was dedicated to Tin Pan Alley, and Paul McCartney's "Silly Love Songs" (Capitol) may have reminded listeners of the music that was once a staple of commercial songwriting.

This look to the past may well be attributable to the demographic shift toward an older population in the United States. In the face of a declining number of teenagers, the music industry perceived a need for offering more music attractive to the adult market. Some radio stations that formerly programmed only "top 40" recordings have already begun to emphasize softer sounds and middle-of-the-road musical styles.

In a country rediscovering dancing as a pleasant as well as healthy form of recreation, disco music continued to grow in popularity. In January *Billboard* magazine sponsored the First Annual International Disco Forum in New York City. Disco, although still young and developing, promised to produce its share of stars even as rock and soul music had in previous years. A novelty number, "Disco Duck" by Rick Dees and his Cast of Idiots (RSO), proved one of the surprise record hits of the year.

Concert Tours. Personal appearances continued to be a major part of the musical scene, with individual performers representing the predominant box office attraction. In August Elton John set what may have been an all-time record by grossing $1,232,000 for seven shows at Madison Square Garden in New York City, and the year's most explosive new performer, Peter Frampton, grossed $432,000 in just three shows at the same arena in October. Neil Diamond and John Denver had highly successful tours, while among the groups, the Beach Boys, Aerosmith, and Paul McCartney and Wings regularly performed to sold-out houses. Among the more unusual singing acts was the premiere appearance at hallowed Carnegie Hall, New York City, of George Burns, at the very young age of 79.

Copyright Law. One of the most important events of the year for composers, lyricists, and publishers

A new cult emerged in 1976 around the glamorous figure of Peter Frampton. The explosive sounds of the Briton's voice and guitar put him in the forefront of the rock scene.

On Feb. 28 the Captain and Tennille (Daryl Dragon and Toni Tennille) accept the Grammy for the 1975 Record of the Year. In July the pair did their prizewinning "Love Will Keep Us Together" at the White House for Queen Elizabeth II of Great Britain.

action from music industry spokesmen. Although the statutory licensing of the heretofore exempt areas of cable television, public television, and jukeboxes was welcomed, the licensing rates were not as high as had been hoped; it was uncertain just how fruitful the return from these sources would ultimately be. The annual licensing charge per jukebox, for example, was to be $8, compared with a fee of over $30 in Europe.

Morality in Songwriting. One issue that gained momentum as the year progressed concerned the extent to which sex- and drug-oriented lyrics and song titles should be allowed broadcast time. Many record producers defended the practice in light of present-day morality and the stress on freedom of expression throughout society, but some broadcasters were prepared to ban records that were clearly suggestive or profane as being harmful to young people. Considered among the more outspoken records were Johnny Taylor's "Disco Lady" (Columbia) and Rod Stewart's "Tonight's the Night" (Warner Brothers). Broadcast veterans were reminded that for many years CBS had banned Cole Porter's classic "Love for Sale" from its stations.

Recordings. The strength of the recording industry in 1976 was amply demonstrated by the fact that there were some 30 recordings in the Platinum Award category (more than 1,000,000 copies sold) and over 180 that earned Gold Award commendations (more than 500,000 copies sold). Heading the charts for the longest periods during the year were Peter Frampton's "Frampton Comes Alive" (A & M) and Stevie Wonder's "Songs in the Key of Life" (Tamla). Rock enthusiasts enjoyed "Fleet-

was the enactment by the U.S. Congress of the long-awaited revision of the Copyright Law, replacing the outmoded law of 1909. Under the new law, all works created after Jan. 1, 1978, were to be protected for the life of the composer and the lyricist and for fifty years thereafter.

Regarding its probable effect on income from performances, the new law met with a mixed re-

McCartney Is Still Flying High

A $50,000,000 scheme to get the Beatles together again fell through, but in the meantime, singer-songwriter Paul McCartney was proving that a rock star's life does not end at 30. In 1976 the 33-year-old McCartney released his sixth post-Beatles album, the third made by his own rock group, Wings. Then he brought Wings—one of whose members is his wife, Linda—to the U.S. for a smash cross-country tour (his first American performances in a decade). In September the McCartneys and Wings made history in Venice, Italy. They became the first modern rock group to make music in Saint Mark's Square and donated the concert's proceeds to help save the ancient city.

Ex-Beatle Paul McCartney.

The popularity of reggae music from the Caribbean continued to grow in 1976. Singer-songwriter Bob Marley, one of the top practitioners, enhanced his mystique late in the year by getting shot and slightly injured by intruders at his Jamaican home.

wood Mac" (Reprise) by the group of the same name.

Among other bestselling records of the year were a number of theme songs from popular television programs: "Theme from S.W.A.T.," "Welcome Back" from "Welcome Back, Kotter," "Happy Days," and "Nadia's Theme" from "The Young and the Restless," a daytime serial. C. W. McCall took advantage of the citizens band radio craze to make a runaway success of "Convoy" (Rocket). Another popular rock single was the Jefferson Starship's "Miracles" (RCA). A novelty instrumental on the top-singles charts for most of the year was "A Fifth of Beethoven" (Private Stock) by Walter Murphy and the Big Apple Band.

Deaths. Connee Boswell, Meyer Davis, Percy Faith, Bobby Hackett, Howlin' Wolf, Johnny Mercer, and Phil Ochs died during the year; *see* OBITUARIES. Other deaths included those of pianist and recording star Jan August (Jan. 17 at 71), rock singer and former Supremes member Florence Ballard (Feb. 22 at 32), songwriters Rube Bloom (March 30 at 73) and Ray Gilbert (March 3 at 63), and rock guitarist Tommy Bolin (Dec. 4 at 25). W.P.

POPULATION STUDY. The debate over the age-old demographic ideas of the British economist Thomas Robert Malthus was renewed with vigor in 1976. Contrary to the prevailing pessimism of recent years, some experts were cautiously optimistic about man's ability to disprove Malthus's famous thesis, put forth in 1798, that population tends to increase much faster than the supply of goods (especially food) available for its needs, thus guaranteeing that average worldwide living standards would remain near subsistence.

Herman Kahn, a noted American intellectual and coauthor of *The Next 200 Years* (published during the year), argued in May that the key to raising living standards was competent and flexible management. He believed the world had enough natural resources and sufficient capacity to improve technology to accommodate an ever-growing global population, which he predicted would reach 15 billion by the year 2176.

Kahn's ideas were echoed in October in a United Nations-sponsored report by an international team of economists. The highly researched study contended that world resources were adequate to support a rapidly increasing population since economic growth was limited not by physical scarcities, but by political and institutional deficiencies. The report called for far-reaching changes in developing countries and for a more equitable distribution of wealth among nations.

One analyst of the short term was less sanguine, however. Clifton R. Wharton, Jr., president of Michigan State University, told the World Food Conference (held in Iowa in June): "The stark fact is that thousands, if not millions, of people in the food-deficit nations are very likely to die of starvation in the next decade before excessive population can be brought under control."

Estimates and Projections. The U.N. estimated total world population in mid-1975 at 3.96 billion, up 71,000,000 from 1974. The combined growth rate of developing nations in 1975 was put at 2.34 percent, indicating that their population would double in thirty years. Industrial countries had an average growth rate of only 0.8 percent, suggesting that their total population would double in eighty-seven years.

See also UNITED STATES OF AMERICA: THE PEOPLE. D.L.N.

PORTUGAL. Portugal was torn by an attempted leftist takeover at the close of 1975 that endangered the democratization process. As 1976 began it was feared the congressional elections planned

TABLE 1
ESTIMATES OF 1975 POPULATION AND VITAL RATES OF MAJOR WORLD REGIONS,
PROJECTED 1975–80 AND 1995–2000

Item	World total	More developed	Less developed	Africa	North America	Latin America	Eastern Asia	Balance of Asia	Europe	Oceania	U.S.S.R.
Population, 1975 (millions)	3,964	1,132	2,832	401	237	324	1,005	1,248	473	21.2	255
Percent distribution of world population (1975)	100.0	28.5	71.5	10.1	6.0	8.2	25.3	31.5	12.0	0.5	6.4
Annual vital rates per 1000 population 1975–80 (estimated)											
Births	31.1	17.4	36.4	45.7	17.5	36.1	24.6	40.7	16.1	25.1	18.4
Deaths	11.9	9.4	12.8	18.0	9.5	8.3	9.1	14.6	10.6	9.0	8.4
Natural increase	19.3	8.0	23.6	27.7	8.0	27.8	15.5	26.1	5.5	16.1	10.0
1995–2000 (medium projection)[1]											
Births	25.1	15.6	27.8	39.1	15.1	29.6	18.1	28.1	15.3	21.2	16.3
Deaths	8.9	9.9	8.6	11.4	9.8	5.7	7.9	8.3	10.4	8.0	9.6
Natural increase	16.2	5.7	19.2	27.7	5.3	23.9	10.2	19.9	4.8	13.2	6.7

[1] Medium projection refers to the future trend considered most plausible in view of past and current circumstances.
Source: United Nations Department of Economic and Social Affairs, *Selected World Demographic Indicators*, 1950–2000. ESA/P/WP, 55, May 28, 1975.

TABLE 2
ESTIMATES OF MID-1975 POPULATION AND CURRENT RATE OF BIRTHS, DEATHS, AND NATURAL INCREASE, SELECTED COUNTRIES

Country	Mid-1975 population (millions)	Rate per 1000 population Births	Deaths	Natural increase	Years at which population doubles at indicated rate
Argentina	25	23	9	14	50
Bangladesh[1]	76.8	50	28	22	32
Brazil	107	37	9	28	25
China (mainland)[1]	839	27	10	17	41
Colombia[1]	24	30–33	9	21–24	31
Egypt	37	36	12	24	29
France	53	15.2	10.4	4.8	144
Germany, Fed. Rep. of	62	9.7	12.1	−2.4	(29)[2]
Great Britain	56	12.4	11.8	0.6	1,155
Hungary	11	18.4	12.4	6	116
India[1]	598	35	16	19	36
Indonesia[1]	131	40–45	18–21	21–24	31
Italy	56	14.8	9.9	4.9	141
Japan	111	17.2	6.4	10.8	64
Kenya	13	49	16	33	21
Korea, Rep. of[1]	35	24–28	8–10	15–18	42
Mexico[1]	60	42	7	35	20
Nigeria[1]	63	49	23	26	27
Pakistan[1]	70	36	12	24	29
Peru[1]	16	41	12	29	24
Philippines[1]	43	36	10	26	27
Poland	34	19	8.7	10.3	67
Singapore	2	17.8	5.1	12.7	55
Spain	35	18.3	8.2	10.1	69
Sri Lanka	14	27.3	8.9	18.4	38
Taiwan	16	23	4.7	18.3	38
Thailand[1]	42	37	9	28	25
Tunisia	6	36	10	26	27
Turkey	39	31–35	11	20–24	32
U.S.	214	14.8	9	5.8	120
U.S.S.R.	254	18.2	9.3	8.9	79
Venezuela[1]	12	36	7	29	24
Yugoslavia	21	18.1	8.6	9.5	73

[1] Rates are estimates based on sample surveys or census data. When data are uncertain, rates are given in a range.
[2] Number of years in which population will be half the present size.
Source: U.N. Population and Vital Statistics Report, Series A, Vol. 28(3), July 1, 1976. However, for the following countries rates are taken from primary country sources considered more recent than the published U.N. data: Colombia, Indonesia, Korea, Philippines, Sri Lanka, Taiwan, Thailand, Tunisia, and Turkey. Recency of data is an important consideration in these countries because birthrates are thought to be declining.

for the spring might have to be postponed. Order prevailed, however, and the elections were held on April 25 as scheduled, with political and military leaders agreeing beforehand to participate in the elections in peace and good faith.

Before the elections the government released several hundred members of the old security police who had been arrested during the 1974 revolution, and most of the military men and leftists implicated in the abortive 1975 revolts.

Election Results. The elections were lively and orderly, with about 85 percent of the qualified voters casting their ballots. The Socialists received 35 percent of the vote and won 106 seats, 26 short of a majority; the Popular Democrats 24 percent with 71 seats; the Social Democratic Center 16 percent; and the Communists 14.5 percent. The elected delegates assembled immediately and approved the constitution. Provisional President Francisco da Costa Gomes signed it at once and Portugal had a democratic government for the first time in half a century.

Next came the election of a constitutional president, which was held June 27. There were three principal candidates: Gen. António Ramalho Eanes, endorsed by all major parties; Adm. José Pinheiro de Azevedo, the prime minister, who had no political support but thought he should run to give the voters a choice; and Maj. Otelo Saraiva de Carvalho, former general and chief of security who had been reduced in rank for his part in the abortive revolt of November, 1975. The Communists, although they did not actively oppose Gen. Eanes, put up Octavio Pato as a civilian candidate.

Gen. Eanes won easily with 61 percent of the vote and took office on July 14, pledging to oppose "demagogic minorities" and to restore law and order.

The newly elected president promptly appointed Mário Soares, 51-year-old Socialist leader, as prime minister. On July 23 Soares swore in a coalition cabinet composed of 11 Socialists, 3 independents, and 3 military men. Most of them had served in previous governments. No Communist was taken into the Soares cabinet. The conservative views of President Eanes and the moderate policies of the prime minister seemed to bring a measure of peace and confidence. Some Portuguese who had left the country during the periods of turmoil came back, among them the former president, Gen. António de Spínola, who had fled to Brazil seventeen months before. In local elections held on Dec. 12 the Socialists won easily, and the Soares government in effect was given a vote of confidence by the people.

The Economy. The Portuguese economy was still in shambles, with runaway inflation and high unemployment. Conditions were aggravated by the influx of Angolan and Cape Verdian refugees, who fled to Portugal when these colonies became independent in 1975. Prime Minister Soares promptly initiated a program of austerity and ordered that lands forcibly taken by peasants during the revolution be returned to their rightful owners. At the same time Soares accelerated the agrarian reforms instituted by the previous government, turning over expropriated lands to the peasants and compensating the owners. These measures met with marked success, and agricul-

The New Team

After nearly fifty years of fascist rule and two years of postrevolutionary chaos, Portuguese voters freely elected a president in June: António Ramalho Eanes, 41, a former army chief of staff who promised to bring order and stability to Portugal's young democracy. For prime minister, Eanes chose a lawyer, 51-year-old Mário Soares, leader of the ruling Socialist Party, to help revive the ailing economy and uphold Portugal's year-old constitution.

President António Ramalho Eanes (right); Prime Minister Mário Soares.

Seen through a window of the White House Oval Office, President Gerald R. Ford works on his State of the Union speech. He delivered it before a joint session of Congress on Jan. 19, 1976.

tural production increased, in some instances by as much as 20 percent.

As part of its austerity program the Soares government imposed higher taxes on all imported goods, particularly luxury items. Other taxes were increased along with transport prices, and a program of mandatory savings bonds was initiated. The Soares programs, however, were being hampered on all sides: by a powerful, aggressive labor movement that was Communist-dominated; by strong opposition on both left and right; and by an ever-watchful military that had not relinquished its hold on the nation.

Foreign Relations. At Strasbourg, France, in September, the European Parliamentary Council admitted Portugal as its nineteenth member.

Portugal granted local autonomy to the Azores and to Madeira, island groups in the Atlantic, to forestall their demands for independence.

Timor, an undeveloped Portuguese colony in Malaysia, was annexed in July by Indonesia, which had occupied the territory after the Portuguese forces were ousted by natives seeking independence.

See STATISTICS OF THE WORLD.   A.R.

PRESIDENT OF THE UNITED STATES. Gerald R. Ford, thirty-eighth President of the United States, was born July 14, 1913, in Omaha, Nebr. In 1976, a year in which substantive affairs of state were overshadowed by domestic politics, President Ford withstood a strong challenge from former California Gov. Ronald Reagan to win the Presidential nomination of the Republican Party. But one of the most remarkable comebacks in the history of American politics fell short as the President was narrowly defeated in November by Democratic candidate Jimmy Carter. This first electoral loss of Ford's career ended his hopes of winning the Presidency in his own right after having succeeded Richard M. Nixon in August, 1974.

Domestic Affairs. Throughout the year the President and the United States Congress continued to spar over domestic and economic policy, with Ford emphasizing inflation curbs while Congress sought to reduce unemployment. Ford was unsympathetic to Democratic spending legislation, vetoing child day care and public works jobs bills. By the end of the year he had vetoed 23 bills, 15 of them while Congress was still in session. The legislators tried to override his vetoes 10 times and succeeded on 4 occasions. In October Ford signed a tax reform measure even though it failed to include his proposal to increase the personal income tax exemption from $750 to $1000. He also signed, with satisfaction, a bill extending federal revenue sharing through fiscal year 1980. His proposed fiscal 1977 budget of $400 billion was passed, with $13 billion added on, by a Congress still willing to be guided by the chief executive on economic matters.

The President proposed no major new legislation in 1976, calling instead for a "new realism" about the limits of government. He counted heavily on a steady economic recovery and made political gains during the first two quarters as production, business, and employment figures showed improvements. But the economic news turned bad in September. At the year's end, as Ford looked back on his domestic record, he regretted most his failure "to turn the economy around as effectively as I had hoped." *See also* CONGRESS OF THE UNITED STATES.

Ford responded to Congressional investigations of U.S. intelligence agencies with a series of executive orders and appointments beginning in February. Central Intelligence Agency (C.I.A.) Director George Bush was given broader authority over all foreign intelligence gathering. Both the C.I.A. and the Federal Bureau of Investigation agreed to observe restrictions on their domestic activities. But Ford balked on the question of stronger independent Congressional oversight of the intelligence agencies. He warned against hamstringing U.S. defense and intelligence capabilities. He also spoke out against Congressional foreign policy initiatives like the cutting off of aid to U.S.-supported forces in the Angolan civil war in January; he stated his belief that the executive branch must be fully empowered to maintain national security and represent the nation in dealings with foreign countries.

The President led the nation in celebrating its 200th anniversary of independence on July 4, participating in several major events over a five-day period. On July 4 he spoke at Valley Forge, Pa., at Independence Hall in Philadelphia, and on board the U.S.S. *Forrestal* in New York harbor. *See* BICENTENNIAL.

International Affairs. The President's greatest foreign policy disappointment of the year was his failure to negotiate a second strategic arms limitation treaty with the Soviet Union. But critics—including, reportedly, Secretary of State Henry A. Kissinger—attributed the failure to Ford's own reluctance to further détente while that policy was under attack by political opponents. The President's greatest diplomatic success was the convening of an international economic summit conference at Dorado Beach, Puerto Rico, June 27–28. Heads of state from six Western nations accepted Ford's invitation to discuss a variety of fiscal, monetary, energy, and trade issues. At the conclusion of the conference, Ford hailed the talks as "a significant step forward in cooperation among industrial democracies."

Appointments. In January Secretary of Labor John Dunlop resigned after Ford vetoed a bill extending picketing rights that Dunlop had supported. Dunlop was replaced by W. J. Usery; *see* CABINET, UNITED STATES. When Daniel P. Moynihan resigned to run for the U.S. Senate, Ford's choice to succeed him as U.S. ambassador to the United Nations was former Pennsylvania Gov. William W. Scranton. The President accepted the resignation of Secretary of Agriculture Earl L. Butz in October. Butz had become a political liability when an obscene joke about Blacks that he told was widely published. *See* PEOPLE IN THE NEWS.

Campaign for the Nomination. Ford's campaign for election to a full term was dogged from the start by controversy and turmoil. His first campaign manager, Howard H. (Bo) Callaway, was forced to resign in March after allegations were made that as secretary of the army he had used his office to extract favored treatment for a Colorado ski resort. Callaway's successor, Rogers C. B. Morton, was replaced in August by James A. Baker 3rd, whose brilliant performance provided some of the Republican Party's few bright moments in 1976.

The challenge for the Republican Presidential nomination that Ronald Reagan offered was a formidable one. Ford started well by beating Reagan in the early primaries. But in March Reagan surprised practically everyone by winning in North Carolina. Reagan then took primaries in Texas, Alabama, Georgia, Indiana, and Nebraska, but the President stopped this succession of victories with a decisive win May 18 in his home state of Michigan. Emphasizing his record of "peace, prosperity, and trust," the President traded primaries with Reagan for the rest of the campaign, losing in California but winning in Ohio in June. Both candidates were just short of the number of pledged delegates needed for nomination at the Republican national convention. In July the balance of power began shifting toward the President, and on Aug. 18 in Kansas City, Mo., Ford was nominated on the first ballot.

Presidential Campaign. Given what they agreed were the President's limited talents as a campaigner, his advisers fashioned a strategy curtailing travel and emphasizing the three televised debates scheduled with Democratic nominee Jimmy

Carter. In what became known as the "rose garden" strategy, Ford stayed in the White House for most of September, dramatizing his incumbency through a series of well-publicized bill signings and other official actions. He soon began to close the wide gap in the polls that separated him from Carter. In the debates the President appeared to most viewers to be calm and trustworthy, but he blundered in the second debate by asserting, contrary to accepted fact, "There is no Soviet domination of Eastern Europe." In the closing weeks the President was forced to endure allegations that when he was a Congressman he diverted campaign contributions to his personal use. The Watergate special prosecutor, to whom the matter had been referred, cleared him of wrongdoing on Oct. 14, but the charges cast a cloud over Ford's integrity, probably his greatest political asset.

Despite all his difficulties, the President narrowed what once had been a 2-to-1 Carter lead in the public-opinion polls to a dead heat. On Nov. 2 the voters elected Carter the thirty-ninth President of the U.S. Carter carried states totaling 297 electoral votes to Ford's 241. His voice gone from the final ten days of campaigning, Ford asked his wife to read his concession statement the next day.

After a nine-day vacation in Palm Springs, Calif., the President turned his attention to the fiscal year 1978 budget and his own future. He placed his suburban Washington home up for sale and said that he planned to build a retirement home in Palm Springs. He was also expected to spend several weeks a year at his condominium in Vail, Colo., lecture occasionally at universities, and remain active in Republican Party politics.

See also ELECTIONS; REPUBLICAN PARTY; UNITED STATES OF AMERICA. T.D.

PRINCE EDWARD ISLAND. See STATISTICS OF THE WORLD.

PRIZES AND AWARDS. The following is a selected listing of prizes awarded during 1976 and the names of the persons who received them. For awards given in specific fields, see the appropriate subject entry, such as LITERATURES OF THE WORLD; MOTION PICTURES.

NOBEL PRIZES

For the first time since the prizes were established seventy-six years ago, all of the winners were citizens of the same country, the United States. The winners and their citations, announced in October, were as follows.

Chemistry. For his studies of the structure and bonding mechanisms of compounds known as boranes:

Lipscomb, William Nunn, Jr. (1919–), American chemist. Educated at the University of Kentucky and the California Institute of Technology, he has taught at the University of Minnesota (1946–59) and, since 1959, at Harvard University. Working with borane compounds, which are made of boron and hydrogen, he used X-ray diffraction and quantum mechanics to determine their geometric structure and predict their reactions. Boranes have potential applications in cancer therapy and polymer chemistry.

Economics. For "his achievements in the fields of consumption analysis, monetary history and theory, and for his demonstration of the complexity of stabilization policy":

Friedman, Milton (1912–), American economist and, since 1946, teacher at the University of Chicago. The school of economic thought he founded there is known as the Chicago School. He was for a while an adviser to President Richard M. Nixon. His principles, which favor deregulation of the economy and a free-floating money exchange rate, have influenced recent government policy. One notable conclusion from his studies is that consumers spend a constant fraction of their income on consumption. Another is that the money supply should be increased at a rate in proportion to the anticipated growth of the economy. Among his writings are *A Theory of the Consumption Function* (1957) and (with Anna Schwartz) *Monetary History of the United States, 1867–1960* (1961).

Literature. For "the human understanding and subtle analysis of contemporary culture that are combined in his work":

Bellow, Saul (1915–), Canadian-born American novelist. A professor of English at the University of Chicago, Bellow has written short stories, nonfiction, and drama, but is best known for his novels, which include *Dangling Man* (1944), *The Victim* (1947), *The Adventures of Augie March* (1953), *Seize the Day* (1956), *Henderson the Rain King* (1959), *Herzog* (1964), *Mr. Sammler's Planet* (1970), and *Humboldt's Gift* (1975). According to the citation that was issued by the prize committee, his work is characterized by "exuberant ideas, flashing irony, hilarious comedy, and burning compassion."

Peace Prize. No peace prize was awarded in 1976.

Physics. For the discovery of a new type of elementary particle named "J" or "psi":

Richter, Burton (1931–), American physicist. In 1956, after earning a PH.D. in physics at the Massachusetts Institute of Technology, he became associated with the high energy physics laboratory at Stanford University. Working at the Stanford linear accelerator with a team of thirty-four other scientists, he produced in 1974 collisions of electrons and positrons that caused the materializ

The 1976 Nobel Prize-winners, all American, at the awards ceremony at Stockholm City Hall in December. They are (from left) Burton Richter, Samuel Ting, William Lipscomb, Baruch Blumberg, Daniel Gajdusek, Saul Bellow, and Milton Friedman.

tion of a new kind of subatomic particle, which he named the psi particle.

Ting, Samuel Chao Chung (1936–), American physicist. Born in Michigan, he was reared in China. After returning to the U.S. and obtaining a PH.D. at the University of Michigan, he worked at the European Nuclear Research Center in Geneva and at Columbia University. In 1967 he joined the Massachusetts Institute of Technology as a professor of physics. In 1974, at the Brookhaven National Laboratory, Long Island, N.Y., he headed an experimental team of fourteen scientists that produced a subnuclear particle, the J particle, by bombarding stationary protons with high energy protons. This discovery was identical to and was made almost simultaneously with the discovery made by the team headed by Richter and named the psi particle.

Physiology or Medicine. For "their discoveries concerning new mechanisms for the origin and dissemination of infectious diseases":

Blumberg, Baruch Samuel (1925–), American biochemist. Holder of an M.D. from Columbia University's College of Physicians and Surgeons and a PH.D. in biochemistry from Oxford University, he became in 1974 a professor of medical genetics at the Institute for Cancer Research of the University of Pennsylvania Medical School. His research led to a test used in screening donated blood for hepatitis viruses and the development of an experimental vaccine for use against the disease.

Gajdusek, Daniel Carleton (1923–), American virologist and pediatrician. A graduate of Harvard Medical School, he did research at the California Institute of Technology before joining the National Institute of Neurological and Communicative Disorders and Stroke in Bethesda, Md., in 1958. His study of kuru, an often fatal disease of the Fore tribe in New Guinea, led to the identification of a very slow-growing virus that causes it;

the study also proved to have implications for the study of other poorly understood diseases.

PULITZER PRIZES

The 1976 prizes were announced on May 3. A special award was given posthumously to Scott Joplin, "the King of Ragtime," for his contribution to American music.

Biography. Richard Warrington Baldwin Lewis, *Edith Wharton: A Biography.*

Commentary. Walter "Red" Smith of the New York *Times* for his sports columns.

Criticism. Alan M. Kriegsman of the Washington *Post* for his writing about dance.

Drama. *A Chorus Line,* conceived, choreographed, and directed by Michael Bennett, book by James Kirkwood and Nicholas Dante, music by Marvin Hamlisch, lyrics by Edward Kleban.

Editorial Cartooning. Tony Auth of the Philadelphia *Inquirer* for work throughout 1975.

Editorial Writing. Philip P. Kerby of the Los Angeles *Times* for editorials against government secrecy and judicial censorship.

Fiction. Saul Bellow, *Humboldt's Gift.*

General Nonfiction. Robert N. Butler, *Why Survive? Being Old in America.*

History. Paul Horgan, *Lamy of Santa Fe.*

Music. Ned Rorem, *Air Music.*

Photography, Feature. The staff of the Louisville (Ky.) *Courier-Journal and Times* for a report on school busing in Louisville.

Photography, Spot News. Stanley Forman of the Boston *Herald American* for a series of photographs of a Boston fire.

Poetry. John Ashbery, *Self-Portrait in a Convex Mirror.*

Public Service. The Anchorage (Alaska) *Daily News* for its revelation of the influence of the Teamsters Union on the politics and economy of Alaska.

Reporting, General Local. Gene Miller of the Miami *Herald* for articles that helped to exonerate two men twice sentenced to death in Florida.

Reporting, International Affairs. Sidney H. Schanberg of the New York *Times* for his coverage of the Communist takeover of Cambodia.

Reporting, National Affairs. James Risser of the Des Moines (Iowa) *Register* for his exposure of large-scale corruption in grain export.

Reporting, Special Local. The staff of the Chicago *Tribune* for its investigation of abuses in federal housing.   F.D.

OTHER PRIZES AND AWARDS

Among the many other awards and prizes distributed during 1976, the following were notable.

Academy of American Poets. Copernicus Award of $10,000 to Robert Penn Warren (for lifetime achievement); $10,000 Academy Fellowship to

Stanley Forman won the 1976 Pulitzer Prize for spot news photography for this vivid action shot of people, plants, and a collapsing fire escape. It first appeared in the Boston *Herald American.*

Robert Hayden (for distinguished achievement); $5000 Edgar Allan Poe Award (to a poet under forty-five) to Charles Wright (for *Bloodlines*); Lamont Poetry Selection to Lisel Mueller (for *The Private Life*).

Bancroft Prizes for American History and Biography. Awards of $4000 each presented by Columbia University to David Brion Davis (for *The Problem of Slavery in the Age of Revolution, 1770–1823*) and R. W.B. Lewis (for *Edith Wharton: A Biography*).

National Arts Club. Gold Medal to R. Buckminster Fuller; Gold Medal for Literature to Norman Mailer.

National Institute of Arts and Letters. The Gold Medal, the institute's highest award, to Leon Edel for biography and Samuel Barber for music; the $10,000 National Medal for Literature to Allen Tate; the Niels Bohr Gold Medal, for contributions to peaceful uses of atomic energy, to Hans A. Bethe; the $5000 E. M. Forster Award to Jon Stallworthy; $2500 Loines Poetry Award to Mona

Van Duyn; $3000 awards to Robert Coover, Robert Craft, E. L. Doctorow, Eugene D. Genovese, Kenneth Koch, Charles Simic, John Simon, Louis Simpson, Susan Sontag, and Louis Zukofsky.

National Medal of Science. Awarded by President Gerald R. Ford to John W. Backus, Manson Benedict, Hans A. Bethe, Shiing-Shen Chern, George B. Dantzig, Hallowell Davis, Paul Gyorgy, Sterling Brown Hendricks, Joseph O. Hirschfelder, William H. Pickering, Louis H. Sarett, Frederick E. Terman, Orville Alvin Vogel, E. Bright Wilson, Jr., and Chien-Hsiung Wu.   L.A.S.

PSYCHOLOGY. Psychological research in 1976 was focused primarily on the workings of the brain.

Alpha Wave Research. It had been reported for several years that the production of alpha waves (8 to 13 cycles-per-sec. brain waves) could be controlled and increased through the use of biofeedback. Volunteers given cues of their own brain wave activity apparently learned to increase the production of those waves. The value of this control was never definitely established, but claims were made that alpha waves were linked to relaxation, tranquility, memory improvement, creativity, and even weight loss.

At the February meeting of the American Association for the Advancement of Science, the results of several years of intensive research on alpha waves were summarized by Martin T. Orne and Stuart K. Wilson of the Unit for Experimental Psychiatry at the University of Pennsylvania. They said that what appears to be voluntary production of alpha waves may be nothing more than a gradual adjustment to a stimulus, usually a light signal, that suppresses alpha. This cue light caused an immediate decrease in alpha in most persons tested, and as a subject grew accustomed to the light, alpha production returned to its original, normal level.

Brain Asymmetry. Research on the differences between the left and right hemispheres of the brain was summed up in October at a conference sponsored by the New York Academy of Sciences. In recent years it became evident that the left hemisphere, which controls the right side of the body, predominates in language-related activities (speech, logic, mathematics, sequential thinking); the right hemisphere has been found predominant in spatial-perceptual abilities (art, music, creative thinking), as well as in emotional responses. Because most people are right handed, it was assumed that most people are "left brained." But research now indicates that up to 40 percent of the population may be right hemisphere oriented or that the two hemispheres may possibly be co-dominant.

Heredity and IQ Levels. Suspicions of fraudulence were strengthened during the year against a classic body of work on heredity and intelligence by the eminent British psychologist Sir Cyril Burt, who died in 1971. Burt's most famous studies were of fifty-three pairs of separately reared identical twins; he reported persistent intelligence quotient (IQ) correlations for every pair despite sometimes markedly different upbringings, thus creating a strong case for inherited mental traits. An examination of these studies in 1972 by Leon Kamin of Princeton University revealed that the tabulated results were so unvarying as to be virtually impossible by mathematical odds. (Arthur Jensen of the University of California, an advocate of Burt's views, confirmed Kamin's findings but said many other researchers' results supported his own stated position that Blacks have an inherited inferior IQ.) In November, 1976, Kamin reported many other deficiencies throughout Burt's works. At the same time, the Sunday *Times* of London declared that Burt had fabricated much of the data, used pseudonyms, and "copublished" with two fictitious collaborators. The recipient of many prizes as well as a knighthood, Burt was so influential that he helped shape a three-tiered school system in England whereby children were assigned to rigid levels according to results of an IQ test given at the age of 11.

The conclusions of Burt and Jensen were also challenged by a 9-year study by Rick Heber and his colleagues at the University of Wisconsin of 20 black children whose mothers were retarded (with IQ's below 75). These children, participating in a preschool enrichment program called the Milwaukee Project, were maintaining above-average IQ's (110–120) after 3 years of normal schooling. Twenty children of identical background who did not enter the program averaged a score of only 80.   R.J.T.

PUBLISHING. New copyright legislation, increased federal funds for book and library programs, and the promise of postal reform all came as good news to the publishing community of the United States in 1976. Independent book publishers continued to merge with each other or with large holding companies. Book sales and magazine advertising revenues increased during the year, but daily newspapers continued to lose readers.

Copyright Legislation. The first comprehensive revision of the nation's copyright law, enacted in 1909, was approved by the U.S. Congress after two decades of controversy and debate. The compromise measure became law shortly after Congress adjourned in October. The archaic 1909 law made no mention of technological developments such as radio, television, recordings, photocopying, microfilming, and computer storage. The revised law was expected to make the U.S. eligible for full membership in the Berne Union, the most important international copyright agreement. Provisions of the new legislation include the following:

Photocopying by teachers, librarians, and archivists—a hotly contested issue—is now subject to strict limitations. The new law permits limited copying of books, magazines, and other works without liability. Wholesale reproductions (as for an entire school system) require royalty payments; systematic reproductions (as a substitute for periodical subscriptions) are forbidden.

Copyright protection will extend through the life of the author, artist, or composer who created the work, plus an additional 50 years. Under the old law, the maximum copyright term was 56 years.

Statutory copyright protection begins at the time of a work's creation, rather than at publication.

Copyright protection will be extended to English-language books and periodicals printed abroad.

Government Funding and Postal Rates. Overriding a Presidential veto, Congress provided higher levels of federal aid to education, including more money for book and library programs. School libraries, for example, will receive $154,330,000 during fiscal year 1977—an increase of $7,000,000 over the year before and $17,000,000 more than the Administration had requested. Publishers, educators, and librarians had demanded the in-

creases, stating that they were essential to existing programs.

Publishers were promised relief from skyrocketing postal rates, which the industry has termed "catastrophic." New legislation passed by Congress in September was designed to moderate future increases for book and magazine mailers and rescue the U.S. Postal Service from its deepening crisis. The measure provided a $1 billion annual subsidy for two years and created a seven-member commission to devise long-term solutions to postal problems. A key provision of the bill required the Postal Service to take into account the "educational, cultural, scientific, and informational value" of mailed materials in setting rates of postage for these materials.

Book Trade. The long-established trend toward publishing-house mergers continued as Doubleday & Co., Inc. (including its book clubs and bookstores), acquired Dell Publishing Co. and its subsidiaries (including Delacorte and Dial Press). Doubleday, perhaps the largest hardcover house, has published about 600 new titles each year. Dell, with a yearly output of some 500 titles, was ranked as one of the biggest paperback publishers.

Announcement was made by CBS, Inc., that it had acquired Fawcett Publications, a privately

From the left: Dustin Hoffman, Carl Bernstein, Bob Woodward, and Robert Redford. Actors Hoffman and Redford played the roles of reporters Bernstein and Woodward in All the President's Men, *the 1976 film version of the reporters' 1975 best-seller. As the year ended, the Washington (D.C.)* Post *reporting team had split up, with nearly $1,000,000 income from their new book* The Final Days *to be divided between them.*

The bomb-shattered car of Don Bolles, in which the Arizona Republic reporter was fatally injured on June 2. Inspired by the gangland-style attack on Bolles, a nationwide team of newsmen came together to carry on his work—a probe of high-level corruption in Arizona.

owned firm established in 1919. (It already owned Holt, Rinehart & Winston, W. B. Saunders Co., the Popular Library paperback line, and a number of magazines including Field and Stream.) Fawcett brought with it two paperback imprints, Gold

---

It Could Have Been a Collector's Item

Early on the morning of Nov. 3 sighs of relief echoed through the offices of the editors of the new Scribner-Bantam English Dictionary. On Sept. 15 they had sent the proofs of their new publication to the printer, in order to meet a January, 1977, publication date. They had decided, however, not to be conservative and list only the 38th President of the U.S., Gerald R. Ford. Through prescience or luck, they also included the 39th President—Jimmy Carter.

Medal and Crest, and several magazines including Woman's Day.

Paperback publishers continued to pay record sums for reprint rights to hardcover books. Avon Books outbid six other paperback houses with its successful offer of $1,550,000 for Simon & Schuster's The Final Days by Bob Woodward and Carl Bernstein. It was the highest price ever paid for paperback rights to a nonfiction book. Bantam Books paid $1,100,000 before publication for Dodd, Mead's Sleeping Murder by the late Agatha Christie. This was a record price for prepublication rights to a work of fiction.

New York City lost a major publishing operation when Time-Life Books transferred its editorial and business offices to Arlington, Va. A spokesman for the book division said that the move was made to avoid high corporate taxes in New York State.

Book sales during the first nine months of 1976 increased over 1975 in all categories except children's books. Bestselling fiction during the year included Trinity by Leon Uris (Doubleday); 1876 by Gore Vidal (Random House); The Deep by Peter Benchley (Doubleday); The Lonely Lady by Harold Robbins (Simon & Schuster); Dolores by Jacqueline Susann (Morrow); A Stranger in the Mirror by Sidney Sheldon (Morrow); and Sleeping Murder by Agatha Christie.

Nonfiction best-sellers included The Final Days by Bob Woodward and Carl Bernstein (Simon & Schuster); A Man Called Intrepid by William Stevenson (Harcourt Brace Jovanovich); World of Our Fathers by Irving Howe (Harcourt Brace Jovanovich); Your Erroneous Zones by Wayne W. Dyer (Funk & Wagnalls); A Year of Beauty and Health by Beverly and Vidal Sassoon (Simon & Schuster); Passages by Gail Sheehy (Dutton); and Roots by Alex Haley (Doubleday).

Periodicals. The magazine industry bounced back from a 1975 slump in advertising revenues. The Publishers Information Bureau reported that magazine advertising revenue for the first ten months of 1976 totaled $1.3 billion—an increase of 22 percent over the same period in 1975 and a record high.

Some of the fastest-growing periodicals in terms of advertising volume were the so-called city magazines (Chicago, Philadelphia, Washingtonian, Los Angeles, The Magazine of Dallas, and Texas Monthly), which have borrowed from the successful format of publisher Clay Felker's New York (circulation 364,000). In February Felker introduced a West Coast version of New York, the Los Angeles biweekly New West. Aiming for an initial circulation of 125,000, he expected to bring his new venture to the break-even point after investing $3,000,000 over a period of three years. *New West* faced its stiffest competition from the established *Los Angeles* magazine (circulation 100,000). In another expansion move, Felker introduced a national edition of his *Village Voice,* the Manhattan weekly that he purchased in 1974.

An exception to the prospering group of city magazines was San Francisco's *City.* The publication folded in February despite a $1,500,000 investment by publisher and film producer Francis Ford Coppola.

For the first time in its fifty-four-year history, Time, Inc., was confronted with a strike of editorial workers in 1976. The company's magazines (*Time, Fortune, Sports Illustrated, People, Money*) continued to publish with the aid of senior editors and administrative employees as more than 60 percent of the firm's 1000 editorial workers walked Newspaper Guild picket lines. The twenty-day strike over working conditions and distribution of wages was settled on June 21.

Newspapers. The New York *Post,* America's oldest continuously published newspaper, was sold in November for approximately $30,000,000 to Australian publisher Rupert Murdoch. Founded in 1801 by Alexander Hamilton and owned since 1939 by Dorothy Schiff, the *Post* became New York's only surviving afternoon daily when the *Journal-American* (Hearst) and *World-Telegram* (Scripps-Howard) folded in 1967. Like most other big-city dailies, the *Post* had lost circulation in recent years, dropping from 700,000 in 1967 to 517,000 in 1975. The new owner added the *Post* to his collection of 83 newspapers and 11 magazines worldwide, including Great Britain's largest-circulation newspaper *News of the World;* the London tabloid *The Sun;* the San Antonio (Texas) *Express and Evening News;* and the weekly U.S. tabloid *The National Star.* Murdoch declared that the *Post* would "continue to maintain its present policies and traditions."

The largest single purchase in U.S. newspaper history was made by 81-year-old Samuel I. Newhouse, who acquired Booth Newspapers Inc., a profitable chain of eight Michigan dailies (combined circulation 500,000), as well as the Sunday supplement *Parade.* Newhouse's investment in the chain was expected to amount to an unprecedented $250,000,000. He also owned 22 other newspapers, 5 magazines, and 10 television and radio stations.

The afternoon Hartford *Times* ceased publication on Oct. 20 after 159 years, leaving Hartford with one daily, the morning *Courant.* From 1972 to 1976 the *Times*'s circulation dropped from 132,000 to 69,000. Hartford was the fifteenth U.S. city to lose at least one newspaper since 1971.

The Wall Street Journal, the country's only national daily with ten printing plants around the U.S., launched a new *Asian Wall Street Journal,* based in Hong Kong. Although the Asian edition had its own staff, it printed much of the material appearing in the New York City edition. Some 40,000 words daily were transmitted from New York to Hong Kong via high-speed computers and satellite circuits.

Newspapers throughout the country continued to change formats as an answer to sharply increased newsprint costs. The New York *Times* reduced its 8-column page, used since 1913, to 6 columns of news and 9 columns of advertising on a page. The new format permitted the *Times* to reduce an 88-page newspaper to 84 pages without any reduction in content, resulting in a newsprint saving of about 5 percent a year. The tabloid New York *Daily News* switched from a 5-column format to one of 4 columns for news and 6 for advertisements. Similar format changes were introduced by newspapers in Baltimore, Chicago, Cincinnati, Cleveland, Denver, Houston, Memphis, Phoenix, Pittsburgh, and Washington.

In its annual statistical roundup, the 1976 edition of *Editor & Publisher International Yearbook* reported that daily newspaper circulation at the end of 1975 had dropped to 60,655,431, its lowest point in ten years. The number of daily newspapers in the U.S. decreased from 1768 in 1974 to 1756 in 1975.

The Bolles Case. The murder in June of Don Bolles, 47-year-old investigative reporter for the *Arizona Republic,* led to an unprecedented experiment in group journalism: a joint investigation of crime and corruption in the state of Arizona. Under the auspices of the Investigative Reporters and Editors Association, eighteen reporters from fifteen newspapers began a three-month investigation late in the year of organized crime in the state. Newspapers as diverse as the Chicago *Tribune,* the Boston *Globe,* and the Eugene (Oreg.) *Register-Guard* contributed reporters. A jointly prepared series of articles was to be written in 1977 based on the results of the investigation. *See* CRIME AND LAW ENFORCEMENT.

Deaths. Paul Gallico, Arnold Gingrich, Peter Lisagor, Leonard Lyons, Benjamin McKelway, and Roy H. Thomson (1st Baron Thomson of Fleet) died during the year; *see* OBITUARIES. Other deaths included those of Freda Kirchwey, editor-publisher of *The Nation* from 1937 to 1955 (Jan. 3 at 82), and publishers Albert R. Leventhal (Jan. 8 at 68) and Joseph W. Lippincott (Oct. 22 at 89).   R.F.

PUERTO RICO. The victory of a pro-statehood candidate in the November, 1976, gubernatorial election had surprising political repercussions.

San Juan Mayor Carlos Romero Barceló (right) meets with U.S. President Gerald R. Ford in June. Five months later he won the governorship of Puerto Rico.

Politics. On Nov. 2 San Juan Mayor Carlos Romero Barceló of the New Progressive Party (P.N.P.) upset incumbent Gov. Rafael Hernández-Colón of the Popular Democratic Party (P.P.D.). In addition to winning the governorship for only the second time since 1940, the P.N.P. made a clean sweep in the election. Candidates of the P.N.P. won mayoralty races in San Juan and Ponce, the two largest cities, and the party took control of both houses of the legislature. The election also proved to be a major setback for the pro-independence movement. The Puerto Rican Independence and Socialist parties together captured only about 6 percent of the vote, little more than in 1972.

On Dec. 31 United States President Gerald R. Ford, who had met with Romero Barceló in June, made a surprising proposal that the U.S. Congress act to make Puerto Rico the fifty-first state. Ford's proposal drew unenthusiastic responses from President-elect Jimmy Carter, from Gov. Hernández-Colón, and from elder statesman and former Gov. Luis Muñoz Marín.

The Economy. Although the island's economy began to recover in 1976 as U.S. industrial activity picked up, the surprise defeat of the P.P.D. was primarily attributed to economic factors. During Hernández-Colón's four years in power, the economy deteriorated considerably, as the island was hit by the worldwide recession and inflation. In addition to canceling development projects, the government had been forced to introduce new taxes and impose a wage freeze on public employees. These austerity measures, coupled with an unemployment rate of nearly 20 percent, contributed to the P.N.P. victory, despite the apparent economic turnaround and reduced inflation in 1976.

Puerto Rico was well received in 1976 in financial markets. A number of state entities, including the Government Development Bank and the Water Resources Authority, received extremely favorable credit terms in issuing and obtaining bonds. Major tax changes also brightened the economic outlook. Puerto Rican industrial incentives were improved, and new U.S. tax regulations permitted U.S. corporations to repatriate at will the earnings they generated in Puerto Rico, free of tax. The U.S. government also passed amendments to the federal food stamp program, allowing Puerto Rico an additional $52,000,000 in food stamps each year.

Independence Movement. Stymied within Puerto Rico, the independence movement gathered some momentum outside the commonwealth. In August a conference of nonaligned nations, meeting in Ceylon (Sri Lanka), called for Puerto Rican independence. A pro-independence rally was held in Philadelphia on July 4. Despite sporadic incidents of violence on the U.S. mainland, activities of pro-independence extremists were greatly reduced in 1976.

See STATISTICS OF THE WORLD. A.K.M.

Q

QATAR. *See* STATISTICS OF THE WORLD.

QUÉBEC. *See* STATISTICS OF THE WORLD.

R

RADIO AND TELEVISION BROADCASTING. The Presidential campaign dominated the airwaves in 1976. Court decisions and the continued ratings war among the three commercial television networks occupied the minds of broadcasters.

Carter Against Ford. Politics was the subject that dominated radio and television during the 1976 election year. From February until June the broadcast networks covered roughly thirty primary elections. Then they set up shop at New York City's Madison Square Garden for the Democratic convention in July and at Kemper Arena in Kansas City, Mo., for the Republican convention in August. From Labor Day until Election Day (Nov. 2) the two candidates—Republican Gerald R. Ford and Democrat Jimmy Carter—crisscrossed the nation, with television camera crews and reporters dogging their every step.

The highlight of the campaign was a series of televised debates between the candidates—three involving the Presidential nominees (Sept. 23 and Oct. 6 and 22) and one (Oct. 15) between the Vice-Presidential contenders, Senators Robert J. Dole and Walter F. Mondale, Republican and Democrat, respectively. The debates, the first since 1960, were made possible by a Federal Communications Commission (F.C.C.) ruling which exempted both press conferences and debates from the "equal time" requirement of Section 315 of the Communications Act of 1934; under this

A Nighttime Soap Opera Loaded with Dirt
The waxy yellow buildup on kitchen floors, impotence, adultery, anti-Semitism, mental breakdown—these are a few of the themes treated on the controversial television serial *Mary Hartman, Mary Hartman,* about a "typical American consumer housewife" coping with life in Fernwood, Ohio. Created by Norman Lear and starring a pigtailed Louise Lasser in the title role, the show premiered in January and was instantly seen by some as a profound comment on American culture, by others as a profound waste of time. Whatever its significance, MH2 attracted a wide audience despite its rejection by major networks and began its second season in October.

Mary Hartman (Louise Lasser) and husband Tom (Greg Mullavey).

A series of three television debates provided the highlights of the 1976 Presidential campaign. President Gerald R. Ford (right) and Jimmy Carter face a panel of newsmen during their first encounter, at Philadelphia's Walnut Street Theater on Sept. 23.

ruling the debates, sponsored by the League of Women Voters, were classed as news events which television was free to cover without having to give other candidates comparable broadcast time. The first of the three 90-min. Presidential debates was marred by an embarrassing 27-min. interruption when a technical failure caused the microphones to go silent.

The Ford campaign spent about $8,500,000 on television and Carter spent $8,000,000—each from a campaign chest of about $22,000,000. The incumbent's television campaign was masterminded by John Deardourff of the advertising agency Bailey, Deardourff & Eyre, and the challenger's by Gerald Rafshoon, an adman from Atlanta.

On election night all three commercial networks remained on the air until well after 3 A.M. (E.S.T.) because of the closeness of the race. Each spent over $3,000,000 on that single evening of broadcast journalism to provide viewers with computer projections and analyses of national, state, and local contests.

Network statisticians estimated that 120,000,000 viewers watched some part of the televised returns, comparable to the 1972 audience but far short of the 142,000,000 people who watched in 1968. Non-network stations around the country increased their proportion of the audience to almost 25 percent, double their normal share, indicating that many viewers were searching for entertainment rather than election news.

Legal Issues. Two court cases were of particular interest to broadcasters during the year. In Los Angeles United States District Judge Warren J. Ferguson ruled on Nov. 3 that the controversial "family viewing" concept, which sought to restrict the hours of 7 to 9 P.M. (E.S.T. and P.S.T.) to programming suitable for the whole family, violated First Amendment guarantees of freedom of speech.

A number of West Coast writers, directors, producers, and actors (backed by the National Citizens Committee for Broadcasting and Action for Children's Television) had claimed in their suit that the F.C.C. had, in effect, coerced the networks and the National Association of Broadcasters into adopting the family hour, and that such action was an unwarranted intrusion by government into the content of television programming. Judge Ferguson agreed. The plaintiffs had, he said, "exposed a joint agreement on the part of the three major networks, the F.C.C. and the National Association of Broadcasters (N.A.B.) to permit one group—the N.A.B. television code review board—to act as a national board of censors for American television. The plaintiffs have evidenced a successful attempt by the F.C.C. to pressure the networks and the N.A.B. into adopting a programming policy that they did not wish to adopt." The N.A.B. appealed the ruling, and all three networks said they would continue to adhere voluntarily to the family viewing plan.

The second court case involved an agreement reached on Nov. 17 between the National Broadcasting Co. (NBC) and the Justice Department to settle NBC's part of a two-year-old antitrust suit against all three networks. The Justice Department had been seeking to restrict networks from sharing either in the ownership of programs they purchased from independent producers or in the profits from syndication and other ancillary rights. NBC agreed to certain formulas to satisfy the Justice Department's objections, but the Columbia Broadcasting System (CBS) and American Broadcasting Co. (ABC) said they would persist in challenging the suit.

New Programs. Most of the new shows for the 1976–77 television season were judged by critics to hold as little promise as those of earlier seasons. ABC had canceled nine shows, including its seven-year veteran "Marcus Welby," along with "The Rookies," "S.W.A.T.," "Harry O," and "Swiss Family Robinson." Among those it inaugurated in the fall were "The Tony Randall Show," "The Captain and Tennille," "The Nancy Walker Show," and "Holmes and Yoyo"; the last two did not survive into 1977. The surprise hit of ABC's season was "Charlie's Angels," an action-adventure series starring three beautiful investigators (played by Farrah Fawcett-Majors, Kate Jackson, and Jaclyn Smith) who work for a private eye never seen on camera. Another hit of the ABC season was a sec-

ond cycle of the miniseries "Rich Man, Poor Man," based on an Irwin Shaw novel. Earlier in the year ABC successfully spun off a nostalgic comedy, "Laverne & Shirley," from its top-rated "Happy Days."

At CBS "Medical Center" (another seven-year veteran) was canceled, as were "Cannon," "Bronk," "Sara," and "Popi." Among the newcomers: "Ball Four," a baseball comedy based on pitcher Jim Bouton's best-selling book of the same name (it was among the earliest casualties); "Alice," an outgrowth of the hit movie *Alice Doesn't Live Here Anymore*; "Executive Suite," a story of life among America's corporate chieftains; and "All's Fair," a Norman Lear comedy series about a middle-aged, conservative male newspaper columnist and a youthful, liberal female photojournalist.

NBC performed the most radical surgery on its old schedule, dropping nine series, adding nine

Fonzie, or "The Fonz," played by Henry Winkler on ABC's "Happy Days," was more than the top attraction on television's top-rated show—he was a culture hero, a beloved wise guy to children and teenagers.

Jaclyn Smith, Farrah Fawcett-Majors, and Kate Jackson (left to right)—three private eyes of eye-catching beauty—made "Charlie's Angels" the most successful of the new fall television programs.

new ones, and shifting time periods on many of its returning shows. Among those canceled: "Joe Forrester," "The Rich Little Show," "Petrocelli," and "Ellery Queen." The new entries included "Van Dyke and Company," a variety show starring Dick Van Dyke (shuffled from one time slot to another and finally canceled); "Baa Baa Black Sheep," a World War II adventure series based on the career of Marine Corps flying ace Maj. Gregory ("Pappy") Boyington; and "Serpico," a police drama based on the Peter Maas book and Sidney Lumet movie of the same name. Also in the NBC schedule were two experiments, "Best Seller" and "The Big Event." The former was a series which adapted such novels as Taylor Caldwell's *Captains and the Kings* and Anton Myrer's *Once an Eagle* into miniseries of 60-min. episodes. "The Big Event" had its most memorable moment in November when it offered the first telecast of the classic film *Gone With the Wind.* The screening attracted the largest audience for any movie in the history of television: a 47.6 Nielsen rating, and a 65 percent share of all the sets in use for a total audience estimated at 110,000,000. "Saturday Night," NBC's hit from the previous season, re-

mained popular despite the departure of performer-writer Chevy Chase.

Awards. The big winner in the 1976 Emmy Awards, presented by the National Academy of Television Arts and Sciences, was ABC, due mostly to its drama special "Eleanor and Franklin." This play set a new record for the number of Emmys handed out to one show—11. ABC ended up with a total of 17 Emmys, compared to 15 for CBS, 11 for NBC, and 6 for the Public Broadcasting Service (PBS).

"The Mary Tyler Moore Show" was voted the outstanding comedy series, and "Police Story" won for outstanding drama series. Other awards went to actors Peter Falk for "Columbo," Jack Albertson for "Chico and the Man," Hal Holbrook for "Sandburg's Lincoln," Anthony Hopkins for "The Lindbergh Kidnapping Case," Rosemary Harris for "Notorious Woman," Susan Clark for "Babe," Kathryn Walker for "The Adams Chronicles," Chevy Chase for "NBC's Saturday Night," Ed Flanders for "A Moon for the Misbegotten," and Gordon Jackson for "Upstairs, Downstairs."

Public Television. The PBS began the year with a new president, Lawrence K. Grossman, who boasted: "Our audiences are up 34 percent at night and 50 percent over two years. This year ... more than 50 percent of television homes are watching public television in the course of a single rating period." Public television's growth was indeed impressive, and Grossman stressed his intention to attract larger audiences. He inaugurated so-called theme nights with individual evenings devoted to the performing arts, variety, specials, drama, or public affairs.

Among public television's better-received offerings of the year were the dramas "Eccentricities of a Nightingale," "Cyrano de Bergerac," and "How Green Was My Valley"; dance programs by the City Center Joffrey Ballet, the Martha Graham Dance Company, and Twyla Tharp; and various musical performances in the "Live from Lincoln Center" series.

One of the most ambitious of public television's efforts was "Visions," produced at KCET in Los Angeles under the supervision of Barbara Schultz. The series was conceived as a drama showcase that would give young American writers an opportunity to be heard on television and to develop their talents. Critical reception to its first year was generally excellent.

Personalities. A number of personnel shifts in the upper echelons of broadcasting surprised the industry in 1976. The most unexpected was the firing by CBS board chairman William S. Paley of his putative heir apparent, 41-year-old Arthur Taylor, from the presidency of CBS. Paley, who at age 75 had headed CBS for 48 years and built it into a $2 billion empire, announced in November that John D. Backe, 44, president of the CBS Publishing Group, would succeed Taylor. Paley also let it be known that he would himself retire in April, 1977, as the company's chief executive officer, while retaining the post of chairman.

What caused the rift? Nobody knew, except that, in the words of one CBS executive, "It was just a case of bad chemistry. The two just didn't get along."

Earlier in the year Robert D. Wood, who had been president of the CBS television network for seven years, resigned to establish a television production company on the West Coast. He was succeeded by 39-year-old Robert Wussler, a news department wunderkind who had supervised, among other events, CBS's coverage of Apollo spaceflights, national political conventions, and election nights.

The most publicized job shift of the year, however, was Barbara Walters' departure from her long tenure as reporter and cohost of NBC's "Today" show and her decision to join ABC News as cohost of an evening news program with Harry Reasoner. Her salary was $5,000,000 for five years, making her the highest paid newscaster on television. At year's end it appeared that her much-publicized arrival had not helped ABC greatly in

---

Archie Bunker, Ph.D.

Listed in the Yale University catalog as English 76-2A, "Literature and Popular Culture," the course covered such recondite matters as the theorem postulated by the "Honeymooners"-"All in the Family" evolutionary pattern. For Yale's English 76-2A was one of the many television-as-literature courses that sprang up during the 1976–77 academic year at institutions from New York University to San Francisco State. As one professor explained, "Television is our culture's most characteristic—and perhaps most serious—form of dramatic art."

The citizens band radio craze that struck the U.S. during the year reached as far as the White House. Betty Ford—wife of the President—tells a "good buddy" that her "handle" is "First Mama."

its bid to attract viewers from competing network news programs. On the other hand, the first of her interview specials (with actress Barbra Streisand and President-elect Jimmy Carter) did attract a wide audience; *see* PEOPLE IN THE NEWS.

At the "Today" show a realignment followed Barbara Walters' departure. Jim Hartz was relieved of his host chores in favor of Tom Brokaw, who had been covering the White House for NBC. And Jane Pauley, a 25-year-old Midwest broadcaster and journalist, was added to the "Today" on-camera team.

Elsewhere on the job front, veteran newsman Daniel Schorr resigned from CBS after his much-publicized dispute with the U.S. House of Representatives. In February the *Village Voice,* a weekly newspaper in New York City, published a report on illegal activities by the Central Intelligence Agency (C.I.A.) that had been prepared by the House Select Committee on Intelligence. Schorr's role in turning the supposedly secret report over to the *Voice* was discovered, and the House Ethics Committee began an elaborate investigation. The committee decided to drop all action against Schorr, but CBS expressed dissatisfaction about Schorr's behavior, and he resigned; *see* CIVIL RIGHTS AND CIVIL LIBERTIES.

Cable Television. Cable television took a few small steps forward during 1976 in its ongoing effort to attain parity with over-the-air broadcasting. Principal among these steps was a 117-page report issued by the staff of the House Communications Subcommittee, titled "Cable Television: Promise Versus Regulatory Performance." The report was decidedly pro-cable and suggested that new legislation recognizing cable television as an important communications medium in its own right was needed; that a rural telecommunications act should be passed, encouraging construction throughout the country of low-powered repeating stations; that cable systems should pay copyright fees for distant stations they import to their customers; that the F.C.C. should abolish all restrictions on pay cable (the added cable service which offers additional programming for extra fees); and that owners of cable systems should not be allowed to own, in the same market, broadcast stations, newspapers, or telephone systems. In April the Ford administration decided not to push for a bill on cable television during 1976, and the subcommittee report had no legislative impact.

Also in April, Robert L. Schmidt, president of the National Cable Television Association, said that he foresaw "continual improvement in the regulatory environment" and "a steady 10 percent growth in subscribers for the next several years."

He forecast an even more dramatic growth for pay cable; he said that it would double by the end of the year, to about 1,200,000 homes, or 11 percent of all cable homes.

Radio. In radio the year's biggest story was NBC's decision to terminate in mid-1977 its syndicated all-news operation called News and Information Service (N.I.S.). After two years in business, N.I.S.'s losses exceeded $10,000,000. The news service simply had not attracted enough station subscribers—and consequently not enough of an audience—to justify its continuation, according to NBC. The network had hoped for 150 subscribing stations and 750,000 listeners by the end of 1976. Instead, it attained only 62 subscribers and an audience of about 200,000.

The radio development which may have the greatest long-term implications was the phenomenal growth of citizens band broadcasting, or CB. By May, 650,000 CB license applications a month were reaching the F.C.C., with at least 15,000,000 sets already in use, most of them in automobiles. Some CB addicts were famous: the wife of the President of the U.S., First Lady Betty Ford, called herself "First Mama" during her brief fling with CB. The CB fad spawned its own jargon, and *The "Official" C.B. Slanguage Language Dictionary* by Lanie Dills became a nationwide best-seller.

Deaths. Death came in 1976 to radio and television personalities Godfrey Cambridge, Paul Ford, Judith Lowry, Ted Mack, and Mary Margaret McBride, and to political commentator Peter Lisagor (*see* OBITUARIES); also to actress Angela Baddeley, Mrs. Bridges of "Upstairs, Downstairs" (Feb. 22 at 71); newscaster H. R. Baukhage (Jan. 31 at 87); announcer Nelson Case (March 24 at 66); and Santos Ortega, Grandpa Hughes of "As the World Turns" (March 10 at 76).

See COMMUNICATIONS.   N.H.

RAILROADS. *See* TRANSPORTATION.

RECORDINGS. American music, long neglected by record manufacturers, came into its own during the Bicentennial year. Many of the commercial labels made substantial contributions to the year-long celebration of this country's musical creativity.

New World Records. Through a grant from the Rockefeller Foundation, a nonprofit company called New World Records was set up to produce a recorded anthology of one hundred long-playing records examining all phases of American music. The records, which were distributed free to 8000 schools and libraries, were packaged with ample and authoritative background notes and covered such diverse areas as band music, bebop, ragtime, and Indian chants. Perhaps the most striking record of all was "Fugues, Fantasia and

A recording by André Watts of a solo piano transcription of George Gershwin's Rhapsody in Blue proved to be one of the year's best-sellers. Much of the American composer's music was rerecorded during the Bicentennial year.

At the age of 94, the still vital Leopold Stokowski conducts a new RCA recording of Gustav Mahler's monumental Second Symphony, the Resurrection.

A New Olympic Record

A high point of the closing ceremonies of the Summer Olympic Games on Aug. 1 was the playing and singing of stirring Canadian music by the Montréal Symphony Orchestra and several massed choirs. Probably very few of the millions who watched and listened were aware that, because of the contract signed by the musicians guild and the Olympic organizing committee, the selections had been prerecorded and the musicians were only pretending to perform. For their masterful pretense they were paid half a million dollars.

Gershwin, who died in 1937. His opera *Porgy and Bess* was recorded complete and uncut by Lorin Maazel and the Cleveland Orchestra on the London label. Although there was no connection between the two, both the recording and the 1976 Broadway production by the Houston Grand Opera Company presented *Porgy* in its original "operatic" form, with its recitatives intact, replacing the spoken dialogue usually resorted to in past productions.

Porgy and Bess was also the subject of an RCA recording in the "Victrola America" series devoted to reissues of material mainly from the 1930's. The *Porgy* selections were sung by Helen Jepson, Lawrence Tibbett, and other luminaries of the period. Among other rereleases in the "Victrola America" series were a recording by Arturo Toscanini and the NBC Symphony of Gershwin's *An American in Paris* and the composer's own 1924 performance of his *Rhapsody in Blue,* accompanied by bandleader Paul Whiteman, who originally commissioned the piece. Another notable recording of Gershwin music was pianist André Watts's interpretation for Columbia of the *Rhapsody in Blue,* in a solo piano version, together with 3 piano preludes and 13 songs.

Variations," a collection of large-scale organ works by such composers as Dudley Buck, Horatio Parker, and John Knowles Paine, grandly played by organist Richard Morris in a church in Buffalo, N.Y. New World Records seemed certain to fill some conspicuous gaps in the documentation of American music.

Gershwin's Year. The most widely represented American composer of the year was George

Contemporaries. Contemporary American composers, as usual, found their most sympathetic

A regal Joan Sutherland is seen on the cover of her latest album, a London recording of Jules Massenet's long-neglected opera Esclarmonde.

"The Concert of the Century," it was dubbed—the May 18 celebration of the 85th birthday of Carnegie Hall in New York City. The Columbia album includes this impromptu chorus: Left to right, Julius Bloom, executive director of the hall, and virtuosos Yehudi Menuhin, Dietrich Fischer-Dieskau, Mstislav Rostropovich, Vladimir Horowitz, Leonard Bernstein, and Isaac Stern.

outlet among the major companies to be on the Columbia label. A set of six records in a "Modern American Music Series" presented works by George Crumb, Morton Subotnick, Morton Feldman, Gunther Schuller, Bruno Maderna, Robert Suderberg, and William Schuman. A splendid recording of Charles Ives's *Songs* was made by soprano Jan DeGaetani and pianist Gilbert Kalish on the Nonesuch label. Jack Beeson's romantic comic opera, *Captain Jinks of the Horse Marines,* which had its premiere in Kansas City, Mo., on Sept. 20, 1975, was issued by RCA with its original cast. And for inveterate collectors of nostalgia, RCA reissued another relic of the musical patriotism of an earlier epoch, the late Paul Robeson's 1940 recording of John Latouche and Earl Robinson's *Ballad for Americans.*

Operatic Recordings. One German opera and a half dozen French works dominated operatic releases. Richard Wagner's *Die Meistersinger* received no fewer than three complete recordings during the year, a remarkable number, considering the length and difficulty of the work. The first, from Philips, was a live performance taped at Bayreuth, Germany, the Wagnerian shrine. It had the advantage of the presence of Karl Ridderbusch, perhaps the finest contemporary exemplar of the leading role of Hans Sachs, the medieval singer-shoemaker. But keen competition was provided before the year's end by a Deutsche Grammo-

phon set conducted by Eugen Jochum, with Dietrich Fischer-Dieskau, and by a London album featuring the Vienna Philharmonic Orchestra under the authoritative direction of Georg Solti.

The upsurge in recordings of French opera might seem unaccountable were it not that several of the works almost simultaneously received New York City performances. London released Jules Massenet's rarely heard *Esclarmonde,* a vehicle for soprano Joan Sutherland on records as well as at the Metropolitan Opera House. Another Metropolitan production, Giacomo Meyerbeer's *Le Prophète,* was similarly reflected in a Columbia recording in which leading parts were sung by Renata Scotto, Marilyn Horne, and James McCracken. Massenet's *Le Cid* was recorded by Columbia during a performance at Carnegie Hall in New York City under the baton of Eve Queler, one of the rising women conductors of recent years.

A third Massenet opera, *Thaïs,* was released by Angel with Beverly Sills in the title role and Lor Maazel not only conducting but playing the s violin in the familiar "Meditation." Gustave Charpentier's *Louise,* perhaps the only true working-class opera, received a long-overdue modern recording from Columbia with Rumanian soprano Ileana Cotrubas in the title role. And what many musicologists regard as the undisputed masterpiece of all French opera, Georges Bizet's *Carmen,* was freshly recorded by Georg Solti in a London version that restored several passages usually deleted.

Orchestral and Solo. Orchestral recordings produced few surprises or revelations during the year, with Gustav Mahler's symphonies continuing to hold the interest of conductors and, presumably, their audiences. Among the year's most stirring Mahler recordings was the Symphony No. 2, the *Resurrection,* issued by RCA in a version conducted by Leopold Stokowski, 94 years old but musically ageless. The late Toscanini, whose recording reissues seem inexhaustible, was represented by an RCA release of performances made during World War II with the Philadelphia Orchestra.

Among pianists, one of the busiest was Lazar Berman, the veteran Soviet artist, who recorded several works for Columbia, including Beethoven's *Appassionata* sonata. Vladimir Horowitz, who had shifted his allegiance from Victor to Columbia, returned to RCA and was represented by live recital performances of Robert Schumann and Alexander Scriabin.

The year's most spectacular instrumental release undoubtedly was Columbia's album devoted to a concert on May 18, 1976, marking the 85th anniversary of Carnegie Hall, at which appearances were made by Horowitz, Yehudi Menuhin, Leonard Bernstein, Isaac Stern, Dietrich Fischer-Dieskau, Mstislav Rostropovich, and many others. Columbia called the album "The Concert of the Century," and while a few critics may have demurred at that judgment, the two-record set nevertheless preserves the glamour, sentiment, and solid achievement of one of the most exciting evenings ever experienced by those fortunate enough to be present.

See also MUSIC; POPULAR MUSIC.   H.K.

RED CROSS. During 1976 the Red Cross conducted relief work in war-torn Lebanon and aided victims of severe earthquakes in Guatemala, Italy, the Philippines, and Turkey.

At the October meetings of the League of Red Cross Societies (L.O.R.C.S.) Board of Governors in Geneva, delegates from ninety-one national societies adopted a new constitution after a week of debate and consideration of 120 amendments. Other subjects discussed were the reunion of families separated by circumstances beyond their

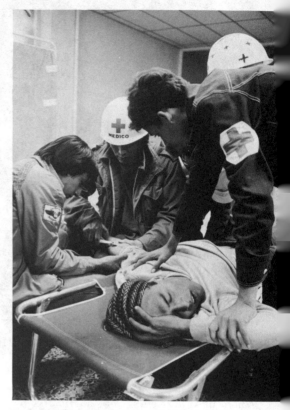

In Guatemala City the Red Cross gives aid to a victim of the devastating earthquake that struck Guatemala on Feb. 4.

control and the need for universal procedures on welfare inquiries at the time of international disasters.

Lebanon. The International Committee of the Red Cross (I.C.R.C.) established a hospital in Beirut staffed with doctors and nurses from Scandinavian Red Cross societies. The I.C.R.C. also sent mobile units to serve victims in outlying areas. From time to time intense fighting closed the Beirut airport, interrupting the airlift of thousands of tons of food and medical supplies from Cyprus. The I.C.R.C. delegation of over 60 people, including 17 doctors and nurses, performed hundreds of surgical operations and treated thousands of outpatients in the hospital, visited prisoners, and handled many health and welfare inquiries from family members in other countries. Distribution of relief supplies benefited all conflict victims without partiality.

Earthquake Relief. Devastating earthquakes struck Central America, Europe, the Middle East, and the Far East during 1976. Approximately 23,000 people were killed and 77,000 injured on Feb. 4 when an earthquake destroyed towns and villages in Guatemala. An appeal by the L.O.R.C.S. brought donations from over seventy national societies, and some neighboring societies sent disaster specialists to assist the victims. Tents, cots, blankets, medicines, and food were flown to Guatemala City, which was heavily damaged. Tent cities were established there and in nineteen areas outside the city. After the emergency phase, the L.O.R.C.S. constructed 10,000 temporary homes for families who could not afford to rebuild. Red Cross assistance, primarily in the form of cash contributions, was also forthcoming after earthquakes rocked northern Italy early in May, the Philippine Islands in August, and eastern Turkey late in November, 1976.

American National Red Cross. Although the last Indochina refugee left Fort Chaffee, Ark., on Dec. 20, 1975, the Refugee Locator Unit at American National Red Cross headquarters continued its efforts for another nine months to reunite families and to provide contact between members of widely separated families in the United States and in other countries. Local chapters helped more than 130,000 Vietnamese and Cambodians begin new lives in a new country during 1976.

A special meeting of the American National Red Cross Board of Governors was held in Portland, Oreg., on May 8, for the sole purpose of considering a report of the Special Financial Planning Committee. It was deemed necessary to reduce programs and services by $5,050,000 in order to operate within a balanced budget. The recreation program, Service in Military Hospitals, was discontinued; the number of personnel in Service at Military Installations was reduced; and most services and programs were concentrated at national headquarters.

Further financial difficulties were caused by Typhoon Pamela, which swept through Guam and the Mariana Islands with 190 m.p.h. winds in late May. Thousands of homes and other structures were smashed, communications were disrupted, and the water system on Guam was knocked out. Few lives were lost, but over 10,000 families needed emergency assistance. This disaster, occurring just after floods in Houston, Texas, and Tulsa, Okla., and the Teton Dam break in Idaho, necessitated a nationwide $10,000,000 disaster fund campaign.

See also ACCIDENTS AND DISASTERS; and separate articles on the individual countries mentioned above.

RELIGION. Along with the daily and weekly rites and the millions of acts of piety and charity that make up the ongoing continuity of religious faiths, 1976 witnessed a number of major developments, particularly in Christianity, the world's largest religion.

CHRISTIANITY

Events concerning the role of women in the church probably had the greatest historical significance. On Sept. 16 in Minneapolis, the General Convention of the Episcopal Church, the United States branch of the Anglican Communion, voted to admit women to the priesthood and make them eligible for election as bishops, starting in 1977. Women previously had been permitted only to be ordained as deacons, which meant that they

PROTESTANT CHURCH MEMBERSHIP	
Religious Group	Inclusive Membership
Baptist Bodies:	
Southern Baptist Convention	12,733,124
National Baptist Convention, U.S.A.[1]	5,500,000
National Baptist Convention of America[1]	2,668,799
American Baptist Churches in the U.S.A.	1,603,033
American Baptist Association	1,071,000
Progressive National Baptist Convention[1]	521,692
Conservative Baptist Association of America	300,000
National Primitive Baptist Convention[1]	250,000
Regular Baptist Churches	250,000
Free Will Baptists	227,434
Baptist Missionary Association of America	215,788
Christian Church (Disciples of Christ)	1,302,164
Christian Churches and Churches of Christ	1,049,816
Church of the Nazarene	441,093
Churches of Christ[1]	2,400,000
The Episcopal Church	2,857,513
Latter-Day Saints:	
Church of Jesus Christ of Latter-day Saints	2,336,715
Reorganized Church of Jesus Christ of Latter Day Saints	157,762
Lutheran Bodies:	
Lutheran Church in America	2,986,078
The Lutheran Church–Missouri Synod	2,763,545
The American Lutheran Church	2,415,687
Wisconsin Evangelical Lutheran Synod	395,440
Methodist Bodies:	
United Methodist Church	9,957,710
African Methodist Episcopal Church[1]	1,166,301
African Methodist Episcopal Zion Church[1]	1,024,974
Christian Methodist Episcopal Church[1]	466,718
Pentecostal Bodies:	
Assemblies of God	1,239,197
Church of God in Christ, International[1]	501,000
Church of God in Christ[1]	425,000
Church of God (Cleveland, Tenn.)	343,249
United Pentecostal Church, International, Inc.	300,000
Presbyterian Bodies:	
United Presbyterian Church in the U.S.A.	2,657,699
Presbyterian Church in the U.S.	878,126
Reformed Churches:	
Reformed Church in America	355,052
Christian Reformed Church	287,503
The Salvation Army	384,817
Seventh-day Adventists	495,699
United Church of Christ	1,818,762

Source: National Council of Churches, *Yearbook of American and Canadian Churches for 1977.*
[1] Noncurrent data, which are statistics compiled in 1974 or earlier.

A Solemn Mass is celebrated on Aug. 1 to open the 41st International Eucharistic Congress. Philadelphia was the site of the congress, the first to be held in the U.S. in fifty years.

could not run self-supporting parishes or lead the full Communion service.

The victory, climaxing years of debate and disagreement, was not won by an overwhelming margin, and a disgruntled minority was unwilling to accept it. Thirty-six bishops served notice that they regarded the decision as invalid. Fifteen conservative organizations, united as a Fellowship of Concerned Churchmen, called a conference for 1977 to discuss whether to leave the denomination. International Anglicanism remained divided in its practice. Canada had voted to permit women priests in 1975 and ordained the first six on Nov. 30, 1976. It was expected to be several years, however, before the Church of England would take the step.

The move toward Anglican women priests raised ecumenical problems. Prior to the U.S. decision, Archbishop of Canterbury F. Donald Coggan, leader of world Anglicanism, released four letters he had exchanged with Pope Paul VI on the issue (in 1975 and 1976). The pontiff cited the "constant practice of the Church, which has imitated Christ in choosing only men; and her living teaching authority which has consistently held that the exclusion of women from the priesthood is in accordance with God's plan for his Church."

With a different emphasis, a 12–5 majority of the Pontifical Biblical Commission stated that the New Testament by itself does not settle the question against women priests. A scholars' study for the U.S. Catholic bishops said that women were ordained as deacons in the early centuries of the church and exercised teaching, liturgical, sacramental, and administrative functions, but that there was no evidence that they were priests as that office was currently understood.

The hierarchy was urged to open the priesthood to women, as well as to married men, by a first-of-a-kind meeting of U.S. Catholics in October at Detroit. Challenging other traditions, the meeting, known as "A Call to Action," urged removal of automatic excommunication for Catholics who divorce and remarry while their first spouses are alive and asked the bishops to recognize the right of married people to decide for themselves what birth control methods to use. The conference, climaxing the U.S. Catholic Bicentennial observance, included 1340 delegates from dioceses and organizations, many of them appointed by bishops, but its recommendations had no legislative force. Archbishop Joseph Bernardin of Cincinnati, president of the National Conference of Catholic Bishops, said that the meeting dealt too hastily with too many topics and that it was unrepresentative because "special-interest groups" had "dominated" the proceedings.

With the Eastern Orthodox churches, the Anglican developments might create an ecumenical impasse. The most productive session of the international Anglican-Orthodox dialogue in many years was held in Moscow, and in the final communiqué the Orthodox participants warned that ordination of women priests would "create a very serious obstacle to the development of our relations in the future."

Among other highlights of that meeting, the Anglicans stated that the phrase "and the Son" (*filioque* in Latin) "has no place in the Nicene Creed." Anglicans have nevertheless traditionally used the phrase that the "Holy Spirit proceeds from the Father and the Son" as it has been used in the Nicene Creed by most Western churches since at least the 11th century.

Prayer Book. The proposed draft for a new *Book of Common Prayer* for the U.S. Episcopal Church also omitted the *filioque* wording, but it was restored upon the insistence of priestly and lay delegates at the General Convention. Conservatives won another partial victory when the vow in the name of the Trinity ("the Father, the Son, and the Holy Ghost"), rather than simply "God," was restored as a possible option in the marriage service. The prayer book version approved by the convention, if given a second endorsement at the 1979 convention, would give the church far more sweeping changes than any revision of the liturgy

since the Episcopal Church was formed in 1789. Besides using updated language, the new book moves from single "common" services to many options. For the Eucharist, for instance, two basic services are offered, with a far wider range of text choices within each, as well as a third free-form service with no specified texts at all. Conservatives, citing what they consider a weakening of doctrine, joined the dissidents over women priests in raising the possibility of some sort of formal schism.

Religion and the Campaign. The U.S. Presidential election led to more religious discussion than at any time since John F. Kennedy became the first Catholic President in 1960. The successful campaign by Jimmy Carter focused attention on the strength of the Evangelical wing of Protestantism. In March, just before the North Carolina primary, Carter worried some and inspired others by telling a home meeting of contributors that in 1967 he had undergone a "deeply profound religious experience" that "changed my life dramatically." Since making a "complete commitment to Christ," he said, "I've had an inner peace and inner conviction and assurance that transformed my life for the better." At a press conference Carter explained that this was nothing "mysterious," but rather "the same kind of experience as millions of people have who do become Christians in a deeply personal way." President Gerald R. Ford and his primary opponent, the former governor of California, Ronald Reagan, told Evangelical media of their Christian commitment as well.

George Gallup, Jr., proclaimed 1976 the "Year of

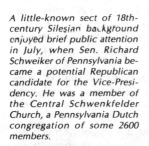

A little-known sect of 18th-century Silesian background enjoyed brief public attention in July, when Sen. Richard Schweiker of Pennsylvania became a potential Republican candidate for the Vice-Presidency. He was a member of the Central Schwenkfelder Church, a Pennsylvania Dutch congregation of some 2600 members.

America's Newest Cardinal

Among the twenty new cardinals installed by Pope Paul VI in May was one American, William Wakefield Baum. A native of Dallas, Texas, and Archbishop of Washington, D.C., since 1973, Baum at 49 became one of the youngest "Princes of the Church" in U.S. history. He has been a strong opponent of racism in his archdiocese, and throughout his career he has advocated more open communication between the Roman Catholic Church and other Judeo-Christian bodies. Baum has strong faith in the future of the Church; in one of the first statements he made after his appointment was announced he said, "I see everywhere signs of a second spring."

Archbishop William Wakefield Baum.

the Evangelical" as he reported a survey in which 34 percent of adult Americans said they had had a turning point when they had committed themselves to Christ. (He also reported that millions of adults had been involved in various Eastern disciplines.) In other Evangelical findings, nearly half of the survey population said they had personally witnessed to others to win them to Christian belief, and 4 out of 10 said that the Bible "is to be taken literally, word for word."

Carter was the first President to be strongly identified with the Southern Baptist Convention, which had become the nation's largest Protestant body (12,733,124 members) through stressing the Bible, evangelism, and generally conservative belief. Carter on two occasions worked briefly as a lay evangelist in Massachusetts and Pennsylvania,

How Many Cubits in a Meter?

Early in October the Good News Bible was published. To the proponents of the metric system and of women's liberation, this was good news indeed. In the new version David slays a Goliath who is nearly 3 meters tall, not 6 cubits and a span, wearing armor weighing not 5000 shekels of brass but 57 kilograms. Many Biblical references to "man" have also been changed. No longer is the "inner man" strengthened by the Holy Spirit; henceforth it is the "inner selves."

and his sister, Ruth Carter Stapleton, had become well known as a "healer of memories" in the interdenominational Neo-Pentecostal movement. Carter's home church in Plains, Ga., where he was a deacon and Sunday school teacher, finally decided after the election to rescind a 1965 vote and open its membership to Blacks, as Carter had urged for years.

It was also the first Presidential election since the U.S. Supreme Court had outlawed virtually all restrictions against abortion, and a Catholic housewife from Long Island, Ellen McCormack, ran in the Democratic primaries to promote the antiabortion cause. Leaders of the National Conference of Catholic Bishops met both Carter and Ford and, despite discussion of many issues, their post-meeting statements emphasized abortion. The bishops found Ford's advocacy of an amendment to permit states to outlaw abortions to be preferable to Carter's stand against any antiabortion amendment, and they so stated. After complaints from within and without the church, the bishops' administrative committee denied that this implied an overall "preference for either candidate or party."

Homosexuality. Church bodies in the U.S. were under continuing pressure to break with age-old tradition and extend moral acceptance to homosexual relationships. The quadrennial General Conference of the United Methodist Church defeated efforts to neutralize the denomination's stand against homosexual acts. The annual General Assembly of the United Presbyterian Church in the U.S.A. declared that it would be "injudicious if not improper" to ordain practicing homosexuals to the ministry. But it also formed a task force on the issue and hinted that future change was possible. The Episcopal convention established a similar study, occasioned in part by a decision by Bishop Paul Moore, Jr., of New York City to ordain an avowed lesbian as a deacon.

The Vatican's Congregation for the Doctrine of the Faith in January issued a "Declaration on Certain Questions Concerning Sexual Ethics"; this stated flatly that all homosexual acts are "intrinsically disordered and can in no case be approved of." The document, which provoked criticism from some theologians, also opposed premarital sex and masturbation. At their November meeting, the U.S. bishops issued a pastoral letter that opposed homosexual activity, extramarital sex, mercy killing, and abortion. It also repeated the traditional strictures on birth control and divorce.

With permission of his Jesuit superiors (but not their endorsement of his views) in New York City, John McNeill published *The Church and the Homosexual*. The book attacked traditional teaching. Father McNeill proposed that the church encourage "a mature homosexual relationship with one partner with the intention of fidelity" for those homosexuals who are unable to become heterosexual. McNeill, who admitted to a homosexual orientation, denied the Vatican's view that homosexual acts are intrinsically immoral and offered a detailed reinterpretation of Bible passages on the subject.

Other Catholic Events. Pope Paul, who reached the age of 79 on Sept. 26, named twenty-one new members of the College of Cardinals, the body that would elect his successor, again decreasing the percentage of Italian members. Among the new cardinals were Aloisio Lorscheider, head of the Brazilian hierarchy; Basil Hume, a former Benedictine abbot who earlier in the year had become Catholic leader of England and Wales; William W. Baum, the ecumenically minded archbishop of Washington, D.C.; Joseph Marie Trinnhu-Khue, archbishop of Hanoi; and Laszlo Lekai of Hungary.

Pope Paul also dealt with a virtual schism of right-wing Catholics led by a French archbishop, Marcel Lefebvre, who opposed the changes of Vatican Council II. Lefebvre was operating a seminary in Econe, Switzerland, despite Vatican orders in 1975 to disband, and during 1976 the Vatican suspended him from episcopal functions for ordaining priests there. Ignoring the suspension, Lefebvre conducted large public Masses using the "Tridentine" Latin rite, an illicit text that was authorized by the 16th-century Council of Trent. Lefebvre termed the new text ordered by Pope Paul in 1969 "a bastard rite." Though Lefebvre opposed the Mass in vernacular languages—the usual form since the council—it was not technically a dispute over using a Latin Mass as such; bishops might authorize Latin Masses, so long as they used the 1969 text.

In the U.S., the last sacramental reform stem-

Some of the more than 200 citizens of Hardenburgh, N.Y., who were ordained in The Universal Life Church by Bishop George McLain (left) in September. The tax-exempt status of "church property" was the alleged motivation for the mass ordination of property owners who were tired of paying large portions of their income to support community services.

Archbishop Marcel Lefebvre of Lille, France. Although Pope Paul VI declared his ordinations invalid, the archbishop continued to celebrate Mass according to a superseded rite and to conduct an irregular seminary in Switzerland, just as if Vatican Council II had never occurred.

ming from the council, a new style for the sacrament of Penance, was introduced in many parishes during Lent. The new form allows the option of face-to-face confession of sins to a priest, usually for longer periods and with more counseling than in the former anonymous confessional box. Called the Rite for Reconciliation, it permits group penance services, but to be sacramental they must include time for individual confessions. Using a form authorized for extraordinary situations, Bishop Carroll Dozier of Memphis, Tenn., held two large services in which sacramental absolution without individual confession was offered as a means of attracting lapsed Catholics.

The number of confessions, as well as Mass attendance, private prayer, per capita contributions, and other signs of church activity, had declined in the U.S. in recent years, according to a controversial book, *Catholic Schools in a Declining Church*. In the book, Father Andrew M. Greeley and two colleagues at the National Opinion Research Center of the University of Chicago compared a 1974 survey of U.S. Catholics with a similar survey in 1963. They found that the trouble was not with the Vatican Council reforms, which were highly popular, but rather with disillusionment with the pope and the hierarchy, especially over the ban on artificial birth control. On the book's main topic, the authors reported highly favorable attitudes toward parochial schools despite a recent

serious drop in enrollment. They traced the problem not so much to rising tuitions as to the lack of schools for Catholics who had moved into suburbs.

From Aug. 1 to Aug. 8 Philadelphia was host to the 41st International Eucharistic Congress. With an estimated cumulative attendance of 1,000,000, it ranked with the Chicago Eucharistic Congress of 1926 among mass U.S. religious spectacles. The congresses began in 1881 with the purpose of encouraging devotion to the Eucharist and the Catholic conception of Christ's "real presence" in the elements of bread and wine. Like other recent congresses, that at Philadelphia combined devotion with wide-ranging discussion of issues in church and society by many Catholic notables. Its primary message, however, concerned world hunger and the need to supply food and aid to impoverished areas of the world.

Eastern Orthodoxy. Representatives of thirteen self-governing churches met in November at Chambesy, Switzerland, and fixed a ten-point agenda for a Great Synod of Orthodox bishops. The agenda included ecumenical relations, the confused status of churches in Western nations, and whether to retain the old Gregorian calendar that makes it impossible to set a common Christian date for Easter. If the synod occurred, it would be the first meeting of its stature since the 8th century and the Orthodox equivalent of Vatican Council II. In another sign of increasing international Orthodox activity, theologians representing the fifteen major theological schools met in August in Athens, the first such gathering since 1936.

Church and State. Ethiopia's military regime in February ousted Patriarch Abuna Tewoflos, head of the Ethiopian Orthodox Church, and charged him with the amassing of a private fortune and other crimes. In July a little-known monk, Aba Melaku Wolde-Mikael, became the first patriarch chosen by election by church leaders rather than appointment by an emperor.

In Rhodesia the churches were deeply involved in the fast-moving political events. The self-exiled Methodist Bishop Abel Muzorewa, a key nationalist leader, returned to Salisbury amid a huge street celebration that underscored his political following. He later participated in the Geneva talks on establishing black majority rule in the former British colony. The white minority regime sentenced Donal Lamont, the Roman Catholic bishop of Umtali, to ten years at hard labor. Lamont had pleaded guilty, admitting he had refused to notify the authorities on the activity of black guerrillas, in order to save the lives of church members and to avoid attacks by white security forces. The day before he was sentenced, a Catholic group headed by the bishop published a 95-page document denouncing Rhodesia's racial policies as immoral.

In Chile, Brazil, and other Latin American nations, Roman Catholic bishops criticized the oppression of human rights through political imprisonment, torture, and murder. Several priests were murdered by unidentified terror squads in Argentina, a Brazilian bishop was kidnapped briefly, and Ecuadorian troops broke up at gunpoint an international Catholic meeting on human rights—all signs of growing tension between Catholicism and military regimes.

In Italy a revision of the concordat between the Vatican and the Italian state was announced at the end of the year.

The World Council of Churches Central Committee gingerly discussed religious repression in the Soviet Union, an isssue that had arisen during the council's 1975 assembly. Just before the committee met in August, research institutes in England, the Netherlands, and Switzerland joined in producing a 100-page dossier on the legal plight of Soviet churches. It stated that "the fundamental laws of the U.S.S.R. must be drastically changed before one can speak of freedom of conscience in the U.S.S.R., before Christians and other believers will be raised from second- to first-class citizens."

In December the ceremony confirming the sainthood of John Neumann, fourth bishop of Philadelphia, was scheduled by Pope Paul VI. On June 19, 1977, Bishop Neumann, a Bohemian-born American who served in the Redemptorist Order in the northeastern U.S. in the middle of the 19th century, will become the first American male saint.

Theology. Rudolf Bultmann, New Testament professor at the University of Marburg, Germany, from 1921 to 1951, died July 30 at the age of 91; see OBITUARIES. His "form criticism" took a skeptical view of the historical reliability of the units of oral tradition about Jesus' words and life that are said to lie behind the written New Testament. Two contemporary German theologians published English translations of major works during the year, the Lutheran Wolfhart Pannenberg (*Theology and the Philosophy of Science*) and the Catholic Hans Küng (*On Being a Christian*).

In the U.S., Evangelical Protestant theologian Carl F. H. Henry released 2 volumes of his projected 4-volume work, *God, Revelation and Au-*

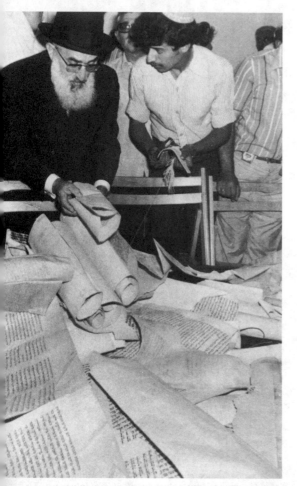

Conflict between Arabs and Jews erupted at religious shrines sacred to both in 1976. These sacred Hebrew scrolls of the Torah from the Jewish section of the Tomb of the Patriarchs (Abraham's Tomb) in Hebron were defiled by indignant Arabs. They claimed that Jews had interrupted the Arabs' own observances at the shrine.

thority: *God Who Speaks and Shows.* On a more polemical level, Henry's successor as editor of *Christianity Today,* Harold Lindsell, came out with a book contending that true "Evangelicals" must believe that the Bible is "inerrant" (totally error free) not just on faith and morals but on details of history, geography, and science. He accused the Southern Baptists and Fuller Theological Seminary in California of drifting toward liberalism. The same issue brought the Lutheran Church-Missouri Synod to schism in December in Chicago, as congregations that favor a "moderate" view of the Bible constituted the new Association of Evangelical Lutheran Churches.

In ecumenical theology, the Catholic-Anglican dialogue in Canada reached agreement that Rome would have to be acknowledged as the prime see of Christianity if unity were to be achieved. In the U.S. theologians from six non-Catholic bodies published an anthology, *A Pope for All Christians? An Inquiry into the Role of Peter in the Modern Church,* describing on what basis their churches could accept the papacy. The Eastern Orthodox theologian, John Meyendorff, proposed the formula reached at the 9th-century Council of Constantinople, in which the Western pope was granted "honorary primacy" but not "jurisdiction" over Eastern churches. The Anglican, Lutheran, Presbyterian, and Methodist writers similarly described a pope with honorary leadership but no churchwide jurisdiction, whereas the Baptist contributor opposed any primacy of person or office in one individual.

JUDAISM

The Central Conference of American Rabbis, at its annual meeting in San Francisco, adopted the document "Reform Judaism: A Centenary Perspective," which some thought would be seen in retrospect as the first new platform for Judaism's liberal branch since the Columbus Platform of 1937. The document professed a strong bond to the state of Israel (Reform was at one time anti-Zionist) and expressed the recent emphasis on Jewish "particularism" and traditional religious observance. The Union of American Hebrew Congregations reported that during 1975 the Reform branch experienced a membership increase of 3 to 5 percent, the largest such gain in many years.

In the Conservative branch, the Rabbinical Assembly's Committee on Jewish Law and Standards reiterated opposition to intermarriage of Jews and Gentiles and restated its position that rabbis "should work to prevent such occurrences." If an intermarriage did occur, it advised the rabbi to encourage the non-Jewish spouse to convert. If that did not happen, the Jewish spouse could be accepted for synagogue membership—but not for synagogue office or honors—so long as there was a pact to raise the children as Jews. On a related topic, a survey of Conservative rabbis found that 42 percent favored positive programs seeking the conversion of Gentiles and that another 50 percent accepted conversion as a valid aspect of rabbinical practice. Only a handful opposed conversion, which in most cases stems from intermarriage.

Despite the improved relations between Roman Catholics and Jews since Vatican II, there were signs of continuing tension. Rabbi Fabian Schonfeld, president of the Rabbinical Council of America (Orthodox), complained to the convention of

Jains of India take part in a ceremony that is held only once in twelve years. To witness the washing and dyeing of the 60-ft. statue of the Jain Saint Gomateshwara, pilgrims journeyed to Mysore from all over India.

A contingent of the more than 3000 members of the Nichiren Shoshu Academy who took part in a colorful parade up the Avenue of the Americas in New York City on July 3. The handsome floats and skillful performances of the academy members, who were attending the 13th annual convention of their worldwide Buddhist group, contributed to New York's Bicentennial celebration.

A sparsely attended Unification Church rally in Yankee stadium in June. The Rev. Sun Myung Moon ended his controversial U.S. ministry in September, with his church facing investigation by the International Relations Committee of the U.S. House of Representatives, as well as charges by some parents that Moon and his followers had brainwashed young adherents to the movement.

that council that the Vatican refused diplomatic recognition of Israel and, at the same time, spoke "sympathetically of those Palestinian terrorists whose program it is to dismember the Jewish state." At the annual meeting of the American Jewish Committee, Father Andrew M. Greeley stated that while relations in the U.S. were generally "excellent," there was "strong and powerful anti-Catholic feeling" among a minority in the Jewish community. Jewish leaders contested Greeley's claim that pro-Catholic feelings among Jews had been declining. The Union of Orthodox Jewish Congregations, responding to a 1975 Vatican decree on Jewish relations, reaffirmed its opposition to any dialogue about religious beliefs.

ISLAM

Sixteen Muslim and 14 Roman Catholic scholars met for 5 days in early February in Tripoli, Libya, on the invitation of Col. Muammar el-Qaddafi, the Libyan strongman. For the scholars it was their most substantive dialogue to date. The progress made was marred, however, by a dispute over the final declaration from the meeting. In the name of "both sides" at the talks it included passages that condemned Zionism as a "racist aggressive movement," endorsed the right of Palestinians "to return to their homeland," and upheld the "Arab nature" of Jerusalem. Upon his return to Rome, Cardinal Sergio Pignedoli, president of the Secretariat for Non-Christians, disassociated the Vatican from these statements.

In America, the Nation of Islam (Black Muslims) continued to move doctrinally toward orthodox Islam under its new leader, Wallace D. Muhammad.

A "World of Islam Festival" in London, funded by Muslim nations but administered by non-Muslim Britons, was one of the most sweeping exhibitions of Islamic art and culture ever assembled.

Security forces in Egypt arrested members of the renascent Muslim Brotherhood for attempted assassination plots. The extremist group sought the establishment of a theocratic Muslim state under strict religious law. In Iran, where the Shi'ite wing of Islam predominates, a revered mullah (teacher), Abolhassan Shamsabadi, was strangled to death. The mullah had criticized the secularizing policies of Shah Mohammed Riza Pahlavi, including the backdating of the national calendar to the start of Cyrus the Great's empire rather than to the Prophet's flight from Mecca, the traditional Muslim date. Although the government was suspected of involvement, police said the murder was sectarian and arrested four followers of another conservative Muslim teacher who had been expelled for fomenting rebellion against the shah.

HINDUISM

Baba ("Father") Muktananda Paramahansa, one of the gurus most recently to teach in the U.S., returned home to India in 1976 after having spent 2 years gathering followers and forming 62 devotional centers. He held a spiritual summit at Switzerland's Maharishi Meditation University with the Maharishi Mahesh Yogi, leader of transcendental meditation. TM, which was presented as a nonreligious technique in some U.S. public schools, met a legal challenge. An interreligious coalition of plaintiffs charged in a U.S. District Court in New Jersey that TM is a form of Hinduism and thus ineligible for public tax support. An-

other Western form of Hinduism, the Hare Krishna movement, was accused in New York City criminal court of entrapping its young disciples. A trial with significant religious freedom overtones was scheduled for 1977.

BUDDHISM

The fourteenth Dalai Lama, exiled temporal ruler of Tibet who is believed to be a reincarnation of the Buddha, delivered his epochal "Wheel of Time" sermon for the sixth and probably last time in his life to a throng in Leh, Kashmir. Because the succeeding Dalai Lama must be discovered in infancy through wondrous signs in Tibet, discussion continued over whether the current Dalai Lama would be the last. The New York *Times* reported from Lhasa, Tibet, that there had been a mass exodus from monasteries and a disappearance of the former evidences of religiosity since the Chinese Communists took control in 1959.

NEWER FAITHS

The leaders of the Church of Jesus Christ of Latter-

An unusual amount of attention was paid to the religious activities of the candidates and their families during the 1976 election year. Ruth Carter Stapleton, an evangelist of the Neo-Pentecostal movement, figured in many news stories. Here (right, foreground) she joins her brother, President-elect Jimmy Carter, his family, and friends in a hymn-sing at the Southern Baptist Church in Plains, Ga., their home congregation.

day Saints (Mormons) had announced that two visions to former church leaders would be added to its scriptures. Both dealt with salvation offered to persons who had not heard the true gospel before they died. The church's world membership had more than quadrupled, to 3,600,000, in the past three decades. To minister to them, President Spencer W. Kimball in 1975 revived the First Quorum of the Seventy, a body which had existed in early Mormonism. In 1976 Kimball expanded its membership to a total of thirty-nine. The church's First Presidency (Kimball and his two counselors) opposed the Equal Rights Amendment to the U.S. Constitution, fearing that it would "stifle many God-given feminine instincts."

Sun Myung Moon, leader and presumed messiah of a Korean cult known as the Unification Church, continued to acquire real estate, headlines, and opponents who accused the group of brainwashing. Despite fervent promotional effort, Moon managed to fill only half of Yankee Stadium for a rally in June. In September he claimed to draw 300,000 persons for a rally at the Washington Monument, six times the official police estimate. At the rally Moon finished his own ministry in the U.S. and left his cult to the direction of native-born leaders.

NEWS HIGHLIGHTS

The American Bible Society in 1976 published the *Good News Bible,* a complete translation in ordinary-level modern English. The New Testament portion, published in 1966, had sold 52,500,000 copies, making it the bestselling paperback of all time. In the emphasis on reader comprehension, familiar phrasings had vanished. "You shall have no other gods before me" becomes simply "Worship no god but me." "I shall not want" turns into "I have everything I need." A translation of the Apocrypha was in preparation for Roman Catholic and Eastern Orthodox use.

Archeologists, meanwhile, were sifting through the 15,000 tablets found at the site of Ebla in northern Syria, a heretofore obscure kingdom dating to 2500 B.C. The tablets, which were dated nearly a millennium before previously discovered records, list many persons and places cited in the Old Testament, and Bible scholars speculated that the full library could rank in significance with the Dead Sea Scrolls, discovered in 1947.

The executive committee of the National Council of Churches in the U.S.A. (N.C.C.) asked a member body, the Orthodox Church in America, to request Rumanian Orthodox Archbishop Valerian Trifa to suspend activity as an Orthodox representative to the N.C.C. governing board. Jewish groups labeled Trifa a war criminal who allegedly incited an anti-Semitic mob that terrorized Jews

in Bucharest in 1941. Trifa also faced federal charges in Detroit that to gain U.S. citizenship he lied about membership in the Rumanian Iron Guard, which advanced Nazi doctrines in the World War II period.

The Rockefeller Foundation issued a critical report on the interdenominational seminaries that have been leaders in U.S. Protestant life and thought. Written by Yale theologian George Lindbeck, with the collaboration of two social scientists from Harvard, Karl Deutsch and Nathan Glazer, the report said that the divinity schools at Yale, Harvard, Vanderbilt, and Chicago universities, and Union Theological Seminary in New York, had become less involved in denominational life than they were earlier. This change was regarded to be partly a result of a current trend toward objective study about religion rather than traditional inculcation of faith and training for the ministry. The document also pointed out that the seminaries were putting less emphasis on course requirements in the Bible, church history, and theology, and replacing them with generalized studies.

The Washington Cathedral (Episcopal) in the District of Columbia, the only traditional Gothic cathedral still under construction in the U.S., marked completion of the nave and side aisles with a dedication ceremony in July in which Queen Elizabeth II of Great Britain, secular head of the Church of England, took part. The cathedral hoped to complete the structure with two final towers in 1980.   R.N.O.

REPUBLICAN PARTY. A divisive struggle for the nomination for President of the United States, followed by defeat in the November elections, made 1976 a bitter year for the Republican Party. President Gerald R. Ford fought off a strong challenge from former Gov. Ronald Reagan of California to win the party Presidential nomination in August, but was defeated in November by Democrat Jimmy Carter. Republicans in the U.S. Congress, outnumbered roughly 2 to 1, supported the President's policies during the year; they helped to sustain six Presidential vetoes in ten attempts to override them and forced the Democrats to compromise on jobs, farm, tax, and housing bills. The November elections left party representation in both the Senate and the House of Representatives for the most part unchanged. *See* PEOPLE IN THE NEWS; PRESIDENT OF THE UNITED STATES.

Ford Against Reagan. Early in the year polls of voters and party leaders alike indicated a close contest for the Presidential nomination between Ford and Reagan. Republicans (about 20 percent of the electorate) admired the Californian for his fervent anti-Communism and his appeal to economic

Elder Statesman
A firm defender of then-President Richard M. Nixon through most of the Watergate affair, Sen. Hugh Scott announced late in 1975 that he had decided to retire and leave Capitol Hill. During 1976, his last year in office, there were allegations that he had received yearly donations from an oil company. But at the age of 77 and after thirty-five years in Congress, Hugh Doggett Scott, Jr., remained a respected elder statesman of his beloved Republican Party. A pipe-smoking moderate, Scott had served in the House of Representatives for sixteen years before winning a Senate seat in 1958. And for his last seven years as a Senator, Scott served as Senate minority leader.

Sen. Hugh Scott of Pennsylvania.

self-reliance and patriotism. Independent voters, a larger group crucial to Republican hopes in the general election, preferred Ford for his incumbency and his more moderate political stance. The President somewhat appeased anti-Soviet feeling among Republicans by expunging the word détente from his vocabulary. The strong economic recovery of the first two quarters also worked to the President's advantage.

Ford narrowly defeated Reagan in the New Hampshire primary on Feb. 24. After winning in Massachusetts, Vermont, Florida, and Illinois, the President looked unbeatable. Reagan finally won a primary in North Carolina on March 23. But after losing in Wisconsin on April 6, Reagan began to experience fund-raising difficulties, and a withdrawal appeared imminent. Suddenly, the challenger's bid caught fire: He swept all the races for delegates in Texas on May 1 and went on that month to victories in Indiana, Georgia, Alabama, Nebraska, Arkansas, Idaho, and Nevada. These primary wins, coupled with successful efforts in states where party caucuses chose delegates, put Reagan in the lead in total pledged delegates. Ford stayed in the race only by pulling out crucial wins in Michigan, Oregon, Kentucky, and Tennessee. The results of the June primaries further clouded the outcome: Ford gained delegates in a close Ohio contest while Reagan won easily in his native California.

In all, Ford won fifteen of the contested primaries and Reagan eleven; but Reagan, owing to his California landslide, led in the total vote by almost 300,000 out of 9,500,000 cast. Tabulations of pledged delegates showed the contenders virtu-

ally tied and both close to a first-ballot nomination.

The Convention. In the weeks before the convention in Kansas City, Mo., President Ford effectively used the prestige of his office in urging the uncommitted delegates to declare in his favor. Reagan, tantalizingly close to victory himself but losing the initiative, decided on a last-minute

Governor-elect James R. Thompson of Illinois and his wife, Jayne Carr, celebrate his election victory on Nov. 2. Political newcomer Thompson easily defeated his Democratic opponent, Michael J. Howlett, and became the Republican Party's most promising new personality.

gamble to make his candidacy more acceptable to moderates. On July 26 he announced that he would select a liberal Republican, Sen. Richard S. Schweiker of Pennsylvania, as his running mate if he won the nomination. The gamble failed. The implausible choice of Schweiker alienated more party conservatives, such as Mississippi delegation chairman Clarke Reed, than it attracted moderates. It also prompted an endorsement of Ford by former Texas Gov. John B. Connally, Jr., a skillful fund-raiser often mentioned as a potential Presidential candidate.

The convention opened on Aug. 16 with a keynote address by Sen. Howard H. Baker, Jr., of Tennessee. On the following day the Reagan forces lost a crucial vote when the convention defeated a proposed rule change that would have required Ford also to announce his Vice-Presidential choice before balloting began. A party platform acceptable to Reaganites was adopted. On Aug. 19 the President was nominated on the first ballot by a vote of 1187 to 1070 for Reagan. Sen. Robert J. Dole of Kansas was selected to be the Vice-Presidential candidate. In accepting the nomination, Ford gave what observers considered the most forceful speech of his career; Reagan then joined him on the podium in a show of unity.

The Campaign. In his acceptance speech the President challenged the Democratic Party nominee Jimmy Carter to debate on television. The debates proved to be the cornerstone of the campaign, which was managed for the Republicans by Houston lawyer James A. Baker 3rd. Ford's self-assurance in the first (Sept. 23) and third (Oct. 22) debates impressed viewers. But a blunder in the second (Oct. 6), when he claimed "there is no Soviet domination of Eastern Europe," probably cost him votes.

Nevertheless, polls showed the underdog Ford-Dole ticket rapidly closing the gap. Perceived by many as a steady, safe leader who had guided the nation through a crisis of confidence, the President sought to cultivate this image and generally kept to the White House until late October. Newsmen summoned to the White House lawn for brief Presidential appearances called it the "Rose Garden campaign." In sharp contrast Dole traveled constantly and made speeches aggressively attacking the opposition. In the final ten days Ford stumped his way across the country in an all-out effort that left him exhausted and voiceless on election eve.

Defeat and Its Aftermath. The Republican comeback campaign fell just short; the national ticket carried twenty-seven states for 241 electoral votes to the Democrats' 297 electoral votes. Even more disappointingly, the party failed to recoup heavy

Ronald Reagan, former governor of California, addresses the Oklahoma State Republican Party Convention in May. The sign held by a delegate presages Reagan's eventual defeat for his party's Presidential nomination.

Congressional losses suffered in the 1974 elections, which were influenced by the Watergate scandal and the resignation of President Richard M. Nixon. Democratic majorities remained undiminished in the Senate and the House of Representatives. Only 2 of the 75 freshman Democratic Congressmen were unseated. One bright spot was the election of Republican James R. Thompson as governor of Illinois. But the Republicans nationally suffered a net loss of one governorship.

While the Republican campaign was widely regarded as a creditable and effective effort against steep odds, the party was left defeated and demoralized at the year's end. Mary Louise Smith announced her resignation as chairman of the Republican National Committee, and a struggle over her replacement ensued. It was obvious to veteran observers of the political scene that such people as Vice-President Nelson A. Rockefeller (called by some the "forgotten Republican of 1976"), John B. Connally, Jr., and Ronald Reagan would have to share the task of rebuilding the party.

See CONGRESS OF THE UNITED STATES; DEMOCRATIC PARTY; ELECTIONS; UNITED STATES OF AMERICA.

W.M.H.

RHODE ISLAND. See STATISTICS OF THE WORLD.

RHODESIA. The year 1976 was marked by intensified diplomatic and military efforts to bring about black-majority rule in Rhodesia.

The year began with meetings between the prime minister, Ian D. Smith, and Joshua Nkomo, the conservative leader of the Zimbabwe African People's Union. After three months, the talks broke down over the question of a timetable for the transfer of power. As the guerrilla war was stepped up and as Rhodesian forces counterattacked with raids into Mozambique against nationalist bases, U.S. Secretary of State Henry A. Kissinger began a series of meetings with spokesmen for the "front-line" African states (Angola, Botswana, Mozambique, Tanzania, and Zambia), and with South Africa's Prime Minister Balthazar J. Vorster. After South Africa declared on May 13 that it would not intervene in Rhodesia to preserve white rule, Smith was under intense diplomatic pressure to agree to the principle of black-majority rule or face economic and military isolation during a greatly expanded guerrilla war. In June the Rhodesian government announced a renewal of the state of emergency and a 40 percent increase in defense expenditures. It was announced shortly thereafter that Rhodesia's white population had decreased by more than 2300 during the first six months of 1976. On Sept. 24, following the completion of a series of meetings between Kissinger and black leaders in Dar es Salaam, Tanzania, and between Kissinger, Vorster, and Smith in Pretoria, South Africa, the Rhodesian prime minister agreed to the Kissinger proposals for the transition to black rule: Majority rule was to come within two years; a biracial interim government would be set up immediately; British legislation would be instituted to hold elections for majority rule and to govern during the transition to independence; there would be an end to economic sanctions; and foreign economic aid would be forthcoming to ensure growth and to protect Whites from losses from expropriation or cancellation of government obligations.

Negotiations began in Geneva on Oct. 28. Great Britain served as sponsor and mediator of the conference. From the onset the black nationalist leaders were divided. Nkomo and Robert Mugabe, a spokesman for the guerrillas in Mozambique, were loosely allied as a "Patriotic Front"; Bishop Abel Muzorewa and Ndabaningi Sithole

White and black Rhodesian soldiers ride together on armed patrol near the Mozambique border in September. Mozambique was accused of harboring black nationalist Rhodesian guerrillas.

In Bulawayo, Southern Rhodesia, supporters of the moderate African National Council celebrate. A conference, intended to formulate plans for black-majority rule in Rhodesia, was scheduled to convene several weeks later.

took more flexible roles. The white delegation held that the Kissinger plan had to be endorsed before the conference could move on to other points, but the Blacks insisted that the details of the interim government had to be settled first and that they must assume power within one year. On Nov. 26, after a one-month deadlock over the date of independence, Nkomo and Mugabe agreed to a British compromise proposal. Independence would be achieved by March 1, 1978, if the details of independence were resolved. Negotiations were deadlocked, however, at the time of the adjournment of the conference, Dec. 14, and no progress was considered likely before its scheduled resumption in mid-January, 1977.

Meanwhile the guerrilla war intensified. As clashes between Rhodesian and Mozambique forces occurred along the border, the Soviet Union stepped up its supply of weapons to the black nationalists, Cuban advisers were reportedly being airlifted from Angola to Mozambique, and the five "front-line" states appeared to be arming for an expanded conflict.

See STATISTICS OF THE WORLD. *See also* AFRICA.   J.T.S.

RICHARDSON, ELLIOT L. *See* PEOPLE IN THE NEWS.
ROCKEFELLER, NELSON A. *See* PEOPLE IN THE NEWS.
RUBBER. *See* MANUFACTURING INDUSTRIES.
RUMANIA. In 1976 President Nicolae Ceauşescu continued to pursue the goal of making Rumania largely independent of control by the Soviet Union. In line with that aim the ruling Commu-

nist Party placed top priority on building up the industrial base of the nation's economy.

Domestically, Ceauşescu maintained tight control over both the Rumanian people and the Communist Party hierarchy. In June and July he conducted an extensive reshuffle within the party and government structures. Among other changes, Ion Coman replaced Ion Ioniţă as the nation's defense minister. No reason for the personnel shifts was given.

Ceauşescu's determination to build Rumania into a strong industrial state was reflected in the new five-year plan. Rumania's blueprint was the most ambitious ever drafted by any Eastern European state, calling for high annual growth rates and the construction of 2700 new factories. By contrast, the plan provided for fairly low increases in wages and for limited production of consumer goods. The government's preoccupation with industry rather than welfare was a source of widespread public discontent.

In international forums Ceauşescu frequently asserted Rumania's independence of Moscow. Speaking at the Soviet Union's Communist Party congress on Feb. 26, he declared that each Communist Party had a right to develop its own policies free of foreign interference. The Rumanian regime took satisfaction from the outcome of a twenty-nine-nation Communist Party conference held in East Berlin, June 29–30. During the gathering the U.S.S.R. reluctantly conceded that no single party could claim leadership of the Communist camp; *see* COMMUNISM.

Ceauşescu handled bilateral relations with the U.S.S.R. with the utmost care. During the summer he visited Soviet Communist Party leader Leonid Brezhnev's vacation retreat in the Crimea. In No-

On Nov. 22 Rumanian President Nicolae Ceauşescu (right) welcomes Soviet Communist Party leader Leonid Brezhnev to Bucharest. It was Brezhnev's first visit to Rumania in a decade.

vember he welcomed Brezhnev to Bucharest for the Soviet leader's first visit to Rumania since 1966.

At the same time Ceauşescu took pains to strengthen relations with both the Third World and Western countries. In August Rumania attended the fifth summit of nonaligned nations in Colombo, Ceylon (Sri Lanka), as a guest, and Ceauşescu harbored hopes that his country might eventually join the nonaligned group. On Nov. 21, just before Brezhnev's arrival, Rumanian officials concluded a ten-year trade pact with visiting United States Commerce Secretary Elliot L. Richardson. The accord was expected to facilitate an increase in commerce between the two nations from $400,000,000 in 1976 to $1 billion by 1980.

See STATISTICS OF THE WORLD.   F.W.

RWANDA. See STATISTICS OF THE WORLD.

S

SAHARA, SPANISH or **WESTERN.** See MOROCCO.
SAMOA. See STATISTICS OF THE WORLD.
SAN MARINO. See STATISTICS OF THE WORLD.
SÃO TOMÉ AND PRÍNCIPE. See STATISTICS OF THE WORLD.
SASKATCHEWAN. See STATISTICS OF THE WORLD.
SAUDI ARABIA. In 1976 King Khalid ibn Abdul-Aziz al-Saud of Saudi Arabia upheld his promise to continue the policies of the late King Faisal. These included enforcement of Islamic moral codes and economic diversification designed to reduce dependence on oil as an export.
Domestic Policies. The major domestic problem for Saudi government planners in 1976 was inflation. It was reported March 2 that the $142 billion five-year plan faced financial difficulties owing to rampant inflation, estimated to be running as high as 50 percent. Economists attributed skyrocketing prices to the phenomenon of "too much money chasing too few goods." Because of such basic operational deficiencies as acute manpower and housing shortages and inadequate port and air facilities, both production and import rates failed to keep pace with the increasing demand for basic as well as luxury commodities. To help curb the rising costs of food and housing the government instituted food price controls on March 21 and contracted for the construction of many modern residential villages. To help offset manpower shortages at all levels, Saudi Arabia hired American and Western European consultants and executives; Egyptians, Palestinians, and Indians for middle-level management positions; and Yemeni, Somali, and Pakistani construction workers.

The 1976–77 budget, approved by the Council of Ministers on June 27, was the same as the 1975–76 budget: $31.4 billion. Of the total, 32.9 percent was earmarked for current expenditure and 67.1 percent for development projects in the social and economic spheres. The defense alloca-

An Arab summit meeting at Riyadh, Saudi Arabia, on Oct. 17. Left to right: Sheikh Sabah al-Salem al-Sabah (Kuwait); Elias Sarkis (Lebanon); Anwar el-Sadat (Egypt); Crown Prince Fahd ibn Abdul-Aziz (Saudi Arabia); Hafez al-Assad (Syria); King Khalid ibn Abdul-Aziz (Saudi Arabia), the host; and Yasir Arafat (Palestine Liberation Organization).

tion for 1976–77 was raised by $2,488,720 to $9.9 billion, or 28 percent of the total budget. After defense, the largest expenditures went toward expansion of communications facilities and public works and housing. Land was broken for the construction of dozens of multimillion-dollar residential and industrial complexes. And, finally, work had begun on ambitious port and irrigation facilities.

Strict social legislation continued to reflect conservative interpretations of Islamic morality codes. Men were warned against wearing their hair too long or marrying non-Saudi women without official permission on pain of losing their jobs or student stipends. A new code of public decency for both women and men was enacted, and schools and other public institutions continued to be segregated by sex.

Regional Developments and Arab Affairs. Because of its wealth, size, and location, Saudi Arabia continued to play a pivotal role in Middle Eastern politics. Saudi mediators played an active role in attempts to settle several regional disputes: the struggle for possession of the former Spanish Sahara, the Egyptian-Syrian rift, the Lebanese civil war, and the war in Oman.

Principal challengers to this regional authority were non-Arab Iran and the radical Islamic state of Libya, both major oil producers. On March 10 the Saudi regime moved to limit Iranian influence in the Arabian Peninsula by establishing diplomatic relations with the People's Democratic Republic of Yemen (South Yemen). King Khalid apparently hoped that if South Yemen withdrew support for the revolutionary movement in Oman, then Iran would no longer be justified in maintaining military forces in the Arab Gulf to protect the sultan of Oman against insurgency. The Iranian military presence was cited as a major reason for increases in defense expenditures.

On July 19 the Saudis entered a solidarity pact with Egypt and the Sudan, establishing "joint organizations and institutions" for military, political, and economic cooperation. Signing of the agreement followed a coup attempt against the Sudanese government, allegedly financed by Libya. Observers felt that the pact was clearly directed against Libya.

Oil and International Politics. Against demands for a price hike by Libya, Iran, and some other oil producers, Saudi Arabia opposed increases in petroleum prices in 1976. Following a meeting of the Organization of Petroleum Exporting Countries (q.v.), or OPEC, in Bali, Indonesia, May 28, Saudi Oil Minister Sheikh Ahmed Zaki al-Yamani expressed satisfaction with OPEC's decision to continue the price freeze and remarked that "nobody can raise oil prices without Saudi Arabia." When the OPEC members met again, however, on Dec. 15–17 in Qatar, Saudi Arabia and the Union of Arab Emirates agreed to a 5 percent hike in their oil prices for the first half of 1977. The other eleven members announced a 10 percent increase for the same period, to be followed on July 1 by an additional 5 percent boost.

See STATISTICS OF THE WORLD. *See also* ARAB LEAGUE; MIDDLE EAST.   S.C.

SCHMIDT, HELMUT. *See* PEOPLE IN THE NEWS.

SCRANTON, WILLIAM W. *See* PEOPLE IN THE NEWS.

SENEGAL. *See* STATISTICS OF THE WORLD.

SEYCHELLES. For Seychelles, 1976 was a year of somewhat reluctant independence. For 182 years Great Britain had ruled the eighty-six islands and islets in the Indian Ocean (their total area is only 107 sq.mi.), and the Seychellois—a racially mixed people descended chiefly from European settlers and African slaves—were in no hurry to gain freedom. But under intense pressure from the Organization of African Unity to put an end to a vestige of British colonialism, the archipelago's political leaders bowed to the inevitable and pressed for independence. In mid-January Britain agreed to end its rule, and shortly after midnight on June 28 the islands formally became the Republic of Seychelles. The republic joined the Commonwealth of Nations immediately upon independence, and it was admitted to the United Nations on Sept. 21.

The economy of the islands, which are known for their beauty, is heavily dependent on tourism. But President James Mancham planned to build Seychelles into a "little Switzerland"—an offshore banking and financial center and possibly a tax haven. As a boost to the economy, Britain agreed to provide development aid totaling $18,700,000 through 1979, with an additional $1,200,000 annually in technical assistance.

According to Mancham, Seychelles would have no army or navy and would remain neutral in foreign affairs. But he stated that if the Soviet Union continued to build its naval power in the Indian Ocean, he would favor a strengthening of the United States presence in the area.

See STATISTICS OF THE WORLD. *See also* COMMONWEALTH OF NATIONS.   R.J.C.

SIERRA LEONE. *See* STATISTICS OF THE WORLD.

SINGAPORE, REPUBLIC OF. During 1976 Prime Minister Lee Kuan Yew continued to mold his tiny island republic into a rigidly disciplined society. In May the Dutch Labor Party, supported by the Labour Party of Great Britain, proposed the expulsion of Lee's ruling People's Action Party (P.A.P.) from the Socialist International because of Singapore's alleged maltreatment of political prisoners. In response Lee charged his critics with naïveté in dealing with Communists and withdrew the P.A.P. from the social-democratic world body.

Lee's tough, law-and-order way of running the country remained popular with Singaporeans, and the major opposition party—the Workers' Party— could make little headway against a government

that had transformed the island into Southeast Asia's biggest economic success. As the economy recovered briskly from the worldwide recession, the government confidently forecast a real economic growth of from 6 to 8 percent for 1976. In general elections held Dec. 23 the P.A.P. won all 69 seats in the parliament.

In foreign policy Singapore maintained close ties with its non-Communist neighbors and with the West. Despite his toughness on domestic Communists, Lee did make some careful approaches to the Communist powers. Economic links with Moscow were strengthened, and in May, Lee made his first trip to Peking. There he told his Chinese hosts that he favored expanded trade between their two countries, but he added that it was premature to talk of establishing formal relations.

See STATISTICS OF THE WORLD.   R.J.C.

SOCIAL SECURITY. The Social Security Administration (S.S.A.), a part of the United States Department of Health, Education, and Welfare, continued in 1976 to operate programs designed to help ensure Americans against economic insecurity. These included old-age, survivors, and disability insurance (OASDI); Medicare; the Supplemental Security Insurance (S.S.I.) program; and the coal miners' black lung benefits program. In addition, the S.S.A. helped administer state-run Medicaid operations.

Considerable controversy was aroused in 1976 by well-documented charges of irregularity and waste in the Medicare and Medicaid programs. Individual members as well as committees of the U.S. Congress carried on extensive investigations of these charges.

OASDI Operations. Cash benefits and lump-sum payments for persons covered under OASDI programs totaled $70.8 billion in the year ended June 30, 1976. In August, 1976, benefits were paid to 32,550,000 persons, who together received $6.3 billion. Retired workers received an average monthly payment of $223, while disabled workers got an average of $244. In May the combined assets of the old-age and survivors trust fund and the disability insurance trust fund were reported to be $44 billion; the great bulk of the assets were in the former fund.

The second automatic cost-of-living increase in benefits, amounting to 6.4 percent, became effective in June. To help cover the increase, the maximum amount of taxable earnings of workers was raised to $16,500, effective Jan. 1, 1977. Tax rates were not raised, however. On the same date the maximum monthly amount a beneficiary may earn without losing benefits was set to rise by $20 to $250.

Maggie Kuhn, national director of the Gray Panthers, testifies in July before a U.S. Senate panel on aging. Her organization, founded in Philadelphia in 1970, worked during the year to build a more favorable attitude toward elderly persons and to end discrimination against them.

In May a federal judge in New York City ruled that a 1972 amendment to the old-age insurance laws, which had ended differential treatment for men and women, discriminated against men who had reached age 62 before 1975. Under the change, since Jan. 1, 1975, all persons, regardless of sex, have had their benefits computed under a single formula when they reached 62, rather than under the dual system favoring women that had previously prevailed. The change had not altered the benefit formula of men already 62 at the end of 1974, thus setting up the discriminatory situation.

Medicare. On June 30, 1976, the tenth anniversary of its establishment, Medicare was providing hospital and medical insurance for about 25,000,000 Americans, including some 2,200,000 disabled persons. During the 1976 fiscal year $12.3 billion was paid out for hospital and related benefits.

Several amendments to the Medicare program were passed during 1976. These included an adjustment of provisions relating to the reimbursement of physicians, a regulation permitting payments to Indian Health Service facilities that met Medicare qualifications, and a measure clarifying

conditions for the reimbursement of patients in Veterans Administration hospitals receiving treatment for chronic kidney disease. In June the U.S. Supreme Court upheld a Medicare provision denying benefits to aliens over 65 years of age who were not permanent residents and who had not lived in the U.S. for at least five years.

S.S.I. and Black Lung Benefits. In September, 1976, 4,275,000 persons received federally administered S.S.I. payments totaling $508,577,000. A cost-of-living increase of 6.4 percent in S.S.I. benefits had taken effect in June.

In January the commissioner of the S.S.A. reported to Congress that since its inception in 1974 the S.S.I. program had made unjustified payments estimated at $574,000,000, of which about $419,000,000 had not been recovered. The official calculated that from January to June, 1975, 11 percent of S.S.I. recipients had been overpaid, 5.7 percent underpaid, and 7.7 percent had been ineligible to receive benefits. The commissioner said that corrective measures, such as increased use of computerized record-keeping, were being taken.

Approximately 473,000 persons received black lung benefits amounting to $74,400,000 in September, 1976, under the Coal Mine Health and Safety Act. The average monthly benefit for miners and their dependents was $281; payments to widows and other survivors averaged $207.

SOMALIA. *See* STATISTICS OF THE WORLD.

SOUTH AFRICA, REPUBLIC OF. The year 1976 was a time of diplomatic setbacks and intensified social unrest within South Africa. Direct challenges were made to the republic's policies of the separation of Blacks (apartheid) and white-minority domination.

Angola and Namibia. As the year began, South Africa had from 4000 to 5000 troops fighting against the Soviet-supported Popular Movement for the Liberation of Angola (M.P.L.A.). When the pro-Western nationalist movements in Angola collapsed (after aid from the United States was cut off), South Africa began to disengage itself from the conflict; by the end of March, all its troops had been withdrawn into Namibia (South-West Africa). There the militant South-West African People's Organization (SWAPO) was stepping up its guerrilla campaign and calling upon Angola, Cuba, and the Soviet Union for aid in its drive for independence from South Africa.

In 1975, bowing to international pressure, South Africa had permitted the opening of multiracial talks on the independence of Namibia. During 1976 these constitutional discussions continued, but by Dec. 17, two years after the United Nations Security Council had condemned South Africa's "illegal occupation" of Namibia, the two sides remained far apart. SWAPO had been recognized by the U.N. as representing the majority of Namibia's Blacks, but South Africa did not recognize SWAPO and refused to negotiate with the organization. Instead, South Africa wanted the several Namibian groups working for independence to agree on their own future course. Efforts by the U.S. to spur negotiations were hampered by the upcoming change in administration, and President-elect Jimmy Carter's views on Namibia had not been made clear.

Rhodesia. South Africa continued for the second year to extricate itself from active participation in

At Umtata, the capital of Africa's newest republic, the South African flag is lowered and Transkei achieves its independence. The new nation, about the size of Denmark, was proclaimed Oct. 26.

the racial conflict in Rhodesia (q.v.). In May the government declared that it would not go to the military aid of Rhodesia's white minority. A conference on majority rule for Rhodesia opened on Oct. 28 in Geneva. Foremost on the agenda was a proposal by U.S. Secretary of State Henry A. Kissinger, suggesting a two-year timetable to accomplish the changeover. South African Prime Minister John Vorster announced his support of Rhodesia's Prime Minister Ian D. Smith but stated on Oct. 31 that he backed the Kissinger plan, at least in principle. By mid-December, however, the talks had made no appreciable progress and were adjourned until mid-January, 1977.

Trouble at Home. Black discontent erupted on June 16, when approximately 10,000 students in Soweto, a black township near Johannesburg, staged a protest against a new regulation requiring the nation's schools to teach all classes in the Afrikaans language. The protest escalated into general rioting and soon spread to neighboring townships and to other major South African cities.

Reprinted from issue of Sept. 13, 1976, of "U.S. News & World Report." © 1976, U.S. News & World Report, Inc.

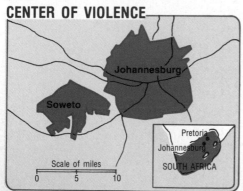

CENTER OF VIOLENCE

Johannesburg

Soweto

Pretoria
Johannesburg
SOUTH AFRICA

Scale of miles
0   5   10

Although the government rescinded the Afrikaans order on July 6, a second wave of riots broke out in mid-July. In late August students organized a three-day work boycott to protest the detention of rioters arrested in June; this was followed by a second boycott in mid-September and another in mid-November. Riots caused by a December boycott of Christmas festivities left more than two dozen dead.

Although many black workers did not participate, the boycotts disrupted economic activity. Scattered incidents of arson, attacks on Whites, and demonstrations continued for the rest of the year. Hundreds of Blacks, many of them students, were killed and thousands more were wounded as police attempted to break up demonstrations. Key figures in the military and the business community responded to the riots with calls for a reassessment of apartheid. Leaders of the tribal regions within South Africa called Bantustans

(black homelands), including the Transkei (q.v.), which attained its independence in October, were equally insistent that black grievances would have to be answered. On Nov. 9, after long and angry debate on apartheid, the U.N. General Assembly voted ten resolutions condemning the republic's racial policies and calling for a complete economic boycott, an arms embargo, the banning of the republic from international sports, and a call to Blacks to seize political power. The vote was carried mainly by African and Arab nations, with the U.S. and its traditional allies voting against the resolution.

See STATISTICS OF THE WORLD. *See also* AFRICA. J.T.S.

SOUTH CAROLINA. *See* STATISTICS OF THE WORLD.
SOUTH DAKOTA. *See* STATISTICS OF THE WORLD.
SPACE TECHNOLOGY. The outstanding space event of the year was the Viking exploration of Mars by the United States, a far more complex undertaking than any previous space activity.
The Viking Mission. Two Viking spacecraft, each

The Mars landscape as it appeared on July 21, the day after the successful landing of Viking I. The view is southeast; the hour is noon, Mars time.

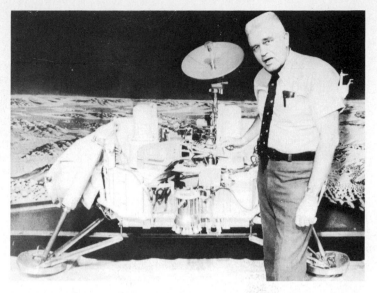

James S. Martin, Viking project manager, with a model of the Mars lander. The complex package contains three biology laboratories, a gas and soil analyzer, two cameras, weather sensors, and a 10-ft. retractable scoop.

ferrying a lander, were launched from the Kennedy Space Center at Cape Canaveral, Fla., on Aug. 20 and Sept. 9, 1975. After a transit of almost 1 billion mi., the first vehicle entered the orbit of Mars on June 19, 1976; the second entered on Aug. 7. They took extensive photographs of the planet from orbit and made direct measurements of the atmosphere. Lander I was detached and parachuted down to the Chryse Planitia basin on July 20, 1976. Because of the more than 200,000,-000-mi. distance between the earth and Mars, telemetry signals to and from the lander took 19 min. each way. Photography of the surface of Mars commenced immediately, and high-resolution black-and-white and color photographs were transmitted to earth. About one week later a trenching scoop was activated to collect soil samples for signs of biological activity. The scoop jammed at first, but the malfunction was corrected from earth by computer instruction. Lander II, identical with the first lander, touched down Sept. 3 in the Utopia Planitia region. Experiments were to continue for a full Martian year, the equivalent of about two earth years.

Luna and the Pioneers. Luna XXIV, a Soviet vehicle launched Aug. 9, drilled the surface of the moon to a depth of 6.6 ft. for a core sample from the previously unexplored Mare Crisium (Sea of Crises). A special robot apparatus broke the slender core into foot-long segments and placed them in a self-sealing container. The spacecraft returned to the Soviet Union on Aug. 22. The core, samples of which were sent to the U.S., bore a record of millions of years of solar activity.

Pioneer X, having swung by Jupiter in December, 1973, crossed Saturn's orbit in February, 1976, and headed out of the solar system toward other stars. Pioneer XI passed Jupiter in December, 1974, and proceeded toward Saturn itself. In December, 1976, the spacecraft disclosed the structure of the sun's magnetic field, a fundamental scientific discovery (*see* ASTRONOMY).

Applications Satellites. On May 4 a unique mirrored ball, 2 ft. in diameter, was launched by the U.S. Called Lageos, for *laser geodynamic satellite*, the inert sphere was placed in a 3600-mi. circular orbit above the earth. The 426 mirrors on its surface were to be used for the reflection of earth-based laser beams, making possible extremely precise measurements of the earth's rotation rate, continental drift, and movements along geological faults. The satellite is expected to last as long as 10,000,000 years. It bears a pictograph message to future earthlings, including the arrangement of the continents as they were 225,000,000 years ago, as they were in 1976, and as they are expected to be 8,400,000 years from now.

The U.S. National Oceanic and Atmospheric Administration (NOAA) commenced operation of an improved polar-orbiting satellite, NOAA-5. An earlier version, NOAA-4, was placed in backup service. Such polar-orbiting spacecraft scan any given spot on the earth twice every 24 hr., returning visual and infrared imagery of cloud cover, sea surface temperature, and other environmental indicators. NOAA also continued to operate two geostationary satellites that provided the national weather maps seen daily on U.S. television news programs. (These satellites have fixed positions in relation to the earth's surface.)

On July 6, Commander Boris Volynov (top) and flight engineer Vitaly Zholobov wave before leaving on their Soyuz 21 mission to rendezvous with a previously launched Soviet space station.

Manned Space Flights. Three Soviet Soyuz cosmonaut missions were conducted during the year. The longest was Soyuz 21, launched July 6 with Col. Boris Volynov and Lt. Col. Vitaly Zholobov on board. Two days later Soyuz 21 docked with the orbiting Salyut 5 space station, which had been launched June 22. Once inside the Salyut, Volynov and Zholobov performed experiments under weightless conditions, including the melting and cooling of metal alloys and studies with plants and fish. The flight ended after 49 days, following a report by the Soviet newspaper *Izvestia* that the cosmonauts had been experiencing "a state of sensory deprivation."

Soyuz 22, launched Sept. 15, was an 8-day flight conducting earth resources photography; the crew were Col. Valery F. Bykovsky and civilian Vladimir Aksenov. Soyuz 23 carried Lt. Col. Vyacheslav Sudov and Lt. Col. Valery Rozhdestvensky into orbit on Oct. 14 to rendezvous with Salyut 5. A docking problem developed, however, and the spacecraft returned two days later.

Space Shuttle Plans. Voyages in the U.S. manned space program remained suspended until 1979, when the Space Shuttle Program was to commence with piloted vehicles that could launch satellites, visit space laboratories, and land back on earth like airplanes. The first of the new space-

craft, named *Enterprise* for the fictional spaceship in the "Star Trek" television series, was presented at a "roll out" ceremony on Sept. 17.

In July the National Aeronautics and Space Administration announced an open competition for 15 pilots and 15 mission specialists for the Space Shuttle Program. Criteria were still being worked out, but pilot applicants were expected to need about 1000 hr. of high-performance flight time and an advanced engineering-related degree. Mission specialists, who were to work primarily with payloads, would need only an engineering-related bachelor's degree. No age limits were to be specified, and women and minority group members were encouraged to apply. The deadline for applications was set at June 30, 1977.

See also COMMUNICATIONS; EARTH AND PLANETARY SCIENCES. F.C.D. III

SPAIN. Agitation against the authoritarian regime of Francisco Franco continued in Spain a year after the dictator's death; 1976 saw strikes and massive protests demanding liberty and amnesty for political prisoners. To assuage the widespread fears of another civil war, Premier Carlos Arias Navarro announced plans for a program of liberalization to be carried out "without haste or undue delay."

Politics. On May 1 Premier Arias outlined his broad legislative program, scheduled to be completed by the end of the year. He urged the Cortes, Spain's legislative body, to pass the necessary laws to accomplish the political evolution of Spain. In June the Cortes approved a bill granting freedom of association and the formation of political parties; the Communist Party, however, remained outlawed. The Cortes, dominated by members held over from the Franco regime, was slow in enacting the liberalizing legislation, and Arias found himself assailed by the conservatives for moving too fast and the liberals for moving too slowly. Tired of the pressure, Arias resigned his post on July 1.

The Council of the Realm, as authorized by the constitution, selected three men from whom the king would choose a premier. King Juan Carlos I appointed Adolfo Suárez González, a 43-year-old cabinet minister and member of the Cortes. Suárez formed what he considered a transition government, in which he kept only the three military ministers from the preceding cabinet. After some prodding, the Cortes on July 13 approved legislation liberalizing the penal code and permitting activities by political parties, which until then had been forbidden. A long-sought general amnesty for political prisoners was decreed and signed by the king on July 30 and some 650 persons were freed. Excluded from the amnesty were people

The End of an Era in Spain
With the abrupt resignation in July of Premier Carlos Arias Navarro, 67, Spain took a step out of the past. To replace Arias, the last premier to serve under Francisco Franco, King Juan Carlos I selected a personal friend, Adolfo Suárez González, 43, who became one of the youngest heads of government in Spanish history. A reform-minded former cabinet member, Suárez won voter approval in November for a plan to convert Spain into a Western-style parliamentary democracy.

Spanish Premiers Carlos Arias Navarro (left) and Adolfo Suárez González.

charged with terrorist acts, most of them Basque separatists.

Constitutional Reforms. On Sept. 11 Suárez took to the radio and television to present to the nation the plan for political reform he had submitted to the Cortes. It was similar to the plan outlined by his predecessor. It provided for a parliament to be elected directly by the people and to be composed of a Congress with 350 deputies, elected for 4 years (1 for each 175,000 inhabitants), and a Senate with 207 members, elected for 6 years (2 for each of the 50 provinces and the enclaves of Melilla and Ceuta in Morocco). In addition, the king would be empowered to appoint additional senators from learned societies and professional corporations. The Congress would have the power to initiate legislation and constitutional reforms, all measures to be approved by the majority of both chambers. The Cortes approved this Political Reform Law on Nov. 18 by a vote of 425 to 59, thereby automatically dissolving itself. In a national referendum on Dec. 15, Spaniards voted overwhelmingly for parliamentary elections to be held in the spring of 1977.

To defuse separatist movements in Catalonia and the Basque country the government appointed committees to study the regional situation and formulate plans to grant some measure of local autonomy.

In the first full year of his reign King Juan Carlos actively promoted the democratization of his country and radiated goodwill. He and Queen Sofia traveled throughout Spain; he held meetings with leaders of the opposition, including the secretary-general of the Socialist Party. In June, during the Bicentennial celebration in the United States, he and the queen paid an official visit.

The Economy. In an address to the nation soon after taking office Premier Suárez called attention to the faltering state of the Spanish economy. He stated that it was beset by both high inflation and unemployment, as well as by a large deficit, which the premier blamed on Spain's political instability. To stimulate exports the peseta was devalued by 10 percent. In October the government froze prices, wages, and dividends for two months. It also imposed an extra 10 percent tax on salaries higher than 1,000,000 pesetas per year and increased the duties on most imported goods. Gasoline prices were increased along with taxes on inheritances and luxury goods. Not only did tourism decline but foreign visitors spent less, thereby depriving Spain of much needed foreign exchange. The Spanish credit remained sound, however, and in July the nation had no appreciable trouble arranging foreign credits in the amount of $1 billion through a consortium of international bankers.

Foreign Relations. On Jan. 24 Spain and the U.S. signed a five-year accord granting the U.S. continued use of air and naval bases in Spain. The U.S. agreed to withdraw its armed atomic submarines from Spanish territory and also agreed to grant an export license for an atomic energy plant to be built near Barcelona.

Also during the year Spain signed a multimillion-dollar contract with Argentina for the construction of ships and port facilities in the South American country.

See STATISTICS OF THE WORLD. A.R.

SPORTS

Briefly in February and again in July, the Olympic Games held the sports spotlight. But during the rest of 1976 there were events astounding enough to catch the attention of the most jaded sports fan. Often they had to do with money . . . or with changes in the rules.

Athletes in the four major team sports—baseball, football, basketball, and hockey—found new freedom in 1976.

The change was most dramatic in major-league baseball, where a new agreement between club owners and players allowed many veteran players to become free agents. A "reentry" draft of 24 such players prompted heavy bidding, and 13 of them signed multiyear contracts worth more than $1,000,000 each.

In professional football, 24 National Football League players became free agents, but the contracts for those who signed with new teams were less lucrative than those attained in baseball. The National Basketball Association agreed to eliminate the option clause, which bound a player to his team after his contract had expired. Almost 15 percent of National Hockey League players became free agents on May 1, but a team that signed one had to compensate his previous team.

The Cincinnati Reds won baseball's World Series for the second straight year. Old champions who regained supremacy were the Boston Celtics in basketball and the Montréal Canadiens in hockey.

It was a year of young heroes. Among the men were 20-year-old Björn Borg in tennis; John Naber, 20, in swimming; Mark Fidrych, 21, in baseball; and Jerry Pate, 22, in golf. Among the women were Nadia Comaneci, 14, in gymnastics; Kornelia Ender, 17, in swimming; Dorothy Hamill, 19, in figure skating; and Chris Evert, 21, in tennis. It was, as usual, a year in which the spotlight fell often upon one veteran boxing champion, Muhammad Ali, still successful and still verbose.

AUTO RACING
Niki Lauda of Austria was critically injured when his Ferrari crashed and caught fire Aug. 1 in the German Grand Prix at Mannheim, West Germany. Fellow drivers pulled him out of the wreckage. Six weeks later, having missed only 3 races, he was competing again, and he failed by 1 point to win the world driving championship for the second straight year. James Hunt of England, driving a McLaren, won 2 of the last 3 of the 16 Grand Prix

races and took the world title. The championship was contested in Europe, the United States, Canada, South America, South Africa, and Japan in Formula One open-cockpit cars. Hunt won 7 races and Lauda 5.

Clay Regazzoni of Switzerland, in a Ferrari, won the first Western Grand Prix of the U.S. on March 28 at Long Beach, Calif. Hunt captured the Cana-

Johnny Rutherford holds up two fingers to signify that he has just won his second victory in the annual Indianapolis 500. Behind him is the championship trophy.

dian Grand Prix on Oct. 3 at Drummondsville, Ontario, and the U.S. Grand Prix on Oct. 10 at Watkins Glen, N.Y.

In the National Association for Stock Car Racing competition, Cale Yarborough of Timmonsville, S.C., Richard Petty of Randleman, N.C., and David Pearson of Spartanburg, S.C., did best. Of the 30 races, Yarborough won 9 in a Chevrolet, Petty 3 in a Dodge, and Pearson 10 in a Mercury. Yarborough became series point champion.

Pearson also won the $343,300 Daytona 500 on Feb. 15 at Daytona Beach, Fla.; the $249,490 World 600 May 30 at Charlotte, N.C., plus 2 major races at Darlington, S.C.; and 2 at Irish Hills, Mich. The Daytona 500, the prestige race of the series, offered sensational racing, with 36 lead changes.

The richest race in history was the $1,037,775 Indianapolis 500 for high horsepower roadsters. It was held on May 30. Johnny Rutherford of Fort Worth, Texas, the 1974 victor, won again in a McLaren with a 4-cylinder Offenhauser engine. The race ended after the 102nd of the scheduled 200 laps because of rain.

BASEBALL

The 1976 major-league season created a high level of excitement both on and off the field, perhaps a carry-over from the excitement generated by the 1975 World Series. The Cincinnati Reds won their second straight National League pennant, the New York Yankees won their first American League pennant in 12 years, and the Reds won 4 straight games from the Yankees as they took the World Series for the second consecutive year.

Aside from the Reds, the division winners were new—the Yankees, the Kansas City (Mo.) Royals, and the Philadelphia Phillies. The season featured attractive new personalities, such as Mark ("The Bird") Fidrych, a rookie pitcher for the Detroit Tigers who talked to the baseball before he pitched it. And there were new, imaginative owners, such as Bill Veeck, who returned to the game with the Chicago White Sox.

Major-league attendance for the 1976 season set an all-time record of 31,318,531 for the 24 teams. In 1977 there would be 26 with the addition to the American League of teams in Seattle and Toronto. According to a United Press International survey, club income in 1976 reached between $150,000,000 and $175,000,000; this included $50,000,000 for television and radio rights.

Johnny Bench, the Cincinnati Reds' slugging catcher, watches a ball he has just hit sail into the left-field stands for a home run in the final game of the 1976 World Series. With Bench's help, the Reds achieved a four-game sweep over the New York Yankees.

NATIONAL LEAGUE

Eastern Division

	W	L	Pct.	GB
Philadelphia Phillies	101	61	.623	—
Pittsburgh Pirates	92	70	.568	9
New York Mets	86	76	.531	15
Chicago Cubs	75	87	.463	26
St. Louis Cardinals	72	90	.444	29
Montréal Expos	55	107	.340	46

Western Division

	W	L	Pct.	GB
Cincinnati Reds	102	60	.630	—
Los Angeles Dodgers	92	70	.568	10
Houston Astros	80	82	.494	22
San Francisco Giants	74	88	.457	28
San Diego Padres	73	89	.451	29
Atlanta Braves	70	92	.432	32

AMERICAN LEAGUE

Eastern Division

	W	L	Pct.	GB
New York Yankees	97	62	.610	—
Baltimore Orioles	88	74	.543	10½
Boston Red Sox	83	79	.512	15½
Cleveland Indians	81	78	.509	16
Detroit Tigers	74	87	.460	24
Milwaukee Brewers	66	95	.410	32

Western Division

	W	L	Pct.	GB
Kansas City Royals	90	72	.556	—
Oakland A's	87	74	.540	2½
Minnesota Twins	85	77	.525	5
California Angels	76	86	.469	14
Texas Rangers	76	86	.469	14
Chicago White Sox	64	97	.398	25½

PENNANT PLAYOFFS

National League—Cincinnati defeated Philadelphia, 3 games to 0

American League—New York defeated Kansas City, 3 games to 2

WORLD SERIES

Cincinnati defeated New York Yankees, 4 games to 0

The Freedom Issue. More significant than all of the statistics for 1976 was the so-called freedom issue. The old reserve clause in the standard player contract bound a player to his team until he retired or the team disposed of him. The 1976 baseball year began with a 17-day lockout of spring training camps, followed by long and bitter negotiations. Finally the club owners and players agreed to a major change in the reserve clause: After 5 years in the major leagues, players could be traded if they wished, and after 6 years they could become free agents.

The owners insisted that hundreds of players would become free agents and the sport would be disrupted. However, when the free-agent draft was held (Nov. 4 in New York City), only 24 players from 13 clubs were available. One of them, Reggie Jackson, signed the most lucrative contract—$2,900,000 for 5 years with the Yankees.

Significantly, 8 free agents were from the Oakland A's, which had won the 5 previous American League Western Division titles and three straight World Series (1972–74). Charles O. Finley, who owned the A's, was known for stormy relationships with players.

On June 15 Finley sold pitcher Vida Blue to the Yankees for $1,500,000 and outfielder Joe Rudi and relief pitcher Rollie Fingers to the Boston Red Sox for $1,000,000 each, only to have Commissioner Bowie Kuhn void the trades as "inconsistent with the best interests of baseball." Finley then sued Kuhn in federal court to reinstate the sales. The A's finished second in their division, 2½ games behind the Royals, but the loss in the free-agent draft of Rudi, Fingers, Bert Campaneris, Gene Tenace, Sal Bando, and others was crushing to the Oakland team.

World Series. The Reds became National League

High-Flying Rookie

First he got down on his hands and knees to pat the dirt on the mound, then he flapped his arms a bit and talked earnestly to the baseball. Using such unorthodox tactics, gangling Mark ("The Bird") Fidrych, 22, pitched his way to a 19–9 season with the lackluster Detroit Tigers and won the American League's Rookie of the Year Award by a mile. A native of Northboro, Mass., The Bird spent two years in the minors before swooping down on the big leagues with his crowd-pleasing antics and elusive fastball. After the season the appreciative Tigers tripled his salary, which had been a minimum-wage $16,000 a year.

The pitching stance of Mark Fidrych.

champions for the fourth time in 7 years. The Phillies' 15½-game lead over the Pittsburgh Pirates dwindled to 3 games before the Philadelphia team started winning again. The Reds defeated the Phillies in the pennant playoff in 3 straight games by scores of 6–3, 6–2, and 7–6.

The Yankees, once the most feared team in baseball, won the American League playoff in the last inning of the last game. A ninth-inning home run by Chris Chambliss sent them into the World Series, where the Reds dispatched them in 4 straight games, 5–1, 4–3, 6–2, and 7–2.

Honors. Bill Madlock of the Chicago Cubs, with .339, repeated as National League batting champion. George Brett of the Royals won the American League title under controversy. In the last inning of the last regular-season game, Brett's fly ball fell in front of left fielder Steve Brye of the Minnesota Twins and rolled to the wall for an inside-the-park home run. The next batter, Hal McRae, Brett's teammate and at that moment the batting leader, grounded out and then shouted angrily at the Minnesota bench. McRae believed manager Gene Mauch of the Twins had ordered Brye to allow Brett to get a hit if possible, and McRae called Mauch's decision racially motivated (Brett is white, McRae black). Mauch denied it. Brett's final average was .3333 to McRae's .3326.

Joe Morgan of the Reds, for the second straight year, and catcher Thurman Munson of the Yankees were voted the most valuable players in their leagues, and catcher Johnny Bench of the Reds was the most valuable player in the World Series. The Cy Young Awards for the outstanding pitchers went to Randy Jones of the San Diego Padres and Jim Palmer of the Baltimore Orioles. Jones and Palmer won 22 games each, more than any other major-league pitcher. Fidrych was the rookie of the year in the American League, and Pat Zachary of the Reds and Butch Metzger of the Padres shared this award in the National League.

Henry Aaron of the Milwaukee Brewers singled in his last time at bat in his last game for the 3771st hit of his 23-year major-league career. Then, at age 42, he retired with 755 home runs (the all-time record), a .305 lifetime batting average, and a new job as vice-president in charge of player development for the Atlanta Braves.

BASKETBALL

The 9-year-old battle between the National Basketball Association (N.B.A.) and the American Basketball Association (A.B.A.) for player talent, and its resultant bidding war that raised salaries to as high as $500,000 a year, ended in 1976. On June 17, less than 2 weeks after the N.B.A. playoffs ended, the leagues merged. The 18 teams of the N.B.A. and 4 of the 6 remaining teams of the A.B.A. formed a 22-team N.B.A. The four A.B.A.

Scott May of Indiana, named the outstanding college basketball player of the year, sinks a foul shot as his team beats Michigan in the finals of the National Collegiate Athletic Association championship tournament.

NATIONAL BASKETBALL ASSOCIATION
1975–76 Regular Season

EASTERN CONFERENCE

Atlantic Division

	W	L	Pct.	GB
Boston Celtics	54	28	.659	—
Buffalo Braves	46	36	.561	8
Philadelphia 76ers	46	36	.561	8
New York Knickerbockers	38	44	.463	16

Central Division

	W	L	Pct.	GB
Cleveland Cavaliers	49	33	.598	—
Washington Bullets	48	34	.585	1
Houston Rockets	40	42	.488	9
New Orleans Jazz	38	44	.463	11
Atlanta Hawks	29	53	.354	20

WESTERN CONFERENCE

Midwest Division

	W	L	Pct.	GB
Milwaukee Bucks	38	44	.463	—
Detroit Pistons	36	46	.439	2
Kansas City Kings	31	51	.378	7
Chicago Bulls	24	58	.293	14

Pacific Division

	W	L	Pct.	GB
Golden State Warriors	59	23	.720	—
Seattle SuperSonics	43	39	.524	16
Phoenix Suns	42	40	.512	17
Los Angeles Lakers	40	42	.488	19
Portland Trail Blazers	37	45	.451	22

PLAYOFFS

Qualifying Round
Buffalo defeated Philadelphia, 2 games to 1
Detroit defeated Milwaukee, 2 games to 1

Eastern Conference Eliminations
Boston defeated Buffalo, 4 games to 2
Cleveland defeated Washington, 4 games to 3

Western Conference Eliminations
Phoenix defeated Seattle, 4 games to 2
Golden State defeated Detroit, 4 games to 2

Conference Finals
Boston defeated Cleveland, 4 games to 2
Phoenix defeated Golden State, 4 games to 3

Championship Finals
Boston defeated Phoenix, 4 games to 2

teams that joined the N.B.A. were the champion New York Nets, based in Uniondale, N.Y.; the Indiana Pacers, who played in Indianapolis; the Denver Nuggets; and the San Antonio Spurs. Each paid $3,200,000 to enter the N.B.A.

AMERICAN BASKETBALL ASSOCIATION
1975–76 Regular Season

	W	L	Pct.	GB
Denver Nuggets	60	24	.714	—
New York Nets	55	29	.655	5
San Antonio Spurs	50	34	.595	10
Kentucky Colonels	46	38	.548	14
Indiana Pacers	39	45	.464	21
Spirits of St. Louis	35	49	.417	25
Virginia Squires	15	68	.181	44½

PLAYOFFS

First Round
New York defeated San Antonio, 4 games to 3
Denver defeated Kentucky, 4 games to 3

Championship Finals
New York defeated Denver, 4 games to 2

The A.B.A., without teams in most of the large U.S. cities, had lost money every year. Of the 10 teams that played in the A.B.A.'s 1975–76 season, the Baltimore Claws disbanded in October, 1975; the San Diego Sails in November, 1975; the Utah Stars in December, 1975; and the Virginia Squires in May, 1976. Of the 6 remaining teams, the Kentucky Colonels and the Utah Rockies (formerly the Spirits of Saint Louis) were excluded from the merger, and each received $3,000,000 in compensation from the 4 other A.B.A. teams.

The merger ended one of two major outstanding antitrust suits against the N.B.A. The out-of-court settlement of a class antitrust action brought by the players association in 1970 ended the other. Agreement was reached when the N.B.A. eliminated the option clause in the standard player contract.

Professional Championships. The Boston Celtics and the New York Nets won the league championships. The Celtics defeated the surprising Phoenix Suns, 4 games to 2, in the N.B.A. playoff finals. The Nets beat Denver, 4 games to 2, in the A.B.A. finals. The players of the year were Kareem Abdul-Jabbar of the Los Angeles Lakers in the N.B.A. and Julius Erving of the Nets in the A.B.A.

Collegiate Winners. Indiana University won its first national championship in 23 years. It defeated the University of Michigan, 86–68, March 29 at Philadelphia in the final game of the National Collegiate Athletic Association tournament. Indiana became only the seventh team to win this title after an undefeated regular season. Rutgers University, the only other major team unbeaten in the regular season, lost to the University of California at Los Angeles, by a score of 106–92, for third place. Scott May of Indiana was named player of the year.

BOATING

The popularity of pleasure boating continued to grow in 1976. Industry spokesmen estimated that $5.3 billion was spent in 1976 on boating goods and services, a $500,000,000 increase over 1975. The nine-day National Boat Show, held in New York City in January, reported record sales of $71,200,000 for boats, engines, and accessories.

Bill Muncey of La Mesa, Calif., drove his boat *Atlas Van Lines* to the unlimited hydroplane title. Joel Halpern of Bronxville, N.Y., won the national offshore title in a 38-ft. Cobra hull with 482-cu.in.-MerCruiser engines capable of generating 1200 hp.

The yacht race of the year was the 3000-mi. transatlantic single-handed race from Plymouth, England, to Newport, R.I. The major winners were Eric Tabarly of France in the 73-ft. ketch *Pen Duick VI,* among big boats, and Michael Birch of

England in the 32-ft. trimaran *The Third Turtle,* among small boats.

BOWLING

Earl Anthony of Tacoma, Wash., Betty Costello of Scranton, Pa., and Betty Morris of Stockton, Calif., dominated the professional bowling tours in 1976.

Anthony led the men for the third straight year. He won 7 tournaments—in Windsor Locks, Conn.; Tamarac, Fla.; Fresno and Norwalk, Calif.; Waukegan, Ill., and Battle Creek and Detroit, Mich. He raised his career total to 27 victories, an all-time record, and he passed $100,000 in career earnings for the second straight year.

In early competition in the women's U.S. Open, Betty Morris rolled a 6-game block of 1564, a world record that included 2 perfect games of 300. She finished second in the U.S. Open and won 8 tournaments, including the Women's International Bowling Congress all-events and the Brunswick world invitation. Betty Costello won 5 tournaments, including the U.S. Open and the Professional Women Bowler's Association na-

Looking fierce, Muhammad Ali misses a right hook against Ken Norton in their championship bout on Sept. 28. Although many observers disputed the decision, Ali retained his title.

tional championship. She, like Betty Morris, earned more than $30,000.

BOXING

Muhammad Ali, of Chicago, Ill., and the world, continued his reign as the outspoken and often outrageous world heavyweight champion. In 1976 he successfully defended his title 4 times in 7 months. Those battles raised his 18-month record to 8 defenses for purses totaling $20,700,000. After his last fight, Ali said he was retiring; a short time later he was discussing his future fight schedule.

Ali, 34, knocked out Jean-Pierre Coopman of Belgium in 5 rounds on Feb. 20 at San Juan, Puerto Rico. Next, he outpointed Jimmy Young of Philadelphia on April 30 at Landover, Md., in a bout much closer than the experts had anticipated. On May 25 Ali knocked out Richard Dunn of England in a 5-round bout held at Munich, West Germany. Finally, for a $6,000,000 purse, he barely outpointed Ken Norton of San Diego. The Norton fight occurred on Sept. 28 at New York City. Meanwhile, on June 25 in Tokyo, Ali had a memorable confrontation in a boxer-wrestler match against Antonio Inoki. There was little action, and the result was a dreary draw. Inoki spent the entire contest on his back kicking Ali's legs. An embarrassed Ali said later, "I wouldn't have done this fight if I'd known he was going to do that."

After the contest Ali's legs were badly swollen— 4 in. around the thighs, 2 in. around the calves. He was hospitalized in Los Angeles with superficial blood clots around the knees, muscle damage, and broken blood vessels; *see* PEOPLE IN THE NEWS.

Carlos Monzon of Argentina retained the world middleweight championship he had first won in 1970, outpointing Rodrigo Valdes of Colombia on June 26 at Monte Carlo. Monzon had not been defeated or even floored in 12 years. Another champion, Roberto Duran of Panama, made the eighth and ninth successful defenses of the lightweight title he had won in 1972.

FOOTBALL

The structure of professional football came under renewed attack by federal courts in 1976. The main victim was the draft of college players, and club owners feared a suicidal bidding war for such college seniors as Tony Dorsett of the University of Pittsburgh and Ricky Bell of the University of Southern California. Dorsett led Pittsburgh to the mythical national college championship.

Professional. The National Football League (N.F.L.) champions were the Oakland Raiders, who defeated the Minnesota Vikings, 32–14, in the Super Bowl on Jan. 9, 1977, at Pasadena, Calif. The N.F.L. had spent a frustrating year as federal courts struck down the Rozelle rule and the college draft, ruling in separate cases that each violated antitrust laws. The Rozelle rule required that a player's former team be compensated when he signed with a new team. Its demise seemed to make little difference; 24 players played out the option year of their contracts and 13 moved to new teams without those teams compensating the players' previous clubs. The college draft was another matter. The draft was devised to allow weaker teams to strengthen themselves, and such teams as the Pittsburgh Steelers were built almost exclusively on draft choices. But in 1976 a federal court struck down the draft, and as 1977 began the N.F.L. had made no decision on how to pro-

ceed with the signing or assigning of college seniors. These and other problems might have been solved by agreement between the league and the N.F.L. Players Association. Although the players' last contract had expired three years before, Ed Garvey, the executive director of the Players Association, preferred to let the guidelines come from the courts rather than from negotiations.

The Steelers had hoped to become the first team to win three consecutive Super Bowl games. Although they lost 4 of their first 5 regular-season games, they won the last 9 to gain the playoffs; then they won their first playoff game. But their comeback ended Dec. 26 in the American Football Conference final at Oakland when the Raiders beat them, 24–7. In the National Football Conference final at Bloomington, Minn., earlier the same day, the Vikings had defeated the Los Ange-

NATIONAL FOOTBALL LEAGUE

AMERICAN CONFERENCE

Eastern Division	W	L	T
Baltimore Colts	11	3	0
New England Patriots	11	3	0
Miami Dolphins	6	8	0
New York Jets	3	11	0
Buffalo Bills	2	12	0

Central Division	W	L	T
Pittsburgh Steelers	10	4	0
Cincinnati Bengals	10	4	0
Cleveland Browns	9	5	0
Houston Oilers	5	9	0

Western Division	W	L	T
Oakland Raiders	13	1	0
Denver Broncos	9	5	0
San Diego Chargers	6	8	0
Kansas City Chiefs	5	9	0
Tampa Bay Buccaneers	0	14	0

NATIONAL CONFERENCE

Eastern Division	W	L	T
Dallas Cowboys	11	3	0
Washington Redskins	10	4	0
St. Louis Cardinals	10	4	0
Philadelphia Eagles	4	10	0
New York Giants	3	11	0

Central Division	W	L	T
Minnesota Vikings	11	2	1
Chicago Bears	7	7	0
Detroit Lions	6	8	0
Green Bay Packers	5	9	0

Western Division	W	L	T
Los Angeles Rams	10	3	1
San Francisco 49ers	8	6	0
Atlanta Falcons	4	10	0
New Orleans Saints	4	10	0
Seattle Seahawks	2	12	0

AMERICAN CONFERENCE PLAYOFFS
First Round
Oakland 24, New England 21
Pittsburgh 40, Baltimore 14

Championship
Oakland 24, Pittsburgh 7

NATIONAL CONFERENCE PLAYOFFS
First Round
Minnesota 35, Washington 20
Los Angeles 14, Dallas 12

Championship
Minnesota 24, Los Angeles 13

SUPER BOWL
Oakland 32, Minnesota 14

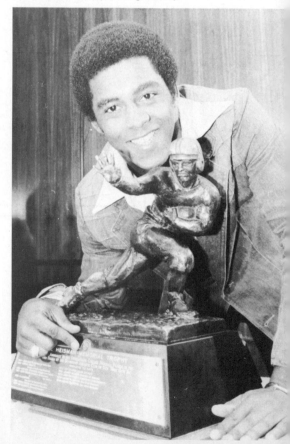

Tony Dorsett, the University of Pittsburgh's running back, with the Heisman trophy awarded to him as college player of the year. Dorsett rushed for more yards in a season and a career and scored more points than any football player in major college history.

Oakland Raiders wide receiver Fred Biletnikoff slides almost to the goal line after a spectacular catch of a forward pass. For this and other catches that led to touchdowns, Biletnikoff was named the most valuable player in the 1977 Super Bowl game.

les Rams, 24–13, scoring a touchdown and a field goal after two blocked kicks. Although both the Raiders and the Vikings had lost their previous Super Bowl appearances, they were truly winning teams. They had the year's best regular-season records: 13–1 for the Raiders and 11–2–1 for the Vikings. In their 14 years with Al Davis (first as coach and then as managing general partner), the Raiders had a regular-season record of 139–46–11, the best in the league. In the 7 seasons since the merger of the N.F.L. with the American Football League, the Vikings had a regular-season record of 75–22–1, the best in the league.

At the other end of the success scale were the Tampa Bay Buccaneers, a new team that lost all 14 of their games—the first time that had ever happened. The Seattle Seahawks, the other expansion team, won 2 of their games.

The players of the year were quarterback Bert Jones of the Baltimore Colts and middle linebacker Jack Lambert of the Steelers, the leading runners O. J. Simpson of the Buffalo Bills and Walter Payton of the Chicago Bears, and the leading passers Ken Stabler of the Raiders and James Harris of the Rams. The coaches of the year were Chuck Fairbanks of the New England Patriots and Paul Wiggin of the Cleveland Browns.

Canadian Professionals. Two of the 9 teams in the Canadian Football League had similar nicknames—the Ottawa Rough Riders and the Saskatchewan Roughriders. They also had similar success, as they won the division titles and met for the Grey Cup on Nov. 28 at Toronto. Ottawa won, 23–20, on a 24-yd. pass from Tom Clements to Tony Gabriel with 20 sec. remaining in the game.

The Canadian league, which had survived with relatively modest attendance, struck a bonanza in 1976. The Montréal Alouettes moved into Olympic Stadium, built for the international Olympic Games, in July, and drew 68,505 spectators for their first game there at prices of as much as $25 per ticket.

College. In 1973 a coach and a player started a four-year campaign to bring football success to the University of Pittsburgh. The year before, Pittsburgh had won 1 game and lost 10. In 1976 the 4-year plan ended in success, as Pittsburgh won all 11 regular-season games and the Sugar Bowl and became the national champion.

The coach was Johnny Majors, the player Tony Dorsett. Majors was a University of Tennessee graduate. Tennessee wanted him to return as coach in 1976, but he would not leave Pittsburgh before Dorsett's senior year. After the 1976 season, when Tennessee once again sought him, Majors accepted a 6-year contract at $50,000 per year.

Dorsett won the 1976 Heisman Trophy as the nation's leading player, after breaking 15 all-time rushing records and tying 3 others. He became the first player in major-college history to rush for

6000 yd. in a career, his 6082 yd. far outdistancing Archie Griffin's record of 5177. Dorsett was a true star: fast, quick, and elusive. In the Sugar Bowl on Jan. 1, 1977, at New Orleans, the University of Georgia keyed its defense to stop Dorsett's running. Despite that, Dorsett ran for 202 yd., a record for postseason bowl games, and led Pittsburgh to a 27–3 victory. In the other major college bowl games, there were two surprises. Southern California and Michigan met in the Rose Bowl at Pasadena, with Southern California winning, 14–6. And Houston beat previously undefeated Maryland, 30–21, in the Cotton Bowl at Dallas.

In their final polls, taken after the bowl games, both the Associated Press and United Press International ranked Pittsburgh first, Southern California second, Michigan third, and Houston fourth.

GOLF

The outstanding golfer of 1976 was a woman. Judy Rankin, 31 years old and a professional for 14 years, became the first woman to earn $100,000 a year in prize money, and she achieved that in 6 months, finishing the year with $150,734. She played on the Ladies Professional Golf Association circuit of 32 tournaments, which carried a record total of $2,800,000 in purses. Judy Rankin won 6 tournaments, JoAnne Carner 4 (including the U.S. Open), Sandra Palmer 3, and Donna Caponi Young 3.

The most successful male professional golfers were Ray Floyd, Jerry Pate, Johnny Miller, Dave Stockton, Ben Crenshaw, Hubert Green, and Jack Nicklaus. Floyd won the Masters and tied for second behind Stockton in the Professional Golfers' Association (P.G.A.) championship. Pate, a professional for 6 months, won the U.S. Open at the age of 22. Crenshaw and Green won 3 tournaments each, Green's on 3 successive weekends in March. Miller won the British Open.

Nicklaus led the men in earnings with $266,438. He won 2 tournaments, including the expanded World Series of Golf, for which the winner's purse of $100,000 was the highest on the P.G.A. tour. (The tour's 44 tournaments were worth a record $9,000,000.) But Nicklaus also had bad days. On Jan. 25, needing a 71 to win the Bing Crosby tournament in Pebble Beach, Calif., he shot an 82. His back nine included two triple bogeys and one double bogey, and once he was buried so deep in a trap that he called people over to show them and laugh with them. On Sept. 10, the week after he won the World Series of Golf, he failed to survive the 36-hole cut in the World Open at Pinehurst, N.C. The Pinehurst cut marked the first time in 105 tournaments in 6 years that Nicklaus had not survived for 72 holes.

Johnny Miller's home was in Napa, Calif., be-

Top woman professional Judy Rankin was the outstanding golfer of the year. She won six top tournaments on the Ladies Professional Golf Association circuit and earned over $150,000 in prize money.

tween the tenth green and the eleventh tee of a course. On Sept. 23 in the Kaiser International Open, with his parents watching from his front lawn, he scored a hole in one on the 182-yd. eleventh hole en route to a course record of 63. Miller, however, finished second to J. C. Snead in the tournament.

HARNESS RACING

A horse named Steve Lobell won the Hambletonian, harness racing's most prestigious race, but he almost paid with his life.

366

The $263,524 Hambletonian, the richest trotting race in history, was held Sept. 4 at Du Quoin, Ill. After the first 3 heats had produced their 3 winners, Steve Lobell won the fourth and final heat and the race. Three hours later he collapsed from heat, exhaustion, and a high fever; a veterinarian and stablehands needed 2 hours to revive him. In the other triple-crown races for 3-year-old trotters, Steve Lobell won the Yonkers Trot but was narrowly beaten by Quick Pay, his stablemate, in the Kentucky Futurity.

In the major races for 3-year-old pacers, Keystone Ore finished first in the Little Brown Jug and Cane Futurity, second in the Messenger Stake and Adios, and third in the Shapiro Stakes, and was voted harness horse of the year. Herve Filion won more races and more money than any other driver.

HORSE RACING

The best thoroughbreds of 1976 were a 6-year-old gelding named Forego and a 3-year-old colt named Bold Forbes. Forego became horse of the year for the third time in a row, and Bold Forbes won both the Kentucky Derby and the Belmont Stakes, 2 of the 3 triple-crown races.

Of his 8 races, Forego won 6; he took 1 second place and 1 third. The gelding earned $491,701 for the year and raised his lifetime earnings to $1,484,997, the third highest earnings in horse-racing history. Carrying 137 lb., the most of his career, he won the year's climactic race, the $283,700 Marlboro Cup (Oct. 2 at Belmont Park) with a spectacular stretch run.

In the $217,700 Kentucky Derby, held May 1 at Churchill Downs, Bold Forbes's fast pace helped him win by a length. When he raced too fast too early in the $182,200 Preakness (May 15 at Pimlico), he finished third; Elocutionist won.

Bold Forbes, with Angel Cordero, Jr., in the saddle, wins the 102nd Kentucky Derby at Churchill Downs on May 1. Honest Pleasure, ridden by Braulio Baeza, finished second.

NATIONAL HOCKEY LEAGUE
1975–76 Regular Season

Prince of Wales Conference

Norris Division	W	L	T	Pts.
Montréal Canadiens	58	11	11	127
Los Angeles Kings	38	33	9	85
Pittsburgh Penguins	35	33	12	82
Detroit Red Wings	26	44	10	62
Washington Capitals	11	59	10	32

Adams Division	W	L	T	Pts.
Boston Bruins	48	15	17	113
Buffalo Sabres	46	21	13	105
Toronto Maple Leafs	34	31	15	83
California Golden Seals	27	42	11	65

Clarence Campbell Conference

Patrick Division	W	L	T	Pts.
Philadelphia Flyers	51	13	16	118
New York Islanders	42	21	17	101
Atlanta Flames	35	33	12	82
New York Rangers	29	42	9	67

Smythe Division	W	L	T	Pts.
Chicago Black Hawks	32	30	18	82
Vancouver Canucks	33	32	15	81
St. Louis Blues	29	37	14	72
Minnesota North Stars	20	53	7	47
Kansas City Scouts	12	56	12	36

STANLEY CUP PLAYOFFS
First Round
Islanders defeated Vancouver, 2 games to 0
Buffalo defeated St. Louis, 2 games to 1
Toronto defeated Pittsburgh, 2 games to 1
Los Angeles defeated Atlanta, 2 games to 0

Second Round
Montréal defeated Chicago, 4 games to 0
Philadelphia defeated Toronto, 4 games to 3
Islanders defeated Buffalo, 4 games to 2
Boston defeated Los Angeles, 4 games to 3

Semifinal Round
Montréal defeated Islanders, 4 games to 1
Philadelphia defeated Boston, 4 games to 1

Championship Finals
Montréal defeated Philadelphia, 4 games to 0

tréal the Canadians took the tournament by winning two consecutive games from Czechoslovakia. The Czechs had won the world amateur championship earlier in the year.

Team Canada included most of the top players in the National Hockey League (N.H.L.) and two (Bobby Hull and Paul Shmyr) from the World Hockey Association (W.H.A.). Among its stars were Bobby Clarke of the Philadelphia Flyers, the N.H.L.'s most valuable player; Guy Lafleur of the Montréal Canadiens, the N.H.L. scoring champion; and Bobby Orr, the N.H.L.'s highest paid and perhaps most talented player. (During the year Mayor Kevin White of Boston likened the 28-year-old Orr to such Boston institutions as Paul Revere's house and the Bunker Hill monument.) But Orr, still recovering from his fifth left-knee operation, played only 10 games for the Boston Bruins during the season. After the season, his contract having expired, he signed with the Black Hawks for $3,000,000 for 6 years, to be paid even if he could not play.

The Canadiens won the N.H.L.'s Stanley Cup playoffs in 13 games, 1 more than the minimum, a feat matched in the W.H.A. by the Winnipeg Jets. The Canadiens defeated the Flyers, who had been the champions for 2 previous seasons, in 4 straight

WORLD HOCKEY ASSOCIATION
1975–76 Regular Season

Canadian Division	W	L	T	Pts.
Winnipeg Jets	52	27	2	106
Québec Nordiques	50	27	4	104
Calgary Cowboys	41	35	4	86
Edmonton Oilers	27	49	5	59
Toronto Toros	24	52	5	53

Eastern Division	W	L	T	Pts.
Indianapolis Racers	35	39	6	76
Cleveland Crusaders	35	40	5	75
New England Whalers	33	40	7	73
Cincinnati Stingers	35	44	1	71

Western Division	W	L	T	Pts.
Houston Aeros	53	27	0	106
Phoenix Roadrunners	39	35	6	84
San Diego Mariners	36	38	6	78
*Minnesota Fighting Saints	30	25	4	64
*Denver/Ottawa	14	26	1	29

*Disbanded during season

WORLD CUP PLAYOFFS
First Round
New England defeated Cleveland, 3 games to 0
San Diego defeated Phoenix, 3 games to 2

Second Round
Winnipeg defeated Edmonton, 4 games to 0
Houston defeated San Diego, 4 games to 2
New England defeated Indianapolis, 4 games to 3
Calgary defeated Québec, 4 games to 1

Semifinal Round
Winnipeg defeated Calgary, 4 games to 1
Houston defeated New England, 4 games to 3

Championship Finals
Winnipeg defeated Houston, 4 games to 0

In the $195,000 Belmont Stakes at Belmont Park on June 5, Bold Forbes led by 6 lengths in the stretch and won by a neck. Then he was idled 4 months with an injured hoof. He raced twice in October and was then retired. His financial record: Bold Forbes had cost $15,200 at a yearling auction, earned $523,035 in his 18-race career, and was syndicated for $4,000,000 for stud duty.

In 1976 Willie Shoemaker became the first jockey to win 7000 races during his career. Both Angel Cordero, Jr., and Sandy Hawley broke the previous record for purse money won by a rider in one year: $4,251,060, which Laffit Pincay, Jr., won in 1974.

ICE HOCKEY

In September, 1976, for the first time, the world's best national teams, professional and amateur, competed in the same tournament, when teams from six nations met for the Canada Cup. Team Canada won the round-robin preliminaries against Czechoslovakia, the Soviet Union, Sweden, the U.S., and Finland. In the finals at Mon-

Team Canada scores a goal against Czechoslovakia in the final game of the Canada Cup ice hockey series. The Canadians won the game in sudden-death overtime by a score of 5–4.

games in the Stanley Cup finals. The Jets swept past the Houston Aeros in 4 consecutive games in the W.H.A. finals, ending the Aeros' 2-year reign.

ICE SKATING

Nineteen-year-old Dorothy Hamill of Riverside, Conn., and 26-year-old John Curry of Great Britain swept the major figure skating honors of the year, including the Olympic and world championships.

Both skaters had been coached in Denver, Colo., by Carlo Fassi, who had coached Peggy Fleming to Olympic and world titles in 1968. When the season ended, both Hamill and Dianne

de Leeuw of the Netherlands, her chief rival, turned professional and signed with ice shows. Curry also retired as an amateur and formed a skating troupe.

In speed skating 25-year-old Sheila Young of Detroit won her third world sprint championship in 4 years and finished third in the world overall championships. She was also a world champion

369

A Game Known as Jai Alai Comes Hurtling North
Beginning early in the summer, Bridgeport and Hartford, Conn., were the unlikely scenes for almost nightly matches of a 300-year-old sport that originated in Europe and took firm hold in Florida as a betting game about fifty years ago: It is called jai alai. At the two Connecticut *frontons* (arenas), the sport (which features players who use long wicker baskets to throw a small hard ball against a distant wall and then catch the 150-m.p.h. rebounds) was an instant hit with fans and a big financial success. In its first six months the Hartford *fronton* generated $3,500,000 in revenues for the state and handled an average of $300,000 in bets six nights a week.

A game of jai alai takes about 15 min. to play; the first who gets 7 points is the winner.

cyclist, and she sold her racing bike for $250 to help pay her fiancé's way to the Winter Olympics. She made it worthwhile by winning 3 medals at Innsbruck, including a gold.

ROWING

East Germany, which dominated the 1975 world rowing championships, was equally strong in the 1976 Olympic Games. The East Germans won 5 gold medals, 1 silver, and 2 bronze in the 8 events for men and 4 gold and 2 silver in the 6 events for women.

The U.S. won 3 Olympic medals. Joan Lind of Long Beach, Calif., took the silver medal in women's single sculls, beaten by a half length by an East German. The Americans also captured the silver medal in men's pairs without coxswain and the bronze in women's eights. The highly regarded American men's eight was eliminated in the trials.

The undefeated Harvard University crew, although it lost 6 men by their graduation, remained the unofficial national college champion. It was Harvard that won the Eastern sprint championship; the University of Washington won the Western sprint title. The University of California, winner of the season-ending Intercollegiate Rowing Association regatta, had lost three times earlier in the year, once to Harvard and twice to Washington.

SKIING

Rosi Mittermaier of West Germany, in her eleventh and last year of international competition, almost swept the major honors for women in 1976. She won two Olympic gold medals and almost won a third, and she captured the World

Cup. Then she retired from skiing to become a designor of sports clothes.

As usual the World Cup series ran from December to March in Europe and North America. The 25-year-old Miss Mittermaier won the women's competition easily. Twenty-year-old Ingemar Stenmark of Sweden took the men's title. Henri Duvillard of France dominated the 21-meet professional circuit.

Austria again won the Nations Cup as the leading amateur team, with the U.S. sixth for the fourth straight year. Of the 53 World Cup competitions, Americans won only 2—the men's giant slalom at Copper Mountain, Colo. (by Greg Jones of Tahoe City, Calif.), and the women's combined at Wengen, Switzerland (by Cindy Nelson of Lutsen, Minn.). Miss Nelson finished eighth overall among women; hers was the highest showing by any American, male or female.

Gustavo Thoeni of Italy, the men's champion 4 times in 5 years, finished third overall. Annemarie Proell Moser of Austria, the women's champion the 5 previous years, temporarily retired and raced automobiles, but she returned to skiing for the 1976–77 season.

SOCCER

The great Brazilian player Pelé had joined the New York Cosmos of the North American Soccer League (N.A.S.L.) in 1975; almost single-handedly he had started soccer on its way to acceptance as a major American spectator sport. The growth of the game continued in 1976, again aided by Pelé.

At the age of 35, Pelé, the leading scorer in soccer history, was the third leading scorer in the league; he also helped his new teammate, Giorgio

Chinaglia of Italy, win the scoring title. With Pelé and the Cosmos helping by attracting large crowds, league attendance averaged 10,300 per game and neared 2,500,000 for the season, both records, although television audiences declined. The American Soccer League (A.S.L.), an older but smaller professional league, averaged 2400 spectators per game.

Both leagues played from April to August. The 20 teams of the N.A.S.L. had mostly foreign players; the members of the A.S.L.'s 11 teams were mostly Americans. The Toronto Metros, 1 of the N.A.S.L.'s 2 Canada-based teams, won the league championship by beating the Minnesota Kicks, 3-0, on Aug. 28 at Seattle. The Los Angeles Skyhawks, 1 of the A.S.L.'s 5 new teams, took their league title with a 2-1 triumph over the New York Apollos. The final game was played Aug. 27 at Los Angeles.

In the major European competition, Anderlecht of Belgium won the European Cup of Cup Winners and Bayern Munich of West Germany won its third consecutive European Champions Cup. Finally, Anderlecht defeated Bayern Munich for the European Supercup. Liverpool of England captured the European Federation Cup and the English League first-division championship.

SWIMMING

John Naber of Menlo Park, Calif., and Kornelia Ender of East Germany won more Olympic medals and broke more world records than any other swimmers in 1976.

Naber was a 20-year-old college junior (at the University of Southern California); Miss Ender was a 17-year-old schoolgirl. Each won 4 gold medals and 1 silver in the Montréal Olympics. Naber broke 4 world records—2 in the backstroke and 2 in relays. Miss Ender broke 5 world records in freestyle, butterfly, backstroke, and individual medley, though her backstroke record lasted only 2 days.

The 6-ft.-6-in. Naber, a friendly, outgoing young man with a delightful sense of humor, even created a grand slam. Never before had a swimmer won the same event in the 5 major meets in the same year. In 1976 Naber won both backstroke races in the Amateur Athletic Union indoor and outdoor and National Collegiate championships, the U.S. Olympic trials, and the Olympic Games.

Other outstanding male swimmers included Brian Goodell, John Hencken, and Jim Montgomery, all of the U.S., and Jonty Skinner, a South African. Petra Thumer and Ulrike Tauber of East Germany were the outstanding women. Shirley Babashoff of Fountain Valley, Calif., the best American woman, swam in 6 Olympic events and won 4 silver medals and 1 gold.

World records were bettered in 13 of the 16 men's swimming events, 11 times by Americans. The 15 women's events produced 14 world records, 12 by East Germans.

TENNIS

For different reasons, Ilie Nastase and Renee Richards created consternation in tennis in 1976.

Nastase, a tempestuous Rumanian, lost to Björn Borg of Sweden in straight sets in the July 3 final of the Wimbledon championships in England and in the Sept. 11 semifinals of the U.S. Open at Forest Hills, N.Y. His ability was overshadowed by his almost constant arguments with opponents, with spectators, and especially with officials. He cursed and he antagonized. As Dave Anderson wrote in the New York *Times,* "He is permitted to get away

Tom Simons of Aspen, Colo., flashes to a new world speed ski record (an average of 117 m.p.h.) at Cervinia, Italy, in July.

371

The young Swedish star Björn Borg strokes a two-handed backhand return in his spectacular straight-set victory over Ilie Nastase in the All-England Championship final at Wimbledon.

with ugly, obscene behavior that would never be tolerated of a lesser player. The difference is that Ilie Nastase sells tickets."

Renee Richards was a 42-year-old resident of La Jolla, Calif. Until a 1975 sex-change operation, she had been Richard Raskind, a physician as well as a ranked player among older men. In 1976 she won a tournament in her hometown, but most women players, fearing for the sport's image and perhaps daunted by Dr. Richards' ability, withdrew from a tournament in South Orange, N.J., in which she played later; *see* PEOPLE IN THE NEWS.

Chris Evert of Fort Lauderdale, Fla., continued to be the outstanding woman player. The 21-year-old Miss Evert defeated Evonne Goolagong of Australia in both the Wimbledon and U.S. Open finals. She passed $1,000,000 in career earnings and did not lose a match from April to November.

Evert also played in World Team Tennis for the Phoenix Racquets, and she was voted both player of the year and rookie of the year. The New York Sets, led by Billie Jean King, won the league championship. In other championships Italy won the Davis Cup for men, and the U.S. won the Federation Cup for women.

Björn Borg's year was marred on Sept. 12 when he lost the U.S. Open final to Jimmy Connors of Belleville, Ill., by scores of 6–4, 3–6, 7–6, and 6–4. At 20 Borg had become the youngest Wimbledon champion in 45 years and the first in 13 years to win without losing a set. He earned so much money that he moved his parents and himself to Monte Carlo to avoid higher taxes in Sweden.

TRACK AND FIELD

By either of two standards—records broken or honors won—American men and East German women did well in the track and field events of 1976. American men won 6 of the 23 gold medals and 19 of a possible 65 total medals in the Olympic Games, the year's major competition. The Olympic champions were Bruce Jenner of San Jose, Calif., in the decathlon; Edwin Moses of Dayton, Ohio, in the 400-m hurdles; Mac Wilkins of San Jose in the discus throw; Arnie Robinson of San Diego, Calif., in the long jump; and the members of both relay teams.

Jenner set a world record of 8618 points for the 10-event, 2-day decathlon. Moses set a world record of 47.64 sec. for the hurdles, a race he had never run until the spring. Wilkins broke an Olympic record, and in the spring he broke the world record 4 times in 1 week.

However, the Americans were shut out of medals in the 100-m dash for the first time since 1928 and in the shot put for the first time since 1936. In addition, an American failed to win the high hurdles for the first time since 1928. Two Americans who were favored to win their Olympic events but were unsuccessful did set new world records during the year. They were Dwight Stones in the high jump and Dave Roberts in the pole vault.

Willie Davenport of Baton Rouge, La., the 33-year-old bronze medalist in the high hurdles, summed it up this way: "America is as good as it was years ago. It's just that the rest of the world has caught up."

The foreign track-and-field stars of the year were Alberto Juantorena of Cuba, Lasse Viren of Finland, and John Walker of New Zealand among the men and Tatyana Kazankina of the Soviet Union and Irena Szewinska of Poland among the women. All were Olympic champions or world record holders or both.   F.L.

SPORTS: THE OLYMPIC GAMES

On land, on the water (and in it), on snow, and on ice the athletes of the 1976 Olympics astonished the world. Even the air was full of them as gymnasts and divers, pole vaulters and ski jumpers performed brilliantly—in spite of pressures political and nonpolitical.

The Summer Games of the twenty-first Olympiad could be remembered as a magnificent sports spectacle that brought together the youth of the world in friendly competition. They were indeed such a spectacle. But it is more likely that they will be remembered for their huge cost and the vast political problems that kept the athletes of almost one fourth of the member nations from competing. The Summer Games were held from July 17 to Aug. 1 in Montréal, Canada's largest and most cosmopolitan city.

The Cost. In 1970, when the International Olympic Committee (I.O.C.) awarded the Games to Montréal, the organizers estimated the total cost at $310,000,000. The actual cost was at least $1.4 billion, and one Canadian official mentioned casually that it might reach $2 billion. The I.O.C., which conducted the quadrennial competition, was angry at the high cost. So were most Canadi-

ans, because they believed they would eventually have to pay the bill. The largest item was the Olympic Stadium, which accommodated 70,000 spectators for opening and closing ceremonies, track and field, and other events. In December, 1974, only nineteen months before the start of the Games, the Montréal organizers finally realized that the Canadian government would not finance the stadium, and they started excavation.

By November, 1975, labor delays had cost 111 workdays and the construction schedule was lagging. The provincial government of Québec took over from the organizers and finished the stadium on time, at a high labor cost. In the final months before the Games, the stadium had 3500 construction workers by day and 1500 by night. Their wages averaged $14 an hour and, working as much overtime as they wished, they earned $1200 to $1500 a week. The stadium alone eventually

He Kept the Flame Burning
Presiding over his first games as president of the International Olympic Committee, Sir Michael Morris, Baron Killanin, kept the Olympic flame burning in spite of hostile crosscurrents. Labor difficulties threatened to cancel the Summer Games, then political disputes led to the absence of Taiwan and many Third World nations from Montréal competition. But the Cambridge-educated Lord Killanin, 62, an energetic Irish businessman, sometime movie producer, and former journalist, insisted that the Games go on. He closed the twenty-first Olympiad with the hope that all nations would compete at the Moscow Olympics in 1980.

Lord Killanin, president of the International Olympic Committee.

cost at least $685,000,000. The nearby Olympic Village cost $85,000,000 and security cost $140,000,-000. The total deficit reached $800,000,000.

Some of the costs were unusual. For example: The organizers spent $1,000,000 more to rent thirty-three cranes than they would have spent to buy them, and security forces spent $1,500,000 for walkie-talkies.

Taiwan. The first political crisis of the Summer Olympics involved the island nation of Taiwan off the coast of China. Taiwan was recognized by the I.O.C. as the Republic of China. The People's Republic of China, or mainland China, was not a member of the I.O.C. and thus could not compete in the Games, but it objected to Taiwan's participation because it considered Taiwan to be a part of China.

Mainland China urged Canada to bar Taiwan. Mainland China was Canada's major overseas customer and in 1975 gave Canada a trade surplus of $320,000,000, of which $307,000,000 was from grain sales. On the other hand, Canada had a $144,000,000 trade deficit with Taiwan in 1975.

Canada refused to let Taiwan compete as the

Republic of China. The I.O.C. was furious that Canada would not accept one of its members, but it said it would not cancel the Olympics. The United States, supporting Taiwan, almost withdrew from the Games. Although its athletes seemed willing to compete under any name, Taiwan finally withdrew.

The New Zealand Question. In 1972 black African nations had threatened to withdraw from the Olympics at Munich unless Rhodesia was barred, because of that African nation's racial policies. Rhodesia was consequently barred. In 1976 the same African nations threatened to withdraw unless New Zealand was barred, because New Zealand's national rugby team was touring South Africa. The I.O.C. had barred South Africa because of its racial practices, but it was reluctant to punish New Zealand. Other nations had also sent athletes to South Africa, and in any case the New Zealand Olympic Committee had no control over rugby.

The New Zealand team stayed and the teams of thirty-one other nations left. Most of them were from Africa; one (Guyana) was from South America. James Gilkes, Guyana's best athlete, attempted unsuccessfully to run in the Olympics under the I.O.C. flag.

The boycott removed such outstanding track

Teams of the competing nations parade in Montréal's new Olympic Stadium and take their places on the field. The opening ceremonies of the twenty-first Olympiad were held on July 17.

The star of the Summer Olympics, Nadia Comaneci, shows her perfect form on the balance beam. The 14-year-old Rumanian gymnast won an astounding 3 gold medals, 1 silver, and 1 bronze.

athletes as Filbert Bayi of Tanzania, cofavorite in the 1500-m run; John Akii-Bua of Uganda, 1972 champion and 1976 favorite in the 400-m hurdles; and Mike Boit of Kenya, cofavorite in the 800-m run.

The boycott forced competition in many sports to be canceled and schedules redrawn. Half of the bouts on some boxing programs were wiped out.

Medals. The competition involved 186 events—and countless races, games, bouts, and matches—in 21 sports. As expected, the nations that won the most medals were the Soviet Union, East Germany, and the U.S.

The U.S.S.R. led all the nations in medals, including gold (47), silver (43), and bronze (35). East Germany was second in gold with 40, and also won 20 silver and 20 bronze. In gold medals the U.S. was third with 34, but the American athletes topped the East Germans with 35 silver and 25 bronze.

The Soviet and American gold-medal totals were similar to their totals in 1972. The East Germans, however, helped by a massive state-supported sports program, doubled their number of gold medals. They dominated women's track and field (9 gold medals in 14 events), women's swim-

ming (11 gold medals in 13 events), and men's and women's rowing (9 gold medals in 14 events). The U.S.S.R. scored heavily in Greco-Roman wrestling (7 gold medals in 10 events), freestyle wrestling (5 gold medals in 10 events), men's gymnastics (4 gold medals in 8 events), and team handball (men's and women's gold medals).

The strong sports for the U.S. were men's swimming (12 gold medals in 13 events), men's track and field (6 gold medals in 23 events), boxing (5 gold medals in 11 events), archery (both gold medals), basketball (regaining the gold medal lost in 1972), and diving (2 gold medals in 4 events).

In addition the Americans made breakthroughs in events in which they had traditionally lagged behind Europeans. They won a silver and a bronze medal in women's rowing, a silver in women's basketball, a bronze in men's gymnastics, and a bronze in judo. These achievements heartened the American officials. But the officials still insisted that they would need money from the federal government, corporations, and indi-

Other women who excelled at Montréal included Kornelia Ender of East Germany, Irena Szewinska of Poland, and Tatyana Kazankina of the U.S.S.R. The 17-year-old Ender won 4 gold medals and 1 silver in swimming. The 30-year-old Szewinska won a gold medal in the 400-m dash, marking the fourth consecutive Olympics in which she won a medal in women's track. Kazankina won two gold medals—for the 800-m and for the 1500-m races.

Among the male track stars was Lasse Viren of Finland, who won the 5000-m and 10,000-m runs, as he had in 1972; this "double double" victory had never before been achieved. The charismatic Bruce Jenner of San Jose, Calif., won the decathlon with a spectacular world-record performance; *see* People in the News. Alberto Juantorena of

Tensed muscles and a bent pole whip Bruce Jenner up and over the pole vault bar in the Olympic decathlon competition. The U.S. athlete set a new world record in winning the ten-event endurance test.

East Germany's great swimmer, Kornelia Ender, happily scans the results board—and learns that she has broken the record in the women's 100-m butterfly race. Her gold medal in this event was 1 of 4 she won at the Olympics.

vidual contributors in order to develop athletes to compete against the constantly improving athletes from the state-supported teams of other countries.

Stars. It was universally agreed that the outstanding athlete of the Summer Olympics was Nadia Comaneci, a 14-year-old Rumanian gymnast (*see* People in the News). Only 4 ft. 11 in. tall and weighing 86 lb., she won 3 gold medals, 1 silver, and 1 bronze, all with a perfection never before seen. Gymnastics performances are rated from 0 to 10 according to execution and difficulty. Only a few of the world's greatest gymnasts had ever received a perfect score of 10. And no 10 had ever been awarded by Olympic judges until 1976, when Comaneci recorded seven 10's on the uneven parallel bars and the balance beam. In 1972, when Olga Korbut of the U.S.S.R. dazzled the world with her performances at the Munich Olympics, gymnastics began to command public attention for the first time. It was front-page news when Comaneci unseated Korbut at the 1976 Olympics. Although Korbut won both a gold and a silver medal in Montréal, she was an almost forgotten figure.

Cuba won the 400-m and 800-m runs, a double victory never before completed in the Olympics. And Willie Davenport, a 33-year-old hurdler from Baton Rouge, La., earned a bronze medal in his fourth Olympics.

John Naber of Menlo Park, Calif., won 4 gold medals and 1 silver in men's swimming and broke world records in both backstroke races. Klaus Dibiasi of Italy won the men's platform diving (after a silver medal in 1964 and gold medals in 1968 and 1972). Vasily Alekseyev of the U.S.S.R. repeated his 1972 triumph in weight lifting. Teofilo Stevenson of Cuba did the same in heavyweight boxing. J. Michael Plumb of Chesapeake City, Md., won a gold and a silver medal in equestrian 3-day competition in his fifth Olympics.

Klaus Dibiasi, a veteran competitor from Italy, shows the form that won him a gold medal in the 10-m platform diving competition. Dibiasi had also won this event in the two previous Olympics.

Alberto Juantorena of Cuba wins the 800-m final in world-record time. He also won the 400-m race, becoming the first man in Olympic history to achieve this double.

Some athletes became stars for reasons other than athletic prowess. Boris Onischenko of the U.S.S.R. was ejected from the pentathlon for using an illegally wired épée. Sergei Nemtsanov, 17, a Soviet diver, first defected to Canada, then decided to return home after all. And two British yachtsmen ceremonially burned their boat after losing a Tempest-class race.

The Winter Olympics. The twelfth annual Winter Olympic Games were held Feb. 4–15 at Innsbruck, Austria. The controversy there was not a new one. When Avery Brundage of Chicago was president of the I.O.C., he wanted the Winter Olympics abolished because, as he said, many of its athletes were receiving illegal payments and were thus professionals. Many European skiers at Innsbruck were reportedly receiving $40,000 to $250,000 a year from manufacturers, governments, and national federations to compete as amateurs.

The Games did, however, go on—with 1054 athletes representing 37 nations. When the Games were over, the U.S.S.R. led in number of medals won, with 13 gold, 6 silver, and 8 bronze. East Germany was next with 7 gold, 5 silver, and 7 bronze. The U.S. made its best showing in 20 years

Left: The only American woman to win a gold medal in speed skating at the Winter Olympics, Sheila Young earned it in the 500-m race. She also earned a silver medal and a bronze.

Opposite page: At 25, Rosi Mittermaier of West Germany was called "Grandma" by her army of adoring fans. But she had enough energy to win two gold medals in the Olympic women's skiing events.

with 3 gold, 3 silver, and 4 bronze. It was surprising because in all of the U.S. there was only one Olympic-size speed-skating rink, one bobsled run, and no luge run at all. American college students played hockey against subsidized teams from European countries, and each of the U.S. figure skaters had to spend $15,000 to $20,000 a year for coaching and practice time on the ice.

The American gold medalists were Sheila Young of Detroit and Peter Mueller of Mequon, Wis., both in speed skating, and Dorothy Hamill of Riverside, Conn., in figure skating. The major American surprise was provided by Bill Koch of Guilford, Vt., who won the silver medal in the men's 30-km cross-country ski race.

The two young Americans, Sheila Young and Dorothy Hamill, charmed the spectators in Austria and the worldwide television audiences. But the most successful—and perhaps the most charming—of all the athletes at Innsbruck was Rosi Mittermaier of West Germany, a 25-year-old Alpine skier. She won the special slalom as expected and the downhill for the first time in her life. Then she attempted an Olympic triple never achieved by a woman. But, in the giant slalom, she missed the gold medal by 0.12 sec., beaten by Kathy Kreiner of Canada.

In men's skiing the gold medalists were Franz Klammer of Austria in the downhill, Piero Gros of Italy in the slalom, and tiny Heini Hemmi of Switzerland in the giant slalom. Klammer's winning effort was a daredevil descent that thrilled the spectators at the scene and the millions who saw it on television.   F.L.

Soviet strongman Vasily Alekseyev triumphantly holds aloft the weighted bar for his gold-medal victory in the super heavyweight class of the Olympic weight-lifting competition. His biggest lift: 562 lb.

SRI LANKA. *See* CEYLON.

STAMPS, POSTAGE. A glance at the issues of 1976 sufficed to show that it was a year of political and social change, as well as a festive year of celebration. Historical milestones, current events, and various cultural commemorations throughout the world appeared on the stamps that served to move letters, postcards, and parcels around the globe.

United Nations Issues. The year 1976 marked the 25th anniversary of the United Nations Postal Administration, and this notable occasion was commemorated with four important new issues. The 30th anniversary of the World Federation of U.N. Associations inspired the design of three new stamps and a souvenir card, calling attention to the social works accomplished by the U.N. and its affiliates. In addition, two colorful commemoratives and a souvenir card honored the World Food Council, and the U.N. Conference on Human Settlements (HABITAT) was hailed by a group of four commemoratives. Also singled out for tribute was the U.N. Conference on Trade and Development.

Worldwide Issues. The American Bicentennial dominated the philatelic scene with some of the most colorful stamps ever issued. Hundreds of new stamps and souvenir sheets honored the United States on the occasion of its 200th birthday, the majority featuring historical paintings of the revolutionary era or scenes representing great battles of the war. Many nations honored great Revolutionary War heroes and outstanding figures

in U.S. history, and several issued stamps illustrating early military uniforms of the revolutionary period. Operation Sail—the visit to the U.S. by the world's great sailing ships—was an internationally acclaimed Bicentennial event, and it was commemorated in the stamps of many countries. The centenary of the invention of the telephone was another widely commemorated occasion. Nations all over the world paid tribute to Alexander Graham Bell and his revolutionary concept in communication. The Innsbruck and Montréal Olympics elicited a philatelic tribute from countries in both the Eastern and Western hemispheres, with stamps featuring Olympic sports events as well as national sports of the various countries. "Europa" stamps, issued to publicize the unity of European postal administrations, have become increasingly popular among topical stamps of the last several years, and in 1976 there were some particularly creative releases. On the basic theme of cultural progress or heritage, twenty-seven nations issued stamps devoted to architectural and other artistic achievements.

United States Issues. The 200th anniversary of the independence of the U.S. was, of course, the most celebrated event of the year. The Fifty State Flag Commemorative Issue was the most unusual release, including in one sheet the flags of all the states arranged in the order of their admission to the union. And each state stamp was also available on a First Day Cover canceled on the first day of issue in that state's capital. A highly praised set of four Bicentennial souvenir sheets was issued to

Outstanding Stamps of 1976. *At the top: A Cook Islands souvenir sheet saluting the American Bicentennial. Second row (left to right): A U.S. group of three stamps that form one picture and a single stamp from Upper Volta, both honoring the Bicentennial. Third row: Bhutan (center) and Poland hail the 1976 Winter Olympics. Fourth row (left to right): Canada commemorates the 1976 Summer Olympics, the United Nations honors the World Federation of U.N. Associations, and the U.S. pays tribute to the Olympics. Bottom row (left to right): Mauritius recalls drought in Africa, Argentina celebrates the 25th anniversary of its national airline, and the Bahama Islands hail the centenary of the telephone.*

coincide with the Seventh U.S. International Philatelic Exhibition held May 29–June 6 in Philadelphia, each with five perforated rectangles usable as stamps. Two featured paintings by American artist John Trumbull: "The Surrender of Lord Cornwallis" and "The Signing of the Declaration of Independence." The other two were reproductions of Emanuel Leutze's "Washington Crossing the Delaware" and William T. Trego's "Washington Reviewing the Troops at Valley Forge." Benjamin Franklin, the Liberty Bell, and the "Spirit of '76" were subjects of some of the other special sets designed to commemorate the historic event. Several creative envelopes were also designed to celebrate the Bicentennial. Four in particular paid tribute to a slice of Americana, saluting the American Homemaker, the American Farmer, the American Doctor, and the American Craftsman. A block of four striking new stamps made up the U.S. Olympic Games issue, saluting the international athletic event held every four years.   L.F.

STATE LEGISLATIVE REVIEW. The following is a summary of actions taken by state legislatures in the United States meeting in regular or special session in 1976.

Taxation. On July 8 New Jersey became the forty-third state to institute a personal income tax when Gov. Brendan T. Byrne signed a measure providing for a graduated levy of 2 to 2.5 percent. The new tax came as a result of a 1973 state supreme court ruling that the heavy reliance in New Jersey on local property taxes to finance public education discriminated against poorer school districts and thus violated the state constitution's mandate of a "thorough and efficient" schooling for every child. Earlier in the year, when the legislators could not agree on a method for raising $374,000,000 to reduce the reliance on property taxes, the court ordered the state's 2500 public schools to be shut on July 1, 1976; they were reopened after the tax measure was enacted. In addition to providing funds for distribution to school systems, the law gave a total of $290,000,000 to municipalities so that they could lower their property tax assessments.

Maine and Nebraska increased their personal income tax rates during the year. State sales taxes were raised in Rhode Island, Tennessee, and Washington. Taxes on gasoline were increased in Connecticut, Idaho, and Kansas. In order to build up a fund to protect its coastal areas, Alaska enacted a tax on oil-terminal facilities constructed to handle the large quantities of petroleum that were to flow from the state's North Slope region after 1977, when the Trans-Alaska Pipeline was scheduled for completion. Tankers would also be taxed.

Despite the nation's ongoing economic troubles, some states were able to reduce selected tax rates. Residential property taxes were lowered not only in New Jersey, but also in Hawaii, Iowa, Louisiana, and Ohio. Colorado, Kentucky, and Utah reduced their personal income tax rates. Tennessee and Utah exempted prescription drugs from their sales taxes. In order to help preserve family farms, inheritance taxes on such units were lowered in Indiana, Minnesota, and Wisconsin.

Medicine. On Sept. 30 California became the first state to enact a measure allowing terminally ill patients to die with "dignity"—by requiring doctors to remove or withhold from them respirators or other "unnatural" and "artificial" life-prolonging machines. The law, set to take effect Jan. 1, 1977, would enable adults to make a "living will" prohibiting the use of life-sustaining mechanisms during the terminal state of an illness. Such a will could be made by a healthy person, in which case the document would have to be renewed every five years, or by an adult diagnosed as terminally ill by at least two physicians. In the latter instance, the will would take effect fourteen days after the diagnosis had been made. A person would be allowed to revoke his living will at any time. The

---

She Is Still Not Telling Her Age

The bones were found in Otter Tail County in Minnesota in the 1920's and judged to be human remains dating back perhaps 10,000 years. Since their discovery they have been known as "Minnesota Man." In March, however, the legislature of the state of Minnesota finally recognized the anatomical facts and ordered an official name change—to "Minnesota Woman."

law specified that life insurance companies could not regard deaths under living wills as suicides, nor could a physician be held liable for a death under such circumstances.

Among the other health-related laws that were passed in 1976 were many new measures designed to lower the cost of medical malpractice insurance. These laws established new statewide insurance pools, reformed existing laws that related to malpractice suits, and more closely regulated doctors to help prevent medical errors.

Several legislatures also enacted measures aimed at tightening the administration of state-federal Medicaid programs, which provide health services to disadvantaged persons. Investigators had uncovered extensive waste in Medicaid operations in a number of states.

Ten states enacted measures allowing pharmacists to substitute cheaper generic drugs for identical brand-name products when filling prescriptions.

Government. For the first time, "sunset" laws, which provide for the automatic termination of certain state agencies unless they are specifically re-funded, were passed by several states. In April Colorado became the first state to adopt such a law, and similar measures were passed by Alabama, Florida, and Louisiana. This legislation was intended to help stem the growth of government by eliminating public bodies that no longer provided necessary services or whose functions had been taken over by other agencies.

Late in the year New York became the forty-ninth state to adopt an "open meeting" law, when it passed legislation opening most meetings of state agencies to the general public. The measure, designed largely to reduce arbitrary decision-making in government and to facilitate public discussion of matters before state bodies, was scheduled to take effect in 1977.

Environmental Protection. Late in the summer California passed sweeping legislation to control growth along its 1000-mi. coastline. The new law put nearly all economic development of the coastal strip, ranging from 3 mi. offshore to about 5 mi. inland, under the jurisdiction of a commission of citizens and public officials. This commission was ordered to preserve natural areas and farmland, to concentrate development in already built-up areas, and to promote public access to the shore.

California also enacted landmark legislation controlling nuclear-generated electric power. Three laws, signed by Gov. Edmund G. Brown, Jr., on June 3, would delay new plant construction until fuel recycling and radioactive waste disposal problems had been resolved and until the feasi-

bility of putting nuclear plants underground had been studied. A citizens' legislative initiative, which would have placed even more stringent controls on nuclear-power development, was soundly defeated in the California primary election on June 8. Similar proposals were rejected by voters in six other states (Arizona, Colorado, Montana, Ohio, Oregon, and Washington) on Nov. 2.

Crime and Punishment. In July the U.S. Supreme Court ruled that the death penalty was a constitutional form of punishment for convicted murderers. But it struck down laws in Louisiana, North Carolina, and Oklahoma that made capital punishment mandatory upon conviction for specified crimes. Louisiana and Oklahoma thereafter passed revised death penalty laws.

Five states enacted measures in 1976 providing compensation for innocent victims of crime. Seventeen states already had such laws. New criminal codes were adopted in Iowa and Maine. The state legislatures of Alabama, Colorado, and Florida passed prison reform acts.

See also SUPREME COURT OF THE UNITED STATES. E.S.K.

STEEL. *See* MANUFACTURING INDUSTRIES.

SUDAN. In 1976 Gaafar Mohammed al-Nimeiry, president of Sudan, faced the third attempted coup of his seven years in office. As Nimeiry arrived at Khartoum airport on July 2, after a visit to the United States and France, gunshots were fired at the presidential party, and grenades and small bombs exploded throughout the city. The government claimed to have killed or arrested all 1000 armed insurrectionists within two days, and announced that they were "foreign mercenaries," trained and sent by Libya.

Early in 1976 there were incidents of unrest in southern Sudan—largely Christian and Black, in contrast to the Arab north—protesting the slow pace of economic development in that region. On Feb. 10 Nimeiry instituted sweeping changes in his cabinet and appointed Rashid Taher as prime minister. Then, on March 3, he announced administrative reforms aimed at improving services and hastening development programs in the south.

Early in 1976 three American companies and one British company began to search for oil in the Red Sea and in south-central Sudan. If the search is successful, the discoveries could bring about sweeping changes in the Sudanese economy, one of the world's most impoverished. Also, as irrigation projects increased the amount of arable land, cotton, long Sudan's principal crop, was giving way to wheat, rice, and other foodstuffs. Experts predicted that as many as 200,000,000 additional

SUPREME COURT OF THE UNITED STATES

acres could be made productive or at least suitable for grazing lands.

See STATISTICS OF THE WORLD. *See also* AFRICA.   S.C.

SUPREME COURT OF THE UNITED STATES, THE. In a busy 1976 calendar the Supreme Court upheld both the constitutionality of the death penalty and federal financing of Presidential election campaigns. Observers noted that the Court showed its solidly conservative makeup in most of its decisions, including many in which the rights of criminal defendants were interpreted more narrowly than in the recent past.

Membership. Throughout 1976 the Court was composed of the following members: Chief Justice Warren E. Burger and Associate Justices (in order of appointment) William J. Brennan, Jr., Potter Stewart, Byron R. White, Thurgood Marshall, Harry A. Blackmun, Lewis F. Powell, Jr., William H. Rehnquist, and John Paul Stevens. Justices Marshall and Brennan were the only remaining liberal holdovers from the 1953–69 tenure of the late Chief Justice Earl Warren. Justice Marshall, 68, suffered a heart attack in July but recovered in time for the convening of the fall term on Oct. 4.

Death Penalty. In a series of historic but equivocal decisions handed down early in July, the Court

Robert Excell White, convicted in Texas of a 1974 murder, was a willing candidate to be the first person executed in the U.S. since 1967. But legal delays, including a December stay of execution issued by the U.S. Supreme Court, put off his date with the electric chair.

upheld the death penalty as a permissible punishment for murder. The Court ruled that capital punishment statutes in Florida, Texas, and Georgia were constitutional, but voided similar statutes in North Carolina, Louisiana, and Oklahoma. In the welter of 200 different opinions, these guidelines for lawmakers emerged: It is unconstitutional to make death the mandatory sentence for a crime, and the sentencing judge or jury must have adequate guidance and information when the death penalty is an option. In the fall term the Court agreed to review more capital punishment cases, implying further clarifications. It also granted stays of execution to two condemned murderers who asked to die speedily: Gary Mark Gilmore in Utah and Robert Excell White in Texas; *see* CRIME AND LAW ENFORCEMENT.

Defendants' Rights. Contending that the needs of society must be balanced against the rights of the individual, the Court restricted the rights of criminal defendants in a number of cases. The issue in each was how broadly to interpret the Fourth Amendment protection against unreasonable search and seizure.

In the most significant of these cases, the Court sharply reduced the power of federal courts to set aside state court convictions that relied on illegally obtained evidence. The Court held that if a defendant is given a "full and fair" chance to argue his Fourth Amendment claim in state courts, he has no further right to raise the issue.

In another case the Court ruled that the Constitution does not require police to obtain warrants before they make arrests in public places, so long as there is "probable cause" to believe that the person being arrested has committed a felony. A later ruling permitted warrantless arrests of suspects pursued from their doorways into their homes.

In other cases dealing with the admissibility of evidence, the Court allowed the government access to personal bank records and ruled that persons can be convicted of selling drugs even if government agents supplied and bought them. It also held that even if evidence seized by state officials is ruled inadmissible in a state trial, the federal government can still use the evidence in a civil proceeding to adjudicate tax liability.

Racial and Sexual Issues. The Burger Court in 1976 generally followed the philosophical lead of its predecessor in cases of racial discrimination and desegregation. It ruled in April that federal courts can order the Department of Housing and Urban Development to create low-cost public housing for minorities in a city's white suburbs if the government has contributed—through public housing programs—to segregation in the city. In June

383

the Court declined to review lower court decisions that ordered busing in the Boston public school system. In December, however, the Court struck down a busing plan for schools in Austin, Texas, suggesting segregation may not be judicially remediable unless a "racially discriminatory purpose" could be proved. Two June decisions struck blows at racial discrimination: The Court ruled that private schools may not exclude Blacks because of race, and it held that laws against discrimination protected Whites as well as non-Whites.

The rights of homosexuals did not fare as well. In March the Court declined to review a North Carolina case in which two men were convicted of breaking a law against homosexual acts. A similar Virginia law was also upheld.

The women's rights movement was dealt a setback by a December ruling. The Court held that employers who offer disability insurance benefits to their employees need not, under federal law, provide such benefits to women who become pregnant.

Civil Liberties. In March the Burger Court, for the first time since the retirement of Chief Justice Warren in 1969, flatly overruled a Warren Court decision that had expanded the constitutional rights of individuals. By a 5-to-3 vote the Court threw out a 1968 decision and held that striking workers do not have a constitutional right to picket their employer's store in a privately owned shopping center. The author of the 1968 majority opinion, Justice Marshall, wrote in dissent that he could not escape the feeling that the Warren Court's ruling had been "laid to rest without ever having been accorded a proper burial." See also LABOR.

Two major decisions had a bearing on freedom of the press: One limited that freedom in libel cases and the other upheld it against judicial gag orders. In the latter decision the Court acted in June to void a Nebraska judge's order barring pretrial news coverage of a murder case. In March the Court limited the protection of the press from libel suits. Previous Court rulings had required public figures to make a much stronger case against a publisher of alleged libel than nonpublic figures. Public figures were, in effect, fair game for the publication of speculation and rumor. But the Court narrowed its definition of "public figure" in a case involving Florida socialite Mary Alice Firestone. She could not be considered a public figure, the Court ruled, even though she was often mentioned in newspaper society columns. See also CIVIL RIGHTS AND CIVIL LIBERTIES.

Other Cases. One of the most eagerly awaited decisions of the year concerned the constitutionality of the 1974 Federal Election Campaign Act. In a series of judgments handed down on Jan. 30, the Court upheld government financing of Presidential campaigns, ceilings on campaign contributions, and contribution disclosure requirements, but struck down expenditure limits (except for Presidential candidates). The Federal Election Commission (F.E.C.) was declared unconstitutional because of the way in which its officers were appointed. The order to void the F.E.C. was stayed twice, finally taking effect March 23; a commission restructured in accordance with Supreme Court directives began operation on May 21.

In other actions the Court upheld a Detroit zoning law designed to restrict pornographic theaters and bookstores. And consumer advocates were cheered by a May ruling that struck down a Virginia statute barring pharmacies from advertising drug prices; this action meant that similar statutes in thirty-three other states would be invalidated, allowing competitive pricing.   M.R.B.

SURINAM. See STATISTICS OF THE WORLD.

King Charles XVI Gustavus and his new bride accept the cheers of their subjects outside the royal castle at Stockholm. At the June 19 wedding Silvia Sommerlath, daughter of a West German businessman, became Queen Silvia of Sweden.

SWAZILAND. *See* STATISTICS OF THE WORLD.

SWEDEN. Forty-four years of rule by socialist governments in Sweden ended on Sept. 19, 1976, when general elections turned out the ruling Social Democrats and replaced them with a Center Party coalition.

Political Developments. In what was widely regarded as a political surprise, the Social Democratic Party was defeated in parliamentary elections for the first time since 1932. Prime Minister Olof Palme and his socialist government resigned on Sept. 20. He was succeeded as prime minister on Oct. 8 by Thorbjörn Fälldin, leader of the Center Party and of a three-party nonsocialist coalition. Fälldin's coalition won only a narrow victory, taking 180 of the 349 seats in parliament. Only 86 of the coalition's seats went to Fälldin's Center Party. By comparison, Palme's Social Democrats won 152 seats and their Communist allies won 17.

The election was not regarded as a decisive rejection of socialism, since many voters were thought to have left the Social Democrats for reasons unrelated to party philosophy. A major issue was the all-out program of the Social Democrats for making Sweden the world's leading user of atomic power by 1985. Fälldin's supporters, opposing the plan, won the backing of environmentalists by promising to shut down the five nuclear power plants already operating in Sweden. Another issue was widespread opposition to a Social Democratic proposal, originated by economist Rudolf Meidner; the plan would eventually have given the workers control of much of Swedish industry. It would have required companies with more than fifty employees to convert 20 percent of their profits into company stock to be contributed to worker funds.

In presenting his coalition cabinet on Oct. 8, Fälldin retreated from his pledge to close nuclear plants. He said his government would require those in charge of the plants to prove by October, 1977, that they had arranged for the safe disposal of radioactive wastes. If parliament decided to phase out the plants before 1978, he promised that he would set up a commission to study the effects of such action.

International Steel Problem. Sweden and other steel-producing nations were hit hard by a worldwide decline in steel demand and specifically by what was considered a United States protectionist policy aimed against steel imports. It was feared that this would result in a cut of $46,000,000 in U.S. imports of Swedish steel, and on Feb. 2 the Swedish government lodged a formal protest with U.S. officials.

U.S. President Gerald R. Ford had warned that he would impose the recommended quotas on specialty steel imports unless Sweden and the other producing countries cut their exports to the U.S. voluntarily. In June, after the exporting countries had made no cutbacks, Ford imposed quotas for a three-year period. The Swedish quota for the first twelve months, like the quotas of other countries, however, actually exceeded total shipments to the U.S. in 1975. The quotas, it was learned, were based on data for the years 1970–75.

The Economy. The 1975 budget of the Palme government, presented at the opening of parliament on Jan. 12, gave high priority to pensions, family aid, labor reforms and benefits, and industrial expansion. In early 1976 industry was in a decline and unemployment was becoming a serious problem. On Jan. 29 the Swedish National Bank reduced the discount rate from 6 percent to 5.5 percent in an effort to bolster the economy by encouraging industrial investment. By the standards of other countries, however, Swedish unemployment was considered minimal. In June there were 62,000 unemployed workers, or 1.5 percent of the work force. By July the figure had declined to 54,000 workers, or 1.3 percent of the labor force. The recession hit especially hard at the shipping industry. Sixty of the approximately 180 ships in the merchant fleet were reported idle by April, and shipowners were requesting $330,000,000 in government aid. Despite the recession, Sweden's per capita income of $6880 in 1975 was second only to Switzerland's $6970, according to data published in July by the Organization for Economic Cooperation and Development.

See STATISTICS OF THE WORLD.　　　　　L.A.S.

SWITZERLAND. Switzerland in 1976 continued its policy of restricting the number of foreigners permitted to work and live in the country. Several cases of espionage involving Swiss and foreign officials came to light during 1976, but details, as usual, were scanty.

Domestic Affairs. Despite what the Swiss regarded as an economic slump, the per capita income in Switzerland during 1975 was the world's highest, at $6970, the Organization for Economic Cooperation and Development reported on July 12. The economic slump and Switzerland's curbs on foreign workers combined to reduce the number of aliens living in the country by 4.9 percent during 1975, according to figures made public in early February, 1976. At that time the total had fallen to 1,012,710, or roughly 15.5 percent of the country's population.

Both the government and the unions had worked out programs to increase the participation of Swiss workers in the management of the companies for which they worked. The proposals were rejected by the nation's voters, however, in a national referendum on March 21. The union plan, which would eventually have given workers equal representation on boards of directors, was defeated by a 2–1 vote. A milder proposal, put forward by the government, was rejected even more resoundingly by a vote of 3–1.

Foreign Relations. In the past Switzerland's geographic, diplomatic, and financial situation made the country a major center of international intrigue. Cloak-and-dagger cases have surfaced frequently, and the year 1976 was no exception. The Justice and Police Ministry disclosed on Aug. 16 that Brig. Jean-Louis Jeanmaire, a former chief of Switzerland's air defense troops, had been arrested on charges of giving secret military data to contacts in the Soviet embassy. Six days later Swiss authorities announced the expulsion of a Soviet diplomat and a Rumanian embassy member for political espionage. On Aug. 30 Switzerland disclosed that the first secretary of the Iranian Mission to the United Nations office at Geneva had also been expelled for "prohibited intelligence activities."

The purchase of 72 United States warplanes (six F-5's and 66 F-5E's) was approved by parliament on March 16 after two years of delays and debates. The plan was ratified despite reports that the Northrop Corp., the U.S. manufacturer of the planes, had made large secret payments to foreign officials in order to secure contracts from their countries.

See STATISTICS OF THE WORLD.   L.A.S.

SYRIA. Inter-Arab politics, and especially the Lebanese civil war, had a profound impact on virtually every aspect of Syrian national life in 1976.

Foreign Affairs. Involvement in neighboring Lebanon's civil war shifted from attempts to mediate between warring factions in January and February to full-scale military intervention by early summer and to responsibility for Arab League peacekeeping efforts in the late fall. Syrian President Hafez al-Assad was expected by most observers to support Muslim leftist and Palestinian factions in Lebanon, as he had during the 1970 civil war in Jordan. When mediation attempts failed, however, Syrian soldiers were sent into Lebanon on March 15 to defend the incumbent rightist regime against an attempted military overthrow led by Lebanese Muslim leftists. On April 9 reinforcements were sent in, and by early June some 6000 heavily armed Syrian troops were committed to battle in Lebanon.

The invasion, according to official Syrian statements, was designed to preserve Lebanon as a secular state and to prevent the partitioning of the country into Muslim and Christian zones. It was a policy that appeared to have at least the tacit agreement of the United States but that was heavily criticized in much of the Arab world, particularly in Iraq and Egypt. Iraqi troops were positioned along the Syrian border in July as a show of strength against Syria's intervention in Lebanon. Syrian criticisms of the Egyptian disengagement agreement with Israel in January were countered in May by Egyptian denunciations of Assad's intervention in Lebanon. The oil-rich states backed Egypt in this dispute, and both Saudi Arabia and Kuwait slowed down their aid payments to Damascus. By August, Jordanian King Hussein I was Assad's only political friend in the Arab world.

By late September, however, Syrian assistance had helped turn the tide of battle in favor of the Lebanese right, so Assad finally succumbed to pressure from both Arab and Soviet leaders to ac-

Syrian President Hafez al-Assad leaves the Elysée Palace in Paris after his June 18 meeting with French President Valéry Giscard d'Estaing.

cept a cease-fire. A long-delayed Arab summit conference convened Oct. 15. It was decided that Syrian forces already in Lebanon, fortified by token units from other Arab states, would become the new Arab League peacekeeping force. This compromise led to a cessation of the fighting, but also left the Syrian army in virtual control of all of Lebanon by the end of the year.

Internal Politics. The war was a devastating blow to the Syrian economy. An ambitious 1976 budget of $4.5 billion had to be trimmed back to about $2.7 billion on May 27, after the cutoff of Iraqi oil supplies and Saudi aid. By late June the war itself was costing an estimated $1,000,000 a day; inflation was running at an annual rate of 20–30 percent, and the steady influx of Lebanese refugees only intensified Syria's economic woes. On Aug. 7

the Syrian pound was devalued to a new rate of 3.90 to the U.S. dollar.

Assad turned to a policy of economic liberalization. The destruction of Lebanese financial facilities caused Syria to allow foreign banks to operate in the country for the first time since 1958. Americans and other Westerners were invited to invest in Syria, and new policies were enacted to help rejuvenate the economic life of the country.

Prime Minister Mahmoud al-Ayubi resigned on Aug. 1. A week later Rahman Abdel Khlefawi, a military man seasoned in inter-Arab affairs and a former premier, formed a new government. It included Syria's first woman cabinet minister, Najah Attar (minister of culture).

See STATISTICS OF THE WORLD. *See also* ARAB LEAGUE; MIDDLE EAST.   S.C.

T

TAIWAN, *or* **FORMOSA,** seat of the Republic of China. Taiwan's domestic politics were tranquil in 1976, and under the leadership of Premier Chiang Ching-kuo the economy staged a stunning comeback. Responding to government measures that included lowering interest rates, easing credits to export industries, and dispatching trade missions throughout the world, the critical foreign trade sector of the island's economy increased by 43 percent during the first eight months of 1976 and registered a surplus of over $250,000,000. The forecast for the full year anticipated a trade volume of more than $15 billion, up from $11.2 billion in 1975, with a 1976 surplus of more than $200,000,-000.

Spurred by the comeback in foreign trade, the economy as a whole grew by leaps and bounds in 1976. The outlook was for a gain of 10 percent in the gross national product (up from 2.8 percent in 1975), based largely on an upturn of 26.5 percent in industrial production during the first three quarters. A six-year economic development plan begun in 1976 called for a total investment of $43 billion, an average annual growth in the economy of 7.5 percent, and a doubling of per capita income—goals which the government expected to reach without major difficulty. Official figures released in 1976 showed Taiwan enjoyed a standard of living second only to Japan in Asia.

Although the Republic of China maintained various kinds of trade and cooperation links with more than 140 countries and regions throughout

the world, it experienced growing isolation in formal diplomatic relations. This trend was underscored by the dispute over participation by Taiwanese athletes at the Olympic Games at Montréal, Canada, during the summer. The International Olympic Committee, under pressure from Canada, refused to allow the team from Taiwan to compete as representatives of the Republic of China. So the Republic of China withdrew from the competition on July 16.

Ties with the United States were reaffirmed during the Presidential debates when President Gerald R. Ford and his Democratic challenger, Jimmy Carter, both pledged to uphold the U.S. commitment to Taiwan. During the year the U.S. withdrew its military advisers from the islands of Quemoy and Matsu, which lie between Taiwan and the Chinese mainland, but stepped up arms shipments to the Nationalists. Observers felt that the overall uncertainty of Taiwan's international position lent credibility to unconfirmed reports that the Republic of China was secretly reprocessing used uranium fuel to produce plutonium for possible nuclear weapons production.

See STATISTICS OF THE WORLD.   T.L.K.

TANZANIA. The depressed economic condition of Tanzania, aggravated by rising oil prices and inflation at home and abroad, continued to be a serious problem in 1976. The government responded with a variety of measures aimed at reducing expenditures and the country's dependency on imports. Government expenditures were further cut by some $6,300,000 when the civil service was reduced by 20 percent. In April the government began to phase out many privately owned retail shops. This measure, it was thought, would facilitate price controls and at the same time reduce oil consumption and reduplication of goods and services. Shop owners designated as superfluous were to be relocated in villages, where they would work in agricultural production. In a related move the armed forces were ordered to begin rounding up the urban unemployed for resettlement in farming villages. The program was only partly successful, as many refused their new assignments and returned to the towns.

In foreign affairs Tanzania continued to focus on the independence movements in southern Africa. President Julius K. Nyerere was an outspoken opponent of United States policy in Angola, and in a September meeting with U.S. Secretary of State Henry Kissinger he called for the U.S. to declare its support for the liberation movements of Rhodesia and South-West Africa, as well as those within South Africa. By the end of 1976 Tanzania had stepped up supplying black nationalists in Rhodesia, and its troops were reported to be bolstering defenses in Mozambique, which had closed its border to Rhodesia.

See STATISTICS OF THE WORLD. *See also* AFRICA. J.T.S.

TECHNOLOGY. Computers began to move rapidly into everyday life in 1976, only five years after the mass production of miniaturized systems became technically possible. Other developments during the year included the use of water as a cutting tool, an innovative light bulb, and a new type of battery designed to bring back the electric car.

Computer Proliferation. Hand-held calculators were purchased by 20,000,000 people in 1976. Microwave ovens with automatic cooking controls made their appearance in 1,600,000 new homes. Electronic games to be played on the living-room television screen were suddenly the latest rage, and an improved version of the digital watch that had come onto the market only two years earlier sold out its stock of about 4,000,000 before the end of the year. Although the public was hardly aware of the fact, all these devices were dependent on the microprocessor, a tiny chip of silicon photoengraved with a complete computer program. Mass production of the microprocessor began in 1972, and in a few short years it had become available for as little as $5. When interconnected with other tiny chips to form a complex system no larger than half a stick of gum, the microprocessor, or minicomputer, cost about

The Pulsar wrist computer functions as both a digital timepiece and a calculator with a memory bank.

$200 and had a capability equivalent to the room-sized computer of only a decade earlier—which sold for several hundred thousand dollars.

Used as independent systems or as terminals for small central computers, microprocessors began to automate many daily activities during 1975 and 1976. New cash registers that showed up in supermarkets could "read" a product by a coded pattern of lines on its label, transmit the name of the item to the store's central computer, and retrieve the day's price and the correct tax while the central computer recorded the sale for inventory control. It was estimated that by 1980 about 20,000 supermarkets would be using the system. In department stores a new plastic tag on clothing and wares was in reality an electronic card that could be read by a computerized cash register similar to that of the supermarkets (and could also signal a detection system at the store's exit if not removed by the cashier). Banks were busily installing terminal microcomputers as cash machines, traffic lights and gasoline pumps operated under computerized control, and many other applications were being brought into direct contact with the public. It was obvious that technology was now ready for the coming age of the computer, limited only by imagination, capital investment, and the continuing concerns about depersonalization, displacement of unskilled workers, and a host of other social effects.

Not all computer activity during the year involved microprocessors. A special need existed for oversized, highly complex computers capable of processing massive amounts of data with many millions of program steps per second. Weather research centers, for example, needed supercomputers to investigate worldwide weather changes both daily and over long stretches of time. For aircraft designers, a supercomputer calculating various wing and body shapes and their interrela-

tionships with air currents could replace the enormously expensive and time-consuming wind-tunnel testing of prototype craft. The Herculean task of dealing with the world's economic variables was another job that could be undertaken by a supercomputer. Missile systems testing for the military, or space flight calculations, were still other obvious applications for a computer with as much high-speed power as could be devised. In 1976 an advanced computer named CRAY-1 (it can run up to 60,000,000 calculations per second) was tested by the Los Alamos Scientific Laboratory in New Mexico for nuclear reactor research. It was built by a specialized firm, Cray Research, Inc. Another CRAY-1 was on order for the National Center for Atmospheric Research in Boulder, Colo. Systems Development Corp. delivered to the U.S. Army ballistic missile center at Huntsville, Ala., the first installment of a new machine that was designed to handle 800,000,000 instructions per second. Even faster computers were already in existence, and development of the technology for computers with a capability of 10 billion instructions per second was getting under way.

Water-Jet Knife. A narrow high-pressure jet of water came into growing use during the year as a cutting tool for trimming automobile brake lining material, for slitting stacks of container cardboard, and for cutting through layers of fabric or leather. Developed in the mid-1960's by scientific researchers, the water jet was considered a curiosity until a few companies recently began to manufacture it as an industrial tool. Its high pressure pump shoots water through a 0.008-in. hole at twice the speed of sound. Some advantages of the water jet

"The Sniff" is an electronic vapor detector developed for the U.S. government by Brookhaven National Laboratory. When explosives manufacturers include a special chemical in their detonating devices, "the Sniff" can detect the chemical—and signal that a bomb is hidden somewhere in the vicinity.

Designed for the family hobby or game room is the new do-it-yourself computer kit. Using a regular television set for the display terminal, it enables the user to devise complex programs for games and mathematical problems.

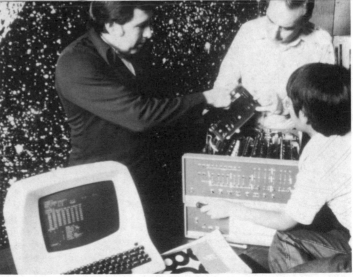

Science Returns to the White House
Confirmed by the Senate in August as head of the newly revived federal Office of Science and Technology Policy, H. Guyford Stever became the first Presidential science adviser since 1973, when Richard M. Nixon abolished the job (presumably because his science staff opposed the Vietnam war). A guided missiles expert and the former president of Carnegie-Mellon University, Stever had been director of the National Science Foundation since 1972. In that capacity he served as adviser to the entire executive branch during the exile of scientists from the White House.

Presidential adviser H. Guyford Stever.

are that it is very fast and precise, does not wear out or need sharpening, and does not create dust or lint. Guided by computerized controls, it can automatically cut the desired shapes for such products as garments or shoes. As reported in *Business Week,* one supplier, Flow Research, Inc.,

This new tool enables scientists to change the basic characteristics of materials, by placing them under pressures as high as those found deep within the earth: at least 8,000,000 lb. per sq.in. It uses two tiny diamond-tipped tungsten carbide pistons; one piston, mounted in a steel ring, is displayed by Francis P. Bundy, a General Electric researcher who gave the apparatus its first successful test.

foresaw a $1 billion industry emerging from a joining of the water jet with computer programming.

Electronic Fluorescent Screw-In Light Bulb. The development of a new household light bulb that lasts ten years and uses only 30 percent of the energy of ordinary bulbs was announced in March by Donald D. Hollister, a California inventor, along with the news that the Energy Research and Development Administration (ERDA) had awarded his small firm, the Lighting Technology Corp., a contract to prepare the bulb for production. The lamp, called Litek, is shaped like an incandescent bulb with a standard screw base, but the lighting device is an adaptation of fluorescent lighting.

In an ordinary fluorescent lamp, electrons pass between electrodes at both ends of a tube and excite mercury atoms to emit ultraviolet rays, which in turn cause a phosphor coating inside the tube to fluoresce. The Litek uses a transistorized circuit in the base of the bulb to supply low-voltage radio-frequency current to a wire coil at the bulb's center. This sets up an electromagnetic field, which energizes the mercury atoms.

Energy savings equivalent to as much as 500,000 bbl of oil per day were considered possible if the new light bulb was to supplant current home lighting. And it was predicted that marketing might come as early as 1978.

Electric-Car Lithium Battery. Researchers at the Lawrence Livermore Laboratory in California were making progress on a new kind of battery that would be able to power a 2000-lb. electric car for 200 mi. at a speed of 60 m.p.h., with a 10-sec.

acceleration from standstill to 40 m.p.h. The system combines a lithium-water-air main battery with a small start-up lithium-water battery. Recharging is not needed until after about 1000 mi. of use; the recharging is done largely by replacing the lithium anodes. The old lithium could then be recycled. Using the current gasoline price and an average rate of 20 mi. per gallon, the researchers estimated that the cost of running both conventional and electric cars would be the same. The advantages of an electric car are that it is pollution free and that it does not use up the dwindling supplies of petroleum. The researchers also pointed out that the price of lithium would be much lower if it were extracted in large quantities.

One obstacle to the development of the car was that in order to produce it either the present automakers would have to change their huge industrial plants or whole new companies and plants would have to be organized. Another problem was that no one yet knew how large-scale lithium processing and handling might affect the environment.   D.G.B., K.E. & M.T.

TELEVISION. See COMMUNICATIONS; RADIO AND TELEVISION BROADCASTING.

TENNESSEE. See STATISTICS OF THE WORLD.

TEXAS. See STATISTICS OF THE WORLD.

TEXTILES. See MANUFACTURING INDUSTRIES.

THAILAND. During 1976 Thailand's three-year experiment with democracy was brought to an end, and the country reverted to military rule.

Electoral Politics. Unable to govern effectively at the head of a shaky coalition government, Prime Minister Kukrit Pramoj dissolved parliament in January and called for elections on April 4. In a bitter campaign that was marred by political murders, Kukrit lost support from the rightists by insisting that virtually all United States troops leave the country by July. His government went down to defeat; Kukrit's brother, Seni Pramoj, became prime minister at the head of a new right-of-center coalition.

The 71-year-old Seni, though pro-American, also favored the troop withdrawal, and in June the U.S. turned over its last two bases—U Thapao Air Base and the Ramasun intelligence station—to the Thais. On July 20 the eleven-year-long American military presence came to an end when the last contingent of troops—the remnant of a force that approached 50,000 during the war in Southeast Asia —left the country. By mutual agreement, 270 U.S. military advisers remained behind.

Military Coup. In September a crisis arose abruptly. It was precipitated by the return from exile of Field Marshal Thanom Kittikachorn, who had fled the country in 1973 after student-led riots had brought down his military government. Seni, under attack from all sides for his indecisiveness in dealing with Thanom's return, resigned as prime minister; then he was persuaded to remain. On Oct. 6 students tried to force Thanom's expulsion by barricading themselves in Bangkok's Thammasat University with a handful of weapons. Heavily armed police and right-wing mobs invaded the campus. In the ensuing melee left-wing students battled right-wing students, while rightist crowds beat suspected leftists savagely. At least 39 students were killed and about 3000 were arrested. As the chaos spread, the military—in a long-expected move—seized control of the country and imposed martial law.

The new junta, headed by Adm. Sa-ngad Chaloryu, promptly abrogated the democratic consti-

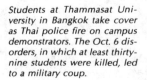

Students at Thammasat University in Bangkok take cover as Thai police fire on campus demonstrators. The Oct. 6 disorders, in which at least thirty-nine students were killed, led to a military coup.

tution, dissolved all political parties, and pledged to preserve the monarchy. In the days that followed the military government carried out a nationwide roundup of suspected Communists, imposed a curfew, and closed the universities. Junta leaders also announced that although elections might be held in four years, the country would not be ready for another attempt at full democracy for sixteen years. Sa-ngad became defense minister and Thanin Kraivichien (a former supreme court chief justice) was named prime minister in the new cabinet. And the government was granted virtually unrestricted powers under a new constitution.

In an attempt to shake the economy out of its doldrums, the new regime reversed the policy of the Seni government and invited foreign investment into the country. Sa-ngad also promised to step up the campaign against Communist guerrillas operating along the Laotian border in the northwest and to encourage the repatriation of the 70,000 Indochinese refugees in Thailand.

Foreign Affairs. The new government expressed a

wish to improve relations with the U.S. and thereby assure itself further military aid. It also pledged to cooperate with Malaysia in fighting the guerrillas in the jungle along their common frontier. After the military coup, Bangkok's relations with the Communist states of Indochina deteriorated sharply, and in December Thai spokesmen accused Vietnam of looking for a pretext to launch an invasion of Thailand.

See STATISTICS OF THE WORLD.   R.J.C.

THEATER. Theater in the United States presented a prevailingly healthy picture in 1976. Broadway and commercial playhouses elsewhere prospered—in some cases setting box office records. Off-Broadway groups and regional companies continued to make the kinds of contributions that have increased their national importance in recent years. With the persistent lack of original scripts deemed commercially promising, Broadway producers relied heavily on revivals, borrowings from regional theaters, and imports. Visitors from abroad included internationally known stars and directors plus several distinguished ensembles.

Broadway and its Imports. Broadway's two biggest hits of the year were comedies. In *California Suite,* a medley of four playlets, Neil Simon applied the format of his 1968 hit *Plaza Suite* to a Beverly Hills locale—with equally amusing results.

The crap-shooting scene from the George Gershwin opera Porgy and Bess. *The locale of the opera is Catfish Row, a black section of Charleston, S.C. This large-scale production of the original uncut version of the American classic was transported to Broadway from Houston, Texas.*

The eye-catching poster for David Rabe's Streamers. *In his bitter comedy, which won the New York Drama Critics' Circle award as the best American play of the 1975–76 season, Rabe defines a streamer as a parachute that fails to open.*

more than $100,000 at the box office in a single week.

Critics generally agreed that the most impressive new American work of the year was Ntozake Shange's "choreopoem" *For Colored Girls Who Have Considered Suicide When the Rainbow Is Enuf.* Acclaimed when first presented Off Broadway at the New York Shakespeare Festival Public Theater, the highly original mingling of words and movement was subsequently transferred to Broadway and achieved hit status. Poetry of a totally different, though no less moving, genre animated *The Belle of Amherst,* by William Luce, a one-woman play in which Julie Harris scored a critical and popular success as New England's famous poet, Emily Dickinson. *Variety,* the show business weekly, chose it as the best play of the season.

Other serious works were made less welcome, both by critics and audiences: Marion Wiesel's adaptation (from the French) of Elie Wiesel's *Zalmen or the Madness of God,* which achieved a mood of exaltation as it celebrated a simple rabbi's spontaneous defiance of Communist tyranny; *Poor Murderer,* Czech playwright Pavel Kohout's symbolistic treatment of a 1902 story by the Russian Leonid Andreyev about the struggle of an actor to obtain his release from a mental institution; *Herzl,* by Dore Schary and Amos Elon, an elabo-

Trish Van Devere and her offstage husband George C. Scott delight each other and the audience in the comedy hit Sly Fox. *Author Larry Gelbart based his romp on the 17th-century classic* Volpone, *by Ben Jonson.*

In *Sly Fox,* which starred George C. Scott in a dual role, Larry Gelbart transferred Ben Jonson's 1603 hit, *Volpone,* from 17th-century Venice to San Francisco of the 1800's and transformed the Elizabethan playwright's caustically comic attack on greed into a broad and ribald farce. By and large, the year's record was spotty. Katharine Hepburn's star power saved Enid Bagnold's *A Matter of Gravity* from sinking under its own weight. Hepburn and Richard Burton (during his temporary appearance in Peter Shaffer's long-running *Equus*) made Broadway financial history: The shows that starred them became the first straight plays to take in

Diane Ladd and Baxter Harris get acquainted in a scene from Lu Ann Hampton Laverty Oberlander, *one of the plays making up* A Texas Trilogy *by Preston Jones. Although critics across the U.S. found much to admire in the three productions, the plays had a disappointingly brief run on Broadway.*

rate biographical drama about the founder of modern Zionism; *I Have a Dream,* Josh Greenfeld's documentary based on the words of Martin Luther King, Jr., with Billy Dee Williams as the late civil rights leader; and *The Runner Stumbles,* Milton Stitt's dramatization of a case history from 1911 in which a Michigan priest was tried for murdering a nun. The last-named production illustrated the growing role of academic and institutional theater in developing scripts. *The Runner Stumbles* went through its preliminary drafts beginning in 1965, when Stitt was a student at the Yale School of Drama. Subsequent revisions were seen at the Berkshire Theater Festival (1971), the Manhattan Theater Club (1974), and the Hartman Theater Company of Stamford, Conn. (1975).

Other imports, besides *Equus, A Matter of Gravity,* and *Poor Murderer,* enriched the U.S. theatrical mixture. The most impressive entry from abroad—and one of the year's major high-

lights—was *No Man's Land,* in which two knights of the British stage, John Gielgud and Ralph Richardson, illuminated the dark reaches of yet another of Harold Pinter's perplexing theatrical enigmas. *Comedians,* featuring an Anglo-American cast, introduced British dramatist Trevor Griffiths to American playgoers with a double-edged comedy about aspiring north-of-England comics and the conflict between cherished craftsmanship and grubby commercialism. Theaters in the U.S. also received visits from such overseas troupes as the Royal Shakespeare Company, the D'Oyly Carte Opera Company, the Abbey Theatre of Ireland, the National Theater of Greece, the Gavella Theater of Zagreb (Yugoslavia), Le Tréteau de Paris, and the Polish Mime Theater.

Musicals and Awards. Among new musicals, the most artistically successful was *Pacific Overtures,* producer-director Harold Prince's blend of Japanese Kabuki and American musical-comedy techniques, with a score by Stephen Sondheim, libretto by John Weidman, scenery by Boris Aronson, and an all-Oriental cast. It won the New York Drama Critics' Circle award as the best musical of the 1975–76 season. The year failed to turn up a successor to the smash hit *A Chorus Line,* which in May added the Pulitzer Prize and in April nine Antoinette Perry awards (Tonys) to its other honors. (Both the two other major 1976 awards—from the Critics' Circle and the Tony committee for the best play—went to *Travesties* by the British author Tom Stoppard.) Among the other musicals, *The Robber Bridegroom,* a country-and-western-style caricature based on a Eudora Welty novella and developed Off Broadway, proved energetically diverting. *Godspell,* an Off-Broadway and international phenomenon since 1971, finally made it to Broadway in 1976.

Revivals. The year's star-topped revivals included Ruth Gordon and Lynn Redgrave in George Bernard Shaw's *Mrs. Warren's Profession,* Ben Gazzara and Colleen Dewhurst in *Who's Afraid of Virginia Woolf* (directed by author Edward Albee), Jason Robards and Zoe Caldwell in Eugene O'Neill's *Long Day's Journey into Night,* Jane Alexander and Richard Kiley in *The Heiress* and Claire Bloom in *The Innocents* (both adapted from novels by Henry James), and Vanessa Redgrave and Pat Hingle in Henrik Ibsen's *The Lady from the Sea.* Richard Chamberlain and Dorothy McGuire headed the cast of Tennessee Williams's *The Night of the Iguana,* one of three Williams plays given major professional productions in New York City in the course of the year. Williams was also represented by *The Eccentricities of a Nightingale,* a drastically revised version of the earlier *Summer and Smoke,* and *27 Wagons Full of*

Cotton, presented by the Phoenix Theatre in a double bill with Arthur Miller's *A Memory of Two Mondays.*

Musicals, too, were reprised in 1976. Broadway welcomed back a 20th-anniversary edition of *My Fair Lady,* the Alan Jay Lerner–Frederick Loewe adaptation of George Bernard Shaw's *Pygmalion,* with Ian Richardson as Higgins, Christine Andreas as Eliza, George Rose as Doolittle, and Robert Coote returning in his original role of Col. Pickering. Producer Joseph Papp drew audiences to Manhattan's Lincoln Center with a new translation of *The Threepenny Opera,* written by Bertolt Brecht and Kurt Weill in 1928. *Going Up* recaptured the charms of a 1919 Otto Harbach–Louis A. Hirsch aviation lark, but it seemed only a pallid reminder of the previous season's *Very Good Eddie,* a Jerome Kern work from the same period. As if to climax this year of backward glances, the record long-run *Fiddler on the Roof* returned to Broadway twelve years after it first opened. Zero Mostel again played Tevye, the poor Russian-Jewish milkman, whose misfortunes have brought riches to so many of those who helped bring him to life on the stage.

Black Artists. Black theater artists contributed repeatedly to the procession of musical hits that already included the previous season's *The Wiz* and *Me and Bessie.* These were followed in 1976 with such notable shows as *Bubbling Brown Sugar,* a guided tour through the jazz high spots of Har-

lem's past; a new, all-black *Guys and Dolls* (Frank Loesser's 1950 hit); the Houston Grand Opera production of George Gershwin's *Porgy and Bess;* and the rousing Vinnette Carroll-Alex Bradford version of the Gospel of Saint Matthew, *Your Arms Too Short To Box with God.*

Failures. The year witnessed several spectacular musical comedy flops. Among the more ambitious were *Home Sweet Homer,* starring Yul Brynner, which raided mythology, got its critical comeuppance, and played on Broadway for one performance; *Rockabye Hamlet,* a Canadian rock extravaganza about the Dane, which seemingly drowned in the din of its own amplification; *Rex,* with music by Richard Rodgers, which dealt ostensibly with the marital and parental troubles of Henry VIII; *1600 Pennsylvania Avenue,* a story of backstairs life at the White House, by Alan Jay Lerner and Leonard Bernstein, which reportedly lost its backers some $1,250,000; and *Music Is,* George Abbott's unsuccessful attempt to repeat with Shakespeare's *Twelfth Night* what he and Rodgers and Lorenz Hart achieved in the 1930's when they turned *The Comedy of Errors* into *The Boys from Syracuse.* It was the 89-year-old Abbott's 118th theatrical venture, as producer, direc-

The National Theatre of Great Britain, on the south bank of the Thames River in London. Built at a cost of more than $26,000,000, the structure houses three separate theaters, two of which (the Olivier and the Lyttleton) opened in 1976.

tor, actor, or author. Earlier in the year, he won the first Lawrence Langner Award (named for the cofounder of the Theatre Guild) "for lifetime achievement in the theater."

Regional Theaters. The increasingly significant role played by regional theaters across the country was illustrated in various ways during 1976. The Arena Stage of Washington, D.C., now in its seventeenth year, became the first non-New York company to receive a Tony award. The Long Wharf Theater of New Haven, Conn., shared with the New York Shakespeare Festival the Critics' Circle award for the best American play: *Streamers,* the third in David Rabe's Vietnam war trilogy. Another striking example of regional theater as a source of new plays occurred with the Broadway premieres of Preston Jones's *A Texas Trilogy,* which originated at the Dallas Theater Center. In the spring of 1976 the center mounted seven new scripts in three days. Among these were Jones's *The Last Meeting of the Knights of the White Magnolia, Lu Ann Hampton Laverty Oberlander,* and *The Oldest Living Graduate.* Although the trilogy failed on Broadway, Jones won praise from hinterland critics as a major new talent.

On the basis of its latest survey covering a twelve-month period, the Theater Communications Group, a national information-exchange service, reported that 11,000,000 patrons attended 1344 productions by 119 resident groups in 60 cities. This represented growth in all departments.

Off Off Broadway. A rising force in the American theater has been Off Off Broadway, a term applied to the small companies operating throughout New York City in lofts, churches, and abandoned movie theaters. In 1976 it continued to be a sounding board for budding playwrights as well as actors. The goal remained good theater rather than profit, and the results were often of Broadway caliber. In addition to the works of young American and British playwrights, playgoers in 1976 were offered Shakespeare, Shaw, and O'Neill and productions of *Dracula* and *Marat/Sade,* as well as a host of others, all at bargain prices. Among the groups whose work critics have praised were the Ensemble Studio Theater, the Manhattan Theater Club, and the Circle Repertory Company.

The changing relationship between Broadway and non-Broadway theater was tersely summed up by Otis L. Guernsey, Jr., in his introduction to *The Ten Best Plays of 1975–76.* Wrote Mr. Guernsey: "Broadway has become no longer an arena but a showcase. . . . Of the eight nonmusical Best Plays [in the current volume], not one originated as a Broadway production." Six came from regional theaters and two from London.

Deaths. Kermit Bloomgarden, Godfrey Cambridge, Lee J. Cobb, Eddie Dowling, Dame Edith Evans, Paul Ford, Margaret Leighton, Jo Mielziner, Paul Robeson, Rosalind Russell, and Dame Sybil Thorndike died during the year; *see* OBITUARIES. Other notable deaths included those of actors Roger Livesey (Feb. 5 at 69) and William Redfield (Aug. 17 at 49); and actresses Angela Baddeley (Feb. 22 at 71), Ruth McDevitt (May 27 at 80), and Ethel Shutta (Feb. 5 at 79).

TOGO. *See* STATISTICS OF THE WORLD.

TONGA. *See* STATISTICS OF THE WORLD.

TRANSKEI. On Oct. 26 the Republic of Transkei became the first South African Bantustan (Bantu homeland) to attain independence. The ceremony was held in Umtata, the capital, where Chief Botha Sigcau was sworn in as president and chief of state; Chief Kaiser D. Matanzima took the oath as prime minister. The nation began to move toward independence in October, 1975, when plans for the new state were approved. In July Matanzima, who was head of the dominant Transkei National Independence Party and leader of the territorial government from 1963 to independence, ordered the arrest of the head of the opposition Democratic Party and eight other party leaders. This move effectively crushed internal opposition to independence.

Formerly a part of South Africa's Cape Province, Transkei covers some 16,500 sq.mi., fronts on the Indian Ocean, and is bordered on the north by Lesotho. The economy is marked by subsistence farming on small plots of land and dependency on South Africa for manufactured goods, jobs, and financial assistance. With unusually fertile land, however, and a 155-mi. stretch of first-rate beaches, Transkei had an economic potential that was exceptionally strong.

Regarded as the homeland for all the Xhosa people, Transkei is inhabited by some 1,700,000 Xhosa. But an additional 1,300,000 Xhosa live in South Africa, many of them having been born there. In May the South African government issued legislation stripping these Xhosa of South African citizenship as of the date of Transkei independence. Although they would be permitted to live and work in South Africa, they technically were part of Transkei and had no political rights in South Africa.

At the end of 1976 no nation other than South Africa had recognized the new state because of worldwide opposition to the South African policy of segregation, or apartheid. Efforts by Transkei to join the Organization of African Unity and the United Nations were also ignored.

See STATISTICS OF THE WORLD. *See also* AFRICA.

J.T.S.

TRANSPORTATION

As the economy revived, traffic picked up—in the air, at sea, on the highways, the railroads, and the mass transportation media. But each mode of transportation had its own special problems.

Automobile sales, which had been most seriously affected by the recent recession, made a strong recovery in 1976 and helped railroads into the black with new-car shipments. Airline travel improved, but the aviation industry had long-range problems that were not easily resolved by increased traffic. Mass transportation and shipping, as usual, made slow gains. The United States government continued its heavy involvement with all the transportation systems, establishing new regulations and increasing financial support.

AUTOMOBILES

The U.S. automobile industry made a strong recovery in 1976 from the two-year slump that had begun abruptly in early 1974 and eased only toward the end of 1975. New-car sales totaled about 9,300,000, up 13 percent from 1975; unemployment in the industry dropped from 274,000 to below 30,000. Foreign car sales, however, remained at about 1,500,000. This was a drop of from 18 percent to 14.3 percent of the U.S. market share, reversing a four-year rise.

Small-Car Decline. The failure of imports to keep pace with the surge in new-car sales reflected not only their higher, less competitive prices but also an unexpected turning away from the small cars that were heavily represented in foreign models. After the rush for subcompacts in the wake of the 1973–74 gasoline shortages, American consumers were either buying the roomier new U.S. compacts or reasserting their taste for the big family car. American subcompacts, which captured 10 percent of total auto sales in 1974, also suffered, falling to 7.1 percent in 1976. To reduce excess small-car capacity, American Motors Corp. slashed prices on its subcompact Gremlins and offered rebates on its slightly larger Pacers; General Motors (GM) rebated its three smallest models, Chevettes, Vegas, and Astres; and Chrysler planned a series of temporary small-car plant closings for early 1977.

1977 Models. Standard-sized and intermediate cars were clearly on the ascendancy in fall sales of the new 1977 models, and by the end of the year they had captured 52 percent of the market, compared with 48 percent a year earlier. GM, most heavily committed to big cars, scaled down all its standard models by an average of 1000 lb. and 10 in. to meet U.S. government mileage standards: By 1978, each automaker's fleetwide average had to be 18 mi. per gallon for highway driving. The new GM Cadillac line, with its smaller-sized Seville, and the scaled-down Pontiac line had exceptionally high sales; the intermediate Oldsmobile Cutlass was the nation's bestselling car. GM ended the year with a 28 percent increase in sales and a record 55.8 percent of the market.

Chrysler increased its total sales by 31 percent with three new models, an intermediate-sized Cordoba and two roomy compacts, the Aspen and Volaré. Ford's volume rose by only 14 percent as a result of a month-long strike at the start of the 1977-model season; its big sellers were the standard-sized Ford and a restyled Granada compact. American Motors suffered a 23 percent drop-off in sales with its line of predominantly small cars. *See* UNITED STATES OF AMERICA: THE ECONOMY.

Meeting Government Standards. U.S. automakers planned to build shorter and lighter cars in all sizes in coming years to increase gasoline mileage, but they were also obliged by law to reduce the emission of noxious fumes. With emission-control devices, however, cars burn more fuel. Efforts to solve this dilemma were varied. Auto engineers were working on reducing gas wastage and exhaust pollutants by means of built-in mini-computer control over such functions as fuel-air mixing, spark firing, transmission shifting, and exhaust-gas recirculation. And meanwhile GM was readying a diesel-engine passenger car for 1978: Diesels burn fuel more efficiently than traditional engines and emit less noxious although sootier fumes. (A Volkswagen diesel Rabbit was due out in the spring of 1977.) Front-wheel drive was another device on its way in the near future, offering lighter-weight cars with more interior space but a less sturdy engine. Ford was to debut a front-wheel-drive Fiesta in the spring of 1977; Chrysler had a front-wheel-drive model due the following fall, and GM's was expected in the fall of 1978.

The last U.S.-built convertible, a Cadillac Eldorado, rolls off the assembly line at the General Motors Detroit plant on April 21. Air conditioning, higher freeway speeds, and safety consciousness had reduced demand for the once popular cars to an uneconomical trickle.

None of these moves, however, was expected to bring the automobile industry into conformity with the stiffer emission standards required for 1978-model cars under the Clean Air Act of 1970. So the manufacturers pressed for an amendment to the act that would give them more time. Meanwhile, the Environmental Protection Agency recalled more than 200,000 of Chrysler's 1975-model cars because a faulty design in the carburetor made it difficult for the autos to maintain current federal emission standards for carbon monoxide.

Air Bags. The air bag, a safety device that inflates on collision, was not made compulsory in 1976, as some had expected, although studies released by the Department of Transportation showed that air bags could save 12,000 lives a year and prevent or reduce 100,000 injuries. Instead, Secretary of Transportation William T. Coleman, Jr., requested that the automobile industry install 500,000 air bags in passenger cars in 1977 and 1978, in order to test their practicality and acceptance by the nation's drivers.

Highways. A strong campaign to expand federal participation in highway maintenance was mounted during the year by the Highway Users Federation, a lobbying group representing the interests of the construction industry, truckers, and automobile and tire makers. Since the mid-1950's, the U.S. has spent roughly $3 billion a year to build the 42,500-mi. system of interstate highways. With the system 88 percent complete, the highway lobby wanted the annual outlays to continue at current levels in order to cover the cost of road repairs. The individual states had been fully responsible for repairs and maintenance until 1976. Then the federal government provided grants of $175,000,000 per year for deteriorating interstate highways. But without far more massive federal

aid, warned the federation, the interstate system was in danger of rapidly breaking down.

AVIATION

Travel on U.S. airlines in 1976 showed a gain of about 14 percent over the previous year despite higher ticket prices. The ten domestic lines and Pan American World Airways (Pan Am) collectively earned almost $400,000,000 during the first three quarters of the year on operating revenues of $11.9 billion, compared with $44,700,000 on revenues of $10.5 billion for the same period in 1975. (The figures were somewhat distorted, however, by a 1976 bookkeeping profit of $103,000,000 taken by Pan Am.)

A commercial aviation record was set during the year by a new, long-range version of the Boeing 747. To herald the start of the service early in the year, Pan Am flew a load of passengers around the world with only two stops in 47 hr.

On July 1, in time for the Bicentennial celebrations in Washington, D.C., the Smithsonian Institution opened the doors of its new National Air and Space Museum, bringing together its historic collection of airplanes and spacecraft. By the end of the year 5,000,000 visitors had made it one of the most popular sites in the nation's capital.

A new discount plan for individual trips to foreign destinations was approved by the Civil Aeronautics Board in October, adding to the several types of bargain travel authorized in 1975 for nonaffiliated groups. Called Advance Booking Charter (ABC), it could lower an economy-flight ticket by about 50 percent. For example, a round-trip fare from New York to London could cost $299 instead of $626, depending on the season.

Concorde. The first regularly scheduled passenger flights by the Concorde, the British-French supersonic transport, were inaugurated on Jan. 21, with

The noise level of the British-French Concorde is recorded by one of twelve meters as it departs from Dulles International Airport near Washington, D.C., in May. In the first six months of monitoring, the supersonic craft proved to be no noisier than ordinary jets on landing (117.9 decibels) but twice as noisy on takeoff (119.8 decibels).

The Greek-owned supertanker Olympic Bravery lies broken off the coast of France after running aground in a January gale. The abandoned hulk represents the biggest dollar loss in shipping history.

a British Airways flight from London to Bahrain in the Persian Gulf and an Air France flight from Paris to Rio de Janeiro. The most important destination for the commercial success of the two airlines, however, was New York City, and this proved to be an elusive goal. U.S. Transportation Secretary William T. Coleman, Jr., gave his approval for scheduled flights to Washington's Dulles and New York's Kennedy airports for a sixteen-month trial period. But the Port Authority of New York and New Jersey, which operates Kennedy,

insisted that the Concorde exceeded the authority's noise regulations and refused it permission to land. Both British Airways and Air France began two weekly flights to the federally operated Dulles airport on May 24 under careful monitoring of noise levels. Despite the 20 percent surcharge above first-class fares, the flights were generally 80 percent to 90 percent full.

Future Aircraft. With the price of jet fuel at record levels and expected to go higher still, and with increasingly stringent airport noise regulations, airlines in 1976 came under more pressure than ever to buy new aircraft that would be quieter and more fuel-efficient. The technology to build such jets was available. The savings in fuel would be enormous, more carefully calculated seating capacity could also reduce costs substantially, and noise levels on the new planes would be extremely low. But no airline was earning enough money to finance a fleet of new planes, the builders could not go ahead with new designs and retooling without sizable orders, and the traditional institutional lenders were unanimous in refusing to invest in new technology programs unless the airline industry's financial health improved markedly over a sustained period of time. No solutions were in sight at the end of the year. But many experts looked toward early proposals for a government-backed arrangement of financing for the next generation of jet planes.

RAILROADS

For the railroad industry, 1976 started on a note of high optimism. In February U.S. President Gerald R. Ford signed into law the Railroad Revitalization and Regulatory Reform Act of 1976, known as the "4-R Act." It set up procedures to encourage and expedite new railroad mergers, instructed the Interstate Commerce Commission (I.C.C.) to permit more rate-making flexibility, and created a mechanism for federal and local subsidization of lightly used branch lines that otherwise would be abandoned. The act also authorized $1 billion in loan guarantees to railroads and ostensibly made available to them $600,000,000 more through government purchase of "redeemable preference shares."

Congress passed the new law in hopes that federal money would make up for the years of neglect and deferred maintenance that had afflicted so much of the railroad industry. But relief was delayed by a controversy over how the $1.6 billion was to be spent. The Transportation Department wanted to direct the money to railroads that would agree to merge or combine traffic on fewer rail lines. But Congress demanded that the money go to the most deserving rehabilitation projects, whether or not a consolidation was involved. Meanwhile, the I.C.C. conducted lengthy hearings on rates. At year's end the railroads had neither the money nor the rate-making freedom the act called for.

Conrail. The new government-funded Consolidated Rail Corp. (Conrail) acquired the properties of Penn Central and the six other bankrupt northeastern and midwestern railroads on April 1. The corporation then began operating the huge merger with far less trouble and confusion than had been originally feared. Conrail was scheduled to receive a total of $2.1 billion over the next five years from its "banker," the quasi-government corporation called the United States Railway Association (U.S.R.A.). The role of the U.S.R.A. was to invest the public money "prudently and wisely" in Conrail, to rehabilitate it into a profitable railroad, and to return the money to the public coffers with interest.

Amtrak. The National Railroad Passenger Corp. (Amtrak), set up by the federal government in 1971, was also supposed to be a profit-making corporation. But after five years it had consumed more than $1 billion in federal subsidies. Under the 4-R Act, Amtrak was to get $1.75 billion over a five-year period beginning early in 1976 for reconstruction of railways along the 450-mi. Northeast Corridor between Boston and Washington, D.C. The Transportation Department, however, held up the start of the program until the fall. At that time a compromise was reached on the pace of the expenditures and 50 percent of the funds were released.

The railroads run by Amtrak had not bought any passenger trains in twenty years, and the domestic passenger-equipment builders had either long since gone out of business or had fallen woefully far behind in technology. By the end of

1976, about 50 percent of Amtrak's short-distance passengers were riding in new equipment; most lines, however, still lacked truly modern stock.

Rail Industry Statistics. Freight traffic on U.S. railroads during 1976 totaled about 795 billion ton-miles, an increase of 5.3 percent over the previous year but still some 7 percent below pre-recession 1973, when 854 billion ton-miles were handled. Setting the comeback pace was a 20 percent increase over 1975 in the shipment of automobiles and automobile parts.

Intercity passenger traffic was up 7 percent as measured by passenger miles, and commuter traffic advanced by 6 percent. Total passenger revenues showed an 11 percent increase over 1975.

Net income for the first nine months of the year totaled $251,500,000, compared with a deficit of $128,500,000 for the corresponding period of 1975. Total employment for the year was expected to equal 1975 levels.

MASS TRANSIT

In 1976 public transportation accounted for only 4 percent of all motorized travel in the U.S., and half of that was concentrated in the New York metropolitan area.

An extensive nationwide study by the Regional Plan Association, partly funded by the federal government, reached two primary conclusions. First, the association concluded that a doubling of mass transportation users would reduce automobile traffic by only 1 percent. Second, the study showed that the concentration of jobs and services in downtown urban areas would be a more effective way to aid public transportation than

A 135-passenger cable car of the Roosevelt Island Tramway, which provides public transportation between a new residential community in the East River and Manhattan. Opened on May 18, it is the first such system in the nation.

The brand new paddle-wheel steamer Mississippi Queen (foreground), with 218 staterooms and a steam calliope, joins its sister boat the Delta Queen on the broad Mississippi River near Vicksburg. Christened on April 30, it was the first overnight passenger steamboat to be built since 1926, when the Delta Queen was launched.

suburban minibuses and other innovative schemes. On existing transit systems, the study reported, improved services and lowered fares attract more users, but the expenses of the improvements are not recouped by the increase in the number of fares. If new systems were constructed, only a few cities—Atlanta, Dallas, Detroit, Houston, Pittsburgh, Los Angeles, and possibly Baltimore—would find full-scale rapid transit cost-effective.

New Funds. The Department of Transportation allocated $1.5 billion for mass transportation during the year and allowed cities the option of diverting some highway money to mass transit uses. Seven major cities received direct aid of $340,000,000 for subway construction and modernization, bus purchases, equipment upgrading, and operating expenses. The seven cities were Baltimore, Boston, Detroit, New York, San Francisco, Seattle, and Washington, D.C.

SHIPS AND SHIPBUILDING

The U.S. active oceangoing merchant fleet stood at 536 vessels as of June 1, 1976, four more than in mid-1975. These figures, however, are somewhat misleading because new ships are bigger and faster than the older ones they replace. The effective size and productivity of the U.S. fleet increased steadily in the 1970's, and the deadweight tonnage of approximately 15,600,000 in the fall of 1976 was well over the 14,400,000 in 1970, when there were 793 ships in service. New orders were expected to add about 70 ships to the merchant fleet by 1980.

Shipbuilding. The trend in commercial construction continued toward building big, high-speed containerships and tankers. Coming into the picture, however, were two new classes of ships. Sixteen specialized liquefied natural gas carriers (LNG's) were either under construction or on order. These ships were specifically designed to bring liquefied natural gas to U.S. ports from for-

eign countries, especially Algeria. In the second class were huge new oceangoing barges. With the same capacity as older merchant vessels, these barges were designed to fill a gap for the shorter trade routes between the major ports serviced by the big, high-speed ships, especially where speed is not critical and port arrangements are not sophisticated. Such a barge could be built for $20,000,000 to $30,000,000, in comparison with the more than $100,000,000 required to build a containership. Another advantage of the barges was that because they are unmanned in transit and are pushed by powerful tugboats, crew sizes average 13 (regular vessels require double or triple that number).

Sailing Ships. The tall sailing ships of twenty-two nations that glided silently into New York harbor on July 3 (see BICENTENNIAL) may have seemed like ghosts out of the past, but to some shipbuilders, a sturdy schooner-rigged four-master could be one answer to rising fuel prices. At a London symposium held in January by the Royal Institution of Naval Architects, it was calculated that a sailing ship of 15,000-ton capacity traveling over a long route would be economically competitive with a steamer of the same tonnage. Such a ship could profitably carry bulk cargo, such as grain. In California work was under way on designs for a modern schooner based on a traditional type of hull; in West Germany a small fleet of computer-controlled square riggers was being seriously contemplated. No one foresaw a massive return to sailing power, but on selected routes and with modern weather forecasting, the sailing ship, retired from international routes in 1957, could become an efficient cargo carrier.

International Trade. On a tonnage basis, the U.S. merchant fleet hauled only about 6 percent of the 1976 U.S. exports and imports. These shipments included coal, grain, fertilizers, and other bulk cargo, and the U.S. fleet includes relatively few ships capable of handling such cargo. For the higher valued cargoes that move in regularly scheduled routes, however, the U.S. carried approximately 30 percent of world tonnage.

At the beginning of the year the U.S. ranked eighth in world oceangoing trade. It followed Liberia, Japan, the United Kingdom, Norway, Greece, Panama, and the Soviet Union. The American ships, however, were generally more modern and efficient than those of other fleets.

Oil Tankers. A rash of Liberian oil-tanker breakups and collisions in U.S. waters in December prompted a U.S. Coast Guard review of the foreign tanker fleets. Among the issues to be examined were aging vessels, hidden ownerships, poor navigational equipment, poorly trained crews, and the lack of double hulls to contain oil in the event of accidents. Tighter regulations for tankers entering U.S. waters were expected to be issued early in 1977.   B.W.

TRINIDAD AND TOBAGO. *See* STATISTICS OF THE WORLD.

TRUDEAU, PIERRE ELLIOTT. *See* PEOPLE IN THE NEWS.

TUNISIA. Despite his failing health and the steady criticism he faced from the Left, President Habib Bourguiba of Tunisia continued to exercise absolute political authority in 1976 through his Destour Socialist Party (D.S.P.).

The most controversial political issue of the year was the increasing conflict between two goals: economic development and free education. Following escalating student protests and widespread campus strikes the National Assembly on Jan. 27 transferred university disciplinary powers to the minister of education, Dris Guiga. Guiga was the author and executor of a policy linking budgets and the number of enrollments in academic programs to the requirements of economic development. On May 28, after a series of demonstrations by students and faculty members, he ordered more stringent sanctions against the academic Left, precipitating a new wave of strikes and arrests. Three days later Bourguiba appointed a new minister of education.

On July 2 Bourguiba opened a two-day meeting of the D.S.P. Central Committee to examine the 1977–81 development budget. The plan envisaged a 7.5 percent annual growth rate and the creation of 100,000 new jobs. Priority was given to the expansion of educational facilities to provide schooling for all boys and 71 percent of all girls within five years. It was expected that $2.7 billion of the budgeted $9.5 billion would have to come from outside sources.

See STATISTICS OF THE WORLD; *see also* MIDDLE EAST.   S.C.

TURKEY. After the political upheaval of 1975, Turkey in 1976 entered a period of relative calm and stability in government. Nevertheless, under the leadership of Premier Süleyman Demirel and his coalition government, the economy continued to falter on problems of unemployment and foreign exchange deficits.

Disaster struck the mountainous eastern region of the country, near Erzurum, in November, when an earthquake killed more than 4000 persons and left additional thousands homeless. The main quake occurred Nov. 24, and small aftershocks were reported for several succeeding days. The worst damage was sustained around the towns of Van and Diyadin, near Turkey's borders with Iran and the Soviet Union. At least 3700 persons were reported dead after the initial shock; many thousands more suffered from injuries or exposure and required immediate medical attention. The relief efforts of Turkish, German, Swiss, British, and American rescue teams were slowed by damage to roads and airfields and by snow and subfreezing temperatures.

The quake came amid efforts to revive the

An armed plainclothes policeman takes shelter behind an armored truck as student violence erupts at the University of Ankara on April 8. Three Turkish students were killed in the rioting and at least 500 were arrested.

economy after the slump of 1975. Increased production accounted for an 82 percent increase in exports for the first six months of 1976 (over the same period of 1975), but total exports still lagged far behind imports. It was feared that the balance-of-payments deficit might lead to devaluation of the Turkish lira, especially since Turkey's most important source of foreign exchange after exports, remittances from workers abroad, was hard hit by unemployment in Western Europe and the resultant return of Turkish workers. In August the Finance Ministry, reporting on rampant unemployment and underemployment, called for "labor intensive investment" to absorb a larger proportion of the labor reserve. The intentions of the coalition government to pursue further industrialization of the country were evident in the fourth five-year plan, announced by Deputy Premier Necmettin Erbakan on July 26. The plan outlined an ambitious industrialization program, with a new emphasis on the development of heavy industry (automobiles, iron, and steel).

The chief opposition to the policies of Demirel's coalition came from the academic community. Political violence on campuses temporarily closed most major universities in January, jeopardizing accreditation for the entire year. At least thirty-four students were killed in clashes with police during the 1975–76 academic year, and 500 students were arrested during a demonstration at the University of Ankara on April 8.

In foreign relations Demirel and his Justice Party pursued a moderate course. On March 26 Turkey agreed to reopen United States military installations, closed in 1975, in exchange for at least $1 billion in military aid from the U.S. An arms embargo, enacted by the U.S. Congress in February, 1975, was eased in June to allow Turkey to receive the aid it needed as a member of the North Atlantic Treaty Organization (NATO). Agreement on guiding principles for negotiations between Turkey and Greece over exploration of the Aegean Sea for oil raised Western hopes for a rapprochement between the two eastern Mediterranean NATO members. (Greece was still troubled, however, by the fact that Turkish troops continued to occupy 40 percent of the Mediterranean island of Cyprus.) Turkish officials complained about relations with other countries, accusing the European Economic Community of dragging its heels in offering monetary aid, freedom of movement to migrant workers, and preferential trade conditions to help revitalize the Turkish economy.

See STATISTICS OF THE WORLD. See also CYPRUS; GREECE; MIDDLE EAST.

S.C.

U

UGANDA. The year 1976 brought some of the severest challenges yet encountered by Idi Amin in his six-year reign as president of Uganda. The once-thriving Ugandan economy was near bankruptcy, with consumption and government spending, investment, and exports all at new lows. Basic foodstuffs were in short supply, and the distribution system in the outlying towns was reported near collapse. Faced with mounting Ugandan debts, Kenya refused to sell Uganda fuel unless it was paid for in advance and in specified foreign currencies. In April, in an effort to keep his armed forces supplied, Amin imposed a blockade on oil being transshipped to Rwanda. The personal power of Amin seemed assured, however. He survived an assassination attempt early in June, and on June 25 the Defense Council proclaimed him president for life.

On June 27 Palestinian guerrillas seized an Air France jetliner shortly after it left Athens bound for Paris and landed it at Entebbe airport. On July 3 Israeli commandos invaded the airport and, in a lightning operation, rescued the passengers and crew, killing twenty Ugandan soldiers during the mission. See ISRAEL; MILITARY AND NAVAL AFFAIRS. While Amin threatened retaliation and demanded Israeli compensation for damages, he himself was accused of having helped the hijackers. Relations deteriorated rapidly between Uganda and Kenya, which had permitted the Israelis to refuel in Nairobi while en route back to Israel, and with Great Britain, which accused Amin of being responsible for the disappearance and probable murder of a British subject, Dora Bloch, who had been a passenger on the Air France flight and who was hospitalized at the time of the rescue operation. (She later disappeared and was presumed dead.) Hundreds of Kenyans working in Uganda were reported to have been arrested, beaten, and, in some instances, executed. On July 28 Britain broke relations with Uganda after most British subjects had evacuated the country. This was the

Big Daddy Retains the Title

In his sixth year as virtual dictator of Uganda, Idi Amin, known as "Big Daddy," continued unchallenged as the most unpredictable leader in equatorial Africa and possibly anywhere else in the world. Diplomacy was his particular arena for the year. A onetime heavyweight boxer, Amin kept threatening to make war on neighboring Kenya—but backed down when Kenyan border guards started an energy crisis by halting all Uganda-bound fuel trucks. But his biggest diplomatic milestone of 1976 came in July. After four years of tense relations with Uganda, the British closed down their embassy in Kampala, thereby severing relations with a Commonwealth nation for the first time in history.

President Idi Amin.

first time Britain had ever cut diplomatic ties with a member of the Commonwealth of Nations (q.v.). Late in July, in protest against Uganda's critical economic condition, senior army commanders demanded Amin's resignation, and students at Makerere University staged a boycott. After a new assassination attempt, Amin struck back, purging more than two dozen high-ranking military officers and placing some 7000 troops under barracks arrest. He also ordered loyal troops into Makerere, where at least 150 students were shot down and hundreds of others were arrested.

On Aug. 7 Amin met with President Jomo Kenyatta of Kenya and agreed to pay outstanding debts, amounting to around $50,000,000. He further agreed to pay for future oil shipments in advance and to end the harassment of Kenyan citizens. The July purge and the August accord permitted Amin to shore up his regime, and conditions within Uganda remained relatively stable for the remainder of the year.

See STATISTICS OF THE WORLD. *See also* AFRICA. J.T.S.

UNION OF ARAB EMIRATES. *See* STATISTICS OF THE WORLD.

UNION OF SOVIET SOCIALIST REPUBLICS. Leonid I. Brezhnev (*see* PEOPLE IN THE NEWS) and the Communist Party colleagues who joined him to overthrow Nikita S. Khrushchev in 1964 remained in power throughout 1976. Domestically, they emphasized ideological orthodoxy and economic growth. In foreign affairs their aim was to extend Soviet influence worldwide while building a firm foundation for Soviet-American détente.

Politics. Communist Party General Secretary Brezhnev, who celebrated his 70th birthday amid much fanfare on Dec. 19, continued to dominate Soviet politics despite recent ill health. In May Brezhnev was promoted to field marshal of the army, the first Soviet leader since Joseph Stalin to hold that rank, which is the nation's highest. Premier Aleksei N. Kosygin, 72, reportedly suffered a stroke in August, but he too remained in office.

The highlight of the political year was the 25th Congress of the Soviet Communist Party, which was held in February and early March. Brezhnev delivered a five-and-one-half-hour address in which he reviewed the nation's domestic and foreign policies. He stressed the need for strengthening "social discipline" at home. In his economic report Brezhnev claimed that the government had made great strides in raising living standards, but he admitted that production of consumer goods had fallen far short of expectations.

During the congress Agriculture Minister Dmitri Polyansky was dropped from the party Politburo; he lost his ministerial post less than two weeks later. Polyansky seemed to be paying the penalty for a disastrous harvest in 1975, when the grain crop was the lowest in a decade. Two officials were promoted to Politburo rank: armaments expert Dmitri Ustinov, 67, and Leningrad party leader Grigory Romanov, who at 53 became the Politburo's youngest member. Less than two months after the congress ended, Soviet Defense Minister Andrei Grechko died of a heart attack (*see* OBITUARIES). Soviet leaders then appointed Ustinov as the nation's first civilian defense minister in half a century. In December, Deputy Foreign Minister Yakov A. Malik, 70, left his post as

Soviet leaders Leonid I. Brezhnev, Nikolai V. Podgorny, Aleksei Kosygin, and Mikhail Suslov (left to right) attend the state funeral of Defense Minister Andrei Grechko, who died in April.

Soviet representative to the United Nations, a job he had held since 1968, to assume new administrative responsibilities in Moscow.

Dissent. Soviet authorities continued to deal harshly with dissent. Even so, a number of well-known dissenters clung to their demands for political liberalization. The eminent nuclear physicist Andrei Sakharov, who was awarded the Nobel Peace Prize in 1975, remained active in his support of lesser-known dissenters, although he had frequent brushes with officials. In an August interview Sakharov admitted that he saw little hope for liberalization even when a new generation of Soviet leaders takes command.

During January adverse publicity in the West led the Soviet government to release dissenter Leonid Plyushch, a Ukrainian mathematician, from custody in a mental hospital. After emigrating with his wife and children to France, Plyushch gave a detailed account of how the Soviet regime commonly imposes terms in mental asylums as punishment for political protest.

Police harassment caused Andrei Amalrik, a dissident writer and historian, to give in to official suggestions that he leave the country. In July Amalrik and his wife departed for the Netherlands. During a visit to the Netherlands that same month, Viktor Korchnoi, the world's second-ranked chess player, also sought political asylum.

In December, pursuant to an agreement mediated by the United States, the Soviet government permitted a leading dissident, Vladimir K. Bukovsky, to leave a prison in the U.S.S.R. for asylum in Great Britain; in exchange, the Chilean government freed Communist Party leader Luis Corvalán

Lepe, who flew to Moscow in time for Brezhnev's birthday celebration.

The Economy. Kosygin delivered a lengthy economic report to the Communist Party Congress on March 1. He outlined the 1976–80 economic plan, which again assigned top priority to heavy industrial production at the expense of light industry and consumer goods. In late October the final version of the plan was presented to the Supreme Soviet by Nikolai Baibakov, chairman of the State Planning Commission. The 1977 growth target for industrial production was set at 5.6 percent, not large by recent standards, but well over the 1976 target of 4.3 percent. Light industry and consumer goods were targeted to grow 4.9 percent in 1977, compared with 2.7 percent in 1976.

One factor that contributed to the nation's ability to set higher economic goals was a bumper harvest in 1976, with a record grain crop of 223,800,000 metric tons. In the hope of repeating if not improving on this successful harvest, the government planned to spend heavily on farming in the new five-year plan. Addressing the party Central Committee in October, Brezhnev announced that $226 billion had been allocated for agriculture through 1980.

Space Program. The Soviet Union conducted several space missions in 1976. During the summer two cosmonauts, Col. Boris Volynov and Lt. Col. Vitaly Zholobov, spent seven weeks aboard the orbiting space station Salyut 5. The primary Soviet space achievement of 1976, however, was a lunar mission in August, when Soviet scientists successfully soft-landed an unmanned spacecraft on the moon. The craft, Luna XXIV, scooped up samples

Dissident author Vladimir Bukovsky was freed from prison and sent into exile by Soviet authorities in December, in exchange for a Chilean Communist Party leader freed by Chilean authorities. Here Bukovsky addresses a press conference in Zürich.

of lunar soil and returned to earth with them on Aug. 22. It was announced in September that Eastern European cosmonauts would participate in Soviet manned space missions beginning in 1978.

Foreign Affairs. In his February report to the party congress, Brezhnev reaffirmed the Soviet commitment to détente with the U.S. He also made it clear, however, that he regarded his nation's interests as global and that his policy was to enlarge Soviet influence wherever possible.

Soviet-American relations were notably cooler than in recent years, and 1976 was the first year since 1971 that no bilateral summit talks were held. During a January visit to Moscow, U.S. Secretary of State Henry A. Kissinger stressed American concern about Soviet intervention in Africa, especially in Angola, where the U.S.S.R. and its Cuban allies were openly supporting the Popular Movement for the Liberation of Angola.

The primary aim of Kissinger's mission was to conclude negotiations on a second bilateral strategic arms limitation treaty. The arms talks became deadlocked, however, and were suspended on Nov. 20 pending the inauguration of Jimmy Carter, the newly elected U.S. President. Meanwhile, U.S.-Soviet economic cooperation continued to increase; the estimated trade volume between the two superpowers in 1976 was $2.5 billion, compared with $172,000,000 in 1971.

Relations between the U.S.S.R. and Japan suffered two setbacks in 1976. In January bilateral talks in Tokyo brought the two countries no closer than ever to signing a World War II peace treaty. Then, in September, a Russian pilot, Lt. Viktor Belenko, defected to Japan with a top-secret MIG-25 jet fighter. The Soviet government protested the granting of U.S. asylum for the officer and, more importantly, the examination of the aircraft by U.S. and Japanese intelligence experts (*see* JAPAN).

Soviet diplomacy in the Third World met with mixed success in 1976. In June the U.S.S.R. and the Philippines announced that they had agreed to establish diplomatic ties. Later in the month, Brezhnev and visiting Prime Minister Indira Gandhi of India issued a declaration reaffirming close relations between their two countries. In October the Soviets signed a twenty-year friendship pact with Angola.

In the Middle East, however, the U.S.S.R. lost ground. In March Egyptian President Anwar el-Sadat abrogated a 1971 friendship treaty with the Soviet Union. A June visit to Moscow by Jordan's King Hussein I ended inconclusively. In addition, Soviet relations with Syria deteriorated in the wake of Syrian military intervention in Lebanon. Moscow's biggest gains were in Libya, a major purchaser of armaments from the Soviet Union.

The U.S.S.R. did maintain a firm grip on Eastern Europe. However, at the 25th Soviet Communist Party Congress and again at a Communist Party conference in East Berlin in June, Western European Communist Party leaders spoke out in favor of liberalization and other policies that differed

A Moscow wall poster portrays British Conservative Party leader Margaret Thatcher as a witch who, having slandered the Soviet Union, now seeks to restore international tensions and wreck détente.

widely from those of the Russian party. At the latter assembly Soviet leaders grudgingly admitted that no one party should lead the Communist camp (see COMMUNISM). Brezhnev reaffirmed this concession in visits to Yugoslavia and Rumania in November.

China was the U.S.S.R.'s major critic in the Communist world. With the death of Chinese leader Mao Tse-tung in September (see OBITUARIES), the Soviets began issuing friendly feelers toward their ideological rival—whether in earnest or for propaganda purposes, Western analysts were not sure. The Chinese response seemed generally negative. In November, however, the two nations resumed talks on border issues after a hiatus of eighteen months.

See STATISTICS OF THE WORLD. See also WARSAW TREATY ORGANIZATION. F.W.

UNITED NATIONS, THE. In contrast to its turbulent predecessor, the year 1976 was a relatively quiet period in the history of the United Nations. It was a year in which issues concerning Africa took precedence over all other matters. Attention was focused on the apartheid, or separate development, policies affecting Blacks in the Republic of South Africa and on the strivings for black majority rule in Rhodesia and in Namibia (South-West Africa).

After an initial veto by the United States, Angola was accepted for U.N. membership on Dec. 1, becoming the 146th member nation. Number 145, Seychelles, had been admitted earlier (Sept. 21), and Western Samoa raised the total U.N. membership to 147 when it was voted in (Dec. 15). Vietnam's application for membership failed once more when the U.S. vetoed the proposal (Nov. 15).

Kurt Waldheim of Austria was reelected on Dec. 7, virtually without opposition, for another five-year term as secretary-general.

The scale of annual assessments was revised by the General Assembly, lowering obligations for 30 countries and raising them for 28 others. The lowest scale was set at 0.02 percent of the operating budget, or about $70,000. The highest was 25 percent, the share paid by the U.S., which amounted to about $95,000,000. The Soviet assessment was 11.33 percent; China, France, West Germany, and Japan were assessed just over 5 percent; and Great Britain's share was 4.44 percent. The budget for fiscal 1977–78 was set at $783,900,000, a 5 percent increase over the preceding year.

On Dec. 15 the General Assembly adopted a West German proposal to draft an international treaty against the taking of hostages. A thirty-five-member committee was set up to write the text of the agreement aimed at curbing international terrorism.

SOUTHERN AFRICA
The problems of the Republic of South Africa were forced on the attention of the U.N. following the riots in Soweto, a Johannesburg suburb, early in the summer. On June 19 the Security Council unanimously condemned South Africa's harsh methods of suppressing the rioting. By Nov. 9 the black African nations, supported by substantial majorities, were able to pass a series of resolutions in the General Assembly condemning various aspects of the South African government's policies regarding Blacks. The most important of

the resolutions—passed by a vote of 108 in favor, 11 against, and 22 abstaining—confirmed the right of black Africans to struggle "by all means" to achieve majority rule in South Africa.

The pressures against the white minority rule of Prime Minister Ian D. Smith in Rhodesia were intensified in March when newly independent Mozambique closed the 800-mi. border it shares with Rhodesia, cutting off Rhodesia's access to the sea. In April the U.N. Security Council unanimously broadened the economic sanctions against Rhodesia that had been in force since 1966. As the year ended, Britain's ambassador to the U.N., Ivor Richard, was hoping to reconvene negotiations in Geneva between Rhodesia's Whites and Blacks. The negotiation sessions, begun in October in an effort to establish a timetable for the assumption of power by Blacks in Rhodesia, were adjourned in December.

Regarding Namibia, the Security Council on Jan. 31 called unanimously for U.N.-supervised elections in that territory. South Africa notified the U.N. in August that the Windhoek constitutional conference, held under South African auspices, had set Dec. 31, 1978, as the date on which Namibia would become fully independent. African leaders denounced the proposal as inadequate and demanded that the Security Council

A small crowd gathers on a gloomy December day as the flag of Angola is raised in front of the United Nations headquarters in New York City. The strife-torn African country had just become the 146th member of the world body.

Ambassador William Scranton raises his hand, indicating a U.S. veto of a proposal to admit Vietnam to membership in the United Nations. The action, taken Nov. 15 in the Security Council, marked the second U.S. veto of the proposal.

endorse sanctions against South Africa. This demand failed on Oct. 19, when the U.S., Britain, and France cast a triple veto against the resolution.

MIDDLE EAST

The problems of the Middle Eastern countries involved the U.N. to a lesser extent in 1976 than they had in previous years. Arab attention was turned to the Lebanese civil war, and African leaders were more preoccupied with achieving black rule in southern Africa.

Israel and the Palestinians. Israel came under considerable pressure over its policies in the areas it had occupied since the 1967 war, even from its staunchest ally, the U.S. On March 25 the U.S. vetoed a draft that would have condemned the policy of Israeli settlements in the areas. On May 26, however, it permitted a majority statement by the Security Council president to stand with its dissent, and on Nov. 11 it joined fourteen other Security Council members in a unanimous condemnation of Israeli administration of the occupied Arab territories.

Regarding the treatment of the Palestinian

problem, the U.S. continued to provide steadfast support to Israel. At the end of January, it vetoed a Security Council resolution that would have favored the establishment of a Palestinian state on the West Bank of the Jordan R. (formerly western Jordan). On May 19, the so-called Palestine Committee, established by the General Assembly in the fall of 1975, produced a two-phase plan that called for total Israeli withdrawal from occupied Arab territories by June 1, 1977; for the return of Palestinian refugees to their homes; and for the establishment of a Palestinian homeland under the leadership of the Palestine Liberation Organization in the evacuated areas. Israel called the plan an attempt to dismantle the Israeli state step by step, and the U.S. used its veto in the Security Council on June 29 to prevent its endorsement. Nevertheless, the General Assembly on Nov. 24 supported the same plan in a vote of 90 in favor, 16 opposed, and 30 abstaining.

In other Mideast-related actions, the Security Council in May and again in November extended the mandate of the U.N. Disengagement Observer Force, serving on the Golan Heights, for another six months. That of the U.N. Emergency Force serving in the Sinai was extended in October for another year.

Oumar Diouf (right) aids a sick child in a small village of western Senegal. Diouf, a chicken farmer, gave two hours of his time each day to treat the townsfolk. UNICEF funds helped to train him as a paramedic and to provide some of his equipment and his medicine.

Cyprus. On the continuing issue of the Greek-Turkish conflict over the partition of Cyprus, the U.N. appeared to be marking time. Twice during the year the mandate of its peacekeeping forces (U.N.F.I.C.Y.P.) there was renewed. Meanwhile in August, a dispute between Greece and Turkey broke out over the potential oil riches on the shelves of the Aegean Sea. On Aug. 25, after some tense days, the Security Council arrived at a compromise measure calling on both sides to resume direct negotiations.

ASSOCIATED AGENCIES

Various agencies of the U.N. were active on the economic front during 1976. The International Bank for Reconstruction and Development, or World Bank, reported a record year in September: Its combined lending was $6.6 billion, an increase of $736,000,000 over the preceding year. The U.N. Development Program (U.N.D.P.), to which $500,000,000 was pledged in new money in the fall, set forth a $2 billion plan for the 1977–81 period for the benefit of developing nations. The World Food Program also reported pledges of $500,000,000, and by April it had appropriated $600,000,000 in food aid. In February a new International Fund for Agricultural Development was established; its target of $1 billion was reached by the end of the year.

The United Nations Children's Fund, or UNICEF, had another fruitful year, approving commitments amounting to over $90,000,000 for projects in 103 countries during 1976. The organization collected $85,000,000 in new pledges during the fall.

In the fall the U.N. Educational, Scientific, and Cultural Organization (UNESCO) held its annual conference in Nairobi, Kenya. By providing for Israeli participation in the activities of the European regional group—blocked since November, 1974, by the Arab nations—and by deferring action on a Soviet proposal that would have allowed state control over the free flow of news, the agency succeeded in reversing a trend that had led Western European nations to become disenchanted with the organization and the U.S. to withhold contributions totaling $40,000,000. However, the price of Israel's readmission was a UNESCO resolution condemning its educational and cultural policies in occupied Arab territories.

Two more conferences were held during the year (at U.N. headquarters) to draft an international law of the sea; once again they were adjourned without substantial progress. Developing nations apparently preferred to adopt a wait-and-see attitude toward the Administration of U.S. President-elect Jimmy Carter on sharing the natural riches of the sea.

Disaster Aid. The U.N.'s ability to provide meaningful humanitarian assistance was further demonstrated at the time of the devastating Guatemalan earthquake in February, which killed 23,000 people and injured 77,000 others. Units from UNICEF, U.N.D.P., the World Health Organization, the Food and Agriculture Organization, and the World Food Program rushed in to help care for the more than 1,000,000 people left homeless. They all worked tirelessly under the guidance of the U.N. Disaster Relief Office.

See also AFRICA; MIDDLE EAST; and separate articles on most of the countries mentioned.   L.H.

UNITED STATES AIR FORCE. See MILITARY AND NAVAL AFFAIRS.

UNITED STATES ARMY. See MILITARY AND NAVAL AFFAIRS.

UNITED STATES COAST GUARD. See MILITARY AND NAVAL AFFAIRS.

UNITED STATES MARINE CORPS. See MILITARY AND NAVAL AFFAIRS.

UNITED STATES NAVY. See MILITARY AND NAVAL AFFAIRS.

UNITED STATES OF AMERICA. The Bicentennial year of the United States was distinctly brighter than its preceding years. A general good humor, most evident during the harmonious Fourth of July celebrations, prevailed in 1976 along with a sense of relief that an era of deceitful government, unpopular war, and economic recession appeared to have ended. The international scene was mostly peaceful, although a conflict in Angola briefly threatened to involve the country in another foreign war. At home heated competition for the Presidential nominations was followed by the defeat of President Gerald R. Ford by a Southern Democrat, Jimmy Carter, who had been virtually unknown in January. The U.S. Congress, in spite of large Democratic majorities, was kept from enacting major legislation by unified Republican minorities and the threat of Presidential vetoes. As if the prestige of politicians had not suffered enough of late, several Congressmen made scandalous headlines with revelations of misconduct. The recession of 1974–75 yielded to improvements in business and agriculture. A pause in the recovery, however, was worrisome, and the year ended with the gloomy possibility of chronic high unemployment and renewed recession.

NATIONAL LIFE

Bicentennial commemorations—from stately observances to tawdry product promotions—filled the land for the first half of 1976. On July 4 the festivities reached a climax: Millions of spectators enjoyed special events in Philadelphia, Washington, D.C., and New York City, and fireworks displays and street fairs were staged in most cities. The mood was festive and happy. Queen Elizabeth II of Great Britain, who arrived on July 6 for a six-day tour of the former colonies, received a warm welcome. After July the fun was over; even politicians omitted Bicentennial references from their rhetoric. But the nation had given itself a grand and fitting birthday party.

There were other occasions for national rejoicing, especially among scientists. Two unmanned spacecraft—Viking I and II—landed on Mars on

President Gerald R. Ford and his children listen in the White House press room on Nov. 3 as First Lady Betty Ford reads a statement conceding the Presidential election. The President had strained his voice in the final days of the campaign. Behind the First Lady are (from left), Steven, the President, Susan, Michael and his wife Gayle, and Jack.

In the first televised debate between Vice-Presidential candidates, Democrat Walter Mondale (left) is matched against Republican Robert Dole. The encounter occurred Oct. 15 in Houston.

July 20 and Sept. 3 and radioed back invaluable data on the planet's soil, atmosphere, and climate. And all five of the 1976 Nobel prizes were won by Americans.

Post-Watergate Ethics. The Watergate scandals and the Congressional investigations of intelligence agency misconduct prompted a closer ethical examination of many of the nation's institutions, including Congress, multinational corporations, and the U.S. Military Academy. Also falling under scrutiny were amateur athletics, the Medicaid program and the medical profession, and the activities of Congressional lobbyists.

In Washington, D.C., politicians responded to the new morality by releasing their recent tax returns and calling upon opponents to do likewise. "Decent" and "honest" became terms of the highest political praise. The year's most sensational scandal was touched off in May when Rep. Wayne L. Hays (D, Ohio) was accused of keeping a mistress on the public payroll. Hays was forced to resign his seat, and other Congressmen faced similar charges. *See* CONGRESS OF THE UNITED STATES.

Health and the Environment. In February medical researchers warned that the nation might soon be in for an epidemic of swine flu, a virus strain thought to be similar to one that infected 200,000,000 people around the world in 1918–19. The Administration decided on a nationwide program of vaccinations, and in April Congress provided funds for this effort. Beginning on Oct. 1 millions of free flu shots were offered to the public, though no confirmed outbreaks of the disease

had occurred. A more mysterious contagion struck Philadelphia in July. Delegates to an American Legion convention and other guests at a hotel became ill, exhibiting severe flulike symptoms. Legionnaires disease, as it was dubbed by baffled health authorities, killed 29 and hospitalized 151 others before it vanished as unaccountably as it had come.

The movement to protect the environment from pollution and misuse recorded both gains and losses. Evidence mounted that the earth's ozone layer was being threatened by fluorocarbons released by certain types of spray cans; a prohibition was imminent. Doubts grew about the safety of the nation's approximately sixty nuclear power plants. The electorate in seven states, however, voted down restrictions on the development of nuclear power. The hardest-fought cause of environmentalists was lost: The British-French supersonic transport jet plane, the Concorde, was granted permission to land at Washington, D.C., for a sixteen-month trial period, in spite of its noisiness and its possibly harmful effects on the upper atmosphere. Secretary of Transportation William T. Coleman, Jr., made the decision in February, including New York City in the experiment. On March 11, however, the New York Port Authority refused to allow the Concorde to land in the New York City area, and at the year's end the ban was still in effect.

An environmental disaster occurred in Idaho on June 5: The Teton Dam, considered unsafe by some engineers during its construction in the early 1970's, collapsed. The suddenly released water

The Bicentennial brings royal visitors to the U.S.: top left, Great Britain's Elizabeth II (center) and Prince Philip (on her left) tour New York City with Mayor Abraham Beame; top right, Hussein I of Jordan and Queen Alia flank President Gerald R. Ford and his wife, Betty, at the White House; bottom right, Spain's Juan Carlos I (third from left) and Queen Sophia (center) visit the Metropolitan Museum of Art, New York City; and below, Charles XVI Gustavus of Sweden inspects the Liberty Bell in Philadelphia's Independence Hall.

drowned fourteen people, flooded 180 sq.mi., and caused about $400,000,000 in damages. A less preventable calamity occurred on July 31 when a flash flood in the Big Thompson R. canyon in Colorado drowned more than 100 people.

In the Headlines. Some familiar names from 1975 cropped up again in 1976. Newspaper heiress Patricia Hearst was convicted on bank robbery charges and later freed on bail pending an appeal. Samuel Bronfman 2nd, son of a liquor magnate, was at the center of a sensational kidnapping trial. Another unusual kidnapping occurred on July 15 near Chowchilla, Calif., when the children on a school bus were abducted and sealed inside a buried truck trailer. The children dug themselves out, and three suspects were soon arrested. See CRIME AND LAW ENFORCEMENT; PEOPLE IN THE NEWS.

The year also marked the death of three rich and singularly powerful Americans: Carlo Gambino, J. Paul Getty, and Howard Hughes. See OBITUARIES.

Sports and Diversions. The sports event of the year was the Montréal Olympics, a summer fixture on most television sets; the young American boxers were a special source of national pride. The New York Yankees sparked major league baseball to a record year in attendance (31,320,592 paid admissions), then succumbed weakly to the Cincinnati Reds in the World Series. Heavyweight boxing champion Muhammad Ali scored a decision over Ken Norton in September.

Some popular motion pictures in 1976 were *All the President's Men, The Omen,* and a remake of *King Kong.* Bestselling books included *Trinity* by Leon Uris and *Roots* by Alex Haley. Legalized gambling in various forms, including state lotteries, bingo, off-track horse-race betting, and casinos, continued to be a growing commercial activity. A new kind of entertainment for travelers, citizens band (CB) radios, became so popular among truck drivers that ordinary car owners bought sets for slang-filled intercommunication. Among children skateboards in a new, more flexible form made a comeback.

GOVERNMENT

"Tonight I report that the State of the Union is better . . . but still not good enough." With these words, spoken in his State of the Union message on Jan. 19, President Ford struck the earnestly optimistic note of his administration in its last year. He went on to urge a generally passive role for government, a "new realism" about what government could accomplish. Warning of the need to keep inflation down, he proposed no major new programs. Sen. Edmund S. Muskie (D, Maine) gave the Democratic reply to Ford's address; he argued that the President "profoundly misunder-

stands" the nation and recommended urgent efforts to get the unemployed back to work. Ford also had critics on his right: Former Gov. Ronald Reagan of California became increasingly critical of the President's leadership as the two struggled for the Republican Presidential nomination. Reagan questioned the soundness of the economic recovery, but his main theme concerned foreign policy. Ford had failed, he said on March 4, "to halt and reverse the diplomatic and military decline of the United States."

One result of Ford's conflict with Congressional liberals like Muskie was legislative stalemate; Congress achieved little of lasting importance during 1976. The challenge to Ford's foreign policy coincided with a year of uneventful drift: Peace prevailed, but détente with the Soviet Union and China was not furthered or clarified by new agreements.

The judicial branch of government dealt with some of the most heated social issues of 1976: busing, abortion, and capital punishment. The busing of students to achieve school desegregation continued to be ordered, though less frequently, by courts in Dallas, Omaha, and elsewhere. A nationwide "right-to-life" movement was the focal point for strong reaction against the legalization of abortion in certain states. A ban on the use of Medicaid funds for abortions was passed by Congress, but a federal district judge ruled the ban unconstitutional in October. In July the U.S. Supreme Court upheld the death penalty as imposed in some recent state criminal codes; see SUPREME COURT OF THE UNITED STATES. This ruling formed the backdrop for the bizarre case of Gary Mark Gilmore, a condemned murderer who sued in the Utah courts to obtain his own prompt execution.

The President Versus Congress. The Democratic leadership in the 94th Congress sought to pass legislation to create jobs, extend government services, and protect consumers and the environment; increased federal expenditures, Democrats argued, would recharge the economy. But the Administration, more concerned about inflation than unemployment, opposed these measures. Ford vetoed fifteen bills during the 1976 session (the threat of veto killed several more); Congress overrode his vetoes only four times. "We have a Democratic Congress," said Ford in justification of his role, "and a Republican President to check their excesses with my vetoes."

Among the important bills enacted were a tax reform measure and a $3.95 billion jobs bill. An Administration-sponsored extension of revenue sharing through fiscal 1980 was also enacted. In the fields of health care, welfare reform, urban reconstruction, energy policy, gun control, and consumer protection, little was achieved.

Intelligence Investigations. The work of the Senate and House committees investigating U.S. intelligence agencies came to an end early in the year. The Senate committee, chaired by Frank Church (D, Idaho), issued its final report in April. It summed up earlier findings of illegal surveillance and political sabotage by the Central Intelligence Agency (C.I.A.) and the Federal Bureau of Investigation (F.B.I.). In May the Senate adopted a key recommendation of the report by creating a permanent Select Committee on Intelligence to oversee the C.I.A. and share surveillance of other intelligence agencies. Meanwhile the House committee voted in January against public release of its report. A draft copy was obtained by newsman Daniel Schorr, who arranged for its publication. In the ensuing protests over the security leak, attention was diverted from the report itself, which focused on abuses of power by the C.I.A. Both the C.I.A. and the F.B.I. admitted past illegalities and undertook to police their own operations more strictly.

Foreign Affairs. Under the guidance of Secretary of State Henry A. Kissinger, U.S. foreign policy remained basically unchanged during a remarkably peaceful year. "Détente" was stricken from President Ford's vocabulary in response to attacks by Reagan and other conservatives, but the policy of avoiding conflict—military and verbal—with the Soviet Union and China remained in effect. Negotiators in the second round of the strategic arms limitation talks (SALT II) with the Soviet Union failed to conclude a treaty. But agreement, according to Ford, was "more than 90 percent" achieved. After the death of Mao Tse-tung in September, Kissinger reaffirmed the long-range U.S. goal of normalizing relations with China.

U.S. diplomatic weight in the Middle East—where peace prevailed except in Lebanon—was increased by the strengthening of ties with Saudi Arabia, Egypt, and other moderate Arab nations. It was hoped that this policy would also reduce the chances of another oil embargo. In U.S.-European relations the chief development was a warning issued by Kissinger in April that the U.S. would look with disfavor on any Communist Party assumption of power in Italy or in any other Western European nation.

Africa was a prime focus of interest. In the first weeks of the year, aid to U.S.-backed forces in the Angolan civil war was cut off by order of Congress. As the Soviet-supported faction gained the upper hand, Kissinger demanded that the U.S.S.R. cease its supply efforts as well, and a Great Power confrontation was briefly threatened. The U.S. vetoed Angola's entry into the United Nations in June in protest against the continuing presence there of Cuban troops, then permitted Angola's entry by abstaining when the vote came up again in November.

American policy toward black Africa took a decisive turn during the year, and a new U.S. commitment to representative democratic rule emerged. Leading a British-U.S. effort to mediate in the conflict over Rhodesia, Kissinger worked out a formula for transferring power to the leaders of the black majority in two years. But a conference in Geneva to work out details of the plan was adjourned at year's end with no appreciable progress.

A dangerous brush with war occurred on Aug. 18 when North Korean soldiers killed two U.S. Army officers in the demilitarized zone between the two Koreas. The victims had been trimming a tree, which was cut down three days later during an American show of force. Tensions mounted as the dictatorships in the North and South alerted troops and threatened war. Talks between the North Koreans and the U.S.-led U.N. Command, however, cooled things off, and an agreement for separating the security forces at the sensitive P'anmunjŏm site was reached on Sept. 6.

Relations with four countries—South Korea, Vietnam, Cuba, and Panama—seemed to be in a process of transition. The increasingly dictatorial rule of South Korean President Park Chung Hee steadily lost support in Washington during the year. Park's suppression of his domestic political opponents was one reason. Another was the revelation that South Korean lobbyists had bestowed cash gifts and other favors on many U.S. Congressmen in recent years to win their influence.

In November the U.S. again vetoed Vietnam's entry into the U.N. while demanding a full accounting of American soldiers missing in Vietnam since the war there ended. Talks leading to normalization of relations, however, were in progress. Cuba announced in October the cancellation of its antihijacking agreement with the U.S. after a Cuban airplane was blown up, allegedly by anti-Castro exiles based in Miami, Fla. The issue of a new treaty governing use of the Panama Canal surfaced repeatedly during the U.S. election campaigns: American conservatives opposed ceding more rights or granting sovereignty over the canal to Panama. That nation and others in Latin America kept demanding a new, less "imperialistic" treaty, but none was concluded.

On Feb. 24 the U.S. Senate approved a bill granting commonwealth status to the northern Mariana Islands in the Pacific. The chain of tiny islands, lying north of Guam, has a population of

Tanzanian President Julius K. Nyerere (center) shares a lighter moment with U.S. Secretary of State Henry A. Kissinger in Dar es Salaam on Sept. 15. Kissinger was beginning a round of talks with southern African leaders.

14,500 inhabitants. If approved by the U.N., it would mark the first new territory added to the U.S. in more than fifty years.

POLITICAL CAMPAIGNS

The year was one of intense political activity in the U.S., culminating in the election of the 95th Congress and the thirty-ninth President, Jimmy Carter.

Financing. For the first time restrictions on campaign expenditures imposed by the Federal Election Campaign Act of 1974 took effect. The sixteen candidates for the major-party nominations were not allowed to accept contributions of more than $1000 per donor. But matching funds distributed by the Federal Election Commission helped to finance their efforts. From March 23 to May 21, however, the candidates went begging while the commission, immobilized by a Supreme Court ruling, was being reconstituted by Congress.

After Ford and Carter were nominated, each of their campaigns was financed by a federal subsidy of $21,800,000. No private contributions were permitted, although the party national committees could and did spend additional amounts. One result was a barely visible Presidential race: Buttons, posters, and bumper stickers were scarcely to be seen. Both Ford and Carter spent over half of their allotted funds on television and radio advertising.

The Primaries. Democrats, with their open field and dozen declared candidates for President, captured most of the headlines during the February–June primary season. Starting with a victory in the Feb. 24 New Hampshire primary, Carter gradually eliminated his opponents. A populist and reformer who eluded the "liberal" label by condemning federal bureaucracy and calling for renewed patriotism, Carter managed to appeal, though not deeply, to a broad range of voters. One by one such opponents as Sen. Birch Bayh (Ind.), Gov. George C. Wallace (Ala.), and Sen. Henry M. Jackson (Wash.) fell by the wayside. Carter's late primary victories in Indiana, Michigan, and Ohio convinced Sen. Hubert H. Hum-

Contenders from California

After a grueling battle through all thirty-one state primaries, former California Gov. Ronald Reagan, 65, narrowly lost his bid for the Republican Presidential nomination. The incumbent California governor, Edmund ("Jerry") Brown, Jr., 38, also won some primaries, but he got started too late to win the Democratic race. The former Jesuit novice did attract attention as a "new generation" politician, and he laid the foundation for a possible future in national politics.

Californians Ronald Reagan (left) and Jerry Brown.

phrey (Minn.), regarded as the hope of a stop-Carter movement, not to enter the race. Liberal Democrats, who had backed Rep. Morris K. Udall (Ariz.) and later Sen. Frank Church (Idaho) and Gov. Edmund G. Brown, Jr. (Calif.), reluctantly fell into line in June to assure Carter of the nomination; see DEMOCRATIC PARTY.

Meanwhile, the Republicans were generating excitement as Reagan mounted a strong conservative challenge to President Ford's candidacy. Reagan was almost counted out after early primary losses, but in May he won primaries in eight states to take a narrow lead in pledged convention delegates. Reagan's personal charm and skillful use of televised speeches made him seem a better bet for November to many Republicans. But Ford belied his image as a plodder by effectively using his office to win over delegates. The economic recovery and prevailing peace worked in his favor, and he was becoming more "Presidential" in manner. The Republican convention in Kansas City, Mo., in August nominated Ford on a close first ballot; see REPUBLICAN PARTY.

Ford Versus Carter. The Democratic ticket—Carter and Sen. Walter F. Mondale of Minnesota—began the campaign with a huge lead in the opinion polls. This lead gradually evaporated as undecideds went Republican. President Ford stayed in the White House most of the campaign until the final ten days. His running mate, Sen. Robert J. Dole of Kansas, campaigned vigorously, as did Mondale and Carter's energetic wife, Rosalynn. Three televised debates between Ford and Carter proved the most memorable events of the campaign, although they probably did not change many minds. The first two debates were widely judged to be marred by statistical one-upmanship, distortions of opponents' views, and distracting mis-

statements of fact. The issues were best discussed in the last debate, held Oct. 22. Ford declared himself for keeping down inflation as the top economic priority, for strengthening national defense, and against any major new government spending programs. Carter advocated reducing unemployment as the top priority, reorganizing the federal bureaucracy, and introducing stronger leadership. Perhaps more important to voters, each man claimed to possess a character worthy of trust.

The Victors. Jimmy Carter was narrowly elected President on Nov. 2, carrying states totaling 297 electoral votes to Ford's 241. The popular vote split 50 percent to Carter, 48 percent to Ford, 1 percent to independent candidate Eugene J. McCarthy, and approximately 1 percent to other minor-party candidates. In a crushing blow to Republican hopes, the Democrats maintained their large majorities in the Senate and the House of Representatives. See ELECTIONS.

Remarking to the nation "We have a lot to learn about one another," President-elect Carter set about naming his cabinet, planning his legislative program, and otherwise preparing to assume power. The new Congress was apparently eager to work with him, yet reluctant to give up its recently asserted independence. It was widely believed that now, with the transition from the Vietnam and Watergate years successfully negotiated, the nation was ready to move again. But in what directions? It was up to the Carter administration to lead the way.   W.M.H.

UNITED STATES OF AMERICA: THE ECONOMY.
Early in 1976 business activity in the United States accelerated, following a relatively slow rate of increase during the last part of 1975. In the spring and summer of 1976, however, the pace of eco-

The donkey, symbol of the Democratic Party, wears a triumphant grin that is strikingly similar to President-elect Jimmy Carter's. The drawing by Don Wright first appeared in the Miami News and was reprinted in Time magazine.

Usually preoccupied New Yorkers pause to study the electronic news display in Times Square. The Dow-Jones stock average topped 1000 in March, and on April 21 the influential index of thirty issues traded on the New York Stock Exchange reached its high for the year, 1011.02.

nomic activity slackened. This slowdown intensified one of the nation's two major continuing economic problems—high unemployment. The jobless rate, which had fallen from 8.3 percent in December, 1975, to 7.3 percent in May, 1976, increased in the following 3 months and stood at 7.9 percent in December. But the more restrained pace of business advance did help to lower the rate of inflation, the country's other major economic problem. During the 12-month period that ended in November, 1976, the consumer price index calculated by the U.S. Department of Labor increased by only 5 percent, the smallest yearly rise calculated since March, 1973.

BUSINESS REVIEW

The performance of the economy in 1976 was indeed erratic. Although national output grew throughout the year, business advanced fitfully.

Economic activity in the opening months of the year was surprisingly strong. The slowness of activity in the autumn of 1975 had led many economists to expect the recovery, which had begun in the spring of 1975, to slide into recession by the spring of 1976. Instead, activity soared in the first quarter, with the gross national product (G.N.P.), the market value of the nation's total output of goods and services, rising by $48 billion. It thus attained an annual level of $1.636 trillion. The G.N.P. adjusted for inflation, or real G.N.P., advanced at an annual rate of 9.2 percent—more than double the nation's recent long-term average rate of advancement.

This abnormal surge stemmed largely from sharply increased consumer spending, which encouraged businessmen to add to their inventories in order to accommodate the increased demand. Consumers stepped up their purchases of goods and services all along the line, with automobile sales leading the way.

The overall consumer inclination to buy had strengthened because employment was increas-

ing rapidly but prices were not. Approximately 1,300,000 persons were added to the employment rolls in the initial 3 months of the year, an extraordinary increase for such a short period. Consumer prices, which had been rising at an annual rate of more than 7 percent in late 1975, increased at a rate of only 2.9 percent in the first quarter of 1976. Food prices actually fell, by an average of 0.8 percent, between February and March.

At the same time businessmen stepped up production to rebuild their depleted stocks and be ready for anticipated high sales levels. The output of factories and mines rose at the rapid annual rate of 12 percent in the first 3 months of 1976. Inventories (goods ready for sale on store shelves and in warehouses), which had been liquidated at the rate of $10 billion in late 1975, were rebuilt at a rate of $13 billion in the first quarter of 1976. **Economic Slowdown.** But the surge of early 1976 did not last. Prices in stores rose more rapidly after March, cutting into the purchasing power of consumers. As a consequence retail demand tapered off, and businessmen slowed down the output of factories, cut back on expansion plans, and hired fewer new employees.

The growth of real G.N.P. slowed to an annual rate of 4.5 percent in the second quarter of the year and to 3.9 percent in the third. The third-quarter figure was held down, in part, by a strike against the huge Ford Motor Co., which caused a production halt from Sept. 14 to mid-October. Under normal circumstances the economic growth attained from April through September would have been viewed as satisfactory. But President Gerald R. Ford and the U.S. Congress had hoped for a faster-than-normal growth rate, in order to reduce the high rate of unemployment.

The Ford administration had sought to achieve an annual growth rate of well over 5 percent. This would not only have reduced the number of unemployed workers, it would also have indicated that production was increasing at a rate sufficient to maintain a low level of inflation by meeting the consumer demands. In addition, more rapid growth would have encouraged businessmen to modernize and expand their plants, and this would have helped to sustain low inflation rates in future years.

The failure of the economy to perform as expected had political as well as economic consequences. Much of the debate during the Presidential race between President Ford and the Democratic Party candidate, former Gov. Jimmy Carter of Georgia, concerned the performance of the U.S. economy. Many political analysts attributed Ford's loss to Carter on Nov. 2 to adverse voter reaction to rising prices and high unemployment.

Economic Upswing. In November the economy began to improve, and it ended the year on a strongly rising trend. The improvement stemmed in part from a resurgence in retail sales, especially of motor vehicles. In 1976 Detroit sold 10,098,173 automobiles, a vast improvement over the 1975 total of 8,628,210. Overall retail sales in December were 3 percent higher than in November; this was the largest monthly increase since early 1972. The number of housing starts, an important indicator of how well the economy is performing, also was at an encouraging level late in the year. In November new housing construction proceeded at an annual rate of 1,705,000 units, an increase of 23 percent over a year earlier. In addition, building-permit authorizations were up 41 percent over the previous year.

Americans favored larger cars in 1976—hence this jam of compacts in an American Motors Corp. (A.M.C.) shipping yard in Kenosha, Wis., in November. Chrysler, Ford, and General Motors enjoyed excellent sales gains during the year, but the sales of small car specialist A.M.C. were down almost 25 percent from 1975.

Another indicator that economic conditions were better late in the year was a strong $15 billion, or 1.1 percent, rise in the annual rate of personal income from October to November. Also, corporate profits reached an annual rate of approximately $150 billion at the end of 1976; this was a considerable increase over the rate established a year earlier. Profits for the entire year of 1976 were about 30 percent higher than they had been in 1975.

Economists pointed to November's record monthly foreign-trade deficit of $906,200,000 as an indication of the relative health of the nation's economy. This record deficit showed that demand was strong in the U.S., in comparison with other leading industrial countries, whose economic problems kept their foreign purchases down. For the first 11 months of 1976 the U.S. had a trade deficit of $5 billion, compared to its surplus of $11.1 billion in all of recession-plagued 1975.

In the final months of 1976 the wholesale prices of some basic commodities, including steel, were increased substantially. This occurred in part because businessmen feared that Jimmy Carter would institute price controls after becoming President in January, 1977. (On Dec. 3, after the steel price rise, Carter said he opposed price controls.) Retail prices were not immediately affected by the upward trend in wholesale prices; in December the cost of food bought at grocery stores was about the same as a year earlier.

Prospects for 1977. In late 1976 the great majority of economists forecast that 1977 would be a strong year, with the real G.N.P. growing by 5.5 percent if some modest stimulation were applied to the economy by the cutting of federal taxes and the expanding of public works programs. And late in December President-elect Carter proposed to do just that, indicating that his advisers believed in a stimulation program that would pump at least $15 billion into the economy during 1977, the first year of his first term in office.

PUBLIC FINANCE

Federal spending for the fiscal year ended June 30, 1976, totaled $365.6 billion, an increase of $41 billion, or 12.6 percent, over the fiscal year 1975. Government receipts for the year rose by only about $19 billion, to $300 billion. As a result the deficit for fiscal 1976 soared to $65.6 billion, considerably larger than the deficit for the previous year, which, at $43.6 billion, was the largest deficit since World War II. The total deficit for the two fiscal years 1975 and 1976 was as large as the combined deficits of the 10 years from 1964 to 1974.

Federal Budget. President Ford, in his economic report to Congress in January, stated that his administration would maintain a budget of moderate economic growth. And, despite the greatly expanded federal deficit, spending in fiscal year 1976 did not rise as fast as it had in the previous year. Outlays for national defense increased $3.7 billion, compared with an advance of $7.9 billion in fiscal year 1975. Spending for international affairs held about steady, and expenditures for social programs, the biggest category in the budget, rose $24 billion in contrast to a $30 billion advance a year earlier. Nevertheless, spending for social programs, at $160.5 billion in fiscal year 1976, had doubled in 4 years.

In an unusual development that was never fully explained, actual federal outlays in 1976 fell considerably below the targets set by President Ford. According to Congressional estimates, spending in the second and third quarters was considerably below the levels projected in the Administration's budget forecast—about $10 billion and $8 billion, respectively. In the fourth quarter, however, expenditure apparently had returned to the level established by the government.

Economic recovery during the 1976 fiscal year resulted in an increased flow of funds to the U.S. Treasury. Individual income tax payments rose by $9.2 billion, to $131.6 billion, compared to a $3.4 billion increase in the 1975 fiscal year.

In 1976 the start of the federal fiscal year was switched to Oct. 1, three months later than in earlier years. To accommodate the change, July through September were labeled as a separate "transition quarter," falling into neither fiscal year 1976 nor fiscal year 1977.

At the end of 1976 both the Administration and Congress anticipated another large budget deficit in fiscal year 1977. The Joint Economic Committee of Congress estimated that the shortfall would reach approximately $65 billion.

Economic Debate. It has become standard practice to use the federal budget, along with the country's money supply, as a means of speeding up or slowing down the economy. During 1976 the Ford administration sought to provide a mild stimulus to help increase the nation's economic growth rate and thus reduce the number of unemployed. Fiscally liberal and fiscally conservative members of Congress debated at length over how much stimulus to apply.

The Congressional debate on federal spending as a tool of economic policy took on an added dimension in fiscal year 1976 as a result of a major change in the legislature's method of dealing with budgetary appropriations. In addition to their existing separate budget committees, the House of Representatives and the Senate maintained a joint Congressional Budget Office (C.B.O.), which

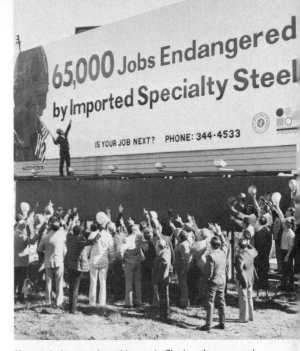

Demonstrations such as this one in Pittsburgh prompted U.S. President Gerald R. Ford to institute quotas on specialty steel imports in June. The imports had led to reduced production of stainless and other specialty steels in the U.S. and caused extensive layoffs.

acted as a counterpart to the President's Office of Management and Budget. Established in 1975 on a trial basis, the C.B.O. played an important role in the economic debate in Washington in 1976 by issuing its own assessments of national economic activity and the amount of stimulus needed to speed up the economy.

Early in the year the C.B.O. took issue with the Administration's policies and recommended a more expansive program, which, in the main, the Congress tried to follow. But in 1976, as in 1975, President Ford vetoed a large number of spending bills passed by Congress.

State and Local Finances. The financial problems of a number of large cities, such as New York, caused them to cut back on their expenditures. But state and local government spending nevertheless continued to grow at a rapid rate in 1976. Experts estimated that outlays were more than 8 percent higher than in 1975. In part this growth was due to a large increase in the amount of federal funds transferred to the states and cities. Under the federal revenue-sharing program, for instance, grants of about $7.2 billion were allocated to state and local governments in the 1976 fiscal year.

State and local governments were forced to

On Sept. 18 a mob of unhappy New Jerseyites gather outside their state capitol in Trenton. They were protesting the newly enacted personal income tax law, designed primarily to raise funds for New Jersey's public schools.

borrow a total of about $22 billion to cover revenue shortfalls. Much of this borrowing was done by selling bonds. Aggregate borrowing at all levels of government accounted for about 40 percent of the nation's total demand for credit.

TAXATION

On Oct. 4 President Ford signed into law the Tax Reform Act of 1976, the most extensive federal tax-revision measure in 20 years. The bill, over 1000 pages long and more than 2 years in the making, covered 19 major categories. One special section repealed or revised obsolete or rarely used sections of the tax code. The bill was expected to increase government revenues by about $1.6 billion in the fiscal year ending Sept. 30, 1977.

Changes for Individuals. The chief benefit for individual taxpayers under the new law was the extension through 1977 of the tax reductions instituted in 1975 and scheduled to expire in mid-1976. These reductions included a $35 tax credit for each exemption listed on an individual's tax return (or, alternatively, a credit of 2 percent of his taxable income up to $9000) and an increase in the standard deduction from his adjusted gross income. In a new departure, working parents were granted a tax credit for a part of their child-care costs. In the past a taxpayer could cite such costs to reduce his taxes only if he itemized his overall tax deductions.

In other changes the new law reduced the taxes that a person 65 or older had to pay on the proceeds from the sale of his residence. A number of provisions regarding retirement savings and pension plans were also altered. For instance, a working person was permitted to open a tax-deferred retirement account in the name of his nonworking spouse. Taxes on most estates valued under $500,000 were eliminated; under the old law levies on these could exceed $100,000.

The total package of tax reductions would save taxpayers a total of $14.35 billion in the 1977 fiscal year, according to calculations made by the Congressional Joint Committee on Internal Revenue Taxation.

Some provisions of the new law, however, increased taxpayer liability. For example, the long-standing deduction of up to $100 of weekly sick pay was eliminated. Also, the holding period necessary to qualify for capital-gains taxes was increased from 6 months to 1 year. (The principle that only about one half of a capital gain is taxed remained.) Much tighter qualifications were established for deducting the expense of using part of one's home as an office.

Severe restrictions were placed on sheltering income from taxation by investing in real estate, oil or natural gas exploration, farming, the production of motion pictures, sports franchises, and some other ventures. For instance, an investor's deduction was limited to the value of the cash he had actually put into such an enterprise. Previously, a taxpayer could deduct first-year losses that greatly exceeded his investment by citing the venture's longer-term expenses.

Income tax deductions were reduced for U.S. citizens living abroad and for nonresident aliens married to citizens or to resident aliens of the U.S. The use of foreign trusts to exempt income from U.S. taxes was prohibited. And the new law reduced to two the number of foreign conventions, seminars, or business meetings for which travel expenses could be deducted.

Corporate Tax Changes. The Tax Reform Act raised the minimum tax for corporations from 10 percent to 15 percent. The rules for deducting foreign tax payments from U.S. taxable income were altered slightly, with the result that firms will have to pay some additional U.S. taxes. Benefits granted for exporting through a Domestic International Sales Corp. were substantially reduced. For the first time, foreign tax credits and export tax benefits would be denied to companies participating in international boycotts, such as the Arab boycott of Israel. Penalties were also imposed on firms that made illegal payments to influence officials in other countries.

The new law also included some tax concessions for corporations. The 10 percent tax credit for money invested in new factory equipment, in effect during 1975 and 1976, was extended through 1980. In a similar move, the 1975–76 tax reduction on the first $50,000 of corporate profits was extended through 1977. And corporations were given tax breaks for buying antipollution devices for their plants or for conducting research into energy-saving techniques.

FINANCIAL REVIEW

Although developments in the nation's major financial markets tended to reflect the erratic course of the U.S. economy in 1976, there were some surprising developments, especially concerning interest rates.

Interest Rates. The behavior of interest rates was in sharp contrast to most past periods of economic advance. The usual pattern has been for interest rates to rise during a period of economic growth as businesses and consumers demand increasing amounts of funds. But in 1976 business demand for funds was slack because firms had a relatively high level of liquid assets, inventory accumulation remained modest, and capital spending programs were stretched out. At the end of the year the total value of outstanding business loans by large commercial banks was slightly below the $120 billion level attained in January. The slack demand for business loans paralleled a lack of aggressiveness by banks toward acquiring large deposits. At the end of 1976 the value of deposits of $100,000 or more held by major commercial banks was down $20 billion from the $83 billion level of late 1975.

A number of steps taken by the Federal Reserve Board (F.R.B.) also reduced pressure on money markets. These measures included a reduction in the reserve requirements of member banks, a cut in the discount rate, and an increase in the rate of growth of the nation's money supply. The F.R.B. seeks to alter the country's total supply of money in several ways in order to meet its overall monetary objectives. The chief method is to change the level of a basic measure of the money supply, or M_1; this measure includes demand deposits in commercial banks and currency in circulation. The F.R.B. also closely monitors another, broader measure of the money supply, M_2; this measure includes time deposits. During 1976 M_1 rose by a relatively modest 5.6 percent. On the other hand, M_2, which many economists consider to have a larger impact on economic growth, rose by a substantial 11.1 percent.

These developments helped to offset the requirements of the U.S. Treasury and American consumers. The Treasury was forced to borrow large sums to finance the huge deficit in the federal budget. Consumers, buoyed by the nation's improved economic outlook, greatly increased their purchases of goods and services, making many such purchases on credit. Total outstanding consumer credit increased by an average of $1.4 billion per month in 1976. At the end of October aggregate consumer credit stood at $173.9 billion, an increase of 10 percent over October, 1975.

The major interest rates were relatively low during most of the year. The prime loan rate, which banks charge their most credit-worthy customers, was changed 8 times in 1976. It began the year at 7.25 percent. Then, from mid-January to early May, a rate of 6.75 percent prevailed. It rose again to 7.5 percent during the following 2 months; then it fell once more. It remained below 7.5 percent for the rest of 1976 and closed the year at 6.25 percent.

Long-term interest rates also were set at relatively low levels during most of the year. For example, the best corporate bonds, which had yielded 8.8 percent late in 1975, were paying 7.9 percent by the end of 1976. The decline in long-term rates was related not only to the ready availability of funds, but also to the falling rate of inflation. With inflation no longer the great problem it had been in recent years, banks felt able to

Charles Schultze testifies before the Senate Banking Committee. President-elect Jimmy Carter had chosen Schultze to head his Council of Economic Advisers.

421

The Old Executive Office Building, Washington, D.C., is the scene of a fireside chat on Dec. 7. James T. Lynn (right), director of the Office of Management and Budget since 1975, explained his duties to Thomas Bertram Lance, whom President-elect Jimmy Carter had just nominated as his successor.

lower the premium added to long-term rates to cover future inflation.

Short-term interest rates stood at 4.6 percent in December, compared to 5.8 percent in January. The trend of these interest rates during 1976 was not smooth. They reacted to the strong first quarter by rising sharply, but thereafter they fell slowly as the economic recovery failed to maintain its pace.

Stock Markets. The nation's fast economic growth in the first quarter of 1976 set in motion expected responses in the major stock markets. The Dow-Jones average of 30 high-grade industrial common stocks traded on the New York Stock Exchange (N.Y.S.E.) had ended 1975 at 852.41. After an upward trend during the first few months of 1976, this closely watched index reached 1011.02 on April 21. This proved to be its high for the year. As economic growth slowed during the spring and summer, stock prices declined. After an intensifying of economic activity in November, the Dow-Jones industrial average rebounded; it closed the year at 1004.65. Overall, the average advanced 152.24 points, or 17 percent, in 1976. It had been a fairly big year for stock trading. Sales on the N.Y.S.E. totaled 5.36 billion shares, an increase of about 14 percent over 1975. And the American Stock Exchange recorded sales of 648,297,321 shares, a jump of approximately 20 percent over 1975.

BANKS AND BANKING

For the nation's banks 1976 was an unusual year. Despite the continued advance in national economic activity, business demand for money was relatively low throughout 1976. Funds injected into the banking system more than covered the

financial needs of borrowers. As a result, interest rates were low during most of the year; thus the income of banks from loans was limited. A surprising number of banks were listed as having financial problems in 1976.

"Problem" Banks. Mainly because of the lingering effects of the 1974–75 recession, evident in the continued high level of defaulted loans, many banks experienced difficulties in 1976 and several were forced out of business.

In January the F.R.B. reported that it was concerned about the condition of 63 bank holding companies. The companies adjudged to have "more serious problems" included the Marine Midland Banks, of New York State, the nation's 13th largest bank, and the First Pennsylvania Corp., the 21st biggest. In addition, 65 state-chartered commercial banks (compared to 38 in 1975) were being watched closely.

In February Comptroller of the Currency James E. Smith informed the Senate Banking Committee that 28 national banks, with assets totaling $11.5 billion, were being monitored by his office. He said that 7 of these banks were in immediate danger of failing because they had low levels of assets compared to liabilities.

Sixteen commercial banks did in fact fail during the year. Most of these were taken over by other banks, and their depositors therefore did not suffer losses. Among the larger banks that closed were Hamilton Bancshares Inc., of Georgia and Tennessee (the third largest bank failure in U.S. history); the American Bank and Trust Co., of New York City; the South Texas State Bank and the Northeast Bank, both of Houston; the First State Bank of Northern California; the First State Bank of Hudson County, New Jersey; and the International City Bank and Trust Co., of New Orleans.

In addition, all thirty-four privately insured Mississippi savings and loan associations were ordered closed on June 20 by the state's legislature. A surge of withdrawals had severely weakened these institutions, which together held $400,000,-000 from about 150,000 depositors. The legislature allowed them to reopen after regaining financial stability, and by early July nineteen were operating again. The lawmakers also required the associations to insure their depositors with the Federal Savings and Loan Insurance Corp. (F.S.L.I.C.) by April, 1977. The overwhelming majority of depositors in state-chartered savings and loan associations in the U.S. were covered by the F.S.L.I.C.; only five states besides Mississippi permitted private insurance.

Despite the difficulties experienced by U.S. banks, public faith in the country's banking system remained high. In a 1976 Gallup Poll, commissioned by the American Bankers Association, 93 percent of the respondents said that they felt their money was safe in a bank. This response was slightly higher than that of a poll taken in 1975.

Federal Regulation. Changes in the regulations that govern a bank's responsibilities in granting mortgages and in upholding consumer interests were instituted during the year. Several states implemented laws requiring banks to disclose the number and value of the home mortgages they made in both urban and suburban areas. This was part of an effort to curb "red lining," the practice of denying mortgages to persons seeking to buy homes in older city areas (outlined in red on a map). In addition, banks in some states were required to give a breakdown by neighborhood of the home-improvement loans they granted.

In 1976 the Federal Trade Commission began to enforce a new "holder in due course" rule. This rule required third-party lenders to assume the responsibility of the seller toward the buyer. In the past, a consumer had been obligated to repay funds borrowed from banks, credit card issuers, or other lending concerns even if the service or merchandise purchased had not conformed to the seller's guarantee. The F.R.B. and many banks opposed the new rule, saying it would disrupt credit operations.

At the beginning of the year President Ford signed a bill extending Regulation Q until March, 1977. This regulation allowed thrift institutions to pay 0.25 percent more interest on deposits than was paid by commercial banks. For the first time this differential became a matter of law; previously the ceiling had been set by federal financial authorities.

Other Banking Developments. In October the shift toward electronic banking, which had gathered momentum in recent years, was slowed by a decision of the U.S. Supreme Court. The Court let stand a lower-court ruling that classified an electronic fund-transfer machine as a bank branch. This decision affected the installation of the machines in states such as Illinois that restrict the establishment of branches by bank holding companies.

Real estate investment trusts continued to founder in 1976 as the real estate market remained depressed and unstable. Especially noteworthy was the failure of the second-largest of these, Continental Mortgage Investors, which owed $550,000,000 to banks. The failure of this trust marked the third largest bankruptcy in U.S. history, outdistanced only by the failure of the Penn Central Transportation Co. in 1970 and of the W. T. Grant Co. in 1975.

At midyear Comptroller of the Currency James E. Smith resigned, with 2 years of his 5-year term still remaining. He had come under fire from some members of Congress for permitting a list of problem banks to be circulated and for advocating the growth of electronic branch banking. Banker Stanley E. Shirk was appointed to replace Smith, but William Proxmire (D, Wis.), chairman of the Senate Banking, Housing, and Urban Affairs Committee, delayed hearings on the appointment. Robert Bloom, the first deputy comptroller

Learning to operate electronic banking machines (such as this one in Pittsburgh) may be easy, but they are in trouble. In 1976 the U.S. Supreme Court agreed that such a machine is actually a branch bank.

for policy, was made acting comptroller, pending the naming of a new comptroller in 1977. W.B.F.

UNITED STATES OF AMERICA: THE PEOPLE. The United States Bureau of the Census estimated late in 1976 that the resident population of the U.S. on July 1, 1976, was 214,659,000. This was a gain of 1,627,000 over the July 1, 1975, figure. Almost all of the growth occurred in two areas. In 1976, for the first time in the 20th century, the South and the West together contained over half of the U.S. population. There were 107,417,000 Southerners and Westerners. Notable increases took place in California and Texas, whose populations in 1976 rose 322,000 and 250,000, respectively, over the 1975 estimates. Several areas recorded drops in population. These included Ohio (with a net loss of 45,000), Indiana (net loss 11,000), and the District of Columbia (net loss 10,000).

Women in the U.S. In 1976 the Census Bureau issued several detailed statistical studies of U.S. women. Among the findings were that females made up 51.3 percent of the nation's population in 1975. Their median age was 30.0 years, compared to 22.4 years in 1900. Life expectancy at birth for females was 75.3 years in 1973, a sharp rise from the 1900 figure, 48.3 years. The increased female longevity was due largely to improved medical care, especially during pregnancy and childbirth. (Life expectancy figures for males were 67.6 years in 1973 and 46.3 years in 1900.)

The Census Bureau noted a sharp increase in women's tendencies to remain single and to have fewer children. For instance, the proportion of women aged 20 to 24 years who were single or divorced was 40 percent in 1975, compared to 28 percent in 1960, just 15 years earlier. Another, even more startling, prediction: The average woman who was of childbearing age in 1975 (between 15 and 44) will produce only 1.8 children in her lifetime. This figure is exactly one half of the 1960 rate.

The bureau also reported a great increase in the number of working women. Between 1950 and 1974 the female work force almost doubled. In 1950, for every 100 men employed full time, 29 women were similarly employed. By 1974 the ratio had increased to 47 women per 100 men. But women tended to earn far lower salaries than men. The median income of full-time female employees in 1974 was $6722, compared to $11,835 for males.

Immigration. According to preliminary statistics, 398,613 immigrants were admitted to the U.S. during the fiscal year ended June 30, 1976. Of that total, some 166,000 entered under the numerical restrictions of the Eastern Hemisphere, and approximately 103,800 were admitted under Western

Hemisphere limitations. Immigrants not subject to numerical restrictions included some 102,000 immediate relatives of U.S. citizens and about 26,800 persons admitted under special provisions of the law. The immigrants included 213,750 females and 184,863 males. Among the principal places of origin were the People's Republic of China and Taiwan, Cuba, the Dominican Republic, Korea, Mexico, and the Philippines.

UNITED STATES DEPARTMENT OF JUSTICE IMMIGRATION AND NATURALIZATION SERVICE WASHINGTON, D.C. PERSONS NATURALIZED, BY COUNTRY OR REGION OF FORMER ALLEGIANCE, YEARS ENDED JUNE 30, 1971 AND 1976		
Country or region of former allegiance	1971	1976
All countries	108,407	142,504
Europe	45,065	49,322
Austria.	627	345
Czechoslovakia	629	1,606
France	1,328	1,006
Germany	8,455	5,056
Greece	2,614	6,595
Hungary	1,438	1,059
Ireland	2,144	1,261
Italy	7,637	8,696
Netherlands	1,428	840
Norway	305	155
Poland.	3,318	2,904
Portugal	1,306	4,117
Spain.	776	902
Switzerland.	508	321
U.S.S.R.	850	518
United Kingdom.	6,983	8,695
Yugoslavia	1,694	3,008
Other Europe	3,025	2,238
Asia.	17,839	46,759
China and Taiwan	2,880	9,326
India	443	3,564
Israel	1,628	1,863
Japan	1,716	1,408
Jordan.	544	1,312
Korea	2,083	7,450
Philippines	5,488	14,765
Other Asia	3,057	7,071
North America	36,941	34,676
Canada	5,915	3,384
Cuba	19,754	15,138
Dominican Republic	752	1,538
Haiti.	554	2,088
Jamaica	500	2,535
Mexico	6,361	5,602
Other North America.	3,105	4,391
South America	5,713	6,764
Argentina	1,459	1,277
Colombia	1,182	1,711
Other South America	3,072	3,776
Africa	795	2,974
Oceania	466	592
U.S. Possessions and Stateless . . .	1,588	1,417

On the other hand, a total of 793,092 aliens were expelled from the U.S. during fiscal year 1976. They were mostly persons who had entered the country without proper authorization. The U.S. Immigration and Naturalization Service estimated that about 400,000 persons enter the U.S. unlawfully each year and that as many as 8,000,000 illegal aliens resided in the country in 1976.

Naturalization. During fiscal year 1976, 142,504 persons became naturalized U.S. citizens, an increase of about 1000 over fiscal year 1975. Of the new citizens, 114,653 were persons naturalized under general provisions of the law requiring 5 years of permanent residence in the U.S.; 22,176 were spouses of children of U.S. citizens; 5631 were military or former military personnel; and 44 were persons naturalized under other provisions of the law. The new citizens included 76,497 females and 66,007 males.

UPPER VOLTA. See STATISTICS OF THE WORLD.

URUGUAY. On June 12, 1976, the armed forces of Uruguay removed President Juan María Bordaberry from office. They allegedly did this because the president wanted to ban political parties and grant himself unrestricted powers for three years after the expiration of his present term (in 1977).

The military leaders, who favored a return to a democratic process, named Vice-President Pedro Alberto Demicheli Lizaso as interim president. And at the same time, they created the National Council, a new corporate body composed of 21 top military officers and the 25 civilian members of the Council of State, for the purpose of selecting a president. The National Council's choice was a 72-year-old lawyer, Aparicio Méndez, who began his five-year term in office on Sept. 1. Under the military leaders' announced plan for return to civilian rule, the two traditional parties—the Colorados and the Blancos—would pick a consensus candidate in the 1981 presidential election. In the elections thereafter each of the two parties would be able to select its own candidate. Ostensibly to prevent Communist infiltration into the parties, Méndez immediately canceled the rights of all current political party leaders (including Bordaberry) to hold public office.

On the economic front the government continued its attack on inflation through restrictive fiscal and monetary policies. Inflation slowed to 45 percent from the 65 percent rate registered in 1975 (consumer prices remained nearly twenty times their 1970 level), and the trade account, helped by strong demand for meat and wool exports, moved into surplus.

See STATISTICS OF THE WORLD.   A.K.M.

UTAH. See STATISTICS OF THE WORLD.

V

VANCE, CYRUS R. See PEOPLE IN THE NEWS.

VENEZUELA. In the midst of his six-year term in office, Venezuelan President Carlos Andrés Pérez pressed onward toward his goal of increasing state participation in the economy. On Jan. 1, 1976, Venezuela became master of its major natural resource, petroleum, when all foreign oil producers officially turned over their facilities to the newly created state oil concern, Petróleos Venezolanos (Petróven), and its satellite facilities. In keeping with the government policy of conserving proved oil reserves, petroleum production remained at or below 2,200,000 bbl per day. Venezuela, which supplies about one third of United States oil imports, continued to advocate higher world prices for crude oil. Along with a majority of the members of the Organization of Petroleum Exporting Countries (q.v.), or OPEC, Venezuela in December announced price increases of 10 percent effective Jan. 1, 1977, and a further 5 percent increase effective July 1, 1977.

The growing economic role that the state had mapped out for itself was clearly indicated in the controversial 1976–80 development plan, which was finally passed in May. The plan called for a total investment of $52 billion over the five-year period, with the state accounting for 53 percent of the total investment. The plan was expected to provide for an average annual growth rate of 8.2 percent in the gross domestic product.

The private sector considered the five-year plan overly ambitious. Nongovernmental leaders also reacted negatively to a bill to control advertising practices, to the imposition of additional price controls to hold down inflation, and to schemes to rationalize the automotive and television manufacturing industries in conformity with Andean Group practices. The 1977 budget, which was released in October, also caused concern because of the large increase in current public expenditures, which would help fuel inflation. The inflation rate, 13 percent in 1975, had been reduced to about 7 percent through most of 1976.

President Pérez visited a number of European countries, the U.S., and the Soviet Union during the year. While in Europe, he promised to help Italy by depositing Venezuelan funds in the country. In a speech before the United Nations General Assembly in November, the president criticized the U.S. for its Third World policies and defended OPEC. During his visit to Moscow, Pérez criticized the U.S.S.R. for its own neglect of the Third World and chided both superpowers for failing to end the arms race. Under an agreement reached with the Soviets, Venezuela would ship oil directly to Cuba.

See STATISTICS OF THE WORLD.   A.K.M.

VERMONT. *See* STATISTICS OF THE WORLD.

VIETNAM, SOCIALIST REPUBLIC OF. For Vietnam, 1976 was a year of reunification, the beginning of a painful process of constructing a single state out of two formerly warring parts.

Politics. After an intense debate at the highest levels of the Vietnamese Workers Party (officially renamed the Communist Party of Vietnam on Dec. 20), the decision was made early in the year to push ahead quickly toward the reunification of North and South Vietnam, which had been politically separate since 1946. On April 25 voters throughout Vietnam went to the polls to elect a National Assembly. In what Radio Hanoi described as a "massive turnout" reaching 99 percent of the eligible voters in some areas, the Vietnamese picked an assembly from candidates chosen by the Communist authorities.

Two months later the 492 members of the National Assembly met in Hanoi, and on July 2 the assembly formally declared the two halves of the country to be one, under the name of the Socialist Republic of Vietnam. The assembly also chose Hanoi as the country's capital and adopted the flag, emblem, and anthem of what had been North Vietnam. With few exceptions, high offices in the unified state were given to Hanoi's long-time leaders, with Pham Van Dong remaining as premier.

In December the first Vietnamese Communist Party congress since 1960 opened in Hanoi. Delegates were welcomed by Le Duan, first secretary of the party and possibly the most powerful man in Vietnam, who then outlined the party's plans for national reconstruction. These included extensive expansion of industry and agriculture, encouragement of foreign trade and investment, and a strengthening of governmental structures, particularly in the south. Premier Pham Van Dong then told the delegates of the government's plans for a massive redistribution of the nation's population, to begin early in 1977. He said that in order to shift surplus labor to places where it was needed people would be moved from the south to the north if necessary. Millions would be forced out of Saigon and other cities and into "new economic zones" in the countryside.

Unification Problems. During most of 1976, Hanoi continued to treat the population of defeated South Vietnam with considerable caution. But observers noted that the "liberation" of a year earlier was beginning to look more and more like an occupation. Southerners were shunted aside as the government in Saigon was taken over almost entirely by northerners. More than 200,000 people

Together Again; Premier Still
A year and a month after North Vietnamese tanks rumbled triumphantly into Saigon, the 492-member National Assembly of the new Socialist Republic of Vietnam declared the country officially reunified, after decades of division and bloodshed. Chosen as premier was Pham Van Dong. At the age of 70, he had already served a twenty-year apprenticeship as premier of North Vietnam. Since his twenties, he had been a Communist and a close collaborator of the North Vietnamese leader Ho Chi Minh. Part of Dong's plans for the reunited nation call for a reshuffling of the country's population of 44,000,000 to move surplus labor to where it can do the most good.

Pham Van Dong, premier of Vietnam.

reportedly remained as political prisoners in "re-education centers."

In the countryside, by Hanoi's own admission, resistance to Communist rule was not entirely eradicated. In Saigon the black market continued to thrive; large numbers of the city's unemployed resisted official pressure to leave for work in the countryside. Toward the end of the year, however, there were clear signs that the Communists were ready to take a tougher line with southerners who resisted their authority.

Foreign Affairs. In November representatives of Vietnam and the United States met in Paris to open their first formal talks since the Communist victory in Indochina. The U.S. delegates refused to discuss the possibility of future economic aid or diplomatic ties until the Vietnamese gave a full accounting of U.S. servicemen listed as missing in action in Vietnam. For the same reason, the U.S. vetoed Vietnam's application for admission to the United Nations in November. In December a se-lect committee of the U.S. House of Representatives reported that none of the missing servicemen was still being held prisoner in Indochina, and that all should be presumed dead.

During the year, a unified Vietnam joined the International Monetary Fund, World Bank, and Asian Development Bank, awarded construction contracts to Western companies, and solicited bids from international oil companies to develop Vietnam's offshore oil resources. Although Hanoi did improve relations with some of the non-Communist states of Southeast Asia, the government also launched bitter attacks on the new military regime in Thailand. Within the Communist world the ties between Hanoi and Moscow—strong to begin with—grew even stronger. China, on the other hand, failed to send a delegation to the December party congress in Hanoi.

See STATISTICS OF THE WORLD.   R.J.C.

VIRGINIA. See STATISTICS OF THE WORLD.

VIRGIN ISLANDS. See STATISTICS OF THE WORLD.

W

WALDHEIM, KURT. See PEOPLE IN THE NEWS.

WALLACE, GEORGE C. See PEOPLE IN THE NEWS.

WALTERS, BARBARA. See PEOPLE IN THE NEWS.

WARSAW TREATY ORGANIZATION, political and military alliance of six Eastern European nations with the Soviet Union. The Warsaw Pact nations held their first formal summit conference since 1974 in Bucharest, Rumania, in November. Communist Party leaders and premiers from the seven member nations were in attendance. As always, the consultations were held in secret. Western analysts believed, however, that among the issues discussed were a preliminary assessment of the possible foreign policy of incoming U.S. President Jimmy Carter, an analysis of China's policy intentions following the death of Chairman Mao Tse-tung (see OBITUARIES), and a common strategy for ongoing talks in Vienna between the Warsaw Pact nations and the North Atlantic Treaty Organization (NATO). The Vienna talks, which had shown little progress since they began in 1973, were supposed to arrive at a formula for mutual East-West military force reductions in central Europe. According to Western sources, there were 777,000 NATO troops and 925,000 Warsaw Pact troops in central Europe in 1976.

At the conclusion of two days of the talks in Bucharest, the leaders of the Warsaw Pact an-nounced on Nov. 26 that they had agreed to create a new committee of foreign ministers for the purpose of improving political collaboration within the alliance. In deference to Rumanian insistence on an independent foreign policy (see RUMANIA), the committee's decisions would evidently not be binding on member nations. In addition, the Communist states came up with a proposal for a new international pact. They suggested that each of the thirty-five nations that in 1975 had signed the final document of the Conference on Security and Cooperation in Europe (the so-called Helsinki agreement) should renounce the first use of nuclear weapons against any of the other signatories. At a meeting that took place in Brussels in December, the NATO foreign ministers, mindful of the numerical superiority of Warsaw Pact conventional forces, rejected the proposal.

Two top Warsaw Pact officials, both Russians, died in 1976: Gen. Sergei Shtemenko, 69, chief of staff of Warsaw Pact Forces, died on April 23; Marshal Ivan Yukubovsky, 64, the Warsaw Pact commander in chief, died on Nov. 30.   F.W.

WASHINGTON. See STATISTICS OF THE WORLD.

WEST INDIES. National elections were held in two of the largest West Indian island nations in 1976.

Politics. In Trinidad and Tobago, Prime Minister Eric Williams and his People's National Movement (P.N.M.) won a fifth five-year term in office. In the Sept. 13 general election the P.N.M. won 24 of 36 seats in the House of Assembly, the newly created United Labor Front won 10 seats, and the Democratic Action Congress secured 2 seats from Tobago. The elections followed the adoption on Aug. 1 of a new republican constitution. Sir Ellis Clarke became the country's first interim president.

In Barbados the ruling Democratic Labor Party (D.L.P.) was ousted in the general election that was held on Sept. 2. The Barbados Labor Party, under the leadership of J. M. G. (Tom) Adams, won 17 seats in the House of Assembly. The D.L.P., which had been in power for fifteen years and whose leader, Errol Barrow, had a strong personal following, won only 7 seats.

In other elections Antigua's Labor Party, headed by Vere Bird, ousted the Progressive Labor Movement government in February. On Anguilla in March the People's Progressive Party, led by Ronald Webster, held onto its parliamentary majority; the island had become a self-governing territory the previous month. Prime Minister Eric Gairy of Grenada was reelected by a narrow margin in December.

The Economy. On the economic front most of the island states fared much better in 1976 than in 1975, as worldwide inflation ebbed and industrial recovery helped boost agricultural export prices and the tourist trade. The sharp drop in the value of the British pound sterling between March and October did, however, create problems for many West Indian states. Some of them cut their ties to sterling, revalued their currencies, and pegged them to the United States dollar.

Although political differences among the twelve members of the Caribbean Common Market (CARICOM) continued to cause problems within the regional trade group, some important agreements were reached that observers felt would help to strengthen the movement. First, members established a new formula for determining whether a product is locally manufactured and thus entitled to certain tariff benefits. Second, progress was made in the ambitious CARICOM aluminum smelter project, to be located in Trinidad and Tobago. Third, the Caribbean Food Corp. was inaugurated in September in Trinidad and Tobago; the company was to coordinate regional agricultural programs, livestock development, and improvement of fishing fleets throughout the region.

See STATISTICS OF THE WORLD. See also JAMAICA.   A.K.M.

WEST VIRGINIA. See STATISTICS OF THE WORLD.
WESTERN SAMOA. See STATISTICS OF THE WORLD.
WILSON, HAROLD. See PEOPLE IN THE NEWS.
WISCONSIN. See STATISTICS OF THE WORLD.
WOMEN. During 1976 women were increasingly active in the economic and political life of the United States. They appeared for the first time as cadets in the major U.S. service academies. Efforts toward ratification of the proposed Equal Rights Amendment (E.R.A.) to the U.S. Constitution became more unified, although no more successful. The right of abortion—a more emotional issue—continued to be upheld by the U.S. Supreme Court. In many foreign countries, the movement to end job discrimination because of sex made significant gains.

Advances and Firsts. The year brought with it the realization that women were rapidly assuming a greater role in the economic life of the nation. Women now made up 41 percent of the labor force, according to the Census Bureau. Of 2,700,-000 workers added to the labor force between September, 1975, and September, 1976, a startling 53 percent were women. The bureau also reported that the number of women holding jobs had almost doubled since 1950, although the median income of women employees was still only 57 percent that of men. The trend toward careers for women was a leading factor in the recent decline in the U.S. birthrate.

Besides factories, offices, and homes, women could be found in many less conventional places

Two cadets prepare to join the 155 other women who became the first of their sex to enter the U.S. Air Force Academy at Colorado Springs, Colo., on June 28. An ironic motto adorns the walkway leading to the orientation area.

Most People Do It for Fun

In December, when *Sports Illustrated* named the sportswomen of the year, golfer Judy Rankin was on the list. She had earned more than $150,000 at her chosen profession in 1976. Although this figure was nowhere near the astronomical earnings of a Jack Nicklaus or a Ben Crenshaw, *Sports Illustrated* pointed out that it *was* higher than the earnings of Sandy Barnhill, who played in fifteen women's tournaments during the year and won $25. (The two golfers who tied for last place on the men's list earned $76.85 each, the magazine noted.)

in 1976. The major U.S. service academies admitted female cadets for the first time in June. About one twelfth of the classes of 1980 at the Army's Military Academy (West Point, N.Y.), the Naval Academy (Annapolis, Md.), and the Air Force Academy (Colorado Springs, Colo.) were women. Few special provisions were needed for the new cadets, who fared about as well as their male counterparts; at the Air Force Academy, for example, 12 of the 157 women admitted in June had departed by Dec. 8, a slightly lower dropout rate than that of the men.

American women broke other barriers in 1976. Of 32 U.S. winners of Rhodes scholarships, 13 were women, eligible for the first time. The New York City Police Department appointed a woman, Capt. Vittoria Renzullo, to head a police precinct. In sports, racing-car driver Janet Guthrie became the first woman to make practice runs for the Indianapolis 500, although she was unable to participate. The Episcopal Church, after much debate, approved the ordination of women. Theo-

logical sexism was also attacked in the new prayer book of American Reform Judaism, *Gates of Prayer,* in which God is still referred to as "He," but "our fathers" becomes "our ancestors" and "mankind" becomes "humanity."

The Abortion Issue. Again in 1976 abortion was a divisive and controversial issue. The U.S. Supreme Court had ruled in 1973 that a woman had a constitutional right to decide whether to have an abortion, but the Court stipulated that this right was "not unqualified." In 1976 decisions, the Court refused to block the payment of Medicaid funds for elective abortions, ruled that states may not require wives to get their husbands' consent for an abortion, and ruled that states may not impose blanket restrictions requiring all single women under the age of 18 to obtain parental consent for an abortion. In another ruling of interest to the women's rights movement, the Court ruled that employers who have disability-compensation plans may, under federal law, refuse to compensate women employees who are absent because of pregnancy.

American women were by no means unanimous in supporting abortion on demand. A strong and vocal antiabortion "right-to-life" movement was led by Ellen McCormack of New York State, who entered most of the Democratic Presidential primaries to publicize her cause. She took 9 percent of the vote in Vermont and 5 percent in Connecticut and Indiana, ending up with 22 delegates at the Democratic Party's national convention in July.

Kenneth C. Edelin, a Boston surgeon convicted of manslaughter in 1975 in connection with a legal abortion he had performed in 1973, won a reversal of his conviction in December.

Politics and the E.R.A. "Equality of rights under the law shall not be denied or abridged by the United States or any state on account of sex." These words, the proposed Twenty-Seventh

Four delegates to the first International Tribunal on Crimes against Women, held in Brussels, Belgium, in March. The conference brought together 1000 women from 28 countries to discuss such problems as rape, wife-beating, and legal discrimination.

Author-researcher Shere Hite refers to a copy of her bestselling 1976 book on female sexuality. She questioned 3000 women, asking them to describe in their own words their sexual feelings, needs, and fears.

Amendment to the U.S. Constitution, formed the central issue and goal of women's rights groups in 1976. In a remarkable show of solidarity, thirty-two women's magazines reached 60,000,000 readers with featured articles on the E.R.A. in their July issues. Publications as diverse as *Redbook, Glamour, Ms., Woman's Day, Family Circle, Essence,* and *Personal Romances* participated in the effort. In addition, a new national bipartisan organization, ERAmerica, was formed to work for ratification of the amendment.

There were both setbacks and advances for the E.R.A. in 1976. A massive lobbying effort by women's groups to persuade the Illinois state legislature to ratify the amendment failed. The Arizona and Louisiana state legislatures also voted against

the E.R.A. But attempts to rescind ratification failed in Colorado, Idaho, Kentucky, New Mexico, South Dakota, and Vermont. Massachusetts adopted a state E.R.A. Four more states, for a total of thirty-eight, must pass the federal amendment before the March, 1979, deadline.

The national elections in November left women's representation in government largely unchanged. The number of women to hold seats in the 95th Congress declined by one to a total of 18, although all 16 incumbent women Representatives who sought reelection won. Once again no woman was elected to the U.S. Senate; Dixy Lee Ray was, however, elected governor of the state of Washington. The number of women holding statewide elective offices increased slightly.

International Events. Courts throughout the world supported women in their fight against job discrimination for reasons of sex, marital status, or family responsibility. In France, India, Israel, Japan, and the U.S., courts voided the requirement of many employers that their women employees be unmarried.

In Italy the 1976 elections brought the first woman to the cabinet of the Italian republic: Minister of Labor Tina Anselmi. Sadake Nakamura Ogata became the highest ranking woman ever to serve in the Japanese foreign service when she was appointed first deputy in her country's thirty-member United Nations diplomatic mission. In France, Françoise Giroud, the secretary of state for the condition of women, submitted a five-year plan designed to raise the status of women closer to equality with men. Giroud became secretary of state for culture in August. In Paris, for the first time in its 700-year history, the Sorbonne had a woman president, Hélène Ahrweiller. Begum Nusrat Bhutto, the wife of the prime minister of Pakistan and a leading international women's rights advocate, announced the inauguration of a "decade of women's liberation" in her country.

See UNITED STATES OF AMERICA: THE PEOPLE: *Women in the U.S.* M.W.B.

WYOMING. *See* STATISTICS OF THE WORLD.

Y

YEMEN ARAB REPUBLIC. Throughout 1976, Col. Ibrahim Mohammed al-Hamadi, chairman of the Military Command Council, focused his attention on problems of economic development in the Yemen Arab Republic (North Yemen) and the

strengthening of the administrative apparatus of the fourteen-year-old republican regime.

North Yemen remained one of the poorest and least-developed regions of the world, increasingly dependent on aid from Arab and Western nations for its fiscal survival. The new budget, approved July 15, allocated $264,000,000 for current and projected expenditures, against a national revenue of only $183,920,000. Despite attempts to boost production of coffee and cotton for export and an increase in remittances from workers abroad, the trade deficit increased by nearly $220,000 during the year.

Grappling with problems of administrative and budgetary mismanagement, al-Hamadi reorganized the cabinet four times during the year. The continued opposition of certain conservative leaders to the republican form of government was manifested late in February, when tribal sheikhs staged a brief uprising.

The Yemen Arab Republic sought closer ties with its conservative northern neighbor, Saudi Arabia, during the year. It was also reported that reunification talks with the People's Democratic Republic of Yemen were held, but apparently no concrete proposals emerged.

See STATISTICS OF THE WORLD   S.C.

YEMEN, PEOPLE'S DEMOCRATIC REPUBLIC OF. The only Marxist state in the largely conservative, oil-rich Arabian Peninsula, the People's Democratic Republic of Yemen (South Yemen) moved to normalize relations with its Arab neighbors in 1976. For years the ideological isolation of the Aden government has been exacerbated by its support for the revolutionary movement in neighboring Oman. Its resources taxed by long military involvement against the Iranian-backed forces of Sultan Qabus bin Said of Oman, the South Yemen government of Premier Ali Nasser Mohammed Hasani negotiated a rapprochement with Iran's rival for regional influence, Saudi Arabia.

On March 10 diplomatic relations were established between South Yemen and Saudi Arabia for the first time. The agreement specified mutual opposition to "foreign influence" in the Arabian Peninsula—presumed by observers to be a reference to the substantial Iranian military presence in Oman. There was widespread speculation that Aden had agreed to withdraw support for the Omani insurrectionists in exchange for Saudi aid and its efforts to persuade Qabus to abandon the war. On March 11 a cease-fire agreement was reached in Oman which, although not totally effective, laid the basis for a gradual de-escalation of the war.

See STATISTICS OF THE WORLD.   S.C.

YOUNG, ANDREW. *See* PEOPLE IN THE NEWS.

YOUTH ACTIVITIES. For the most part, young people in the United States in 1976 shared the interests and concerns of the general population: the national elections, the economic crunch, and environmental problems. Although the much-dis-

---

"You Gotta Be a Football Hero"

A nationwide poll of 500 male and female pupils in grades 5 through 12 produced interesting results. Published in August, it listed the 50 individuals most admired by the students. Number one was football star O. J. Simpson. Second was a rock'n'roll singer, Elton John, and third was Neil Armstrong, the former astronaut. Down the list at ninth was U.S. Secretary of State Henry A. Kissinger. And his boss? President Gerald R. Ford placed thirteenth.

---

cussed generation gap did not disappear altogether, the differences that set youths as a group apart in recent times seemed blurred.

The New Generation. In the two preceding national election years, protests over the Vietnam war and environmental demonstrations galvanized large numbers of the young in the U.S. By contrast, not a single recognizable "youth issue" surfaced during the 1976 Presidential campaign. There was some suggestion that a post-Watergate generation had "turned off" on politics. Yet campaign organizers for both the Democratic and Republican parties reported young volunteers signing up in droves (at least one third of President Gerald R. Ford's primary campaign workers were recruited out of high schools and colleges). Like their elders, the younger political activists this time around interested themselves less in ideology or rhetoric and more in the character of the candidates.

Delegates to the first Young Men's Christian Association World Youth Peace Conference chat before convening in Palacios, Texas, on Nov. 7. Some 225 delegates from 60 countries attended the conference.

If the anti-Establishment alienation of the recent past appeared muted, there was little to suggest that young Americans had made a full swing back to the "silent generation" of the 1950's. The marks of the "permissive 1960's" remained. Studies indicated that among teenage girls in 1976, approximately half were virgins. One in every five births in the U.S. was attributed to teenage romances. And at least half of the American teenage population had tried marijuana, though most studies indicated that the use of hard drugs such as heroin and LSD had declined. Curiously, many national magazines began publishing warnings of rising teenage alcoholism and, particularly among teenage girls, increased cigarette smoking.

Still, the overall trend among American youth was to place less emphasis on "doing your own thing" than on coping with the problems of the real world. Foremost among these problems were jobs and careers. With diminishing confidence in a college degree as a guarantee of a well-paying career, the percentage of U.S. high school graduates going on to higher education seemed to have stabilized at between 50 and 55 percent. Paradoxically enough, a Northwestern University study during the spring found improved job prospects for college graduates in selected fields, notably engineering, business administration, accountancy, and law.

Who's Got a Job? Most American youths did find jobs, but far too many did not, as the jobless rate among teenagers remained alarmingly high. While the overall unemployment rate climbed to 8.1 percent late in the year, the corresponding figure for unemployed youths between the ages of 16 and 19 stood two and a half times higher. Among black youths, traditionally the hardest hit, the figure hovered around 40 percent; *see* NE-GROES IN THE UNITED STATES. And those numbers did not include many young people, perhaps as many as 200,000, who had given up job hunting.

To attack the chronic youth unemployment problem, groups of educators, labor leaders, businessmen, and government officials met throughout the year to seek remedies. One such session in May at the Eleanor Roosevelt Institute of Hyde Park, N.Y., heard former U.S. Secretary of Labor Willard W. Wirtz warn that joblessness among American youths was likely to remain at unacceptably high levels, even under conditions of "full employment" among adults. Wirtz was among many during the year who advocated the establishment of universal youth service programs, under which every teenager would perform voluntary community service or work on conservation projects. In November Robert T. Hall of President-elect Jimmy Carter's transition team

Pat Sloan, equipped with mandatory helmet and protective pads, takes a spill at a new skateboard park in Carlsbad, Calif. Such parks were a response to the great skateboard revival of 1976.

indicated that an additional $1 billion might be necessary on top of the $2 billion spent annually on federal youth job programs to tackle the hardcore problem.

Crime and the Young. Visions of aimless, jobless youth on a rampage were given some credence by sporadic outbursts of youth-gang violence in many large U.S. cities during the summer. In Chicago six young thugs held up motorists stalled on a flooded freeway. In Detroit youth-gang terror culminated in a spate of muggings (and one reported case of rape) at a Cobo Hall rock concert. A similar outburst during the Muhammad Ali-Ken Norton boxing match in September made headlines in New York City. There, as in San Francisco, youth-gang violence invaded even the Chinatowns, communities supposedly long free of juvenile delinquency.

Overall, figures released by the Federal Bureau of Investigation in 1976 showed that in the period 1970–75, crimes committed by teenagers rose 54 percent (compared to 41 percent for the general population). In 1975, 43 percent of those arrested for serious crimes were 18 years old or under and 75 percent were 24 or under.

The steady climb in juvenile violence brought stern responses in some cases. Detroit met its youth-gang problem with a police crackdown and curfew. In New York State the state legislature enacted a law permitting family court judges to impose two-year minimum sentences on 14- and 15-

year-olds found guilty of murder, arson, or kid-napping. For the first time judges were directed to consider the need to protect society along with the welfare and rehabilitation of errant youths.   D.C.

YUGOSLAVIA. President Josip Broz Tito, 84, the founder of Communist Yugoslavia and the world's oldest chief of state, was afflicted in September by an acute liver ailment. The Yugoslav leader soon recovered from his illness, however, and on the whole he was able to count 1976 as a successful year for his unique brand of independent Communism.

Politics. In preparation for the day when he would no longer be able to play a personal role in holding together Yugoslavia's disparate ethnic groups, Tito continued to deal harshly with dissent in all forms. The government conducted dozens of political trials, and Tito defended such prosecutions by stating that "there are enemies who don't want Yugoslavia to exist as an independent nation." In March a former deputy premier of Croatia was among those convicted of pro-Soviet conspiracy. Two months later a Soviet woman was found guilty of spying on behalf of the Soviet Union. In July the regime convicted a pro-Soviet Yugoslav émigré, Vlado Dapcevic, who had evidently been kidnapped by Titoist agents during a visit to Rumania in 1975.

The Economy. The country was hard hit by a continuing recession in 1976, but inflation slowed and the economy enjoyed a modest upswing toward the end of the year. On July 20 the Yugoslav parliament adopted a new five-year plan (for the years 1976–80), calling for annual growth rates of 7 to 8 percent in industrial production and 6 percent in real personal income.

In May one of the biggest engineering enterprises ever carried out in Yugoslavia, the Belgrade-Bar rail line, reached completion. The 292-mi. line, which took twenty-four years to build, links the national capital, in landlocked Serbia, with the Adriatic coastal port of Bar.

Foreign Affairs. In his relations with the Soviet Union, President Tito made every effort to win assurances that Moscow would respect Yugoslav independence after his death. The Soviets acquiesced to Tito's demands on two occasions. During a Communist Party summit conference in East Berlin in June, the U.S.S.R. dropped its claim of being the arbiter and leader of world Communism (*see* COMMUNISM). Then, on a trip to Belgrade during November, Soviet Communist Party General Secretary Leonid Brezhnev reiterated past pledges of noninterference in Yugoslav affairs, although he and Tito disagreed sharply on many policy issues.

Tito continued to develop ties with the nations of the Third World. Yugoslavia was a prime organizer of the summit conference of nonaligned states that took place in Ceylon (Sri Lanka) during August. The Yugoslav president also consulted with Third World leaders on numerous other occasions.

Relations with the United States were mixed during 1976. Yugoslavia was angered when U.S. officials gave in to Croatian terrorist demands for the publication of certain Croatian nationalist propaganda statements. The demands had been made during the hijacking of a TWA jet in September; *see* CRIME AND LAW ENFORCEMENT. Tito's government was also irked several weeks later when Yugoslavia became an issue between President Gerald R. Ford and Democratic Party Presidential candidate Jimmy Carter, who differed over the hypothetical question of whether the U.S. should go to war if the Soviet Union invaded Yugoslavia after Tito's death (Carter said it should not). In November, however, the Yugoslavs were pleased by remarks made by the visiting U.S. Commerce Secretary, Elliot L. Richardson, who reaffirmed Washington's support for "the independence, nonalignment, and integrity of Yugoslavia."

See STATISTICS OF THE WORLD.   F.W.

YUKON TERRITORY. *See* STATISTICS OF THE WORLD.

Members of a rescue team survey the wreckage left by the worst midair crash in aviation history. On Sept. 10 a Yugoslav DC-9 collided with a British Airways Trident high over the Zagreb region, killing 176 people—all the passengers and crew members of the two planes.

Z

ZAIRE, REPUBLIC OF. President Mobutu Sese Seko of Zaire suffered a dramatic reversal in his foreign policy in 1976. The 46-year-old Mobutu had actively supported the National Front for the Liberation of Angola (F.N.L.A.) against the Soviet- and Cuban-backed Popular Movement for the Liberation of Angola (M.P.L.A.). After the mid-January collapse of the F.N.L.A., hostile M.P.L.A. forces stood along Zaire's trade routes that crossed Cabinda to ports on the Atlantic Ocean. In an effort toward rapprochement, Mobutu joined Agostinho Neto of the M.P.L.A. in Brazzaville on Feb. 28, to issue a joint communiqué in which Zaire recognized the M.P.L.A. government of Angola. In exchange for Zaire's promise to restrain or expel F.N.L.A. members and to repatriate upward of 1,000,000 Angolan refugees, Neto agreed to guarantee Zaire's access to the Benguela railroad, a vital link between Zaire and the Atlantic. Although relations between the two countries improved, Mobutu moved ahead with plans to purchase $50,000,000 worth of U.S. weapons.

The Zaire economy in 1976 was reeling under a 62 percent decline in the worldwide price of copper, Zaire's chief export. In March an effort was made to remedy this setback with a 42.1 percent devaluation of the national currency. Although encouraging foreign buyers, it caused import prices to nearly double. Compounding Zaire's economic woes were an annual inflation rate of about 40 percent and a balance of payments deficit that in 1975 reached more than $500,000,000. Zaire had borrowed extensively and owed about $3 billion, including $800,000,000 to private lenders in the United States. On June 17 eleven major creditor nations agreed to reschedule the debts, permitting a ten-year period of repayments.

See STATISTICS OF THE WORLD. *See also* AFRICA.   J.T.S.

ZAMBIA. In 1976 the low price of copper on the world market and the conflicts in southern Africa severely damaged the Zambian economy. The use of the Benguela railroad, connecting landlocked Zambia with the Atlantic port of Lobito, in Angola, was disrupted by the Angolan civil war. More than one third of the copper produced in Zambia in 1976 had to be stockpiled after the newly opened Tanzam railroad, linking its copper mines with the port city of Dar es Salaam, Tanzania, was unable to handle the accumulated freight. A possible alternative route, transshipment through Rhodesia to ports in Mozambique, was blocked when Mozambique sealed its border, following an incursion by Rhodesian troops. On Jan. 30 the government announced that costs, including transportation, exceeded current market prices for copper. It then issued an austere budget for the remainder of 1976. Expenditures were slashed by $136,000,000 to a total of $842,000,000, and immediate price increases were imposed on most consumer goods.

Zambia continued to provide bases and support for Rhodesian and Namibian black nationalists, and President Kenneth D. Kaunda played a significant role in the negotiations aimed at forcing a settlement of the Rhodesian crisis. More than thirteen clashes were reported in 1976 between South African and Zambian troops along the Namibian border. These actions required the Zambian government to use its dwindling cash reserves to bolster its defenses.

See STATISTICS OF THE WORLD. *See also* AFRICA.   J.T.S.

ZOOLOGY. *See* LIFE SCIENCES.

In 1976 the Tanzam railroad, built by African and Chinese laborers, began limited operations. Unfortunately it proved incapable of transporting the enormous stockpiles of Zambian copper, destined for the port of Dar es Salaam.

STATISTICS OF THE WORLD

in the tables on the following pages will be found the latest available statistics on

Nation Capital	Population	Type of Government	Heads of Government	Currency Value in U.S. Dollars	GNP (000,000)	GNP (per capita)
AFGHANISTAN Kabul	19,280,000 318,094	Republic	President and Prime Minister: Lt. Gen. Mohammad Daud Khan	Afghani 0.022	$ 1,620	$ 100
ALBANIA Tiranë	2,480,000 171,000	People's republic	Presidium Chairman: Haxhi Lleshi Chairman, Council of Ministers: Mehmet Shehu	Lek 0.24	1,260	530
ALGERIA Algiers	16,780,000 1,200,000	Republic	President and Prime Minister: Col. Houari Boumédienne	Dinar 0.24	9,840	650
ANGOLA Luanda	5,800,000 480,613	People's republic	President: Agostinho Neto Prime Minister: Lopo do Nascimento	Escudo 0.037	3,370	580
ARGENTINA Buenos Aires	25,380,000 2,976,000	Federal republic	President: Lt. Gen. Jorge Rafael Videla	Peso 0.0071	46,900	1,900
AUSTRALIA Canberra	13,500,000 166,101	Federal parliamentary state (C)	Governor-General: Sir John Kerr Prime Minister: Malcolm Fraser	Dollar 1.02	63,450	4,760
AUSTRIA Vienna	7,520,000 1,614,841	Federal republic	President: Rudolf Kirchschläger Chancellor: Bruno Kreisky	Schilling 0.058	30,480	4,050
BAHAMAS Nassau	200,000 3,233	Parliamentary state (C)	Governor-General: Sir Milo B. Butler Prime Minister: Lynden O. Pindling	Dollar 1.00	490	2,460
BAHRAIN Manama	260,000 110,000	Emirate	Emir: Isa bin Sulman al-Khalifah Prime Minister: Khalifah bin Sulman al-Khalifah	Dinar 2.53	550	2,250
BANGLADESH Dacca	76,820,000 1,132,373	Republic (C)	President: Abusadat Mohammad Sayem	Taka 0.062	7,260	100
BARBADOS Bridgetown	250,000 88,097	Parliamentary state (C)	Acting Governor-General: Sir William Douglas Prime Minister: J. M. G. Adams	Dollar 0.50	270	1,110

THE COUNTRIES OF THE WORLD

Imports / Exports	Revenue / Expenditure	Elementary Schools: Teachers / Students	Secondary Schools: Teachers / Students	Colleges and Universities:[1] Institutions / Students
$ 209,022,000	$ 242,977,000	16,293	8,247	1,264
173,355,000	216,022,000	621,437	170,519	9,399
NA	1,150,000,000	20,555	3,030	1,153
NA	1,092,600,000	518,002	85,441	28,668
4,035,000,000	5,332,120,000	55,763	14,950	2,881
4,259,000,000	5,297,930,000	2,409,367	384,001	30,070
624,000,000	530,251,000	11,343	3,987	324
1,218,000,000	507,040,000	485,955	67,230	2,660
3,656,000,000	4,168,800,000	183,796	148,213	38,964
3,931,000,000	4,699,200,000	3,485,495	1,125,715	423,824
9,811,000,000	17,868,000,000	70,911	65,211	10,984
11,575,000,000	21,855,400,000	1,811,027	1,042,384	208,149
9,391,000,000	10,458,400,000	25,241	48,067	9,349
7,518,000,000	11,008,500,000	520,761	858,751	78,787
1,565,000,000	115,244,000	751[1]	600	NA
3,416,000,000	117,110,000	34,097	21,609	3,000
445,596,000[2]	339,418,000	2,126	752	67
181,712,000[2]	339,418,000	43,409	17,548	689
710,000,000	744,427,000	155,023	94,132	7,201
311,000,000	1,232,290,000	7,750,000	2,265,469	117,603
204,000,000	86,027,000	NA	NA	111
85,000,000	119,436,000	39,132	30,182	1,028

Nation Capital	Population	Type of Government	Heads of Government	Currency Value in U.S. Dollars	GNP (000,000)	GNP (per capita)
BELGIUM . . . . Brussels	9,800,000 1,054,970	. . . . Constitutional monarchy	. . King: . . . . Baudouin Premier: Léo Tindemans	. . . Franc 0.026	$ 51,080	. . . . $5,210
BHUTAN . . . . Thimphu	1,145,000 10,000	. . . . Limited . . . . monarchy	. . King: . . . . Jigme Singye Wangchuk	. . . Ngultrum 0.11	80	70
BOLIVIA . . . . Sucre La Paz	5,630,000 106,590 605,200	. . . . Republic	. . President: . . . . Col. Hugo Banzer Suárez	. . . Peso 0.05	1,390	250
BOTSWANA . . . . Gaborone	690,000 30,000	. . . . Republic . . . . . . (C)	. . President: . . . . Sir Seretse Khama	. . . Pula 1.15	180	270
BRAZIL . . . . .107,140,000 Brasília	107,140,000 272,002	. . . . Federal . . . . . . republic	. . President: . . . . Gen. Ernesto Geisel	. . . Cruzeiro 0.093	93,180	900
BULGARIA . . . . Sofia	8,720,000 937,069	. . . . People's . . . . . . republic	. . Chairman, Council of State: . . . . . . Todor Zhivkov Chairman, Council of Ministers: Stanko Todorov	. . . Lev 1.03	15,390	1,770
BURMA . . . . Rangoon	31,240,000 2,055,365	. . . . Socialist . . . . republic	. . President: . . . . U Ne Win Premier: U Sein Win	. . . Kyat 0.15	2,710	90
BURUNDI . . . . Bujumbura	3,760,000 78,810	. . . . Republic	. . President: . . . . Col. Jean-Baptiste Bagaza Premier: Lt. Col. Édouard Nzambimana	. . . Franc 0.011	300	80
CAMBODIA . . . . (DEMOCRATIC KAMPUCHEA) Phnom Penh	8,110,000 650,000	. . . . Republic	. . Presidium Chairman: . . . . Khieu Samphan Acting Premier: Nuon Chea	. . . Riel NA	570	70
CAMEROON . . . . Yaoundé	6,400,000 274,399	. . . . Republic	. . President: . . . . Ahmadou Ahidjo Prime Minister: Paul Biya	. . . CFA Franc 0.0041	1,650	260
CANADA . . . . Ottawa	22,830,000 302,345	. . . . Federal . . . . . . parliamentary state	. . Governor-General: . . . . Jules Léger Prime Minister: Pierre Elliott Trudeau	. . . Dollar 1.03	136,570	6,080
CAPE VERDE . . . . Praia	290,000 4,054	. . . . Republic	. . President: . . . . Aristides M. Pereira Premier: Maj. Pedro Pires	. . . Escudo 0.032	NA	NA
CENTRAL AFRICAN . . . . . REPUBLIC Bangui	2,610,000 187,000	. . . . Republic	. . President: . . . . Gen. Salah Eddine Ahmed Bokassa Prime Minister: Ange Patassé	. . . CFA Franc 0.0041	350	200
CEYLON (SRI LANKA) . . . Colombo	13,990,000 618,000	. . . . Republic . . . . . . (C)	. . President: . . . . William Gopallawa Prime Minister: Sirimavo R. D. Bandaranaike	. . . Rupee 0.12	1,790	130
CHAD . . . . N'Djamena	4,030,000 179,000	. . . . Republic	. . President and Premier: . . . . Gen. Félix Malloum	. . . CFA Franc 0.0041	360	90
CHILE . . . . Santiago	10,250,000 1,759,087	. . . . Republic	. . President: . . . . Gen. Augusto Pinochet Ugarte	. . . Peso 0.08	8,490	820
CHINA, PEOPLE'S . . . . . .838,800,000 REPUBLIC OF Peking	838,800,000 7,570,000	. . . . People's republic	. . Premier: . . . . Hua Kuo-feng	. . . Yuan 0.51	245,840	300
COLOMBIA . . . . Bogotá	23,540,000 2,850,000	. . . . Republic	. . President: . . . . Alfonso López Michelsen	. . . Peso 0.029	11,630	510

Imports / Exports	Revenue / Expenditure	Elementary Schools: Teachers / Students	Secondary Schools: Teachers / Students	Colleges and Universities:[1] Institutions / Students
$30,691,000,000[3]	$16,066,300,000	NA	NA	NA
28,807,000,000[3]	18,022,600,000	1,023,670	802,215	148,628
NA	3,777,990	492[4]	[4]	*
NA	9,493,000	11,420[4]	[4]	*
256,000,000	284,450,000	33,084	20,461	2,727
548,000,000	314,650,000	769,968	592,636	27,352
175,003,000	62,257,100	3,047	727	40
112,802,000	216,531,000	103,711	12,245	244
13,558,000,000	9,418,560,000	525,658	372,237	59,760
8,656,000,000	7,875,720,000	14,082,098	5,588,583	785,159
5,408,000,000	9,741,480,000	47,667	25,143	9,667
4,691,000,000	9,722,340,000	992,835	382,689	121,798
125,000,000	2,167,110,000	74,266	26,332	3,989
158,000,000	2,324,190,000	3,300,153	871,880	56,310
62,000,000	37,955,500	4,980	876	108
32,000,000	33,396,800	179,286	9,586	490
NA	13,818,100	20,374	2,468	1,164
NA	43,030,300	479,616	104,900	9,988
599,000,000	311,403,000	19,719	NA	328
447,000,000	311,403,000	1,014,135	108,425	4,484
34,306,000,000	25,130,100,000	277,450[4]	[4]	48,055
31,881,000,000	26,286,300,000	5,610,063[4]	[4]	592,267
32,238,500	10,924,500	1,078	186	*
1,849,800	6,116,050	63,734	3,712	*
46,000,000[5]	70,677,700	2,987	585	NA
48,000,000[5]	77,400,700	193,866	16,588	380
680,798,000	659,406,000	100,098[4]	[4]	2,453
509,918,000	970,180,000	1,539,473	1,149,536	19,286
92,000,000	89,996,300	2,540	NA	85
37,000,000	89,996,300	198,030	12,918	605
1,911,000,000	535,164,000	67,963	26,637	NA
2,480,000,000	623,388,000	2,320,502	452,456	144,165
7,400,000,000	NA	NA	NA	NA
6,300,000,000	NA	NA	NA	NA
1,558,000,000	993,563,000	87,623[1]	47,419	13,875
1,358,000,000	1,111,490,000	3,173,994[1]	911,419	124,236

439

Nation Capital	Population	Type of Government	Heads of Government	Currency Value in U.S. Dollars	GNP (000,000)	GNP (per capita)
COMORO ISLANDS . . . . Moroni	310,000 12,000	Republic	President: Ali Soilih Premier: Abdallah Mohamed	CFA Franc 0.0041	$ 28	$ 103
CONGO, REPUBLIC OF . . Brazzaville	1,350,000 289,700	People's republic	President: Maj. Marien Ngouabi Premier: Maj. Louis Sylvain Goma	CFA Franc 0.0041	470	390
COSTA RICA . . . . San José	1,970,000 215,441	Republic	President: Daniel Oduber Quirós	Colón 0.12	1,520	790
CUBA . . . . Havana	9,090,000 1,130,634	Socialist republic	President: Osvaldo Dorticós Torrado Premier: Maj. Fidel Castro Ruz	Peso 1.21	5,780	640
CYPRUS . . . . Nicosia	640,000 116,125	Republic (C)	President: Archbishop Makarios III	Pound 2.41	850	1,310
CZECHOSLOVAKIA . . . . Prague	14,800,000 1,095,615	Federal socialist republic	President: Gustáv Husák Premier: Lubomír Štrougal	Koruna 0.19	47,270	3,220
DAHOMEY (BENIN) . . . . Porto-Novo	3,110,000 100,000	People's republic	President: Lt. Col. Mathieu Kérékou	CFA Franc 0.0041	370	120
DENMARK . . . . Copenhagen	5,060,000 562,405	Constitutional monarchy	Queen: Margaret II Premier: Anker Jørgensen	Krone 0.17	29,390	5,820
DOMINICAN REPUBLIC . Santo Domingo	4,700,000 671,402	Republic	President: Joaquín Balaguer	Peso 1.00	2,710	590
ECUADOR . . . . Quito	6,730,000 557,113	Republic	President: Vice-Admiral Alfredo Poveda Burbano	Sucre 0.04	3,200	460
EGYPT, ARAB REPUBLIC OF Cairo	37,230,000 5,126,000	Republic	President: Anwar el-Sadat Prime Minister: Gen. Mamdouh Muhammad Salem	Pound 2.56	10,090	280
EL SALVADOR . . . . San Salvador	4,010,000 388,498	Republic	President: Col. Arturo Armando Molina Barraza	Colón 0.40	1,540	390
EQUATORIAL GUINEA . . . Malabo	310,000 19,341	Republic	President: Francisco Macías Nguema	Ekuele 0.015	80	260
ETHIOPIA . . . . Addis Ababa	27,950,000 1,083,420	Republic	Chairman, Provisional Military Council: Brig. Gen. Tafari Banti	Dollar 0.48	2,550	90
FIJI . . . . Suva	570,000 60,000	Parliamentary state (C)	Governor-General: Ratu Sir George K. Cakobau Prime Minister: Ratu Sir Kamisese K. T. Mara	Dollar 1.10	410	720
FINLAND . . . . Helsinki	4,710,000 502,383	Republic	President: Urho K. Kekkonen Prime Minister: Martti J. Miettunen	Markka 0.26	19,350	4,130
FRANCE . . . . Paris	52,910,000 2,290,900	Republic	President: Valéry Giscard d'Estaing Premier: Raymond Barre	Franc 0.20	272,410	5,190

Imports Exports	Revenue Expenditure	Elementary Schools: Teachers Students	Secondary Schools: Teachers Students	Colleges and Universities:[1] Institutions Students
$ 14,311,800 4,698,380	$ 8,710,240 8,710,240	554 23,194	128 3,197	* *
125,000,000[5] 85,000,000[5]	231,895,000 231,895,000	4,650 293,138	1,681 72,517	145 2,098
637,000,000 454,000,000	208,421,000 248,932,000	12,643 367,901	4,449 106,511	NA 24,256
2,446,000,000 2,680,000,000	2,718,000,000 2,718,000,000	78,451 1,925,700	37,577 613,800	5,725 76,900
306,000,000 151,000,000	121,993,000 164,225,000	2,219[6] 78,479	2,523 57,794	74 679
9,081,000,000 8,358,000,000	44,180,000,000 43,414,500,000	96,781 1,890,081	24,103 397,492	20,557 135,874
113,000,000 53,000,000	56,183,000 61,074,600	4,708 244,032	NA 40,768	119 1,911
10,366,000,000 8,716,000,000	9,651,990,000 9,713,660,000	52,812[4] 554,578	[4] 372,529	NA 103,553
773,000,000 895,000,000	473,600,000 494,500,000	15,216 833,439	5,647 121,833	1,709 37,538
943,000,000 884,000,000	509,280,000 473,840,000	28,885 1,117,569	15,099 268,388	NA 43,743
3,951,000,000 1,402,000,000	2,026,830,000 2,350,110,000	100,119 4,096,863	64,083 1,710,165	18,143 351,522
562,000,000 463,000,000	238,680,000 197,160,000	15,727 618,428	1,662 35,603	1,620 20,034
21,152,400 25,017,900	10,188,300 16,288,400	630 35,977	175 6,014	* *
310,000,000 238,000,000	562,153,000 649,268,000	18,646 859,831	6,929 190,922	434 6,474
273,000,000 169,000,000	104,125,000 111,000,000	4,229 135,092	1,327 28,423	NA 1,348
7,602,000,000 5,487,000,000	7,302,870,000 7,446,470,000	21,248 393,242	35,419 516,979	5,698 66,690
54,247,000,000 52,214,000,000	50,519,300,000 60,042,300,000	255,919 6,367,523	264,144 5,029,242	38,000 763,980

Nation Capital	Population	Type of Government	Heads of Government	Currency Value in U.S. Dollars	GNP (000,000)	GNP (per capita)
GABON REPUBLIC Libreville	530,000 75,000	Republic	President: Omar Bongo Premier: Léon Mébiane	CFA Franc 0.0041	$ 820	$1,560
GAMBIA, THE Banjul	520,000 41,047	Republic (C)	President: Sir Dawda K. Jawara	Dalasi 0.42	80	170
GERMAN DEMOCRATIC REPUBLIC Berlin	16,850,000 1,094,147	Socialist republic	Chairman, Council of State: Erich Honecker Chairman, Council of Ministers: Willi Stoph	Mark 0.39	58,880	3,430
GERMANY, FEDERAL REPUBLIC OF Bonn	61,830,000 283,260	Federal republic	President: Walter Scheel Chancellor: Helmut Schmidt	Deutsche Mark 0.41	365,220	5,890
GHANA Accra	9,870,000 564,194	Republic	Chairman, Supreme Military Council: Col. Ignatius K. Acheampong	Cedi 0.87	3,310	350
GREAT BRITAIN London	55,960,000 7,281,080	Limited monarchy (C)	Queen: Elizabeth II Prime Minister: James Callaghan	Pound 1.69	188,630	3,360
GREECE Athens	9,050,000 867,023	Republic	President: Constantine Tsatsos Premier: Constantine Karamanlis	Drachma 0.027	17,680	1,970
GRENADA St. George's	100,000 7,303	Parliamentary state (C)	Governor-General: Sir Leo de Gale Prime Minister: Eric M. Gairy	Dollar 0.42	30	300
GUATEMALA Guatemala City	5,540,000 706,920	Republic	President: Gen. Kjell Eugenio Laugerud García	Quetzal 1.00	3,010	570
GUINEA, REPUBLIC OF Conakry	4,420,000 525,671	Republic	President: Sékou Touré Premier: Louis Lansana Beavogui	Syli 0.048	660	120
GUINEA-BISSAU Bissau	530,000 65,000	Republic	President: Luis de Almeida Cabral Chief State Commissioner: Francisco Mendes	Peso 0.032	127	227
GUYANA Georgetown	790,000 99,989	Republic (C)	President: Arthur Chung Prime Minister: L. F. S. Burnham	Dollar 0.39	370	470
HAITI Port-au-Prince	4,580,000 458,675	Republic	President: Jean-Claude Duvalier	Gourde 0.20	640	140
HONDURAS Tegucigalpa	3,040,000 270,645	Republic	President: Col. Juan Alberto Melgar Castro	Lempira 0.50	990	340
HUNGARY Budapest	10,540,000 2,047,000	People's republic	Chairman, Presidential Council: Pál Losonczi Chairman, Council of Ministers: György Lázár	Forint 0.12	22,410	2,140
ICELAND Reykjavík	220,000 84,856	Republic	President: Kristján Eldjárn Prime Minister: Geir Hallgrímsson	Króna 0.0054	1,220	5,550

Imports / Exports	Revenue / Expenditure	Elementary Schools: Teachers / Students	Secondary Schools: Teachers / Students	Colleges and Universities:[1] Institutions / Students
$ 469,000,000[5]	$ 348,575,000	2,339	NA	NA
942,000,000[5]	78,940,500	114,732	18,555	555
60,000,000	13,722,700	742	311	*
49,000,000	24,249,800	20,724	5,907	*
11,290,000,000	42,712,200,000	155,932[7]	NA	31,176
10,088,000,000	42,160,000,000	2,725,372[7]	468,080	325,113
75,565,000,000	49,367,600,000	269,310	314,497	93,841
91,620,000,000	59,171,200,000	6,499,824	5,076,139	729,207
805,000,000	607,391,000	50,153	5,440[1]	952
720,000,000	857,826,000	1,454,999	94,781[1]	7,466
53,262,000,000	56,354,400,000	280,919	269,000	NA
43,760,000,000	69,055,500,000	6,316,180	4,364,347	626,634
5,457,000,000	3,096,660,000	28,427	NA	5,177
2,288,000,000	3,313,360,000	913,972	638,718	84,603
18,676,400	18,565,400	884	198	*
8,725,490	18,565,400	29,795	5,068	*
700,000,000	279,600,000	16,163	5,906	1,191
586,000,000	322,900,000	571,308	104,494	21,878
79,155,600	197,889,000	4,698	2,785	NA
70,360,500	197,889,000	169,132	63,409	1,974
41,660,200	21,382,000	1,148	176	*
3,055,610	20,449,100	48,007	4,133	*
342,000,000	191,838,000	4,077	2,989	231
359,000,000	193,361,000	132,023	67,853	2,307
100,000,000	43,320,000	8,470	1,735	211
72,000,000	43,320,000	336,511	51,174	2,100
400,000,000	117,850,000	13,045	3,184	617
283,000,000	147,550,000	460,744	62,136	9,226
7,176,000,000	37,425,100,000	65,687	13,749	11,601
6,091,000,000	38,004,400,000	1,039,586	374,569	103,390
487,000,000	278,838,000	1,466[8]	2,102	410
308,000,000	276,495,000	27,046	24,693	2,429

Nation Capital	Population	Type of Government	Heads of Government	Currency Value in U.S. Dollars	GNP (000,000)	GNP (per capita)
INDIA New Delhi	598,100,000 301,801	Federal republic (C)	President: Fakhruddin Ali Ahmed Prime Minister: Indira Gandhi	Rupee 0.11	$ 78,990	$ 130
INDONESIA Djakarta	129,000,000 4,576,009	Republic	President and Prime Minister: Gen. Suharto	Rupiah 0.0024	18,600	150
IRAN Tehran	33,020,000 3,774,048	Constitutional monarchy	Shah: Mohammed Riza Pahlavi Prime Minister: Amir Abbas Hoveida	Rial 0.014	35,120	1,060
IRAQ Baghdad	11,120,000 2,800,000	Republic	President and Prime Minister: Field Marshal Ahmed Hassan al-Bakr	Dinar 3.38	10,400	970
IRELAND Dublin	3,130,000 566,034	Republic	President: Patrick J. Hillery Prime Minister: Liam Cosgrave	Pound 1.68	7,330	2,370
ISRAEL Jerusalem	3,370,000 344,200	Republic	President: Ephraim Katzir Prime Minister: Itzhak Rabin	Pound 0.12	11,150	3,380
ITALY Rome	55,810,000 2,856,309	Republic	President: Giovanni Leone Premier: Giulio Andreotti	Lira 0.0012	153,300	2,770
IVORY COAST Abidjan	4,890,000 500,000	Republic	President: Félix Houphouët-Boigny	CFA Franc 0.0041	2,570	420
JAMAICA Kingston	2,030,000 111,879	Parliamentary state (C)	Governor-General: Florizel A. Glasspole Prime Minister: Michael N. Manley	Dollar 1.10	2,270	1,140
JAPAN Tokyo	110,950,000 8,678,642	Constitutional monarchy	Emperor: Hirohito Prime Minister: Takeo Miki	Yen 0.0034	425,880	3,880
JORDAN Amman	2,700,000 615,000	Constitutional monarchy	King: Hussein I Prime Minister: Mudar Badran	Dinar 3.01	1,040	400
KENYA Nairobi	13,400,000 630,000	Republic (C)	President: Jomo Kenyatta	Shilling 0.12	2,580	200
KOREA, DEMOCRATIC PEOPLE'S REPUBLIC OF P'yŏngyang	15,850,000 1,500,000	People's republic	President: Marshal Kim Il Sung Premier: Pak Sung Chul	Won 0.97	5,960	390
KOREA, REPUBLIC OF Seoul	33,950,000 6,884,000	Republic	President: Park Chung Hee Premier: Choi Kyu Hah	Won 0.0021	15,800	470
KUWAIT Al Kuwait	1,000,000 80,405	Constitutional emirate	Emir: Sheikh Sabah al-Salem al-Sabah Prime Minister: Sheikh Jaber al-Ahmad al-Sabah	Dinar 3.42	10,830	11,640
LAOS (LAO PEOPLE'S DEMOCRATIC REPUBLIC) Vientiane	3,300,000 176,637	People's republic	President: Prince Souphanouvong Prime Minister: Kaysone Phoumvihan	Liberation kip 0.005	220	70

Imports Exports	Revenue Expenditure	Elementary Schools: Teachers Students	Secondary Schools: Teachers Students	Colleges and Universities:[1] Institutions Students
$ 6,094,000,000	$ 9,458,540,000	1,602,515	523,341	119,000
4,365,000,000	12,079,400,000	78,000,000	8,400,000	2,540,000
4,708,000,000	6,014,690,000	418,000	168,847	NA
7,103,000,000	6,589,630,000	12,982,600	2,208,194	329,000
10,343,000,000	19,918,600,000	120,017	60,120	10,475
20,249,000,000	20,233,600,000	3,646,421	1,778,469	123,114
2,365,000,000	2,001,350,000	58,455	16,145	2,843
7,278,000,000	2,769,970,000	1,408,929	404,634	65,481
3,768,000,000	2,012,610,000	17,249	20,760	3,149
3,177,000,000	2,427,080,000	535,845	252,677	31,737
4,140,000,000	6,041,660,000	37,476	15,774	9,127
1,835,000,000	8,520,000,000	527,165	148,708	70,431
38,366,000,000	33,281,800,000	245,628	402,336	50,662
34,821,000,000	37,574,400,000	4,968,900	4,415,387	846,897
1,127,000,000	439,654,000	13,158	NA	368
1,181,000,000	439,654,000	606,263	92,614	6,034
1,113,000,000	576,165,000	9,383	2,524	638
707,000,000	1,009,650,000	441,145	80,254	8,413
57,881,000,000	85,114,600,000	395,062	486,902	167,525
55,844,000,000	89,524,900,000	9,816,536	8,983,762	2,007,870
731,000,000	624,242,000	9,418	6,088	488
158,000,000	660,606,000	352,696	125,928	8,186
938,000,000[9]	593,505,000	56,543	8,203	NA
496,000,000[9]	520,716,000	1,816,017	186,467	9,896
800,000,000	11,214,200,000	100,000[4]		NA
600,000,000	11,214,200,000	1,500,000	1,200,000	300,000
7,275,000,000	2,698,690,000	107,436	77,389	12,671
4,948,000,000	2,954,380,000	5,618,768	2,936,042	250,233
2,263,000,000	3,314,570,000	5,811	8,303	399
8,991,000,000	1,983,770,000	96,163	86,131	5,303
57,000,000	22,475,500	7,340	1,104	136
5,000,000	47,394,300	274,067	20,819	875

Nation Capital	Population	Type of Government	Heads of Government	Currency Value in U.S. Dollars	GNP (000,000)	GNP (per capita)
LEBANON Beirut	2,870,000 474,870	Republic	President: Elias Sarkis Premier: Rashid Karami	Pound 0.39	$ 3,300	$1,080
LESOTHO Maseru	1,040,000 13,312	Limited monarchy	King: Moshoeshoe II Prime Minister: Chief Leabua Jonathan	South African rand 1.15	150	120
LIBERIA Monrovia	1,710,000 171,580	Republic	President: William R. Tolbert, Jr.	Dollar 1.00	500	330
LIBYA Tripoli	2,440,000 245,000	Republic	Chairman, Revolutionary Command Council: Col. Muammar el-Qaddafi Premier: Maj. Abdul Salam Jalloud	Dinar 3.38	7,530	3,360
LIECHTENSTEIN Vaduz	23,949 4,472	Constitutional monarchy	Sovereign: Prince Francis Joseph II Chief of Government: Walter Kieber	Swiss franc 0.40	NA	NA
LUXEMBOURG Luxembourg	360,000 78,400	Constitutional monarchy	Grand Duke: Jean Prime Minister: Gaston Thorn	Franc 0.027	1,990	5,690
MALAGASY REPUBLIC (DEMOCRATIC REPUBLIC OF MADAGASCAR) Tananarive	8,020,000 366,530	Socialist republic	President: Lt. Comdr. Didier Ratsiraka Premier: Justin Rakotoniaina	Franc 0.0041	1,440	170
MALAWI Lilongwe	5,040,000 86,900	Republic (C)	President: Hastings Kamuzu Banda	Kwacha 1.09	630	130
MALAYSIA Kuala Lumpur	11,900,000 451,977	Federal constitutional monarchy (C)	Supreme Head of State: Tuanku Yahya Putra Prime Minister: Datuk Hussein bin Onn	Ringgit (Dollar) 0.40	7,610	660
MALDIVES, REPUBLIC OF Male	120,000 15,000	Republic	President and Prime Minister: Amir Ibrahim Nasir	Rupee 0.12	10	92
MALI, REPUBLIC OF Bamako	5,700,000 196,800	Republic	President: Col. Moussa Traoré	Franc 0.002	410	70
MALTA Valletta	330,000 14,049	Republic (C)	President: Sir Anthony J. Mamo Prime Minister: Dominic Mintoff	Pound 2.30	455	1,377
MAURITANIA, ISLAMIC REPUBLIC OF Nouakchott	1,320,000 100,000	Republic	President: Moktar Ould Daddah	Ouguiya 0.022	290	230
MAURITIUS Port Louis	860,000 138,355	Parliamentary state (C)	Governor-General: Sir Raman Osman Prime Minister: Sir Seewoosagur Ramgoolam	Rupee 0.15	420	480
MEXICO Mexico City	60,150,000 8,299,209	Federal republic	President: José López Portillo	Peso 0.045	58,130	1,000
MONACO Monaco-Ville	24,000 1,685	Constitutional monarchy	Prince: Rainier III Minister of State: André Saint-Mleux	French franc 0.20	NA	NA
MONGOLIAN PEOPLE'S REPUBLIC Ulan Bator	1,440,000 310,000	People's republic	Presidium Chairman: Yumzhagiyin Tsedenbal Chairman, Council of Ministers: Jambyn Batmönh	Tugrik 0.30	860	620

Imports Exports	Revenue Expenditure	Elementary Schools: Teachers Students	Secondary Schools: Teachers Students	Colleges and Universities:[1] Institutions Students
$1,333,000,000	$ 724,050,000	NA	NA	2,759
589,000,000	724,050,000	497,723	174,711	44,296
90,137,000	25,016,300	3,951	780	127
13,855,700	23,213,400	187,459	13,565	724
331,000,000	124,200,000	4,111	1,140	180
406,000,000	124,500,000	149,687	27,937	2,214
2,762,000,000	3,262,770,000	22,842	9,697	NA
8,265,000,000	4,396,480,000	522,473	128,579	9,590
NA	66,083,500	82	106	41
210,772,000	66,062,500	2,053	1,525	1,039
1,878,790,000	719,486,000	1,857	1,481	169
2,081,360,000	776,291,000	35,589	20,339	458
286,000,000	319,503,000	15,553	5,906	260
244,000,000	420,304,000	1,004,447	114,487	6,683
248,000,000	87,876,200	10,287	857	156
136,000,000	147,971,000	537,301	16,894	1,086
3,888,000,000[10]	1,880,110,000	57,312	29,074	2,080
4,126,000,000[10]	2,664,820,000	1,808,720	772,761	28,000
4,378,000	NA	35	26	*
3,426,000	3,305,990	926	336	*
127,000,000	65,249,100	7,848	NA	151
42,000,000	65,249,100	276,307	11,329	731
376,000,000	174,533,000	1,718	2,285	305
167,000,000	199,051,000	32,569	29,670	1,420
170,000,000	72,170,900	1,585	NA	*
181,000,000	72,170,900	35,049	4,444	*
331,000,000	151,118,000	5,264	2,200	173
306,000,000	156,667,000	154,830	56,914	1,295
6,631,000,000	27,732,700,000	242,029	93,159	33,971
2,909,000,000	27,732,700,000	11,026,175	1,613,229	408,704
NA	73,617,600	57	203	*
NA	86,358,000	1,556	2,017	*
115,000,000	883,875,000	4,144	7,423	725
82,500,000	879,437,000	127,986	175,488	8,900

447

Nation / Capital	Population	Type of Government	Heads of Government	Currency Value in U.S. Dollars	GNP (000,000)	GNP (per capita)
MOROCCO Rabat	17,310,000 367,600	Constitutional monarchy	King: Hassan II Prime Minister: Ahmed Osman	Dirham 0.22	$ 6,940	$ 430
MOZAMBIQUE Maputo	9,240,000 354,684	People's republic	President: Samora M. Machel	Escudo 0.032	3,590	420
NAURU Yaren	7,128 NA	Republic	President: Hammer DeRoburt	Australian dollar 1.02	NA	NA
NEPAL Kathmandu	12,570,000 150,402	Constitutional monarchy	King: Birendra Bir Bikram Shah Dev Prime Minister: Tulsi Giri	Rupee 0.08	1,310	110
NETHERLANDS Amsterdam	13,650,000 757,958	Constitutional monarchy	Queen: Juliana Prime Minister: Joop M. den Uyl	Guilder 0.39	66,060	4,880
NEW ZEALAND Wellington	3,090,000 141,100	Parliamentary state (C)	Governor-General: Sir Edward Denis Blundell Prime Minister: Robert D. Muldoon	Dollar 0.93	12,440	4,100
NICARAGUA Managua	2,160,000 313,400	Republic	President: Gen. Anastasio Somoza Debayle	Córdoba 0.14	1,310	650
NIGER, REPUBLIC OF Niamey	4,600,000 102,000	Republic	President, Supreme Military Council: Lt. Col. Seyni Kountché	CFA Franc 0.0041	470	100
NIGERIA, FEDERATION OF Lagos	62,930,000 900,969	Federal republic (C)	Head, Supreme Military Council: Lt. Gen. Olusegun Obasanjo	Naira 1.59	17,830	240
NORWAY Oslo	4,010,000 465,337	Constitutional monarchy	King: Olaf V Prime Minister: Odvar Nordli	Krone 0.19	21,070	5,280
OMAN Muscat	770,000 15,000	Sultanate	Sultan: Qabus bin Said	Rial 2.90	930	1,250
PAKISTAN Islamabad	70,260,000 77,000	Federal republic	President: Chaudhri Fazal Elahi Prime Minister: Zulfikar Ali Bhutto	Rupee 0.10	8,770	130
PANAMA Panamá	1,670,000 441,090	Republic	President: Demetrio Basilio Lakas Bahas Chief of Government: Gen. Omar Torrijos Herrera	Balboa 1.00	1,640	1,010
PAPUA NEW GUINEA Port Moresby	2,760,000 104,500	Parliamentary state (C)	Governor-General: Sir John Guise Prime Minister: Michael T. Somare	Kina 1.07	1,150	440
PARAGUAY Asunción	2,650,000 417,152	Republic	President: Gen. Alfredo Stroessner	Guaraní 0.0079	1,200	480
PERU Lima	15,870,000 2,862,197	Republic	President: Gen. Francisco Morales Bermúdez Prime Minister: Gen. Guillermo Arbulú Galliani	Sol 0.015	10,670	710
PHILIPPINES, REPUBLIC OF THE Manila	42,510,000 1,438,252	Republic	President and Prime Minister: Ferdinand E. Marcos	Peso 0.13	13,030	310

448

Imports Exports	Revenue Expenditure	Elementary Schools: Teachers Students	Secondary Schools: Teachers Students	Colleges and Universities:[1] Institutions Students
$ 2,560,000,000 1,542,000,000	$ 1,752,530,000 1,966,020,000	37,368[1] 1,506,500	20,226 433,358	1,737 25,525
462,000,000 297,000,000	456,242,000 452,085,000	10,800 605,000	2,000 45,000	200 2,300
20,833,300 35,714,200	37,895,600 36,275,400	88 1,440	33 475	* *
10,589,500 12,788,900	90,880,500 164,857,000	18,074 392,229	7,749 216,309	1,499 19,198
34,573,000,000 35,075,000,000	23,254,100,000 28,380,000,000	50,988 1,454,971	NA 1,387,571	NA 247,964
3,152,000,000 2,152,000,000	3,463,100,000 4,118,560,000	20,086 523,673	10,980 208,596	3,214 47,953
517,000,000 376,000,000	194,306,000 285,937,000	8,139 305,690	1,916 61,084	694 11,618
96,000,000 53,000,000	64,859,800 64,859,800	2,736 110,437	539 11,108	40 280
6,103,000,000 8,078,000,000	8,380,400,000 2,746,130,000	136,142 4,662,400	20,448 516,658	3,459 23,228
9,718,000,000 7,207,000,000	7,299,450,000 8,762,450,000	19,109 375,004	28,415 334,969	5,300 56,664
392,524,000 864,012,000	1,467,400,000 1,467,400,000	1,164 35,290	48 419	* *
2,125,000,000 1,005,000,000	1,780,990,000 3,103,330,000	117,000 4,657,000	91,908 1,767,357	3,790 107,757
867,000,000 272,000,000	271,400,000 392,600,000	10,731 328,460	5,803 123,404	999 24,204
516,000,000 476,000,000	465,809,000 453,349,000	7,545 236,024	1,906 38,676	313 2,823
186,000,000 187,000,000	128,831,000 146,059,000	14,506 451,530	6,499 66,746	1,529 12,212
1,531,000,000 1,514,000,000	1,378,880,000 1,741,880,000	74,013 2,865,334	39,024 911,866	11,426 159,339
3,375,000,000 2,241,000,000	2,310,280,000 2,986,530,000	255,561 7,784,150	56,019 1,910,625	32,651 678,343

449

Nation Capital	Population	Type of Government	Heads of Government	Currency Value in U.S. Dollars	GNP (000,000)	GNP (per capita)
POLAND Warsaw	34,020,000 1,436,100	People's republic	Chairman, Council of State: Henryk Jabłoński Chairman, Council of Ministers: Piotr Jaroszewicz	Złoty 0.30	$82,440	$2,450
PORTUGAL Lisbon	8,760,000 761,500	Socialist republic	President: Gen. António Ramalho Eanes Prime Minister: Mário Soares	Escudo 0.032	13,930	1,540
QATAR Doha	180,000 130,000	Constitutional emirate	Emir and Prime Minister: Sheikh Khalifa bin Hamad al-Thani	Riyal 0.25	1,110	5,830
RHODESIA Salisbury	6,310,000 555,000	Unilaterally declared republic	President: John J. Wrathall Prime Minister: Ian D. Smith	Dollar 1.60	2,930	480
RUMANIA Bucharest	21,250,000 1,565,872	Socialist republic	President: Nicolae Ceauşescu Chairman, Council of Ministers: Manea Manescu	Leu 0.083	18,227	910
RWANDA Kigali	4,200,000 60,000	Republic	Head of State and President, Council of Ministers: Maj. Gen. Juvénal Habyalimana	Franc 0.011	330	80
SAN MARINO San Marino	20,000 4,423	Republic	Co-Regents: Primo Bugli IV Virgilio Cardelli Secretary of State for Foreign and Political Affairs: Gian-Carlo Ghironzi	Italian lira Vatican City lira 0.0012	NA	NA
SÃO TOMÉ and **PRÍNCIPE** São Tomé	80,000 17,400	Republic	President: Manuel Pinto da Costa Premier: Miguel Trouvoada	Escudo 0.032	47	588
SAUDI ARABIA Riyadh	8,697,000 350,000	Monarchy	King and Prime Minister: Khalid ibn Abdul-Aziz	Riyal 0.28	16,690	2,080
SENEGAL, **REPUBLIC OF** Dakar	4,140,000 714,100	Republic	President: Léopold Sédar Senghor Premier: Abdou Diouf	CFA Franc 0.0041	1,310	320
SEYCHELLES Victoria	60,000 15,000	Republic (C)	President: James R. M. Mancham Prime Minister: F. Albert René	Rupee 0.15	NA	NA
SIERRA LEONE Freetown	2,710,000 274,000	Republic (C)	President: Siaka P. Stevens Prime Minister: Christian A. Kamara-Taylor	Leone 0.89	520	180
SINGAPORE, **REPUBLIC OF** Singapore	2,250,000 1,327,500	Republic (C)	President: Benjamin Henry Sheares Prime Minister: Lee Kuan Yew	Dollar 0.40	4,700	2,120
SOMALIA Mogadishu	3,170,000 230,000	Republic	President: Maj. Gen. Muhammad Siad Barre	Shilling 0.16	260	80
SOUTH AFRICA, **REPUBLIC OF** Cape Town Pretoria	25,470,000 691,296 543,950	Republic	President: Nicolaas Diederichs Prime Minister: Balthazar J. Vorster	Rand 1.15	29,210	1,200

Imports Exports	Revenue Expenditure	Elementary Schools: Teachers Students	Secondary Schools: Teachers Students	Colleges and Universities:[1] Institutions Students
$12,536,000,000	$21,686,700,000	199,600	35,500	45,000
10,283,000,000	21,500,000,000	4,447,500	992,300	521,900
3,840,000,000	2,828,000,000	48,352	22,748	3,676
1,939,000,000	4,140,000,000	1,191,477	377,405	58,605
270,838,000	1,392,340,000	1,024	625	*
2,304,020,000	489,308,000	20,237	7,368	*
541,000,000	677,757,000	21,983	4,370	202
652,000,000	756,797,000	863,877	82,814	1,355
5,144,000,000	48,853,100,000	139,790	31,766	15,690
4,874,000,000	48,853,100,000	2,889,946	707,767	187,889
58,000,000	35,062,400	7,777	834	109
35,000,000	40,553,600	398,000	10,500	1,019
NA	34,991,200	99	90	*
NA	34,991,200	1,692	1,115	*
9,568,840	6,338,440	303	116	*
12,484,100	6,326,660	10,015	2,370	*
3,473,000,000	27,675,200,000	26,592	10,295	1,454
31,088,000,000	12,885,300,000	570,697	148,753	14,882
559,000,000	427,769,000	6,294	3,118	NA
451,000,000	427,769,000	283,276	66,644	7,773
28,992,400	16,560,600	428	190	*
1,954,540	16,287,800	10,232	3,926	*
187,000,000	99,564,900	5,599	1,871	268
131,000,000	107,052,000	176,658	37,550	1,476
8,133,000,000	1,063,250,000	10,972	7,341	1,680
5,376,000,000	1,062,770,000	337,816	180,427	17,802
129,000,000	105,957,000	1,789	1,870	51
65,000,000	92,613,100	69,493	40,662	958
7,589,000,000	7,135,000,000	140,695[4]	[4]	15,663
5,315,000,000	8,011,310,000	5,427,682[4]	[4]	175,855

Nation Capital	Population	Type of Government	Heads of Government	Currency Value in U.S. Dollars	GNP (000,000)	GNP (per capita)
SPAIN Madrid	35,470,000 3,634,000	Monarchy	King: Juan Carlos I President, Council of Ministers: Adolfo Suárez González	Peseta 0.015	$68,650	$1,960
SUDAN, DEMOCRATIC REPUBLIC OF Khartoum	17,760,000 321,666	Republic	President: Maj. Gen. Gaafar Mohammed al-Nimeiry	Pound 2.87	2,560	150
SURINAM Paramaribo	420,000 151,500	Republic	President: Johann H. E. Ferrier Prime Minister: Henck A. E. Arron	Guilder 0.56	348	870
SWAZILAND Mbabane	490,000 20,800	Monarchy (C)	King: Sobhuza II Prime Minister: Col. Maphevu Dlamini	Lilangeni 1.15	190	400
SWEDEN Stockholm	8,200,000 671,226	Constitutional monarchy	King: Charles XVI Gustavus Prime Minister: Thorbjörn Fälldin	Krona 0.23	54,850	6,720
SWITZERLAND Bern	6,400,000 154,700	Federal republic	President: Rudolf Gnägi	Franc 0.41	43,110	6,650
SYRIA Damascus	7,350,000 836,668	Socialist republic	President: Gen. Hafez al-Assad Premier: Maj. Gen. Abdel Rahman Khlefawi	Pound 0.27	3,480	490
TAIWAN (FORMOSA) Taipei	16,171,569 2,046,878	Republic	President: Yen Chia-kan Premier: Chiang Ching-kuo	New Taiwan dollar 0.026	11,370	720
TANZANIA, UNITED REPUBLIC OF Dar es Salaam	15,160,000 396,700	Republic (C)	President: Julius K. Nyerere Prime Minister: Rashidi M. Kawawa	Shilling 0.12	2,060	140
THAILAND Bangkok	41,870,000 2,213,522	Limited monarchy	King: Bhumibol Adulyadej Prime Minister: Thanin Kraivichien	Baht 0.049	12,140	300
TOGO, REPUBLIC OF Lomé	2,220,000 214,200	Republic	President: Gen. Gnassingbe Eyadéma	CFA Franc 0.0041	460	210
TONGA Nuku'alofa	100,000 25,000	Constitutional monarchy (C)	King: Taufa'ahau Tupou IV Prime Minister: Prince Fatafehi Tu'ipelehake	Pa'anga 1.25	15	167
TRANSKEI Umtata	1,751,000 24,838	Republic	President: Chief Botha Sigcau Prime Minister: Chief Kaiser D. Matanzima	Rand 1.15	NA	NA
TRINIDAD and TOBAGO Port-of-Spain	1,070,000 65,400	Republic (C)	President: Sir Ellis E. I. Clarke Prime Minister: Eric E. Williams	Dollar 0.42	1,590	1,490
TUNISIA Tunis	5,770,000 468,997	Republic	President: Habib Bourguiba Premier: Hédi Nouira	Dinar 2.30	3,080	550
TURKEY Ankara	39,180,000 1,522,350	Republic	President: Fahri Korutürk Premier: Süleyman Demirel	Lira 0.062	26,800	690

Imports Exports	Revenue Expenditure	Elementary Schools: Teachers Students	Secondary Schools: Teachers Students	Colleges and Universities:[1] Institutions Students
$16,097,000,000	$10,941,900,000	196,216	76,617	27,909
7,691,000,000	10,941,900,000	5,774,929	1,290,972	406,398
887,000,000	968,696,000	28,129	9,766	1,351
443,000,000	874,497,000	1,082,601	230,699	20,054
218,487,000	198,211,000	5,271	475	NA
235,294,000	226,327,000	136,363	4,680	2,138
115,429,000	41,865,300	2,220	NA	NA
175,498,000	35,607,800	86,110	15,147	269
17,874,000,000	19,574,700,000	39,833	55,826	NA
17,439,000,000	21,792,200,000	671,651	528,765	131,614
13,305,000,000	4,926,790,000	22,500	NA	5,075
12,957,000,000	5,101,640,000	561,645	499,457	60,329
1,669,000,000	1,564,320,000	30,850	21,712	NA
930,000,000	2,822,160,000	1,133,515	431,013	53,369
6,966,000,000	2,876,440,000	61,560	56,386	13,292
5,639,000,000	2,269,650,000	2,390,645	1,426,077	281,983
714,000,000[9]	508,314,000[11]	23,580	2,518	353
349,000,000[9]	801,063,000[11]	1,126,165	52,305	2,683
3,143,000,000	2,356,270,000	212,114	42,336	NA
2,485,000,000	2,911,020,000	6,385,468	907,111	72,030
109,000,000	136,062,000	5,627	1,335	156
189,000,000	136,062,000	329,443	48,415	1,471
17,640,200	6,242,600	641	510	*
6,807,460	6,845,750	16,688	10,552	*
NA	NA	10,000[4]	[4]	*
NA	102,353,000	518,928[4]	[4]	*
1,470,000,000	511,308,000	6,408	1,343	420
1,754,000,000	546,160,000	227,580	28,457	2,600
1,422,000,000	608,374,000	22,225	9,364	1,019
855,000,000	608,374,000	910,532	196,647	13,723
4,640,000,000	9,222,440,000	156,476	57,199	11,773
1,401,000,000	10,001,300,000	5,324,707	1,516,880	185,285

Nation Capital	Population	Type of Government	Heads of Government	Currency Value in U.S. Dollars	GNP (000,000)	GNP (per capita)
UGANDA............. Kampala	11,550,000.... 330,700	.Republic...... (C)	.President:...................... Field Marshal Idi Amin	.Shilling......... 0.12	$ 1,780....	$ 160
UNION OF ARAB .... **EMIRATES** Abu Dhabi	220,000.... 60,000	.Federal....... state	.President:...................... Sheikh Zaid bin Sultan al-Nahayan Prime Minister: Sheikh Maktum bin Rashid al-Maktum	.Dirham 0.25	4,590....	13,500
UNION OF SOVIET ...... **SOCIALIST REPUBLICS** Moscow	254,380,000.... 7,635,000	.Federal....... socialist republic	.Presidium Chairman:............ Nikolai V. Podgorny Chairman, Council of Ministers: Aleksei N. Kosygin	.Ruble 1.33	580,750....	2,300
UNITED STATES .... Washington, D.C.	213,610,000.... 734,000	.Federal....... republic	.President:...................... Gerald R. Ford	.Dollar .... 1,406,610....		6,640
UPPER VOLTA, ... **REPUBLIC OF** Ouagadougou	6,030,000.... 130,000	.Republic......	.President and Premier:.......... Gen. Sangoulé Lamizana	.CFA Franc...... 0.0041	470....	80
URUGUAY .... Montevideo	3,060,000.... 1,229,748	.Republic......	.President:...................... Aparicio Méndez	.Peso........... 0.31	3,210....	1,060
VENEZUELA .... Caracas	11,990,000.... 1,035,499	.Federal....... republic	.President:...................... Carlos Andrés Pérez	.Bolivar........ 0.23	19,830....	1,710
VIETNAM, SOCIALIST ... **REPUBLIC OF** Hanoi	43,450,000.... 1,378,335	.Socialist..... republic	.President:...................... Ton Duc Thang Premier: Pham Van Dong	.Dong.......... NA	6,440....	146
WESTERN SAMOA ...... Apia	150,000.... 30,300	.Constitutional monarchy (C)	.Head of State:................. Malietoa Tanumafili II Prime Minister: Tupuola Taisi Efi	.Tala.......... 1.22	40....	280
YEMEN ARAB .... **REPUBLIC** San'a	6,670,000.... 134,600	.Republic......	.Chairman, Military Command...... Council: Col. Ibrahim Mohammed al-Hamadi Prime Minister: Abdul-Aziz Abdul-Ghani	.Rial 0.22	740....	120
YEMEN, PEOPLE'S ...... **DEMOCRATIC REPUBLIC OF** Aden	1,690,000.... 264,326	.People's...... republic	.Chairman, Presidential Council: ... Salem Rubayi Ali Prime Minister: Ali Nasser Mohammed Hasani	.Dinar.......... 2.90	200....	120
YUGOSLAVIA .... Belgrade	21,350,000.... 746,105	.Federal....... socialist republic	.President:...................... Marshal Tito President, Federal Executive Council: Džemal Bijedić	.Dinar.......... 0.055	25,430....	1,200
ZAIRE, REPUBLIC OF ... Kinshasa	24,900,000.... 2,008,352	.Republic......	.President:...................... Gen. Mobutu Sese Seko	.Zaire.......... 1.14	3,650....	150
ZAMBIA............... Lusaka	4,900,000.... 415,000	.Republic...... (C)	.President:...................... Kenneth D. Kaunda Prime Minister: Elijah H. K. Mudenda	.Kwacha 1.55	2,310....	480

Imports / Exports	Revenue / Expenditure	Elementary Schools: Teachers / Students	Secondary Schools: Teachers / Students	Colleges and Universities:[1] Institutions / Students
$ 133,000,000[9]	$ 192,148,000	24,032	2,842	470
263,000,000[9]	318,083,000	786,227	60,129	4,018
1,760,000,000	424,943,000	1,225	1,112	*
7,305,000,000	424,943,000	32,022	21,695	*
36,969,000,000	296,684,000,000	2,417,000[4]	[4]	302,000
33,310,000,000	296,419,000,000	38,375,000	10,004,200	4,671,000
102,984,000,000	297,520,000,000	1,276,000	1,086,000	10,577,000
106,157,000,000	349,372,000,000	31,100,000	15,400,000	8,800,000
114,000,000	49,813,000	2,775	615	40
36,000,000	49,813,000	124,966	14,416	436
487,000,000	363,686,000	13,908	NA	2,315
382,000,000	488,153,000	356,514	193,958	26,280
5,359,000,000	9,472,420,000	58,457	30,913	11,228
10,214,000,000	7,389,950,000	1,924,040	584,211	161,054
NA	NA	NA	NA	NA
NA	NA	10,584,311[12]	[12]	[12]
36,000,000	13,191,800	NA	NA	30
7,000,000	15,335,500	30,388	10,914	129
190,000,000	83,169,300	4,053	594	42
13,000,000	118,316,000	154,607	10,886	950
187,000,000	44,415,100	6,355	1,480	75
203,000,000	65,813,500	183,744	31,216	383
7,697,000,000	3,707,250,000	126,327	21,801	19,197
4,061,000,000	3,659,880,000	2,869,344	728,608	359,651
780,000,000	1,077,240,000	80,481	NA	1,442
1,359,000,000	1,090,810,000	3,292,020	320,404	16,053
783,000,000	1,000,930,000	16,920	3,280	NA
1,401,000,000	1,174,040,000	809,796	68,551	3,958

1. Figure is for public schools only.
2. Excluding petroleum.
3. Including Luxembourg.
4. Only one figure, for combined elementary and secondary education, is available.
5. Excluding trade with other members of the Customs and Economic Union of Central Africa (Central African Republic, Republic of Congo, Gabon, Cameroon).
6. Excluding teachers in Turkish-Cypriot schools.
7. Figure is for ten-year polytechnical high schools.
8. Including preschool teachers.
9. Excluding trade with other members of the East African Community (Kenya, Tanzania, Uganda).
10. Including trade among the States of Malaysia.
11. Excluding Zanzibar.
12. Only one figure, for students at all levels, is available.

State Capital	Population	Per Capita Personal income	Governor Lieutenant-Governor	Revenue Expenditure	Roads (Miles)	Railways (Miles)
ALABAMA Montgomery	3,665,000 133,386	$4,643	George C. Wallace (D) Jere L. Beasley (D)	$ 2,089,570,000 2,049,795,000	86,415	4,543
ALASKA Juneau	382,000 6,050	9,448	Jay S. Hammond (R) Lowell Thomas, Jr. (R)	622,301,000 797,754,000	9,848	547
ARIZONA Phoenix	2,270,000 581,562	5,355	Raul H. Castro (D) *	1,419,017,000 1,459,718,000	52,105	2,034
ARKANSAS Little Rock	2,109,000 132,483	4,620	David H. Pryor (D) Joe Purcell (D)	1,138,889,000 1,135,590,000	78,110	3,559
CALIFORNIA Sacramento	21,520,000 254,413	6,593	Edmund G. Brown, Jr. (D) Mervyn M. Dymally (D)	15,562,855,000 15,271,687,000	169,616	7,317
COLORADO Denver	2,583,000 514,678	5,985	Richard D. Lamm (D) George L. Brown (D)	1,650,599,000 1,616,188,000	84,324	3,457
CONNECTICUT Hartford	3,117,000 158,017	6,973	Ella T. Grasso (D) Robert K. Killian (D)	1,747,292,000 1,930,237,000	18,853	656
DELAWARE Dover	582,000 17,488	6,748	Sherman W. Tribbitt (D) Eugene D. Bookhammer (R)	522,360,000 514,979,000	5,160	291
DISTRICT OF COLUMBIA *	702,000 *	7,742	Mayor: Walter E. Washington (D)	* *	1,102	30
FLORIDA Tallahassee	8,421,000 71,897	5,638	Reubin O'D. Askew (D) J. H. Williams II (D)	4,253,460,000 4,528,405,000	98,091	4,107
GEORGIA Atlanta	4,970,000 496,973	5,086	George D. Busbee (D) Zell Miller (D)	2,706,370,000 2,764,481,000	100,589	5,408
HAWAII Honolulu	887,000 324,871	6,658	George R. Ariyoshi (D) Nelson K. Doi (D)	982,344,000 1,082,473,000	3,681	0
IDAHO Boise	831,000 74,990	5,159	Cecil D. Andrus (D) John V. Evans (D)	527,557,000 536,390,000	56,514	2,633
ILLINOIS Springfield	11,229,000 91,753	6,789	Dan Walker (D) Neil F. Hartigan (D)	6,788,895,000 7,119,197,000	131,130	10,572
INDIANA Indianapolis	5,302,000 744,624	5,653	Otis R. Bowen (R) Robert D. Orr (R)	2,901,780,000 2,706,998,000	91,406	6,374
IOWA Des Moines	2,870,000 200,587	6,077	Robert D. Ray (R) Arthur A. Neu (R)	1,765,907,000 1,770,611,000	112,832	7,587
KANSAS Topeka	2,310,000 125,011	6,023	Robert F. Bennett (R) Shelby Smith (R)	1,278,662,000 1,228,422,000	134,724	7,616

THE STATES AND OUTLYING AREAS OF THE UNITED STATES

Radio Stations	Television Stations	Daily Newspapers	Public Elementary Schools: Teachers Students	Public Secondary Schools: Teachers Students	Colleges & Universities: Institutions Students
196	17	24	17,240 384,947	18,140 374,399	56 146,653
21	7	7	2,011 51,094	2,079 38,201	9 13,831
73	11	14	15,287 349,831	6,432 143,164	22 139,631
134	8	34	10,406 242,794	10,272 213,909	29 61,977
388	53	122	113,500 2,653,818	74,000 1,765,753	247 1,404,866
99	11	27	12,865 302,216	13,335 266,912	39 130,275
59	5	28	19,793 403,494	15,681 248,955	46 145,053
16	0	3	2,677 64,512	3,672 62,964	10 29,956
14	6	2	3,982 72,019	2,960 57,950	18 83,704
290	27	51	36,908 793,708	35,082 757,665	74 295,703
250	18	37	30,584 653,771	20,127 436,521	66 165,595
29	10	4	4,900 93,342	3,624 83,088	12 37,677
53	6	16	3,998 99,922	4,566 96,694	9 35,347
241	24	88	63,423 1,538,579	47,845 731,313	147 481,260
170	17	80	25,700 653,891	26,584 572,317	64 198,964
128	13	42	16,150 322,297	16,353 289,814	63 106,458
92	12	52	12,892 246,328	12,681 201,736	52 115,266

State Capital	Population	Per Capita Personal Income	Governor Lieutenant-Governor	Revenue Expenditure	Roads (Miles)	Railways (Miles)
KENTUCKY	3,428,000	$ 4,871	Julian M. Carroll (D)	$ 2,184,711,000	69,933	3,516
Frankfort	21,356		Thelma L. Stovall (D)	2,032,510,000		
LOUISIANA	3,841,000	4,904	Edwin W. Edwards (D)	2,609,465,000	54,260	3,683
Baton Rouge	165,963		James E. Fitzmorris, Jr. (D)	2,585,136,000		
MAINE	1,070,000	4,786	James B. Longley (Ind.)	701,636,000	21,544	1,665
Augusta	21,945		*	736,675,000		
MARYLAND	4,144,000	6,474	Marvin Mandel (D)	2,778,211,000	27,428	1,091
Annapolis	29,592		Blair Lee III (D)	3,136,475,000		
MASSACHUSETTS	5,809,000	6,114	Michael S. Dukakis (D)	3,724,025,000	31,369	1,405
Boston	641,071		Thomas P. O'Neill III (D)	4,360,815,000		
MICHIGAN	9,104,000	6,173	William G. Milliken (R)	5,973,800,000	118,591	5,963
Lansing	131,546		James J. Damman (R)	6,499,624,000		
MINNESOTA	3,965,000	5,807	Wendell R. Anderson (D)	3,214,365,000	128,334	7,366
St. Paul	309,980		Rudy Perpich (DFL)	2,922,116,000		
MISSISSIPPI	2,354,000	4,052	Charles C. Finch (D)	1,435,692,000	66,950	3,644
Jackson	153,968		Evelyn Gandy (D)	1,433,630,000		
MISSOURI	4,778,000	5,510	Christopher S. Bond (R)	2,158,568,000	116,724	6,062
Jefferson City	32,407		William C. Phelps (R)	2,219,820,000		
MONTANA	753,000	5,422	Thomas L. Judge (D)	505,749,000	78,205	4,898
Helena	22,730		Bill Christiansen (D)	476,517,000		
NEBRASKA	1,553,000	6,087	J. James Exon (D)	790,594,000	97,798	5,415
Lincoln	149,518		Gerald T. Whelan (D)	818,798,000		
NEVADA	610,000	6,647	Mike O'Callaghan (D)	434,321,000	49,655	1,573
Carson City	15,468		Robert E. Rose (D)	411,571,000		
NEW HAMPSHIRE	822,000	5,315	Meldrim Thomson, Jr. (R)	368,869,000	15,156	752
Concord	30,022		*	433,954,000		
NEW JERSEY	7,336,000	6,722	Brendan T. Byrne (D)	3,854,833,000	32,704	1,687
Trenton	104,638		*	4,325,766,000		
NEW MEXICO	1,168,000	4,775	Jerry Apodaca (D)	1,004,947,000	70,198	2,057
Santa Fe	41,167		Robert E. Ferguson (D)	857,584,000		
NEW YORK	18,083,000	6,564	Hugh L. Carey (D)	14,857,537,000	107,743	5,310
Albany	115,781		Mary Anne Krupsak (D)	15,704,675,000		
NORTH CAROLINA	5,469,000	4,952	James E. Holshouser, Jr. (R)	3,247,883,000	88,624	4,115
Raleigh	121,577		James B. Hunt, Jr. (D)	3,226,479,000		
NORTH DAKOTA	643,000	5,737	Arthur A. Link (D)	551,255,000	105,934	5,070
Bismarck	34,703		Wayne G. Sanstead (D)	464,387,000		
OHIO	10,690,000	5,810	James A. Rhodes (R)	5,111,134,000	110,247	7,727
Columbus	539,677		Richard F. Celeste (D)	5,449,408,000		
OKLAHOMA	2,766,000	5,250	David L. Boren (D)	1,657,683,000	108,465	4,944
Oklahoma City	366,481		George Nigh (D)	1,536,607,000		
OREGON	2,329,000	5,769	Robert W. Straub (D)	1,534,872,000	103,884	3,043
Salem	68,296		*	1,499,491,000		
PENNSYLVANIA	11,862,000	5,943	Milton J. Shapp (D)	7,236,912,000	114,868	8,020
Harrisburg	68,061		Ernest P. Kline (D)	7,933,758,000		
RHODE ISLAND	927,000	5,841	Philip W. Noel (D)	644,446,000	5,475	139
Providence	179,213		J. Joseph Garrahy (D)	656,013,000		
SOUTH CAROLINA	2,848,000	4,618	James B. Edwards (R)	1,704,761,000	60,631	3,034
Columbia	113,542		W. Brantley Harvey, Jr. (D)	1,854,946,000		

Radio Stations	Television Stations	Daily Newspapers	Public Elementary Schools: Teachers Students	Public Secondary Schools: Teachers Students	Colleges & Universities: Institutions Students
186	12	27	19,400 429,258	11,850 262,354	38 113,629
137	17	26	22,600 592,479	18,355 254,723	30 148,355
54	7	9	7,141 172,350	4,673 78,581	25 37,516
84	7	13	22,039 459,731	22,034 421,196	52 175,622
102	10	46	29,200 813,410	31,750 385,000	119 356,362
216	21	54	48,500 1,090,003	43,000 983,285	93 414,450
142	11	31	21,060 426,779	25,150 453,165	66 176,011
155	11	23	13,100 285,865	10,480 226,542	45 87,743
165	23	57	24,623 514,997	23,860 450,363	81 205,929
54	12	11	4,945 114,646	3,700 57,142	12 29,812
69	15	19	9,400 167,440	8,800 148,229	30 66,040
32	7	9	2,978 72,839	2,752 66,906	6 20,916
42	4	9	4,565 103,392	3,870 71,205	24 37,190
64	4	29	48,000 924,000	31,300 534,000	64 264,655
76	8	20	6,582 133,681	6,191 140,931	17 50,542
274	29	77	88,900 1,753,293	100,800 1,647,921	285 990,196
281	18	52	33,973 817,537	17,500 367,459	114 187,155
35	12	10	4,785 59,829	2,925 71,502	15 26,641
241	27	95	54,745 1,365,523	50,790 927,124	129 367,776
106	9	53	15,360 320,077	13,800 274,730	44 131,558
104	13	22	11,671 274,099	10,433 203,460	43 112,148
291	23	105	52,900 1,128,946	60,400 1,117,272	175 429,628
22	2	7	5,277 101,491	4,052 74,826	13 61,716
151	12	19	16,291 382,693	10,889 247,036	55 121,265

State Capital	Population	Per Capita Personal Income	Governor Lieutenant-Governor	Revenue Expenditure	Roads (Miles)	Railways (Miles)
SOUTH DAKOTA Pierre	686,000 9,699	$ 4,924	Richard F. Kneip (D) Harvey Wollman (D)	$ 398,414,000 406,779,000	82,532	3,351
TENNESSEE Nashville	4,214,000 448,003	4,895	Ray Blanton (D) John S. Wilder (D)	2,037,298,000 2,187,759,000	81,042	3,184
TEXAS Austin	12,488,000 251,808	5,631	Dolph Briscoe (D) William P. Hobby (D)	6,250,160,000 5,754,523,000	253,795	13,306
UTAH Salt Lake City	1,228,000 175,885	4,923	Calvin L. Rampton (D) Clyde L. Miller (D)	786,663,000 809,336,000	48,387	1,726
VERMONT Montpelier	476,000 8,609	4,960	Thomas P. Salmon (D) Brian D. Burns (D)	397,929,000 411,128,000	13,836	716
VIRGINIA Richmond	5,032,000 249,621	5,785	Mills E. Godwin, Jr. (R) John N. Dalton (R)	2,917,520,000 3,040,962,000	62,423	3,875
WASHINGTON Olympia	3,612,000 23,111	6,247	Daniel J. Evans (R) John A. Cherberg (D)	2,631,677,000 2,665,762,000	81,530	4,767
WEST VIRGINIA Charleston	1,821,000 71,505	4,918	Arch A. Moore, Jr. (R) *	1,300,647,000 1,230,731,000	36,465	3,494
WISCONSIN Madison	4,609,000 173,258	5,669	Patrick J. Lucey (D) Martin J. Schreiber (D)	3,310,232,000 3,406,685,000	104,720	5,808
WYOMING Cheyenne	390,000 40,914	6,131	Ed Herschler (D) *	336,743,000 300,645,000	31,857	1,779

OUTLYING AREAS OF THE U.S.

Area Capital	Population	Status	Governor Lieutenant-Governor	Revenue Expenditure	Roads (Miles)	Railways (Miles)
AMERICAN SAMOA Pago Pago	30,000 2,451	Unorganized, unincorporated territory	Acting Governor: Frank Barnett	$ 33,921,000 33,921,000	71	0
GUAM Agaña	100,000 2,119	Unincorporated territory	Ricardo J. Bordallo Rudolph G. Sablan	112,630,000 99,070,000	230	0
PANAMA CANAL ZONE Balboa Heights (headquarters)	46,000 232	Army-administered territory	Maj. Gen. David S. Parker Col. Charles I. McGinnis	69,431,000 67,928,000	144	48
PUERTO RICO San Juan	3,090,000 452,749	Commonwealth	Rafael Hernández-Colón	2,148,986,085 2,099,775,108	10,456	60
TRUST TERRITORY OF THE PACIFIC ISLANDS Tanapag (administrative center)	120,000 654	U.N. trust territory	Acting High Commissioner: Peter T. Coleman	79,605,496 62,812,448	NA	0
VIRGIN ISLANDS Charlotte Amalie	65,000 12,220	Unincorporated territory	Cyril E. King Juan Luis	126,212,500 126,212,500	510	0

Radio Stations	Television Stations	Daily Newspapers	Public Elementary Schools: Teachers Students	Public Secondary Schools: Teachers Students	Colleges & Universities: Institutions Students
44	.10	13	5,375 99,844	3,013 51,373	17 29,359
220	.17	34	24,004 537,793	15,274 339,133	67 169,050
424	.57	.114	71,996 1,517,060	63,973 1,295,828	145 550,002
44	3	5	6,350 163,453	6,165 146,255	14 74,295
24	2	8	3,100 63,090	3,259 41,784	23 27,977
192	.15	33	32,400 665,606	24,150 438,063	73 220,231
133	.15	22	18,740 398,825	14,770 386,624	47 173,165
87	9	29	10,563 229,919	8,644 174,200	28 70,378
182	.18	35	26,720 541,563	23,540 422,656	58 179,444
32	3	9	2,200 44,140	2,360 44,044	8 15,539

Radio Stations	Television Stations	Daily Newspapers	Public Elementary & Secondary School Teachers	Public School Students: Elementary Secondary	Higher Education: Institutions Students
1	1	.1	342	8,022 2,097	1 689
2	1	.1	1,229	17,009 11,582	1 3,363
1	1	.0	406	5,964 4,923	1 1,590
79	.10	3	.25,796	.466,737 230,422	24 91,135
8	1	.0	1,946	30,746 7,748	1 31
5	3	.4	1,408	15,844 8,668	1 1,985

The material in the table has been prepared with the kind assistance of Statistics Canada. It should be noted that all dollar figures are in Canadian dollars. The figures for schools include elementary and secondary schools; the institutions above the secondary school level include professional and technical schools, colleges, and universities.

Province Capital	Population	Per Capita Personal Income	Premier Lieutenant-Governor	Revenue Expenditure
ALBERTA	1,826,000	$6,064	Peter Lougheed	$3,494,100,000
Edmonton	542,845		Ralph Steinhauer	2,929,300,000
BRITISH COLUMBIA	2,491,000	6,272	William Bennett	3,550,200,000
Victoria	212,466		Walter S. Owen	3,502,500,000
MANITOBA	1,028,000	5,635	Edward R. Schreyer	1,271,400,000
Winnipeg	570,725		Francis L. Jobin	1,358,300,000
NEW BRUNSWICK	688,000	4,498	Richard B. Hatfield	886,600,000
Fredericton	44,572		Hédard J. Robichaud	957,000,000
NEWFOUNDLAND	557,000	4,027	Frank Moores	805,000,000
St. John's	140,883		Gordon A. Winter	928,400,000
NORTHWEST TERRITORIES	38,000	5,678[1]	Commissioner:	158,200,000
Yellowknife	8,195		Stuart Hodgson	158,900,000
NOVA SCOTIA	832,000	4,625	Gerald A. Regan	974,100,000
Halifax	261,366		Clarence L. Gosse	1,006,400,000
ONTARIO	8,331,000	6,431	William G. Davis	9,801,900,000
Toronto	2,753,112		Pauline E. McGibbon	11,084,000,000
PRINCE EDWARD ISLAND	120,000	4,008	Alexander B. Campbell	194,500,000
Charlottetown	19,133		Gordon L. Bennett	198,700,000
QUÉBEC	6,243,000	5,312	René Lévesque	9,220,800,000
Québec	543,193		Hugues Lapointe	9,261,700,000
SASKATCHEWAN	935,000	5,971	Allan Blakeney	1,254,200,000
Regina	148,965		George Porteous	1,265,600,000
YUKON TERRITORY	21,000	5,678[1]	Commissioner:	57,000,000
Whitehorse	13,045		James Smith	64,300,000

1. Figure is combined average for Northwest Territories and Yukon Territory.

THE PROVINCES AND TERRITORIES OF CANADA

Roads (Miles)	Railways (Miles)	Radio Stations	Television Stations	Daily Newspapers	Schools: Teachers Enrollment	Post-secondary: Institutions Enrollment
94,957	6,227	38	12	7	24,219 448,801	24 47,223
38,204	4,787	64	9	19	27,765 566,236	24 48,815
47,175	4,744	24	6	8	12,514 242,729	13 21,705
13,967	1,665	18	4	6	7,970 166,114	12 12,455
6,945	944	26	7	3	7,674 158,240	7 8,154
991	129	13	0	0	685 12,484	0 0
16,939	1,247	27	5	6	11,006 205,072	24 20,782
98,595	9,847	136	27	51	95,983 2,058,371	54 220,160
3,392	254	4	1	3	1,483 27,911	3 2,175
66,115	5,409	96	22	14	77,120 1,486,288	84 193,974
128,626	8,561	25	8	4	11,283 228,218	9 16,824
2,412	58	2	1	0	285 4,975	0 0

KEY TO
SIGNED ARTICLES

The following is a partial list of contributors to this Yearbook. The initials at the end of an article are those of the author, or authors, of the article.

A.A.A., AMADIO ANTONIO ARBOLEDA, B.S., M.S.
Publishing Consultant, University of Tokyo Press and United Nations University. Coeditor of *Scholarly Publishing in Asia* and other books.

A.K.M., ALICE KERR MOORHEAD, B.A., M.B.A.
Assistant editor, *Business Latin America.*

A.K.R., ALEXANDER KEENE RATENSKY, B.A., M.ARCH.
Assistant Professor of Architecture, City College of New York.

A.M., ALAN McGOWAN, B.E.
President, Scientists' Institute for Public Information.

A.R., AGAPITO REY, B.S., M.A., PH.D.
Former Professor of Spanish, University of Arizona. Coauthor of *The Rediscovery of New Mexico* and other books.

A.S., ANDREW SOLTIS, B.A.
Chess Columnist, New York *Post.* Second Vice-President, Marshall Chess Club. International chess master, 1974. U.S. Intercollegiate chess champion, 1969. Author of *The Best Games of Boris Spassky* and other books.

B.K.C., BRENNA KATZ CLARKE, B.S., M.S., PH.D.
Lecturer in English Literature and Drama, St. Patrick's College, Dublin.

B.M.P., B. M. PARKER, B.A., M.A., PH.D.
Instructor of English, John Abbott College, Québec.

B.Q., BENJAMIN QUARLES, B.A., M.A., PH.D.
Lecturer in History, Morgan State University. Author of *Black Abolitionists* and other books.

B.R., BEA RIEMSCHNEIDER, B.A.
Assistant Editor, *Archaeology.*

B.W., BRENTON WELLING, B.A.
Associate Editor, *Business Week.*

C.B., CATHARINE BROWNE, B.S.
Former Writer, European Community Information Service, Washington, D.C.

C.C., CARLOTTA CONNELLY, A.B., M.A.
Former Teacher, Bureau of Indian Affairs, Hopi Reservation.

C.H., CHARLES HAGEN, A.B., M.F.A.
Managing Editor, *Afterimage.*

C.O.P., C. OTIS PORT
Engineering Editor, *Modern Plastics.*

C.P., CARL PROUJAN, B.S.
Editorial Director, Science Department, Scholastic Magazines, Inc. Author of *Secrets of the Sea.*

D.C., DANIEL CHU, B.A.
Associate Editor, *People.*

D.G.B., DALE G. BURRIER, E.E.
Managing Editor, *Industrial Research.* President, Valpo Tech Alumni Association.

D.G.S., DUNCAN G. STECK, B.S.
Account Executive, Anna M. Rosenberg Associates, public relations firm.

D.J.H., DONALD J. HARVEY, B.A., M.A., PH.D.
Professor of History at Hunter College, City University of New York. Consultant, Rockefeller Foundation Humanities Fellowships. Author of *France Since the Revolution.*

D.L.N., DOROTHY L. NORTMAN, M.A.
Staff Associate, Demographic Division, The Population Council, New York. Author of publications on family planning.

D.M., DERWENT MAY, M.A.
Literary Editor, *The Listener.* Author of *Dear Parson* and *The Professionals.*

D.Mac., DONNARAE MacCANN, B.A., M.L.S.
Freelance Consultant and Writer. Coauthor of *The Black American in Books for Children* and *The Child's First Books.*

D.P., DON PERETZ, B.A., M.A., PH.D.
Professor of Political Science and Director of the Southwest Asia-North Africa Program, State University of New York at Binghamton. Author of *Middle East Reader* and other books and articles.

D.R.B., DOROTHY R. BRODIN, B.A., M.A., PH.D.
Professor, Herbert H. Lehman College, City University of New York. Author of *Marcel Aymé* and other books.

D.T.A., DENNIS T. AVERY, B.A., M.S.
Special Assistant, Commodity Futures Trading Commission.

E.A.C., EDWIN A. COOK, B.A., PH.D.
Associate Professor of Anthropology, Southern Illinois University. Editor, *American Anthropologist.*

E.S.K., ELAINE STUART KNAPP, B.A.
Editor, *State Government News, State Headlines.*

F.C., FRANCES CERRA, B.S., M.S.
Consumer Reporter, New York *Times.*

F.C.D. III, FREDERICK C. DURANT III
Assistant Director for Astronautics, National Air and Space Museum, Smithsonian Institution.

F.C.H., FRED C. HESS, A.B., M.A., ED.D.
Professor of Physical Science, State University of New York Maritime College, and Former Science Editor, WPIX–TV, New York.

F.D., FREDERICK DRIMMER, B.A., M.A.
Former Faculty Member, College of the City of New York. Author of *Very Special People* and other books.

F.L., FRANK LITSKY, B.S.
Assistant Sports Editor, New York *Times,* and President, Track Writers Association.

F.L.K., FRANK L. KENNEY, B.S.
Public Information Specialist, Fish and Wildlife Service, U.S. Department of the Interior.

F.U.J., FREYA U. JESCHKE
Librarian, Goethe House, New York City.

F.W., FAY WILLEY, A.B., A.M.
Associate Editor, International Department, *Newsweek.*

G.H., GEOFFREY HORN, B.A., M.A.
Supervising Editor, Funk & Wagnalls Yearbook. Freelance writer and editor.

H.K., HERBERT KUPFERBERG, B.A., M.A., M.S.
Senior Editor, *Parade,* and Music Critic, *National Observer.* Author of *The Mendelssohns* and other books.

H.T.H., HENRY T. HOPKINS, B.A.E., M.A.E.
Director, San Francisco Museum of Modern Art.

I.K., I. KEPARS, B.A., A.L.A.A.
Chief Reference Librarian, Australian Reference, National Library of Australia. Editor, *Australian Books.*

I.S., IVAN SANDERS, B.A., M.A., PH.D.
Assistant Professor of English, Suffolk County Community College.

J.A.B., JEAN A. BORGER, B.A.
Manager of Officer Services, Bureau of Public Information, American Dental Association.

J.B., JOHN BEAUFORT
New York Drama Critic, *The Christian Science Monitor.*

J.deS., JORGE DE SENA, M.SC., *Livre-Docente,* PH.D.
Professor of Portuguese and Comparative Literature, Chairman of the Department of Spanish and Portuguese, and Chairman of the Comparative Literature Program, University of California at Santa Barbara.

J.F.M., JOSEPH F. MANGAN, B.B.A.
Assistant Professor, The College of Insurance. Consulting editor, Werbel Publishing Co.

J.G., JOHN GRIBBIN, D.SC., M.SC., PH.D.
Visiting Fellow, Science Policy Research Unit, University of Sussex.

J.Gr., JOHN GRAHAM, B.A.
Editor, *Rubber Age.*

J.N., JOHN NORMAN, B.A., M.A., PH.D.
Professor of History and Government, Pace University. State Factfinder, Connecticut Board of Mediation and Arbitration.

J.T.S., JAMES T. SABIN, B.S., M.A., PH.D.
Vice-President, Editorial, Greenwood Press.

J.V.O'G., JAMES V. O'GARA, JR., B.S., M.A.
Editor-at-Large, *Advertising Age.*

J.W.R., JAMES WILLIS ROBB, A.B., A.M., PH.D.
Professor of Romance Languages, George Washington University. Author of *El Estilo de Alfonso Reyes.*

K.B.H., KENNETH B. HIGBIE, B.S.
Chief, Division of Solid Wastes, Bureau of Mines, U.S. Department of the Interior.

K.E., KATHERINE ELLIOTT, M.R.C.S. (Eng.), L.R.C.P. (London).
Assistant Director, The Ciba Foundation. Chairman, Health Panel of the Intermediate Technology Development Group.

L.A.S., LESTER A. SOBEL, B.B.A.
Editor, Vice-President, Facts On File, Inc. Author of *Russia's Rulers: The Khrushchev Period* and other books.

L.F., LUCILLE FOY, B.A.
Director of Public Relations and Advertising, Minkus Stamp & Publishing Co.

L.H., LOUIS HALASZ, J.D.
United Nations Correspondent, International Feature Service. Lecturer on International Affairs.

L.S., LOUIS SNYDER, B.A.
Press Representative, Opera Company of Boston. Former Music Critic, *The Christian Science Monitor.*

M.H., MARION HENDELSON
Merchandising and Fashion Consultant, Claire M. Lang Associates. Former Lecturer, Merchandising, Laboratory Institute of Merchandising.

M.J.C., MICHAEL J. CUSACK
Editor, *Science World,* Scholastic Magazines, Inc.

M.R.B., MILTON R. BENJAMIN, B.A.
General Editor, *Newsweek.*

M.T., MURRAY TUROFF, B.A., PH.D.
Director, Computerized Conferencing and Communications Center, New Jersey Institute of Technology. Associate Professor of Computer and Information Sciences.

M.W.B., MYRNA WEINER BRESKIN, B.A.
Editing Manager, McGraw-Hill.

N.A., NORMAN ACTON, B.S.
Secretary-General, Rehabilitation International. Chairman, Council of World Organizations Interested in the Handicapped. Editor, *International Rehabilitation Review.*

N.H., NEIL HICKEY, B.A.
New York Bureau Chief, *TV Guide.*

N.P., NEAL PRONEK, B.B.A.
Managing Editor, T.F.H. Publications, Inc., and *Tropical Fish Hobbyist.*

N.T.G., NANCY TRILLING GOLDNER, B.A.
Dance Critic, *The Christian Science Monitor, Dance News,* and *The Nation.*

O.A.L., ORO ANAHORY-LIBROWICZ, B.A., M.A., PH.D.
Lecturer in Spanish, Concordia University. Coeditor, *Information Proche-Orient.*

P.D.B., PETER D. BEITCHMAN, A.B., M.A.
Director, Education and Community Affairs, Association of New York Neighborhood Health Centers.

R.F., RUSSELL FREEDMAN, B.A.
Faculty Member, The New School for Social Research. Author of *Growing Up Wild* and other books.

R.G.G., RICHARD G. GUNDLACH, B.S.
Communications Editor, *Electronics.*

R.J.C., RAYMOND J. CARROLL, B.A.
General Editor and United Nations Correspondent, *Newsweek*

R.J.S., ROBERT J. SHAW, B.S., B.A.
Freelance writer. Author of *Libraries: Building for the Future.*

R.J.T., ROBERT J. TROTTER, B.S.
Behavioral Sciences Editor, *Science News Magazine.*

R.N.O., RICHARD N. OSTLING, A.B., M.S., M.A.
Religion Editor, *Time.* Former President, Religion Newswriters Association. Author of *Secrecy in the Church.*

R.P.P., RAYMOND P. POINCELOT, B.A., PH.D.
Associate Biochemist, Connecticut Agricultural Experiment Station, Department of Biochemistry.

R.R.H., ROBERT R. HUNTLEY, B.S., M.D.
Chairman, Department of Community Medicine and International Health, Georgetown University School of Medicine. President, Georgetown University Community Health Plan, Inc.

R.W.B., RICHARD W. BROWN, B.F.A.
Professor, Motion Picture Studies, The New School for Social Research. Host of NBC–TV series, *Filmmakers on Filmmaking.*

R.W.S., RUTH W. STIDGER, B.A.
Associate Editor, *World Construction.* Coauthor of *Inflation Management* and other books.

S.A.K., SERGE A. KORFF, A.B., M.A., PH.D. Professor of Physics, New York University. Former President, New York Academy of Sciences.

S.C., SHEILA CARAPICO, B.A. Ph.D. candidate, Department of Political Science, State University of New York, Binghamton.

S.C.L., STEPHEN C. LEWIS, B.A., M.A., PH.D. Chairman, Humanities Division, Suffolk County Community College. Coauthor of *Focus on the Written Word.*

S.J.A., STEPHEN J. ACKERMAN, J.D. Lecturer, Department of Community Medicine and International Health, Georgetown University School of Medicine.

T.D., THOMAS DEFRANK, B.A., M.A. Correspondent, *Newsweek.*

T.H.J., THOMAS H. JOYCE, B.A. Labor Correspondent, *Newsweek.* Former White House Correspondent, The Detroit *News.*

T.L.K., THOMAS L. KENNEDY, A.B., M.A., PH.D. Professor of History, Washington State University. Author of articles on China.

T.W.D., THOMAS W. DAVIS, B.SC., M.SC., PH.D. Professor Emeritus, New York University.

W.B.F., WILLIAM B. FRANKLIN, B.S., M.S. Editor, *Business Outlook,* and Special Correspondent, *London Economist.* Author of *Current Business Trends* and other books.

W.E.M., WILLIAM E. METCALF, A.B., A.M., PH.D. Assistant Curator of Roman and Byzantine Coins, The American Numismatic Society.

W.J.B., WALTER J. BOCK, B.S., PH.D. Professor of Evolutionary Biology, Columbia University. Author of publications on evolution.

W.J.G., WILLIAM J. GILSTRAP, B.A. Former Associate Economist, Chemical Bank.

W.M.H., W. M. HAVIGHURST, B.A. Supervising Editor, Funk & Wagnalls Yearbook. Former Humanities Editor, Cadillac Modern Encyclopedia. Former Editor, American Heritage Dictionary.

W.P., WILLIAM PERRY, B.A., M.A. Music Director, Museum of Modern Art. Executive Producer, *Anyone for Tennyson?* series, PBS.

ACKNOWLEDGMENTS

Below is a list of organizations whom we want to thank for their assistance in compiling this Yearbook.

Department of the Census, U.S. Department of Commerce

Social Security Administration, U.S. Department of Health, Education, and Welfare

U.S. Immigration and Naturalization Service

American Red Cross

National Council of Churches

National Safety Council

Organization for Economic Cooperation and Development

PICTURE CREDITS

130 Wide World
131 UPI
132 Yoshida/Sygma
133 Wide World
135 UPI
136 *Both:* Martha Swope
137 The New York Times
138 *Top, Left:* UPI; *Top, Right:* Pictorial Parade; *Bottom:* Wide World
139 The New York Post
142 *Top:* NASA; *Bottom:* Cornell University
144 George Plafker/U.S. Geological Survey
145 Scripps Institution of Oceanography
146 University of Delaware
147 *Both:* The American Mathematical Society
148 *Top:* Wide World; *Bottom:* UPI
150 Wide World
151 University of Michigan
152 *Left:* UPI; *Right:* Wide World
153 *Clockwise from Upper Left:* UPI; UPI; UPI; Wide World; Wide World
157 Litton Industries
158 Wide World
159 Sohio
160 *Both:* U.S. Department of Commerce
161 *Top:* Wide World; *Bottom:* U.S. Army Corps of Engineers
162 University of Maine/Prof. Charles D. Richards
164 *Left:* UPI; *Right:* Wide World
165 *Left:* Vauthey/Sygma; *Right:* Men's Fashion Association
168 *Top:* Nogues/Sygma; *Bottom:* French Embassy
169 Pictorial Parade
170 Wide World
171 UPI
172 Wide World
173 UPI
174 Keystone
175 UPI
176 *Top:* Keystone; *Bottom:* British Information
180 UPI
181 UPI
182 UPI
184 Chemical & Engineering News
185 University of Utah Medical Center
186 Public Broadcasting System
189 George Ortez/N.E.W.S.
190 Tigua Indian Community
191 UPI
193 Grumman Corporation
195 UPI
196 *Top:* Wide World; *Bottom:* UPI
198 Wide World
200 Wide World
201 UPI
204 Wide World
206 *Both:* UPI
207 UPI
209 UPI
210 Wide World
213 Brookhaven National Laboratory
214 University of Michigan
216 Forest, J., et al, *Science,* Vol 192, pp. 884, Fig. 1, 28 May 1976. Copyright 1976 by the American Association for the Advancement of Science.
217 Woods Hole Oceanographic Institute
218 Schecter/Schwei
219 Jill Krementz
220 Blackglama
221 Jill Krementz
222 Wide World
223 Photo Trends
224 Henri Dauman/Magnum
225 German Information Center
226 *Both:* Sekai Bunka
228 Jill Krementz
229 Wide World
230 Anne de Brunhoff/Knopf
232 Magna Distributing Corporation
233 Photo Trends
234 UPI
235 Spiewak & Sons
236 DuPont

237 UPI
239 UPI
240 Wide World
241 UPI
242 *Top:* UPI; *Bottom:* Wide World
243 U.S. Navy
245 Wide World
247 Wide World
248 UPI
249 Michael Norcia/Keystone
250 Twentieth Century Fox
251 *Both:* UPI
252 Wide World
253 Richard Braaten/Kennedy Center
254 Wide World
255 *Top:* Jack Mitchell/The Opera Company of Boston; *Bottom:* Columbia Records
257 UPI
258 *Top:* UPI; *Bottom:* Wide World
259 UPI
261 NATO
262 Wide World
264 *Top and Bottom:* Wide World; *Middle:* Keystone
265 *Clockwise from Upper Left:* Wide World; Wide World; Photo Trends
266 *Both:* Wide World
267 *Top:* Pictorial Parade; *Bottom:* UPI
268 Wide World
269 *Top:* Keystone; *Bottom:* Photo Trends
270 *Top:* UPI; *Bottom:* Photo Trends
271 *Both:* Wide World
272 *Top:* Keystone; *Bottom:* Photo Trends
273 Wide World
275 *Top:* Vanguard Records; *Bottom:* Photo Trends
276 Wide World
277 Wide World
279 Wide World
281 Wide World
282 Wide World
283 *Top:* UPI; *Bottom:* Wide World
284 UPI
285 UPI
286 *Top:* UPI; *Bottom:* Keystone
287 Wide World
288 *Left:* Keystone; *Right:* UPI
289 Brack/Black Star
291 UPI
292 Wide World
293 Wide World
294 *Both:* Keystone
295 Wide World
296 German Information Center
297 *Left:* Wide World; *Right:* UPI
298 *Top:* ABC; *Bottom:* Keystone
299 UPI
300 *Top:* T.F.H. Publications, Inc.; *Bottom:* Evelyn Shafer
302 Eastman Kodak
303 *Top:* American Federation of the Arts; *Bottom:* Cover photograph of *People of Kau* by Leni Riefenstahl. First published in Germany by Paul List Verlag under the title *Die Nuba von Kau.* © 1976 by Leni Riefenstahl. English translation copyright © 1976 by William Collins Sons & Company Ltd. By permission of Harper & Row, Publishers, Inc.
304 Imogen Cunningham/The New York Public Library
305 Wide World
306 NASA
307 Keystone
308 Ken Regan/Camera 5
309 *Top:* UPI; *Bottom:* Wide World
310 Island Records
312 *Left:* Sygma; *Right:* Mendonca/Sygma
313 UPI
316 Gunner/Sipa Press/Black Star
317 Stanley Forman/Boston Herald American
319 Wide World
320 Lud Keaton/Arizona Republic
322 UPI
323 WNEW-TV
324 UPI
325 Wide World

326 Wide World
327 Newsweek–Susan McElhinney
329 *Top:* WNET; *Bottom:* RCA
330 London Records
331 Wide World
332 Carland/Red Cross
334 Wide World
335 The Central Schwenkfelder Church
336 UPI
337 Wide World
338 Keystone
339 Wide World
340 UPI
341 *Top:* Photo Trends; *Bottom:* Jack Lipkins
342 Gould/Keystone
343 Liaison
345 *Both:* Wide World
346 UPI
347 Wide World
348 Wide World
349 Wide World
350 Wide World
352 U.S. Senate
353 UPI
354 NASA
355 UPI
356 UPI
357 *Both:* UPI
358 Neil Leifer–Sports Illustrated/© Time,-Inc.
359 Dick Raphael–Sports Illustrated/© Time, Inc.
360 Detroit Tigers
361 James Drake–Sports Illustrated/© Time, Inc.
363 UPI
364 Wide World
365 Tony Triolo–Sports Illustrated/© Time, Inc.
366 John G. Zimmerman–Sports Illustrated/© Time, Inc.
367 UPI
369 Manny Millan–Sports Illustrated/© Time, Inc.
370 Florida News Bureau
371 Wide World
372 Co Rentmeester–Sports Illustrated/© Time, Inc.
373 Wide World
374 Frank Wilcox/Image Bank
375 Neil Leifer–Sports Illustrated/© Time, Inc.
376 *Top:* Heinz Kluetmeier–Sports Illustrated/© Time, Inc.;
   Bottom: Walter Iooss, Jr.–Sports Illustrated/© Time, Inc.
377 *Top:* Neil Leifer–Sports Illustrated/© Time, Inc.; *Bottom:*
   Heinz Kluetmeier–Sports Illustrated/© Time, Inc.
378 *Both:* Jerry Cooke–Sports Illustrated/© Time, Inc.

379 Neil Leifer–Sports Illustrated/© Time, Inc.
380 Minkus Stamp Co.
383 Wide World
384 Black Star
386 Pictorial Parade
388 Tiffany & Company
389 *Top:* Brookhaven National Laboratory; *Bottom:* Byte Shops,
   Inc.
390 *Top:* National Science Foundation; *Bottom:* General
   Electric
391 UPI
392 Martha Swope
393 *Top:* Lincoln Center; *Bottom:* Dubuskey/Schulman
394 Krawitz
395 Denys Lasdun & Partners
398 Wide World
399 *Top:* UPI; *Bottom:* Wide World
400 UPI
401 Delta Queen Steamboat Company
402 UPI
404 Wide World
405 Wide World
406 *Top:* Keystone; *Bottom:* Wide World
407 United Nations/Saw Lwin
408 *Top:* United Nations/Saw Lwin; *Bottom:* Brian
   Alpert/Keystone
409 Wide World
410 Wide World
411 UPI
412 *Clockwise from Upper Left:* Michael Norcia/Keystone;
   Pictorial Parade; Peter L. Gould/Keystone; UPI
415 *All:* UPI
416 Don Wright/© 1976 New York Times Special Features
417 UPI
418 UPI
419 Specialty Steel Industry of the U.S. and United
   Steelworkers of America
420 Wide World
421 Wide World
422 UPI
423 Wide World
426 Wide World
428 Wide World
429 Keystone
430 UPI
431 YMCA
432 UPI
433 Wide World
434 UPI

INDEX TO THE 1977 YEARBOOK
EVENTS OF 1976

INTRODUCTION

This Index is a comprehensive listing of persons, organizations, and events that are discussed in the 1977 Yearbook. Entries in **boldface** letters indicate subjects on which the Yearbook has an individual article. Entries in lightface type are to individual references within articles. In either type of entry, the letters a and b refer, respectively, to the left and right column of the page cited. If no letter follows a page number, the reference is to text that is printed across the full width of a page. Only the first significant mention of a subject in a given article has been included in the Index.

In a main entry such as **Australia:** 91a, the number refers to the page on which the article begins. The succeeding lightface page numbers refer to other text discussions in page order of the volume. If, however, as in **Congress of the United States:** 120a, Elections, 154b, another title precedes the second page reference, the discussion is located in the titled subentry in the page location mentioned. In the case of comprehensive articles such as the **United States of America,** reference is made to the page location of the beginning of the article, and a few selected major topics of the year are referred to by title and page location. The discussion of foreign relations of the United States in that article may be augmented by reference to separate articles on the countries and international organizations concerned.

When an Index entry is followed by the abbreviation **illus.,** the reference is to a caption and picture on the page mentioned. If more than one page reference is given in a lightface entry, the first page number provides the most extensive information on that subject.

LIST OF ABBREVIATIONS USED IN THE INDEX

CB   Citizens Band (radio)
Co.   Company
COMECON   Council for Mutual Economic Assistance
Corp.   Corporation
E.C.   European Communities
I.R.A.   Irish Republican Army

NATO   North Atlantic Treaty Organization
O.A.S.   Organization of American States
O.E.C.D.   Organization for Economic Cooperation and Development

OPEC   Organization of Petroleum Exporting Countries
U.N.   United Nations
U.S.   United States
U.S.S.R.   Union of Soviet Socialist Republics

473

474